The Beginning Elementary School Teacher In Action

by

R. C. Bradley and F. E. Halstead

1974

International Standard Book Number 0-8418-4486-0
Library of Congress Catalog Card Number 74-77091
Copyright © 1974, The University Press

Printed in the United States of America
THE UNIVERSITY PRESS
Wolfe City, Texas 75496

Preface

Anyone having served anywhere in the ranks of teaching in the turn of the "70's" knows that expectations for prospective and experienced teachers have changed. This is not a "bandwagon" book. The reader will find the collection of articles immersed in powerful descriptions depicting the teacher as first, a person; second, a teacher. A major purpose of this book is to bridge these two gaps.

Research evidence reveals that unless a teacher makes changes in his *teaching style* and *instructional strategies* during the first four years of his on-the-job experience, it is unlikely if he will make dynamic changes in the future. Consequently, these authors have sought to focus at the onset upon new, significant *strategies* of teaching which beginning teachers should seek to acquire earlier in their professional careers. To mention a few, these strategies include: individualization and personalization of instruction, teaching children to think, teacher competencies, and classroom management expertise.

To this writing, rarely have beginning teachers explored their obligations to handicapped children in the regular classroom. Currently, there is a "shift of emphasis" from placing *exceptional* children all day in special rooms and schools to, providing them with opportunities to be assigned to mainstream classes for at least a portion of the school day. A portion of this textbook deals with selected types of exceptional cases with whom the novice teacher will be expected to deal.

The National AESP has written and adopted a resolution to do away with traditional grade cards in every elementary school throughout the nation; therefore, the sections about parent-teacher interviews, evaluation, and community leadership should be especially valuable.

A unique feature of this book stems from the concerted opinion of the authors as they selected its provocative contents. That is, beginning teachers can learn to do what experienced teachers are, or should be doing. Beginning teachers at the undergraduate levels all too often have been the "leftouts" in pre-professional training. Consequently, these textbook contents will help the beginning teacher enter his profession with a strategy which he can identify as his own, and to be proud of it, as he seeks to make his own valuable contribution to modern youth.

Contrary to popular opinion, there should not be a "hands off" policy to the use of techniques; skills, and knowledges generally resigned only to special service personnel. The more a teacher knows about these techniques and the use to which specialists put them, the more likely he can follow the advice of a professional counselor, guidance specialist, or psychologist. In no instance, however, should any untrained person seek to manipulate the highly refined skills that only these persons have been trained to conduct and induce. But at times there are general knowledges that even the beginning teacher must call upon in a given situation. Thus the purpose of the selections, which focus upon the teacher as one who must draw from counselor and guidance skills, will help fill this void. The beginning teacher, with or without training, will be the best school psychologist some children will ever have. This concept must not go overlooked nor without fuller exploration.

The rising tide of teacher militancy, professional negotiations, political involvement, and legal obligations of the teacher, necessitates a direct involvement of the beginning teacher in discussions of school law before he ever goes on the job. The articles presented in Chapter XIV give the teacher a very clear picture of "tort liability" from contributory negligence to unavoidable accidents in which a student suffers physical damage or wherein teacher-student rights are breached.

This book adds another dimension to professional commitment. As with any other job situation, how a person feels about himself, his work, and his clients has much to do with how he does his professional task. The work in this section states more than the fact that a teacher should feel committed to his professional choice, but ways to achieve this commitment are cited.

Summarily, this book is aimed at increasing the productive thinking of the beginning teacher. It should provide a climate which provides the reader with continuous opportunities to develop criteria against which he might measure himself as a prospective teacher. A large measure of the contents of this book can be used by a novice teacher in a "self-directed" fashion. But the essence of its contents can be more adequately fulfilled if it is used under the direction of the professional educator who anchors to it his own wisdom and expertise.

In the teaching profession no man stands alone. Nevertheless, where one stands and how he stands is self-selected. The prophet Ezekiel stated:

> I fell upon my face and I heard a voice of one that spake. And he said unto me, son of man, stand upon thy feet, and I will speak unto thee.
>
> And the spirit entered into me when he spake unto me, and set me upon my feet, that I heard him that spake unto me.

Symbolically, as in the language of the Bible, the experienced teacher cannot learn or teach in a passive position, neither can the beginning teacher. No doubt one of the greatest aids a starting teacher can give himself is the *state of mind* that encourages him to, "stand on his feet!"

F. E. H.
R. C. B.

Acknowledgments

We are grateful to our friends and colleagues who read the manuscript and contributed suggestions and criticism. Special thanks to teachers of teachers,—the cooperating teachers of public elementary schools and their administrators, who offered timely and provocative assistance and information. Great appreciation likewise is expressed to the junior and senior level student teachers at North Texas State University who shared with us their feelings and experience.

Lastly, to the authors and publishers who granted permission to reprint their copyrighted materials, we acknowledge our greatest debt.

F. E. Halstead
R. C. Bradley

Dedication

to

Nadine and Marilyn

Table of Contents

Chapter I

The Teacher

Teaching has been generally considered as a process of transferring information and skill from the living to the living by the living. But today teaching has become more than that, the teacher is first, *a person.* The modern teacher is the result of human skill and know-how rather than the product of hope and chance. Although one's innate personality is more influential in his success as a teacher, good teachers are not born good teachers. The honored position must be achieved through proper preparation and experience.

The contents of this Chapter will serve to show the reader that any beginning teacher plans for a profession rather than for a job. The professional preparation for teaching should be based upon an anticipation of a long career rather than a trial period because the demands are not only time consuming but strenuous.

Whatever the college student does in his preprofessional training depends largely upon his personal expectations of a teacher. The work which follows was selected on the basis that its historical, descriptive, and analytical nature would be most helpful to the beginning teacher's perceptions of the significance of *the teacher*, *teaching*, and *the profession.*

SCHOOL is for . . .
LAUNCHING YOUR NEW CAREER

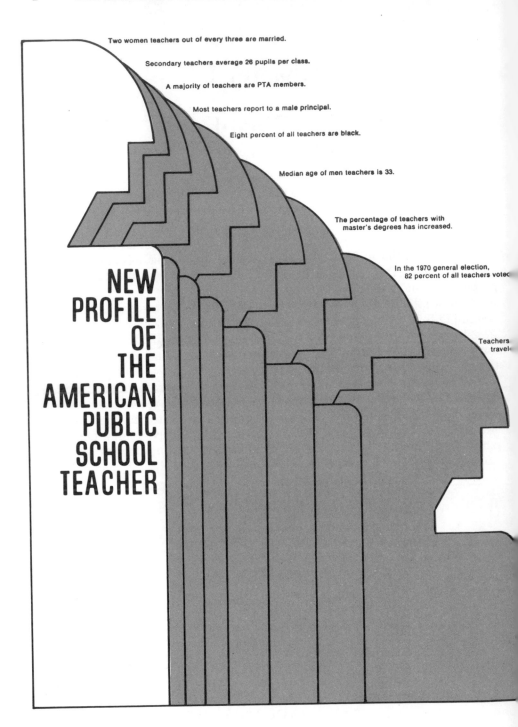

NEW
PROFILE
OF
THE
AMERICAN
PUBLIC
SCHOOL
TEACHER

Two women teachers out of every three are married.

Secondary teachers average 26 pupils per class.

A majority of teachers are PTA members.

Most teachers report to a male principal.

Eight percent of all teachers are black.

Median age of men teachers is 33.

The percentage of teachers with master's degrees has increased.

In the 1970 general election, 82 percent of all teachers voted

Teachers travel

New Profile Of The American Public School Teacher

NEA RESEARCH DIVISION

Teachers are younger, better educated (but less experienced), and better paid than they were 10 years ago. They still work as many hours a week both in and out of school as they used to and teach as many days of the year, but they spend fewer hours on unpaid work and have fewer extra nonteaching days of duty. They have slightly smaller classes, are less likely to be misassigned, and are more likely to have a duty-free lunch period than in the past. They are less likely to join organizations (although very likely to participate in political elections) and more likely to own or be buying their own homes and two cars.

These are some of the changes in the teaching profession during the 1960's that came to light in a recent study by the NEA Research Division. Every 5 years, the Division conducts a comprehensive survey of the American teaching profession by means of a questionnaire sent to a nationwide sample of teachers in public elementary and secondary schools. Topics covered range from details of the teacher's assignment to facts about his family and outside activities. The latest survey, made in spring 1971, received an 84 percent response from the teachers questioned. This article presents some of the major findings about what has happened to the teaching profession in the 1960's and where it stands at the beginning of the 1970's.

Who are the teachers of America?

The 1960's have seen some changes in the teaching population, including the following:

• The median age of teachers has dropped from 41 years in 1961 to 35 years in 1971. Men still have a median age of 33, but women have become progressively younger; their median age fell from 45½ to 40 between 1961 and 1966 and to 37 in the last 5 years.

NEA Research Division. "New Profile of the American Public School Teacher." *Today's Education.* May 1972. 61:14-17.

• The percentage of men teachers in the profession has increased from 31 to 34 percent since 1966. More elementary teachers and more older teachers (age 50 or older) are now men.

• More teachers are married, an increase from 68 to 72 percent in 10 years. Four men out of 5 and 2 women out of 3 are married.

• The "old maid schoolteacher" was already a thing of the past in 1961, but single women in the profession have since decreased in percent from 17 to 14.

• The percentage of men with working wives has increased from 32 to 45 percent in the last 10 years, and the percentage of men with wives employed in full-time teaching has increased from 17 to 21 percent in the last 5 years.

• Women teachers tend to come from families of higher occupational and educational status than men. The percentage of women whose fathers were business or professional men has increased from 38 to 45 percent since 1961, compared with a constant 34 percent of men from such background. The mothers of 3 in 10 women, compared with 2 in 10 men, went to college.

Men and women teachers exhibit different and changing career patterns:

• The experience of men teachers has *increased* from a median of 7 years to a median of 8 years in the course of the 1960's, but the experience of women has *decreased* from 14 to 8 years in median terms since 1961.

• Two-thirds of all women teachers began teaching either within the past 5 years or more than 20 years ago. In contrast, 6 in 10 men began teaching within the last 10 years.

• The percentage of women teachers who have had a break in service has decreased from 53 to 40 percent since 1961, and the percentage of women with a break in service for marriage or homemaking has decreased from 17 to 10 percent since 1966. However, nearly 1 woman in 5 continues to report a break in service for maternity or child rearing, and 5 percent of women teaching in 1970-71 planned to drop out in 1971-72 for homemaking and/or child rearing.

Within the profession, positions held by teachers reflect traditional sex identification of occupational roles:

• Only 1 man in 4 teaches in elementary school and less than 1 percent of all men teach grade 3 or below. In contrast, two-thirds of all women are elementary teachers, and one-third teach grade 3 or below. Conversely, 42 percent of men, compared with 18 percent of women, are senior high teachers.

• In secondary schools, the largest percentage of women teach English, while greater percentages of men than women teach science and social studies.

• The principalship is a male preserve. Two-thirds of all teachers are female, but 89 percent of all teachers report to a male principal. In elementary schools, 84 percent of teachers are women, but 80 percent of elementary teachers have men for principals. In secondary schools, 99 percent of teachers indicate that their principals are men.

Where teachers are

The nation's public school teachers are distributed among different types of communities:

• The largest proportion of teachers, 45 percent, are in school systems enrolling 3,000-24,999 pupils; 28 percent teach in large systems with 25,000 or more enrollment and 27 percent in small systems with less than 3,000 enrollment.

• More than one-third of all teachers teach in urban schools, more than half teach in suburban communities or small towns, and about 1 teacher in 8 is in a rural school. Two teachers in 10 are in large cities with a population of 250,000 or more, about half of them teaching in inner-city schools.

• Three teachers in 8 report that a majority of the pupils they teach come from the lower middle class; 2 in 8 report mainly pupils from the upper middle and upper classes; and 1 teacher in 6 indicates that a majority of his pupils are lower class in socioeconomic status. The rest report mixed economic classes among their pupils.

• Although 8 percent of teachers identify themselves as black and 6 percent report that they have a black principal, 12 percent report that half or more of the pupils they teach are black.

• In large systems, 29 percent of teachers teach in the inner city, 28 percent report that half or more of their pupils are black, and 29 percent that a majority of their pupils are lower class in socioeconomic status.

• Six teachers in 10 live within the boundaries of the school systems that employ them, but only 1 teacher in 3 lives within the attendance area of the school where he is teaching. In large systems, only 17 percent of teachers live within the attendance area of their schools, compared with 36 percent in medium-sized systems and 50 percent in small systems.

Teachers, like the rest of the population, are mobile:

• Only 29 percent of 1971 teachers were living in the communities where they had lived as children, a decrease from 33 percent in 1961. Recent newcomers to their communities increased from 11 to 15 percent in the same 10 years.

• About half of all teachers have taught in more than one school system. Three teachers in 8 have taught in a different system in the same state where they currently teach, and 1 teacher in 5 has taught in another state.

- Five percent of those teaching in 1970-71 planned to teach in a different school system in 1971-72.

Progress and problems in teaching conditions

Improvement has occurred in a number of areas of teaching conditions, but evidence of continuing problems also exists:

- The percentage of teachers teaching at least part of the time in grades or subjects outside their major field of preparation has decreased from 31 to 23 percent since 1961. However, correction of misassignment has taken place where least needed: Fewer teachers are teaching some but less than half of their time out of field, but 1 teacher in 7 continues to be so seriously misassigned that he is teaching 50 percent or more of the time outside his field.

- The mean size of classes taught by elementary teachers has crept downward at a snail's pace from 29 pupils per class in 1961, to 28 in 1966, to 27 in 1971. Secondary teachers average 26 pupils per class, down from 27 in 1966 and 1961, but the mean number of pupils they teach per day is still over 130.

- Secondary teachers' unassigned periods have increased from a mean of 4 to a mean of 5 per week in the last five years, but 1 secondary teacher in 5, as in 1961, has no unassigned periods at all.

- Data on lunch periods show a victory for teachers in the second half of the 1960's. The percentage of teachers eating lunch with their pupils, which *increased* from 39 to 47 percent between 1961 and 1966, *decreased* to 31 percent in 1971. In 1966, fewer than 4 elementary teachers in 10 had a duty-free lunch period; in 1971, 6 in 10 had a duty-free lunch.

- The mean total working week for teachers is still 47 hours, as at the beginning of the 1960's. However, the mean number of hours spent by teachers on non-compensated school-related activities has decreased from 11 to 8 per week in the last 5 years.

- Teachers still teach a mean of 181 days a year, but their mean number of nonteaching days of contract has dropped from 5 to 4 since 1966.

Teachers' professional qualifications

Academic preparation of teachers has improved greatly during the 1960's:

- Nondegree teachers have almost entirely disappeared from the profession. In 1961, 15 percent of teachers did not even have a bachelor's degree; now 97 percent have at least a bachelor's degree.

- The percentage of teachers with bachelor's degrees increased in the first half of the decade; the percentage with master's degrees, in the second half. Forty-two percent of men and 19 percent of women have a master's degree or 6 years of preparation.

Teachers also show a strong interest in continuing education and professional growth:

- In the last 3 years, 61 percent of teachers have earned a mean of 14 semester hours of college credit beyond the bachelor's degree.
- Six teachers in 10 have participated in workshops sponsored by their school systems during the last 3 years.
- Six percent of 1971 teachers had had sabbatical leave for study, travel, or other purposes at some time since fall 1968.

Outside activities

Teachers' participation in organizational activities has declined in the past decade, but they continue to show a high degree of interest in activities that have professional relevance:

- Percentages of teachers who are members of churches, political parties, youth-serving groups, fraternal organizations, women's groups, men's service clubs, and parent teacher associations have decreased during the 1960's especially among younger teachers.
- The mean number of hours per week that teachers give to working for organizations during the school year has decreased from 2 to 1 in the past 5 years. The percentage of teachers who do not give time to working for organizations has increased from 33 to 41 percent in the past 10 years.
- A majority of teachers, however, are members of local, state, and national educational associations, and more than half of all secondary teachers are members of subject-matter or professional special-interest associations. Despite the decrease since 1966, a majority of teachers also are still PTA members.
- Teachers are travelers. Apart from 4 percent who have traveled on sabbatical leave in the last 3 years, 26 percent have undertaken other educational travel in the last 3 years, and 35 percent traveled during the 1970 summer vacation.

Data on teachers and politics include the following:

- Formal membership in political party organizations dropped drastically from 31 to 13 percent between 1961 and 1971.
- However, 82 percent of teachers voted in the general election in 1970 and 75 percent voted in primary elections.
- By a ratio of 6 to 4, teachers who classify their political philosophy as conservative or tending to be conservative outnumber those who either are or tend to be liberal.

● Forty-three percent of teachers classify themselves as Democrats and 34 percent as Republicans, but 22 percent report that they are not affiliated with any political party. More than a third of teachers under age 30 have no party affiliation.

Economic status

Teachers have to some extent participated in the rising affluence of the American middle class during the 1960's, but differences in salaries continue to leave a number of lower-paid teachers:

● The mean annual salary reported by teachers has increased from $5,264 in 1961 to $9,261 in 1971.

● Since 1966, teachers who own or are buying their own homes have increased from 62 to 67 percent, and teacher families with 2 or more cars have risen from 37 to 47 percent.

● Teachers in small school systems have a mean salary that is more than $1,000 lower than the mean salary of teachers in medium or large systems.

● The mean salary of Southeastern teachers is approximately $2,500 less than the mean salary of Northeastern teachers.

●Women continue to have lower salaries than men; however, a larger proportion of men have master's degrees. Although the percent of increase in the mean salary of men and women teachers has been similar over the past decade, the dollar amount of difference has increased.

● As in 1966, 1 out of every 6 teachers with a master's or higher degree has a lower salary than the mean salary of teachers with a bachelor's degree or less.

Few teachers rely entirely on their salaries as teachers to support themselves and their families:

● Teachers with income in addition to their teaching salary have increased in percent from 51 to 57 between 1961 and 1971. In 1971, 81 percent of men averaged about $1,900 in extra income, and 44 percent of women averaged just over $1,000. The percentage of women earning extra income during the summer or school year or both has doubled in the last 10 years.

● Although women have lower salaries than men and fewer of them have extra income, the combined total income of married women teachers and their husbands averaging $18,510, is higher than the $15,006 averaged by married men teachers and their wives.

● The teacher's salary represents an average of 52 percent of total household income for the families of married women and 72 percent of total income in the households of married men.

A Concept of Teaching*

B. OTHANEL SMITH

It is well understood that words can be defined to satisfy the purpose of the individual who uses them. For this reason many controversies center in the meaning of terms. The literature of education is filled with claims and counter claims about the meaning of "education." One authority defines education as growth; another says it is the cultivation of intellectual virtues; and still another claims that education is the means by which civilization is transmitted from one generation to another. These definitions are controversial because each one is packed with a set of preferences about what is to be taught, how it is to be taught, who is to be educated, and so on. And conducting the controversy consists in unpacking the definitions—each side pointing out what the opposing view commits us to, what it denies or fails to include, and at the same time claiming its own conception to be more defensible and desirable.

The word "teaching" is used in various ways also, and definitions of it often lead to or underlie controversial discussions in pedagogical circles. While the unpacking of various definitions of "teaching" would be an interesting undertaking, it is not our purpose to do so in this article. We shall attempt to undercut conventional definitions by developing a descriptive rather than a normative concept of teaching and to distinguish it from other concepts with which it is often confused.

Definitions of Teaching

Three uses of the word "teaching" are found in ordinary discourse.

*The analysis reported herein was made pursuant to a contract with the United States Office of Education, Department of Health, Education, and Welfare.

Dr. Smith is the author of *Research on Teaching to Develop Critical Thinking*, a report published in 1960 by the University of Illinois Press.

Smith, B. Othanel. "A Concept of Teaching." *Teachers College Record.* February 1960. 61:229-241.

First, it is used to refer to that which is taught, as a doctrine or body of knowledge. In the expression "the teachings of the church" reference is made to a body of ideas or a system of beliefs. Second, "teaching" is used to refer to an occupation or a profession—the profession of one who instructs or educates. And finally, "teaching" is used to refer to ways of making something known to others, usually in the routine of a school.

We are concerned here with the third of these uses and shall disregard the first two altogether. "Teaching" in this third sense has been defined in the following ways:

> Teaching: arrangement and manipulation of a situation in which there are gaps or obstructions which an individual will seek to overcome and from which he will learn in the course of doing so.[1]

> Teaching: intimate contact between a more mature personality and a less mature which is designed to further the education of the latter.[2]

> Teaching: impartation of knowledge to an individual by another in a school.[3]

From a generic standpoint, each of these definitions suffers from the same defect. It smuggles in its own particular view of how teaching is to be carried on. All are question-begging definitions, for they answer in advance the very question which research on teaching seeks to answer. The first of these definitions commits us to the view that the individual learns by engaging in problem solving, and that he is motivated to learn by involvement in an unsettled state of affairs for which he has no ready-made response. To teach is to engage and direct the pupil in problem-solving. Once we accept this definition, we commit ourselves to a chain of propositions identified with a particular theory of education.

The second definition just as surely, though perhaps less obviously, incorporates a theory of didactics. Teaching, we are told, consists in contacts between two individuals, one more mature than the other. The contacts are to be intimate and designed to advance the education of the less mature person. Education, in the view of the author of this defini-

---

[1] Adapted from John Brubacher, *Modern Philosophies of Education* (New York: McGraw-Hill, 1939), p. 108.
[2] Henry C. Morrison, *Basic Principles of Education* (Boston: Houghton Mifflin, 1934), p. 41.
[3] Adapted from common usage.

tion, is the development of the individual through learning, and learning in turn is defined as an adaptive process. Intimate contact supposedly requires the presence of one person in the company of the other. To unpack this definition of teaching would again bring to view a theory of education.

We are no better off when we turn to the last of these three concepts. The definition of teaching as the impartation of knowledge is typically used by persons who think of education as the cultivation of the mind, the mind being thought of as an accumulation of information—factual, theoretical, and practical. Teaching, according to this definition, typically takes on the character of lecturing.

To say that the foregoing definitions are question-begging is to say that teaching is confused with didactics. The way in which teaching is or can be performed is mistaken for teaching itself. In its generic sense, teaching is a system of actions intended to induce learning. So defined, teaching is observed to be everywhere the same, irrespective of the cultural context in which it occurs. But these actions may be performed differently from culture to culture or from one individual to another within the same culture, depending upon the state of knowledge about teaching, and the teacher's pedagogical knowledge and skill. Didactics, or the science and art of teaching, are not the same as the actions which they treat. And a definition of teaching as such, which packs a set of biases about how these actions are to be conducted, confuses teaching with its science and its art.

Teaching and Learning
Distinguished

Furthermore, teaching is frequently assimilated to learning. The belief that teaching necessarily entails learning is widely held, and is expressed in more than one book on pedagogical method. As one of our most distinguished authorities says, unless the child learns the teacher has not taught.[4] Then he goes ahead to say that teaching is to learning as selling is to buying, apparently on the assumption that if there is no buying, there can have been no selling. At first, this binding of teaching

---

[4] William H. Kilpatrick, *Foundations of Method* (New York: MacMillan, 1926, p. 268). See also John Dewey, *How We Think*, Rev. ed. (New York: D.C. Heath, 1934), p. 35f.

and learning together after the fashion of selling and buying seems plausible enough. But the analogy will not bear inspection, although it does highlight the responsibility of the teacher and the importance of active endeavor by the pupil.

To begin examination of the idea that teaching entails learning, let us note first of all that teaching and selling each involve some sort of interaction. We do, perform or accomplish many acts unaided. We race, hunt, and sing without the assistance of anyone. But there are actions which can be performed only in association with other persons. We can do business only if there is somebody to do business with. We can negotiate if there is someone to carry on negotiations with, and not otherwise. Likewise we can carry on the activities of selling only if there is someone who will buy our product and we can teach only if there is somebody whom we may instruct. Were there no buyers, there could be no sellers. Unless there were pupils, there could be no teachers. Such verbs as *negotiate*, *sell*, and *teach* signify proceedings between two or more individuals, involving some sort of deliberation with adjustment of mutual claims and interests in expectation that some result will issue. Lacking a process of interaction there can be neither teacher nor pupil just as there can be neither seller nor buyer.

Beyond this point, the analogy between teaching and selling begins to break down. To see how this is so, let us spell out the analogy. There are four elements in the selling-buying operation: a seller, a buyer, the act of selling, and the act of buying. Similarly, in the teaching-learning combination we find a teacher, a pupil, the action of teaching, and the activities of learning. To say that a teacher is to teaching as a seller is to selling, while not strictly correct, does not do violence to either of these relations. The qualifying expression "not strictly correct" is inserted because there are several different actions which we expect of a teacher: making assignments, grading papers, showing how to do something, telling why something is the case, and so on. But there is little more than one sort of behavior predictable from the statement that one is a seller; namely, that he gives something in return for a consideration, usually money. Looking further we find that learning is not coordinate with buying, because the relation of pupil to learning is not the same sort of thing as buyer to buying. We can say that a buyer is to buying as a pupil is to "pupiling," but the parallel breaks down when we say "as a pupil is to learning." "Pupiling," if there were such a word, would be required by the analogy to mean receiving instruction just as "buying" means receiving something in return for an agreed-upon price. Nor are we any better off if we substitute "learner" for "pupil," since "learner" is defined as one who receives instruction.

Furthermore, the relation between selling and buying is not the same as that between teaching and learning. The statement "I am selling X and someone is buying it from me" is implicitly tautological. It is clear from common usage that in order to be selling something someone must be buying. It would be contradictory to say "I am selling X but no one is buying it,"* or to say "I am buying X from so and so but he is not selling it." If you state "I am selling X" you are stating only part of what you mean, for implicit in this statement is the idea that someone is buying it. On the other hand, "I am teaching X (meaning, say, mathematics) to A and he is learning it" is not tautological. It is not contradictory to say "I am teaching X to A but he is not learning it." Nor is it contradictory to assert "A is learning X but no one is teaching it to him." "I taught X to A" means that I showed A how to do X, or told him such and such about X. This expression does not include the idea that A learned from me how to do X. It is thus not repeating the idea to add it to the expression. Hence "I taught X to A" says something different from "I taught X to A and he learned X." However, the parallel suggested in the paragraph above is logically similar to that between buying and selling. To assert "I am teaching X (mathematics) and he is 'pupiling' it" (meaning he is receiving my instruction), would be tautological. It would then be contradictory to say "I am teaching X (mathematics) and he is not 'pupiling' it" (meaning he is not receiving my instruction). To give instruction would seem to entail receiving it. It would likewise be contradictory to say "He received instruction, but no one gave him instruction."

The difference between teaching and learning may be further explored by reference to the distinction which Ryle makes between what he calls task words and achievement or success words.[5] Task words are those which express activities such as *racing, treating, traveling*, and *hunting*. The corresponding achievement words are *win, cure, arrive*, and *find. Teaching* is a task word and *learn* is the parallel achievement word. Achievement words signify occurrences or episodes. Thus one wins, arrives, or finds at a particular moment, or a cure is effected at a partic-

---

*There is a sense in which it would not be contradictory to say, "I am selling X but no one is buying it." For example, "I have been selling cars all day but nobody bought one" is not self-contradictory. But in this case it would be more precise to say "I have been *trying* to sell cars," etc., meaning I have been doing things intended to result in the sale of cars.

[5] Gilbert Ryle, *The Concept of Mind* (London: Hutchinson House, 1952), pp. 149-52.

ular time. Nevertheless, some achievement verbs express a continued process. A boat is launched at a particular instant but it is held at the dock for inspection. On the other hand, task verbs always signify some sort of activity or extended proceedings. We can say of a task such as play, treat, or teach that it is performed skillfully, carefully, successfully, or ineffectively. We may play the game successfully or unsuccessfully, but we cannot win unsuccessfully. We may treat a patient skillfully or unskillfully, but the restoring of health is neither skillful nor unskillful. It makes sense to say that we teach unsuccessfully. But it is self-contradictory to say we learned French unsuccessfully.

Teaching as a System
of Actions

That learning does not necessarily issue from teaching, that teaching is one thing and learning is quite another, is significant for pedagogical research. It enables us to analyze the concept of teaching without becoming entangled in the web of arguments about the processes and conditions of learning; in short, to carry on investigations of teaching in its own right. Teaching, like learning, has its own forms, its own constituent elements, its own regularities. It takes place under specifiable conditions—time limits, authority relations, individual abilities, institutional structures, and so on. What is needed for scientific inquiry is a concept which recognizes teaching as a distinctive phenomenon general enough to embrace normative definitions (see page 10) as special cases.

The word "teacher" is a dispositional term in the sense that under specifiable conditions—classroom, pupils, and so forth—the individual referred to as a teacher tends to behave in characteristic ways. He may explain something with the expectation that what he says will be remembered by the pupil; he may draw a diagram and point out certain features of it, emphasizing that these are to be remembered; he may read from a book and ask a pupil to interpret the passage; and so on. When the teacher behaves in these and many other ways, we say he is teaching. To repeat, teaching thus conceived may be defined as a system of actions directed to pupils. These actions are varied in form and content and they are related to the behavior of pupils, whose actions are in turn related to those of the teacher. From the execution of these actions and interactions of teacher and pupil, learning occurs. But learning, being an acquired disposition to behave in particular ways in particular circumstances, is neither action nor behavior, though it is exhibited in actions. The theoretical conception of teaching we propose to present will include all the actions of teachers necessary to explain and to predict the behavior of pupils and the occurrence of learning, though such explaining and predicting cannot be made from these actions alone.

It is to be kept in mind that the actions which constitute teaching, as defined in this discussion, take place in and are influenced by an environment which typically contains such social factors as mores, organizational structures, and cultural resources, as well as physical objects, persons, and so forth. But this environment is excluded from our conception of teaching, not because it is unimportant or irrelevant to teaching, but because it is not a part of the concept of teaching. Teaching is doubtless related the the mores and to social structures, but it is not the same sort of thing.

To explicate the concept of teaching we shall resort to a model which draws upon the psychological paradigm developed by Tolman,[6] although the psychological features of his model are of little interest to us here. All the variables involved in and related to the actions which make up teaching can be classified into three categories, but the actions themselves belong to only one of these. Although their particular contents continue to be controversial, the categories themselves have been well established in the behavioral sciences. They are (1) independent variables, (2) dependent variables, and (3) intervening variables. By referring to the model it can be easily seen that the actions of teaching belong to the first of these categories, and the actions of pupils to the second. Learning, as achievement, is an intervening variable. The index of its presence is pupil behavior, and this behavior is a dependent variable.

In the course of teaching, these variables are related in various ways. In so far as these relations can be postulated, described, and verified, teaching can be shaped in terms of empirically tested principles. While it is not possible here to deal concretely with these relations, we can discuss them in a very general way. In the model, the arrows indicate the direction of causal influences. The teacher's actions are followed by postulated states, events, or processes in the pupil and are represented by the intervening variables. Then, as a result of these variables, the pupil behaves in one or more of the ways indicated in the dependent variables column. The teacher can see the pupil's behavior, but he cannot see the postulated events and processes; that is, he cannot observe interests,

Edward C. Tolman, "A Psychological Model," in *Toward a General Theory of Social Action*, Edited by Talcott Parsons and Edward A Shils (Cambridge: Harvard University Press, 1952), pp. 279-302.

A PEDAGOGICAL MODEL

I INDEPENDENT VARIABLES *(Teacher)*	III INTERVENING VARIABLES *(Pupils)*	II DEPENDENT VARIABLES *(Pupils)*
⟶	⟶	
(1) Linguistic behavior	These variables consist of postulated explan-	(1) Linguistic behavior
(2) Performative behavior	atory entities and proc- esses such as memories, beliefs, needs, infer-	(2) Performative behavior
(3) Expressive behavior	ences, and associative mechanisms.	(3) Expressive behavior

motives, needs, beliefs, and the like. But these psychological entities and processes are present by implication in the behavior of the pupil. The teacher may therefore infer these psychological factors from the pupil's behavior, and in some instances he actually does infer them, although he may not be aware that he is doing so. Thus the teacher often infers from the reactions of the pupil that he is interested, or that he wants to do so and so, or the contrary.

Our model does not depict the ebb and flow of teaching, nor does it give a complete schema of the cycle of giving and taking instruction, hereafter referred to as the teaching cycle. To complete the picture the model must be extended to the right in duplicate form. Thus extended, the model would show that the pupil's actions bring into operation the teacher's intervening variables. These variables in turn lead to teacher actions, and at this point the whole cycle begins again. In this way the process of teaching is continued until the teacher believes either that the pupil has achieved what the teacher intended or that it is not profitable to continue teaching at the moment.

The foregoing analysis enables us to describe the teaching cycle, to mark off units of this cycle, and to distinguish the act of teaching from the act of receiving instruction. The teaching cycle is symbolized as follows:

$$\| P_t \to D_t \to R_t \| \to P_p \to D_p \to R_p \| \to P_t \to D_t \to R_t \| \to P_p \to D_p \to R_p \| -$$
$$P_t \to D_t \to R_t \| \to P_p \to D_p \to R_p \| \cdots\cdots\cdots\cdots\cdots\cdots \to \text{achievemen}$$

where P_t is the teacher's perception of the pupil's behavior; D is the teacher's diagnosis of the pupil's state of interest, readiness, knowledge, and the like, made by inference from the behavior of the pupil; and R_t is the action taken by the teacher in light of his diagnosis; and where P_p is the pupil's perception of the teacher's behavior; D_p is the pupil's diagnosis of the teacher's state of interest, what he is saying, and so on, as inferred from the teacher's behavior; and R_p is the reaction of the pupil to the actions of the teacher.

Each unit marked off by the double vertical lines is an instance of the teaching cycle. Each one consists of a teacher-pupil interaction. Within this teaching cycle are two subunits divided by the single vertical line. The subunit $P_t \rightarrow D_t \rightarrow R_t$ is what we refer to as an act of teaching; the subunit $P_p \rightarrow D_p \rightarrow R_p$ is what we call the act of taking instruction. These are reciprocating acts, and when performed under proper conditions they issue in achievement.

Teaching, according to our schema, does entail someone to give instruction as well as someone to take it. If a pupil is working on an assignment, he is probably learning. But no teaching is going on. No one is acting toward the pupil as a teacher. However, teaching acts can occur, though in abbreviated form, without the physical presence of pupils. For example, a teacher giving instruction over a television network is not in the physical presence of pupils. He can even be cut off the air by a mechanical difficulty, and being unaware that anything has happened, continue to teach. In a case like this the teacher is shaping his instructional behavior to some generalized pupil group anyway, and the fact that he is off the air consequently makes no difference.

Of course actual classroom teaching is not as simple as our schema. For one thing, more than one pupil is usually involved in classroom teaching. The teacher typically addresses himself to the entire class rather than to a single pupil. Even when he appears to be talking to a single pupil, he usually speaks for the benefit of the whole class. His perception of pupil behavior is likely to be some sort of generalized picture, and his diagnosis a hunch as to the general state of the class as a whole. Finally, his actions are likely to be shaped more by these general considerations and by his habits than by the psychological requirements of any one pupil.

The fact that classroom teaching is more complex than our pedagogical model is no criticism of the model. One of the advantages of models is that they give a simplified picture of the phenomenon they depict. However, the fact that our symbolic schema and verbal performances in the classroom are isomorphic is borne out by our descriptive studies of classroom teaching. By taping classroom discourse and analyzing it into pedagogically neutral units called episodes we have established a context within which to view verbal exchanges comprising the teaching cycle. Acts of teaching as well as acts of taking instruction can be clearly distinguished in the episodic structure.

Our knowledge of the act of teaching as well as that of taking instruction is meager. Neither of these acts has been investigated sufficiently to justify, from a scientific standpoint, fundamental changes in teaching. We have considerable knowledge of how human learning occurs, although much of it comes by extrapolation from studies of animal learning. The amount of adjustment in our current theories of learning which verbal behavior and cognitive processes may require is something about which we can only guess. We do not even know how accurately our learning theory describes what occurs in the act of taking instruction. Be that as it may, the act of teaching has received far less attention than its central role in pedagogy would seem to require.

The Variables

Intervening variables consist of constructs, or postulated entities and processes, which stand between the independent and dependent variables and are functionally related to them. The independent variables—the teacher's actions—are conceived to be causal factors which evoke or bring into operation postulated entities and processes, and these in turn are connected by a set of functions to the dependent variables—to the behavior of pupils. An account of these variables would involve us in psychological theory, and consequently, in one of the most controversial areas of the behavioral sciences. In the heyday of radical behaviorism, postulation of entities and processes between stimulus and response was frowned upon. Even Thorndike's postulation of physiological entities and processes was believed to be unnecessary to the explanation of learning. In recent years, however, different schools of psychology have assumed, each in its own way, whatever processes and entities seem to afford the most plausible explanation. To a large extent, differences in schools of psychology hinge upon differences in their conceptual postulations. Fortunately our task is a modest one, requiring us to delin-

---

[7] B. Othanel Smith and Others, *A Study of the Logic of Teaching.* A report on the first phase of a five-year research project. United States Office of Education. Dittoed 1959.

For a more detailed treatment see "The Analysis of Classroom Discourse: A Method and Its Uses," by Mary Jane Aschner (Unpublished Doctor's Dissertation, University of Illinois, 1958).

eate only the variables of our model. Were we to develop completely a general theory of teaching, we would be required to set forth a set of intervening variables, and to show their postulated causal connections with both independent and dependent variables of our model.

The independent variables consist of linguistic, performative, and expressive behaviors. These behaviors are essential elements of the concept of teaching and are not to be confused with the dependent variables, which are the behaviors identified with the act of taking instruction and are functionally associated with learning.

To continue our discussion of independent variables, teaching acts consist largely in verbal behavior, in what is done with and to pupils through the medium of words. But the fact that language is the primary medium of instruction is not as important as the things we do with language. For if we are to understand teaching, we must know what the actions are that we perform linguistically. Furthermore, it may be supposed that changes in the effectiveness of instruction will follow upon changes in the execution of such verbal actions.

What are the sorts of actions we perform with language in the classroom? First, there is a group of actions which have to do with the performance of what we shall call logically relevant—subject to logical appraisal—tasks. The teacher is called upon to deal with questions whose answers involve logical operations. For example, the teacher defines terms. To define a term is to perform a logical operation. If he gives a classificatory definition such as "A triangle is a plane figure with three sides," the teacher names the class of things (plane figure) to which triangles belong and then gives the attributes (three sides) which distinguish triangles from all other plane figures. We will describe only briefly a few of the logically relevant actions which are found in didactic verbal behavior.[8]

Defining. In general, definitions are rules for using words. There are several ways to define words, depending upon the rules. Among these ways are classificatory, operational, relational, and nominal definitions.

Classifying. To classify is to put something in a category. The teacher classifies implicitly when he defines, describes, or explains. But

---

[8] For a more extended discussion of these verbal actions see Smith and Others, *op. cit.* It should be noted that there are different dimensions of verbal behavior which cannot be discussed here. The teacher not only makes assertions about objects, but also talks about language itself. To ask "What is the author comparing X to?" in a given passage is to direct the pupil's attention to an object, event, and so forth, while to ask "Is this passage a metaphor?" is to ask about language itself. To ask for a definition is one thing, and to ask what a definition *is* is quite another thing.

the logic of classification is far more involved than the mere verbal act of asserting "X is a Y." Its logic becomes explicit when the teacher attempts to tell why he classifies X as a Y. He is then expected to set forth the criteria (rules) he uses and to show that they apply in the particular case.

Explaining. Explanations are called for when an event or a state of affairs is to be accounted for. To explain is to set forth an antecedent condition of which the particular event to be accounted for is taken as the effect, or else to give the rules or facts which are used to tell why decisions or judgments were made or actions taken. There are at least six different kinds of explanations: mechanical, causal, sequent, procedural, teleological, and normative.

Conditional Inferring. In conditional inferring, a set of conditions is described and the teacher then gives the consequent—the effect, result, or outcome. Sometimes the conditions are fairly simple, so that the path from the conditions to a conclusion is easily followed and the logical connection between the conditions and the outcome is fairly explicit. In other instances the path is complex, involving a number of steps, and is difficult to connect logically with the conditions.

Comparing and Contrasting. In this sort of verbal action two or more things—actions, factors, objects, processes—are compared; or else something is given and the teacher attempts to interpret it by describing another familiar object or process to which it is compared. Such comparative relations can often be expressed in terms of transitivity and symmetry.

Valuating. To perform the act of valuating, the teacher rates some object, expression, event, or action, let us say, as to its truth and the like. If he gives the complete operation of valuating, the teacher will set forth the reasons for his rating.

Designating. To designate is to identify something by name, word, or symbol. The verbal action here consists in citing instances or examples of a group of things or in giving the name of a particular thing or class of things.

Other Actions. In addition to the foregoing actions, there are verbal actions less closely related perhaps to logical operations. The teacher states theorems, rules, beliefs. He reports what was stated in a book, or verbally by someone. He states something to be the case; for example, that the date and place of a particular event were thus and so.[9]

---

[9] Our own studies of classroom discourse in English, social studies, science, and mathematics show that episodes involving definitions make up about 4 per cent of the total number of episodes; classifying about 3 per cent; explaining about 13 per cent; conditional inferring about 7 per cent; comparing and contrasting about 3 per cent; valuating about 5 per cent; designating about 15 per cent; and others 50 per cent.

The second group of actions which teachers perform with words is called directive action. In the moment-to-moment tasks of the classroom the teacher is called upon to tell pupils what to do in the performance of some operation or the practice of a motor skill. He may observe a pupil's mistake in the practice of typing and tell him what to do to correct it, just as on the playing field he may tell a player what to do to improve his tackling. He may tell a pupil in the laboratory that a piece of apparatus is to be set up in a particular way, or that he has made an error in reasoning which can be corrected in such and such a way. These verbal actions are all directive in the sense that they instruct the pupil in what he is to do. There are other directive actions which are less specific and only suggest the direction in which the pupil is to move. Verbal actions of this sort always frame a situation in a general way. For example, a teacher may tell a group of pupils that they are to take a trip by automobile and that they need to know how much the gasoline will cost in order to pro-rate the expense among members of the class. He then asks what they need to know in order to find out the cost of the gasoline. In this case, the teacher sets a situation and suggests the line along which the pupils are to work.

In both of these sorts of saying and telling the teacher does not intend that the pupil learn what he says. The pupil is not expected to say back to the teacher, in either the same or different words, what the teacher himself said. In the case of learning motor skills, he does expect the pupil to do what he is told, and thereby to effect changes in his performance. If the pupil forgets entirely what the teacher said, it does not matter so long as the pupil's performance is improved. The same is true with respect to less specific directives, as in the case of the automobile trip. The pupils most certainly will forget all about the situation laid before them by the teacher. This is not what the teacher wishes them to remember. His hope is that the pupils will learn how to analyze a situation and to decide upon the relevant factors in the course of working it out. This use of language is quite different from the expository uses discussed above. There the pupil is expected to remember what the teacher says and to repeat it in his own words in a subsequent situation. If the teacher says that the law of gravity is so and so and that it can be expressed mathematically thus and so, he expects the pupil to remember what he has said and to be able to say the same thing in his own words when he is called upon to do it.

Finally, the teacher performs admonitory acts. He praises and commends; blames and reprimands. He recommends, advises, and enjoins. He says to a pupil, "That is good." He may say to another, "That is not up to your ability. You could have done better." He may say, "You got yourself into this difficulty. You have only yourself to blame." He may suggest some course of action as the way out of the trouble. He may enjoin the pupil to remember so and so when he comes up against a particular sort of situation in the future. These kinds of verbal acts may effect psychological reinforcements or extinctions depending upon the particular admonitory act and the circumstances in which it occurs. They are conventionally understood to be taken for their social or emotional impact upon the pupil rather than for their cognitive content.

We turn now to consider those independent variables of our model which are nonverbal. The first set of these we call performative actions that is, actions which are performed for assumed or understood purposes but which are not linguistic. They may be accompanied by verbal behavior but they are themselves mere motor performances. These actions serve to *show* rather than to *tell* something to pupils, and the showing is done by manipulating objects. The teacher shows a pupil how to do something—say, how to regulate a Bunsen burner—by performing the act himself. At the same time, he may say, "Here is the way to do it—you turn this to control the amount of air," and so forth. But the saying is itself directive verbal behavior and not performative in our sense. The act of turning the element of the apparatus, and thus showing the relation between the turning and the color of the flame, is what we refer to as performative behavior. In such cases it is assumed that the pupil is to learn how to perform this action himself, so that the next time he will be able to adjust the burner without the aid of the teacher.

Numerous instances of this type of performative behavior can be found in the day-to-day work of the teacher. In some situations, however, the teacher engages in performative actions which the pupil is not expected to learn, for their purpose is to facilitate the learning of something else. For example, the teacher performs a demonstration in a science class to show the lines of force in a magnetic field. He goes through the usual operations of putting the appropriate piece of paper over a magnet and then sprinkling iron filings on the paper. Of course the pupils may learn from their observation of the teacher how to do the demonstration themselves. But the purpose of the performance is to show the magnetic field rather than how to carry out the demonstration.

The second set of nonverbal variables is what we call expressive behavior. These behaviors are illustrated in bodily posture, facial expression, tone of voice, expression of the eyes, and other ways. Typically they are neither purposeful nor addressed to anyone. In this respect they differ significantly from both verbal and performative actions, which we always understood as being directed to someone or to a group. Nevertheless, expressive behaviors function in teaching because they are taken by pupils as signs of the psychological state of the teacher. In this sense expressive behaviors are natural signs, like the things we call clouds, lightning, rivers. We take them as signifying something—as a cloud is a sign of rain.

Turning now to the dependent variables of our model—those which make up the instruction-taking part of the teaching cycle—we find a parallel between these variables and the independent ones. The pupil performs linguistic actions. He defines, explains, valuates, and so on, just as the teacher does. He performs these actions at the teacher's suggestion, or often even voluntarily. However, the pupil's purpose is not to instruct anyone, but to bear witness that he is taking instruction—that he understands what is happening or that he is taking part in (accepting or dissenting from) what is going on.

Directive verbal behavior of the pupil occurs infrequently, and usually on occasions when he plays the role of teacher, as chairman of class discussion, for example. The same observation holds for admonitory behavior. Classroom conventions do not permit the pupil to praise, blame, or advise the teacher with respect to his work, but this does happen on occasion. A pupil may complain that the teacher has been unfair, but he is not likely to say either to another pupil or to a teacher, "Your explanation was splendid." Such verbal behavior is odd and is likely to be ill received by the pupils as well as by the teacher.

While the pupil exhibits performative behavior (nonverbal behavior carried on for a purpose), he does so typically to practice the actions themselves rather than to instruct anyone. Thus he engages in performative actions when he sets up laboratory equipment, takes part in athletic events, and so on. Actions of this nature under the direct tutelage of the teacher are part of the teaching cycle. If they occur outside of teacher-pupil interaction, they are simply ways of study and practice.

The expressive behavior of the pupil is the same as that of the teacher. The pupil smiles or frowns; he slumps or sits erect in his seat; his voice is firm and convincing or weak and uncertain. Such behavior in the pupil, even more often than in the teacher, is not addressed to anyone. It is not typically intended to communicate. Nevertheless, it functions as signs to the teacher—as the skies, clouds, and winds are signs to the skipper at sea. The posture of the pupil, the light in his eyes, or the frown on his face tell the teacher who can read them about his feelings, intentions, and ideas.

The Language of
Didactics

By "didactics" is meant, of course, the science or art of teaching, and not teaching itself. When we speak of what we know about how teaching is to be conducted we have reference to didactics. The language of didactics traditionally is marked by such terms as "method," "drill," "interest," "learning situation." Discussions of teaching as such are carried on in the terms of the lecture method, problem method, project method, supervised study method. Much of the research on teaching has been framed in terms of these various doctrines. Is the problem method more effective than the lecture method? Is the project method more effective than the recitation method?

Numerous experiments to find answers to these and similar questions have produced only inconclusive results. This fact is often attributed to inadequate control of experimental conditions and to the complexity of the phenomenon itself. No one can doubt the strength of these claims. Nevertheless, the fact that teaching itself has never been analyzed apart from the context of doctrine may contribute to failure to control relevant factors. Has not our theorizing about teaching, even for experimental purposes, become clouded with commitments to the very words we use to discuss teaching?

If what we just said about pedagogical theorizing is only partly correct, it suggests that a new way of talking about didactic questions is in order. Perhaps a new approach to the study of teaching will emerge if we abandon the term "method," which is associated with such heavy-laden terms as "induction," "deduction," and "problem-solving"—terms for which everyone has his own preconceptions and predilections. If we cut through the verbal curtain and look at actual instructional operations in the classroom, we find them to be different from what our linguistic commitments lead us to believe. We see that teachers do many things which cannot be neatly fitted into the traditional theories of pedagogy. For example, at one time a teacher sets up a verbal situation from which he can move in a number of directions, depending upon his assessment of the way his pupils are psychologically deployed. At another time he sets up a nonverbal state of affairs and invites his pupils to explore it, to tell how it can be handled, and so forth. On another occasion a pupil may execute a verbal maneuver to counter the teacher's move. The teacher may then outflank the pupil, leaving one or more members of the class to meet the challenge.

We need studies of the sorts of positions teachers assume, and what maneuvers and detailed actions they take under varying circumstances and with different sorts of materials. If these were made, it would be appropriate to speak of the strategies and tactics of teaching. From such descriptive studies we might then go on to develop experimental as well as more nearly adequate theoretical didactics.

What Is Teaching?
One Viewpoint

MARIE M. HUGHES

PSYCHOLOGISTS, other researchers, and curriculum workers are in agreement that a most important variable in the classroom is that of the teacher.

The teacher behavior in the classroom that is most pervasive and continuous is, of course, the verbal action. The verbal and the nonverbal behavior of teachers is, according to Mary Aschner, "the language of responsible actions designed to influence the behavior of those under instruction" (1).

Indispensable data then for a description and analysis of teaching are verbatim records of what the teacher said and did and the response made by a child or group, including children's initiatory actions directed toward the teacher.

Data of This Study

The date of this study (2) were secured from 41 elementary teachers—7 men and 34 women. These teachers had classrooms in 19 buildings in 8 school districts.

The representativeness of the group may be judged from the fact they received their training degrees in 22 different states. Their age range was 25 to 50 years; their teaching experience, 5 years to 30 years; with a bimodal distribution at the ninth and fifteenth years. They were career teachers and judged good by supervisory and consultant staff members.

Three 30-minute records were secured from each of the teachers by two observers working at one time in the classroom with the teacher's cooperation and knowledge of the exact time the observers would arrive to take the record. In general, the records were taken several days apart.

Hughes, Marie M. "What is Teaching? One Viewpoint." *Educational Leadership.* January 1962. 19:251-259.

A brief episode from one 30-minute record may provide a more adequate picture of the data with which we worked:

Record No. 2620, page 2:

> T.: Carl, do you remember the day you came to school and said you could play a tune on the piano? It was a tune we all knew and so we sang it with you. You found out you could play the same tune on the tone bells. I wonder if you'd play the same tune for us today.
>
> T.: My! We liked to sing with you. Can we start our music time by your playing again and our singing with you? Why don't you play it on the tone bells?
>
> Carl: I'd like to play it on the piano.
>
> T.: Well, all right, you may play it on the piano if you'd rather. Do you want to play it all through once or shall we start right off together?
>
> Carl: I'll play it through. (Played on piano "Mary Had a Little Lamb" with one hand.)
>
> T.: That was very nice!
>
> Carl: I think you could sing with me.
>
> T.: All right, we'd be glad to. (Carl played and children sang.) Thank you, Carl.
>
> Carl: You could even do all of it.
>
> T.: You mean we could sing all of the verses?
>
> Carl: I can even do "followed her to school one day . . . etc."
>
> T.: I'm sure you can, Carl. Thank you very much.

What does the teacher do? It is obvious that there is a wide repertoire of behavior open to the teacher.

> The teacher *tells* people what to do.
>
> The teacher *sets* goals, the specifics of attention. "Today, we shall do the 25 problems on page 90."
>
> The teacher *gives* directions. "Take your books out and open them to page 90." "Do not write your name."
>
> The teacher *reprimands.* "Take your seat, Johnny."
>
> The teacher *accuses.* "You didn't work very hard."
>
> The teacher *admonishes.* This is, of course, before anything happens. "Don't forget to close the door." "Make sure you look up your words."
>
> The teacher *supports* and *encourages.* "That's nice." "Good." "Fine." "OK." "I knew you could do it."
>
> The teacher *grants* or *denies* requests.
>
> The teacher *clarifies* and *elaborates* on the problem or content under discussion.
>
> The teacher *asks* questions.
>
> The teacher *gives* cues.

There are many ways to categorize or organize the verbal behavior and non-verbal behavior of a teacher. It is the point of view of this investigator that the superior-subordinate relationship in the teacher-learner situation, with its culturally bestowed power position over the child, makes it impossible for the teacher to act in the classroom without performing a *function* for some child, group, or the entire class as recipients. It is the teacher who holds the power to give aid or withhold aid; to judge and to punish; to gratify or to deny; to accept or to ignore the response of a child.

Actually, children who are not participants in a given episode of interaction with the teacher do respond to his behavior (3, 4).

The presumptuousness of looking at teacher behavior from the standpoint of functions performed for the child is recognized. The 30-minute consecutive record often made it possible to follow actions and reactions through an episode, and many times several episodes. In addition, for a four year period there has been consistent effort through interviews and paper and pencil tests to discover children's views of typical classroom situations. To date, responses have been secured from

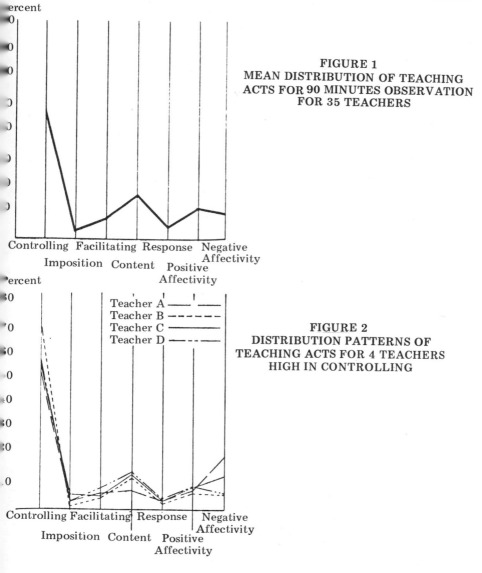

FIGURE 1
MEAN DISTRIBUTION OF TEACHING
ACTS FOR 90 MINUTES OBSERVATION
FOR 35 TEACHERS

FIGURE 2
DISTRIBUTION PATTERNS OF
TEACHING ACTS FOR 4 TEACHERS
HIGH IN CONTROLLING

some 1400 fifth and sixth graders in three states (5, 6). Interviews have been held with younger children, and with junior high youths.

As expected, children react in an individual manner; however, there is a great range of intensity of reaction. In general, there is a high degree of emotionality, with children responding to elements in the situations that were not intended or foreseen by adults. Another tentative finding was that for any given teacher behavior, from 7 to 20 percent of those to whom it was directed appeared to make no response. They were not involved or they failed to identify with the situation when given the opportunity in interviews or paper and pencil test. The mode for this noninvolvement was 14 percent. Most of the teachers are, of course, aware of the phenomenon of one or more children seeming not to be "with it."

Description of Teaching

Figure 1 presents the mean distribution of teaching acts performed by the teachers during three 30-minute periods of teaching. It is immediately clear that the largest number of teaching acts falls within the category of controlling functions. Figures 2 and 3 present the mean distributions of teaching acts for teachers who are among the highest and those who are among the lowest in the exercise of control in the classroom. Since the present report is devoted largely to an exposition of Controlling Functions, and the Development of Content, a brief definition of the other categories may be useful.

Teacher Imposition: These are acts where the teacher projects himself into the situation. For example: In a few classrooms without

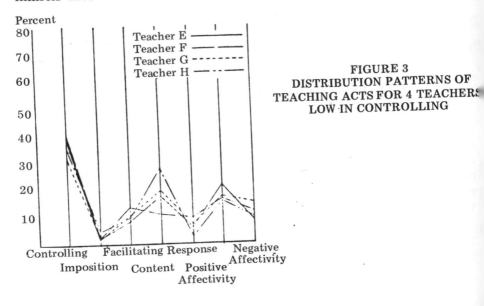

FIGURE 3
DISTRIBUTION PATTERNS OF
TEACHING ACTS FOR 4 TEACHERS
LOW IN CONTROLLING

routine procedures for supplies, the teacher might say over and over again, "Keep your seat, I'll bring it to you." Another is the expression of evaluation; e.g., on reading a story in a foreign locale, "Their names are certainly queer." Moralizing is another act that falls in this category. As may be noted in the figures, very few teaching acts fall in this category.

Facilitating: These acts may be thought of as management functions that are relatively neutral. All statements that designate time, change of schedule and so forth. Those information seeking acts that are non-evaluative; that is, the child is free to have or not have it, e.g.: "Who brought lunch money?" Rhetorical questions of "Wasn't that fun?" "Did you enjoy it?" "We're finished, aren't we?" Such questions, if they evoke a response, secure a chorus of "yes" or "no" as expected. More often than not the teacher does not wait for an answer.

These management functions differentiate least among teachers and are the most stable with a teacher's series of records.

Personal Response includes meeting the individual requests of children, listening to their personal interests and experiences unrelated to the content under consideration.

These are all positive responses and most often are interactions between a teacher and a single child.

Positive and Negative Functions need little comment since they are the praise and reproof categories. It is realized that the use of positive and negative reinforcement controls behavior; however, by their very nature these teaching acts are, as a group, more affectivity-laden. Therefore, it was deemed desirable to trace them out separately.

Although space does not permit an elaboration of these last three categories, it is hypothesized that they have much to do with the personal liking or not liking of the teacher. There is something in a personal response that conveys the idea, "You count—you are important enough for me to listen to you, and to do something just for you."

Approval and acceptance were expressed most often in a stereo-typed manner: "Fine," "Yes," "O.K.," "Good," "All right." Such expressions without a definite referent served the purpose of allaying tension. It was one way of saying, "All is well."

It is hypothesized that the acceptance of reprimands of any degree of intensity depends to a large extent on the teacher's use of *public criteria*. If he makes clear the elements in the situation that call for certain required behavior, children may protest, but they can accept the reprimand as just. Consistency of teacher behavior is another element in fairness.

In general, more acts of positive affectivity were recorded for teachers than of negative affectivity; however, Figure 2, depicting teachers high in control, shows two teachers who were more negative than positive in their teaching. The gross differences in distribution of teaching acts shown in Figures 2 and 3 suggest that the classroom is quite different for the children in attendance.

Controlling Functions

Our study showed that the teaching acts most frequently performed were those of control. By control, reference is not limited to discipline. Since these teachers were considered good teachers, their classes were well organized and generally attentive. By control is meant goal setting, directing the children to the precise thing to which they give attention. Not only is the content named for children, but they are held to a specific answer and processes of working. Such control is firm and pervasive. In many classrooms the control might be considered implacable. Sixty-eight percent of the teachers had one or more of their records with 50 percent or more of their teaching acts categorized as controlling.

The teacher most often wanted only *one* answer and refused all others. For example, a third grade was reporting on books read, then classifying them according to theme. One little girl made a few remarks about her book and then said, "It's a fantasy." The teacher immediately replied, "You mean imaginative, don't you?" No reward for the use of a divergent word or a suggestion of any relationship of differentiation between the two.

The control of content is exercised by the teacher in the structure of the *what* to give attention to. In a third grade arithmetic class each child had a foot rule. The teacher structured the group by saying. "Today, we are going to study the middle line. What is it called?" Several children answered. "One-third," "a fourth," "a half." One boy was busy measuring some paper on his desk and said, "This is 6¼ inches." (Correct) The teacher replied, "Just the middle line today. We just talk about the half."

As long as the question or statement that structures the class or the individual requires but *one* answer, the teacher is in absolute control. Nothing more may properly occur until the next question is asked. Such structure of content appears to evoke memory but little more in mental activity.

When structure is open, more than one answer is possible. Indeed, there may not be an absolutely right answer. For example, "What might happen if the new highway went across the state by one route instead of another?" Closed structure of content resulted in question and answer between teacher and class—it was strictly recitation. Open structure, with more than one answer possible, resulted in participation of several pupils before re-entry of the teacher in the situation. In other words, more ideas were generated and more pupils became involved in the work.

Control as Regulation of Who

Another phase of controlling behavior is that of regulating who will do what; answer questions, give the report, take lunch money to the office, etc. Such regulation can serve indirectly as punishment or as reward.

"Your work is finished, so you take the books to Mrs. Jones." At least a criterion of choice, "your work is done," is made public. In one episode the children were sharing their stories with one another and the teacher regulated after each story with, "Whom shall I choose, whom shall I ask to go next?" A child would then be named. As teacher choices followed one another, the excitement mounted over the who was to be next and not over the content of the stories.

Other teachers set up some *neutral* manner of regulating. "Write your names on the board when you are ready and we shall take them in order." Another teacher had children put a slip on a spindle. Their stories were then read in order of completion. Some teachers made charts of committees who worked at the various housekeeping and management chores a week at a time.

We found in one sixth grade that the students considered the teacher unfair. He was perplexed, so we tried to find out why this perception. It turned out that Lou and Hazel always got to answer the telephone. They sat next to the office and could answer without moving about unduly. This fact had not been shared with the children; consequently, all they saw was unfairness.

The use of *Public Criteria* for the controlling actions of the teacher is suggestive. It ameliorates the power of the teacher. It gives the authority an impersonal embodiment.

Control Over Many Activities

The controls exercised are expressed in all kinds of activities. It was difficult to get hold of the criteria used by teachers in their expression of control.

A child was making cut-out paper pears to be placed in a cornucopia poster filled with fruits and vegetables. The teacher said, "Why don't you make them bigger?"

> Child: I made them like they are on my grandfather's farm.
> T.: Get the picture from my desk and make them big like that.

The teacher judged in cases of altercation or conflict of interest. Incidentally, the conflict of interest was frequently between teacher and child or group. To illustrate, a teacher said:

> T.: Who do you wish to have help you with your reading?
> Child: Madeline.
> T.: How about Susan?
> Child: Jane.
> T.: Let's see. Mary would be a good one. Yes, go sit with Mary.

A junior high school teacher working with the English class putting out a paper said:

> T.: Here are some interesting things about the Navy that we could put in the paper. Who wants to write it?
> Agnes: I will. I read it and thought the boys might like it.
> T.: No, you already have three things in. I'll write it myself.

We hypothesize that consistent use of *Public Criteria* might aid in reducing the conflicts with authority. *Public Criteria* are situationally placed:

> T.: There is time for *one* story before noon.
> T.: We had trouble with a certain kind of problem yesterday; therefore, we will work on similar problems today.
> T.: The children using the saws are on the barn committee and must have them until they finish; therefore, you have to wait.

Public Criteria can also express the conventions and accepted ways of doing. "You have too many erasures on your paper to read it easily," instead of "I won't take a paper that looks like that."

Place of Controlling Functions

This investigator believes that it is the business of the teacher to manage (control, if you prefer) the classroom so that learning for all the children present may proceed. Controlling functions will undoubtedly constitute between 30 and 40 percent of a teacher's behavior; however, the power component may be ameliorated through the use of:

> Open-structure that permits some choice or requires more than one answer.
> Increased Regulation (*who* is to respond) that is neutral or done with public criteria that expresses the reason for the choice.
> Directions that are clear with limits set to reduce repetition of directions and lessen the number of reprimands.
> Rules that are group developed, situationally oriented, and enforceable. They should make sense to children.

Development of Content

There is a relationship between the development of content and the nature of the control exercised by structure. When the structure permits no exploration on the part of children it serves to delimit and restrict.

A primary class was reading about a baby elephant. They discussed its age and other things pertaining to the picture of the baby elephant. Finally Ben spoke up and said:

> Ben: Look, here is an elephant with a tusk.
> T.: Yes, that elephant is on the other page. Read this page and find out what Baby Elephant did when she got to the monkey cage.

It might have been profitable to raise the question why one elephant had tusks and the other did not. It can be hypothesized that the mental processes evoked by the different situations are likewise different.

In another class the teacher and class were looking at a large map of the two hemispheres, when one child asked where the local town was. The teacher replied, "It is about here, but can't be seen on this map. I'll get you one and you can find it and other towns you know."

The teaching acts that develop content elaborate and add to the content or problem under consideration. Response is made to the data placed in the situation by the children. It is believed that children involved in content have something to say. They are encouraged in this by the teacher who respects their efforts. The teacher *stimulates* by offering several suggestions of ideas or of activities that might be done. The choice of doing, however, remains with the child. (It is, of course, proper to give a direction or an assignment, which then would be an act of control.)

Evaluation that keeps content as a referent is in this category. To illustrate, "You have used several kinds of sentence structure in your composition. Very good." The phrase, "That's good," spoken after a child has read the composition does not tell him whether he was good to have written it at all, or good to have read it, or just good to have gotten through the episode. In terms of compositions, he has received nothing definite that helps him move ahead with his writing. He has received teacher approval. With most of the evaluation made in the form of generalized approval or disapproval, such expressions foster dependence on teacher instead of judgment and interest in the content.

If children and youth are to become interested in subject matter for its own sake, do they not need to link their own sake, do they not need to link their own experience and make their own personal inquiry in relationship to it? If children are not listened to, how can one know what concepts are developed or what interpretations are made?

An upper grade discussion had been going on concerning early California Indians.

> T.: Incidentally, did the California Indians have a pretty easy life?
> Arthur: No.
> T.: Yes they did, Arthur. Don't you remember? Who can tell me about it?

What logic was Arthur using in his reply? Was it strictly subjective, "I wouldn't have liked it," or had he assessed the situation with some judgment?

When do children use a variety of mental processes such as making comparisons, explaining with some logic, noting relationships, generalizing from a series of data? What kind of questions and teacher responses evoke what mental activity (7)?

Perhaps teachers need to develop what might be called *creative use of interruptions.*

Not long ago a mother reported the disgust of her kindergarten son whose teacher allegedly told him that he couldn't talk about dinosaurs until third grade. The child had been to the Dinosaur Monument and Museum with his family. While there, the father had bought each boy a book which had been read at home.

One can conjecture all kinds of reasons why the teacher did not wish to get off on dinosaurs. However, the question remains, "In what situations do teachers act in ways that children can see them as people who *aid* in their personal quest for knowing? Since this child's dinosaurs were tied to Vernal, Utah, it might have been very stimulating to listen to his story and also mention the Berea Tar Pits within the city of Los Angeles, as another locale where bones had been found.

It is, of course, possible that the child wanted attention only. Even so, the school can meet such personal needs of children through the use of their explorations and inquiries in the development of content. It is suggested that children's questions and remarks be integrated with the lesson plan of the teacher.

The present study of teaching found that the most prevalent series of teaching acts were in question-answer test or recitation situations. Far too many such situations were spent in working for the specific answer wanted by the teacher.

Of the total group of 41, only 3 teachers had all of their records with 20 or more of their teaching acts in this category of development of content. Seventy-four percent of all records had 20 percent or less of teaching acts falling in this category of exploration, amplification, utilization of children's questions and remarks, evaluation and stimulation. This category has been described as working with the content or problem and called *development of content.*

Some relationships of one category to another may be of interest. Development of Content and Negative Affectivity correlate—.42 significant at the .001 level in social studies. This relationship is not unexpected, since teachers who use many acts of Negative Affectivity are not responsive to children's ideas and explorations even in subject matter.

Personal Response is correlated—.35 with Controlling and a —.38 with Negative Affectivity. Again, this is not unexpected and it holds for all records regardless of kind of work the classes were doing.

The point of view expressed in this report is that teaching may be described in terms of functions the teacher behavior, verbal and non-verbal, performs for the child, group or class to whom it is directed. It was found possible to categorize such teaching acts in seven categories: Controlling, Imposition, Facilitating, Development of Content, Personal Response, Positive Affectivity, and Negative Affectivity.

Control of the class was exercised in varied activities, but particularly in terms of *what* to give attention to and *who* was to do what; also, the how of doing was prescribed and enforced.

Management of the classroom for learning is the teacher's job; therefore, control functions are necessary. It was suggested, however, that the power component the teacher holds may be reduced with changes in verbal behavior.

In dealing with subject matter, little attention was given to children's exploratory remarks or their questions. The questions teachers used for structure were usually closed; that is, asked for one *right* answer. It was suggested that one right answer evoked the use of recall as a mental process instead of stimulating a larger range of mental activity.

It was suggested that *responsiveness* on the part of the teacher to children's remarks, questions, personal experience (data they place in the situation), would lead them to greater involvement in content (subject matter) and stimulate use of higher mental processes.

Teachers demonstrated different patterns in teaching. Different patterns do affect the learning of children (8, 9).

BIBLIOGRAPHY

1. MARY JANE ASCHNER. "The Language of Teaching." In: *Language and Concepts in Education*, Edited by O. Smith and R. Ennis. Chicago: Rand McNally Co., 1961. 124 p.

2. MARIE M. HUGHES and ASSOCIATES. *The Assessment of the Quality of Teaching: A Research Report.* U.S. Office of Education Cooperative Research Project No. 353. Salt Lake City: The University of Utah, 1959.

3. J. KOUNIN, and P. GUMP. "The Ripple Effect in Discipline." *The Elementary School Journal*, Fall 1958, p. 158-62.

4. J. KOUNIN *et. al.* "Explorations in Classroom Management." *Journal of Teacher Education*, June 1961, p. 235-46.

5. ARTHUR CARIN. "Children's Perceptions of Selected Classroom Situations." Doctoral Dissertation, University of Utah. June 1959.

6. ELENA DE VANEY. "Perceptions Among Teachers and Students of Varying Cultural Backgrounds." Doctoral Dissertation, University of Utah. October 1960.

7. M. J. McCUE ASCHNER. "Asking Questions to Trigger Thinking." *NEA Journal*, September 1961, p. 44-46.

8. NED FLANDERS. *Teacher Influence: An Interaction Analysis.* U.S. Office of Education Cooperative Research Project No. 397. Minneapolis: University of Minnesota, 1960.

9. PAULINE SEARS. "What Happens to Pupils Within the Classroom of Elementary Schools." Paper read at American Educational Research Association meeting, Los Angeles, June 30, 1960.

A Model for Learner Success

A. BERT WEBB

Two of the foremost causes of difficulty in today's classrooms are lack of adequate lesson preparation by teachers and failure to provide students with alternative learning experiences. Although teachers generally subscribe to the assumption that planning is essential to success in teaching and learning, many tend to overlook the necessity of developing specific goals. A large number of those who do plan for instruction are remiss in their efforts because they tend to work on a limited day-to-day basis. Under these circumstances, there is little or no evidence of clear direction or adequate feedback regarding the success or failure of the learning experiences which are provided. Thus, if comprehensive feedback is not available, teachers tend to rely on "feelings" that a given lesson is successful or unsuccessful.

When operating at this level, teachers often move all students from one lesson to the next without providing perplexed learners with an opportunity to "redeem" themselves. Consequently, learner difficulties are ignored or undetected, and provisions are not made for eventual success. As a result many teachers become reinforced in their belief that only a small percentage of their students is capable of success.

An Instructional Model*

Every teacher has the responsibility to become familiar with at least one planning technique which reflects basic principles of instruction. One reliable approach to instruction is drawn from a model which provides systematic reference to essential parts of the overall process.

---

*A sequel to this work appears in *The Clearing House* (May 1972) entitled, "Learner Success: A Sequel." In this summary of research, Dr. Bert Webb utilizes the principles of the model.

Webb, A. Bert. "A Model for Learner Success." *The Clearing House.* May 1972. 46:540-544.

The model calls for pre-planning, selection of instructional procedures, measurement, prescription, and evaluation. The last two, prescription and evaluation, are frequently neglected because many teachers tend to become preoccupied with test scores and grades.

In order to clarify the purposes of the instructional model and to emphasize the importance of its ingredients, a brief discussion of each element is presented. Following this discussion, a simple device is submitted for the reader to consider as a guide to lesson preparation. Figure 1 is a representation of the model which reflects consideration for various learning styles.

Pre-planning

Typically, this step is characterized by reading several pages in a text and deciding which portions to use and which to omit. But the model suggests that a teacher be more sophisticated in deciding what to teach. Consequently, the teacher is called upon to consider three fundamental items: learner needs, environmental factors, and instructional objectives. It should become apparent to the reader that the model may be utilized by individuals or by teams of teachers. In determining learner needs, consideration is given to previous experience regarding the given concept under study. This may be done by developing pre-tests, by reference to standardized scores, or by any other accessible means.
The major concern, however, is to identify current levels of achievement for all learners being affected by the process.

Next, it is important to identify environmental factors which may dictate limitations or lend themselves to resourceful utilization. Such factors are time, space, materials available, sources of information, finances, personnel, etc. By considering these factors, one may make more realistic decisions about projected expectations of learner accomplishment.

The third factor to be considered in the pre-planning stage is the statement of objectives. The objectives should be specific and reasonable. Each objective should include a minimum level of acceptable performance which may be expected of learners and the conditions under which learners should be able to perform their tasks.[1]

Selection of Instructional Procedures

Teachers are called upon to make two kinds of decisions: what to

---

[1] *Writing Behavioral Objectives, an* inexpensive paperback by David E. Hernandez, is a valuable guide for teachers who wish to know more about the mechanics of stating objectives.

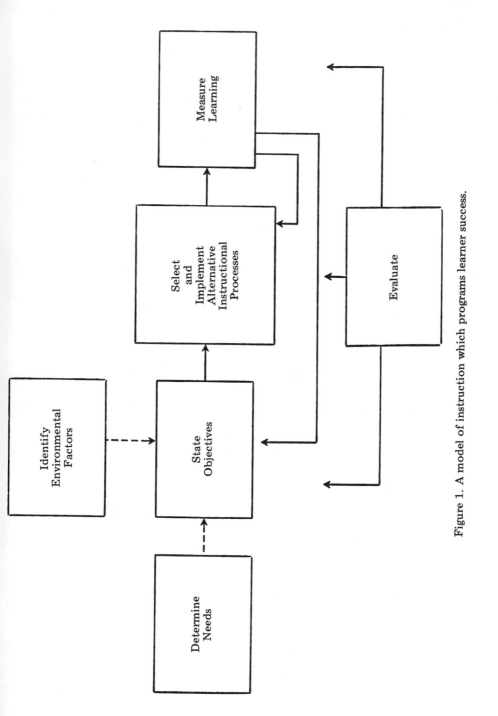

Figure 1. A model of instruction which programs learner success.

teach, and how to teach it. The pre-planning stage of this model provides important items for the teacher to consider when deciding what to teach. The process of instruction component is the stage in which the teacher decides how to teach it. Using this model, he may organize his instruction to fit a conventional classroom setting or a diversified approach, depending upon the nature of his own situation. This model may be utilized equally as well in either case, regardless of the organizational structure.

In making his instructional decisions, the teacher must consider the appropriateness of such techniques as lecture, question-answer, group process, discovery, independent study, audiotapes, videotapes, films, filmstrips, slides, unipacs, readings, field trips, simulation, laboratory work, direct experiences, etc. The decision to utilize any given method of instruction should be based upon previous decisions regarding the instructional environment. Alternative approaches are provided so that participants may progress in accordance with their own unique learning styles or preferences. In the event of difficulty, other alternatives may be selected in order to provide additional opportunity for success.

Measurement and Prescription

This component of the model is crucial. It is in this realm that many teachers are derelict in their duty. Generally, upon completion of an instructional task, the teacher applies some form of measurement and "gives" grades. He then directs the attention of his students toward another unit of study . . . and leaves many of them stranded between previously stated objectives and the intended goals. He is frequently quite willing to begin another lesson on a false assumption that the previous lesson was successful, or on an assumption that there is "not enough time" to reteach a given concept. Essentially, then, the teacher's behavior reflects his values. If he were to examine his values he would address himself to these questions:

(1) Do I attempt to build upon learner weaknesses (known or unknown)?
(2) Is my purpose only to "cover material," or is it to facilitate successful learning experiences for as many of my students as possible?

Measurement, according to this model, should be applied at reasonable intervals to determine the level of learner goal attainment. The measuring device should be designed to assess achievement in accordance with expectations which are delineated in the statement of objectives.

The process of prescribing alternative learning experiences for those who experience difficulty during their initial efforts to reach the prespecified goals greatly expands their probability of success. The teacher is charged with the responsibility of assuming that many of these "stragglers" are capable of achieving the objectives if given further opportunity to do so.

Essentially, this process places the teacher in a position to do something with assessment results rather than merely to assign grades. It gives him an opportunity to pinpoint learner weaknesses and to prove that he really *wants* his pupils to achieve certain goals. By identifying learner deficiencies in a given situation, the teacher may prescribe certain activities designed to redirect perplexed students through various similar learning experiences which lead to the original instructional goals. Thus, the unsuccessful learner has additional opportunities to reach predetermined goals and to experience success, even though the success may come more slowly than that of other pupils.

After all, instructional endeavors should not be reduced to contests between learners and the clock or among the learners themselves. For in those situations, emphasis seems to be placed upon failure rather than on success. Learners are pitted against each other, with some "winning" and many portrayed as losers. It seems much more humane to structure learning experiences in such a way that those who do not achieve as rapidly as others still have access to the same learning goals as their peers. Why not give them more than one opportunity to grasp a concept? *Individual progress* is a teacher's concern, not competitive comparison. Prescriptive instruction makes goal attainment accessible to nearly all; but one-shot, group-oriented instruction is suitable only for a few.

Evaluation

Evaluation should be comprehensive and continuous. It should be used to pinpoint possible instructional weaknesses, as well as to isolate discrepancies between objectives and outcomes. In other words, evaluation of the instructional process should tell the teacher whether he directs learning experiences as he desires. It also provides feedback to him regarding the adequacy of his measuring devices and the appropriateness of the objectives. Consequently, by using evaluation as an integral part of this model, the teacher is able to make modifications which enable him to improve his effectiveness.

Lesson Planning

Now, where does lesson planning fit into the scheme as presented in the model? It is a simple matter of asking five questions which are derived from the model of instruction. In planning for instruction, the teacher should organize his units and/or lessons around the following questions:

(1) *What do I want to accomplish?* To answer this question, the teacher must state his objectives clearly.
(2) *How do I want to accomplish it?* Here, the teacher must draw upon his resources so that he may decide which process or processes to use.
(3) *What materials am I going to use?* Once again, a resourceful teacher utilizes reliable instructional aids to achieve his goals.
(4) *How do I know if I accomplished my task?* The teacher constructs measuring devices which are derived from his answer to the first question. These devices provide him with valuable information regarding the success or failure of his endeavors. They also provide him with sources of learner deficiencies.
(5) *If I have not accomplished my task with each pupil, what must I do now?* Here, the teacher decides whether learning problems occurred as a result of unrealistic teacher expectations, inadequate instruction, or learner difficulty. He then employs prescriptive instruction so that original or revised goals may be attained.

These five simple questions may serve as the skeleton of a unit of study or as the outline of a daily lesson plan. However, a caveat is in order; the teacher is reminded that greatest benefits will not be derived unless the complete outline is used. He must plan wisely, select instructional procedures and materials appropriately, measure and evaluate accurately, *and* he must be willing to prescribe additional learning experiences which are designed to promote learner success.

REFERENCES

1. BLOOM B. S., J. T. HASTINGS, and G. F. MADAUS. *Handbook on Formative and Summative Evaluation of Student Learning.* New York: McGraw-Hill, 1971.

2. CARROLL, JOHN B. "A Model for School Learning," *Teachers College Record*, 1963, Vol. 64, pp. 723-733.

3. HERNANDEZ, DAVID E. *Writing Behavioral Objectives*, New York: Barnes and Noble, 1971.

4. HOUGH, JOHN B. "Ideas for the Development of Programs Relating to Interaction Analysis." Unpublished report, Projects to Advance Creativity in Education Conference, Tustin, Michigan, August 23-25, 1966.

5. WEBB, A. BERT. "Effects of the Use of Behavioral Objectives and Criterion Evaluation Upon the Classroom Progress of Adolescents." Unpublished Doctor's dissertation, The University of Tennessee, 1971.

The Human In The System

LOUIS J. RUBIN

In America, success in school is closely linked with vocational opportunity and, in turn, with material affluence during adulthood. Whether a boy is destined to fill gas tanks or debate in a courtroom is in large measure determined by the number of years he spends in school. What is learned, how much is learned, and the amount of emotional scar tissue that is accumulated in the process all are secondary; the object of the game is to acquire the degrees which are the price of admission to well-paid occupations and the "good life." That much of the money which ultimately rewards success in school may, in time, be spent on psychiatrists, pills, and various other forms of anxiety-control does not seem to be important. Nor is the possibility that a man who fills gas tanks may lead a thoroughly satisfying life, and a lawyer may be a desperately unhappy person, of any consequence. In our way of things it generally is considered better to be rich than poor—and if affluence alone mattered, it probably would be.

Because of the tie between schooling and earning power, the expectations of parents regarding the education of their children are largely conditioned by the social ethos, and their standards for judging the quality of schools are clearly drawn. In the eyes of parents, completing school (irrespective of whatever it is that is completed) is crucial. Thus, good schools are recognized as ones which enable their students to go further in the educational hierarchy, and bad schools are ones which do not. Consider for example, that although drop-outs sometimes are happier after they leave school, their parents invariably are disappointed.

The use of the school system as a control-value for entry into desirable vocations, coupled with the aspirations parents have for their children, results in a great emphasis on acquiring information and passing tests in the classroom—on cognitive instruction. It is scarcely surprising,

Rubin, Louis J. "The Human in the System." *California Elementary Administrator.* December 1970. 34:19-21.

therefore, that most teachers are predominantly interested in the kind of learning that can be measured on standardized tests. For a teacher's reputation and esteem depend upon equipping students to score well on such tests. Reducing a child's anxiety or enhancing his self-concept, on the other hand, do not carry much of a reputational pay-off. In the typical classroom, resultingly, the cognitive goals are the chief thing and the stage is set for drill, repetition, and occasionally, the mastery of test-taking for emotional repression.

Children, however, are not so made. Whereas the teacher strives for knowledge of book, the child strives for knowledge of self. Whereas the teacher—at the day's end—counts the number of pages covered, the child counts his good and bad experiences. Whereas the teacher worries about intellectual gains, the child worries about emotional losses. There is, in short, a fundamental conflict of interest between teacher and pupil in the schoolroom. One is driven by the god of cognition and the other by the god of effect. What students are after, in other words, is a feeling of personal adequacy. They want to be liked by their teacher, accepted by their peers, and applauded by their parents; they want, in sum, *to be winners rather than losers*. So, when kids do learn, it is not so much because they prize the subject-matter, but because they fear the loss of the success symbols which are withheld when they do not learn.

The consequences of all this are of course often disastrous. Even with the winners—with children who successfully perform the required cognitive tricks—a great opportunity is lost. Instead of using cognitive insight as a springboard to emotional growth, instead of searching-out a sane balance between feelings and facts, teachers settle for half-best. And for the losers, school becomes an intensely destructive experience. It breeds a familiarity with failure and a growing sense of impotence: once the student falls far enough behind, there is little hope of ever catching up. We have produced, through all this, a vast number of children who hate school, who doubt their capacities, and who, for the remainder of their lives, may be defeated by a defective self-concept.

The New Scene?

Currently, a radical answer to this problem is reflected in the spate of "new schools" which recently have arisen. Much about them is commendable and, in instances, they well may point the way for the "old schools." Although these counter-school movements vary from place to place, most of the schools take humaneness and freedom as their cardinal principles. Emotional support is a first order of business, there often is a sensitive effort to avoid needless trauma, and the child is free to pursue his own interests. The learning environment (at least in the best of the lot) is clearly more therapeutic than in the majority of regular schools. But with respect to the other side of the educational obligation, the expansion of intellect, their effectiveness is becoming increasingly questionable. If the children of the free schools do not learn something of man's accumulated wisdom, if they cannot add a column of figures properly, they too will fail both themselves and their society. They may not, for example, forever be able to resist the temptations of good jobs and affluence. And, as their tutors hope, if they are to become agents of social reform during their adulthood, a well-informed mind will surely not be a disadvantage. Put another way, in their present shape, the new schools may be a different kind of excess rather than an authentic alternative.

Social institutions, the school among them, must of necessity undergo constant readjustments. Not only does the nature of the human predicament shift from time to time, technical capabilities grow increasingly sophisticated, and the society periodically displays a willingness to deal anew with pervasive problems from the past which have remained unresolved. Schools, consequently, will always be faced with the need to deal with their own weaknesses, for howsoever good their quality, the changing social scene will continue to make realignments necessary. The present time is no exception to this historical condition. Although today's schools are better than any which have existed before, they suffer nevertheless from a variety of infirmities, some of which could not have been foreseen a generation ago. Parts of the curriculum have become archaic; teaching—once an authentic helping profession—has in cases reduced itself to uninspired routine; a growing bureaucracy has found it increasingly difficult to be responsive to the diverse demands of a pluralistic public; and, crucially, the system itself has been unable to adjust rapidly enough to the extraordinary character of the current youth generation. Definitively different from any previous generation, a subculture unto itself, youth has found it both more important and more difficult to gratify psychological needs. It is thus more vulnerable to, and more fearful of, the pain and emasculation which accompany sustained anxiety. It is perhaps for this reason that the young are so profoundly interested in their own emotional lives.

The natural linkage between emotion and intellect is hardly a new idea. Its importance has long been acknowledged in the literature. Consider, for example, these words of Prescott, written fully thirty-two years ago:

"Schools must help children to understand the nature of social conflicts, to recognize the rights of others in the struggle for security, to tolerate reasonable social experimentation aimed at ameliorating suffering and insecurity, and to accept personal responsibilities and a share in the burden of caring for the unfortunate and underprivileged. These seem to be the essential elements of educational policy necessary to social integration.

"Schools also have a differential function varying from individual to individual. They must seek the personal adjustment of children who are thwarted or insecure under immediate conditions. They must help some to develop fortitude to endure that which simply cannot be changed. They must guide individual adolescents into socially useful forms of self-realization and assist them in the discovery of means for rich and satisfying experience. . . . Schools must be reorganized to avoid being, themselves, the cause of frustration, or loss of status, of unrealizable ambitions, of deep resentment against social authority, of repeated humiliation. To accomplish their differential aims, the schools often must stand as a buffer between the child and some social processes. They must be of definite assistance to children who are misunderstood, exploited, incompetent, or underprivileged. This is no easy task. The social order itself is greatly confused and the future is quite obscure."[1]

The Ritual of Polarizing

The end destination, therefore, is a point on which there is widespread agreement; *it is the question of route that is open to dispute.* My own conviction is that the answer lies in cultivating what is most simply described as a wise and humane teacher—one sensitive to the connective tissue between mind and spirit. We must indeed be accountable, to ourselves and the social order; machines and instructional systems, to be sure, do have their place; but it is the humane teacher who best can negotiate the delicate compromise between the free school, where a child can spend his days kicking a can or throwing pebbles, and the establishment school, where often a child must put aside feeling, imagination, and creativity in order to survive.

It is not a mere middle-of-the-road policy that is argued for here. Rather, it is for a conception of learning which respects the inseparability of rational thought and emotional experience. A skillful teacher can draw forth the psychological overtones of an intellectual

---

[1] Daniel A. Prescott, "Emotion and the Educative Process," American Council on Education: Washington, D.C., 1938.

problem and, conversely, the intellectual insights which illuminate and clarify an emotional hang-up. Such a teacher is neither compelled to make use of blind walks, nude encounter groups, and other faithless rites—nor to seek educational salvation in the memorization of a list of the world's largest rivers. The cultivation of such wise and humane teachers and the construction of a school system which permits them to survive are together the twin challenges we face.

As the movement to reform education mounts, a major controversy has been kindled. The roots of the dispute lie in the long-standing conflict between utilitarianism and humanism. Whenever the question of changing human behavior arises, the morality and efficacy of manipulation soon become critical issues. Maturation—the psychological and intellectual torque of human growth—is, in essence, the transitional process between a nurturing environment and self-sufficiency. Are we therefore to trust in the sanative benefits of healthy experience, or are we to place our faith in scientific precision and assume that human behavior—because it is predictable—can be shaped and controlled by calculated intervention?

There are no sure answers, save for the fact that each position offers advantages and disadvantages. Human behavior *is* lawful. No action is without its cause. And the causes—the energizing forces which govern our conduct—rarely are simplistic. They are, instead, a complicated mix of perception, attitude, belief, value, and identity. Because reward and punishment are powerful incentives, they can indeed be used to regulate human action. If we wish, we can tame the spirit of leaders (and followers) as effectively as we train dogs and parrots. The question is, however, whether such training is ethical or permanent, and whether it destroys something that is peculiarly human.

Manipulation vs. Self-Direction

If we resist the temptation to manipulate people's behavior, we can also stimulate change through the psychodynamics of self-evaluation. By making it possible for an individual to increase his awareness, to gain new insights which enlarge his sense of options, we unleash the human capacity to resolve problems creatively. Such creative freedom is the seminal element of growth, for in authentic growth each man is responsible only to himself.

The difference between self-directed growth and other-directed conditioning is therefore clear. Both spawn behavioral change, but in the former impulse stems from the desire and will to become more adequate, and in the latter it stems from the bribe of reward or the threat of punishment.

We can program people as surely as we program machines and obtain machine-like precision, but in so doing, we also will obtain machine-like insensitivity and rigidity. Machines, even magnificent ones, must be readjusted again and again as circumstances require. The free human spirit, in contrast, is self-adjusting.

We look to our leaders for the vision of something better, and for the strength and imagination to take us from where we are to where we should be. Thus, the control of one's destiny is the indispensable precondition of leadership. But the purpose of programming is to impose constraints, while the purpose of leadership is to shatter them. One therefore destroys the other.

I do not mean by these warnings to imply that the science of behaviorism is without merit. The careful observation and recording of behavior need not interfere with imagination, free thought, and the expression of feelings. Once observed, however, we often attribute cause to the wrong stimulus. For example, the child may find the behavior itself intrinsically more satisfying than the nickel which is offered as a reward. It is also true, of course, that every teacher seeks to influence the behavior of the children in her charge, and that the children, like their adult counterparts, respond to the reinforcements which follow their actions. If we wish pupils to learn a particular behavior it would be senseless to deny the laws of operant conditioning. Unless great care is taken, however, we may unintentionally teach, as well, some bad notions, and we may find that the child's inalienable right to teacher affection has been subverted into the bribery of a conditional pay-off. The pitfalls rather than the potency of the behavioristic method should give us pause.

On Target

To return to the opening theme, then, four predominant needs provide a setting in which to consider the use of instructional systems: *first*, the need to conceive of schooling, not as a period of vocational preparation, but as a stream of events which cut deeply into the child's experiential record, leaving permanent markings; *second*, the need to conjoin intellectual development with the regular psychological exercise that builds strong emotional muscle; *third*, the need to invent alternative approaches to learning, borrowing all that is wholesome from the new experimental schools; and *fourth*, the need to capitalize as often as possible upon self-directed growth, progressively lessening reliance upon manipulative conditioning.

Good learning systems ensure that pupils reach predetermined objectives which lead to change in behavior. As such, they are immensely valuable. Properly engineered systems aim at a clearly defined target, marshal the most powerful resources available, make due allowances for the situational constraints in which the learning is to be accomplished, and provide a means for ascertaining whether the goal has been reached. Construed in this way, a learning system benefits equally the third-grade teacher who wants her students to learn elementary computational skills and the superintendent who wants to decrease drug consumption among high school students. Good systems, in short, increase the precision and efficiency of expended energy.

The wise administrator, therefore, does well to harness systems theory to his task. It should be remembered, however, that *an incomplete system is no system at all*. A teaching program, a computer, an evaluation scheme, a technique for individualizing instruction—all are but pieces of a potential whole. Only when they are integrated, when in concert they constitute a skillfully organized set of procedures that produce a specified end, do they create a legitimate system. The abiding danger, self-evidently, is that if any of the essential components are left out or misused, the worth of the system is destroyed. Systems, by definition, cannot be used piecemeal. And it is also clear that even a potent system, in and of itself, is no guarantee of educational quality. A good system, deployed toward a bad end, is a double tragedy; for when this is the case an undesirable goal is accomplished with spectacular proficiency. It is insufficient, consequently, to think of the system alone; system and objective must be judged in a body.

Learning is a natural whole, the parts of which support one another in some inexplicable way. Disciplined and systematic study, the free flow of imagination, and the search for the inner peace of emotional stability are branches of the same tree. All feed the school's highest ambition: the enrichment of the person's life so that joy, satisfaction, and meaning transcend what is simply existence. To cut off one branch in favor of another would be to commit the fatal error.

Let us by all means put our instructional systems to good use. So too can we exploit what psychologists have learned about behavioral change. But let us, at the same time, guard against mindless authoritarianism, against the destruction of independent thought, and against the substitution of habit and routine for the inward freedom that so easily is lost.

Chapter II

The Novice Teacher And His First Position

Elementary education majors in the 70's are faced with a challenge which comparatively few teachers have experienced in the past—that of actually attaining a teaching position when they graduate. The fact is that students are graduating from colleges of education at a far greater rate than the need for teachers in the public schools has evolved. The challenge to the elementary major of the 70's desirous of attaining any position in teaching is to become fully acquainted with the procedures most likely to be beneficial to him as an applicant. Since professors often treat this aspect rather briefly, this Chapter will provide the reader with several specific steps for gaining the teaching position for which he has prepared.

The question of greatest concern to most novice teachers after securing a teaching position is "how do I begin the school year?". Few beginning teachers have had the opportunity to experience the opening—or the closing—of an elementary school year during their student teaching assignment. Since most student teachers simply adapted to routines established by the regular classroom teacher over a long period of time, it is little wonder that the beginning teacher exhibits an unusually high concern over this phenomenon. Therefore, the authors have included several articles to assist the novice in his preparation for those first few days on the job.

How To Find The Job You Want In Education

DANIEL FRIEDMAN

If you are a teacher who has remained in one school system for a number of years and quite suddenly you want to change your position, or if you are seeking employment in education for the first time, you may feel uncertain about how to proceed. Some of the many considerations involved are discussed here.

Developing a job-seeking philosophy. Such a philosophy is usually not stated but is implicit in the actions and inactions of the applicant. The following suggestions may be useful.

1. An application for a position should always be submitted in good faith. Never apply for a job which you would not accept if offered.
2. Schools and their personnel practices vary greatly. Seek connection with those systems that interest you most.
3. Always conduct yourself with dignity and in a professional manner.
4. Do not allow yourself to feel rejected by letters of refusal. The chosen candidate may be better qualified. Or the choice may be based on factors over which you have no control.
5. Start your efforts as early as possible. Although the peak number of positions-open listings occurs in April and May, many are known before then.
6. Of course you will notify your present employer and respect the contract, written or verbal, that you have with him.

Learning about available positions. The following list of sources of information on job openings may be helpful.

1. College and university placement bureaus (most commonly used).
2. Local school and/or county districts; personal contacts.
3. NEA Search is a computer-based locator and referral service for matching job applicants and teacher vacancies. Write to NEA Headquarters, 1201 Sixteenth St., N.W., Washington, D.C. 20036, for application forms.
4. Magazines: *Saturday Review*—classified section; state journals of education—single ads; organs of educational associations and societies in your field of specialization.
5. Newspapers: *The New York Times*, Teacher Openings section (third Sunday of each month); the local newspapers—classified and other advertisements.
6. State and federal education departments.
7. Teacher employment agencies—private, state, and federal. (These agencies advertise in educational periodicals and are listed in telephone directories.)
8. For further information, read "How to Obtain a Teaching Job," a chapter in *Manual of Certification Requirements for School Personnel in the United States*—a 1967 book; NEA; list price $5.00.
9. *For administrators.* The magazine *Nation's Schools* lists staff changes in its "About People" section; *The School Administrator*, an AASA (American Assn. of School Administrators) monthly publication, lists some staff changes in the section "Here and There"; *American School Board Journal* lists staff changes in its "Administrative News" section.

Applying for a position. Once you have found out about several openings that you might fill, what do you do?

1. The accepted procedure is to write a letter to the prospective employer indicating: (a) your interest in a specific position and your availability; (b) your education, experience, and personal data (frequently listed on a separate resume sheet); (c) where your credentials may be obtained.
2. Do not call the employer. Usually your letter will be answered within two weeks. This may be a confirmation of the receipt of your letter, a request for an interview, and/or an application form. The latter should be filled out and returned promptly.
3. Be certain that your credentials are up-to-date. Mention recent work experiences and include letters of reference from recent employers. If you have no credentials file, get one.

Most colleges have a placement office to serve their graduates. If you wish, you may use a private agency. Either of these will save your time, that of persons who recommend you, and that of prospective employers.

Participating in the interview. There's no need to dread this aspect of changing employment. The following points are worth some consideration in advance.

1. Observe the usual conventions about appearance, punctuality, and remembering names.
2. Try to assess the personality of the interviewer. What can you do or say to establish rapport?
3. Do not be overconfident and at no time talk down to the interviewer. Try not to disagree with him but at the same time do not be self-effacing. Temper all judgments but take a firm stand when appropriate.
4. Stress the experiences and accomplishments that set you apart from others.
5. Aim to project a mature, even-tempered, flexible, open-minded image.
6. Be prepared to give a five-minute thumbnail sketch of your background.
7. Answer questions honestly.
8. Be prepared for the role-reversal period (usually coming near the end of the interview) when you may be called on to question the interviewer.
9. Leave the discussion of salary to the interviewer. But if he does not introduce the subject, you can do so just prior to the close of the interview.

Deciding which position to accept. An offered contract can be held for several days in most cases. Assuming several positions are offered, base your decision on the following factors:

1. What is the potential for professional growth?
2. How challenging is the position?
3. How satisfied will you be after a year or more?
4. Do supervisory practices in the system seem suited to your personality and way of teaching?
5. Salary, a traditional measuring factor, should be evaluated in terms not only of actual money but also of fringe benefits.

Keeping a level head. To find the right job requires time and effort. Begin your search early. Remain calm and confident. Bear in mind that education needs you as much as you need a position in your chosen field.

What Your Placement Office Should Mean To You

RONALD E. WALTON

Over the past several decades, the process of recruiting teachers has grown from an informal, non-structured procedure to a highly sophisticated, well-organized program in most school systems. With the phenomenal growth of school districts, administrators have discovered that it is necessary to enter the arena of competition if quality teachers are to be attracted and retained by the local system.

Running parallel to the growth of teacher recruitment programs has been the development of services offered by Bureaus of Educational Placement or Teacher Placement. School systems have come to rely heavily in filling vacancies on the advice and counsel of placement officials on the college and university campus. Some of the reasons for this reliance are discussed in the paragraphs which follow.

Of the reasons involved in the increased confidence of school officials in Educational Placement Bureaus, one should be of special interest to the prospective teacher. The profit motive is all-important in the method of operation of the private employment agency. This motive is absent, of course, with campus placement bureaus.

It is only logical that a private placement service must make money if it is to remain in business. Therefore, monetary considerations often take precedence over the candidate's suitability for a particular position. This, coupled with the fact that most beginning or experienced teachers can ill-afford that percentage cut from the first year's salary on the new job, makes dealing with the private placement agency less than desirable.

A second reason for a strengthened relationship between public

Walton, Ronald E. "What Your Placement Office Should Mean to you." *ASCUS*. 1969 Annual. Pp. 9-10.

school employing officials and college placement bureaus is related directly to the belief and knowledge that a candidate will be recommended only for those positions for which he is qualified. And "qualified" in this case is not limited to matters of certification, but includes the broader connotation of matching candidates to specific positions in specific school systems.

Just as the registrant has certain preferences in the placement process, such as size of school district desired, geographical consider- ations, etc., likewise the school district has certain preferences with respect to the characteristics sought in employing teachers. School administrators have confidence in the ability of university placement officials to prevent the mis-match from taking place in recommending candidates for positions.

A third aspect of the service offered by placement officials which is of vital importance to school personnel officials is the integrity of the credentials. Although many school districts have highly developed patterns of screening applicants for teaching positions, the fact still remains that a good set of credentials from the college placement office serves as a positive factor in the final decision-making process.

To the personnel director of a school system, the college placement credentials represent the written record. A well-organized, neatly composed, and up-to-date set of papers may be responsible for creating the impression needed to cinch the job. On the other hand, a carelessly accumulated, inaccurate set of credentials may well spell defeat for the applicant.

A concern which is equally important to the prospective teacher and the employing official, is the counseling service provided by the college placement bureau. Except for those registrants who are pinpointed geographically, the task of selecting the proper position is not a simple one. There are few individuals or agencies any better equipped to be of assistance in this process than the college placement office.

Placement counselors are generally well-informed in matters of certi- fication, tenure laws, salary schedules, reciprocity, etc. In addition, the placement bureau office usually maintains a complete, up-to-date file of recruitment brochures which will answer many of the registrants ques- tions relative to a specific school district. In this respect, the registrant can certainly consider the placement office a valuable resource. Simulta- neously, the local school official can rest assured that the prospective teacher has been given accurate information about teaching in his community or state.

To further illustrate what was previously mentioned as the changing nature of teacher recruitment procedures, and to emphasize the importance of the placement bureau in this process, perhaps a brief description of the mode of operation of most school district personnel offices would be appropriate.

Most school systems classify the applicants for positions into three categories: the walk-in, the write-in, and the recommended. The walk-in is the individual who just happens to be in town and decides to drop by the personnel office to see about a teaching position. He may or may not be able to talk with the personnel director since there were no advanced arrangements made by the applicant. He is generally given an application form by the office secretary which he either fills out on the spot or returns at a later date. Quite obviously, the chances of this individual receiving serious consideration for a job are slim. The reaction of the personnel director is generally that this may well be characteristic of this individual's performance as a teacher—hap-hazard and ill-planned.

The write-in candidate also has some rather imposing odds to overcome in order to be a front-running applicant. The very fact that the individual has to resort to writing a letter of application may indicate that the distance between the applicant and the school system is great enough that a personal interview may not be possible. Few school districts are willing to fill vacancies with individuals who have not been seen personally. On the other hand, if distance is not really a limiting factor, but the individual just decides to write a letter of inquiry, in more instances than not, the response will be a form letter accompanied by an application. The only problem here is that the district may have several file drawers of such inquiries without any real knowledge as to which applicants are worthy of serious consideration.

If, however, the school system has a vacancy which it reports to the Teacher Placement Bureau, and in return receives several sets of credentials to review, the reaction of the personnel director to the recommended candidates is going to be quite different from that of the previous two categories. Because of the completeness of the credentials and the implicit faith most public school officials have in the quality of the recommendations of placement counselors, the registrant suggested by the teacher placement bureau will find himself in strong contention for a position with the district of his choice.

Your placement bureau should mean a great deal to your present state of security relative to seeking and finding the right job, and to your professional future. It is no longer safe to assume that one can land a job via the "string pulling" route. If a district hires on that basis, it could be labeled as a questionable place to teach. Therefore, the prospective teacher will need assistance of the highest level in obtaining that first teaching position. The writer proposes that this kind of assistance is available from college placement bureaus.

As a practicing school administrator, the very best advice which can be given to college seniors about to enter the teaching profession is to register with the college placement bureau, keep the bureau informed as your specific plans for locating are formulated, and follow the bureau's instructions relative to acknowledging notices sent describing certain positions available. By following this advice, the interests of both the registrant and the school district will be effectively served by the college placement bureau.

SCHOOL is for . . .
PROFESSIONAL GOAL SETTING

*A letter directed to a prospective employer is a vital
step toward securing a good teaching position. What will
your letters communicate about you as a potential candidate for a
teaching position? Can you sell yourself?*

Do Your Letters Sell You?

HAROLD REGIER and LODA NEWCOMB

Inquiry Letter

The inquiry letter, one tool of position seeking, is a means of finding vacancies. The letter asks: Is a teaching vacancy for which I am qualified anticipated? The inquiry is *not an application for a position.* Generally it is directed to school administrators in a specific geographical area and asks whether vacancies exist or are expected. It requests procedures to be followed for applying if the school is seeking candidates in your field.

The letter should clearly indicate that this is an *inquiry* and should include such information as teaching level and assignment desired, degree and/or date of completion, major and minor teaching fields, and other qualifications based on education and experience. Mention that credentials are on file and available at your college or university placement office. Naturally, the credentials should be prepared in advance of your letter writing and be available immediately upon request by an administrator.

Usually the smaller school-district and college administrators respond to inquiries by giving information about positions vacant or by reporting that they have no vacancies in your field. Large school systems which have vacancies in most teaching fields each year, usually send an application form and literature about their schools and communities

Regier, Harold., and Newcomb, Loda. "Do Your Letters Sell You?" *ASCUS.* 197
Annual. Pp. 9-10.

Complete and return the application form immediately so that your name will be placed on the list of available candidates. Carefully follow instructions in completing the application form.

Candidates should not be surprised if some of their letters of inquiry remain unanswered. Shortage of clerical assistance and many inquiries in some areas of the country result in few acknowledgments of letters received.

Application Letter

Writing a suitable application letter that will attract attention and give you an opportunity to interview administrators is the first step in securing a position. The application letter is only one of the vital steps, but it may create the first impression of your ability to communicate and may determine whether you are considered for employment. The first impression may be either favorable or unfavorable. From your letter the administrator may learn many things about you so keep him, his interests, and his needs in mind as you write.

Placement personnel will provide you with additional information about writing letters. Construct your letter so that it reflects your abilities and works for you. Administrators look for creativity and orignality in teachers they employ. Your letter should reflect these qualities.

Good-quality stationery is essential in writing any business letter. White business paper, usually bond, 8½" x 11" and an envelope of a standard size is appropriate. A typewritten one-page letter with the writer's complete address and an ink signature is recommended. After you write the letter, study it carefully to make sure the content is clear and concise and that spelling, English usage, and punctuation are correct. Determine whether the letter appears neat, clean, and correctly spaced. Does the letter sound like you, not someone else? Have an impersonal advisor review your letter, suggest improvements, and make corrections. Keep in systematic order carbon copies of letters you write since you will need this information for future reference.

The full name and the title of the school administrator should be used if this information is available. Obtain the correct spelling of names. Either the placement office or the library will have directories to assist you in securing the name of the superintendent of schools, the director of personnel, or the appropriate college official. When your letter requests a reply, enclose an addressed, stamped envelope.

The content of the letter should be clear and concise with an opening paragraph that includes a statement of your reason for writing the letter, the type of position for which you are applying, and the source of the information that a vacancy exists. Write short paragraphs for ease in reading. Give brief statements about your qualifications, major and minor fields, work experience, military status, location and date of your student teaching, and other experiences that qualify you for the position. Always include personal data, giving facts rather than generalizations about yourself. Avoid requesting a certain salary. Most schools can pay only amounts specified on their salary schedules. If you are a public school teacher, indicate either whether you hold a certificate or what certificate, credential, or license you can secure upon graduation.

In your application you may present items that reveal your human side. Discuss prior experience, if any, and tell about your interests and hobbies. Mention that your credentials (confidential file) are available and give the complete address of your college placement office.

If at all possible make yourself available for a personal interview. If the place is some distance away, state when you can most conveniently travel to the community. Often interviews are scheduled during vacations or weekends. Generally you should try to interview as early as possible after your application letter and credentials have been reviewed by school employers.

Data Sheet

A data sheet or resume is sometimes used by a candidate who has more information to transmit than he can incorporate in a one-page application letter. The letter is then shortened and the data page added. A brief application letter and a data sheet make a better impression than a lengthy letter. Candidates with considerable experience, lists of activities, publications, military experience, and other personal information helpful in describing qualifications, use the data sheet for convenience. Again, the name of the placement bureau where your credentials are on file should be listed on either the data sheet or the letter. A sample data sheet may be helpful as a guide, but the candidate should prepare one to meet his needs. An impression of how systematic and orderly you are is communicated by the form and the style you use in preparing these materials.

Follow-up Letter

To follow up on previous communications, including on-campus interviews, candidates need to write letters. To thank the interviewer for his time and for the opportunity of being interviewed, the candidate usually writes a letter within a week and restates his interest in a position in the district. Briefly reviewing his qualifications for the type of position in which he is interested is helpful. Any additional information not mentioned during the interview may be included. This effort aids in keeping the administrator interested in you as a candidate. If the district supplied you with an application form, complete and mail it with this letter. All suggestions about exercising care in writing letters also apply to the application form.

Acceptance Letter

An offer of a position should be acknowledged promptly by writing a letter of acceptance, provided you are convinced that this is the position you desire. Generally the terms of the agreement are restated in the letter to make sure that there is mutual understanding; include the position, the period of contract, the place, and the salary. Sign the contract or the offer and return the school's copy with your acceptance letter. If the school has enclosed other instructions, read them very carefully. Other materials such as loyalty oaths and withholding tax forms should be returned at the appropriate time. Note deadline dates in the instructions so that the contract and the other forms you are to return will reach the school office before the dates specified.

Delay Letter

Sometimes a candidate is not ready to accept an offer but is interested in the position. A letter stating an interest is appropriate; but, if there is a delay, a clear statement of the reason for it should be given. The request may be for a time extension beyond the two-week deadline stated in the job offer or the official contract. Or a candidate may wish more information about the school, the community, or the assignment. In some cases several offers are being considered simultaneously and additional time is desired. Some schools will not give time extensions, so the candidate must reach a decision regarding the offer at once. This may be the time to use the telephone to discuss the matter with the official making the offer and to seek assistance by consulting a placement counselor.

Schools and colleges vary in employment policies. Some districts give the candidate a specific period in which to accept or reject an offer. The administrator may want to continue looking for a teacher if you are looking for other jobs. Consequently, the school policy does not provide for the granting of an extension of time. Some districts are very flexible and hold positions open for a reasonable time. Competition for teachers in critical fields prompts many administrators to give the candidate a brief period in which to accept the offer. If he does not accept it, they want to contact other potential candidates immediately.

Rejection Letter

Rejecting an offer of a position requires a tactful letter expressing appreciation for the offer and for the school's confidence in you. Clearly state that the position offered *is not being accepted.* The reason for rejection may or may not be given, depending on circumstances causing the candidate to refuse the position. A positive statement to keep the door open for future consideration is always wise. The employer may at some future date be in a location where you will want to apply for a position he has vacant. Remember that superintendents and college administrators, as well as teachers, move from position to position.

Be sure to return the contract or the offer if you are refusing the position.

Conclusion

Your letter may or may not help you secure the desired teaching position that is open. To achieve your goal, the appearance of your letter and its contents must sell the administrators on the idea that you will be a successful teacher in that school and an asset to the community. Your placement office has personnel to help you if you have special problems in communicating with administrators. Effective communication depends upon the reader's receiving the message you intend to convey in your letter. By following the above suggestions regarding letter writing, by being as original as possible, and by establishing a friendly relationship with school officials, you will aid yourself in advancing professionally.

Preparing for Your School Interview

DR. DONALD L. BECHTEL

HOW CAN YOU enhance your chances of being selected for a position?

First, decide that you are truly interested in the available position. Most schools send some pamphlets, perhaps a student handbook, or other materials about their school system and community to prospective candidates. This information should be studied carefully. Next, seek additional information about the school system and community by consulting reference books, and acquaintances familiar with the system, and by talking with educators familiar with the school district. If, on the basis of this initial information, you are not interested in the position, notify the superintendent and proceed to investigate other job opportunities. Interviewing for a position with little or no genuine interest should be avoided as it wastes everyone's time.

To prepare for the interview develop in advance a list of pertinent questions to ask the interviewer. Don't be afraid to refer to a list while being interviewed. The following types of questions might be prepared:

School Organization. What organizational patterns are found in the district (graded, non-graded)? Are these patterns developed around student needs? What innovative organizational patterns are evident?

School Policy. What are some of the major school policies? Are school policies developed around specific problems to meet specific educational needs?

The Instructional Program. How is the instructional program organized (departmentalization of instruction by subject matter, individualized study, team teaching)? What learning resources and special

Bechtel, Donald L. "Preparing Your School Interview." *School and Community.* March 1972. 57:8.

services are available to teachers (curriculum consultants, guidance services, media, library resources, learning centers)? What funds are available for learning resources? To what extent do teachers participate in the curriculum development?

Testing and Evaluation. What is the school district's philosophy on the testing, evaluation and grading of students? What systems are used to report student achievement (report cards, conferences)? What is the nature and extent of testing carried on by the school in evaluating student achievement?

In-Service and Professional Growth Opportunities. What types of in-service programs have been recently developed? What opportunities are available for continuing professional growth in the area?

Teacher Welfare. What methods are used in determining salary and fringe benefits for teachers? What is the policy on promotion and advancement in the system? Does the salary schedule compare favorably with other school systems in the area?

Listen carefully to the initial presentation of the interviewer. If, after the initial presentation, important unanswered questions remain, refer to your previously formulated list of questions to obtain additional information.

Teacher candidates are sometimes reluctant to ask a number of questions—sometimes because of tension, and sometimes because they feel that perhaps the wrong impression might be conveyed to the interviewer. Generally speaking, a candidate who asks a series of well-formulated questions during the interview gives the interviewer the image of a well informed, conscientious professional. This impression may determine which of two equally competent candidates will be offered a contract.

The most effective interviews are those in which communication flows between interviewer and interviewee. One unwritten rule is that the interviewer should engage in about 60 percent of the talking. In this way, the interviewer has the opportunity to make his presentation, allowing sufficient time for the interviewee to make comments and ask questions.

Because of limited time or distance, an administrator may feel it impossible to conduct a personal interview and may decide on an interview by telephone. While telephone interviews may be successful, they should be avoided if possible. By visiting the school, talking with the superintendent and perhaps other school officials, you gain more information than is possible by telephone. Likewise, the interviewer is able to learn much more about you by a personal interview.

After the interview, evaluate the strengths and weaknesses of the interview. If you are selected for the position, try to determine what factors influenced the decision. If another was chosen, evaluate what went wrong. Perhaps you responded too little, perhaps too much, maybe to some questions in the wrong way. Perhaps the problem was either too much or too little enthusiasm. In any case, evaluating the success or failure of an interview can give valuable insight into how to modify or strengthen interviewing procedures in the future.

SCHOOL is for . . .
SHARING YOUR LIFE

Teacher Contracts–Bane or Blessing?

EVART W. ARDIS

In the public school systems of the United States, teacher contracts are required in all of the 50 states and the District of Columbia. For the purposes of this article, the discussion will be limited to the contract as it applies to the beginning teacher, who normally would be signing his first contractual agreement.

What is a contract? The contract, as it applies to teachers, is a written agreement between the board of education and the teacher for performing a specific task for a specified period. This agreement is enforceable by law. Contracts vary considerably, from one covering a short, vague statement of conditions, to a lengthy document spelling out the provisions in detail. Usually the contract is only as lengthy as is necessary to cover the desired requirements of the employer and the employee and is not too difficult to understand.

What are the ethics and responsibilities involved in signing teacher contracts? The school district, almost without exception, is legally held to the provisions of the contract. If the teacher performs his duties as specified, he can be reasonably assured that the terms of the contract will be fulfilled.

The teacher, likewise, has a legal and ethical responsibility to see that the terms of the contract are fulfilled. A contract becomes meaningless if either party feels that the agreement, or any part of it, can be disregarded. In addition, there is the moral, ethical and professional responsibility to see that the educational program is not disrupted once the school year has started.

The beginning teacher should be cautious in signing a contract, especially if this is the first experience with one. Legal language can be

Ardis, Evart W. "Teacher Contracts—Bane or Blessing? *ASCUS.* 1968 Annual. Pp. 7-9.

confusing, and the new teacher may not understand what rightly should be included in the contract. Discussing the contents of the first contract with someone knowledgeable in this area can be helpful. The contract should not be signed until one is reasonably sure the position and the contract fit the specifications desired by the teacher.

The teacher should "break" a contract only when it is absolutely necessary. Some new teachers may sign a contract as early as January or February to start teaching the following fall. It is possible that, in the meantime, many "better" opportunities, such as more salary or a better teaching situation, will be brought to his attention. One should never break a contract for these reasons. This is unprofessional and does not contribute to one's record. There are school districts where one will find provisions in a teacher contract for terminating the agreement, such as a 30-day "clause" or a 60-day "clause". This is usually not a very satisfactory contract, as it can be terminated by either signatory.

"Breaking" a contract is justified only in such emergency cases for women teachers as marriage, pregnancy and illness. Under any circumstances, terminating a contract should be done in agreement with the superintendent of schools or the director of personnel well ahead of the time the teacher expects to leave.

Various forms of contracts. Throughout the country, one may find various types of teacher contracts used by boards of education. Some of the ones most commonly found are:

1. The regular one-year or two-year contract still most commonly used by most school districts.
2. The continuing contract, which is issued after a probationary period or after a teacher has attained tenure status. The contract itself will provide for possible changes each year, such as salary adjustments.
3. Probationary contracts are generally provided for the period of time up to when the teacher is eligible for a permanent contract. Some school districts have a probationary period of a year or so for the new teacher, during which time he must prove himself to be successful.
4. Temporary contracts are sometimes used where the teacher's services are needed for a portion of the year. Usually this is when the regular teacher has had to leave for one reason or another.
5. Substitute teacher contracts are used in some school districts, especially in the larger systems, where substitutes are not known personally and where a large number are utilized.

Letter of Intent. A letter of intent is a non-legal agreement, which some school districts may use in lieu of a contract until such time as the legal contract can be issued. Other districts may have a different name for an agreement of this kind.

The letter of intent is usually used in two kinds of situations. One is in the situation in which a school recruiter wishes to hire a candidate, and he is not empowered to issue the legal contract. The letter of intent, in this case, will serve the purpose of the contract. Another situation where it may be used is the one in which a legal contract, for one reason or another, cannot be issued at the usual time of the school year—March, April, or May. A letter of intent may be issued until such time as the legal contract can be made available:

A teacher should use caution in signing a letter of intent. This document has value only in a situation where the teacher has complete confidence in the integrity of the employing officials.

When are contracts issued? There is no specific time when teacher contracts are issued by a school district, although one will find them forthcoming under three conditions in regard to time. First, there will be the time when a new teacher is being hired. This, of course, may be any time of the year. Second, boards of education are usually ready to issue contracts when the yearly budget is finalized to the extent that they know the financial situation for the following year, probably in March, April, or May. Third, after the conditions for a contract have been negotiated by a teacher-organization and school board negotiating teams. This may be at any time of the school year, but is most likely to be in the spring or early summer. The negotiated contract, or parts of it, may extend for a period longer than one year.

Tenure Provisions. In many states, tenure provisions for public school teachers have been enacted into law by state legislatures. In other states, individual school districts have adopted provisions for tenure for their particular teachers. These provisions for tenure vary considerably from state to state or from school district to school district. However, in general, after a probationary period of two or three years of successful teaching, a teacher is placed on permanent tenure. An evaluation during the probationary period of teaching is made which will either justify tenure or termination of employment. Tenure will continue under normal conditions until such time as the teacher leaves the job or until the teacher can no longer serve satisfactorily.

Professional Negotiations. In recent years, a new means for determining the contents of teachers' contracts has arisen in many states. This is called professional negotiation. Under this process, the board of education, or its representatives, negotiates with representatives of the teaching staff on nearly all school matters which affect teachers, including salary policy, conditions of work, and so forth.

HINTS
To A Beginning Teacher ...

Success for the entire year may
depend on the way you get
started on that first day of school

R. C. BRADLEY

Here are some hints and ideas for a beginning teacher. Remember, these notes are only a sampling of those ideas, thoughts, attitudes, and school record data a beginning teacher would like to know. Also keep in mind that the information given is only one person's opinion subject to critical review and alteration. This information represents those things I would have like to have understood before starting the first day teaching in an elementary school. Since I have taught in primary, intermediate, and upper grade levels, I have come to the conclusion that one must isolate that criteria pertaining to his level of teaching. I, too, have faced the problem of "What is expected of me the first day of school?" I hope this will help you.

Before the First Day

A. Understand the grading system used in your school and the promotion or retention policies.

B. Be aware of how to keep the attendance report by the week, month and year. This will help you keep all "first" records accurately and completely; thus, making the end of the year reports much easier to fill out. Find out holidays to be counted "in attendance" and whether or not if a child is absent the day before the holiday he should be counted

Bradley, R. C. "Hints to a Beginning Teacher." *School and Community.* November 1957. 44:18-19.

absent on the holiday also.

C. Have an estimated number of the children to be in your class so you will have enough desks and chairs available. This is most important in grades one through four, as the children are looking forward to having their own "home", so to speak, and they will be disappointed if it is not there waiting for them.

D. Know the books (and workbooks) that the Board of Education *will not* purchase, but are used by the school system and find out where the children may purchase them and the approximate cost. It is best to have one list only of items that you or the school consider important and necessary—send it home by all children the same day—eliminating parental criticism that schools are always calling for something every day. Also the use of only one list is convenient for teachers, students and parents. It helps the parent and student by permitting them to buy all supplies at one time; it helps the teacher by having all students obtain the teaching aids at once. Also the pupil feels better when he has the same articles as Johnny or Suzie. It helps the teacher to find those pupils who cannot furnish their own materials or workbooks. The teacher may then want to contact an organization that would be willing to help these children (PTA, business organization or professional organization).

E. Talk to your principal about discipline. What is the policy of handling difficult boys and girls if they become a major problem?

F. Become familiar with your playground schedule as well as the noon duty or extra-curricular activities expected of you. Find out the policy or regulations about students leaving the school grounds during school hours. (This is found in the School Handbook if your school has written one.)

G. Ask the procedure when it is necessary for you to be absent.

H. Ask your principal if you should follow the Course of Study in your daily plans or use it only as a Guide.

I. Understand health policies of your school. Is a note required for children to enter school after short or long illnesses? Teach yourself to recognize impetigo, cold sores, measles, etc. It is not your duty to diagnose or be a doctor, but it helps to tactfully suggest medical attention. Always, unless an emergency, avoid applying any medicine yourself. *Never* give medicine internally to a child unless permission is given in writing and signed by the parent or doctor. (This prescription is to safeguard your own health in public education.)

J. Although you probably will not find time to teach basic subject matter on the first day, you should plan plenty of varied activities on this day as well as for days to come. Lapses in a variety of activity are invitations to discipline problems. Give children something to do for the next day too. This starts a rapid discipline of themselves toward school procedures which have escaped them over the vacation.

K. You should have your room as neat and organized as possible before the first day. Children, although they will not at all times show it, like a well organized classroom, and will help to keep it that way.

The First Day

The big rush is here. Accept it. Don't worry about trivial things. Spend your time helping children to become adjusted to their classroom desk, library, school, etc. You will, however, be setting the stage for a most perfect year. Know your setting and dialogue well for this first impression is important to both student and parent. This came back to me in a round-a-bout way one year. The children were talking and one said to his parent, "You know, I'm going to like him. He seemed so happy and smiled at me today." Well, this doesn't seem like much, but it certainly does tell us what they expect. Isn't this something that is so easy to give?

The first day as nearly as possible you will try to get as much permanent record information as possible. If children living in a certain zone, according to the permanent record information, are to be the only persons coming to your school, double-check the addresses to be certain they are now enrolled in the right school. If in doubt, check with the principal. Some parents insist their children are to go to this school. You know better according to the address, so invite them down to talk the situation over with the principal as it is his duty to solve these problems. This will seem as if it is a big problem to you but your principal has been through this many times and it will just put him in shape for the day. Then perhaps you should go back to your room as there are some things your principal may want to say in confidence to these irate parents.

You usually will be furnished an enrollment form to use. If you are not, be certain the first day to find out the following information: student's name, parent's name, present address, phone number, resident or non-resident pupil, birth date (year, month and day), family doctor, a religious preference. It is most important to find early in the school year the religious preference of your students. Some religious denominations will not allow their members to stay in the classroom for the Lord's Prayer, Pledge of Allegiance to the Flag, rhythm activities, etc. Choose with caution your opening exercises. Even if you find you must read aloud "The Bible" to the students, do so without comments on your "readings." Your comment is your interpretation which probably shall differ from that of another. I believe it is the duty of the Church and Sunday School to teach their beliefs peculiar to their own denomination.

This belief of mine has avoided for me many unjustified and disfavorable circumstances that have been encountered by fellow workers. However, I do teach those "Truths" basic to all religions.

Many parents will bring their children to you for enrollment. They will tell you how nice Johnny is (and he is probably a pill, look out!) or how much special help he will need. This is your opportunity—let them know how nice it is to see parents interested in the progress of their boys and girls. Show confidence to these parents at all times. Even if in doubt. There are always established teachers that will help you with some problem or your principal will help you if you will only ask. Ask for help before you need it—then you soon find you needed little help—you needed only someone to help understand the problems, and how to solve them will soon develop naturally.

If parents the first day stand around or bother you, until you develop more confidence know of a room beforehand that they might wait until you dismiss the children. Be tactful about inviting them to wait in this room until you have rounded up the routine work that needs to be done today. They will understand. However, be certain they understand that they just "must" come back and visit when regular school sessions get underway. The parents want to feel "wanted" the same as their child. Just think for a moment, this child they brought to you is the most important possession they have. The parents want the most capable and confident teacher they can have for their child. You would want the same. You can be that teacher, and when you recognize this, you are, then, the best teacher for that child. Your attitude to the entire school enterprise is the best teaching equipment you have at your immediate command.

The first day is not too soon to talk with the children about the fire drill or drills. Explain their purpose as a safety measure and make it a game to be the most orderly and efficient of the school to leave and re-enter the building properly. Award them a little free time or something to instill in their minds a responsibility to themselves, school, and teacher. Ten minutes of free time, I have found, make many free of injury for life. Be certain you can operate the Emergency Fire Extinguisher by yourself. Is your first aid kit properly supplied?

After you have explained about some activities you hope to accomplish with your students throughout the year, ask them if there are any questions about this year's school work. We, as teachers, forget that we are not to supply both questions and answers all of the time. Student participation and organization can be developed readily in lower grades if we have understanding parents, students, administrators, and a patient teacher.

At the scheduled dismissal time help your students find the right bus until they become acquainted with the procedure. This could be considered the principal's task, however, he is judging you on your thoughtfulness and your capabilities of becoming a capable teacher. I dare say, it will be most helpful to all concerned.

As you teach, remember please—perhaps you cannot change the Destiny of the World, but you can affect the destiny of boys and girls entrusted to your care and guidance who will soon traverse this earth. You and I must not fail to meet their needs.

SCHOOL is for . . .
ADVENTURING BEYOND CLASSROOM WALLS

Chapter III

The Beginning Teacher And His Instructional Strategies

What strategies of teaching should the beginning teacher seek for direct application to his own teaching style? First, the teacher needs to construct for himself two sets of cognitive maps by which he wishes to guide the process of learning: (a) the map of the basic ideas and concepts that the study of selected topics is to produce, and (b) of the nature of intellectual skills involved and of the ways in which these selected skills are mastered.

Secondly, the teacher must acquire the role of "question-asking" rather than "answer-giving". Cognitive operations are stimulated only as pupils *search*, *invent*, and *discover* the processes by which to deal with the tasks proposed by carefully designed questions. Thirdly, the concept of learning as applied in this book has its real emphasis upon sampling judiciously the specific instances which are valid examples of certain ideas and concepts rather than merely "covering" content. Finally, the wise novice teacher understands and accepts the fact that it takes both time and practice to acquire new skills in thinking. This is especially important when preceding instruction has cultivated habits which are inconsistent with processes required in *analytical*, *critical*, and *creative thinking*.

One source of evidence for the need of this Chapter is found in the absence of published material concerned with *strategies for teachers.* Effective teaching does not come about in a hit-or-miss fashion, each teacher must seek to design his own strategy of teaching. By drawing from several strategies no doubt he will come up with a design he can truly live with and thereby increase purposefully his *instructional power.*

Learning Begins With a ?uestion

HARRY K. DORSETT

One of my favorite teachers, Harry Emerson Fosdick, once said that the compliment he most appreciated from his preaching was from a woman who came by at the conclusion of a sermon and confided, "You raised so many questions this morning that I almost passed out in excitement."

It is so difficult to get teachers to ask instead of to tell. Most lesson plans are an outline of facts and ideas to be memorized. Stimulating and provocative questions would make these facts and ideas significant and meaningful.

The simplest and most useless question, to borrow a term from the legal profession, is the leading question: "Does the river Nile overflow its banks?"; "If a man and boy are see-sawing, will he balance his end?"; "How long did the Seven Years War Last?"; "Was Anthony's date with Cleopatra the greatest date in history?"; "Which Boswell wrote the life of Samuel Johnson, James or Connie?" The only justification for this type of question is to permit reticent pupils to participate in class dialogue.

Only a mite higher on the totem pole is the drill or pumping question: "What takes the dative?"; "What is the population of Timbuctoo?"; "How many furlongs in 180 yards?"; "Who was the little boy in the bulrushes?"; "What are the chief exports of Barcelona?" This type of interrogation never leaves one palsied with ecstacy. And yet most of the questions one hears in the classroom fall into this category. All should be thrown in the wastepaper basket and teachers who ask them should be sued for malpractice of profession.

Dorsett, Harry K. "Learning Begins with a ?uestion." *North Carolina Education.* January 1972. 2:25, 35-36.

Humor is important in the classroom; there are questions that have no other purpose than to amuse: "When Little Bo-Peep lost her sheep, was it deductible?"; "Was Eve framed?"; As one flea said to another, "Shall we walk or take a dog?"; "Does being crazy help you play the oboe?"; "Could you start a fine library by leaving out the works of Jane Austin?"

Occasionally, one hears compound questions: "Who sent what against England during whose reign and for what purpose?"; What should you pay for how much to give to whom?" One question at a time, pretty please, with whipped cream and cherries.

If students are not merely asked to compare, the comparison question can be a dilly: "Should the good man get the good girl?"; "If Lincoln were living today would he be a Republican?"; "Would the atomic bomb have been dropped on white people?"; "Is democracy more quickly achieved by revolution than by evolution?"; "Why can jazz turn a neat profit when the best music must depend on alms?"; "Is the world worse off than when you came into it?"; "Do people know what they want more than they used to?"; "Are poets the greatest liars?"; "Would you rather marry a neat, cross woman than an untidy, good-natured woman?"; "Was there more justification in chopping off the head of Louis XIV than Charles I?"; "If you were a snowflake would you rather go across a barn or into a tree?"; "Should a young person be tolerant of an intolerant old person?"; "Can the black man, who has been matured by suffering, help bring maturity to the white man?" This type of question is not popular with get-through-the-day-teachers.

In deductive questioning you proceed from the general to the specific; in inductive you arrive at the general from the specific. An art teacher displays a braser. In an instant the silence is lighted up. "What is it?" "What is it called?" "How did it get its name?" "What is it made of?" "How was it made?" "Who uses it?" "Could I use it?" These are inductive questions that would normally come from students if teachers would only encourage them to ask. But since most teachers are dedicated to stodginess, they continue to ask the traditional deductive questions such as, "What principles are involved in the making of a braser?" and "How could we make a better braser?"

In the rhetorical question the response desired is an unarticulated feeling or attitude: "Who can deliver the vote of a free people?"; "Do Edens exist in order to be lost?"; "How big is your dream of America?" "Do four freedoms include the freedom to be free?"; "If there were no grief to hollow out our hearts, where would there be room for joy?" "What if life itself is the sweetheart?"; "Must people perish in torment to save those who have no imagination?"; "Why should anyone starve?" "Can a person be moral and at the same time insensitive to another person?"; "How can the kingdom of God come when people won't even let happiness come?"; "What can it profit a man to gain the whole world and come to his property with a gastric ulcer and bifocals?" The rhetorical questions provide a dramatic experience, can tremendously influence emotions. We should never forget that the intellect, after all, is but a speck afloat on a sea of emotion.

The impossible-to-answer question emphasizes the fact that there are questions worth perusing although one can never find *the* answer: "What is truth?"; "Is there purpose in the universe?"; "What is beauty?"; "Is space only what we perceive it to be?"; "What is the good life?"; "Is time infinite?" On such questions we need to resist the inclination to make up our minds to give meaning to our lives.

It is only through challenging, thought-provoking questions that you discover you have wings: "What should I do about the 250,000 in the world who are in jail today because of their beliefs?"; "How can an open society have secret agencies?"; "Why is class so important when we pretend we have none?"; "Would Christ be a member of the First Baptist Church?"; "What experience have you had with ghosts?"; "How does a fly land on the ceiling?"; "Was Hamlet crazy?"; "What was the world doing the day you were born?"; "What is the most important thing we can think about this minute?"; "What mute, inglorious Miltons have you known?"; "Suppose you had 24 hours to live, what would you do?"; "What if Cleopatra's nose had been a quarter of an inch longer?"; "Do murder and cruelty reach a saturation point or grow greater with each fresh crime?"; "Is the right to privacy the greatest right of civilized man?"; "What are the chances that history has a meaning?"; "Do you lose something when you learn something?"; "How far can a free society go in regulating inflammatory expression?"; "What are the two most important words in your vocabulary?"; "Who speaks for the United States?"; "Are revolutions caused by those who try to stop them?"; "Are we responsible for the evils in the world that we have never made?"

Questions should have a personal quality, should contribute to making one an intellectual peeping-Tom. Most, if not all, learning begins with a question in the mind of a student. If the student has a question, this question should take precedence. If he doesn't, it is up to the teacher to supply it.

The average child of four asks over 200 questions every day. A research study indicated that high school students ask one question per month. When a child returns from school each day his parents should inquire regarding what important questions he asked that day in school. I believe that it was Jesus who said, "Those who question shall reign."

The Art of Asking Questions

R. C. BRADLEY

A central part of all learning activity is the asking of questions. Possibly less attention is given to the preparation of questions for learning activities than educators would care to admit. Nevertheless, questions are of major import both to classroom teachers and to pupils. The task set by a question prior to actual reading of a selection not only gives a "mind set" to that content, but should help the pupil to determine the rate at which he will consume the material.

Preliminary Questioning

For instance, if sixth grade pupils were about to read a lesson in social studies dealing with the Civil War, what the teacher does through preliminary questioning is an important factor in determining what the pupil learns and the rate at which he learns it. For example, the question, "What caused the Civil War?", calls for the pupil to attend to what the book says, while, "What are some possible explanations of the Civil War?", suggests that the pupil is expected to read with some deliberation and meditation. In the former question he seeks facts as quickly as he can secure them; in the latter, he reads more deliberately and uses the author's facts as a basis for extending and expressing his own ideas.

Productive reading, as this author conceives it, is thinking which the individual does "on his own" as he reads. Not all independent thinking should fall into a structure or mold for guidance purposes; it is the teacher's responsibility, however, to explore the various cognitive processes necessary to help the pupil improve his ability to read. It is with a few selected samples of questions for guiding pupils during the reading act that this article purports to deal.

Bradley, R. C. "The Art of Asking Questions." *North Carolina Education.* November 1966. 61:14, 32-34.

Type of Thinking

With Respect to the Learner, What Do Questions Determine? The structure of questions prior to the reading act is most important in that these questions (1) determine the type of thinking skill the child will employ in searching for and attacking the selection or passage; (2) involve the thinking skills one may learn simultaneously as he performs the reading act; and, (3) determine the range or scope of information that one will confine himself to within a selection at a given moment or period of time.

A major instructional deficiency with intermediate grade pupils is the fact that the purpose for which they read a selection is more often set by the teacher. The deficiency may stem in part from the atmosphere of the large class which inhibits the individual from freely asking many questions before he starts to read. Certainly it could stem from a sheer lack of question-asking practice by the pupil and his training in how to ask pertinent questions. In part it may reflect the absence of an adequate skill in question-asking, or even the lack of a strong enough *mind set* in readiness to ask questions.

Information and Memory

What Types of Questions Need to be Structured for the Reader's Benefit? First, the teacher will want to acquaint his pupils with nformational or memory questions. (*e.g.* In reading this selection you will find three causes of the Civil War. What are they?). Questions of this type are of one answer usually; sheer recall, convergent responses; no equivocation. Nearly 81 percent of the questions used in classrooms are short one-answer questions. Such questions only *point* to cognitive thinking.

Second, the teacher needs to look at a higher level of questioning which requires the child to *synthesize* the ideas he reads. (*e.g.* Were there any avenues of agreement or values held in common between the North and South as to the purposes for which they were fighting?). Questions of this type call for the child to check categories of knowledge he now has, and require that he read with some depth in order to regroup some skills and extend his ideas as gaps are bridged in his thinking processes.

Making Inferences

Third, there is need for the development of questions which direct the child to use skills in *making of inferences. (e.g.* What position might

Abraham Lincoln take with respect to Civil Right's issues if he were living today?). Noteworthy here is the fact that a type of reading is called for in which the thinking process is allowed some degree of flexibility. There is no right response. The less evaluative or exact an answer sought from a pupil, the higher the level of comprehension and quality of reaction. In other words, a very high level of response should be expected from questions of the third type because one must transform what he knows to the question as cited. Very rarely do we find questions of this type flowing before or after the reading of a selected passage.

Fourth, we need to develop questions which use skills in *predicting consequences* (creative and divergent thinking skills). (*e.g.* If the South had won the Civil War, how might this have affected the historical development of our country from that time to the present?). Here we have established facts predicated upon previous learnings. The pupil must take an independent variable that is known and predict on that basis what outcomes might have been. "If" these things be true, *then* this should follow. Questions of this type "lift" the level of thinking of the pupil.

Feelings and Emotions

Fifth, attention should be given a portion of the class time to questions that deal with *feelings* and *emotions*. (*e.g.* How would you feel if you had to fight your own brother during a time of war? Do you feel the cause of the war and its outcomes were just?). Unless we take to the reading lesson opportunities for pupils to respond with feeling and emotion, they may not react any differently to the various types of new questions that we structure than they did to the previous, traditional types.

What is the Pupil's Responsibility to the Questioning Act? First, accurate listening is essential if children are going to read to find out answers to questions of the first type (memory skills) since this involves following the thread of a discussion; following directions correctly; repeating orally or in writing exactly what has been said; and summarizing accurately.

Second, pupils must read, discuss, and listen to an argument in order to answer it, seek evidence on which to form an opinion on controversial questions, or require sources of evidence to support facts.

Reserve Judgment

Third, for making of inferences one must reserve judgment until all the facts are read; misleading statements must be detected; and some opportunity must be sought to express self-creatively.

Fourth, in predicting consequences pupils must read to find out unspecified information on a topic in which new or related ideas may occur; seek to determine sincerity or bias of the writer; analyze and synthesize information so valid judgments may be made and outcomes expected can be more logically forecast.

Lastly, as one becomes sensitive to his own feelings and emotions, he senses the beauty of words and ideas, responds with feeling to the skill of their arrangement, and watches for indefinite, emotionalized terms.

Who asks questions before the reading act in the classroom? Nearly two-thirds of the time it is the teacher. What kinds of questions are pupils asking the other one-third of the time? For the most part such things as, "What page are we on?"; "Where's my book, Miss Smith?"; "What were we supposed to do?".

Who should be asking most of the questions to determine the purpose for which one reads? Probably the pupils under the sound guidance of the teacher. If we are going to reverse the traditional process, then we are going to need to teach differently. As teachers look at the questions they ask, it may be found that children who miss questions from some content area on a Wednesday test get the same questions again on Friday. If we teach children to read wisely, they will be able to think in terms of the several types of questions herein mentioned as they read for meaning.

The relationships between the categories of questions suggested in this article for determining the type of reading skill to apply are similar to that between colors on a spectrum. There, the colors of red, orange, yellow, green, blue, indigo, and violet are plainly visible. Between each color, one finds an area that is neither one nor the other . . . but a part of both. The same is true of the categories of questioning. One's difficulty in classifying any question before, during, or after the reading act, however, should in no way be a detraction from the quality of the question that needs to be asked.

It is my contention that teachers who spend considerable time on the improvement of the types of questions they pose will be those who help pupils to ask relevant questions.

After all, this is what education is about: teacher helps pupil to learn!

Stimulus Variation In The Classroom

ROY SANDERS

All of the things we teachers do in the classroom—the way we talk, gesture, move about, erase the chalkboard—are stimuli which impinge upon the sense receptors of the student. The more varied this stimuli is, the better the teaching.

Constant repetition of the same stimulus, no matter how intriguing or curiosity-provoking it may have been initially, produces lethargy in the subject. For example, we pay little if any attention to the ticking of a clock; indeed, if we do, we soon become drowsy. But the uncivilized person, upon first experiencing the "ticking box," becomes wildly excited and listens intently to each tick.

The more varied the stimuli the more alert and interested the student and the better our teaching. The point at which this generalization ceases to be true is when the teacher's goal becomes that of keeping his students entertained and interested by means of varied stimuli rather than that of employing a variety of stimuli to realize educational objectives.

Conversely, the less varied the stimuli the less alert and less interested the student. We have only to recall the teacher who stood immobile behind the lectern, only his lips moving and his voice exhibiting little variation in tone, pitch or volume. His students doodled, wrote letters, fidgeted, yawned or slept through his lectures.

In a recent study Yamamoto, *et al.*, asked students to suggest adjectives descriptive of the best and the worst teachers. (1,467) Heading the list for good teachers were such adjectives as *knowledgeable*, *well-informed*, *enthusiastic* and *dynamic*, and for the worst teachers the

Sanders, Roy. "Stimulus Variation in the Classroom." *School and Community.* February 1972. 58:36-37.

adjectives *dull, boring, monotonous, lazy* and *unenthusiastic.* This study points up quite clearly the importance of varying the stimulus in the classroom. The enthusiastic and dynamic teacher is continually varying the stimulus. He is moving about the room; he is working with different groups and individuals; he is using a variety of materials, procedures and media; he is using fresh, vivid illustrations and examples; he is seeking participation and involvement by the class; he is interested in his students and their needs; and he is enthusiastic about teaching. The dull, boring, monotonous teacher, on the other hand, varies the stimulus much less frequently. He sits behind his desk or stands behind his lectern, keeps his students "busy," and uses the same tired procedures month after month and year after year. [1]

From kindergarten through graduate school the teacher is the focal point in most classrooms. This does not mean that such an arrangement is necessary or desirable for effective teaching. Indeed, some of the best teaching I have ever witnessed occurred in classrooms where one had to take a second look to distinguish the teacher from the students. But the fact is that we teachers usually find ourselves in front of the room explaining, relating, discussing, illustrating—in short, lecturing. The over-used lecture might become a more acceptable teaching method if stimulus variation accompanied its use.

What can the teacher do to vary the stimulus? Let's begin with the voice. He can adjust the volume so that he can easily be heard in the back of the room; he can vary the tone and pitch to produce a live, vibrant quality; and he can emphasize key words and phrases. Nothing induces sleep like listening to a lecture given in a low-pitched monotone with inadequate volume and little if any emphasis upon key words. Lack of enthusiasm is reflected by dullness in speech. If one has little enthusiasm for what he is doing or saying, his performance will almost surely be lacklustre. Donald Ecroyd points out possible reasons for dull performances in his stimulating little book *Speech in the Classroom:*

"The person whose speech is dull because of pitch patterns or the person who has a monotonous voice has probably either failed to grasp the real meaning of what he is trying to say, or has not (for one reason or

1. Yamamoto, Kaoru, Douglas J. Pederson, Roger Opdahl, Harry Dangel, Charles E. Townsend, Marilyn Berger Paleologos, and Alva N. Smith, "As They See It: Culling Impressions from Teachers in Preparation," *The Journal of Teacher Education,* Vol. 20, Winter 1969, pp. 465-75.

another) permitted himself to become involved or enthusiastic." (2, 39-40)

Gesturing can be useful, not only to vary the stimulus but also to get the point across. The latter is accomplished by such gestures as ticking off points on the fingers, "first of all," "secondly," "thirdly," etc., or banging one's fist into his palm or rapping on the desk as he says, "Now this is important, class," or "Let's all be sure we get this point."

Another stimulus variation is that of appealing to as many of the senses as possible. Most lecturers appeal only to the sense of hearing with the result that students frequently let their attention wander. The teacher can switch from the aural sense to the visual by asking the students to look at a diagram or model, or he can refer to the visual aid in such a way that students must look at it if they are to follow the development of the concept.

Another effective stimulus variation is pausing. Too often we teachers hurry from one point to another as though the quality of our instruction was being measured by the quantity of our verbiage. We seem to be in a race to get a predetermined amount of material covered. Our teaching would be greatly improved if we paused occasionally, allowing students to assimilate new ideas, relate new material to old, analyze and evaluate what has been presented, and prepare for the introduction of new ideas.

Such a simple procedure as moving from one side of the desk to the other provides some variation. Of course, if one is chained to his lecture notes, even this simple stimulus variation becomes almost impossible. But even in this situation one can provide variation by maintaining good eye contact with all areas of the classroom; varying tone, pitch and volume of one's voice; pausing occasionally for students to think about new concepts; and emphasizing key words or phrases.

Another source of stimulus variation is the use of different media. Many of us rely almost entirely upon the chalkboard for illustrations, outlines, etc. We overlook other media such as overhead projectors, flannel boards, magnetic and electric boards, opaque projectors, graphs, models, maps, globes, exhibits, artifacts, pictures, and a host of others. The chalkboard is an important medium but its overuse makes it less effective at times than other media. Parenthetically, I might mention that the chalkboard provides greater variation of stimulus if different colors of chalk are used now and then.

2. Ecroyd, Donald H., *Speech in the Classroom*, (Englewood Cliffs, N.J.: Prentice-Hall, Inc.) 1960

Verbal reinforcement also should be varied. Too often we use only one or two words or phrases of reinforcement, and students soon come to expect the same words of praise or encouragement regardless of their accomplishments. As a result, they view them as routine and mechanistic, and they pay little or no attention to them. Perhaps it would be better to give no reinforcement at all than to mouth the same expression routinely after each student response as though the reinforcement was a necessary hindrance to be gotten out of the way before another gem of wisdom could proceed from the teacher. There is no reason to limit ourselves to such expressions of approval as "fine," "very good," and "yes." Madsen and Madsen (3, 116-18) list some sixty-odd words and sentences of approval. The important thing, however, is not the number of expressions used but rather the sincerity and wholeheartedness with which they are expressed.

Perhaps the most important kind of stimulus variation in the classroom is that of student participation. Here the focus is upon the student—what he is doing while he is learning. The student may give a class demonstration or explain a theorem; several students may role-play a situation of interest to all the class; the class may discuss an issue which elicits a great deal of student-teacher and student-student interchange; or several groups of students may work on problems or projects simultaneously. The key is action, and action is a synonym for stimulus variation.

SCHOOL is for . . .
CRITICAL THINKING

3. Madsen, Charles H., Jr., and Clifford K. Madsen, *Teaching/Discipline*, (Boston: Allyn and Bacon, Inc.) 1970.

A Simulation Experience
In The Middle School

CHESTER W. DUGGER

Simulating actual situations is one way to student involvemen which closely approximates the work of real scientists. When student begin to experience situations, frustrations, and elations like thos experienced by real men and women engaged in scientifically relatec occupations, the learning experience becomes open-ended, and anythin; can happen. Moreover, facts and theories gain significance as the studen actually uses them.

The following simulation experience was devised by the author, anc it has been used successfully at the middle school level. It gives student an opportunity to use measurement skills to solve a practical problem; i emphasizes and offers practice in research design; it integrates scienc and economics; and it provides information relative to vocationa guidance.

At the conclusion of a unit on measurement the teacher enlisted th help of a friend who was a practicing chemical engineer. On th following day the engineer was introduced to the class and addressed th students:

Ladies and gentlemen, I understand that we have in this room some of the finest chemists in the land. I represent M-Salt Company and have been commissioned by my company to enlist your help in solving a problem. You see, our geologists have located a huge salt deposit. This deposit is situated near a large metropolitan area. Within this area tremendous quantities of salt are consumed. A team of economists from our company has indicated that, since this area of consumption is located at considerable distance from other salt deposits, it may be economically feasible to use the salt source newly discovered.

Dugger, Chester W. "A Simulation Experience in the Middle School." *The Science Teacher.* March 1972. 9:70-71.

There is one major problem which we must solve before we can continue. This is where all of you come in. Unfortunately, the salt which we have found is mixed with sand. We very much need your help to determine: (a) what percentage of salt and sand are in the mixture by weight, and (b) what is the least expensive means for separating the salt from the sand.

I have brought samples of the mixture with me so that you may begin your investigations at once. I will keep in touch with you through Mr. Davis (your teacher), who will be your plant manager. Keep me posted on your findings.

When the engineer left, a discussion began concerning the problem and how the class might go about solving it. The teacher explained that the first step was to consider various possible extraction procedures; second, to perform preliminary tests concerning these procedures; and third, to formulate a functional research design. The importance of the research design was emphasized as a means to insure that each contingency had been considered and provided for.

The class decided to break into teams and to tackle the problem independently. The work was begun.

It was obvious from the first that most of the students were interested and eager to get going; still, there were a few who just could not seem to get involved. Although these students did make half-hearted attempts to get started, early signs of frustration began to appear. In these cases the teacher provided support when and where it was needed.

He soon found that reaction to frustration takes many forms and that apparent disinterest was often related to uncertainty.

Initial investigations were, for the most part, of the trial-and-error variety. One group considered and rejected the use of sieves. Another considered the possibility of separation procedures based on differences in weight. Eventually one group after another began to consider the possibility of dissolving the salt in water. This suggested other questions. How could the salt solution be separated from the sand? How could one be sure that all of the salt had been extracted?

Considerable time went into discovery, experimentation, and rejection efforts. Gradually, however, a definite research design began to emerge.

Some procedures were hotly debated. For example, one student suggested that the salt-sand mixture could be repeatedly rinsed and the rinse water collected. When the rinse water no longer tasted salty, one could assume that most of the salt had been extracted. Another student earnestly rejected the "taste test" on the grounds that it "Just doesn't seem scientific!"

Most of the groups quickly forgot about the teacher's suggestion that the research design be put in a "step-by-step" written form. Later, some of these groups had to do over parts of their procedure because some vital step had been overlooked.

Several students came to the teacher seeking information as to how "percentage by weight" might be found. The teacher went through the procedure with several students, but with the understanding that these students would act as consultants if the question should arise again, which it did.

When the final research results were submitted to the plant manager they were accepted only if the completed research design accompanied them. The teacher could quickly check the design to see whether a legitimate procedure had been used. The results themselves were monitored roughly by the fact that the mixtures had been prepared using constant volumes of salt and sand. Where legitimate procedures were followed, the results seldom varied more than plus or minus two grams for a 40-gram sample.

Final results concerning the salt-sand ratio were obtained within three days, but this was only the beginning. A preferred extraction method had to be devised. Discussion led to a suggested procedure, practical on a commercial scale, which included the use of mixing tanks, settling tanks, and evaporation ponds.

Several students volunteered to make drawings of the proposed extraction plant. When the drawings were reviewed, it was noted that the best drawing would probably include ideas from several of the drawings. A committee was formed to make this combination and to construct a model.

When the model was tested, and all the data were collected, the class prepared a full report. The salt company representative was invited back, and the report was presented. The class made use of the extraction plant model, charts, graphs, overlays, and other visuals to add clarity to its report. Estimates concerning amounts of water, electricity, and other raw materials were reported, and land-use requirements were specified.

The visitor was visibly pleased and impressed by the students' work and he began his response by saying so. He then reintroduced himself to the class as a chemical engineer. He indicated that the report he had just witnessed was very like a report he had recently made to a chemical company in the immediate area. He emphasized repeatedly that this class had been doing exactly what many chemical engineers do. He then discussed the different types of jobs available in his chosen field. He noted the educational requirements, chances for advancement, salary levels, and advantages and disadvantages for a considerable number of related occupations. A lengthy question-and-answer period followed.

On the next day the teacher entered the classroom a bit late, walked to the front of the room, and began:

Ladies and gentlemen, I understand that we have in this room some of the finest economists in the nation. I have with me some data concerning a proposed salt mining and marketing business operation.

Friendly groans trickled through the classroom as the students began to roll up their mental sleeves for a new adventure.

SCHOOL is for . . .
LEARNING BY
OBSERVING

Roles Goals And Failure

WILLIAM GLASSER, M.D.

Quite a few years have passed since I, as consulting psychiatrist at the Ventura School for older delinquent girls in California, first began putting together my ideas about schools and kids and education. I've set forth these ideas in some of my books, and a surprising number of teachers who have tried them out find they work. Only recently, however, did I discover the theory which explains why these methods are effective.

An interview with Marshall McLuhan in the March 1969 issue of *Playboy* seemed to suggest the answer. When asked why there is so much turmoil in high schools and colleges, McLuhan replied that today's students are searching for a *role not a goal.* By role I mean an identity, a belief in who they are which is not directly tied to what they do.

I'd like to make a small alteration in what McLuhan said and put it this way: Students are searching for an identity or a role *before* a goal. By contrast, I look back at my own pre-World War II school days and ask myself what I was searching for in school, and I can tell you it wasn't for my identity. I was looking for a way to make it through school! I was searching for answers that would give me security in the form of good grades, a diploma, and a job—not for ways to satisfy my human or role needs. That was my goal, and that's the way it was for most people then. The schools said, "You do what we tell you to do when we tell you to do it, and if you don't, you fail." The serious, hard-working, student did, of course, get his diploma (the goal) and also some recognition (his role), but *the goal came first.* That is the way it was then and generally is now. Schools still say that the goal, the task, and what we teach must

---

Dr. Glasser is author of *Schools Without Failure* (1969) and *The Identity Society* (1972).

Glasser, William. "Roles, Goals, and Failure." *Today's Education.* October 1971. 60:20-21, 62.

take precedence; the student must subordinate himself and what he feels—his role and identity—to the job we say has to be done.

Today, in an era of affluence and the promised easy life of the fantasy world of television, young people no longer accept this traditional sequence. Students want their roles to precede—if only briefly —what they believe they should or must do. They say, "We want a little pat on the head, a little recognition as a person before we start the job and we want this to continue as we work." But after kindergarten, schools continue to demand that the work come first: "We'll recognize you as a person only *after* you do our job."

It's this idea which I believe causes the trouble and the lack of motivation plaguing so many of today's young people. Kindergarten is the only place where we accept kids as people, and they succeed in kindergarten. If they don't learn everything we had planned, we still value them and we don't get too upset.

First grade? Well, that's different. After all, we've got to teach them to read. The teacher says to the little kid, "Read!" His parents say, "Read!" The community says, "Read!" And if the child doesn't, we fail him.

Usually he takes the failure personally because he is role-oriented. He thinks we not only failed him in reading but as a human being. When this happens, he starts behaving totally as a failure. He stops almost all schoolwork and often becomes a discipline problem in order to gain some recognition, if only as a failure.

We figure out lots of excuses for why he's not reading—his eyes don't track, he reads backwards or sideways. But the real reason is that he sees himself as a failure   and he sees no sense in reading. Yet we keep telling him, "Read! Write! Do arithmetic! Sit still! Keep quiet! Shut up! Learn!" and when he doesn't we say he's lazy or educationally handicapped.

We find all kinds of sophisticated explanations for why he isn't learning. We buy all kinds of complicated equipment and establish special classes to help him learn—*but nothing much happens because he believes he is a failure, and failures get attention and recognition only by failing and misbehaving.*

The conditions which produce so many failures in our schools appear to be related to changes which came abruptly after World War II. The reasons for these changes include the possibility that, for the first time, the world can be fused into a meaningless blob by the bomb.

More recently, the war in Vietnam has played roulette with young people's lives. Its goals do not seem a reasonable price to pay for giving up a chance to achieve the good life that now seems possible. In much of the Western world, essential material goods are virtually assured for vast numbers of people so that economic survival is no longer the driving force it was at one time. Recent moves in our culture to give human rights priority over property rights have also contributed to change.

The television industry has known about the new focus on role or identity from at least 1951 (although I didn't find out about it until 1969) and through their recognition of McLuhan's "role not goal" they've been able to sell items of no utility as well as items of negative utility, such as cigarettes. If television can do that, surely we ought to be able to get kids to learn something with as much utility as reading.

But, unlike the world about them, schools say: "Achieve the goal we set for you or we will give no consideration to you and your role." To be sure, some kids will work for goals in school but they have enough role reinforcement in their homes to compensate for not having it at school. They *know* who they are.

In our previous goal-oriented society, success and failure were mostly tied to economic success or failure, economic security or insecurity, and in most cases, this actually meant survival or nonsurvival. These were the basics of the depression years when people were actually starving. We accepted this state of affairs by saying, "It's too bad, but that's the way things have always been and always will be." We were forced to be so concerned about our own security that we couldn't concern ourselves with others.

All that has changed at every level of society. Business *must* be concerned or it will find profits dropping. Politicians who do not rein-force the role of their constituents (assuming the latter are economically secure) will lose votes. Our changed society demands that we care for other people as people. Lonely people or those who have no one to care for them think of themselves as failures and become a burden on society.

To follow that thought, today everyone wants a role first, but there are two possible kinds of roles. Individuals can believe they're successful and competent human beings or they can believe they're failures. From countless discussions with groups of students, I have determined that even in relatively good high schools only half the kids feel they're successful; the rest consider themselves failures. In high schools in depressed areas, I have found that as few as 5 percent of the students believe they are successful. I don't think those who now consider themselves failures came to school feeling that way. They learned they were failures as they moved through school. Once they feel they're failures, they reinforce this belief by doing nothing or by resorting to delinquency. Then we threaten or punish, which reinforces their failure

I believe we have two ways of stopping this destructive process: first, by not failing kids and, second, by making friends with them. Being friendly with a person reinforces his role as a successful human being. When a person feels he's accepted and worthwhile in another's eyes, effective communication begins to take place and constructive things begin to happen.

Industry has known this ever since it found out people were changing—about the end of World War II. To make more money, industry replaced the hard sell with the soft sell. It began to tell a prospective customer, "We care about you. We think you're a good person and we want to help you become a better one."

Schools haven't yet learned this lesson. That's what they have to work toward; that's what I'm trying to help teachers do.

Teachers can become effectively involved with kids in a number of ways. A structured, well-planned class meeting each day is a good starter. I'm not talking about the ordinary class discussion. I'm talking about a meeting keyed to behaving in thoughtful, socially responsible ways. I'm talking about a meeting in which logical, orderly thinking takes priority. I'm talking about a meeting which involves everyone in the room—one in which kids learn to care for and respect each other and where meaningful participation takes precedence over the teacher's "right answer."

I'm concerned about bringing relevance, thinking, and involvement into the school by helping teachers learn to care for and become friends with the kids with whom they work. Our society needs successful, achieving people. We can develop such people only if we concern ourselves with the children with whom we work, letting them know that we like them as individuals—as people—that we do feel their humanity is of primary importance, that we want to know them as friends, and that we want to work with them to help all of us grow toward our maximum potential as human beings.

If we make this change, learning can become a joyful and exciting experience, both for the children and those of us responsible for working with them.

Room For Intellectual Wiggles

Teachers can cultivate curious minds in their
students by providing . . .

R. C. BRADLEY

Efficient teaching isn't measured totally by the depth of chalk dust accumulated in the blackboard tray at the end of the day.

But neither is there assurance that unused boards (teaching *per se*) reduce the intellectual fallout that is resultant from having acquired only particles of concepts or the dust of antiquated facts which currently seem to cloud the minds of some children who once had the zest to learn.

Someday in the very near future one of the major prerequisites for identifying the ideal teacher will be his courage to be curious. Educators must examine their own ranks if they are to cultivate and preserve curious minds for carrying on the dynamic work in the affluent society which they live in and serve.

Pupils will really study and learn when they want to.

But if success in school is necessary simply to win the approval of parents or teachers, or to obtain the desired diploma, then another less significant type of incentive to learn prevails.

Too often the school subject is not of real interest to the pupil, some parents and teachers appear indifferent to his school success, and he can graduate merely by maintaining a decent attendance and behavior record.

What then moves one to study?

Children's school experiences often become fear-inducing stimuli because it is quite common for a child who is achieving success in school

Bradley, R. C. "Room for Intellectual Wiggles." *The Texas Outlook.* April 1968
52:54-55, 68.

work to be afraid of failing a test, of being demoted, or failing to gain the approval of his teacher. The less probable the occurrence of a catastrophe, the greater the fear seems to be.

Rare also is the educator who cares as much about intellectual curiosity as he does about orderly classroom management. We stubbornly hang on to marking schemes, report cards, and book report themes with utter disregard for maturation of children in our teaching.

To plan activities and learnings regardless of the child's interest is selfish and destructive. Thus, the scared fighter may be the best fighter, but the scared learner is always a poor learner.

Curiosity Appears

As the term curiosity is normally used, it means someone is wanting to find something out. If this were all that one needed to say about curiosity, then one could identify an instance of it whenever a pupil asked a question, or engaged in exploratory behavior.

While curious pupils do want to find things out, set themselves a problem, curiosity is not necessarily a characteristic of problem-solving behavior.

When someone is striving to achieve a particular goal or purpose such as looking for a book, or seeking ways to solve a problem, we do not assign his exploratory questions or behavior to curiosity though he does want to find something out. The stronger the pupil's drive or goal is, the less likely he is of exhibiting marks of curiosity.

Pupils are curious, then, when they are relieved of the pressures of strong needs or preconceived goals, and when they truly want to find things out. (Pupils who ask questions do so often to please the teacher.) Yet, there is little need for pupils to be taught how to solve intellectual problems if they aren't first curious about them.

Stimuli

Children seek out stimuli for two reasons. First, for novelty, surprise, and change; and second, to relieve a disturbance within them caused by lack of information.

For this latter reason, their exploratory behavior responses may become *specific*. These responses may be so specific that they fall into a special category called *epistemic* motivation.

Thinking is a form of epistemic behavior if it is motivated by conflicts in ideas, attitudes, or beliefs. One reason a child asks so many questions is to gain information so that behavior can be guided in the future.

When children react to novelty or newness they exhibit *diversive* responses, ones which have been observed in animals. Scientists report that rats seem to tire of running through the same old maze. If they are allowed to try a new one, they will choose it.

Psychologists have found that the higher the degree of complexity offered by stimuli, the longer and stronger the response. It has long been known that a baby likes to look at changing leaf patterns and fancy wallpaper. When pairs of patterns were placed side by side in the baby's field of vision, he spent more time looking at the complex forms. This is also true of adults.

Another significant facet of teaching is to develop a skill for keeping some learning incongruous, or inconsistent, with what has been taught previously. Sometimes a completely new stimulus or activity provokes excitement, alertness, and perhaps even flight.

For example, have you ever seen a cat undergo the new experience of hearing a recorded human voice or cat's meow from the stereo speaker? The cat hears the voice or meow but it is not coming from a human or an animal as far as he is concerned. The visual and auditory stimuli are incongruous. The cat is torn between dashing from the room and investigating the speaker further.

Teachers would do well if they would provide their pupils the opportunity to explore intermittently during the school year selected ideas which may be incongruent with previous learnings or which are so new in structure that their learning power reaches greater depth and breadth.

Cultivate Curiosity

Until the spark of curiosity is lit, there is little guarantee that learning is taking place. Facts and knowledge are of little value when they are acquired by being pushed into the mind. Their strongest anchorage for future recall is the interest with which facts were received.

Problems of Curiosity

Are there specific dangers involved in letting children explore only those things about which they are curious?

For one thing, the curious thinker may not be popular.

For if he does not trust his own ideas, why should others believe in him?

Quite likely he will never receive the just guidance he deserves because oftentimes the teacher finds himself in a position of uneasiness since his ideas are subjected to challenge, ridicule, and mistrust.

Curiosity is immediate and very easily satisfied, so the child with his unsystematic curiosity is not necessarily going to use the right criteria to determine whether the information he has obtained is true or false. And the process used may limit his exploring the question fully. (It can be considered illogical when one concerns himself with whether or not the curiosity venture will bear fruitful results.)

Moreover, children may want to explore issues that are not necessarily a responsibility of school personnel.

To keep children curious the teacher must be eager to keep them in a state of wonderment about that which they learn. This is done in part by varying the content, giving the old experiences a new twist, and sprinkling the fields of learning with recent findings.

If curiosity is to be truly cultivated, the students must be allowed to talk about things other than graded subjects. There needs to be room to "intellectually wiggle" in our elementary schools, to get some thinking room in our minds, and then to be wise enough to take up the slack and wiggle again.

For too long we've been trying to teach children to be curious (forgetting that by their very nature they are anyway), rather than helping them to find out how to be curious or what interesting things can come from having a curious mind.

At this point, it is important to add that to be curious only, without having curiosity rewarded, is like putting on one's Sunday best with nowhere to go. For without satisfaction, one might as well let his ideas wither and die before his energies are spent.

We've got to do away with the nonsense theory that children have six elementary years, six secondary years, and four college years to learn only what the school prescribes.

When all children learn the same things and are expected to think alike, no one profits very much. But when a child is allowed to explore something unique to him which has aroused his curiosity, then learning takes on a new meaning.

A Teacher's Responsibility

The teacher will find it a rewarding experience to keep the spark of curiosity ignited in his pupils, and keeping that spark ignited may mean the difference between a child's success or failure. Teachers will find that it has always been the curious ones who have made major contributions in this world—those who were willing to go a step beyond the chalk dust curtain.

The teacher's knowledge of a child's powers for being curious must lead to an enlargement of his mental vision or interest will wane and the essence of that for which one strives becomes a clouded memory. Therefore, the modern teacher must take on a new image, that of innovator, seeker, and sharer of new ideas.

If we do not seek to improve this image the fault of not having curious minds to unlock the pathway to planets beyond this earth will not be "in our stars, but in ourselves" and man's mind will become weaker because of it.

SCHOOL is for . . .
LEARNING and THINKING
about IDEAS, VALUES,
and THINGS

Strategies For Developing An Elementary School Child's Powers Of Thinking

DR. R. C. BRADLEY

In my visits to many elementary schools across this country it is not uncommon for me to ask sixth grade children this question: "Have you had any lessons in your elementary school experience which have dealt with 'how to think?' " In the last five years the more prevalent answers have ranged from "No!" to "What do you mean by that?" No doubt much thinking is going on in the elementary school but shouldn't children be able to pinpoint it? Schools are for thinking and thinking can mean many things. To identify specific *thinking operations* is not an easy function but it is with this task that this author purports to deal.

The thought processes which follow, comprise a list that is suggestive rather than inclusive. It is hoped that these ideas will aid the elementary teacher in giving emphasis to thinking.

Observing. When an elementary school child *observes* he should be taught to record certain of his observations. This means that his teacher helps him to devise criteria to use in checking what is being noted with possible expectations. In devising this criteria sometimes it is necessary to make several observations and to let those become the criteria for making more defined observations.

As one looks he perceives, and from watching intently, comes a greater accuracy of observation. The process should be disciplined by purpose.

Classifying. Children should learn about systems of classification. As a child classifies objects he is perceiving the order in things about him.

Bradley, R. C. *Strategies for Developing an Elementary School Child's Powers of Thinking.* A Bassi Association Monograph Publication: Denton, Texas. August 1971. 1:1-4.

He must take things apart in his mind (analysis) and put them together again (synthesis) to make order out of the world. When a child is asked to look for commonalty in or among groups, he is having an experience in classification as a thought process.

Comparing. As a child observes two or more objects, ideas, or processes he may only look for likenesses or differences. The pupil who is trained in making comparisons is one who looks for *interrelationships* in addition to observing what is present in one idea yet absent in another.

Interpreting. As a child reads he is experiencing meaning, that is, he is putting meaning into the printed page as well as getting meaning out of it. The pupil who is skilled in interpreting finds it possible to check his inferences against the facts. Previously acquired facts support the interpretation he has presented.

Perceiving Assumptions. In the absence of factual support, one learns to make rather wise judgments, namely, something is true or probably true, false or probably false according to previous wise learnings and investigations. When one doesn't know for sure, he assumes from making a sum total of all of his perceptions that seem pertinent to the matter at hand.

Hypothesizing. Hunches or ideas can be built into hypotheses. Although tentative and provisional, an hypothesis is a possible solution to a problem. Elementary pupils can be taught how to make a preliminary intellectual test of the ideas they encounter. Formulating hypotheses is but one step of this thought operation since consequences must be explored if a given belief is entertained.

Criticizing. The untrained child may look for defects or short-comings when he is asked to criticize a piece of work, while the trained child provides a basis for what he is saying—he can present his criteria used in making the judgment. The trained child recognizes that when he is asked to criticize, he must first create a standard against which to defend his judgment. The person well versed in how to criticize something accurately, recognizes that he must have a *basis* for what he is saying; he can defend his position for he has thought about it before criticism is offered.

Summarizing. Children are usually good fact finders; they look for detail. When a child is taught to look for key episodes, to find the major structure, to identify the more relevant material, he is experiencing the summarization process. When the pupil is trained in summarizing his vocabulary includes such words as: essential, pertinent, significant, relevant, important, major, and inclusive. When summarizing, a child is in the process of synthesizing the material, determining relevant ideas from irrelevant ones, and ultimately finishes the task by restating the most essential points in a meaningful and organized fashion.

Imagining. This thought process is perhaps the most misused skill and yet the most used skill in the elementary school. It is misused when a teacher expects the child to perform a thought act that is anchored to his real world. When the teacher asks a child to *imagine* he should not expect the child to present supporting data. If a child recognizes that when he uses his imagination he is to go beyond his real world, to perceive in the mind what has not been wholly experienced, to roam in fancy, to make mental pictures, to think beyond his experiences, truly he is one who is imagining as he should have been trained to do.

Implementation of Thought Processes. The typical teaching act must be altered if children are going to learn how to think. The work to be learned must be rich, of high quality, worthy of being thought about. These specific concepts must be honored:

a) *seek rich, new content.* Much of what is taught to children in schools today is known to them prior to instruction.

b) *Plan for "dissonance" in the teaching act.* The wise teacher keeps the pupils somewhat off-balance between what they think is going to happen and what actually does take place in the learning situation.

c) *Collect "gap-fillers."* Newspaper clippings, poetry, excerpts from good books, film strips, pictures, commercial transparencies, and other related media should be immediately accessible to the children and/or teacher. These interesting ideas should be interwoven into the daily lessons.

d) *Use "novelty" in the instructional act.* The use of novel ideas creates a new mental set for most children. An unusual event or a twist of newness to an old point stirs some children to think in higher order.

e) *Refine question-making skills.* The types of questions a teacher asks determine the cognitive skills a pupil will employ, the linear range of data and information to be covered, and the cognitive skills a pupil should be expected to learn.

Strategies to Employ. Thinking is a complicated process and it takes a number of strategies in order that pupils can encounter its various aspects. The exemplars which follow will serve as illustrations for involving children in various thought operations.

*Underline one of the first five words in each of the following statements which you think makes it the truest statement.

1. All, Most, Many, Some, No poor people work harder than rich people.
2. All, Most, Many, Some, No pupils are happier in schools today than the pupils living in past periods.
3. All, Most, Many, Some, No things that we learn we learn only in school.
4. All, Most, Many, Some, No dogs are bigger than cats.
5. All, Most, Many, Some, No American elementary pupils hold parttime jobs after school.

*From the questions below you are to select the one item which would be more difficult to prove than the other four. In the space provided place your numbered selection.

(5) 1. Which of the following would be most difficult to prove true or false? (1) In Mexico the government is a republic, (2) Our nation's schools are superior to Spanish-American schools, (3) The United States has a Rocket base in Hawaii, (4) Our country trades with Argentina, (5) The principles contained in the Monroe Doctrine are out of date.

*In answering this question what seems to be a safe assumption?

Bob went to the store and bought two pencils for 10 cents. What was the cost of each pencil? (If you said 5 cents; you made a false assumption since one pencil was a compass pencil for 3 cents and the other was a red pencil for grading tests worth 7 cents.).

*What can you infer from this statement: "If heaven isn't really beyond our grasp, what is it really for?"

*In the parentheses below place an F for Fact and an O for Opinion.

(F) Oklahoma is North of Texas.
(O) High taxes increase the prosperity of our country.
(O) War is likely under any kind of social system.
(F) Generally it can be shown that a crisis brings out the best in people.
(O) The Indians are better off today than they were before white men came to North America.

*Select some table or graph in the light of the level of young children you are teaching and ask them to draw conclusions from it based on questions you provide them on mimeographed sheets of paper. Insert these directions: This is a worksheet to test your ability to draw conclusions from statistical data. In making your decisions you are to consider only the evidence given in the table (or graph) and to see if there are any logical trends which may be reasonably inferred from the data.

Answer Symbols: Numbers only please.

1. If the evidence alone is sufficient to make the statement true;
2. If the evidence alone is sufficient to indicate that likely the statement is true;
3. If the evidence alone is not sufficient to indicate any degree of positiveness or falsity;
4. If the evidence alone is sufficient to indicate the statement is probably a false one;
5. If the evidence alone is sufficient to make the statement false because it is actually contradicted in the table (or graph).

The above mentioned procedure gives a pupil experience in placing one of the numbers before the dozen or so questions that a teacher has structured as a result of an analysis of the table or graph.

*Grasping the *meaning* of statements beyond the actual facts presented is a very important skill or ability, particularly in the social sciences, since much reading investigation and research is essential to the final product, an oral report.

Student directions: Let us assume that the information below is true, and if so, then it is possible to establish other facts using the ones in this paragraph as a basis for one's reasoning. You are in the thought operation of *drawing inferences. Caution:* there is always a limit to the number or kinds of facts which can be adequately and properly inferred from any statement.

Put . . .

T—if the statement can be inferred as TRUE from the paragraph

F—if the statement may be inferred as UNTRUE and the work in the paragraph implies it is false.

N—if no inference can be drawn about it from the context.

Paragraph A

The list of necessities for the poor free laborer in ancient Rome was very small. He needed about fifteen bushels of wheat every year. About the only meat he had to eat was that which the priests gave away after a sacrifice on holidays. He needed about a penny's worth of oil and another penny's worth of wine each day; his small daily portion of vegetables cost this much again. A pound of cheese cost somewhat more, but would last for several days. These foods made up the pattern of his usual menu. The wool for the two tunics he needed each year cost about $1. Half this much would pay for a pair of sandals which he seldom wore. The state supplied amusements on holidays free of charge and also supported the free public baths, where friends could gather. If he was out of work the state would also supply him with grain. Therefore it was possible for the poor freeman to live and also to have a wife if his wife would spin and weave. (Abridged and edited from T. Frank, *History of Rome,* 1923, p. 389-90.).

Questions on Paragraph A:

(N) 1. Many rich Romans were cruel to their slaves.
(T) 2. Conditions for living by Roman laborers were very poor.
(F) 3. The Romans diet consisted of cheeses and green vegetables, since their religion denied their eating of meat.
(F) 4. Roman laborers made their own clothes.
(N) 5. Roman slaves were much better off than free laborers.
(T) 6. The wife of the laborer generally made her husband's clothes.
(F) 7. Priests expressed little interest in the welfare of the poor.

*Purchase two sacks of marshmallows. In one sack drop powdered alum. Then mix the two sacks together and place these on a large serving tray. Pass these out among the pupils and ask them to observe them, to make inference regarding them, and to hypothesize about them. (Those receiving the ones with powdered alum will say of course, "I have marshmallows!" Upon tasting them, however, to their amazement, discover they do not taste like marshmallows. Consequently, they must formulate another hypothesis and cite other assumptions.).

*To help children imagine ask them to respond to such questions as: (1) What would happen if we had to face a week when there was no sun? (2) Pretend that all electricity was cut off in the world for 48 hours. What might be the result? (3) You are on an unknown island and can make one call home, what would you say that would help your parents, airplane pilots, missing persons bureau, or the like to find you?

*Take a raw potato and hold it in your left hand. Place a soda straw in your right hand. Raise the soda straw high enough that you can drive it forcefully into the potato. Did it go? On the next try, as you get close in the drive toward the potato, cap your thumb over the top end of the soda straw while continuing your drive into the potato. What happened? What caused the straw to go on through without breaking? (The air literally blasts a hole through the potato.).

Summary. There is no real reason to teach *thinking* apart from any subject, nevertheless children must have experiences in it. The prudent teacher will seek to develop thinking operations along with knowledge and understanding in various fields rather than attempting to teach it always as a separate entity. If one does not intermittently run a check, however, some thought skills may be left out entirely. This may mean that the novice teacher will want to devise a plan in which a running account is made by the week concerning the types of thought skills that were emphasized. Unless one does seek to look at each thought operation to be taught, he may go several weeks by-passing (or perhaps not even teaching one thought skill at all) significant thought processes which a child should be encountering.

Someday, in the life of this writer, it is hoped that he will visit some elementary classrooms and when he asks, "Have you had any lessons on thinking?" Some pupil will respond, "My teacher says I'm a better 'inference maker' than 'fact finder'." Then he will know that elementary schools truly are for thinking.

A Teaching Strategy for Culturally Deprived Pupils: Cognitive and Motivational Considerations

DAVID P. AUSUBEL

The possibility of arresting and reversing the course of intellectual retardation in the culturally deprived pupil depends largely on providing him with an optimal learning environment as early as possible in the course of his educational career. If the limiting effects of prolonged cultural deprivation on the development of verbal intelligence and on the acquisition of verbal knowledge are to be at least partially overcome, better-than-average strategies of teaching are obviously necessary in terms of both general effectiveness and specific appropriateness for his particular learning situation. Yet precisely the opposite state of affairs typically prevails: the learning environment of the culturally deprived child is both generally inferior and specifically inappropriate. His cumulative intellectual deficit, therefore, almost invariably reflects, in part, the cumulative impact of a continuing and consistently deficient learning environment, as well as his emotional and motivational reaction to this environment. Thus, much of the lower-class child's alienation from the school is not so much a reflection of discriminatory or rejecting attitudes on the part of teachers and other school personnel—although the importance of this factor should not be underestimated; it is in greater measure a reflection of the cumulative effects of a curriculum that is too demanding of him, and of the resulting load of frustration,

Ausubel, David P. "A Teaching Strategy for Culturally Deprived Pupils: Cognitive and Motivational Considerations." *The School Review.* Winter 1963. 71:454-463.

confusion, demoralization, resentment, and impaired self-confidence that he must bear.

Cognitive Considerations

An effective and appropriate teaching strategy for the culturally deprived child must therefore emphasize these three considerations: *(a)* the selection of initial learning material geared to the learner's existing state of readiness; *(b)* mastery and consolidation of all ongoing learning tasks before new tasks are introduced, so as to provide the necessary foundation for successful sequential learning and to prevent unreadiness for future learning tasks; and *(c)* the use of structured learning materials optimally organized to facilitate efficient sequential learning. Attention to these three factors can go a long way toward insuring effective learning for the first time, and toward restoring the child's educational morale and confidence in his ability to learn. Later possible consequences are partial restoration of both intrinsic and extrinsic motivation for academic achievement, diminution of anti-intellectualism, and decreased alienation from the school to the point where his studies make sense and he sees some purpose in learning. In my opinion, of all the available teaching strategies, programmed instruction, minus the teaching-machine format, has the greatest potentialities for meeting the aforementioned three criteria of an effective and appropriate approach to the teaching of culturally deprived pupils.

Readiness.—A curriculum that takes the readiness of the culturally deprived child into account always takes as its starting point his existing knowledge and sophistication in the various subject-matter areas and intellectual skills, no matter how far down the scale this happens to be. This policy demands rigid elimination of all subject matter that he cannot economically assimilate on the basis of his current level of cognitive sophistication. It presupposes emphasis on his acquisition of the basic intellectual skills before any attempt is made to teach him algebra, geometry, literature, and foreign languages. However, in many urban high schools and junior high schools today, pupils who cannot read at a third-grade level and who cannot speak or write grammatically or perform simple arithmetical computations are subjected to irregular French verbs, Shakespearean drama, and geometrical theorems. Nothing more educationally futile or better calculated to destroy educational morale could be imagined!

In the terms of readiness for a given level of school work, a child is no less ready because of a history of cultural deprivation, chroni academic failure, and exposure to an unsuitable curriculum than because of deficient intellectual endowment. Hence, realistic recognition of this fact is not undemocratic, reactionary, or evidence of social class bias, of intellectual snobbery, of a "soft," patronizing approach, or a belief in the inherent uneducability of lower-class children. Neither is it indicative of a desire to surrender to the culturally deprived child's current intellectual level, to perpetuate the status quo, or to institute a double, class-oriented standard of education. It is merely a necessary first step in preparing him to cope with more advanced subject matter, and hence in eventually reducing existing social class differentials in academic achievement. To set the same *initial* standards and expectations for the academically retarded culturally deprived child as for the non-retarded middle- or lower-class child is automatically to insure the former's failure and to widen prevailing discrepancies between social class groups.

Consolidation.—By insisting on consolidation or mastery of ongoing lessons before new material is introduced, we make sure of continued readiness and success in sequentially organized learning. Abundant experimental research has confirmed the proposition that prior learnings are not transferable to new learning tasks unless they are first over-learned.[1] Overlearning, in turn, requires an adequate number of adequately spaced repetitions and reviews, sufficient intratask repetitiveness prior to intra- and intertask diversification,[2] and opportunity for differential practice of the more difficult components of a task. Frequent testing and provision of feedback, especially with test items demanding fine discrimination among alternatives varying in degrees of correctness, also enhance consolidation by confirming, clarifying, and correcting previous learnings. Lastly, in view of the fact that the culturally deprived child tends to learn more slowly than his non-deprived peers, self-pacing helps to facilitate consolidation.

Structured, sequential materials.—The principal advantage of programmed instruction, apart from the fact that it furthers consolidation, is its careful sequential arrangement and gradation of difficulty which insures that each attained increment in learning serves as an appropriate foundation and anchoring post for the learning and retention of subsequent items in the ordered sequence.[3] Adequate programming of materials also presupposes maximum attention to such matters as lucidity, organization, and the explanatory and integrative power of substantive content. It is helpful, for example, if sequential materials are so organized that they become progressively more differentiated in terms of generality and inclusiveness, and if similarities and differences between the current learning task and previous learnings are explicitly delineated.[4] Both of these aims can be accomplished by using an advance organizer or brief introductory passage before each new unit of material, which both makes available relevant explanatory principles at a high level of abstraction and increases discriminability. Programmed instruction can also be especially adapted to meet the greater needs of culturally deprived pupils for concrete-empirical props in learning relational propositions.

Although programmed instruction in general is particularly well suited to the needs of the culturally deprived child, I cannot recommend the small-frame format characteristic of teaching-machine programs and most programmed textbooks. In terms of both the logical requirements of meaningful learning and the actual size of the task that can be conveniently accommodated by the learner, the frame length typically used by teaching machines is artifically and unnecessarily abbreviated. It tends to fragment the ideas presented in the program so that their inter-relationships are obscured and their logical structure is destroyed.[5] Hence it is relatively easy for less able students to master each granulated step of a given program without understanding the logical relationships and development of the concepts presented.[6] In my opinion, therefore, the traditional textbook format or oral didactic exposition that follows the programming principles outlined above, supplemented by frequent self-scoring and feedback-giving tests, is far superior to the teaching-machine approach for the actual presentation of subject-matter content.[7]

Motivational Considerations

Thus far I have considered various environmental factors that induce retardation in the culturally deprived child's intellectual growth, as well as different cognitive techniques of counteracting and reversing such retardation. These factors and techniques, however, do not operate in a motivational vacuum. Although it is possible separately to consider cognitive and motivational aspects of learning for purposes of theoretical analysis, they are nonetheless inseparably intertwined in any real-life learning situation. For example, school failure and loss of confidence resulting from an inappropriate curriculum further depress the culturally deprived pupil's motivation to learn and thereby increase his existing learning and intellectual deficit. Similarly, although a number of practice and task variables are potentially important for effective learning in a programmed instruction context, appropriate manipulation of these variables can, in the final analysis, only insure successful long-term learning of subject matter provided that the individual is adequately motivated.

Doing without being interested in what one is doing results in relatively little permanent learning, since it is reasonable to suppose that only those materials can be meaningfully incorporated on a long-term basis into an individual's structure of knowledge that are relevant to areas of concern in his psychological field. Learners who have little need to know and understand quite naturally expend little learning effort; manifest an insufficiently meaningful learning set; fail to develop precise meanings, to reconcile new ideas with existing concepts, and to formulate new propositions in their own words; and do not devote enough time and energy to practice and review. Material is therefore never sufficiently consolidated to form an adequate foundation for sequential learning.

The problem of reversibility exists in regard to the motivational as well as in regard to the cognitive status of the culturally deprived pupil, inasmuch as his environment typically stunts not only his intellectual development, but also the development of appropriate motivations for academic achievement. Motivations for learning, like cognitive abilities, are only potential rather than inherent or endogenous capacities in human beings; their actual development is invariably dependent upon adequate environmental stimulation. Cognitive drive or intrinsic motivation to learn, for example, is probably derived in a very general sense from curiosity tendencies and from related predispositions to explore, manipulate, and cope with the environment; but these tendencies and predispositions are only actualized as a result of successful exercise and the anticipation of future satisfying consequences from further exercise and as a result of internalization of the values of those significant persons in the family and subcultural community with whom the child identifies.

Intrinsic motivation.—The development of cognitive drive or of intrinsic motivation for learning, that is, the acquisition of knowledge as an end in itself or for its own sake, is, in my opinion, the most promising motivational strategy which we can adopt in relation to the culturally deprived child. It is true, of course, in view of the anti-intellectualism and pragmatic attitude toward education that is characteristic of lower-class ideology,[8] that superficially better case can be made for the alternative strategy of appealing to the incentives to job acquisition, retention, and advancement that now apply so saliently to continuing education because of the rapid rate of technological change. Actually, however, intrinsic motivation for learning is more potent, relevant, durable, and easier to arouse than its extrinsic counterpart. Meaningful school learning, in contrast to most kinds of laboratory learning, requires relatively little effort or extrinsic incentive, and, when successful, furnishes its own reward. In most instances of school learning, cognitive drive is also the only immediately relevant motivation, since the greater part of school learning cannot be rationalized as necessary for meeting the demands of daily living. Furthermore, it does not lose its relevance or potency in later adult life when utilitarian and career advancement considerations are no longer applicable. Lastly, as we know from the high dropout rate among culturally deprived high-school youth, appeals to extrinsic motivation are not very effective. Among other reasons, the latter situation reflects a limited time perspective focused primarily on the present; a character structure that is oriented more to immediate than delayed gratification of needs; the lack of strong internalized needs for and anxiety about high academic and vocational achievement, as part of the prevailing family, peer group, and community ideology;[9] and the seeming unreality and impossibility of attaining the rewards of prolonged striving and self-denial in view of current living conditions and family circumstances, previous lack of school success, and the discriminatory attitudes of middle-class society.[10]

If we wish to develop the cognitive drive so that it remains viable during the school years and in adult life, it is necessary to move still further away from the educational doctrine of gearing the curriculum to the spontaneously expressed interests, current concerns, and life-adjustment problems of pupils. Although it is undoubtedly unrealistic and even undesirable in our culture to eschew entirely the utilitarian, ego-enhancement, and anxiety-reduction motivations for learning, we must place increasingly greater emphasis upon the value of knowing and understanding as goals in their own right, quite apart from any practical benefits they may confer. Instead of denigrating subject-matter knowledge, we must discover more efficient methods of fostering the long-term acquisition or meaningful and usable bodies of knowledge, and of developing appropriate intrinsic motivations for such learning.

It must be conceded at the outset that culturally deprived children typically manifest little intrinsic motivation to learn. They come from family and cultural environments in which the veneration of learning for its own sake is not a conspicuous value, and in which there is little or no tradition of scholarship. Moreover, they have not been notably successful in their previous learning efforts in school. Nevertheless we need not necessarily despair of motivating them to learn for intrinsic reasons. Psychologists have been emphasizing the motivation-learning and the interest-activity sequences of cause and effect for so long that they tend to overlook their reciprocal aspects. Since motivation is not an indispensable condition for short-term and limited-quantity learning, it is not necessary to postpone learning activities until appropriate interests and motivations have been developed. Frequently the best way of motivating an unmotivated pupil is to ignore his motivational state for the time being and concentrate on teaching him as effectively as possible. Much to his surprise and to his teacher's, he will learn despite his lack of motivation; and from the satisfaction of learning he will character-istically develop the motivation to learn more.

Paradoxically, therefore, we may discover that the most effective method of developing intrinsic motivation to learn is to focus on the cognitive rather than on the motivational aspects of learning, and to rely on the motivation that is developed retroactively from successful educational achievement. This is particularly true when a teacher is able to generate contagious excitement and enthusiasm about the subject he teaches, and when he is the kind of person with whom culturally deprived children can identify. Recruiting more men teachers and dramatizing the lives and exploits of cultural, intellectual, and scientific heroes can also enhance the process of identification. At the same time, of course, we can attempt to combat the anti-intellectualism and lack of cultural tradition in the home through programs of adult education and cultural enrichment.

Extrinsic motivation.—The emphasis I have placed on intrinsic motivation for learning should not be interpreted to mean that I deny the importance of developing extrinsic motivations. The need for ego enhancement, status, and prestige through achievement, the inter-nalization of long-term vocational aspirations, and the development of such implementing traits as responsibility, initiative, self-denial, frustration tolerance, impulse control, and the ability to postpone immediate hedonistic gratification are, after all, traditional hallmarks of personality maturation in our culture; and educational aspirations and achievement are both necessary prerequisites for, and way-station prototypes of, their vocational counterparts. Hence, in addition to encouraging intrinsic motivation for learning, it is also necessary to foster ego-enhancement and career-advancement motivations for academic achievement.

As previously pointed out, however, the current situation with respect to developing adequate motivations for higher academic and vocational achievement among culturally deprived children is not very encouraging. But just as in the case of cognitive drive, much extrinsic motivation for academic success can be generated retroactively from the experience of current success in schoolwork. Intensive counseling can also compensate greatly for the absence of appropriate home, community, and peer-group support and expectations for the develop-ment of long-term vocational ambitions. In a sense counselors must be prepared to act *in loco parentis* in this situation. By identifying with a mature, stable, striving, and successful male adult figure, culturally deprived boys can be encouraged to internalize long-term and realistic aspirations, as well as to develop the mature personality traits necessary for their implementation. Hence, as a result of achieving current ego-enhancement in the school setting, obtaining positive encouragement and practical guidance in the counseling relationship, and experiencing less rejection and discrimination at the hands of school personnel, higher vocational aspirations appear to lie more realistically within their grasp. Further encouragement to strive for more ambitious academic and vocational goals can be provided by making available abundant scholarship aid to universities, to community colleges, and to technical institutes; by eliminating the color, ethnic, and class bar in housing, education, and employment; by acquainting culturally deprived youth with examples of successful professional persons originating from their own racial, ethnic, and class backgrounds; and by involving parents sympathetically in the newly fostered ambitions of their children. The success of the Higher Horizons project indicates that an energetic program organized along the lines outlined above can do much to reverse the effects of cultural deprivation on the development of extrinsic motivations for academic and vocational achievement.

NOTES

[1] See R. W. Bruce, "Conditions of Transfer of Training," *Journal of Experimental Psychology*, XVI (1933), 343-61; C. P. Duncan, "Transfer in Motor Learning as a Function of Degree of First-task Learning and Inter-task Similarity," *Experimental Psychology*, XLV (1953), 1-11, and his "Transfer after Training with Single versus Multiple Tasks," *Journal of Experimental Psychology*, LV (1958), 63-72; L. Morrisett and C. I. Hovland, "A Comparison of Three Varieties of Training in Human Problem Solving," *Journal of Experimental Psychology*, LV (1958), 52-55; and J. M. Sassenrath, "Learning without Awareness and Transfer of Learning Sets," *Journal of Educational Psychology*, L (1959), 202-12.

[2] See Duncan, "Transfer after Training with Single versus Multiple Tasks," *op. cit.*; Morrisett and Hovland, *op. cit.*; and Sassenrath, *op. cit.*

[3] D. P. Ausubel and D. Fitzgerald, "Organizer, General Background, and Antecedent Learning Variables in Sequential Verbal Learning," *Journal of Educational Psychology*, LIII (1962), 243-49.

[4] D. P. Ausubel, "The Use of Advance Organizers in the Learning and Retention of Meaningful Verbal Learning," *Journal of Educational Psychology*, LI (1960), 267-72; D. P. Ausubel and D. Fitzgerald, "The Role of Discriminability in Meaningful Verbal Learning and Retention," *Journal of Educational Psychology*, LII (1961), 266-74, and their "Organizer, General Background, and Antecedent Learning Variables in Sequential Verbal Learning," *op. cit.*

[5] S. L. Pressey, "Basic Unresolved Teaching-Machine Problems," *Theory into Practice*, I (1962), 30-37.

[6] D. G. Beane, "A Comparison of Linear and Branching Techniques of Programed Instruction in Plane Geometry" ("Technical Report," No. 1 [Urbana: Training Research Laboratory, University of Illinois, July 1962]).

[7] Pressey, *op. cit.*,

[8] F. Riessman, *The Culturally Deprived Child* (New York: Harper & Bros., 1962).

[9] A. Davis, "Child Training and Social Class," *Child Behavior and Development*, ed. R. G. Barker, J. S. Kounin, and H. F. Wright (New York: McGraw-Hill Book Co., 1963), pp. 607-20.

[10] *Ibid.*

Chapter IV

The Teacher as a Personalizer of Instruction

Introduction*

Many schools have taken steps to *individualize* instruction for their children. Yet this is but a first step; *personalization* is the second. More often than not, when a school authority boasts individualized instruction for all children, he speaks of:

    a) some form of school organization (team teaching, non-gradedness, open concept schemes)
    b) the selection of certain "educational packages" or graded materials supposedly designed for specific learning problems, and
    c) other related *hardware-software* materials designed for use with specific, predetermined types of children.

In other words, as school people talk about individualizing instruction they typically speak in terms of manipulating materials, changing of school organizational patterns (i.e.; moving from self-contained classroom units to open area constructs), and placing some burden of responsibility on the child for determining how fast he will progress in the new arrangement (e.g.; *contracts* by the pupil for specific amounts of academic units of work). But schools do more than individualize instruction,—they must personalize their instruction in light of their knowledge regarding the talents, curiosity, intellect, interest, background, personal needs, and powers of each scholastic.

A new concept in education is *Personalized Instruction.* It entails not only the humanizing of education but a new term "cooperative planning of a child's *educational program.*" No doubt the term has been coined as a result of the observation that learning has become

---

*Written especially for this volume by R. C. Bradley, January 1, 1974.

113

fragmentized, mini-lessons are being designed, and what was once thought to be a necessary sequence to learning is receiving a strong, hard look by educationalists, practitioners, and research oriented persons.

When a teacher seeks to *personalize* instruction, he becomes a penetrating person. The school success of a child is more closely related to some special effort of his teacher to inspire him to succeed than it is to specific instructional procedures. For example, many evidences are available to indicate that by all professional rights some children were so handicapped in physical, social, psychological, and mental ways they should likely never be able to read, but their will power and the remedial teacher's power of instruction and motivation caused them to learn in spite of those inabilities.

The phenomenon of individual differences has created instructional problems for teachers for a long time and the efforts to deal with those problems have generally been through organizational structure (non-gradedness, team teaching, open concept designs), not essentially *personalization*. Aiding teachers in the personalization of instruction is a worthy goal to which more schools might dedicate inservice programs and faculty meetings, and it is with this purpose that this author purports to deal.

Personalized Versus Individualized Instruction

Individualized instruction is "custom-tailored" instruction designed to fit a particular learner. In providing individualized instruction the teacher concerns himself with knowledge of a pupil's individual differences. He recognizes that the learner has a pattern and rhythm of growth peculiar to the individual. Notable differences exist between individuals, in speed of learning, energy output, depth of feeling, and facility of insight.

Personalized instruction is likewise based upon individual variations of the learner but its power comes from penetrating more deeply a child's perceptions of such understandings as these: how he feels about the consequences of what is being learned, what he believes he can learn to do better, how to identify personally the best way he learns, how to determine personally under the auspices of his teacher what is relevant for his personal program of instruction, and how to develop means through which he understands his own reactions of "self" and what his teacher is seeking to do to make his school life happier, easier, and educatively more profitable.

When one individualizes instruction more likely his judgments of the educational program are based more upon variations in learning habits between learners (individualization) than upon individual variations *within* learners. Personalized learning is directed toward *intra*-individual variations, that is, variation of learning habits within each specific child.

In individualized instruction one does not assume that each student's instruction comes in isolation, nor does it mean each pupil is on a separate subject. In personalized instruction, however, the teacher is directing his attention, comments, and instructional strategies to *one* child. One behaves quite differently when teaching a *single* pupil;—to meet his personal needs one must recognize that each pupil is an individual (unlike all other pupils, a dynamic, changing organism). One can individualize assignments to meet a child's basic surface needs, but it is the personalized, deep-rooted instruction which makes a difference in the learner. How a child feels about his subject likely governs how much he does and learns about it.

It seems noteworthy to mention that of a college graduate class of 40 experienced teachers who were asked to teach a single child only five appeared with an educational program written out as the instructional guidelines for use with their child. Typically, experienced people assume that work with an individual requires less planning than it does for a whole class.

In personalized instruction the teacher is sensitive to how things seem to his pupils rather than being exclusively concerned with concrete events. When a teacher works with one child he applies beliefs and understandings to particular persons, rather than applying facts to dozens of people in the abstract. His acute sensitivity to the personal needs of the youngster helps the learner to feel: identified with rather than apart from others; basically adequate rather than untrustworthy; as worthy rather than unworthy; and wanted rather than unwanted. It is apparent that these characteristics influence the extent to which a child responds to instruction even though it has already been individualized for him. Summarily, *personalized* instruction complements the various individualization processes.

Teacher-Pupil Planning of a Child's Educational Program

For some time we have known that a person participates in a stronger degree if he has been a part of the planning. Certainly the teacher will offer guidance and direction in planning of a child's personal educational program for such help is mandatory. Moreover, as a child plans with the teacher, he commits himself to carrying out the plan they have cooperatively worked out. It is in this planning stage that the teacher intermittently bombards the child with such questions as:

1. Do you know the skill that is necessary to do this drill?
2. How long do you think we should spend on this area?
3. What means should we use to evaluate your progress?
4. Would you prefer to do this option or that?

At every turn the teacher supplies essential information to the child as they plan. He is very helpful in helping the pupil become self-directed; he promotes self-direction; he helps each student to know himself, to establish goals, to make plans and to carry them out. When a child is involved in planning his own educational program he learns to simultaneously make judgments about the effectiveness of present procedures and how to devise better ones if they are needed.

While the personalized educational program of a child is being planned, the teacher is helping a pupil find something by which to live. He should want a child to know values people hold, to be able to understand and accept differences, to discover values which are significant to him. As the teacher becomes this personal, it is more likely that a child will find a deeper commitment to school life which in turn gives purpose and meaning to life itself.

If the major function of a formal education is to help people develop a skill for continuing their own education after they leave the school setting, a teacher who performs the role of increasing self-direction makes a major contribution.

How Does One Personalize Instruction?

BE SUPPORTIVE IN COMMENTS TO PUPILS

Consider this school setting. A child is asked to go to the chalkboard to work an arithmetic problem. In any individualized assignment the work has already been selected on the basis of these knowledges about the child: maturity, intelligence, background experiences, and prior skills. Typically, the teacher says, "Fred, go to the board and work problem 7, *I know you can do it!*" In personalized instruction the teacher remarks to the same child and setting: "Fred, go to the board and do problem 7; *I don't know whether you can work it or not!*" In the former statement, if the pupil cannot work the arithmetic problem, he merely demonstrates the fact that what the teacher perceived to be true, was not true. He could not work it. He failed his teacher. He feels beaten academically, socially, and intellectually. However, the latter statement helps a child to recognize two basic feelings:

(1) If he could not work it, then it is still alright because the personalized remark by his teacher indicated that she doubted if he could do it anyway.
(2) If he does work the problem, then the pupil wins twice—
   (a) he surprised his teacher who believed he could not do it and,
   (b) he pleased himself because he may not have been sure that he could get it right in the first place.

He achieves. He is proud. He pleased his teacher.

LOOK FOR THE EMOTIONAL SIDE OF THE QUESTION

Bobby slams his book, pushes it off his desk, and states: "I hate arithmetic and I'm not working any more problems." Teacher A walks over, picks up the book, places it before Bobby, and with firmness in her voice states: "You get to work on this page and I mean right now!"

Teacher B, seeking to personalize her work with Bobby, reaches down to the floor, picks up the book, takes it to her desk and returns to Bobby, then states: "I suspect I know how you feel. Recently when I had on my Sunday clothes, and had a flat tire to change, the task seemed unbearable. Arithmetic is difficult for you isn't it?" Likely Teacher B will be able to find that it is not only arithmetic that has caused the problem but there are in addition other obstacles to overcome if Bobby is to return to his arithmetic work by tomorrow. Note that Teacher B removed from Bobby's vision his seemingly distasteful obstacle, the arithmetic book.

It is the wise teacher who is able to move his thoughts and a pupil's inner self from feelings of inadequacy to convictions that one can succeed and overcome environmental or intra-variable conflicts. In personalized instruction both the teacher and the pupil seek to discern the emotional aspects of a problem from the academic or skill oriented factors evidenced in the conflict.

SEEK TO CLEAR UP EACH CHILD'S MISCONCEPTIONS

In planning a child's personal educational program, some content and structure of his work should deal with his own misconceptions. Recently some first graders were asked, "Where does syrup come from?" One pupil said, "Aunt Jemima"; another said, "From corn—the green giant has something to do with it."; a little girl said, "I don't know Miss Smith, but it's made in a log cabin."

After all of these weird answers a little boy finally gave rise to: "I'm not sure, but I saw on Walt Disney something that makes me think it comes from trees!" His red-faced, freckle-faced buddy nudged him in the side and said, "Man, You've got to be kiddin!" It takes little probing in a

2 or 3 minute private conference with a child to find out something of those things which he believes to be worthy of treatment in his personalized program of instruction. Listen for misconceptions. Seek to clear them up.

PROMOTE THE IDEA THAT ONE'S PERSONAL PROGRAM OF INSTRUCTION IS DIRECTED TOWARD IMPROVING LIFE INSIDE AND OUTSIDE OF SCHOOL

At a very early age too many children do not see the school as a place of relevancy. They view it as being cold, impersonal, and unrelated to their real life. At least a portion of one day a week ought to be dedicated to helping youngsters find out what life is really like. The teacher might place himself in the role of an original researcher and ask a child in a private session what it is that he is struggling to be, what is his purpose, what can be done by the school to help him achieve his purposes. Personalized comments should be directed toward helping a child perceive what difference he makes as a person to homelife, school life, and other areas wherein he works, plays, and allocates his time.

Since the individual resides in a given environment, his *self* must interact with it. However, a part of this environment is the pupil himself. Personalized conferences can be an adjunct to a child's instructional program. An intermediate level child can be presented with the view that an individual has many selves: the self he really believes he is, the self he realistically aspires to be, the ideal self, the self he hopes to be, the self he thinks others see, the self he fears he might be now.

The teacher's task is not to try to fuse all of these *selves* but to help a child personally recognize that he can make a conscious differentiation of one's self from all others.

There are external factors which teachers control daily in their work with children but it is a different instructional task when one attempts to help a child preserve his own self-concepts. A child who can answer these four basic questions has profited from personalized instruction: (1) Who am I? (2) What am I? (3) How strong am I? (5) What is my place? These questions not only help a child relate to his environment but provide him with criteria that will help him make sense out of the world around him.

KEEP CHILD CURIOSITY ALIVE

The general principles of how to be curious may be learned through books, activities, and experiences obtained both at home and school, but the zest, the burning desire, the color, the tone, and the feel of the spirit which makes it live in us, must all be caught from those in whom it already lives. Curiosity helps one (a) explore an avenue of learning until the mind produces a new idea; (b) as one extends his curiosity bent nature he does so by destroying bad ideas and then replacing them with more adequate ideas; (c) curiosity helps one find disorder in order, and likely the more worthy findings are in the essence of the work itself.

In a third grade class children passed over the point as shown in pictures that many Japanese farm houses had straw roofs. At seatwork time the teacher personalized her work by asking a rather curious type of student why most of the houses had straw roofs in all pictures shown at social studies period. The child really didn't know but as a result of the personal follow-up by his teacher, this same child came in two days later with the following report.

> Straw can be bundled to keep out the rain. It costs less than roofs like most people have in our neighborhood. Rice paddy farmers have much straw left after harvesting the rice. I think it is good that they use straw since it is left-over and doesn't cost them anything.

Why didn't the teacher ask this question during social studies class? Because she knew of a child in her group who needed the opportunity to explore something on his own successfully. Likewise, she gave him some personal attention designed to make him curious enough to look into the problem. Moreover, the teacher knew that when the report came back it would be worthy of sharing at another time with the whole group. The teacher who deals with keeping a pupil's mind fresh and curious is breaking away from the traditional, routine school experience.

Through personalized attention a child is allowed to dream, to give vent to imagination, to respond to its calling, and to seek understanding out of its mysticism. The way to encourage curiosity is to applaud and reward it.

COMPLETE THE LEARNING CYCLE

It is possible for a teacher to offer individualized instruction, yet unknowingly, neglect a very important personalized aspect of a child's educational program. Consider this diagram of an acceptable instructional act:

*(Content) Subject or Skill to be learned	(Method) Activity or experience	(Evaluation) Test to determine extent of achievement

*A Partial Learning Cycle

Generally it has been an acceptable practice to present content to pupils through a chosen method and then to test in written form the extent to which learning took place. However, it should be remembered that the learning cycle is not completed until the pupil is provided with an opportunity to use his information or newly acquired skill on fresh, rich, new content.

Until the instructional act of the teacher becomes so personalized that it reaches the child through helping him to complete the learning cycle, it seems reasonable to assume some children will learn to respond to a test and neglect personal application of what has been learned. For those teachers who seek to complete the learning cycle their efforts can be schematically shown as follows:

**	Teach content (Pre-test)	Through Method	Test	Provide New Content	Re-test

**A Complete Learning Cycle

There are significant ways, other than through written tests, from which one can learn whether or not a pupil has achieved the proficiency sought in the lesson. For example, these include the teacher's observation of a finished art project, listening to oral comments and responses to questions, and witnessing other related overt behaviors of children. Once the teacher perceives that the child has learned, he prepares an assignment to which the child is expected to apply his newly acquired knowledge or skill. Consequently, personalized instruction does not rest upon "teacher exposure" to knowledge but "student disclosure" of what he has actually learned.

HUMANIZING INSTRUCTION

Individualized instruction does not mean there is always a one-to-one teacher-pupil correspondence, but teachers who effectively personalize instruction do give each child some independent study and help on a one-to-one relationship.

To allow for the uniqueness of pupils, that is, to adjust for individual differences, is an essential and laudable aim. But to strive for *personalization* of individualized instruction is the ideal objective, to be striven for but only approximated. One way of personalizing instruction is to make a commitment to involvement with pupils. That is, helping pupils to search out the implications of ideas, to find out what they mean from the child's point of view, to value and glory in them.

Seeking uniqueness in teaching simply by individualization of instruction does not preclude the fact that many persons simply need to become more competent in doing their respective jobs. Individualization of instruction is a task of the competent teacher, however, individualizing work experiences of children without an accrument of *personalization* is of little consequence.

SCHOOL is for . . .
FULLFILMENT of
INWARD DESIRES

Individualized Instruction

JAMES E. EISELE

Much has been written in recent years about individualized instruction, and there is some evidence to indicate that a variety of attempts have been made in the schools to foster instruction that can be termed individualized. Gibbons (1) for example, lists numerous proposals for individualized programs, under ten major categories and excluding those in specific subject areas, which have been made, and used to some extent, during this century. Individualization of instruction is, indeed, a major topic of the hour.

In spite of this avowed popularity, however, little has been accomplished by way of breaking from traditional lock-step, group centered instruction in the vast majority of classrooms. The impact, in terms of numbers of students experiencing individualized instruction, of those programs enumerated by Gibbons, has been negligible. In other words,

> . . . much more lip service than implementation is given individualizing instruction. In fact, it is quite safe to say that nothing is more discussed, yet has less done about it than individualization of instruction. (2)

There appears to be ample evidence that the individualization of instruction is not occurring to any marked degree, in spite of a widely recognized need for the practice. This leads to the question, "Why?" Why have more teachers not attempted to meet the needs of individuals in their classrooms. If they are trying, why are they not succeeding to a noticeable degree? With a drop-out rate which claims a high percentage of students before they reach the end of twelfth grade, and with the lack of relevancy in the curriculum becoming a national rallying point for students of all ages during the past decade, there is ample evidence that individual needs and interests are **not** being satisfied.

Eisele, James E. "Individualized Instruction." *Contemporary Education.* October 1971. 43:16-20. Reprinted with the permission of the author and Indiana State University.

Something must be done to close the gap between theory and practice in education. Data being collected (3) suggest that even among classroom teachers and school administrators there is considerable discrepancy between statements about individualized instruction with which they agree, in theory, and the degree to which these statements are carried out in practice. This, it seems, would beg the issue. How can the practice of individualizing instruction become commonplace rather than the exception?

There are few simple solutions to complex problems of teaching and learning. However, it would appear that two major obstacles exist. The first problem, which is heard over and over again, is a lack of knowledge of just exactly what is individualized instruction. Confusion between individualization and independent study, classroom grouping, and other instructional techniques is common. Teachers and other professionals have shown a keen desire to answer this question by attending conferences on the subject and reading numerous articles and books.

The second problem which seems to exist is a general inability to get started" on some practical level of individualization. This is sub-divided into problems of what to do first, what help is necessary, and what kind of materials are needed. Of course, finding the answers to these questions is no guarantee that the goal of individualization will be realized overnight, but they will make it more likely to occur.

This paper takes the point of view that the resolution of these problems will have the best chance of emerging if they are addressed systematically. That is, if the entire process of individualized instruction were to be conceptualized, analyzed, and synthesized into a logical flow of activities, there would be a better chance of providing answers to the above questions and solutions to the problems, while also giving educators a point of entry into the process—a way of proceeding.

This paper focuses on developing a conceptual framework for viewing individualized instruction—a way of explaining what it is. Every effort is made to draw this conceptualization from the literature and research from the field, although extensive documentation is omitted for readability and because of the common acceptance of many established findings. This framework can then be analyzed into subcomponents and their interactions and synthesized into a logical flow of inputs, operations, decisions, and outputs.

What is Individualized Instruction?

That individualized instruction is not the same thing as independent study bears constant repetition. More accurately, individualized instruction "has reference to the steps taken to meet the needs of pupils . . ." (4) and perhaps the worst thing that could be done in this regard is to isolate students from one another for all time during their years of formal education, in the name of individualized instruction.

Recognition that the needs of individuals should be considered in determining what they should learn is gaining strength. In the foreword to the A.S.C.D. yearbook on individualized instruction Kimball Wiles states:

> . . . The 1962 yearbook . . . was a statement of the thesis that the individual perceives, interprets, and integrates uniquely in terms of his previous experiences and present needs and purposes. School programs not based on this premise are not significant, relevant or even helpful to many students. (5)

Most, but certainly not all, educational theorists and practitioners would agree with Wiles' statement. For those who would agree, a necessary component of individualizing instruction is the identification of students' needs. That is, a thorough and systematic effort must be made to diagnose students' needs in light of external and internal criteria. These criteria may be drawn from many sources, but the focus for the curriculum and instruction must be drawn upon the **individual student** in relation to these criteria.

A need may be defined as the difference between where and what student is and where and what the criteria suggest he might become. However, an important point to stress is that both of these dimensions are severely subject to the individual's perception of them. The individual perceives himself in a certain way; that is, everyone has some idea of what he is and where he is. Furthermore, each individual interprets and perceives the standards which are set before him in his own way. Therefore, a determination of students' needs is not something which can be made without reference to the individual if it is to serve as a basis for meaningful instruction.

Identifying the needs of students enables the teacher to make instruction purposeful; and almost everyone agrees that instruction should have purpose. Since instruction is really a process of facilitating changes in students' behavior, these purposes should be student oriented and not statements of what the teacher should do. Tyler stated it best when he said:

> Since the real purpose of education is not to have the instructor perform certain activities but to bring about significant changes in the students' patterns of behavior, it becomes important to recognize that any statement of the objectives of the school should be a statement of changes to take place in students.(6)

In addition to being stated as learner behaviors, objectives should relate to the needs and interests of individuals. Of course, this is implied by previous statements to the effect that a necessary component of instruction is the identification of needs. This serves the purpose of specifying goals which students consider important, interesting, and worthwhile. A recent study shows that objectives which teachers considered important and interesting for students agree little with those that students considered so. However, through cooperation these differences were essentially eliminated. (7) All necessary precaution must be taken to avoid premature feelings that, "We know what the students need." Careful planning is necessary to insure that objectives be relevant and worthwhile. This implies, of course, that objectives will vary considerably among individuals according to their needs.

Once individual objectives are determined and specified, students can be grouped for instruction according to common goals. This is not at all atypical, even in more traditional classrooms. Students seeking to attain common goals are often found working in various kinds of sub-groups—large or small—as well as independently. Grouping according to common objectives is one way of handling classroom logistics.

Another major component of individualizing instruction, however, deals with grouping and sub-grouping of students according to the way in which each learner can best attain a specified goal. Hence, five students, all aiming for the same objective, can be working in groups smaller than the whole at differentiated learning tasks. Hunter summarizes this concept concisely:

> Each individual finds that some learning behaviors are more productive for him than others. Some children learn more quickly if they read, some need to listen, others find it easiest to learn if they talk about the material. (6)

It is a complex process to ascertain how a student may learn best. Individual styles of learning depend upon a number of characteristics of the learner about which educators presently know very little. This need not obstruct the differentiation of learning tasks on certain bases about which there is available knowledge, and it must serve as a basis for research on other characteristics.

Individualization of instruction should be extended to a fourth major component, evaluation. Evaluation is primarily concerned with progress in attaining specified goals. The procedures for evaluation are varied for students according to the objectives toward which they were aiming. The progress which has been made, particularly evidence that a goal has been attained, becomes part of the data which are used to ascertain needs and specifying subsequent objectives.

Also, evaluation serves the purpose of determining the effectiveness and efficiency of the instructional procedures being used. Thus evaluation not only helps determine subsequent goals, but also to alter and adjust procedures for attaining the same goals. The trend toward accountability in education should result in placing considerably more emphasis on this aspect of evaluation.

Evaluation procedures should be employed in consideration of still another factor, individual learner characteristics. Even when two or more students are pursuing identical objectives it may be necessary to utilize different forms of evaluation because of the unique characteristics of each individual.

A Model

Although four components are specified above, they often are seen operating as a single process. This is because the interaction and interrelationships between the four components are much greater than would appear in the above description. That is, teachers do not perform functions related to only one component at a time and in the sequence in which they are presented. Instead, movement between the components is extremely flexible, as it should be.

Several of the relationships between components can be shown through the use of a simple model. The diagram in Illustration I is a visual representation of what may take place during instruction which emphasizes individualization.

Arrows facing in either direction in the model indicate that backtracking can and does occur. For example, during involvement in an actual learning activity, someone might make the decision to change the objective. This could apply between any steps of the model. Further, the crossed lines with arrows indicate that any two components of the model could be connected to one another. For example, a decision might be

ILLUSTRATION I

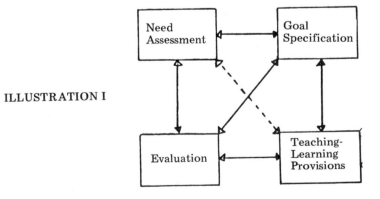

made that the greatest apparent need of the student would be to become involved in an on-going activity, omitting the formal specification of objective (actually, in this case, the objective "to become involved in the activity," is also quite apparent, though perhaps unstated).

The basic model would operate according to the following conception. The teacher collects information about several aspects of students' background. The data are presented in such a way as to provide as accurate a picture as possible of each student's educational profile. Also provided are various criteria or standards, to which the student can compare his profile. These standards may represent norms or points other than norms. Based upon the differences between the profile and the standards to which a comparison is finally made, a need is identified. In turn, goals and preconditions to the goals are specified. Pretesting is done to locate the exact point at which the student is working, and then instructional procedures are selected which are best suited for each individual to achieve his own objectives. Evaluation is conducted both during and after instruction in order to determine what should be done next. The cycle has no beginning or ending—students are always involved in the process whether in school or out, and they will always be involved as long as the brain continues to function.

Conclusion

The use of the model for individualizing instruction described in this paper is hardly universal. To use the procedures stated or implied requires the performance of numerous functions. Among these functions would be at least the following.

(1) Data must be gathered on several aspects of human behavior.
(2) Criteria for comparing student profiles must be identified and selected.
(3) Students must be counseled regarding their status and possible alternatives to that status.
(4) General goals must be identified and specified for achieving desired behavioral status.
(5) Preconditions to the general goals must be stated.
(6) Performance criteria for the preconditions must be ascertained.
(7) Pretesting on the resulting behavioral objectives must be done.
(8) Appropriate learning tasks must be determined.
(9) Instructional procedures must be created or identified.
(10) Procedures must be implemented and monitored.
(11) Post-testing must be done.
(12) Comparisons must be made between pre- and post-tests.
(13) Judgments must be made about the students' progress and the efficiency and effectiveness of instruction.

Multiplying these functions by the number of students for which a teacher is responsible compounds the problem. In many cases only a total revamping of the entire operation of the educational institution will permit such a program to prevail. In other instances minor adjustments will suffice.

In order to move toward this kind of instruction, however, more help is needed. Perhaps most importantly, this model requires further analysis into greater detail, with more precise delineation of sub-components and their interactions, and further specifications of required inputs, operations, and decisions, and the expected outputs. Reorganization and redesign of the existing institutional and professional provisions could then be accomplished in light of recognized needs for effective and efficient instruction.

REFERENCES

1. GIBBONS, MAURICE. "What is Individualized Instruction," *Interchange*, Vol. 1, No. 2, 1970, 28-52.

2. KEUSCHER, ROBERT E. "Why Individualize Instruction," in Howes, Virgil M. (ed.), *Individualization of Instruction*, New York: The Macmillan Company, 1970, p. 7.

3. Unpublished data in the author's file.

4. CLYMER, THEODORE, and NOLAN C. KEARNEY. "Curricula and Instructional Provisions for Individual Differences," Henry, Nelson B. (ed.), *Individualizing Instruction*, 61st Yearbook of the N.S.S.E., Part 1, Chicago: University of Chicago Press, 1962, p. 268.

5. DOLL, RONALD C. *Individualizing Instruction*, 1964 Yearbook of the A.S.C.D., Washington: The Association, 1964, vii.

6. TYLER, RALPH W. *Basic Principles of Curriculum and Instruction*, Chicago: University of Chicago Press, 1949, p. 44.

7. BIANCHI, GORDAN B. *A Descriptive Comparison of the Differences Among Instructional Objectives Which Are Formulated and Selected With and Without the Participation of Students*, unpublished doctoral dissertation, Buffalo: State University of New York at Buffalo, 1970.

8. HUNTER, MADELINE. "Individualized Instruction," *Instructor*, March 1970, p. 58.

Individualized Contracting in the Elementary Classroom

CHARLES D. SCHMITZ and ELIZABETH A. SCHMITZ

This year one of the goals of the Columbia public schools was to further implement a program of individualized instruction within each classroom.

With individualization as the goal, an exciting method was developed by the authors which can be implemented in any elementary classroom. The practical application of this method of individualized contracting can take any shape and go as far as any teacher decides is appropriate for his class.

Problems With Traditional Approach

The program was first introduced at Benton elementary school in Columbia in the third grade classroom of Elizabeth Schmitz. This classroom provided an excellent test situation because it contained a typical heterogeneous grouping of children with a wide range in ability levels, scholastic achievement, socio-economic background, racial origins and energy levels. In September, 1971, the members of the class were functioning at such different levels that it was necessary to have three math groups, two spelling groups, and three reading groups. Several students went to special reading and speech classes. As a result, there was very little time left to devote to language, creative writing, science, social studies or fine arts.

Another difficulty before the class started the contract system was the children's inability to get along with one another in the classroom. They could not work together in any of the traditional groupings. Because of this, the first step was to use a sociometric test in order to identify the possible source of the problem. A sociometric analysis of the classroom indicates the cliques in the class, who the popular children are,

Schmitz, Charles D., and Schmitz, Elizabeth A. "Individualized Contracting in the Elementary Classroom." *School and Community.* May 1972. 58:14-15, 23.

129

as well as who the isolates are. By the use of Dr. Irvin Cockriel's (Asst. Professor, College of Education, University of Missouri-Columbia) new computerized sociometric analysis, it was discovered that there were only five members of the class that ranked above ten points when the question was asked, "Who would you like to work with?" This was done on a three-point scale, meaning that each child had three choices ranked from first choice (3 points) to third choice (1 point). On the other hand, there were six complete isolates who were not chosen by anyone.

Working Units

Utilizing the information gathered from the sociometric analysis, the classroom was ready to take on a new shape. It was then possible to set up the "working units." A "working unit" is a group of three or four children who can function well together with each one contributing and helping one another.

Each working unit in the third grade class was set up with one complete isolate and one member of the class who ranked above ten points on the sociogram. The units were then filled with one or two of the students with whom the isolates indicated a desire to work. The desks were arranged in clusters so that the working units could easily operate as a group. This created an informal atmosphere which would make learning seem easier and more enjoyable.

Implementation

The class was not orientated to working units or individualized assignments, so the next step was for each child to fill out a somewhat structured contract form. Basically, the contract lists the subject areas and leaves room for the students to fill in the assignments they want to do and a place to put a check mark next to each assignment completed. The learning environment immediately changes from a "have to" to a "get to" or "want to" attitude.

The length of the contract period is determined by the needs of the learning situation and the maturity of the students in the third grade class. The first contract period starts on Monday morning and ends on Tuesday afternoon with the last contract period beginning on Thursday morning and ending Friday in the afternoon. This leaves Wednesday open to be called a "play day." Wednesday is a day for subject area games which reinforce learning, for the entire class to share ideas, or for class instruction activities which bring the class back together as a whole group.

For each contract period a general plan of lessons with suggested choices for each subject area is placed on the blackboard. This excludes reading, which is not implemented into the third grade system, because the structure of the basal reading series used in the third grade follows a definite plan. It will be necessary to have good teacher aides, excellent physical facilities, easy access to all levels of reading materials, continual testing with analysis, and profile charts to successfully individualize reading in the primary grades.

After the suggested choices are placed on the blackboard, all of the alternatives are discussed before the students choose. Some of the choices can be verbally emphasized so that the students will know their importance. These choices are by no means mandatory, they are only meant to give the students a good starting point. From there, the students can create an unlimited number of ideas for their tasks. When each child has decided what he is going to do and has filled out his contract forms, he must discuss his choices with the teacher before approval is given. As soon as the student has received approval, he begins working. Group instruction can begin as soon as all of the working contracts have been approved. Since the working units can function without the teacher, the teacher has more time to teach small groups and individual children.

Working Examples and Scheduling

At this point the teacher can individualize the lessons to any extent he wishes. For example, in the third grade classroom in which the plan was implemented, social studies is totally individualized. Each student reads the textbook at his own rate and then decides what he wants to do with what he has learned. Some make posters illustrating an interesting lesson, some make notebooks, others put on plays, and some just discuss the material with a group of other students and the teacher.

On the other hand, mathematics in this classroom is taught in three groups. Each group is assigned a minimum number of pages. Each student then chooses the problems he will do. To give the students greater freedom in their choice of mathematical tasks, a large number of dittos and games are made to accompany each lesson. This enables the teacher to keep a small number of controlled groups in any subject for teaching purposes.

Each of the three groups in math meets with the teacher for about

30 minutes per day. At this time the lessons are explained, questions answered, board work is done, and short tests may be given to see if the group is ready to move on to the next mathematical idea.

When the group work is completed, the students are free to proceed on their contracts. They do not have to do the mathematical tasks immediately after the group lessons. If a student needs a break from math, he can study science or language. Later he can return to the math lessons refreshed.

Each student has approximately three hours a day to work on his contracts. No restrictions are put on how or when he does a certain subject. At any time during the day, activities in all subjects could be taking place.

In budgeting his time, a student may over-estimate his abilities or under-estimate the time necessary to complete a certain task. In this case the student is free to complete the unfinished work at home. No homework, as such, is ever assigned. However, all of the students at one time or another find it helpful to take work home.

As each student finishes his lessons in one area he checks off the appropriate assignments and continues into another area of study. Each contract period emphasizes a different area of study. In this way the student can concentrate his hardest efforts in one area at a time.

Each student is responsible for all of his papers and contract forms. This gives him a chance to organize all of his work and see how much he has accomplished and how much he has left to complete.

Checking Each Contract

When the two day contract period is up, a checking time is scheduled during an art project or seat-work craft time. During this period the teacher and each individual student meet and go over all of the work. All papers are graded and discussed with the pupil. Each area of study is reviewed to see what each student has learned and where he needs help. The child knows if his contract is complete or if he must do more work to earn his token and star. Tokens are given for contracts completed and turned in on time. The children save them to earn things such as baby fish, flower seeds, gum or games. The stars are earned for completing a contract, whether it is turned in on time or not, and placed on an honor card displayed on each student's desk. The completed contract forms are attached to the papers, and each student is responsible for filing his forms in the class file box.

Results

Students know how well they have done in each area of study, and what they need to work harder on. Each student displays a great sense of pride and accomplishment with each completed contract. The successful completion of a contract motivates him to work even harder on the next one. He feels the responsibility of deciding what is important and what he will do. This encourages him to complete more work, as well as do a better job. In the third grade classroom in which this plan was implemented, the work load has increased more than 33 percent.

All of the children have learned how to budget their time and organize their tasks in order to complete each contract. Daydreaming and time wasting has been minimized. Each contract also helps the student make a realistic evaluation of himself. He decides what he can do, as well as what he actually will do.

Enthusiasm seems to be growing each day. Instead of the normal "middle-of-the-year blues," the entire class is active and excited about coming to school just to participate and learn. An example of their involvement is their choice of what they want to buy with their tokens. Instead of candy or toys, which are available for a small number of tokens, the students are so excited about the class aquarium and terranium they save all of their tokens to earn fish or garden seeds. In sharing time students tell how fish breathe or why plants grow rather than the usual "I got a model car for my birthday."

One of the major changes in the classroom is in the students' interaction with each other. They have found new friendships by working together. This is evidenced by a follow-up sociometric analysis. After three months, the number of complete isolates has fallen from six to four. No longer is one student embarrassed because of his constant failure to keep up. Since each student works at his own pace, each attains success. Since the contract system was initiated, there has been nearly 100 percent completion of all tasks by all children.

Valuing as a Dimension of the Educational Process

DR. ROBERT LEROY McCLARIN

What is Valuing?

What is its significance for Education?

In order to explain the process of valuing, it will be necessary to define such words as value, valuing, valuation, and reflective thinking. In doing so, reference will be made to several books written by John Dewey. Special note is made of the book titled *Theory of Valuation* by Dewey, since it provides an in-depth treatment of the theoretical bases for the process discussed in this article.

Definitions

To value means primarily to prize, to esteem; but secondarily it means to apprize, to estimate. It means that is, the act of cherishing something, holding it dear, and also the act of passing judgment upon the nature and amount of its value as compared with something else. To value in the latter sense is to valuate or evaluate (1).

The word "value" as Dewey used it, cannot be separated from the effort and the activity that produces that value. To apprize, to estimate, indicates that there is an act of passing judgment, as opposed to, to prize, to esteem, which indicates an object has intrinsic value in and of itself.

The word "valuing" suggests an on-going activity involved in the formation of a value and an existing process by which a value is established. "Valuation" refers to the total process of forming a

McClarin, Robert L., "Valuing as a Dimension of the Educational Process." *PEP Journal.* Summer 1971. 10:4-9.

judgment by ourselves in relation to the many influences upon us, be they intellectual, material, or personal. This judgment is arrived at, in part, through the secondary process of reflective thought.

In the book *How We Think*, Dewey outlines this reflective process in five steps:

1. Perplexity about the unknown elements of a situation.
2. Interpretation of the givens.
3. Examination of all factors needed for clarification.
4. Elaboration of a hypothesis.
5. Testing of the hypothesis (2).

These steps can be seen to correspond with the processes of experimental method and scientific method. All of these terms were used interchangeably by Dewey in his writings. When he wrote about one of these methods, despite which term he used, he was referring to the basic five points listed above.

What is Valuing?

Valuing is an on-going reorganization process that takes place within the individual as that individual deals with his desires, problems, and aspirations; to the end of achieving a "valued" decision on a course of action.

A value derives its beginning and momentum from our human "organic tendencies and acquired habits"(3). When a problem arises, or a conflict of habits occurs, we become conscious of the conflict and desires are formed. In the course of living, and therefore learning, all people will encounter problems. Impulses and desires will determine a directional movement. They furnish the focus around which reorganization begins. (The process of valuation is based on this assumption.) Impulses define the peering, the searching, the inquiring. "Each conflicting habit and impulse takes its turn in projecting itself upon the screen of imagination" (4). Each projection embodies an end in view, those conditions which will alleviate the problem. This end in view gives further direction to the reflective thought process by leading to an examination of all factors surrounding the problem. In this way the desires are directed inward to the individual. If fulfilled outwardly, failure through contact with the environment might result.

An act overtly tried out is irrevocable, its consequences cannot be blotted out. An act tried out in imagination is not final or fatal. It is retrievable (5).

In defining the problem and examining all influencing factors, subject matter, old habits, and past valuations, will be used as content. As a result of this deliberation, hypotheses should evolve that try to unify all competing tendencies, desires, and impulses in a modified direction towards the ends in view. The consequences of each hypothesis are projected on the mind to determine the actions and possible reactions. Any hypothesis that contains consequences that would harm the individual or not allow the individual to continue to evaluate, would be discarded. This final step is extremely important to Dewey's philosophy and distinguishes valuing from other reflective theories such as experimental method, scientific method, reflective thinking, and problem solving. Any decision or valuation made must allow for the individual to continue the valuing process. A good judgment might in addition be defined as "an activity when conflict and entanglement of various incompatible impulses and habits terminate in a unified, orderly release in action"(6).

George Geiger seems to have hit the point squarely when he wrote the following:

> We come upon the logic of practical judgments. This process does not of itself have to be reflective, since the choices leading to value can be arbitrary or whimsical; but when the process of making judgments is understood, then the possibility of options other than those of caprice and authority becomes that much more real.
>
> What Dewey is saying is, once more, that skill is the sole alternative to luck. When conflicting wants present themselves, something has to be done—something will be done. Choice cannot be eliminated, nor can values fail to arise. Dewey is proposing that intelligence can be substituted for arbitrary choice. This is not intended to be simply an honorific statement. By intelligent choice he understands the control of means in order to reach and test ends in view, using the funded knowledge of previous ends-means relations. This is what it is to be rational, what is unique in the value or goodness of reflection; it permits us to solve problems and not disguise them or pass them by(7).

With this directive, Dewey is urging us to develop skill in using the process of valuation to help increase the meaning of present experience. Each valuation made is but one small step toward the development of a value judgment. A value judgment comprises a number of decisions, all interrelated and organized into a unified whole. Developing the skill of forming these judgments and organizing them into a unified value system within each individual is a problem area which most of our schools have chosen to ignore. Alice Meil sums up the state of research when she wrote about the education of our desires, a prerequisite to the process of valuing.

We do not know too well how to educate the desires of people. This is an area in which much experimentation is required. We are certain only of profitable direction of effort, which are the replacement of empty verbalizations with generalizations upon actual experience and the uses of many media for presenting ideas(8).

Behaviors Involved in the Valuing Process

From the readings on Valuation, a series of assumptions were made concerning the behaviors involved in the valuing process and the features of the environment in which valuation can take place. Louis Raths made several of these assumptions by defining a value as requiring these seven behaviors:

1. Choosing freely; (the choice of value must be made by the student in order to be valued.)
2. Choosing from among alternatives; (An understanding of other possibilities must be present before the decision is valid.)
3. Choosing after thoughtful consideration of the consequences of each alternative; (The choice made must have in view what the actual consequences will be.)
4. Prizing and cherishing; (The student must view his decision as a good one and must be happy with it.)
5. Affirming: (The student must openly affirm this choice.)
6. Acting upon choices; (The value selected must influence his life.)
7. Repeating;(9) (The value must be a repetitive force and it must be applicable in many situations.)

From Dewey's writings can be deduced a series of behaviors needed to fulfill valuation. Given below is a list of behaviors in a possible sequential pattern ranging from the initial contact with the problem to the action taken to solve the problem.

1. THE STUDENT ENCOUNTERS A PROBLEM SITUATION. This may be a situation which arouses the student to a consciousness of his present mode of behavior, may be an obstacle or block to present behavior, or may be a situation involving a conflict of habits and personal choice for its solution.
2. THE STUDENT HAS DESIRES THAT RESPOND TO THE PROBLEM SITUATION. He envisions what conditions, if brought into existence, would unify the elements of the situation and provide a solution to the problem. Here desires act as impulses that direct the student in solving the problem.
3. THE STUDENT CAN STATE THE ENDS IN VIEW OR THE ANTICIPATED RESULTS OF DESIRE. These anticipated results are those elements which, actualized, can unify and solve the problem. Once stated, they act as directional means to the formation of a solution.
4. THE STUDENT WILL FEEL PERPLEXED ABOUT THE UNKNOWN ELEMENTS SURROUNDING THE PROBLEM IN LIGHT OF THE ENDS IN VIEW. The student will see voids in the problem situation,

which, if filled as suggested by the ends in view, would solve the problem.

5. THE STUDENT CAN MAKE A COMPLETE EXAMINATION OF ALL FACTORS NEEDED FOR CLARIFICATION. Knowledge gained through old habits, past experience, and subject matter are brought to bear on the problem and its many facets.

6. THE STUDENT CAN USE THE GIVENS IN A REORDERING AND RESTRUCTURING FASHION TO GAIN NEW INSIGHT INTO THE PROBLEM.

7. THE STUDENT CAN DEVELOP HYPOTHESES THAT MIGHT LEAD TO THE UNIFICATION OF ALL ELEMENTS IN THE PROBLEM. A hypothesis is a proposition of means and ends that offer a solution to a problem.

8. THE STUDENT TESTS EACH HYPOTHESIS BY COMPARING THE CONSEQUENCES OF THE HYPOTHESIS WITH THE ENDS IN VIEW. If the consequences do not agree with the ends in view, a judgment or adjustment must be made based on one of the following:
   a.) There is need for more thought and reflection.
   b.) The ends in view were unrealistic or unachievable, or were both.
   c.) The means were not suitable to the problem.
   d.) The problem was not real or inappropriate for solving.
   If the consequences coincide, or nearly coincide, judgment can be made by selecting a hypothesis for action.

9. THE STUDENT TAKES ACTION IN THE FORM OF APPROPRIATE BEHAVIOR COINCIDING WITH THE CHOICE MADE. A good solution solves the problem without further enlarging it, unifies all elements in a modified direction, and allows for future valuings based on the consequences attained.

Significance for Education

The valuing process, as described above, can be used to support and encourage freedom and commitment in students and, therefore, in adults. This can be accomplished by structuring all teaching-learning situations on the behaviors given for valuing. Both Dewey and Raths provide theoretical assumptions concerning these behaviors. Raths, Harmin, and Simon cite research that indicates positive results.

Carl Rogers gives a perspective of the success of valuing in achieving the freedom and commitment needed by adults if they are to become fully functioning human beings. Rogers writes about freedom and commitment in the following manner. Of freedom he says,

> I see this freedom of which I am speaking . . . as existing in a different dimension than the determined sequence of cause and effect. I regard it as a freedom which exists in the subjective person, a freedom which he courageously uses to live his potentialities(10).

On commitment he comments,

> This commitment is more than a decision. It is the functioning of an individual who is searching for the directions which are emerging within himself(11).

In referring to the aforementioned behaviors described by Raths and Dewey, one sees that each behavior listed, when actualized by a student, will be an expression of his freedom and commitment—freedom, because he is dealing with his own unique problem; commitment, because he believes that the best decision is based on his feelings and past experiences.

The students will gain valuable concepts from using the valuing process. For example: for a student to form a judgment about action, it may be necessary for him to revise part or all of his original goal in favor of more realistic goals. The ability of the student to do this and to understand what he is doing is basic to the completion of the process. From such an experience the student would begin to understand that goals and objectives are not fixed, but can be freely chosen.

> To free curiosity; to permit individuals to go charging off in new directions dictated by their own interests; to unleash the sense of inquiry; to open everything to questioning and exploration; to recognize that everything is in process of change—here is an experience(12).

Teachers and students might come to see that learning, in an everchanging environment, must by nature be fluid. The goals that are important today may be altered tomorrow. The value judgments of yesterday may not be applicable to today's problems. Similarly, the types of activities used to achieve those objectives cannot be fixed in any type of formula approach because they may vary with the individual.

The valuing process could be described as a continuing reorganization of all that is felt and known by an individual. A person experiencing subsequent problems will certainly need to rely on previous judgments as a starting point for the new reorganization process. In the classroom, a skilled teacher would be able to see corallary problems with which the student could deal. The student might similarly see these areas as he progresses through his initial judgment. The teacher, in conjunction with the student, must plan for the next step and allow for the next step to occur.

> Almost every choice faced by men and women, by children and youth, as they deal with their problems of everyday living, demands a value judgment. Every aspect of life can make a potential contribution to building sound judgments(13).

The school and the classroom contribute one aspect in the life of a child. Within this environment that child will have problems and desires. These problems and desires can be dealt with through valuation and brought to a conscious level where they can be examined. These judgments can then make valuable contributions to the future judgments that each student will make.

In every description of valuing, reference is made to the need for the individual to be happy and committed to his choice. Such commitment may be evidenced by the action taken and by the repetition of that action. This is the factor that sets valuation above that which is referred to as reflective thinking, scientific process, problem solving, and experimental method. Edward Krug, writing about reflective thinking, gives the main point to be considered.

> Reflective thinking can lead one to a correct conclusion as to which course of action should be adopted to accomplish a particular result, but it does not by itself indicate whether one kind of result or purpose is more desirable than another(14).

Reflective thought, scientific method, and all the others, can be practiced in the classroom on isolated areas of study with no hint of whether the purpose for which students strive is of value, of whether the goal selected means anything to the student. Worse yet, these methods could be presented as a formula approach which could be considered an end in and of itself. This, however, is not valuation as Dewey described it, and it is not part of the dimension of valuation.

Valuing Broadens the Base of Educational Objectives

This paper is part of an initial attempt to develop the theoretical concept of valuing into a useful tool; a tool that will enable education to broaden its base of objectives and to produce individuals ready, in many ways, for community life. Louise Berman put it this way:

> A conceptualization of the curriculum must encompass several ingredients. First, it must be based upon an adequate view of man, a conception that is broad enough to account for a wide range of behaviors(15).

Some of these broader educational goals are discussed in more detail in the following paragraphs.

Valuation offers students a means to organize their thinking processes. "If young people do not learn to think while in school, it is fair to ask: How are they to keep on learning?"(16).

> No one doubts, theoretically, the importance of fostering in school good habits of thinking. But apart from the fact that the acknowledgment is not so great in practice as in theory, there is not adequate theoretical recognition that all which the school can do and need for pupils, so far as their minds are concerned, is to develop their ability to think(17).

We cannot dispute the fact that thinking is a major goal of education today. The tools to handle this immense task, however, have not been available. Valuation uses reflective thinking as its base, and a student given sufficient encouragement and freedom will, through practice, begin to see a process of thought organization developing. The type of thinking that will be an end product will, because of the nature of valuation as an individual process, be independent thinking not vulnerable to manipulation. It cannot, however, be so independent that it isolates the individual from society. There must be a unity of purpose in all the individual does. Each person must examine the consequences of his thoughts in view of their effect on him as well as on others. Similarly, he must take into account the consequences of the behavior of others on him.

Valuation will help students achieve the skills necessary to solve problems. Problem solving can be a difficult task for a child. A decision cannot be made until necessary facts are determined. The young child must rely on others for ideas and will receive both "good" and "bad" opinions. His decisions must inevitably be based on the information he obtains and the experiences he has encountered.

Problem solving does not come naturally to us, but must be built through reinforcement and encouragement. (All types of learning behaviors could be included in this statement.) Some parents try to achieve some success in this area during their child's preschool years. That the school then ignores this new skill and does not develop it further is one of the crimes perpetrated by education. The most the school does, in general, is to indicate a formula approach. Valuation is an alternative that gives students practice in solving problems. Without this practice, the student will enter into any number of blind alleys whenever problem solving is required as it is in everday life.

> The actual process of thought is neither smooth nor sequential. Thought-in-process includes innumerable errors and corrections, digressions, discussions ending in blind alleys, the laborious trial of guesses, the tedious process of evaluating and validating. Terms must be defined and redefined: schemes for classifying one's ideas must be made and often scrapped. There are analysis, selections, and discrimination of ideas. Many, many errors and concensus appear before the problem is solved.(18).

The school must do more in this area of problem solving. To let a student stumble into society without a thorough background in this skill is asking for an extension of what is becoming known as our sick society—a society made up of individuals concerned about themselves and a society that puts off the solution of problems, in fact, leaves the problems for another generation to solve.

Valuation offers a means to the development of a value system in an individual and to subsequent redirection of modes of behavior. In our schools problem solving has always been thought of in an academic sense and the little that has been done, had been directed toward the solution of academic problems. The whole realm of value judgments has been ignored completely except in situations calling for identification and imitation and those using pleasure and pain tactics to mold behavior. Valuation deals with the solution of problems in all areas of human endeavor. In valuation, each problem is a personal one that has been selected by the student for solution. In achieving this solution, the student is making use not only of factual academic information, but also of information concerning himself and the nature of his feelings. By solving this problem the student learns about himself and his abilities at the same time that he learns the facts necessary to achieve a solution.

Further research in the area of valuing may help in the development of a science of values. Teachers must begin to plan for value development in the classroom. In order to do this, there is a need for research into those qualities which should be looked for and achieved by the student as part of the process. The different elements of the climate must similarly be specified.

> There appears to be no necessary reason why the criteria implicit in such judging may not be raised to the level of conscious formulation and thus made available for refinement and further development. Just as the science of metallurgy arose out of the art of working with metals, so a science of valuation must find its formulations in our daily acts of valuing(19).

Reflections

A major goal of education is to help students achieve mastery of a process of education that will enable them to continue their education beyond formal schooling. The above statement implies that the "object and reward of learning is continued capacity for growth"(20). What has been expressed up to this point is that valuation, as a process, can help a student gain this more meaningful type of education.

Such an education will stress the organization of a student's thinking processes, consciously provide experiences in solving meaningful problems, and strive toward the goal of developing a whole person useful to society and characterized by the beginnings of a unified value system. Research will be needed upon which these new school objectives can be based, with the ultimate goal of establishing a science of values.

The role of the teacher in carrying out these new objectives is an area that needs a new imaginative look. As an indication of one point of view, this quotation from Hullfish and Smith's book titled *Reflective Thinking*, gives this interesting point made in an article by Irwin Edman:

> There are just a few things a teacher can do, and only that for the sensitive and the spirited. He can initiate enthusiasms, clear paths, and inculcate discipline. He can communicate a passion and a method, no more(21).

The point made by the authors Hullfish and Smith following this statement is, "What else is there?"

> The communication of a method of coming at life in reflective terms, coupled with a passion for doing so, is what the shooting is all about. This is a proper aim of a teacher in a free society(22).

1. JOHN DEWEY, *Democracy and Education* (New York: MacMillan Co., 1916) p. 238.

2. JOHN DEWEY, *How We Think* (Boston: D. C. Heath and Co., 1910), pp. 106-114.

3. JOHN DEWEY, *Theory of Valuation* (Chicago: University of Chicago Press, 1939), p. 29.

4. JOHN DEWEY, *Human Nature and Conduct* (New York: Henry Holt Co., 1922), p. 190.

5. *Ibid.*

6. *Ibid.*, p. 120.

7. GEORGE GEIGER, *John Dewey in Perspective* (New York: Oxford University Press, 1958), pp. 57-58.

8. ALICE MEIL, *Changing the Curriculum, A Social Process* (New York: Appleton-Century-Crofts, Inc., 1960), p. 25.

9. LOUIS E. RATHS, MERRILL HARMIN, and SIDNEY B. SIMON, *Values and Teaching* (Columbus: Charles E. Merrill Books, Inc., 1966), pp. 28-30.

10. CARL R. ROGERS, *Freedom to Learn* (Columbus: Charles E. Merrill Publishing Company, 1969), p. 265.

11. *Ibid.*, p. 273.

12. *Ibid.*, p. 105.

13. FLORENCE B. STRATEMEYER and OTHERS, *Developing a Curriculum for Modern Living* (New York: Bureau of Publications, Teachers College, Columbia University, 1957), p. 48.

14. EDWARD KRUG, *Curriculum Planning* (New York: Harper and Brothers Publishing, 1957), p. 64.

15. LOUISE M. BERMAN, *New Priorities in the Curriculum* (Columbus: Charles E. Merrill Publishing Company, 1968), p. 2.

16. RATHS, HARMIN, SIMON, p. 3.

17. DEWEY, *Democracy and Education*, p. 179.

18. WILLIAM H. BURTON, ROLAND B. KIMBALL, and RICHARD L. WING, *Education for Effective Thinking* (New York: Appleton-Century-Crofts, Inc., 1960), p. 25.

19. RATHS, HARMIN, SIMON, pp. 95-96.

20. DEWEY, *Democracy and Education*, p. 100.

21. IRWIN EDMAN, "The Art of Teaching," *New York Times Magazine*, (May 25, 1941), p. 7.

22. H. GORDON HULLFISH and PHILIP G. SMITH, *Reflective Thinking* (New York: Dodd, Mead and Co., 1961), p. 22.

SCHOOL is for . . .
SHARING VALUES

Self- Concept Development in the Reading Program

SHIRLEY BERRETTA

Aware teachers have probably always known that emotional factors play an important part in a child's success in learning to read. Nearly thirty years ago, Arthur Gates (1941) estimated from his clinical experience that 75 per cent of the children with severe reading disabilities showed personality maladjustment. Since that time the relationship between reading failure and various personality maladjustments has been explored in a number of research studies.

Of all the areas of personality correlated with reading achievement, one factor, self concept, seems to be particularly useful for reading teachers. It may be worthwhile to look at the meaning of self concept before exploring ways in which the reading teacher may help in the development of positive self concept.

The Influence of Self Concept on Reading

According to Sullivan, the self is made up of "reflected appraisals." These "reflected appraisals" come from the child's parents, teachers, and significant others. A child who, for whatever reason, develops negative self perceptions may see himself as an inadequate reader, incapable of learning, or just generally inadequate. Children with negative self images may be filled with fear of failure and terrified of new experiences. Some may be restless, unable to concentrate, and anxious under pressure of time limits. Others may be quiet and withdrawn. Failure in reading may be among these behavioral manifestations of poor self concepts.

Berretta, Shirley. "Self-Concept in the Reading Program." *The Reading Teacher.* December 1970. 24:232-238. Reprinted with permission of the International Reading Association and Shirley Berretta.

There are carefully designed studies that clearly show the relationship between self concept and reading. One study that indicates a cause-effect relationship between self concept and reading achievement is the doctoral dissertation of Mary Lamy (1963). In this study, measurements of self perception were made during kindergarten prior to reading instruction and during the first grade. Self perception scores correlated as highly with reading achievement as did intelligence scores. Together the two scores were found to be better predictors of reading success than either score taken separately. Because Lamy's study shows a positive relationship between reading achievement and self perceptions that were inferred during kindergarten—*before reading instruction*—it gives strong support to the idea that self perceptions are causal factors in reading success and failure.

Other research has also supported the relationship between self concept and reading achievement. Wattenberg and Clifford (1964) found that measures of self concept during kindergarten are predictive of reading achievement. Giuliani (1968) found self concept as well as verbal-mental ability significantly related to reading readiness. Toller (1968) compared self evaluations of achieving readers with those of retarded readers. She found significant differences in favor of achievers on acceptance, adequacy, personal and social self, security, number of problems, and consistency of view of self.

Self-Concept Development in the Reading Program

Research supports the idea that an adequate self concept is an important component of successful reading. The self concept, then, may be thought of in the same way as basic skills, such as, vocabulary building, recognition skills, and word attack techniques, each of which is an important element of successful reading. In order to explore methods of promoting adequate self concepts, it is necessary to relate these methods to an integrated reading approach.

The methods of developing self concept will be set in the context of an individualized approach to reading. However, these methods need not be confined to the individualized approach. They may be used easily in a nongraded organization or even adapted for use in a more traditional reading program.

Rationale for the Individualized Approach

The objective of the individualized approach to reading is the fullest development of the student's skills and capacities. This approach is unique in that skills are developed by the flexible use of methods adapted to the learning style of the individual child. It also aims at developing greater and more lasting interest in reading than some traditional reading approaches. "The healthy child is naturally active and he is engaged almost continually while awake in an active exploration of his environment. He seeks from that environment those experiences that are consistent with his maturity and his needs" (1959, P. 89). Discussing self-selection, Olson (1959) wrote: "Throughout nature there is a strong tendency for life to be sustained by the self-selection of an environment appropriate to the needs of the plant, animal, or human being" (P. 90). Olson described pacing as "the acts on the part of the teacher which insure that each child is provided with the materials upon which he can thrive and also . . . the attitude which expects from the child only that which he can yield at his stage of maturity" (P. 94).

Self-Concept Development and the Sensitive Teacher

What can the teacher do to promote adequate self concepts in children? The reading teacher is not in a position to provide psychotherapy for severely disturbed children. However, she must consider personality factors as one influence on reading achievement. Some children may require help from outside the school before any reading program can be effective. However, there are many children within the normal range who have self perceptions that limit their success in reading. It is the child who sees himself as inadequate or in inconsistent ways that is a concern of the reading teacher who uses an individualized approach.

The sensitive teacher is the most important element in helping the child with negative self perceptions. The reading teacher must be highly skilled in the area of sensitive relating to the child as well as in reading instruction. Sensitive relating is experiential in nature and cannot be captured in words on paper. Writing about sensitivity is like writing about the skill of sailing. One can describe the skills involved in sailing, but there is a certain sensitivity that a person develops to the wind and the adjusting of his sails that cannot be adequately described. It is possible, however, to describe some attitudinal and behavioral aspects of the sensitive teacher.

The attitudes, personality, and skill of the teacher are the most important factors in the individualized approach. Barbe (1961) quoted Jacobs as saying: "Individualized reading starts not with procedures but with a creative, perceptive teacher—one who believes that children want to learn; who thinks with children rather than for them; who basically respects the individual behavior of every youngster; who works with children in orderly but not rigid ways" (P. 19).

EXPERIENCE OF SUCCESS AND MEANING. The sensitive teacher knows that experience of success and a sense of meaning in learning is essential for the growing child. Successful experience is one of the surest ways of achieving positive self perceptions. It is unnecessary for a child to experience failure in reading. An aware teacher once said, "It's not where you are that counts in this class, it's where you go from where you are now that's important." It seems that with this kind of attitude every individual can go someplace.

The flexibility and variety of books used in the individualized approach allows the teacher to modify the learning material to fit the individual level of the child. By selecting from a range of books and activities, the teacher can help a child have experiences in which he can succeed. Each child may be challenged, not overwhelmed with threat. As a child develops his reading ability he realistically comes to see himself as one who can do things, as one who can be successful. Consistent communication of confidence from the teacher helps him to see that what he does is valued. This attitude helps the child to clarify his particular goals in reading and to start work toward them. It helps him to fulfill his learning potentialities.

In addition to meeting the level of ability of a child, it is important that tasks have meaning for him. When a child does not see any personal meaning in something, it becomes very difficult for him to learn it. Repeated experiences of this nature may cause him to see himself as lacking in ability to learn. New skills come to have meaning for a child when he can see these skills as consistent with his perceptions of self.

In order to provide experiences that have personal meaning, the teacher should be concerned with the child's interests. In some instances this is simply a matter of allowing the child freedom to select his own reading material. Other times the teacher may need to help a child learn to make choices and help him become aware of what is available for him to choose. Some children see themselves in such a helpless way that they are unable to make decisions about anything. Such a child might be helpless to answer the question, "What are you interested in reading today?" But offered a choice between two stories briefly described he can probably select one. A sensitive teacher would have done some ground work to learn some of the child's interests. As time goes on, the teacher offers more choices and moves toward helping the child to learn to select and assume responsibility for his own activities. Learning to make satisfying choices in reading may help him to see himself as capable of decisions in other areas of his life.

In addition to helping children follow their own interests, the teacher may stimulate new interest through a wide variety of books and activities. The scope of activities which may be used is virtually unlimited. A display, report, or oral reading by one child may stimulate other students to read. A panel can be a springboard for class discussion. Children may use puppets or dolls for making book reviews interesting. Many aids such as those suggested by Brogan and Fox (1961) can be used to make the learning experience vital:

> The classroom must be set up primarily as a place for active learning, with the focus on "doing centers, not just looking centers" ... [with] bulletin boards that truly communicate, the Work Table, painting and clay centers, the Make-It Table, toys and gadgets, science materials, radio and television, the Writer's Table, the puppet theater, the house, the cooking center, the victrola, filmstrips and films, and ... the Library Corner or Reading Center (Pp. 219-220).

Within a classroom such as this, students may prepare materials for their conferences with the teacher or the sharing period with other students and conduct group projects and self expressive activities.

THE INDIVIDUAL CONFERENCE. A sensitive teacher can use the individual conference to help develop positive self perceptions as well as develop reading skills. Using the individual conference does not imply that the teacher discard her role of reading instructor. In fact, the individualized program demands an extremely thorough knowledge of all skills so the teacher will be prepared to help with any skill at the appropriate time for the child.

The individual conference may take the place of the traditional reading circle. The child usually meets individually with the teacher and reads something that he has selected. The teacher observes both oral and silent reading skills to check the child's understanding of word meanings as well as sight vocabulary. She checks his comprehension by questions or by discussion and instructs in the necessary skills. Through the teacher's guidance the child gains awareness of his strengths and weaknesses and makes plans for developing skills. With opportunity for practice and correction in the privacy of a conference with his teacher, a child progresses at his own rate.

Each child is encouraged to select, from the range of materials, those books which he wants to read. The teacher may suggest ways in which the child can share his reading with others in the class. Sometimes the students are scheduled for their conferences once a week. Other times they ask for individual time as they feel a need.

Barbe (1961) has recognized the potentiality of the individual conference as something more than reading instruction. He wrote: "The individual conference is essentially a counseling session. The classroom teacher who has no formal training in counseling, as such, would do well to examine some of the literature on counseling techniques, as well as spend some time in in-service training developing this particular skill (P. 48)."

The individual conference provides the teacher with an opportunity to establish a warm and accepting relationship with the student. Through the individual conference the teacher and the child can develop a mutual trust and respect. It gives her an opportunity to relate to the child in a way that will help him develop a positive self image. Rogers (1962) stated that it is the quality of the helping relationship that is most growth producing.

In the individual conference the teacher is in a position to listen attentively to what the child is saying. This is not only a strong rein-forcement for his reading, but it communicates some positive things to him. It says that he is a valuable person, that he is worthy of being heard, that what he has to say is important. Many children, when trying to verbalize, have been neglected or rejected by busy parents and come to think of themselves as not having anything worthwhile to contribute. A child with a negative self concept may find that his teacher is the first person who listens to him.

SMALL GROUPS. Another aspect of the individualized reading program that adapts itself to development of positive self perception is the small group. Grouping in the individualized program differs from the skill-oriented ability groups of other approaches. Small groups are important, not only in helping students with their skills and sharing their reading, but also for helping children gain positive perceptions of themselves—as social selves and learners. In a small group the teacher is a key to how well the group functions. Her role is that of facilitator of discussion rather than that of lecturer. Along with stimulating discussion of reading, the teacher may encourage students to relate reading to their personal experiences. It is very important that the teacher serve as a model of acceptance and warmth so that the children may emulate this attitude and develop a climate in which each child can express himself and feel valued.

The small group experience provides a life-like situation for children to gain feedback about self and to learn to fulfill needs in socially accepted ways. As children interact with their classmates they may become aware of many choices and alternate ways of behaving.

Conclusion

For years the word "individual" has been taught, yet many programs are designed for administrative convenience. We realize the importance of good mental health, yet emotional development is rarely an intentional part of a curriculum. Self concept is as much a factor in reading success as intelligence or mastery of basic skills. A program integrating reading instruction and development of positive self perceptions is exciting because if offers the promise of meeting individual needs for learning and for good emotional development.

REFERENCES

BARBE, W. *Educator's Guide to Personalized Reading Instruction.* Englewood Cliffs, N. J.: Prentice-Hall, 1961.

BROGAN, PEGGY, and FOX, LORENE. *Helping Children Read.* New York: Holt Rinehart and Winston, 1961.

GATES, A. The Role of Personality Maladjustment in Reading Disability. *Journal of Genetic Psychology,* 1941, 59, 77-83.

GIULIANI, G. The Relationship of Self-Concept and Verbal-Mental Ability to Levels of Reading Readiness Amongst Kindergarten Children. *Dissertation Abstracts,* 1968, 28, 3866B.

LAMY, MARY. Relationship of Self-Perceptions of Early Primary Children to Achievement in Reading. *Dissertation Abstracts,* 1963, 24, 628-629.

OLSON, W. Seeking, Self Selection and Pacing in the Use of Books by Children. In Jeannett Veatch (Ed.) *Individualizing Your Reading Program.* New York: C. P. Putnam's Sons, 1959.

ROGERS, C. The Interpersonal Relationship: the Core of Guidance. *Harvard Educational Review,* 1962, 32, 416-429.

TOLLER, GLADYS. Certain Aspects of the Self Evaluations Made by Achieving and Retarded Readers of Average and Above Average Intelligence. *Dissertation Abstracts,* 1968, 28, 976A.

WATTENBERG, W., and CLIFFORD, CLARE. Relation of Self-Concepts to Beginning Achievement in Reading. In W. Durr (Ed.) *Reading Instruction: Dimensions and Issues.* Boston: Houghton Mifflin, 1967.

Chapter V

The Teacher As A Classroom Management Expert

When speaking of the teacher as a classroom manager, thoughts often turn to terms such as discipline, pupil control, corporal punishment, and orderliness. Beginning teachers have in the past, gained most of their ratings as "good teachers" to the extent that they could "control their youngsters". Although corporal punishment in the form of spanking is not totally condemned by the authors, it is strongly recommended that the beginning teacher consider it one of the alternatives far down his list when attempting to manage the classroom for the most effective learning.

The ability of the classroom teacher to establish an effective environment for learning requires the acquisition of insights which go beyond that simply of techniques for controlling misbehavior. A broader concept of classroom management requires the beginning teacher to examine the self concept and its relationship to a pupil's behavior and his academic achievement. Some basic principles for dealing with children are provided to help the new teacher reexamine his understanding of the principles of growth and development previously encountered in child development study and apply them to the implementation of positive reinforcement techniques suggested by Alice Behre (winter 1970) in "Road Signs to a Successful Journey."

The vital nature of effective classroom management in the creation of a climate for maximum learning for pupils—physically, socially, emotionally, and intellectually—mandates that the beginning teacher develop a teaching style with which he feels comfortable and which has evolved from a thorough understanding of the principles of human learning and motivation.

Basic Principles In Dealing With Children

DR. RUDOLF DREIKURS

Golden Rule: "Do unto others as you would have others do unto you." This is the basis of democracy, since it implies equality of individuals.

Mutual Respect: Based upon the assumption of equality, is the inalienable right of all human beings. No one should take advantage of another—neither adult nor child should be a slave or a tyrant.

Encouragement: Implies faith in the child as he is, not in his potentiality. A child misbehaves only when he is discouraged and believes he cannot succeed by useful means. The child needs encouragement as a plant needs water.

Reward and punishment are outdated. A child soon considers a reward his right and demands a reward for everything. He considers that punishment gives him the right to punish others, and the retaliation of children is usually more effective than the punishment of adults.

Natural consequences, utilizing the reality of the situation rather than personal power, can exert the necessary pressure to stimulate proper motivation. Only in moments of real danger is it necessary to protect the child from the natural consequences of his disturbing behavior.

Action instead of words in times of conflict. Children tend to become "mother-deaf" and act only when raised voices imply some impending action, and then respond only momentarily. Usually the child knows very well what is expected of him. Talking should be restricted to friendly conversations and not used as disciplinary means.

Withdrawal—effective counteraction. Withdrawal is not surrender and is most effective when the child demands undue attention or tries to

Dreikurs, Rudolf. "Basic Principles in Dealing With Children." *Minnesota Elementary School Principal.* December 1970. 6:27-28.

involve one in a power contest. He gets no satisfaction in being annoying if nobody pays attention.

Withdrawal from the provocation, not from the child. Don't talk in moments of conflict, but friendly conversation and pleasant contacts are essential. Have fun and play together. The less attention the child gets when he disturbs, the more he needs when he is cooperative.

Don't interfere in children's fights. By allowing children to resolve their own conflicts, they learn to get along better together. Many fights are provoked to get the adult involved and by separating the children or acting as judge, we fall for their provocation, thereby stimulating them to fight more.

Take time for training and teaching the child essential skills and habits. If a mother does not have time for such training, she will spend more time correcting an untrained child.

Never do for a child what he can do for himself. A "dependent" child is a demanding child. Most adults underestimate the abilities of children. Children become irresponsible only when we fail to give them opportunities to take on responsibility.

Understanding the child's goal. Every action of a child has a purpose. His basic aim is to have his place in the group. A well-behaved and well-adjusted child has found his way toward social acceptance by conforming with the requirements of the group and by making his own useful contributions to it. The misbehaving child is still trying, in a mistaken way, to gain social status.

The four goals of a child's misbehavior. The child is usually unaware of his goals. His behavior, though illogical to others, is consistent with his own orientation.

    No. 1—Attention getting . . . . wants attention and service

    No. 2—Power . . . . .wants to be the boss

    No. 3—Revenge . . . . wants to hurt us

    No. 4—Display of inadequacy . . . . .wants to be left alone

Our reactions to a child's misbehavior patterns:

    No. 1—Feel annoyed . . . . wants to remind and to coax

    No. 2—Feel provoked . . . . "you can't get away with this!"

    No. 3—Feel deeply hurt . . . . "I'll get even!"

    No. 4—Feel despair . . . . "I don't know what to do!'

Fallacy of first impulse. By acting on our first impulse, we tend to testify the child's misbehavior patterns, rather than to correct them.

Minimize mistakes. Making mistakes is human. We must have the courage to be imperfect. Build on strength, not on weakness.

Danger of pity. Feeling sorry for the child, while natural, often add harm to an already tragic situation and the child may be more harmed by the pity than by the actual tragedy. Life's satisfactions depend on one's ability to take things in stride. Feeling sorry for someone leads to his self-pity and to the belief that life owes him something.

Don't be concerned with what others do, but accept responsibility for what we can do. By utilizing the full potential of our constructive influence, we do not have to worry about what others may do to the child. Compensation for the mistakes of others is unwise and over-protection may rob the child of his own courage and resourcefulness.

A family council gives every member of the family a chance to express himself freely in all matters pertaining to the family as a whole and to participate in the responsibilities each member has for the welfare of the family. It is truly education for democracy and should not become a place for parents to "preach" or impose their will on children, nor should it deteriorate into a "gripe" session. The emphasis should be on "What can WE do?"

Have fun together and thereby help develop a relationship based on mutual respect, love and affection, mutual confidence and trust, and feeling of belonging. Playing together, working together, sharing interesting and exciting experiences lead to the kind of closeness which is essential for cooperation.

SCHOOL is for . . .
PUPIL PLANNING

Top Priority:
Understanding Self And Others

DON DINKMEYER

Prompted by general unrest in society, the prevailing spirit of the times, and the revolution of the young, educators are looking closely at their purposes and their products. Are we developing individuals who are able to cope with the problems of living in a democracy? Are we developing individuals who are able to interact effectively with one another? Increasing polarization between the young and the old, black and white, conservative and liberal, suggests that there is a breakdown in communication. Educators might well investigate the discrepancy between their goals and their products.

The generally accepted objectives of education suggest that teachers should be concerned with the development of the whole child. In practice teachers are concerned with the whole child—as long as he does not come to school. Teachers accept the concept of the whole child, but they are not ready to deal with the child's social immaturities, his feelings of inadequacy, his anger, his joy, and his exuberance. Many teachers prefer to treat the child as a receptacle into which they can pour knowledge that can be inspected at regular intervals on test days.

Published statements of objectives almost inevitably list purposes that embrace social and emotional as well as intellectual development. However, a close look at the classroom and the interactions which occur there suggests that there is an overwhelming emphasis on acquiring knowledge.

The Taxonomy of Educational Objectives: Affective Domain provided a scholarly presentation of educational objectives in the affective area (1). However, despite educators' interest in affect, there is little evidence that teachers are truly involved in developing and utilizing

Dinkmeyer, Don. "Top Priority: Understanding Self and Others." *The Elementary School Journal.* November 1971. 72:62-71. Reprinted by permission of the author and the University of Chicago Press, © copyright 1971.

educational programs that focus on feelings and human behavior.

Certainly there have been some educational efforts in this area, notably *Self Enhancing Education* (2), a program to motivate learners by using twelve self-enhancing processes. Another pioneer effort is *A Teaching Program in Human Behavior and Mental Health* by Ralph Ojemann (3). However, no program has been widely accepted by administrators, curriculum directors, and teachers as a high priority area of instruction. We say we are interested in the development of the whole child, but our actions speak louder than our words.

The lack of required, sequentially developed programs in self-understanding and human behavior testifies to an educational paradox. We have taught children almost everything in school except to understand and accept themselves, and to function more effectively in human relationships. Can we assume that this type of understanding develops by osmosis or magic?

Some teachers would rather talk about the whole child than be confronted with his feelings, his thoughts, beliefs, and values. If this is not true, why do so many teachers emphasize cognitive, intellectual, and academic learning? Standardized achievement tests and tests prepared by classroom teachers betray what we really value.

Visit a classroom and see what occasionally happens when the teacher is faced with the whole child and his feelings. Here is what happened in one classroom:

> Teacher: Now we will open our books and do the ten problems on page 33.
> Johnny: I don't feel like it.
> Teacher: Johnny, open your book and get started.
> Johnny: I hate math!
> Teacher: Get started now, or I am going to give you extra work.
> Johnny: I'm not going to do it.

In this vignette we see considerable affect on the part of the child and the teacher. However, the affect is not dealt with. The child still has strong feelings, fears, or anxieties that keep him from operating more effectively.

The denial of feelings and attitudes in the classroom is not rare. Teachers generally lack the preparation to accept feelings in the classroom. Flanders and Amidon (4) found that acceptance of feelings accounted for only .005 per cent of the verbal interaction in the classroom.

I am not suggesting that teachers are not interested in developing better relationships with children. On the contrary, Witmer and Cottingham (5) found evidence that teachers are interested in increasing their guidance skills and in providing guidance activities. Witmer and

Cottingham concluded from their research that the teacher in the elementary school is a major source and activating force for most of the guidance practices in the school. Since the teacher has about a thousand hours a year with the pupils, why do we permit the guidance responsibilities of the classroom teacher to depend on her interests and preferences? The teacher does not have a choice about whether she teaches arithmetic or language arts each day. Why are guidance experiences often completely at the teacher's option?

The lack of regularly programmed experiences in this area bears investigation. Those who have encouraged teachers to experiment with programs in human behavior have found that teachers are interested. Why, then, the lack of programs?

Certainly teacher education programs must bear part of the responsibility for this gap. Traditionally, they have not taught skills that would help classroom teachers facilitate group discussions of personal and social problems. Teacher education programs have not acquainted prospective teachers with sources of materials in the form of open-ended stories, discussion starters, and other devices to encourage interaction. Teacher education programs have not provided students with supervised experiences in using procedures such as puppetry or role-playing as guidance tools.

Teachers who are highly motivated in this area have found it difficult to acquire planned experiences to develop an understanding of self and others.

We can expect some critics to brush aside the study of self and human relations as a frill. Yet research shows growing evidence that feelings of self-adequacy and the self-concept are significant in school achievement. The evidence indicates that few factors are more important to the child's academic success than his evaluation and acceptance of himself. Research tells us that children who come to school with negative self-concepts have difficulty in learning. Wattenberg and Clifford wrote: "In general, the measures of self-concept and the ratings of ego strength made at the beginning of kindergarten prove to be somewhat more predictive of reading achievement two years later than was the measure of mental ability" (6). Walsh (7), Coopersmith (8), and Fink (9) all found that the child who had an adequate self-concept was more effective socially and academically. Combs and Soper (10) also found a significant relationship between feelings of adequacy and educational achievement. They made the discouraging discovery that the longer the child was in school, the lower his self-esteem. Lamy (11) reported that the best single predictor of beginning reading achievement in first grade was the child's perception of self in kindergarten. Lewis, Lovell, and Jessee (12) demonstrated that achievement increased when the interpersonal relationship between the teacher and the child was perceived as therapeutic. Sears and Sherman (13) summarized their research by presenting a model that clearly delineates the link between affective and cognitive variables. The authors illustrated the interrelationship through case studies.

Research indicates that affect and cognition are inextricably present in every learning situation. The learner's development suffers when his feelings and emotions are ignored. Our educational systems appear to discourage creativity and spontaneity. Schools must be reorganized to encourage creative, flexible, and spontaneous interaction that results in achievement-oriented behavior.

Affective development can no longer be left to chance. Educational experiences in understanding self and others are not an interesting innovation. Experiences of this kind are basic to the educational process. The child who harbors feelings of inadequacy functions ineffectively. The child who must cope with disruptive emotions or poor social relations does not progress academically.

Administrators formerly assigned personal and social development to specialists. However, specialists can no longer be the only personnel concerned with emotions, feelings, and human relationships.

Teachers must be equipped to function in classroom guidance. They are "where the action is" and hence are accessible to the total child. To function effectively the teacher must:

- risk being involved with personal relationships
- extend himself to listen, hear and care
- empathize with what children experience
- understand what they say
- help them develop self-understanding—and commitment, involvement, action programs [14:314].

The feelings that accompany learning have a profound effect on the results of learning. If a child has positive feelings, he becomes motivated, involved, energized, and makes lasting gains. If a child has negative feelings, he participates very little or withdraws. He must be forced, and he dismisses what he learns as soon as external controls are withdrawn.

Motivation, affect, and learning cannot be separated. In the past, emotions have been considered primarily as disruptive forces. We think of anxiety, fear, anger, hatred, and hostility as emotions that inhibit learning. We seldom recognize that they are always present and must be dealt with if the learner is to become involved. We must become aware that emotions can energize, renew, and restore the learner. To recognize the positive force of emotions, one need only visit a classroom that is lush with emotional feelings and another that is arid and sterile.

In the days when autocratic methods in education were

unchallenged, perhaps it was possible to stifle emotions. The effect on the child's development was debilitating despite the notion that silence and learning were synonymous. With the increasing challenges from youth for equality and the insistence on democratic participation in decision-making, we are recognizing that autocratic processes can no longer survive in the classroom any more than on the political scene.

Teachers must ask whether their philosophy, their methods, and their evaluation instruments are directed at developing human beings or at teaching subject matter. The development of fully functioning human beings is not an incidental by-product of the educational process. The development of fully functioning human beings is the central purpose of the educational process.

Some may ask why the classroom teacher should be involved in this type of instructional activity. She must be involved because guidance and education serve the same ends. Only as the child understands himself, his needs, his purposes, and his goals is he free to become involved and committed to the educational process. Guidance and instruction must be understood as interdependent and complementary. Any valid learning experience has a guidance component. However, it is in the classroom that the child copes with both the work and the social tasks of life. It is in the classroom, then, that affect and cognition must be integrated. Materials and programs that offer significant experiences to actualize human potential must be incorporated into the educational scene.

Planned experiences that personalize and humanize the educational experience are essential. Every intellectual experience is immersed in feelings. We can no longer deny this fact. Our challenge is to use feelings in a positive way to energize the educational process.

Developing Understanding of Self and Others is an educational program that focuses on the development of purposeful behavior that is personally significant and socially satisfying (15). The program helps the child with the self and with the social components of living. Experiences are designed to help the child become more aware of himself as a social being. The program helps the individual understand the purposive and causal nature of human relationships. As he becomes aware of his own purposes and goals, he becomes able to function more effectively with others and more involved in the educational process.

In *Developing Understanding of Self and Others* developmental tasks provide the goals for guidance and education. The program offers experiences with eight developmental tasks that the normal individual faces in his development. All children need help with these tasks. Some children need more help than others. The purpose of the program is to provide experience in understanding and coping with the eight tasks:

1. Self-identity, self-acceptance, developing an adequate self-image and feelings of adequacy.

2. Learning a giving-receiving pattern of affection.
3. Learning to develop mutuality, moving from being self-centered to effective peer relations.
4. Learning to become reasonably independent, to develop self-control.
5. Learning to become purposeful, to seek the resources and responsibilities of the world, to become involved, and to respond to challenge with resourcefulness.
6. Learning to be competent, to achieve, to think of self as capable of mastery.
7. Learning to be emotionally flexible and resourceful.
8. Learning to make value judgments and choices, and to accept the consequences of one's choices.

The program, which focuses on normal developmental problems, is based on a set of lessons and experiences for the entire class. The lessons are to be conducted in a democratic atmosphere that encourages full participation by the children. Each child is encouraged to share his feelings, attitudes, and reactions. It is essential for the teacher to stress that there are no right answers and no wrong answers. The teacher must be capable of hearing the individual's feelings and perceptions. She is not called upon for judgmental transactions and evaluations of pupil's contributions.

To reach children who have unique learning styles, the program uses varied media and modes. They include recorded stories, music, open-ended stories, discussion starters, lessons on puppetry, role-playing activities, art, and experiential activities.

A typical week in the program uses each of these activities. However, plans for using the material are flexible. Each teacher knows her class, individual and group needs, and the type of activity that appears to be most interesting and productive. Thus, feedback from the class determines the order of activity and the amount of time spent on a particular facet of the lesson.

Each unit includes a complete cycle of activities. One cycle of activities includes a story, a poster, a problem situation, a role-playing activity, puppetry, and supplementary activities.

The first unit in *Developing Understanding of Self and Others* is titled "Understanding and Accepting Self." A song "I'm Glad That I Am Me" and a poster "I Am the Only Me in the World" are designed to develop self-identity and self-acceptance. The story "The Red and White Bluebird" directs discussion to accepting ourselves as we are. Each child is encouraged to make a "ME" button or badge to symbolize his uniqueness.

The unit "Understanding Feelings" helps children deal with giving-and-receiving patterns of affection, and offers children an opportunity to talk about positive and negative feelings. The story "Gordo and Molly" directs discussions to sharing. A role-playing activity "Let's All Share" gives children a chance to enact and express feelings about sharing. The open-ended story "Flopsie Is Afraid" presents a problem situation to help children discuss what they can do to understand and help others who are fearful.

"Understanding Others" is the title of the unit on peer relations. The puppetry activity "Special" provides an example of unacceptable behavior. The activity centers on a girl who demands special treatment. The children are encouraged to be aware of the selfishness of being special and to think of ways to deal with such behavior.

The unit "Understanding Independence" is designed to help children learn to function without constant supervision. The story "Good Guy and Old Lazy" raises the question "Should one do one's best, or should one do only what is required?" The role-playing activity "Big Trouble" deals with the temptation to be irresponsible and the consequences of irresponsibility. *The Lazy Beaver*, a story about laziness and courage, can be read to the children (16).

Unit 5 "Understanding Goals and Purposeful Behavior" is concerned with understanding the purposeful nature of behavior. A problem situation "Tina and the Class Play" is a vignette about a child who hesitates to start because she is afraid she might fail. The poster in this unit is titled "It Takes Courage To Try." As supplementary reading, teachers may read to the class *The Little Engine That Could* (17).

The unit "Understanding Mastery, Competence, and Resourcefulness" focuses on learning to be competent and to think of self as capable of mastery. The story "Duso and Squeaker" tells about a young dolphin who is not so competent as Duso the Dolphin. The discussion after the story gives children an opportunity to list their achievements and to build confidence in their own ability. Puppet activity titled "John Won't Try" gives children an opportunity to experience the roles of the child who is eager to try, the child who tries and makes mistakes, and the child who refuses to try.

Unit 7 "Understanding Emotional Maturity" is concerned with emotional flexibility and resourcefulness. The activities explore the purposive nature of emotions and emphasize courageous and effective responses to stress and change. The story "The New House" discusses problems in a common experience, changing one's residence. The problem situation "A New Teacher" opens discussion on reasons why change is upsetting. The puppet activity "The Doctor" deals with the common anxiety of seeing doctors and dentists, initiates discussion of fears, and elicits ways to cope with fear.

The final unit "Understanding Choices and Consequences" has stories about honesty and fairness. One poster is titled "Each of Us Is Important." "Mary's New Friend" is a problem situation that deals with prejudice and how we are more alike than different.

The material is concerned with enhancing self-understanding, awareness of self and others, and purposeful motivational involvement in the tasks of life. The experiences are designed to build a positive self-concept and feelings of adequacy. The child becomes aware of the feeling area of his life. He learns that behavior is caused and purposive. He learns that there are reasons why human beings act as they do.

In teaching the lessons the teacher should allow for spontaneity and for creative thought and expression by the children. The lessons must involve the full range of human experiences, feelings, beliefs, and behavior. Sometimes a lesson stimulates a child to discuss a concern that is pertinent to him or his group, but does not appear to be the major purpose set forth in the lesson guide. The teacher is directed to link the problem situations in the lessons with current concerns in the classroom. The primary purpose is to help children apply their experiences to current life problems.

The program *Developing Understanding of Self and Others* provides a procedure for personalizing and making the educational experience meaningful. The school becomes concerned with the real priorities—children and their concerns, their self-identity, their feelings of adequacy, their emotional needs, social challenges, development of independence, and purposeful behavior. The child has experiences that help him become emotionally flexible and resourceful. He learns to think of himself as capable of achievement. He becomes involved in making value judgments and choices, and in accepting the consequences of his decisions. He matures as a total being.

Giving priority to individuals, then, places an emphasis on the real goal of education—the development of a fully functioning human being.

REFERENCES

1. DAVID R. KRATHWOHL, BENJAMIN S. BLOOM, and BERTRAM B. MASIA. *Taxonomy of Educational Objectives, Handbook II: Affective Domain.* New York: David McKay Company, 1964.

2. NORMA RANDOLPH and WILLIAM HOWE. *Self Enhancing Education.* Palo Alto, California: Sanford Press, 1966.

3. RALPH OJEMANN. *A Teaching Program in Human Behavior and Mental Health.* Cleveland, Ohio: Educational Research Council of America (n.d.).

4. N. A. FLANDERS and E. J. AMIDON. "The Role of the Teacher in the Classroom." Minneapolis, Minnesota: Minneapolis Association for Productive Teaching, Inc. 1967.

5. M. WITMER and H. COTTINGHAM. "The Teacher's Role and Guidance Functions as Reported by Elementary Teachers," *Elementary School Guidance and Counseling,* 5 (October, 1970), 12-21.

6. W. WATTENBERG and C. CLIFFORD. "Relationship of Self-Concepts to Beginning Achievement in Reading," *Child Development, 35* (1964), 461-67.

7. A. WALSH. *Self-Concepts of Bright Boys with Learning Difficulties.* New York, New York: Teachers College, Columbia University, 1956.

8. S. COOPERSMITH. "A Method for Determining Types of Self-Esteem," *Journal of Abnormal Social Psychology, 59* (July, 1959), 87-94.

9. M. B. FINK. "Self-Concept as It Relates to Academic Underachievement," *California Journal of Educational Research, 13* (March, 1962), 57-62.

10. ARTHUR W. COMBS and DANIEL W. SOPER. *The Relationship of Child Perceptions to Achievement and Behavior in the Early School Years.* Cooperative Research Project No. 814. Gainesville, Florida: University of Florida, 1963.

11. M. W. LAMY. "Relationship of Self-Perceptions of Early Primary Children to Achievement in Reading," *Human Development Readings in Research.* Edited by I. J. Gordon. Chicago: Scott, Foresman, 1965.

12. WILLIAM LEWIS, JOHN T. LOVELL, and B. E. JESSEE. Interpersonal Relationship and Pupil Progress," *Personnel and Guidance Journal, 44* (December, 1965), 396-401.

13. P. SEARS and B. SHERMAN. *In Pursuit of Self-Esteem.* Belmont California: Wadsworth Publishing Company, 1964.

14. DON DINKMEYER. "The Teacher as Counselor: Therapeutic Approaches to Understanding Self and Others," *Childhood Education, 46* (March, 1970), 314-17.

15. DON DINKMEYER. *Developing Understanding of Self and Others* (DUSO). Circle Pines, Minnesota: American Guidance Service, 1970.

16. VERNON BOWEN. *The Lazy Beaver.* New York: David McKay Company, 1948.

17. WATTY PIPER. *The Little Engine That Could.* New York: Platt and Munk, 1945.

Changing Behavior By Personalizing Learning

FOREST J. FRANSEN and JOANNE LANDHOLM

Everything we do today seems to have a price tag attached to it. We think very little about venturing a million dollars to prospect on Mount Ararat for the remains of Noah's ark. Jet airliners cost three to five million apiece. As a nation we spend billions of dollars to explore space. Spending for educational programs, however- especially those designed to develop wholesome individuals with adequate interpersonal skills—is done reluctantly and often insufficiently. For this reason alone, a program which will help to develop these skills with no more expenditure than that provided in the normal school budget becomes an anomaly. Just such a program was instituted at Thomas A. Edison Elementary School, Denver, Colorado, using its present staff and facilities.

The program evolved from a new approach to the use of multi-disciplinary teams. The historical use of such teams depends upon gathering together a group of school specialists—nurse, psychologist, social worker, principal, and teacher—to direct the knowledge and skills of their various disciplines to the solution of pupils' problems. However, experience over many years has resulted in diminutive returns. We at Edison School arc not suggesting that each of these disciplines isn't important or that they fail to perform a function which is important or supportive to the educational process. Not at all! We merely recommend a redirection of these disciplines to involve children more directly than heretofore. It isn't enough to gather literally reams of background information on a child in trouble. Dr. William Glasser points out this fact in his book *Reality Therapy*. He says that we should be more concerned with the present and future than with the past. In other words DO IT and do it with children. We at Edison School want to share our experi-

Fransen, Forest J., and Landholm, Joanne. "Changing Behavior by Personalizing Learning." *The Journal of School Health.* February 1971. 41:70-73.

ences in this area.

We initiated our program by having a recommended authority in the field of mental health talk to our entire staff. We learned that Dr. Walter J. Limbacher, director, Resource Development branch, Division of Psychiatric Services, Denver (Colorado) General Hospital, was such a resource. Dr. Limbacher provided background information and emphasized the need for school persons to do something to improve interpersonal feelings among children. His publications *Mental Health* and a 4th grade pupils' booklet *Here I am* proved to be excellent references. He also held two after-school sessions with the Edison staff.

From this beginning Edison School's staff began to formulate plans and develop a program. We began by sounding out and getting commitments from those representing the disciplines within our school. Everyone responded enthusiastically.

A letter was sent to parents informing them that their child would be involved. We assumed that there would not be any objection and suggested that they call the principal for further details. The few parents who have inquired have in all cases given their support. As one mother put it, "Good Luck." The principal has on several occasions informed the PTA and local community leaders.

Our experience has covered the past two semesters. Those representing the various disciplines at the school experimented with different groupings and combinations of children during the first semester.

DISCIPLINES	CHILDREN INCLUDED	DAYS AND TIME
social worker & nurse team	eight 6th grade girls	every Tuesday for 50 minutes for 12 weeks
principal & nurse team	ten 4th grade boys and girls	every Thursday for 50 minutes for 12 weeks
social worker, teacher assistant, and counselor from community Mental Health Clinic	fifteen 5th grade boys and girls	every Thursday for 50 minutes for 12 weeks
teacher assistant	eight 5th grade boys	every Thursday for 50 minutes for 12 weeks
social worker	eight 5th grade girls	every Thursday for 50 minutes for 12 weeks
principal & nurse	twelve 5th grade boys and girls	every Thursday for 50 minutes for 12 weeks
teacher assistant and coordinator of nursing	twelve 5th grade boys and girls	every Thursday for 50 minutes for 12 weeks
social worker and teacher	twelve 5th grade boys and girls	every Thursday for 50 minutes for 12 weeks

This school year we concentrated on the fifth grade. We wanted to give this group discussion experience to all of the fifth grade. To do this, we have organized our groups in this way.

This latter schedule represents one full class of fifth graders. Since we have three fifth grades, we will arrange for three sessions during the year with the goal of giving every fifth grade pupil this experience.

What were our purposes in personalizing learning? We would feel a great accomplishment if the following could be reached, even in part:

1. To effect a change in behavior
2. To improve self-image
3. To effect an improved climate in group living

Since the group sessions could provide a new experience for most of the children, we felt some structuring would be necessary.

At our first session we explained to the children that the purpose of the meeting was to give them an opportunity to talk with a group about "their concerns." Various positive reactions were observed when the children were told they would not be marked on their performance in the sessions. The following guidelines for their own behavior in the group were set up:

1. No need to raise your hand for permission to talk, but let one person at a time talk.
2. Keep discussions among ourselves. No need to discuss outside the group, except with parents.
3. Make up any school work you miss by having attended sessions.

Various techniques were used for acquainting the children with each other. They would tell what they knew about the person sitting next to them. We discovered that the comments made were generally superficial, relating to such things as hair color, female or male, and color of clothes. Even though they were daily in class with one another, they found they really did not know much about each other. Each pupil was given an opportunity to talk about himself. They shared such information as where they were born, schools attended, difficulties with siblings, where their fathers worked (some did not know what type of work their fathers did, only that they worked), and their hobbies. The leaders also shared their past and at all times would "level" with the group. A fifth grade girl in her first meeting with the group talked about a recent trip to California. She was extremely verbal and concerned about an exposure of siblings to "weed" and "paint- and glue-sniffing." The tone of the group seemed very emphatic as she spoke. She held their attention for over ten minutes without interruption. Another group took turns "mirroring" each other. Two pupils would sit facing each other. One would describe how he saw the other pupil, and that pupil would attempt to reflect the gestures and motions the other made. The group members were observing and quick to comment about nervous tendencies, forgetting to look directly at the person, and agreed that communication did take place using the sense of sight. They also agreed a person could learn more about each other when they could "talk together."

The pupils discussed the types of things they would like to talk about. They listed ten to twelve topics on a chalk board and then voted for whichever they would discuss first. Usually they were ready to proceed to a new topic each week. Their last session included topics such as (1) Illness—real or fake, (2) Teachers, (3) Marks—why they were necessary, their reaction, and parents' reactions, (4) Communism, (5) Dreams, (6) Honesty, (7) Fighting—peers and siblings, (8) Fears, (9) Mistreatment of animals, (10) Drugs, (11) Temper, and (12) Friendship.

Various techniques were used for opening the discussions each week. A ten-minute filmstrip on "sharing" set the stage for the group's discussion that day. Use of a tape recorder to record and present material from Dr. Limbacher's book *Mental Health* proved very effective in the discussion of "fears." This audio aid helped to improve the children's listening skills as well as to stimulate discussion. We would take about two paragraphs of material and then *pose* a question, "Has this ever happened to you?"

Midway through the sessions we gave each pupil a worksheet listing items they were to number as to importance—one to fifteen. A problem was then read to them about a space ship, lost from a mother ship, and the children were to rank the items they would need for survival. This experiment was one suggested in the NEA Journal. We asked the children first to work individually on one worksheet and divided them into two groups of five afterward to work out the same problem. These fourth graders became involved in challenging each other as to which items should be most important and which least. Children from both groups scored higher working in a group than working individually, a result which the experiment was meant to show.

The principal's recent trip to Germany provided the springboard for a discussion of communism. Pupils responded with many questions about slides he had taken. Two of the children were obsessed by the fact that people tried to cross through the Berlin Wall by hiding under trucks. "Checkpoint Charlie" also brought forth many comments. The children were quick to note and comment on the differences between their life in the United States and what they saw on the slides.

Talking about dreams turned into a game of "Who Can Top This?" We injected facts about dreaming taken from psychology reference books and from Dr. Limbacher's material in *Mental Health*.

Role-playing was a favorite activity among the children. We opened the discussion about report card marks with the principal playing the role of a boy who hid his report card from his mother. The nurse played the role of the mother who felt that disciplinary action must be taken and then worked out a system with the child to help him improve the marks and still have time for "fun" things.

Four group members picked the role-playing method for opening discussion on illness—real or fake. They portrayed two children in a family—one of whom received attention, as she was really ill, and the other who pretended to be sick to gain attention. When the pretender really became ill, no one believed her. The children asked permission to present their skit for the rest of their 4th grade class. The skit worked out so well that they presented it in an assembly, first to grades 1-3 and then to grades 4-6. The girl who played the role of the mother was a girl who had previously feigned illness to get out of class. One teacher whom she had had difficulty communicating with said later, "I couldn't believe my eyes. She is really coming around."

We are continually evaluating our group sessions. Prior to the sessions we review the pupils' cumulative folders for family information and comments from teachers about the history of previous participation in class. Dividing the group in half, with each of us taking five or six children to observe alerts us to any changes in behavior that are occuring. After each session we discuss what has evolved and comment on individual involvement and participation that day. We are quite honest with each other and evaluate our own performance too. Behavior changes? Yes, we are seeing them, and now some teachers are commenting that they are noticing some positive changes among the children who have been involved in the groups.

During a recent parent-teacher conference, a parent made a favorable comment, and now the principal is receiving support from the PTA board members in regard to the group meetings. Communication is increasing, attitudes are changing favorably, self-images are improving, and so are report card marks. In the health office the school nurse observed that some of the children who were known for feigning illness were still stopping to see her. However, the nature of the call was now much different. Several children came to ask questions about the group. Some asked her help in doing some role-playing, while others expressed their happiness being in the group. Instead of the visits being during class periods, they are becoming "before-and-after-school" visits. The principal has also noticed increased contact with these children. One girl stopped him to say, "You know me better than anyone else in the school, huh?" Others visit his office to talk about ideas for the group. These children are quick to speak to us while passing in the halls, and seem pleased when we can refer to them by name.

The children have a chance to evaluate each other too. Without any early announcement we have them arrange their chairs in a straight line. We number the chairs, with number one being the chair for the pupil who participated most during the discussion that day. The last chair is for the pupil who participated the least. The children move each other (one at a time, without talking) by taking the child's arm. After allowing a few minutes for position changing, we ask them to stop to evaluate what they have done. The groups have been excellent in their selection of placements, and the children who occupy the first and last places are able to say that that is where they feel they belong. We always comment that on another day, during another discussion, the placement could be quite different. In our experiences with this technique we find the pupil in the last chair usually increases his participation and involvement during the following sessions.

In one group we had one pupil who was quite disruptive. We called two other group members in and told them we were concerned about one of our group who was acting in an unfavorable way. The two children were quick both to tell us they also were concerned about one member and to identify the pupil. We asked if they had any suggestions that might help him. They thought they could take care of it by talking to this boy. Later that day in our meeting, they sat next to this boy. Whenever he started to disrupt the group one or the other simply put his hand on the boy's knee. This act quieted him.

The children also filled out a questionnaire. Included were questions such as (1) What do you like most about the group meetings, and what do you like least? (2) Do you feel differently about yourself since being in the group? (3) Were the meetings anything like what you expected? (4) What about the size of the group? (5) Have the meetings helped you learn more about your friends? (6) Have you had a chance to discuss things that you couldn't discuss elsewhere?

We have met with the other group leaders periodically to share ideas and talk about our goals, and to evaluate our progress in attaining these goals. We find that our own enthusiasm has remained as high as when we started the group sessions, and we are constantly searching for new ideas in working with these children.

The pupils who haven't been involved stop to ask when it will be their turn, so we feel there must be some communication going on between these pupils and those already participating. Those who have participated are asking if there will be more sessions.

Our final meeting with the children is a "surprise" day. We have ice cream treats and evaluate what we liked and disliked in the group.

The multiple problems in our schools today prompt us to examine more efficient and effective ways to use our specialists in the field of education. We would propose, as we have described in detail in this article, a sharing of the skill which each discipline possesses with groups of children rather than with individuals. We believe it is more effective, a better use of the tax dollar, and a way to secure community approval.

REFERENCES

1. GLASSER, WILLIAM, *Reality Therapy.* New York, 1965.

2. LIMBACHER, WALTER J., *Here I Am—Dimensions of Personality.* Dayton; George A. Pflaum, 1969.

3. LIMBACHER, WALTER J., *Mental Health.* Dayton; George A. Pflaum, 1967.

4. LUKE, BARBARA "Lost on the Moon; A Decision-Making Problem." NTL Institute for Applied Behavioral Science, *National Education Association* (February, 1969) pp. 55-56.

SCHOOL is for . . .
TESTING YOUR
STRENGTHS

Road Signs To A Successful Journey

Happiness Is Being A Positive Teacher

ALICE C. BEHRE

The positive approach does work! It not only helps the child to enjoy school and to learn more, it makes the teacher's day more pleasant and makes it possible for her to enjoy better relationships with her students. The positive approach is simple and easy to use. It is built on the basic principle that all people repeat the behaviors that are rewarding to them. In a classroom setting, the teacher's attention is often the greatest reward possible. Therefore, the behaviors receiving the most attention from the teacher are those most frequently repeated. The teacher using a positive approach pays attention to those behaviors she wants continued.

Sometimes it seems easier to notice and respond to inappropriate behaviors. Teachers may do it almost unconsciously. If Tommy is the boy who is always talking, always out of his seat, and never working, Tommy's name might very well be mentioned most often during the day by remarks such as "Tommy, sit down", "Tommy, get to work", etc. Tommy probably can find no reason to change his behavior. He is being amply rewarded by a huge share of the teacher's attention.

The following suggestions might serve as a guide for initiating or reinforcing the positive approach.

1. The teacher and the class make specific and definite rules that everyone understands. Rules should be:

   a. Short and to the point.
   b. Stated in a positive way.

Behre, Alice C. "Road Signs to a Successful Journey." *Maryland Department of Elementary School Principals.* Winter 1970. 11:26-27.

"Stay in your seat during reading" rather than "Don't walk around the room during reading".

  c. Varied for different activities such as work, study, play periods.

2. The teacher shows her approval for appropriate behavior; this is the crux of positive classroom control and the teacher's motto might be "CATCH THEM BEING GOOD".

Tommy finds it difficult to stay in his seat. The teacher watches for times when he is in his seat and then really lets him have it—the attention—by verbal praise, smiles, a nod, or special privileges.

Another method is to give attention to desirable behavior that is incompatible with the undesirable behavior going on. While Tommy is out of his seat, the teacher gives attention and praise to children near Tommy who are sitting down.

Some children need more praise than others. If they haven't been taught discipline earlier, the positive teacher's first priority is to teach that good things happen only when behavior is appropriate. The undisciplined, the immature, and the forgetter need more praise.

3. Ignore disruptive behavior unless someone is getting hurt. The teacher gives her attention only to those who are working. If a disruptive child shows improvement, this improvement merits attention. The ultimate desired behavior must be reached by small steps.

4. Punishment may be necessary if the unwanted behavior is very intense or so frequent that there is no desired behavior to notice. Punishment rarely changes behavior; it may halt a behavior temporarily, but that undesirable behavior will resume and persist after the punishment has taken place.

If punishment is necessary, isolation can be the solution. If the student is isolated from his class and teacher, he loses all opportunity to receive attention. Unfortunately, there are few locations convenient for a child to spend a few minutes alone, so this practice is not always possible. If punishment is used, it must be accompanied by the use of attention to those behaviors incompatible with the punished behavior.

5. The positive approach requires consistency. If the teacher gives her attention to Tommy on Monday only when he's sitting in his seat, she can't reverse and give him attention on Tuesday for being out of his seat. This will confuse Tommy and will not help to reduce the number of times he gets up.

6. Attention must be immediate. If Tommy sits in his seat working quietly from 9:30 to 9:45 AM, he must be rewarded at that time. If the teacher waits until lunch time, she will have lost her opportunity to increase Tommy's sitting down behavior.

Verbal praise or teacher approval has been mentioned most often as the rewarding agent. For some children this may not be enough to change behavior. Other activities that might be used as rewards for strengthening behavior might be:

Using games and puzzles	Candy
Being first in line	Trinkets
Letter to parents	Extra Recess
Reward from parents	Class Party
Helping in other classes	Helping Teacher
Special Class privileges	Special Art time

The teacher and the class can make an almost limitless list. Social attention or praise will eventually become more rewarding than tangibles.

In summary—the teacher who uses the positive approach:

1. Makes definite rules,
2. Pays attention to desirable behavior,
3. Ignores undesirable behavior.

The positive approach works equally well with one individual or with an entire class. The teacher must analyze the situation, decide which undesirable behaviors she wants to eliminate, which desirable behaviors she wants to increase, and proceed from them positively!

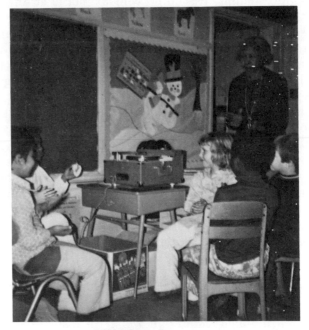

SCHOOL is for . . .
TAKING TURNS

Chapter VI

The Teacher As Curriculum Implementor

The knowledge explosion has made it impossible for any individual to possess more than a fractional part of all the knowledge known to man today. The curricular content of the elementary school has continued to expand at every level of learning while the length of the school day as well as the school year have changed little. Your challenge as a beginning teacher is one of developing *a personal philosophy of education* which takes into account the needs of our democratic society, the unique needs of individual pupils, and the physical conditions under which you and your pupils must operate for maximum learning to take place.

It has long been recognized by educators that once the teacher takes charge of a group of youngsters, decisions concerning what each child will master, how much time he will be allowed in order to attain this mastery, and what type of activity or modes of learning will most likely insure that the concept or skill will be attained are the major responsibilities of the classroom teacher. The challenge indeed appears awesome; yet, the decisions you make daily in the implementation of the curriculum for the maximum growth of each of your pupils is the creative responsibility of a truly professional teacher, a position which you have been working four years or more to attain.

The central theme of this Chapter is concerned with the implementation of the curriculum as a process for rational thinking. Although teachers' manuals and curriculum guides will be beneficial to you as a beginning teacher, the challenge of assessing current national concerns and implementing relevant considerations such as environmental education into your existing curricula requires you to be an informed and responsible professional teacher who understands the purpose of elementary education in the United States as it exists today. This is your challenge as you seek to be a true facilitator of learning for your pupils in the years ahead.

The Teacher as a Curriculum Maker

CHARLES R. MAY

New national studies are raising critical questions about the role of the teacher in curriculum making. I believe that all teachers are basically interested in improving themselves and in doing a good job. However, this does not mean that all teachers perform at the same level. In fact, teachers generally perform at three different levels and, consequently, assume three different roles in curriculum making.

These three roles can be seen as points on a continuum. At one end of the continuum is the teacher who is a "manipulator." Teachers at this level are manipulated by curriculum planners and by the textbooks they use. In turn, these teachers manipulate their students in much the same way. While operating at this level, teachers do those tasks which have been determined for them. Consequently, the decisions that they make are those delegated to them. For the most part, those decisions are restricted to their immediate area of operation—their classrooms.

This pattern would indicate that others have the responsibility for planning the curriculum, and the function of teachers is to see that this planning is carried out in their classrooms. Therefore, "covering the content" in the ways determined by the curriculum planners and textbook writers is the main responsibility of these teachers.

Teachers operating at the manipulative level behave more like technicians than members of a profession. In accepting a minor role in curriculum decision making, these teachers relinquish the status of a professional person. I have not always held this view. For example, in my first year of teaching, I found myself overly dependent upon my textbook and the ideas of others. The teacher, I felt, was the "doer," putting into operation the plans of the experts. I reasoned that the expert had the time, knowledge, and experience to determine and organize the content

May, Charles R. (Indiana State University) "The Teacher as Curriculum Maker. *Ohio Schools.* December 1965. 43:12-13, 45.

and methods which teachers should use in their teaching. Thus, if a teacher could read the teacher's guide that accompanied a textbook, he should do at least an average job of teaching.

This view, I now believe, restricts the teacher to a minor role in curriculum decision making. Primarily, the tasks given a teacher at this level are those of serving on textbook committees and deciding which of several activities suggested by the experts should be used in teaching a lesson. Teachers who are interested in becoming professional people, however, are not satisfied to operate at this minor level of decision making, nor are they willing to be manipulated by others.

Toward the middle of the continuum are teachers operating at a level above the manipulative stage. These teachers have no need to use their textbooks and teacher's guides as though they were recipes or blueprints. They have an understanding of the textbook author's purposes and philosophy. Furthermore, they have an understanding of children's needs and interests. With these insights, they know when and where to supplement or deviate from the text. In other words, the teacher at this level is a "source" just as the textbook or curriculum guide is a source of content and method.

This level is therefore characterized by teachers who take an interest in curriculum planning. Frequently such planning is carried out through committees and through in-service workshops. At this level, the administration often assumes the leadership role. The following conditions foster this level of activity: time during school hours for planning, encouragement, guidance, recognition, and putting the results of planning into operation.

From my own experience, I found operating at the source level much more satisfying than operating at the manipulative level. Although there is security in following the textbook and in doing the suggested activities, this level of operation proves to be rather routine and unimaginative. Therefore, as I gained knowledge and experience, I changed my emphasis from covering the text to that of using learning activities designed to meet the needs and interest of my students. As a result, I found my role in curriculum decision making changing also. For example, in teaching reading I switched from a basal textbook approach to an individualized approach, which required me to make many of the decisions that had formerly been made by the textbook authors. But because I knew my students, our reading objectives, and the variety of methods we could use, I was secure in using this approach. The reactions of the students toward reading revealed that the change was desirable, especially for that particular class.

Working at the source level requires much of the teacher; many more demands are placed on him. But the rewards are greater, too.

Primarily, it is the difference in knowing that one is working as a professional person rather than as a technician.

At the opposite end of the continuum is the process level. Teachers operating at this level are fully professional. These teachers are characterized by a sound understanding of the following: teaching objectives, content, and methods. Moreover, they are aware of children's needs and interests. They are further characterized by their "open" attitude toward experience, their view of living and learning as a process, and their belief in the worth of each individual. They have a positive attitude toward themselves, their profession, and mankind in general.

A teacher at this level is considered as a "process" person. He views his function as that of bringing "raw materials" of learning—including himself—into the classroom. Together the teacher and the students then build concepts and understandings from this "raw material." Each student is involved in the process.

Teachers operating at this level have a vital part in curriculum planning. They assume leadership roles along with the administrators in making revisions in the curriculum. They are, indeed, the most important people involved in curriculum planning. By utilizing research and experimental studies, these teachers determine the best educational procedures and then work to incorporate these procedures into the curriculum.

As we mature and grow as a profession there will be fewer teachers operating at the manipulative level and more will come to function at the source and process levels. I am convinced that the type of teacher training that our future teachers now receive will shape more professional attitudes both toward teaching and toward the teacher's responsibilities in curriculum making.

SCHOOL is for . . .
CURIOSITY
STIMULATION

Subject Matter with a Focus on Values

SIDNEY B. SIMON* and MERRILL HARMIN

How increasingly irrelevant the schools seem! Social conflicts range all around us and the schools (the universities, too) go trotting down their "bland" alleys and continue to devote teaching time to grammar drills, the founding of Jamestown, and the urgent problem of how tall the flag pole is if its shadow is fifty feet at high noon.

If only we could see that the confrontation of high noon is here now, and if any drills are in order, perhaps they ought to be riot drills. If we must measure shadows, let them be the shadows of de facto segregation which cloud our land.

Of course this is not easy. Almost all of us feel tremendous ambivalence as we wrestle with that question of just how much of the standard subject matter of the school is to be set aside to make room for dealing with the current concerns of our society. We can all too quickly cite the fact that these problems are not the school's fault, and that they are too big, too all-encompassing to be tackled in school anyhow. Or we say we have other obligations, like teaching our students the inheritance of man's intellectual past.

What a school budgets time and money for, however, tell what it prizes. What and who it rewards tell what it cherishes. What the school asks on its true and false questions says more than almost anything else what it cares about, and just now, with the heavy emphasis upon college

*Sidney B. Simon, Associate Professor of Curriculum and Instruction, Temple University, Philadelphia, Pennsylvania; and Merrill Harmin, Associate Professor, Southern Illinois University, Edwardsville.

Simon, Sidney B., and Harmin, Merrill. "Subject Matter With a Focus on Values." *Educational Leadership*. October 1968. 26:34-37. For information about current values clarification materials or nation-wide training workshops, contact Values Associates, Box 43, Amherst, Mass. 01002.

entrance, the schools care most deeply about putting in more subject matter.

We are not going into that weary either/or argument about subject matter *or* play-play-play. We have nothing against subject matter, per se. We do have an urgent need, however, to make subject matter more relevant, and to us, relevancy means that the subject matter *must* illumine a student's values. Louis Raths puts it this way: "The function of information is to inform. To inform what? To inform our values."

Three Levels

Information which stays merely at the level of filling in the holes of a crossword puzzle, or name-dropping at a suburban cocktail party is information which we really do not need. So much of schooling is at this facts-for-facts level. There is a second level, a higher level, engagingly presented by Bruner, and this is called the concept level. We believe that there is still a higher level, a level which makes use of facts and concepts, but which goes well beyond them in the direction of penetrating a student's life. This we call the *values level.*

Let us look at an example to make this point. Take the favorite social studies topic, "The United States Constitution." We can teach this at the fact level, the concept level, or the values level.

I. *Fact Level* (U. S. Constitution)

1. Information about where and when the Constitution was drawn up
2. Who was involved and which colonies wanted what in it
3. Information about how it differed from the Articles of Confederation
4. Data on what was in the preamble and perhaps asking the class to memorize it
5. A list of the first 10 amendments and why they were called the Bill of Rights
6. The order in which the colonies ratified the document.

The above items should be fairly familiar facts to most of us, although we have probably forgotten the specifics. At one time this topic was presented to us in an organized manner, each fact building upon fact. Unfortunately, it was difficult to remember then and it still is hard to retain. It was of interest to only a few students and of little use even to them in any relevant search for values which might enlighten living in today's world.

Thus, many teachers tried to teach the Constitution at the *concept* level, encouraged by Bruner and followers.

II. *Concept Level* (U. S. Constitution)

1. Our Constitution as a landmark in the evolving concept of democratic forms of government
2. The concept of "compromise" and how it operated in reconciling the economic forces of the period
3. The motives of the signers and the constituencies all representatives are obligated to serve
4. The social injustices which the Bill of Rights attempted to correct
5. The concept of amendment and how it has operated in state legislatures and in Congress
6. The Constitution today as seen in the actions of the Supreme Court and the American Civil Liberties Union, etc.

The above "subject matter" will be seen as the basis for good teaching. It attempts to build relationships between random facts and to pull together generalizations supported by data. Many educators would be proud to have this kind of teaching going on in their schools, but we would argue that this approach is simply not good enough for these complex times. Let us look now at the *values* level, that third level to which subject matter needs to be lifted.

III. *Values Level* (U. S. Constitution)

1. What rights and guarantees do you have in your family? Who serves as the Supreme Court in disputes?
2. Have you ever written a letter to the editor of a newspaper or magazine?
3. Many student governments are really token governments controlled by the "mother country," i.e., the administration. Is this true in your school? What can you do about it? If not you, who should do it?
4. Should the editorial board of your school newspaper have the final say about what is printed in it? How do you reconcile the fact that the community will judge the school, a tax supported institution, by what is printed in the school paper?
5. When was the last time you signed a petition? Have you ever been the person to draw one up? What did the last sign you carried on a picket line say?
6. Where do you stand on wire tapping, financial aid to parochial schools, censorship of pornographic magazines, or the right of a barber to decide if he wants to cut a Negro's hair?

This kind of teaching is not for the faint-hearted. It often hits at the guts, but if we are to see the school as more than a place from which we issue the press release each spring which tells which colleges our students made, then we must do more teaching at this third level, this values level.

Let us be clear that teachers are not to throw out facts and concepts. Obviously, these are essential if we are to have anything to base our values upon. On the other hand, let us say forcefully that Levels I and II, no matter how brilliantly taught, do not clarify students' values. That third level has to be consciously and consistently pushed.

To Inform Our Values

Here is another example to argue for our third level point of view. Take Shakespeare's *Hamlet*. It is a good example for three reasons. It is taught universally, it is universally taught badly, and it is a play particularly ripe with values-teaching possibilities.

I. *Fact Level (Hamlet)*

1. Information on the year the play was written, and the sequence it occupies in Shakespeare's works
2. What country did Rosencranz and Guildenstern come from?
3. How did Hamlet's father die? How do we know that?
4. What is the relationship between Hamlet and Queen Gertrude? Between Hamlet and Polonius? and Ophelia?
5. Identify these quotations and explain why Shakespeare put them in the play
6. What is Hamlet's tragic flaw?
7. Who are all the people dead at the end of the play?

The above list is not meant to be all-inclusive by any means. Many other facts and details would be stressed by different teachers. Most teachers, however, feel at ease with such material. Students have been trained to feel comfortable with it, too. They know how to give the teacher what he wants on the kinds of questions which will be asked on tests. (True or False: Ophelia died from an overdose of rosemary?)

Teachers who are more aware will more often be teaching at the second level, the concept level.

II. *Concept Level (Hamlet)*

1. The concept of tragedy as opposed to comedy and how Shakespeare departed from the Aristotelian concepts of drama
2. To understand the various thematic threads of: incest, indecision, revenge, etc.
3. To know the dramaturgy behind the "play within a play" concept
4. The concept of "ghost" as it was understood by an Elizabethan audience
5. Psychological concepts which motivate Hamlet, Gertrude, Laertes, etc.
6. The various ways *Hamlet* has been played by the great Shakespearean actors.

Again, our lists are merely suggestive. It should, however, be quite apparent that this kind of teaching is much more lively and meaningful as compared with the survey of routine facts or going over the play line for line. Nevertheless, it is a serious error *not* to take your teaching to that third level, the values level. *Hamlet* is so very well-suited to help students develop the skills of clarifying their values and evaluating their lives. We believe that questions like the ones below should help students to do this.

III. *Values Level (Hamlet)*

1. King Claudius supposedly killed to get ahead. How far will you go to get what you want?
2. Laertes hears his father's advice, and it comes out a string of cliches. What kind of advice do you get which falls on *your* deaf ears?
3. Part of *Hamlet* is about the obligation of a son to seek revenge for his father. Where do you stand on that kind of act?
4. Hamlet is cruel to Ophelia. In what ways have you ever been cruel to members of the opposite sex? When have you been the recipient? Is cruelty an essential part of love to you?
5. What are some things about which you are having trouble making up your mind? Where will you go for help? Whom do you trust? How will you know that you have made a wise decision?
6. What kind of son or daughter do you want to be?
7. Death is a regular happening in *Hamlet*. How close have you ever come to death? What part of you responds to a news story of death on the highway, death in Vietnam?

It might be well to take a look at the third level, the values level, questions posed here. For one thing, the questions have a heavy component of "you" in them. Among these "you" questions there are some which invite a student to examine alternatives and to follow out the consequences. Some search for elements of pride in his choices. All of them, hopefully, cause him to look more closely at his present life, to see it as related to the subject matter he is studying. Some of the alternatives show that the subject matter could be pertinent to his personal existence. This is essential, this linking of the facts and concepts to the choices and decisions in the student's real life, at least if we are serious about teaching for the clarification of values.[1]

Among these "you" questions there are several which get the student to look at what he is actually *doing* in his life. The questions about the United States Constitution at the third level illustrate this clearly. This action emphasis is very important in the search for values. Many of the social conflicts of our time rage on because so many of us have a giant gap between what we "say" and what we "do." For many of us this gap is a chasm.

These are troubled and confused times in which to grow up. To live life with integrity becomes more and more difficult for more and more people. The threads of alienation which are increasingly woven into our youth must give us all deep concern.

For more on the values theory which supports this article, see: Louis E. Raths, Merrill Harmin, and Sidney B. Simon. *Values and Teaching.* Columbus: Charles E. Merrill Books, Inc., 1966.

We must demand of the subject matter we teach that it make us more than politely erudite. We must insist that it relate to students' lives. It must pertain to the realities of life in this complex and confusing time. Subject matter which is lifted to that third level, that values level, will give us a fighting chance. We must not be guilty of ignoring Dag Hammarskjold's warning: "In modern times we are in danger of taking facts for knowledge, and knowledge for wisdom."

SCHOOL is for . . .
DEVELOPING
NEW CONCEPTS

The Teacher and Method: The DEVELOPMENTAL METHOD

DR. BRADLEY LOOMER and CAROLYN JONES

The developmental method of instruction is probably best exemplified by the mathematics program. Emphasis within this method is focused on the logical structure that mathematics provides.

Dr. Herbert Spitzer, former director of University Elementary School, suggests there is a difference between the explanatory method of teaching and the developmental method. In general the explanatory method is based on the premise that pupil understanding and mastery of facts and processes will be superior if the facts and processes are explained to the pupil before he engages in other exercises similar to the presented problem. The developmental method employs the belief that logical pupil-problem situations and exercises provide a more meaningful approach to teaching mathematics. In this case the pupil must utilize the skills and knowledge he already possesses to discover new skills and new knowledge.

Critical examination of the developmental method in mathematics shows its relationship to the problem solving approaches used in other curricular areas. In the teaching of reading, social studies, science, and other areas as well, the teacher attempts to create a situation in which the pupil is trying to find the answers to questions. It appears logical to then assume that mathematical instruction, to be most successful, should be directed toward trying to solve a problem.

Spitzer[1] has identified the following as the most distinctive features of the developmental method:

Loomer, Bradley, and Jones, Carolyn. "The Teacher and Method: The Developmental Method." *The Iowa Elementary Principal.* Winter 1971. 5:8-10.

1. A "figure it out" or "problem solving" type of approach to learning is used.
2. Each area of arithmetic content is introduced through work problems in which a need for, or a use of, the new principle is exhibited.
3. New facts, terms, and arithmetic procedures are developed from pupil experiences originating from and relating to these introductory word problems.
4. Pupil activity is emphasized through frequent use of directions such as "find the answer by any method" and "show that the answer is correct."
5. These instructions elicit solutions of varying quality as well as different rates of progress.
6. The differentiation of instruction achieved in this way makes formal separation of the class into groups unnecessary.
7. Pupil experience is used as the basis for mastery study and a variety of specific study procedures are supplied.
8. Understanding is fostered by requesting that the answer be found by more than one way and through use of drawings, number line, evaluations, and reviews.

The figure it out or problem solving approach allows each child to develop those skills that work best for him. It encourages self-development by its emphasis on each child's approach to solving the problem. No generalized version is expected to be utilized by the class members. Discovery should come as each child investigates and attempts to draw conclusions. Information pieced together by the child is much more meaningful than some external approach suggested by the teacher.

It is quite important to realize that the child is placed in a situation where he sees a use for certain knowledge and then is encouraged to figure out his own way to obtain this knowledge. During this discovery or incubation state the pupil will attempt to make self-discoveries under the teacher's guidance. New problems will be brought into the educational process through familiar settings. The child is thus given the opportunity to comprehend the new in terms of old knowledge. Conceivably the students could spend an entire period searching for a solution. All teachers should be patient and not try to show the student while at the same time allowing the pupil to enjoy the thrill of discovery. If the pupil cannot cope with the problem, we are asking him to do something for which he does not have sufficient background. In this case, the pupils should back up to much simpler problems and attempt to discover solutions and relations at a less complex level until he has mastered the missing concept.

There are many natural and desirable problem situations which arise within the room. These are quite useful because they represent themselves as being genuine to the pupil. Word problems that are utilized should be chosen from the objects and experiences that are familiar to the students. Word problems are employed because they represent a meaningful whole to the pupils. Some representative statements of word problems follow:

Representative Word Problems

1. Mr. Johnson would like to have five committees work with him in designing play areas for the school. How many people, using this class, will be on each committee?
2. Sally has charged her daily lunch in the school cafeteria for three days. If the charge is 35c per meal, how much does Sally owe the cafeteria manager?
3. The fourth graders will entertain the third graders at a Halloween Party. If there are 30 pupils in third grade and each one will receive 3 cookies, how many dozen cookies will the fourth grade need?

Real and genuine problems are interesting and challenge the attention of the pupil. They provide the identification with the problem for students.

When new facts, terms, and mathematical procedures are taught a systematic, pupil-accented approach will be used. Children are not told but guided to their discovery and re-discovery. Results will be verified and reverified until understanding is acquired.

When any new term, process, or fact is introduced the following general format is employed:

1. Usually five or six problems involving the process or fact are presented to the students.
2. The pupils are directed to determine and write the number question to each problem.
3. Those who are capable are instructed to write the answers and if time permits, show that their solutions are correct. This usually involves drawings and diagrams.
4. Individual solutions are placed on the board and discussed. A statement is written which relates to the purpose of the lesson which is a new process, term, or fact. For example, if the process is multiplication a written statement such as "five threes equal fifteen" is appropriate.
5. Further discussion will lead to a shortening of the above statements to read "five 3's = 15."
6. The mathematical text is now consulted to find a way or method to write the statement in algorism form (5 x 3 = 15) and for examining various procedures for presenting multiplication in this example.

The developmental method allows each child to utilize whatever knowledge of facts and concepts that he has at his disposal. Emphasis is on providing situations where the pupil questions, suggests, gathers ideas, tests his own solutions, and challenges the solutions of others in the classroom. It is the express purpose of this method to force the student to develop new facts and terms for himself. This procedure strengthens the creative thinking power of each child giving him the opportunity to think both inductively and deductively.

Children are encouraged to show evidence of their qualitative thinking through the employment of drawings, diagrams, and objects to support their solutions. The child's ability to represent the problem by concrete drawings gives proof of his ability to truly understand the process.

It is well to mention the fact that the use of multiple ways of finding the answers to given problems provides each student with the opportunity to work with materials and at rates that are in keeping with his ability. This directly provides the teacher with an avenue for keeping the group together for most instruction and at the same time allowing pupils to work at different levels and speeds. Pupils frequently profit from working on the same topics. This is true when new topics are introduced, mastery exercises are utilized, and in many other occasions. Thus, pupils could be working on many differentiated levels but also participate in many common activities on a daily basis such as evaluation or in the discussion of a unique or special solution to problems. The differentiated approach serves to keep many of the undesirable aspects of total grouping for arithmetic out of the classroom.

Mastery of a process has always received attention in schools. In too many cases, drill has received much more emphasis than necessary. There are few situations where an automatic and instantaneous response is both necessary and desirable. It is suggested that drill for mastery come only after the student has had ample time to understand the fact or process and senses the true need for knowing it automatically. In many cases drill will be unnecessary because through the process of discovery, re-discovery, and verification will come mastery. If drill is to be used to affect mastery it is of utmost importance that the drill be made functional for the pupil.

Meaning and understanding are two aspects emphasized within the developmental method. If meaning and understanding are not stressed, the mathematics program runs the danger of emphasizing only the narrow computational objective of mathematics. True understanding of numbers and their operations may take a long time. Some students may remain at a low level of understanding for an extended period of time. Others will move more quickly. The teacher should allow and encourage procedures that are meaningful to the student. Allowing pupils to employ a self-designed but longer procedure promotes learning. Longer procedures, if they aid understanding and provide meaning, are preferred to shorter ones which lack meaning for many pupils.

Most modern mathematics programs emphasize the following principles of teaching mathematics: (1) discovery, (2) generalization, and

(3) testing by applying the learned material to new situations. In providing the path for discovery the pupils should be given the opportunity to have experiences with real and concrete objects. Through the usage of concrete objects will come the natural progression from discovery to solution to generalization to mastery as evidenced by being able to apply the learned material in new *situations*.

SCHOOL is for . . .
HARMONIZING

---

[1] Herbert F. Spitzer, *The Teaching of Arithmetic*, (Chicago: Houghton-Mifflin Company, 1961), p. 9

Multimedia

RON PAYNE

Recently, certain groups have been asking more proper questions about learning rather than merely theorizing about teaching. These groups have seen the instructor as a communicator. He is an individual who must be concerned with his effectiveness and ability to convey a message, and according to their reasoning, there is no disgrace if he is a poor orator. They have found that little learning occurs during the processes of mere telling.

One member of this group, Dr. David K. Berlo, has conceived a model of communication. He points to a "source" who encodes a "message" made up of contents with a certain unique structure. The source sends the message through one or more channels (the five senses) to a "receiver" who must decode the message. The receiver's success in decoding the message determines the effectiveness of the source. Dr. Berlo points out that the more channels used to convey a message the more likely the chance for successful communication.

In the rays from the light shed by Dr. Berlo, many educators have shown their concern for students by turning to educational media. Seven points which represent the value of educational media have been set forth in the Encyclopedia of Educational Research.

1. They supply a concrete basis for conceptual thinking and hence reduce meaningless word-responses of students.
2. They have a high degree of interest for students.
3. They make learning more permanent.
4. They offer a reality of experience which stimulates self-activity on the part of pupils.
5. They develop a continuity of thought; this is especially true of motion pictures.
6. They contribute to growth of meaning and hence to vocabulary development.
7. They provide experiences not easily obtained through other materials and contribute to the efficiency, depth, and variety of learning.

Out of this concern for the student, and in keeping with the seven values of educational media, a new idea is in a final phase of formulation.

Payne, Ron. "Multimedia." *The Oklahoma Teacher.* May 1972. 53:15-16.

This idea, called "multimedia" attempts to stimulate the student to achieve new heights of learning by the creation of a complete environment. This approach borrows from the Berlo concept in that multimedia utilizes several channels to convey a message.

Consequently, a multimedia classroom is one that contains two or more types of media for communicating information to the student, as well as providing some measure of control to the instructor as he manages the learning environment. It is a conscious overlapping of several stimuli to produce a total environment.

The typical multimedia classroom will have capabilities of projecting films, slides, videotapes, off-the-air or CCTV, and transparencies with all projectors behind a rear screen. In addition, tape recorders and TV cameras are available in most installations. Room lights should be controlled from the lectern manually or mechanically and the lights may be colored to augment the creation of desired moods and overall conditions. They should be controlled by rheostat to facilitate dimming them to a soft glow or increasing them to a full brilliance.

A multimedia classroom can be an excellent apparatus to present the student with the three main types of learning experiences. Audio and still photographs may achieve a symbolic experience while motion pictures and sound may provide a vicarious experience. And by the utilization of both symbolic and vicarious experiences, it is possible to either simulate or produce a direct learning experience which is recognized by Edgar Dale and others as the most preferred type of learning experience.

In this connection, Thompson calls on teachers to assume new roles not unlike that of an apothecary. He suggests that instructors must be able to "diagnose" the deficiencies of his students and then be able to "prescribe" certain experiences to eradicate these deficiencies. And multimedia presentation seem to be a good way of providing those experiences.

However, there are two ways to look at multimedia classrooms. One way is to view it as a room full of equipment. Another is as a tool waiting to help the instructor who spends the extra effort to achieve the purposes of multimedia presentations. And as intimated earlier, the purpose of multimedia is to increase communication effectiveness by utilizing more than one channel to convey a message.

In the physical usage of multimedia classrooms, there are four ways of putting the room to work:

1. Independent. The lecturer controls each piece of equipment from the lectern while each piece is independent of the other.
2. Manual. The lecturer uses one control button to operate equipment as he reads a script.

3. Semiautomatic. The lecturer uses no control buttons because equipment operation is programmed. The script is recorded or read live and the lecturer can stop the presentation at any time to digress.
4. Automatic. The lecture is on audio tape and equipment operation is programmed. No participation on the part of the instructor is undertaken during the presentation.

There are disadvantages that impair the use of multimedia classrooms. Instructors have found that when equipment is not stored in the room proper, it is easier to use the old-fashioned lecture. By the inherent nature of the program,   there must be a large staff on hand to help instructors wanting the benefits of the room. A large amount of preparation time must be spent for a single presentation. As an extra stab, the cost of the room as a whole is a deterrent to small colleges and many public schools.

However, multimedia classrooms do afford instructors the chance to be creative. Several avenues of learning are opened to pursue. By giving the instructor control over the environment of the student, he can better manage the learning situation. In addition, multimedia classrooms fit successfully into a systems approach strategy.

These six points should be considered in implementing multimedia classrooms.

1. Multimedia classrooms enable instructors to realize the goal of quality in large class instruction—but not without effort.
2. Effective utilization requires that the instructor be assisted by several technicians.
3. Appropriate use of the room requires planning and rehearsal time far in excess of that used in preparing for a lecture.
4. Unless the instructor finds some sort of reward for this travail, he is likely to retreat to the practice of using the room for lecture.
5. Faculty enthusiasm is the key to realization of values of the "improved" instructional environment in the MM classroom.
6. This enthusiasm is intimately connected to the provision of released time for faculty.

Concept Learning In Science

MILTON O. PELLA

Concepts have been cited as the products of scientific processes, as the basis for further scientific studies, and at times as the knowledge that is applied by the technologist. Concepts in and of science, according to some educators, are to be the desired outcomes of science instruction.

Concepts are important not only because they are the warp and woof of science, but also because they provide the possessor with a means of coping with the development of knowledge in the future. It seems that one way known to provide for maximum coverage of old and new knowledge is through the development of a classification system. The formation of concepts or conceptual schemes is one method of classification which results in such economical use of human intelligence. As stated by Philip Phenix:

> The only satisfactory answer to the crisis in learning lies in the formulation and persistent use of key concepts. . . .
> Key concepts probably should not be taught explicitly and directly, at least to beginners. It does mean that particular items of knowledge should be selected and used with an eye to their exemplification of the basic concepts of the field.
> Ineffective teaching and learning, according to this thesis, are due in no small degree either to the failure to understand the need for comprehensive organizing concepts and their function in the economy of learning or to using the wrong key concepts (e.g., mistaken idea of what science really is).
> It is claimed that some concepts of high generality can be found which will provide truer insight into a field than could be gained by mere heaping up of isolated scraps of information. As knowledge develops the organizing principles change—old disciplines decline and new fields open up. Discovery of powerful key concepts applicable to a given group of ideas is the best way of defining a field of knowledge. [9]

Concept formation results in a simplification of past, present, and future experiences, because individual facts become parts of the ideas. *A*

Pella, Milton O. "Concept Learning in Science." *The Science Teacher.* December 1966. 33:31-34.

concept may be viewed initially as a summary of the essential charac-teristics of a group of ideas and/or facts that epitomize important common features or factors from a larger number of ideas. Because of their comprehensive nature, concepts are useful to the individual in gaining some grasp of a much larger field of knowledge than he has personally experienced. He is able to interpret and assimilate new infor-mation into the old schemes through the modification of existing concepts.

What is a Concept?

Reflection upon the nature of a concept given here "initially" reveals that such a definition is not fruitful in answering teaching-learning questions. There is need for a more specific definition or description before the many questions essential to teaching and learning concepts may be studied; there is need for an epistomology of concepts so that intelligent communication is possible. A first attempt to develop a definition or description leads to the question "Are concepts in all disciplinary areas the same?" Is the concept "mother" in a social sense the same as "mother" in a biological sense? Are these two parts of the same concept "mother"? Does the social concept "mother" depend upon higher level emotional factors than does the biological concept "mother"? Are the concepts of citizen, revolution, Uncle Sam, love, hate, etc., structurally similar, not in elements, but in design, to the concepts of force, mass, time, electron, atom, cell, living things, etc.? These questions lead nowhere—their answers are included in the basic question.

Such questions, however, do have value in that they suggest that some concepts have been identified. A fruitful procedure may be to examine certain science concepts for the purpose of determining their individual characteristics. A list may be made of their individual origins, nature, etc., and then the items may be compared.

A concept of "insect" is used as example *A:*

An insect is an animal with six legs and three main body divisions. This statement

1. is a symbolic representation.
2. is a decision made by man.
3. is a decision based upon human experience with natural phenomena.
4. is an abstraction from a field of experience.
5. is a generalization that includes more than a field of personal experi-ence.

6. involves the conscious or rational relating of facts. (The facts that are alike are placed together; the facts are classified.)
7. describes a man-made idea.
8. describes an idea that may exist at various levels of complexity (incomplete and complete metamorphosis).
9. is useful in making predictions and unifying information.

Example *B:*

A force is a push or pull which tends to change the motion of a body. This statement

1. is a symbolic representation.
2. is a decision made by man.
3. is a decision based upon human experience with natural phenomena.
4. is an abstraction from a field of experience.
5. is a generalization that includes more than the field of personal experience.
6. involves the conscious or rational relating of facts. (The push or pull is correlated with a change in motion.)
7. describes a man-made idea.
8. describes an idea that may exist at various levels of complexity (contact and noncontact forces).
9. is useful in making predictions and interpretations.

Example *C:*

An atom is the smallest particle of an element possible and is composed of electrons, protons, neutrons, and other particles. This statement

1. is a symbolic representation.
2. is a decision made by man.
3. is a decision that is not based upon direct human experience with natural phenomena.
4. is an abstraction of a created idea. (It is a verbal symbol representing a mechanical model.)
5. is a generalization that includes more than a field of personal experience.
6. involves the conscious or rational relating of facts. (The intent is to explain rather than describe human experience.)
7. describes a man-made idea.
8. describes an idea that may exist at various levels of complexity (atom as a unit or atom as an aggregrate of units).
9. is useful in making predictions and interpretations.

A comparison of these three concepts reveals many similarities and a few differences. There is one difference between concepts *A* and *B*; concept *A* is concerned with the classification of facts, and concept *B* is concerned with the correlation of facts: if *a* then *b*. Concept *C* is different from *A* and *B* in two ways:

Concepts A and B are

1. Abstractions from a field of direct experience
2. Descriptions of human experience

Concept C is

1. Abstraction of a created idea.
2. Explanation of human experiences. This type of analysis may be repeated with other concepts, such as:
   1. Matter occupies space and has mass.
   2. A vertebrate is an animal with a backbone and an internal skeleton.
   3. The digestive system is a group of organs with the common functions of preparing food for assimilation.
   4. Spermatophyte plants form seeds.
   5. Matter may be changed by adding or subtracting energy.
   6. The structure of the digestive system of animals varies.
   7. Digestion is the process of changing food from an insoluble to a soluble form.
   8. The electrical current in a circuit varies with the resistance if the voltage is constant.
   9. Matter is made up of particles called atoms.
   10. The structure and habits of animals are adaptations that are the result of evolutionary development.
   11. In the process of digestion, the molecular structure of the elements contained in the food is changed.
   12. Light is an electromagnetic wave.

Note that 1 to 4 are similar to concept *A*, 5 to 8 are similar to concept *B*, and 9 to 12 are similar to concept *C*. Concepts of type *A* could be labeled as *classificational*, concepts of type *B* could be labeled as *correlational*, and concepts of type *C* could be labeled as *theoretical*. Concepts of type *C* go beyond sensory experience or facts, yet fit the human reasoning that has been tempered or indoctrinated by facts. One outstanding similarity is that all are "created by man" from direct real experience or from other created "ideas" that may be the result of real experience.

Before elaborating on the similarities, another source of information may be examined: definitions or descriptions given by other individuals concerned with the problem. Here is a selection of such definitions:

A concept is an idea, a mental image of an action or thing, a generalization about related data. It is an understanding of the immediate based upon the impact of present impressions on past experience, usually labeled with a verbal symbol or symbols. [7]

Every concept is an apperceptive system: a mass of experience functioning in a condensed form. [1]

When an element common to many experiences is not merely recognized when it appears, but (1) is thought of without being perceived, and (2) is capable of being combined in thought with other elements, it becomes a concept of general meaning and application. To be a general concept the element must be something for consciousness apart from its perceptual setting and it must be applicable to a different setting. [6]

A concept is a network of significant inferences by which one goes beyond the set of observed critical properties exhibited by an object or event to the class identity of the object or event in question, and thence to additional references about other unobserved properties of the object or event. The working definition of a concept is the network of inferences that are or may be set into play by an act of categorization. [2]

Physical concepts are free creations of the human mind, and are not, however it may seem, uniquely determined by the external world. [5]

A concept is a psychological phenomenon, complete description of which will be contained someday in a theory of explaining the numerous empirical laws involving the concept. [8]

We have a concept when we recognize a group of situations which have a resemblance or common element. We usually give a name or label to the group. [4]

A concept deals with the meaning an individual attaches to a word or symbol rather than the mere fact that any given symbol is associated with any given object. [10]

Conceptual schemes are more or less general systems of abstract propositions of empirical references which shape the determinate conditions under which empirical phenomena are related among themselves. [3]

The variability with some similarity is noted in these definitions and in many others which can be found in the literature. The next step in the attempt to describe or define a concept is a second examination of the place of concepts in science.

The ambition and hope held in the last century that science could offer a photographic replica or true image of reality have been abandoned. Science as understood today has two major assignments: (1) the description of certain phenomena in the world of experience and (2) the establishment of general principles for their prediction and for provision of a system of concepts that assist in their explanation. The system of concepts that facilitates description of phenomena is largely *classificational* in nature, the system of concepts that facilitates prediction is largely *correlational* in character, and the system of concepts that facilitates the explanation of phenomena is made up of *theories* of verbal, mechanical, or mathematical varieties.

The selection or development of concepts from the chaotic diversity of sense experience is determined by many factors other than the facts themselves. One factor may be the sequence of receipt of the sensory experiences that were the result of uncontrolled observations of natural phenomena or the result of experiments. A second factor may be the cultural pattern of the time and its effect on subconscious patterns of thought.

These two notions result in the demand for consideration of the belief held by some that the meaning of a concept is identical with the procedure that led to its formulation. Is it possible that the redefinition of concepts or the meaning attributed to a given concept has some part of its origin in the changing sense of values accepted by the scientific community? The historical record of such concepts as "force" and "electron" give some credence to a positive answer.

Characterizing a Concept

A list of the characteristics of concepts in science based on the preceding statements may now be risked.

1. Concepts are ideas possessed by individuals or groups. They are a type of symbolism.
2. Concepts of any particular object, phenomena, or process exist in a continuum from simple to complex.
3. Concepts emerge as a result of experience with more than one object, phenomenon, or fact. They are generalizations.
4. Concepts are the result of abstract thinking that embraces the many experiences.
5. Concepts involve the relating of facts or supposed facts to each other by the individual.
6. Concepts are not always based upon a physical encounter.
7. Concepts are not inherent in nature or reality.
8. Concepts are not photographic images of reality.
9. Concepts are neither true nor false; they are, rather, adequate or inadequate.
10. Concepts have five primary relationships: relations to people, relations to things, relations to other concepts, relations within conceptual systems, and relations to processes.
11. Concepts are useful in making predictions and interpretations.
12. The individual concepts formed in any area may be determined by the sequence of the sensory experience received or available.
13. The individual concepts formed in any area may be determined by the cultural pattern at the time of formulation. As the culture changes, the meaning and value of a given concept may change.
14. The nature of a concept may be determined by the procedure that led to its formulation.
15. Concepts and conceptual schemes are rendered inadequate as a result of new knowledge and must undergo constant revision.

Concepts and Teaching

It is reasonable that these 15 recognizable characteristics of concepts should be carefully considered in the process of teaching and learning where the concern is not essentially the development of personal concepts of the creative variety but rather the development of concepts of product and process acceptable to the discipline of which they are a part. The continuation of science in any culture must depend upon transmission of the accumulated knowledge and strategies of science from one generation to another. The emphasis on concept development in science has been important and is becoming increasingly important with the rapid growth of knowledge. It is the one way known to provide the maximum coverage of knowledge because it is a kind of classification or summarizing system which results in the conservation of human intelligence. To go further, it may be said that a conceptual scheme is a summary of the essential characteristics of a group of concepts that epitomize important common features or factors from the larger group of concepts. Because of their comprehensive nature, concepts enable the possessor to have some grasp of a much larger field of knowledge than he has personally experienced. He is able to interpret the new and to assimilate it into the old through the modification of existing concepts. The current product and process concepts of science are the heritage of each generation.

Concepts may be taught or formulated by indoctrination, induction, deduction, extrapolation, interpolation, analysis, synthesis, and probably other means.

With reference to the development of science concepts with children, the following questions are asked:

1. How important is the level of mental development of the child to learning *classificational, correlational* and *theoretical* concepts?
2. How important is the intensity of the physical encounter which the learner has with the facts from which a concept is formulated?
3. How important to the learner is extensive physical encounter with the facts from which a concept is formulated?
4. How important to the learner is the sequence of the stimuli offered?
5. How representative of the total class covered by the concept must the stimuli offered be?
6. How remote from reality may the stimuli be for individuals of different experiential maturity?
7. When in their lives can learners utilize facts or ideas not based on physical reality?
8. To what extent is the cultural background of the learner a factor in concept learning?
9. How important are the procedures involving telling, demonstrating, or laboratory experience in concept learning?
10. Is it reasonable to expect learners of all school ages to develop concepts of the classificational, correlational, and theoretical varieties at some level during each year of their educational preparation?
11. Is it reasonable to expect the learner to discover a concept as a result of free inquiry?
12. How important is the vocabulary and language development of the learner in concept development?
13. Should we be satisfied with allowing pupils to formulate their own concepts whether or not they conform to those accepted by the discipline?
14. How deeply imbedded is the problem of transfer in concept learning?

These questions have been probed slightly by Piaget, Inhelder, Gagne, Loveall, and others; however, they are far from answered. The answers are fundamental to effective teaching, curriculum design, and teacher training. Surely it may be speculated that concept learning depends upon the characteristics of the learner and the circumstances under which he is guided.

What evidence is sought out to indicate that a specific concept has been developed or accepted by the learner? To date all that seems to be known is included in the words "transfer" and "verbalization." Are these valid?

Research is the avenue to determining whether the basic thoughts are credible. Much of this should and can be performed in the classrooms of the schools of this nation. This will lead to the answer to a more important question, "How do children of different ages, cultural backgrounds, and abilities learn concepts in science?" This is far more fundamental than "How do we teach concepts in science?"

REFERENCES

1. BAGLEY, WILLIAM CHANDLER. *The Educative Process.* Macmillan, New York 1905. p. 144.

2. BRUNER, JEROME S.; GOODNOW, JACQUELINE J.; and AUSTIN, GEORGE A. *A Study of Thinking.* Science Editions, Inc., New York. 1956. p. 244.

3. CONANT, J. B. *Science and Common Sense.* Yale University Press, Oxford. 1951. p. 25.

4. CRONBACH, LEE J. *Educational Psychology.* Harcourt, Brace & Co., New York. 1954. p. 281.

5. EINSTEIN, ALBERT, and INFELD, LEOPOLD. *The Evolution of Physics.* Simon and Schuster, New York. 1938. p. 33.

6. HOBHOUSE, LEONARD TRELAWNEY. *Mind in Evolution.* Macmillan, London. 1901. p. 329.

7. KRANZER, HERMAN C. "Children and Their Science Teachers." *Journal of Research in Science Teaching 1:181; 1963.*

8. MELTON, A. W. Editor. *Categories of Human Learning.* Academic Press, New York. 1964. p. 226.

9. PHENIX, PHILIP H. "Key Concepts and the Crisis in Learning." *Teachers College Record* 58:137-43; December 1956.

10. WOODRUFF, ASAHEL DAVIS. *The Psychology of Teaching.* Longmans, Green & Co., New York. 1951. p. 285.

Reading Is For Thinking

DR. R. C. BRADLEY

One of the surest ways to build in a child a permanent attachment for reading is to ensure the perception that *reading is for thinking*. The major purpose of this Monograph will be to focus upon the question: *How can we teach children to think through reading—to acquire the power of independent thought?*

Dewey has already established one truth about pupil learning: *thinking, as distinct from fact assimilation and verbalization, is most likely to occur when the learner makes over, or otherwise uses, knowledge and/or skill in the course of his further learning* (2, p. 776). Likewise, one reads to "grasp with the mind", and what is obtained finally amalgamates into *wisdom*. The major task of the school is: *teaching people to think* (3, p. 26).

When a child demonstrates some measure of his ability to make the right decision in personal and social affairs, the extent of his *wisdom* has been personified. Reading and thinking leads to higher level decisions; namely, *wisdom*.

Reading and Interpreting

When a child is asked to read and then interpret what he has read, this procedure involves an intensive effort of thinking *through* the precise meaning of the author. When one interprets he engages in a creative type of thinking simply because the ideas on the page must be built anew in his own mind. Obviously minds of readers differ, consequently, the informed mind will bring forth higher thought levels than will be entertained by one who has had limited experiences.

An excellent place to deal with interpretative skills is an understanding of metaphorical language. For example, in *Five Little Peppers*

Bradley, R. C. *Reading is for Thinking.* A Bassi Association Monograph Publication: Denton, Texas. October 1971. 1:1-4.

and How They Grew, Margaret Sidney states: "It was just on the edge of twilight." Thus the child must interpret the figure which borrows from space to describe time.

Reading and Integration

Pupils are always integrating information; that is, "putting together" words, concepts, images, and ideas. Perceptually, mere reading does not always cause things "to add up." Rather, a moment of insight will bring forth new perceptions sometimes based on unrelated types of information. For example, while one watches the TV program *Wild Kingdom,* his evaluations of it may come from prior scientific work or certain knowledge about animal life gained from reading in various resource books. Integrating what one reads, hears, or sees is a process unique to each individual.

In the book, *Profiles of Courage,* by John Kennedy, samplings of information about great men are discussed but the book itself helps one to *experience* great faith and courage. Each reader makes his own connections with past knowledge and experience. The *connections* heighten the emotional impact of the book and the intentions of the writer.

Reading and Curiosity

To encourage children to think, the prudent teacher will help each child develop a strategy of conquest. One can find the answer to his questions by reading widely but he must also learn to think deeply; to analyze his findings with good judgment and discrimination.

Pupils who are curious have vigorous minds. The child who exhibits strong moves to be curious: (a) asks more and better questions, (b) selects more outgoing, adventurous, investigatory stories, (c) needs more general information about the world in which he lives, (d) devours many specific facts of an unusual nature, (e) takes pleasure in reacting positively to the unbalanced and unfamiliar, (f) persists longer at the reading act, and (g) reads a wide variety of materials to satisfy his many interests.

The classroom teacher has a dual role as far as satisfying the reading activities of the curious reader. First, the child should be allowed, encouraged, and expected to read much information in specific areas of interest; and secondly, wherein new horizons can be explored, new interests developed, fresh ideas revealed, and new insights developed—such tasks are also the role of the teacher.

Reading and Creativity

A child must be taught how to develop sets of criteria which can be used to test the authenticity of what has been revealed to him through reading. That is, the creative reader comes to the printed page with a set of values and information against which he tests what he is reading. If he does not have knowledge of this fact, the teacher must help him devise the type of criteria which will help him to make wise decisions and judgments about that which has been read.

If a child does have criteria for judgmental purposes, he revises his values and corrects his information if the reading material appears valid to him. Through reading and thinking, points of concern can be studied and clarified.

When a child thinks about what has been read, no doubt he accepts, rejects, raises questions, makes inferences, and comes to some acceptable (at least to him) tentative conclusions. He separates himself, cognitively speaking, from the decisions arrived at by the author. He becomes caught up in independent conclusions, acts which necessitate the suspension of judgment, and ultimately finds himself weighing ideas. More importantly, he discovers he must trust the author. He must honor the facts, seek out "between the line" meanings, and recognize his own biases. Moreover, he educates his mind simultaneously to "read with a guarded trust."

Reading and Precise Thinking

Oftentimes children are asked to read their textbooks before they have training in how to get understanding from what is read. For example, although these expressions might be found falling quite regularly within adult conversations, the child who encounters these expressions in his reading materials is often at a loss as to their meaning.

the golden rule	the patience of Job
Doubting Thomas	was reasonable doubt
Faith of Abraham	snowed under with work
the wisdom of Solomon	

A major portion of the aforementioned words deals with Biblical meanings. Lamentably, a teacher must recognize that many boys and girls may have grown up without hearing references to the Bible. Consequently, a teacher must help each child to attach meaning to *figures of speech.*

A further illustration can be found in *Miracle on 34th Street.* After Fred had promised Kris Kringle his freedom, going the very limit of using details as modes of proving him competent, Mr. Kringle deliberately failed the test he was given. Fred had *"talked himself way out on a long, long limb,* and now he felt it cracking." Sometime later, yet before Mr. Kringle's trial, Mr. Sawyer *"placed himself in a frying pan and . . . was squirming and wriggling to get out."* In a later episode depicting Fred talking with his girl friend, Fred states: "Well, *it all boils down to this:* You don't have faith in me."

Literal meaning of words sometimes found in italics will be of no help to a child unless the teacher instructs the reader in how to take meaning to them. A pupil who is untrained is likely to take seriously something that the author wanted his reader to take humorously.

Types of Figures of Speech

A figure of speech is a departure from the direct method of saying a thing in order to make it more eyecatching, meaningful, beautiful, fanciful, or effective. A few samples follow:

(1) *Simile:* the writer expresses a likeness between two things that in most respects are totally unlike. E.g., "After the swim yesterday, I'm *stiff as a board."*

(2) *Metaphor:* the writer emits an implied comparison but omits such words as "as", "like", etc. E.g., "She has a *heart of gold."*

(3) *Hyperbole:* the writer uses exaggeration for effect. E.G., "You are *fast as lightning,* and as *silent as the night* itself."

(4) *Personification:* the writer endows inanimate objects with human attributes. E.G., "Love won", "Duty calls", etc.

(5) *Irony:* the writer uses subtle sarcasm. E.G., "That's the *earliest* you've ever come in *late!"* "You're a *fine* specimen for others to look up to."

The brevity of this Monograph will not allow a discussion of alliteration (repetition of sound), onomatopoeia (adaptation of sound) antithesis (idea contrasts), and other types of significant figures o speech. Nevertheless, they should be studied.

Reading and Vocabulary Power

Tracing words to their original sources can be fascinating to inte mediate level pupils. Not only is there the entertainment factor, but studying the history of a particular word provides valuable aid in spelling and word meaning.

Consider these samples: (1) The word, *abundance,* comes from Latin AB(from) and UNDA(wave). Since water is plentiful, anything appearing in wave-like quantities would be abundant; (2) *alphabet,* first two letters in Greek are ALPHA and BETA. (3) *boycott,* Captain Boycott was an agent for an Irish landlord who charged his tenants high rent. As a result of high rent, the collector Boycott was subjected to social isolation as a protest by the people. (4) *quarantine,* a long time ago when a person had a communicable disease, he was required to stay indoors for 40 (quaranta) days. Today the period is shorter, but the ARA combination has not changed.

Summary

A child has a set of perceptual powers that he takes to reading. These powers of thinking are increased through the right types of reading experiences. Words are used to describe concept systems. Cognitively speaking, words are not difficult but ideas are sometimes hard to grasp. As the pupil reads for understanding his thought processes should serve as a facilitating organization of experience inside his central nervous system. A child receives meaning not from the printed page but from his intellectual and perceptive powers, *the powers of thinking and reasoning.*

Thoughts (thinking skills) applied to words one reads evoke concepts. At times, no doubt, what one reads also brings forth new thinking operations and new conceptual processes. When a child reads, *what* he reads should serve to evoke concepts—it is a wise teacher who makes certain that the selections assigned for silent and oral reading are of the structure which assures the reader that concepts are there to be evoked.

As Cushenberry states, "Pupils can be aided materially in learning to read critically. A mere knowledge of the importance of critical reading is not enough to inspire that they know how to apply the skill (1, p. 96)." Most children need direct training in *reading for thinking.*

BIBLIOGRAPHY

1. CUSHENBERRY, DONALD C. *Reading Improvement in the Elementary School.* West Nyack, N.Y.: Parker Publishing Company, 1969. P. 96.

2. DEWEY, JOHN. *Democracy and Education.* New York: MacMillan Company, 1961. P. 776.

3. PATON, JAMES M. "Teaching People to Think." *The Journal of Educational Thought.* April, 1967. 1:15-30.

Closing the Environmental Education Gap

CLAUDE D. CROWLEY

The winds of change always seem to whip up more work, and it is now plain that the gusts of environmental concern that raised little dust devils a few years ago have turned into a strong and steady gale. As a result, teachers are under pressure to give more time and energy to environmental education.

But to expect educators to overcome decades of limited emphasis on the environment and suddenly to come forth with full-grown programs of environmental education is unrealistic. At the classroom level this means we have a serious environmental education gap. And the gap closers will be those teaching now, not those who are training to be teachers.

The dean of the College of Education at the University of Texas at Austin has said, "If all teachers colleges in America had the best possible programs in operation right now, we would still be faced with an environmental education gap for some years ahead. Why? It takes time for new teachers to be absorbed into the system, so delay between today's training and tomorrow's improved teaching is a natural thing. ... Those who are now teaching ... are the ones who will be carrying the conservation education responsibility for the foreseeable future."

Some school systems have plans to build the entire curriculum around the environment, but here, too, educators see years of delay.

"Our hope is to eventually have environmental education as the core of a reorganized curriculum," says a science specialist in the Washington, DC, public schools. "And I emphasize the *eventually* because a major curriculum development is a fantastically expensive process, not only in money but in time and in the number of expert people who must be involved."

Crowley, Claude D. "Closing the Environmental Education Gap." *Today's Education.* April 1972. 61:24-25.

Yet environmental education will not wait. Growing environmental complexities are at the door of each school each day as the children swarm out. We are bombarded by newspaper and magazine articles, editorials, TV documentaries, and public service announcements on pollution, conservation, and environmental matters. Penetrating questions come from concerned—and even frightened—pupils.

What's a teacher to do? One answer is to use the people already in your community who are trained in environmental specialties. Almost every school has within a telephone's ring people who can give rational, factual, usable information about our air, water, soil, and animal life—in short, the environment. These people can help with ideas, literature, resource specialists, and perhaps with land on which to do outdoor lab work.

The first requirement in utilizing qualified "outsiders" is to know who they are and where they can be found. Governmental agencies (including the county extension director) that have offices in a locality will be listed in the telephone book under "United States Government," " State of," and " County Government." The chamber of commerce may be able to direct teachers to local chapters of conservation organizations, such as the National Audubon Society and the National Wildlife Federation. Here are just a few other sources that will yield help to teachers at almost any location and that may suggest other ideas on where to get outside assistance:

The Soil Conservation Service of the U. S. Department of Agriculture has resource people that include soil conservationists, biologists, soil scientists, and other specialists. SCS people can help schools plan and develop conservation measures on schoolgrounds in harmony with educational needs. Local and state SCS offices can furnish reference materials.

The U. S. Department of the Interior has many bureaus that may be able to help your locality. Some of these are the Bureau of Mines, the Geological Survey, the Bureau of Indian Affairs, and the U. S. Fish and Wildlife Service.

The county extension director or county agent has access to literature and information on many environmental subjects.

If there is a national or state park or a national or state forest nearby, the employees will be conservation-minded people who are willing to help. Many such public facilities employ naturalists who can give specialized assistance.

If you live and work near a national park or landmark, you will certainly want to know more about the National Environmental Study Area program (NESA) of the National Park Service. This program involves designating certain federal lands for environmental education. NEA's Environmental Education Project has been conducting workshops for teachers and resource management personnel on selected NESA sites during the current school year and is preparing a booklet under contract to the National Park Service on "How To Conduct an Environmental Study Area Workshop." This should be available by summer.

The National Park Service also has funded the development of the NEED program (National Environmental Education Development). Materials currently available for fifth and sixth grades are not intended as an additional course of study. Rather, the program encourages integrating environmental learning into the regular curriculum. (For additional information about either of these programs, address inquiries to the Office of Environmental Interpretation, National Park Service, Washington, DC 20240.)

You may be pleasantly surprised to find that the manager of your local sewage disposal plant is an ardent conservationist, intent on operating his plant in the most efficient manner possible to minimize pollution. A visit to the treatment plant can be a fascinating way to study one environmental problem—and what your community is doing about it.

Contact the person in your city who is in charge of solid waste disposal. He can enlighten you and your pupils about the size of the problem, present methods of dealing with it, and future plans for your area.

Many industries are working hard to overcome pollution and environmental damage. If there is a sizable industry near you, contact its public relations office about literature, films, and people who can explain the industry's environmental program.

Organizations can help. In every state, the Soil Conservation Society of America has chapters that carry out local conservation projects and have access to literature and expert assistance. Garden clubs and city or county councils of garden clubs may help a school or teacher with materials for environmental studies or exhibits. Some clubs will lend a hand in the development of outdoor study sites.

The National Association of Conservation Districts (NACD) has a conservation film rental library consisting of about 150 titles, many of which are suitable for classroom use. A free catalog can be obtained by writing to the NACD Environmental Film Service, P. O. Box 855, League City, Texas 77573.

So there you are. Experts predict that effective institutional adjustment to heavier environmental education demands may take years. Meanwhile, back at the school, the teacher faces the problem now, not later.

Closing the environmental education gap at the classroom level will occur faster if teachers and conservationists get together, but the

nitiative must come from the teacher. Conservationists and environ-
ment-related professional people are increasingly aware of the educational and social implications of their work, but their primary concern is
n their own field. They are willing to share their knowledge and skills-
—with the public in general and schools in particular—if they are asked.

SCHOOL is for . . .
ROLE PLAYING

Chapter VII

The Teacher As Communicator

Communication is the "cement" of any organization and especially of school organizations and classrooms. Understanding of communication begins largely as a matter of human relationships. Communication is an effort on the part of two persons or more to link their lives at a point, to bridge a gap in understanding between them, to send and receive thoughts that have reasonably similar meanings for each of them. The pupil's grasp of content will be determined in large measure by the success of the teacher in communicating it. Parental regard for the school rests primarily upon what the teacher communicates daily to their children.

Whether it be communicating directly with students, the several publics found in most school communities, parents in interview situations, speech-making, or community forums, the way the sender and receiver *perceive each other* is of utmost significance in the process. The old cliche of "what you do speaks louder than your words" should not be taken lightly by classroom teachers. One's *nonverbal* behavior transmits a positive or negative attitude to the receiver of the message. Consequently, new teachers must be concerned about both *verbal* and *nonverbal* patterns of behavior. Each article that follows should generate a new idea about communication. Each should be considered carefully for what it means in terms of improving the communicative behavior of the on-the-job teacher.

Teacher Patterns of Communication*

JOHN M. KEAN

The dialogue between teachers and pupils in the classroom has borne the brunt of diverse research efforts for several decades. Discordant as this may seem to classroom artists, educational researchers have begun to categorize classroom interaction into forms usable for analysis and for conscious deliberation about the effects of this interaction upon learning.

Teachers' language has been central to this research; yet little has been done to dimension the teachers' language and to look at its pattern or its style in the way that one would look at the language of a book, film, or any other medium. Yet, the classroom language does appear to be different—peculiar to the instructional situation. The following quote taken from the transcript of a teacher's classroom language illustrates the uniqueness of classroom talk:

> Be sure when you make your "P" that you don't get a loop in the side. Look at your capital "P". No loop. See, in your small "p" you have that loop but not in your capital "P". Boys and girls, look at the board for a minute. Make your capital "P". Start your swing up, down, back up on the same line. No loop in the capital "P". Some of you are getting it confused with the small "p" where you do have your loop. No loop in the capital "P". R , how can you write if your paper is not out of your notebook and flat on your desk? That isn't your best writing position.

Showing this kind of monologue to a teacher who has never listened to himself can be frightening. To the lay reader, such language would

*The research discussed in this paper was supported by the Cooperative Research Program of the Office of Education, U. S. Dept. of Health, Education, and Welfare, Project S-331. The final report was submitted August, 1966. For more specific information write to the author, University of Wisconsin, 606 State Street, Madison, Wisconsin 53703.

Kean, John. "Teacher Patterns of Communication." *Education.* October 1966. 87:78-82.

seem as bad as that used by Batman. In fact, hearing a tape recording of oneself spewing forth the above might lead to some kind of neurosis.

For many years, teachers have acted as if language had some mystical power that brooked no interference. Once teachers had worked their way through college, passed a speech-proficiency test, and worked with children, their natural ability with language would somehow suffice in the classroom.

Yet at the same time, teachers have worried about the deterioration of their language ability. They have suspected that the language of their classroom is not the same as that heard and used by the children outside of school. At the same time language arts experts have requested them to always keep their vocabulary and sentence structure a little "higher" than the children's so that there will be incentive for the children to improve, others have told them not to talk down to children. Meanwhile, supervisors judge teachers on how fluently they speak, or how well they communicate, or how acceptable their speech is. This confusing pattern has developed with no information about how teachers do speak.

Additionally, many of the recently delineated dimensions of teacher behavior (e.g., logical operations used, habitual expressions) are probably dependent upon the language structure employed by the teacher. Indeed, any research involving verbal behavior inevitably involves language as an unmanipulated independent variable.

A number of verbal behavior theories (e.g., 2,3,4,5,6) have hypothesized that a relationship does exist between cognitive behavior and language structure. Coupled to this is the import of teacher's language upon children's language. Brown and Bellugi's (7) finding that mothers "edit" their children's sentences to syntactically correct ones, while leaving basic forms unchanged, suggest that teachers of young children might use a similar strategy in developing the linguistic structures of the children. And although some assert that children's basic language structure is established by the time they enter school (8, 9), the role of the teacher cannot be passed over since children's oral language continues to develop until adolescence (10).

Findings that concept learning and problem solving are related to the language in which questions are asked (3), the report that linguistic forms linked to social class induce differential learning (11, 12), and the indication that children use different linguistic structures intra- and extramurally (13) all demand the investigation of the role of the teacher's language.

To describe teachers' language according to its structure would seem to be an ideal way to begin. A study of the language of five second-grade teachers and five fifth-grade teachers in a suburban Ohio school district was undertaken to explore the possibilities of this kind of research. Each teacher's classroom oral language was tape recorded (with remote equipment) for 40 minutes on each of five different days. The last four 40 minute periods were pooled for each teacher and transcribed to provide the data needed to look at the teacher's language. Linguistic criteria similar to those employed for the study of children's language (8, 14) were used in order that language data might be comparable and that later studies of teacher-pupil language might be facilitated.

Results of the Study

Since the study was exploratory, the basic treatment was descriptive. Generally, the teachers' amount of language (number or words used for 160 minutes) ranged from 9,249 to 16,244 with no significant difference attributable to grade levels. For all of these words, the teachers produced an average of 1,753 communication units (shortest possible grammatically terminable units). This in itself is an interessting finding. The average for second grade was 1,734, and for fith grade, 1,773, suggesting that little or no difference can be attributed to the grade level with which the teacher is dealing.

Obviously, no conclusion can be based on such a limited sample, but there is certainly justification to ask why teachers at the different grade levels do not differ in the number of things they express to children, albeit this measure is one of quantity and not quality.

Teachers' use of mazes (unintelligible tangles of language, garbles, etc., that occur when one is thinking on his feet, or is tired) was also analyzed. Teachers at either grade level used these infrequently, perhaps because by dint of experience, teachers are extremely fluent or they are seldom challenged in class or their lessons are very well planned, or they "think before they speak" in the manner that they are always asking children to do.

As one measure of style, a vocabulary diversity measure, the type token ratio, was run on a stratified random sample of the total pages of transcript so that a 2000 word sample was obtained for each teacher. The mean different number of words was 825 for second-gradeteachers and 857 for fifth-grade teachers, again no significant difference. This result may be attributable to subject and/or materials being used, but it may also suggest that we need to look more carefully at the impact of classroom vocabulary. For instance, why would the amounts be so similar when the range of subject matter discussed in fifth grade would appear to be so much greater than that in second grade?

When the transcripts were analyzed as to the use made of basic structural (sentence) patterns, again no difference was found between the two grade levels. The most frequently used patterns by all teachers are represented by the following types: "Your adjective," partial; "What did you put there, R. . . .?" question; "You know that," subject—transitive verb—transitive verb complement; "Let's do it later," requests, commands; "Now it could be a nimble girl," subject—linking verb—linking verb complement; "He is in the office," subject—linking verb.

No differences in pattern usage were noted for either group. Although the above patterns were the most frequently used, at least twenty-four different word order types were noted. Little meaning can be attributed to such findings except that, all encouragements for children to vary their sentences to the contrary, teachers depend almost entirely upon the most common patterns. Notably absent from the list of frequently used patterns are those containing inner and outer complements ("He gave *me* the paper" and "He called it *Henry*") and the passive voice pattern.

Since the teachers were expected to use all of the relatively few structural patterns, some of the components within patterns were also analyzed. Teachers at both levels depended almost entirely upon nouns and pronouns for subjects and for complements, although they did use some clauses in the latter position. For movable adverbial elements, they were somewhat less restricted, making use of phrases, clauses, and combinations of these as well as single words.

The last major analysis was of the teachers' use of subordinating clauses. Again, no essential difference was noted between grade levels. Teachers tended to subordinate frequently sometimes including five and six subordinate clauses within one sentence. A typical example containing three dependent clauses is the following: "I think that we should all read as loudly as we can because with this machine going, you can't hear very well."

In total, thirty-one scores were obtained. Of these, twenty-four with variability sufficient to permit intercorrelation and to satisfy product moment correlation criteria were used to study oral language relationships. A number of these scores were not given interpretive consideration. Some correlations did prove worthy of further study. Fifteen were directional to one grade or the other, while three others were actually reversed at the different grade levels. For example, second grade teachers who used the linking verb sentence pattern more had a smaller average number of words in mazes.

There does not overtly appear to be a reason for this correlation. However, a deeper analysis of the relation of this particular structure to the meanings conveyed by it or to the context in which it is used may possibly suggest reasons for the inverse correlation in relation to the way children process and learn information.

Conclusion

The work that has been done on the structure of teachers' language serves only to highlight the necessity for greater understanding of the influences of teacher-language on pupils' learning to use the structure of the English language. The study has provided information about the structure of teachers' language that needs to be compared with knowledge about children's language. For instance, what structures are used most by children; by teachers? What is the real effect of teachers' language compared to the language of television or of parents or of peers upon the development of the child's language structure, subsequent to entering school? Indeed, can the teacher exert any influence along these lines?

The assumption has always been that "impeccable" language of the teacher was important, that a teacher who used poor language structures (or poor grammar) was a bad, even disgraceful, influence upon children. No concern was even given to questions of reality in language learning.

Much is being learned about children's language, much that will have important implications for schooling, but it would seem particularly important to attend to the teacher's language. We might surmise, perhaps, that teachers' language does differ from children's language, particularly those children who come from different cultural backgrounds.

We have assumed that children's language could be modified or extended to fit the school situation (witness project Head-Start), but we have not considered the actual differences in either quantitative or qualitative terms to assess how much either children or teachers might need to change their language in order to communicate in the classroom. The teacher's classroom language is not only a means of teaching language to the children, but also a primary screen through which most school-learned concepts pass.

We might wonder how teachers modify their language in order to communicate with children. Simply by changing the structure of one person's language, responses from another person can be changed. Language is indeed, the most prominent unseen shaper of what happens to children in school. When one accepts the idea that style of oral verbal language controls to some extent what the hearer will acquire from it, then one must weigh carefully the almost complete emphasis on this one form of teaching in the school. Particularly in this age of inquiry and self-actualization, the language prerogatives of the classroom cannot be based on vague assumptions about adult control over language. A whole new field, psycholinguistics, offers ample opportunity for teachers to better understand how their language "fits" the language of the children they teach.

REFERENCES

1. MAYER, MARTIN. *The Schools* (New York: Doubleday, 1963), p. 22.

2. AUSUBEL, DAVID P. *The Psychology of Meaningful Verbal Learning: An Introduction to School Learning* (New York: Grune and Stratton, 1963).

3. CARROLL, JOHN B. "Some Psychological Effects of Language Structure," *Psychopathology of Communication.* Paul H. Hock and Joseph Zubin, eds. (New York: Grune and Stratton, 1958), pp. 28-36.

4. SAPIR, EDWARD. *Language: An Introduction to the Study of Speech* (New York: Harcourt, Brace and Co., Inc., 1921).

5. VYGOTSKY, LES S. *Thought and Language* (Cambridge, Mass.: Massachusetts Institute of Technology Press, 1962).

6. WHORF, BENJAMIN. *Language, Thought, and Reality: Selected Writings* (New York: John Wiley and Sons, 1956).

7. BROWN, ROGER and BELLUGI, URSULA. "Three Processes in the Child's Acquisition of Syntax," *Harvard Educational Review,* Vol. 34 (Spring, 1964), pp. 133-151.

8. LOBAN, WALTER D. *The Language of Elementary School Children.* National Council of Teachers of English, Research Report No. 1 (Campaign, Illinois: the Council, 1963.)

9. MILLER, WARD and ERWIN, SUSAN. "The Development of Grammar in Child Language," *The Acquisition of Language.* Ursula Bellugi and Roger Brown, eds. Monograph of the Society for Research in Child Development No. 29, 1964, pp. 9-34.

10. HOCKETT, C. F. "Age Grading and Linguistic Change," *Language,* Vol. 26 (Spring 1950), pp. 449-557.

11. BERNSTEIN, BASIL. 'Social Class and Linguistic Development: A Theory of Social Learning," *Education, Economy, and Society.* A. H. Halsey, Jean Floud, and C. A. Anderson, eds. (New York: The Macmillan Company, 1961), pp. 288-314.

12. BERNSTEIN, BASIL. "Social Class, Linguistic Codes and Grammatical Elements," *Language and Speech,* Vol. 5 (October-December 1962), pp. 221-40.

13. JOOS, MARTIN. "Language and the School Child." *Harvard Education Review,* Vol. 34. (Spring 1964), pp. 203-10.

14. STRICKLAND, RUTH G. "The Language of Elementary School Children: Its Relationship to the Language of Reading Textbooks and the Quality of Reading of Selected Children," *Indiana University School of Education Bulletin,* Vol. 38 (July 1962), pp. 1-131.

15. RILING, MILDRED E. *Oral and Written Language of Children in Grades 4 and 6 Compared with the Language of Their Textbooks.* U. S. Department of Health Education, and Welfare, Office of Education, Cooperative Research Project No 2410 (Durant, Oklahoma: Southeastern State College, 1965) pp. 190.

Sharpening Your Communicative Skills

GEORGE DEMOS and BRUCE GRANT

One of the counselor's primary tasks is to communicate to others—students, teachers, parents, etc. Thus it is of the utmost importance that he communicate well. Here in capsule form is a functional frame of reference for counselors, teachers, administrators, and all others who have an investment in communication.

If you are transferring your thoughts to others, you are communicating. However, *communicating* includes the implication of making your thoughts *known* to others. This is the hurdle that too often many persons fail to surmount in communicating.

Causes of Faulty Communication

Let's examine the major causes of faulty communication in the usual forms of verbal exchanges.

I. Semantic Errors
  1. Using a vocabulary beyond the level of comprehension of listeners
  2. Speaking in the jargon of an occupation, discipline, hobby, or special interest
II. Speaking Technique Errors
  1. Talking too fast or too slowly
  2. Speaking too loudly or too softly
  3. Saying too much or too little
  4. Straying from subject
III. Listening Errors
  1. Not paying attention to what is being said
  2. Thinking about what you want to say while attempting to concentrate on what is being said by another
  3. Neglecting to ask questions when clarification is needed

Demos, George., and Grant, Bruce. "Sharpening Your Communicative Skills." *Education.* November 1966. 87:174-176.

IV. Psychological Errors
   1. Monopolizing the conversation
   2. Staying within your frame of reference and ignoring that of others
   3. Becoming hostile if the thoughts of others disagree with yours
   4. Becoming afraid if concepts are introduced which threaten your self-esteem or value system

Approaches for Improvement

A perusal of these factors contributing to faulty communication is apt to be disturbing, for there appears to be a formidable task involved in circumventing these blocks to understanding. Nevertheless, much progress can be made by any of us who *want* to communicate. To eliminate the contributors to poor communication there are some possible approaches for improvement. Prior to initiating these procedures it would be prudent for you to meet two standards:

I. Want strongly enough to *understand what others think* to be willing to pay the price of achieving this goal.
II. Want strongly enough to have others *understand what you think* to be willing to pay the price of achieving this goal.

Unless you can answer each of the foregoing criteria with an emphatic "yes," forget the proposition of enhancing your communicative skills. If you can respond "yes" to these criteria, proceed towards accomplishing the following goals:

I. To Eliminate Semantic Errors:
   1. Use words familiar to your listeners, or define those words you suspect they do not have in their vocabulary.[1]
   2. Abandon jargon except when conferring with people who use and understand it.
II. To Eliminate Speaking Errors:
   1. Avoid talking too rapidly by not trying "to cover too much ground."
   2. To correct speaking too slowly, recognize that if you are to deal with your subject matter adequately in a specified period of time, it is necessary to accelerate word usage; this is facilitated by "knowing your subject."
   3. Speaking too loudly or too softly can be adjusted by "turning up or down" the volume of your voice to meet the requirements of

---

[1] The exception to this practice is any situation in which you are functioning as a teacher or attempting to educate your listeners. Here you have a responsibility to use words appropriate to what you are attempting to accomplish.

the moment; it helps to be sensitive to the way others respond to your voice.

4. Reduction of redundancy and repetition may be achieved by challenging yourself to cover a point succinctly and remembering that the other fellow may want a chance to reply to what you are saying.

5. If you are to overcome excessive briefness, know what your purpose is when you begin talking and allow sufficient time to say as much as needs to be said.

III. To Eliminate Listening Errors:

1. If your attention wanders from what is being said, ask pertinent questions designed to determine the speaker's frame of reference. Or, if your concentration is diluted by problems which keep intruding into your consciousness, excuse yourself and attempt to deal with those difficulties.

2. Whenever you cannot focus on the words being spoken because of what you wish to say yourself, realize that a wise reply must be based upon the comprehension of the thought to which you are responding.

3. Failure to seek clarification by questioning can be circumvented by learning more about whatever is being discussed. Usually, when you *know* your subject, questions flow freely if they are accompanied by interest.

IV. To Eliminate Psychological Errors:

1. To avoid dominating the conversation, practice the principle of "do unto others what you would have them do unto you."

2. Moving from your frame of reference to that of others is primarily a matter of switching your attention from yourself to others; talk to help them—not you.

3. When you are alerted to anger emerging within you, analyze *why* you feel as you do. Similarly, if your self-esteem or value system is threatened, self-analysis is needed. If the hostility or fears do not yield to your intellectual probing, or the feelings persist contrary to logic or reasonable expectations, you may need professional help in understanding.

In conclusion, two guiding principles are offered for your consideration in seeking the improvement of communication techniques or skills.

I. *Talk less; listen more.*

II. Listen as if you were going to be required to respond verbatim to whatever is being said.

Nonverbal: The Language Of Sensitivity

CHARLES M. GALLOWAY

The nonverbal is indeed the language of sensitivity. It is the age-old language of lovers, that sublime communication without words. It is the language of the content, a knowing smile, an exchanged glance that tells more—much, much more than words can ever say. It is the frown that makes one feel guilty; the silent anger that emits a tenseness so real that it can almost be touched. It is that obscure, yet emphatic meaning behind the silence that thunders its message. The nonverbal is so complicated that it can convey an entire attitude, yet so simple that when a head nods or shakes everyone understands. All human relationships involve meanings that are more than words, and the nonverbal exposes the truth in these relationships.

We are just beginning to understand the subtle influences of the nonverbal between teacher and student. The teacher's nonverbal behavior seems to be integral in the formation of student attitudes toward school. Students often see and understand nonverbal behaviors that escape the awareness and sensitivity of adults. Here is an example that was offered by Elise Schilder, a perceptive elementary teacher.

Mrs. Johnson heard the door slam as Keith ran into the house from school.

"Guess what, Mom? My teacher likes me."

"Why, what did she say to you, Keith?"

"She didn' say nothin' but I know she likes me, really! She smiled at me when I was readin' and she put her arms around me. Gee—I like school!"

A few houses down the street, Mrs. Turner looked out the front door and saw her son, David, kicking a stone up the sidewalk, mumbling angrily to himself.

Galloway, Charles M. "Nonverbal: The Language of Sensitivity." *Theory Into Practice.* October 1971. 10:227-230.

"Why are you late, David? What's wrong?"

"I hate that ol' icky school. I hate it. I hate, I hate it. And I hate my teacher. She don't like me."

"How do you know she doesn't? Did something happen?"

"Yeah. I was readin' and Miss Brown kept lookin' at me. Then she clicked her tongue like this—tsk, tsk, tsk. And she told Keith to read. She put her arm around him! I hate her. I don't wanna go to school no more."

Would a teacher deliberately put-down David because he didn't read well. I think not. What was said to him without words? Plenty. Will the singular events that Keith and David experienced set the pace and direction of their school lives from now on? Probably not. Nevertheless, if Keith's teacher continues to be unaware of the effects of her behavior, harmful results can gradually accrue. This is especially true if a pattern of relationship between teacher and student becomes firmly established. While no single event causes a lasting value or attitude, a series of similar events can. Add to this the likelihood of teacher unawareness and you have an outcome which may never be remedied.

Reading the behavior of another or sensing the appropriate thing to do is not always easy. Knowing how another person feels is much more difficult than is apparent. Sensitive responses are not necessarily available. But more importantly, a person may not recognize what he has to do.

A teacher had just returned from a long day at school. He was tired and emotionally drained. Taking an easy chair in his living room, he turned his attention to the evening newspaper. Although he had warmly greeted his family, his three-year-old daughter found her way to his side. She took the remaining space in his chair, whispering, "Daddy, I love you."

He replied, "I know you do," thinking "that's sweet."

Within a few seconds, she insisted, "Daddy, I love you so much."

With that restatement, he exclaimed, "I love you, too, honey."

Now she snuggled up much closer, making it most difficult for him to read the paper. He didn't want to turn away from her in his chair, although it would have made reading easier. He knew this movement might be interpreted as rejection. So he remained in his somewhat uncomfortable position.

At this moment she gave him a kiss on the cheek and was almost sitting in his lap. Softly, she said, "Daddy, I missed you."

"Sugar, I missed you too," he repeated.

By now the paper was completely disarrayed in his hands and he hadn't the faintest notion of what he was reading. He turned his full attention to her, gave her a squeeze, and put his right arm around her.

Responding to those silent cues, she remained still and quiet. In that second, he wondered if he was going to be able to read the paper at all.

A moment before, his adolescent son had entered the room to sit nearby. He realized that his son was there but he chose not to acknowledge his presence. Without knowing how, he somehow realized that his son knew what was going on. For a brief second he didn't know what to do. But the paper no longer seemed important. He decided to look at his son without appearing gushy and with a glance that suggested, we men stick together. Winking back, his son expressed without a word, "Dad, we know you had a long day, but we want to be with you." Except for a quick, few sensitive seconds, he could have missed it all.

Long before a child learns to speak, he forms a picture of himself from how he is treated. He knows when the arms around him are supportive. He feels how he is lifted and handled. Facial displays, touch, and vocal tones mean something. They do not go unnoticed. The child cannot verbalize his feelings but he knows; he feels. His sensitivity to others is astonishingly accurate. The meaning of human contact is understood and later he will understand the words that accompany these messages.

People of all ages can be heard to say, "You know what I mean." During a conversation, people also repeatedly say "you know," or "I mean." These phrases may be uttered as many as a dozen times during a single conversation. Anytime we talk we scurry for words that capture our meaning. We want to be understood. We have great faith in words. But we don't always say what we mean or mean what we say.

In a classic children's book, *Horton, The Elephant* by Dr. Seuss, Horton assigns himself the improbable task of hatching an egg. After taking a position on a bird's nest (the mother has gone to Florida), Horton repeats these words again and again: "I meant what I said, and I said what I meant; an elephant is faithful one-hundred percent." Horton meant what he said, his actions followed his words. He didn't desert the nest and the egg hatched into a flying elephant. People mean what they say too. But sometimes they don't. And therein lies the rub.

If we lived in a perfect world of saying what we meant and meaning what we said, then a language of nonverbal sensitivity would be nonexistent. When words are unclear and seem like masked messengers of meaning, we then search for the essence of what is meant. This language of sensitivity emerges because words are inadequate expressions of our full meaning.

Not only do words fail to carry the full intent and meaning of what we say, they aren't as effective as nonverbal expressions. A head nod gives assurance. A warm glance expresses love. Focused attention suggests that we are listening. A gesture qualifies a word. Eye contact closes interpersonal distance. Touching has its own meaning. Our actions speak so elegantly, words have to take a backseat.

We must not believe that all we do is verbalize. An adult can tell a child that he is dumb, ugly, dirty, or unimportant without a single word. And without question, the child understands. It is these kinds of non-verbal messages which are so devastating and which we are most likely to overlook. Indeed, we often express evaluations without words that we would never have the courage to state verbally.

In spite of this tendency, I am convinced that teachers and parents do not deliberately set out to put down the young. They do it unwittingly. No malicious intent exists. As adults, we are simply unaware of the many, many messages we send. And sometimes it's what we don't do that counts the most. A poignant example of this kind of omission occurred a few years ago. I had gone to a large city school to observe student behavior. I had been to the school many times so the teachers knew me well. I was there to observe specific students for an entire school day. I noticed that these students looked at teachers but teachers did not necessarily look back. This was true, even though the students had different teachers for every class period. From class to class these students trudged to their seats, but their presence was never acknowl-edged. These students were not spoken to, nor were they visually con-tacted by any teacher. It's hard to imagine that students can come to school, spend the day with several teachers, and never be recognized. Treated as nonpersons or nonentities, the school might as well have declared that they didn't exist. This is a tragic reality, but it's true. I am thoroughly convinced that none of these teachers deliberately or inten-tionally excluded these students, but isolation and subtle rejection occurred nonetheless. Imagine the loneliness and alienation that was experienced. We shouldn't be too surprised later when a student acts out his feelings with all the vehemence and energy he can muster. He won't be able to verbalize the reasons why, but the feelings within him will cry out for recognition and self-esteem.

In spite of an absence of contact with some students, teachers managed to view other students differently. When teachers talked, they looked at some students to suggest that everything was going well. In these instances, mutual glances were exchanged between teacher and students in a positive manner. It was assumed that these students under-stood the lesson. But there were all kinds of visual discriminations going on and the differences in eye contact were amazing. Eyes that looked up or down transmitted, "I reject you." Eyes that avoided contact suggested, "You are not included." Eyes that stared at students revealed, "I dislike you." As I sat there watching all of this, I mused that these teachers didn't know what was happening. I thought, "They would be appalled if they knew." I was sure that their reaction would be one of disbelief. So that I won't be misunderstood, let's make it clear: these teachers were not unlike teachers anywhere. They were doing their job as they saw it.

In the face of these unforeseen consequences, teachers often ask, "What can I do? How can I improve my nonverbal influence?" Most teachers want a precise routine of the right moves to make. They want to become practiced in the exact science of body movement and expression. But I usually steer clear of formulas. Exact prescriptions of what every teacher should do seems too static and stereotyped. Teachers must learn what their own expression equipment means to them and to others. I see nonverbal behaviors and expressions as true extensions of the person. I don't wish to create artificial manners and maneuvers. My view minimizes technical training and maximizes self-discovery and self-development.

A recent book, *The Teacher Moves*, by Barbara Grant and Dorothy Hennings describes the nonverbal motions and clues that they believe are essential to improving teaching performance. Their book outlines in specific detail the way teachers move nonverbally and suggests a series of experiments teachers might try to improve teaching. All of this is appropriate. By providing a systematic way to study nonverbal movements, Grant and Hennings' discussion of nonverbal clues provides a legitimate means to change nonverbal patterns and actions. They suggest the use of an inventory which they have developed for creating an awareness of the non-verbal.

If possible, I would want every teacher and adult to be a student of his own nonverbal activity. Teachers could fill-out the Grant-Hennings inventory; they could be video-taped to see themselves; they could obtain feedback from a confidant; they could introspectively analyze their own nonverbal actions. All of these should be used by a teacher to understand himself better.

But an emphasis should not be placed on external moves which are disconnected from the internal realness one is. When nonverbal movements and expressions become artificial techniques for convincing others, then no one benefits. Neither teacher nor student. For the same difficulty between teacher and student emerges again. This is the disparity between what a teacher is and what he pretends to be. For too long, we have viewed teaching as a ritualistic ceremony with precise techniques. It becomes too easy to act on a stage of pretense and to play a game of human contact that smothers realness. When we say that the language of sensitivity between us is nonverbal, we mean to say that the authentic and the real will prevail. We can pretend that this isn't true, but nonverbal actions speak for themselves. It is to the fidelity of human experience that nonverbal meanings have value.

Nonverbal Communication

CHARLES M. GALLOWAY

A SHORT COURSE by **DR. CHARLES GALLOWAY**, a foremost authority
in a major phase of instruction now attracting serious attention . . . .
Do the assignments section by section. You'll find a new ability to
control this vital part of your teaching skills!

When second-grade teacher Ruth Harris was getting dressed for
school one dull Monday, she hesitated between a black suit and a bright
print dress. Choosing the print, she thought, "It will brighten the day for
me and the children." Things did seem to go well all day. . . .

As Paul Trask entered the school building, he saw the principal at
the end of the hall. Expecting a smile and a wave, he was surprised to get
a curt nod and the sight of a disappearing back. Paul wondered what
could be wrong. . . .

Annette Webster looked at her fourth-year arithmetic group as they
bent over the problem she had presented to them. She noticed Chris
scowling at his paper and biting his lip and moved to help him. . . .

What happened with these teachers? Each one either sent or received
a message without saying or hearing a word. What happened was **nonverbal communication.**

Nonverbal communication is behavior that conveys meaning without
words. It can be symbolic or nonsymbolic, spontaneous or managed. It
can be expressive, transmitting emotion; or it can be informative, transmitting facts. It can be as specific as a gesture or as general as the
atmosphere of a room. It can be either dynamic or static.

Nonverbal communication takes a certain amount of time and
occurs at a certain tempo. It can be quick or slow. It can be negative or
positive—something that doesn't happen as well as something that does.
Or it can be a combination of any of these—and there's even a non-verbal
component in verbalisms.

All human beings are compelled to send and receive messages. They try
constantly to discover information which lessens confusion or increases

Galloway, Charles M. "Nonverbal Communication." *Instructor*. April 1968.
77:37-42. Reprinted from INSTRUCTOR, copyright 1968, the Instructor Publications, Inc., used by permission.

understanding. When messages are carried by words, the participators are consciously aware of hearing or seeing the words. But nonverbal communication is given much less conscious thought. The operations of giving information through nonverbal action and reading the meaning of another person's nonverbal behavior usually occur without deliberate reflection.

The clothing you wear, your posture, or how you walk transmits a message to others. You may be saying, "I am a teacher; I am meeting your expectations (and mine) of how a teacher should look." Depending on your emotional needs, you may also be trying to say, "I am an alert, modern teacher," or even, "I may be a teacher, but at heart I'm a swinger!"

So we can say that nonverbal clues are evident in any situation where people are with other people. In fact, the most subtle and covert kinds of information can be discovered in this way. Here are three examples:

Nonverbal phenomena establish the status of interaction. At a party you are talking to someone, but his eyes are following someone else around the room. His posture and manner indicate his desire to be off. What conclusion do you come to?

Nonverbal behavior indicates what the other person thinks of us. You are discussing a controversial topic with a small group. Everyone is reacting politely, but you are aware of those who approve of your ideas and those who disagree. How do you know?

Nonverbal clues are used to check the reliability of what is said. You had mailed a coupon indicating interest in an expensive set of books. The man who shows up at your door is poorly groomed and shifty-eyed. Although his credentials seem in order, you hesitate even to let him in. The significance of nonverbal behavior in the classroom is an idea about teaching that is growing in importance. Until now, it has seldom been recognized or understood, at least in a formal, specific way. Now persons interested in improving the teaching act are studying the implications of nonverbal communication—implications that are important for you to understand.

Assignments

▶ 1. Think of at least one classroom situation in which of each the three conditions described above occurred.
▶ 2. Review the last two days of school. Can you recall an incident in which a child's behavior belied his remarks?
▶ 3. When a nonverbal cue disagrees with or contradicts a verbal remark,

we tend to accept the nonverbal message as representative of the real meaning. Discuss why this occurs.

Nonverbal phenomena

Nonverbal behavior consists of such events as facial expression, posture, gestures, movement, even the arrangement of space or objects around the behaver. It involves use of the body, use of space, and even the use of time.

Although we are often unaware of the process, we are very conscious of the eloquence of nonverbal cues. We all agree that "actions speak louder than words," and realize that *how* we say something can be as important as *what* we say. We also know the feeling of being "in tune" with someone—immediately understanding him and having him understand us.

Most of us believe that the most personal and valid kinds of information are discovered by what we call intuition. What really happens is that we subconsciously respond to nonverbal clues transmitted by other persons.

During the school day, many graphic portrayals of nonverbal phenomena occur. Here are some common ones, and as you read them, think about your class. Undoubtedly you will recall many examples like them, and will be able to add others.

Substitute Expression—A child shrugs his shoulder in an "I don't know." manner after being accousted in the hallway for running. Probably this means he feels guilty at being caught, yet he hesitates to engage the teacher in a verbal debate. This is especially true if his verbal defense is likely to be employed against him later in the conversation. One of the places events like this occur repeatedly is in inner-city schools, where children are already conditioned to express their frustrations and defiance in a nonverbal way.

Qualifying Expression—Ann says, "I don't sing well," but what does she mean? Stated one way, it suggests that she *does* sing well; or it may mean that she *would like* to sing well; or, that she truly *does not* sing well. The intent of verbal remarks is usually qualified through intonation and inflection. Facial expressions and gestures also qualify verbal language.

Nonverbal Symbolic—John observed the teacher watching him. Now he is painting with large dramatic strokes, one eye on the teacher, hoping she will look his way again. When we know we are being observed, our behavior is designed to have intent or purpose for the observer. It symbolizes our thoughts or intentions. Eyes alone may beckon or reject. Many gestures and facial expressions symbolize our deepest feelings.

Nonverbal Nonsymbolic—You are watching a child who is observing another child, totally unaware that you are watching him. His behavior is considered nonsymbolic since it is free of overt intent. When you observe the unobserved observer, it is a profound process—for his reactions are genuinely his own with no desire to create an impression. Observing a person who is unaware of our presence is both informative and fun.

Attentive or Inattentive—Your students are pretending to listen while their minds wander in fields of fantasy, and when they respond it is in a bored fashion. Nonverbally they are being inattentive. As an experienced teacher, you are able to detect such reactions and use them to change the pace and direction of what is being taught. Observing when students are involved and interested and when they are not is a skill that teachers learn. But teachers vary widely in their ability or willingness to use these pupil reactions as directions for their own behavior.

There are other nonverbal occurrences, but these are good ones to start with. Undoubtedly you can add other specific types from your own experiences.

Assignments

▶ 1. Identify children in your class who typically react nonverbally to either reprimand or approval. Do you know what they are really trying to communicate?

▶ 2. Experiment with positive body and facial qualifying expressions, especially when you feel a need to support a request or judgment you are making.

▶ 3. Think of a nonsymbolic situation in which your observation was later confirmed; another one which later proved wrong.

Classroom Cues

Nonverbal behavior is not limited to personal practices. Many classroom phenomena serve as nonverbal communicators. Their impact on the course and direction of an activity can strongly affect the contextual meaning that is derived from it.

Methods of distributing materials can affect the activity that follows; the way a group is formed influences its practices; even the degree of neatness required suggests behavior to the pupil.

Nonverbal cues either reinforce or minimize verbal messages. They become the focus of attention and *carry conviction that lingers long after the verbal event has passed.* Why this is so is difficult to answer, but the strong influence of nonverbal cues is unmistakable.

Classroom phenomena often play a more significant role in students' learning than the formal teaching which takes place. In any classroom, the extent and duration of teacher-pupil contacts are great. It is vital to have mutual understanding in the exchange of the messages that are nonverbal in character and import.

Consider phenomena that are typical of any classroom:

USE OF SPACE—Classrooms are divided into territories. Both teacher and students occupy space. Some arrangements of territorial rights are traditional, with the teacher's desk at the front of the room and students seated in rows. Other arrangements are more imaginative. Some uses of space are fluid, others are static.

Space arrangement shows the teacher's priorities—what she thinks important; what she thinks about her children; how she envisions her own position. A change in a spatial arrangement influences the potential meaning of a learning context.

TEACHER TRAVEL—Where and when a teacher chooses to travel in a classroom is significant. In the past, teachers usually moved around their own desks as if they were isles of security. They rarely ventured into territories of student residence, unless they wished to check up on or monitor seatwork. Today that picture has changed. Some teachers have done away with desks; others have put them in less focal places.

To move toward or away from students signifies relationships. Teachers may avoid some students or frequent the work areas of others. All of those movements have meaning that students recognize.

USE OF TIME—How teachers use their time indicates the value and importance they place on types of work, on subject areas, and on acceptable activities. Spending little or no time on a topic indicates a lack of interest in or knowledge about it so that even little children are aware of teachers' preferences.

Teachers often fail to recognize the implications of their use of time. One teacher spends two hours marking papers. A teacher in the next room spends the same amount of time in helping children mark their own papers. Certainly these teachers have different concepts of evaluation and it is revealed by their uses of time.

CONTROL MANEUVERS—Teachers engage in various nonverbal tactics to control the behavior of students. These silent expressions serve as events reminding students of teacher expectations. Some typical examples of nonverbal maneuvers: the teacher indicates inability to hear due to classroom noise; places finger to lips; stands with hands on hips and stares in silence; scans room to see who is not working; records in grade book while student is making a report. Negative maneuvers tend to "put children in their place." Similarly, positive maneuvers can give encouragement, help a child overcome fear, put a nervous child at ease, or resolve a tense situation.

As the teacher works to establish better classroom phenomena, he must be careful to avoid *incongruity*. This is an event where there is a contradiction between what is said and what is done, and it may occur many times in a day. The thing to remember about an incongruity is that it is nonverbal behavior that makes the impression that is most lasting and most difficult to overcome.

Incongruous behaviors occur frequently during times of praise or encouragement. Teachers use words such as "good" or "nice job" but the praise can appear false or unbelievable. When we are not honest with children, it is the nonverbal clues that trip us up.

Nonverbal phenomena should not be thought of primarily in negative terms. Many classrooms are well arranged. The teacher's approach to an activity provides excellent motivation. Or, through meeting a child's eyes or with a small gesture, a teacher builds confidence. Such nonverbal events can be highly conducive to good classroom climate.

Nonverbal qualities that contribute to effective classroom interaction are suggested:

Attention—The event of listening to pupils when they talk. This is essential. When a teacher fails to listen, a pupil is likely to believe that what he says is unimportant.

Reception—Behavioral evidence that a teacher is listening, by maintaining eye contact while a pupil is talking. The event of attending to pupils when they talk assures pupils and encourages them to believe that their verbal communication is valued by the teacher.

Reinforcement—a look or gesture to reinforce approval of an act by a student. Not only the timid but also the seemingly forward child may need reinforcement if he is to go ahead on his own.

Facilitation—A movement toward a student for the purpose of helping or assisting. Teachers quite often detect needs or unexpressed feelings by students, and initiate a move toward the student to alleviate his concern. Teachers engage in such events because, either consciously or subconsciously, they have become sensitive to the nonverbal cues given by their students.

We all recognize that expressive cues are fleeting and transitory. Nonetheless, they transmit emotion and feeling, and are detected as indications of meaning far more quickly than speech. *It is the appearance of such cues that especially suggests to others the attitudes we hold at a given time.* Therefore, they are particularly important in establishing the classroom environment and in working out good rapport with each child.

Assignments

▶ 1. Draw some alternate layouts for your classroom. List changes in nonverbal phenomena that each layout would imply.

2. Make a two-day study of how often you contact each child in any of many ways. Keep a list of children's names and devise a simple code to indicate times of approving or disapproving, individual or group sharing, listening, or other interaction.

Feedback

Improving classroom nonverbal behavior is not easy, especially in discovering incongruity. Yet we probably all agree that such improvement should be a conscious goal for any teacher.

One enlightening and sometimes disconcerting way to check your present behavior is by watching yourself on film or video-tape. Another way is to listen to the comments and suggestions of an observer whose judgment you trust. A teacher's major source of feedback, however, is the responses of students.

To become more knowledgeable about the nonverbal reactions of your youngsters to your behavior is a difficult quest. Even when you begin to recognize the reactions, it is naive to believe that change is imminently possible. Most of us have been observing and behaving in patterned ways for a long time. Ridding oneself of past habits and attitudes is a difficult undertaking and must be a continuing process.

The best way to start is to develop an attitude of *openness*. Openness to one's experience and the realization that a rich and available source of data exists in the classroom is crucial. Openness is necessary if an improvement of perceptual skills and style of behaving is to be effected.

Assuming that a teacher has an open attitude toward self and others, the steps for becoming better informed involve *awareness, understanding*, and *acceptance*. To be aware is to observe more fully and to be open to the nonverbal reactions of others and oneself. To understand implies the need to analyze the meaning of your observations and to suspend judgment until you are reasonably certain of their real meaning. To accept is to acknowledge that your behavior means what it does to students, even though the meaning is not what you intended to imply.

This last step is especially difficult because most of us do not like to admit even to ourselves that others perceive us differently. But once you can accept what your behavior represents to others, the door is open to behaving differently. (Does it seem odd to be talking about the *behavior* of teachers? That is a word usually reserved for children, yet the teacher's conduct in the classroom is of vital importance to every child.) In being open to nonverbal cues, it is useful to recognize behavior as a cultural, social, and psychological phenomenon. The behavior of a teacher or of students arises from experiences that have been learned over a period of time. Here are some points to consider as you view students' reactions:

Similar experiences can mean different things. A pat on the back to one child may imply friendliness and support, whereas to another exactly the same behavior may be interpreted as an aggressive and threatening gesture. Similarly, an aggressive act by a child may be in defiance of controls, or in response to something in your classroom climate that has encouraged him to go ahead on his own.

Reaction to physical contact varies. To some children who are accustomed to adults' maintaining a physical distance from them, too close a proximity by the teacher might well stifle and embarrass. Conversely, other children prefer the close contact and warmth of teacher-pupil contacts. One broad cultural understanding among us that you may not have realized is that we do not stand too close to one another while talking in public. When the appropriate distance is broken, talking ceases.

Nonverbal expressions among racial, ethnic, and social classes can differ markedly. Similarly, the behaviors of suburban, rural, and inner-city children vary. The teacher must be sensitive to behavior differences and seek to learn what they imply rather than coming to premature conclusions.

Meeting expectations appears to be a development ability. If meeting expectations is a learned process, it explains why the behavior of young children appears so unaffected and natural. Much of their behavior is spontaneous and unrehearsed. With older children, activities of pretending to listen in class, appearing busy during seatwork assignments, and putting on a front of seeming to be interested, may all be games that they have learned to play.

There are perhaps many such games that children learn to play in school, and the longer they go to school the better their skills develop. This is a necessary step in preparing for adult roles; but on the other hand, children who do need help may be able to conceal their need.

Responsiveness may be misleading. Parents who want their children to succeed often stress the importance of "pleasing the teacher." In actuality, the student less overt in his responsiveness may be more receptive to what is going on. Nonverbal clues are the best way to judge responsiveness.

Deprived children may be incapable of meeting the behavioral expectations of the teacher. They may neither understand the rules of the school game nor be able to control their behavior satisfactorily. Indeed, many teachers do not facilitate their fumbling efforts, but, rather, try to catch them in the act. Such students need practice in what it means to be a student.

Awareness of the behavior of yourself and your students and what it means does not come all at once. Interpretations change as realization increases. But the processes of awareness and realization are concomitant. You perceive to greater depths, you are more attuned to those around you, and you begin to employ nonverbal clues for positive purposes. Having opened the door, you realize you have the ability to change and improve.

Assignments

▶ 1. A company selling video-tape recorders may be willing to give a demonstration of its product in your school. Volunteer to be photographed. It may take courage! Or make a class movie, letting children take footage with a movie camera. (Don't try to be in the film. Chances are you will be automatically included.) Study it to see how your nonverbal behavior could improve.

2. Make a study of the feedback at times when you are an observer— for example, of children's reactions to the librarian, music teacher, or other classroom visitors.

3. Discuss feedback in a teachers' meeting. Let teachers anonymously mark profile sheets showing impressions they have of other teachers, including yourself. (The results may amaze you.)

Experimenting

Since nonverbal communication is so basic and certainly old as mankind, why the recent interest in its role in education? Are teachers now expected to search for hidden meanings behind everything that happens in their classrooms? Must they become overly sensitive to ordinary behavior? Not at all.

Teachers need not set out to discover meanings that lurk in the subterranean caverns of the mind. Indeed, they shouldn't. Instead, the purpose is to become more aware of nonverbal cues because they operate as a silent language to influence teacher-student understandings and interactions. And it is through these understandings and interactions in the classroom that the business of teaching and learning goes forward.

Your final assignment in your nonverbal course is an invitation to experiment in every phase of classroom nonverbal communication. The possibilities are limitless:

▶ 1. If you customarily work with small groups of children, experiment with the spread of the chairs. When the chairs are touching each other, do children react differently from when they are a foot apart? What about two feet? Does it make a difference whether you sit on a higher chair or one the same height?

▶ 2. Nonverbal acts are often preferable to words, and many studies show that the teacher's voice is heard far too often. Without telling the children of your intentions, experiment with giving nonverbal instead of verbal directions. Use devices such as a tap of a bell to tell children you want their attention, or the flick of lights to show that a period is about to end.

▶ 3. Make a definite attempt to react more effectively to signals. A kindergarten teacher found that she could avoid calamity by observing more closely a boy with bathroom problems. The child chewing his pencil may be hoping you will come to his desk. Or, the one wanting to sharpen his pencil may be lacking an idea to write about.

▶ 4. Try to match your degree of nonverbal behavior to the child's and examine the results. For instance, sometimes teachers tend to be overarticulate with a nonarticulate child, subconsciously compensating for his lack. In contrast, a child who sits quietly beside the teacher may be getting warmth and comfort from the teacher's sitting quietly beside him. Matching the nonverbal behavior of a child is a kind of approval.

▶ 5. Experiment with light and heat—both important factors in classroom climate. Some teachers flick the switch as soon as they open the door, yet in most classrooms, any artificial light is not necessary on a normal day. Light affects mood, and so does heat. Deliberate changes in temperature can also be an effective device for changing classroom atmosphere.

▶ 6. Use nonverbal displays. The old adage that a picture is worth a thousand words applies in establishing classroom climate, especially if you employ humor and relaxation. One teacher experimented with two signs. The first said, "Pick up paper and put it in the wastebasket." The second was a silhouette of a child neatly dropping paper in the wastebasket. The second proved to be by far the better reminder.

▶ 7. Provide opportunities for children to express emotions by nonverbal means. Pantomimes are not only highly expressive for the actors but also give teachers insight into their feelings and emotions. Various forms of rhythm and creative dance are good nonverbal expressions, and so of course are all types of art work.

▶ 8. Talk about nonverbal patterns with your children, but do it astutely. Give them the opportunity to express themselves about nonverbal behavior on the part of adults that gives them pleasure or causes them frustrations.

▶ 9. Increase your practice of looking students in the eye. Experiment with glance exchanges for individual-to-individual contact.

▶ 10. Increase the frequency of your relevant gestures. They are an excellent way of underlining points you are trying to make.

▶ 11. Check your relevancy by checking your degree of effectiveness in transmitting ideas. This is not easy to do but it is especially important. Do you often feel misunderstood? Does a particular point you tried to make fail to get across? Your nonverbal behavior may have an incongruity that cancels out the effectiveness of your words.

▶ 12. Experiment with new movement patterns. Things you have been doing, do differently for a while. You may be making yourself too

available or not available enough. Be sure, however, that your accessibility is not just a sneaky way to maintain close supervision.
▶ 13. Let children experiment with furniture arrangement that involves group interaction. One teacher tried putting desks in groups of four with the children facing each other. Two days later the desks were reversed so that this time the children faced away from each other.
▶ 14. Individualize your attention. You can't listen to all of the children all of the time, so experiment with listening very intently to a child for a brief period. As long as he is talking, look directly at him.

These suggested experiments aren't new. You've known about them all before. What's new is the emphasis on their nonverbal aspects. Considering them from this new point of view can help you understand their impact. Your goal is to use nonverbal communication more effectively in your quest for better ways of teaching.

In this initial exposure to the subject of Nonverbal Communication, you have been introduced to the importance of silent messages and subtle cues. The value of self-observation has been emphasized and the significance of feedback stressed. To be better understood and to better understand remains a continuous task for us all; attending to the non-verbal aspects of action, reaction, and interaction facilitates our efforts. While no shortcut to full meaning is ever available to us, an openness to nonverbal cues does enhance our chances of knowing.

After you have had the experience of engaging in the assignments and trying the experiments, you will find that your sensitivity to non-verbal phenomena has increased. One of your first responses will be a feeling of amazement that nonverbal communication can make such a difference in the classroom—and elsewhere. You will be struck by the lasting influence it has in human affairs. Becoming aware of the non-verbal events occurring around you can be an exciting and enlarging experience in achieving a better understanding of yourself and your world.

Research

SAMUEL WEINTRAUB

Teachers reading:
quantity and quality

If the number of members belonging to a professional organization and the power to attract crowds were the major criteria for measuring interest in a particular activity, reading would rank among the most popular pastimes in the United States, with teachers leading in the pursuit of it. The phenomenal growth of the International Reading Association is but one manifestation of this interest. Professional education meetings in which reading is the topic often draw a standing-room-only audience. Adults outside of the teaching profession, too, are vitally concerned with reading, as evidenced by the attendance at PTA meetings when reading is the focus as well as by the increasing enrollments in adult reading courses.

Why are teachers so interested in the topic? One would hope it might be in part because they themselves are avid readers. Certainly it is the goal of reading teachers everywhere to develop permanent interest in reading in their students. Hopefully, we do not send out as an end product only people who *can* read but, equally important, individuals who *do* read. Yet Asheim (1956) stated that as a nation "Americans . . . are not serious readers."

Jacobs (1956) says of the teacher who would promote permanent reading interests in his pupils, "Such a teacher has felt the import of reading in his own living . . . " It seems logical that a teacher can best develop the habit of reading in pupils if he himself is an habitual reader. It also seems that a teacher can best develop an interest in *serious* reading if he himself is a *serious* reader. This column is devoted to exploring answers to two major questions: Do teachers read? And, if so, what do teachers read?

Weintraub, Samuel. "Teachers Reading: Quantity and Quality." *The Reading Teacher.* October 1967. 21:67-71. Reprinted with permission of the International Reading Association and Samuel Weintraub.

Historically considered, one of the first studies investigating these questions was reported by Waples (1933). His comments are of more than passing interest if teachers' attitudes are transmitted to pupils: "The subjects of most concern to public school teachers indicated a conventional and insufficient awareness of social issues confronting the next generation. Teachers and, more importantly, teachers in training were found to be insufficiently concerned with socially important topics." Waples continued by observing that social attitudes of teachers were much like those of the population at large and could be criticized "as provincial, conventional, or sensational." His findings on teachers in training are similar in vein. He implied that the latter group would be better prepared as teachers if exciting reading focusing on important social problems were an essential part of their undergraduate program.

Some thirty years later, Odland and Ilstrup (1963) asked whether future teachers would read. They surveyed the reading habits of undergraduate students in a children's literature course. Of the almost 350 students, 10 per cent had read no books in the six months preceding their study. About 30 per cent had read five or more books in the previous six-month period, while the other 60 per cent were in between these two extremes in the number of books read. Some read magazines only and completely neglected books. The personal reading habits of these students were similar to those reported for college students in other studies. Odland and Istrup state ". . . there would seem to be basis for asking if the adults who accept the responsibility of teaching young children the values of reading really consider reading a valuable medium of communication" (1963, Pp. 83-87).

Balow investigated the magazine reading of graduate and undergraduate students in education and of college graduates in arts. He concluded that:

> . . . these teachers and prospective teachers apparently are reading essentially non-scholarly magazines. Escape reading predominates. Journals of political comment, of ideas, or of such difficulty . . . that the readers would have to struggle for understanding are conspicuously absent. To the extent that periodical reading reflects a desire for knowledge, these education students show little interest in the realm of ideas, whether it be literature, art, science, or politics (1961, Pp. 57-59).

Perhaps if teachers do not read widely in the areas of personal reading or in reading matter related to important social values, they do considerable reading in professional literature. Approximately twenty-five years ago, Simpson (1942) looked at the reading patterns of 746 teachers and administrators. He found that ". . . little or no professional reading to help solve school problems is done by the teacher or administrator." The findings of the study showed that 40 per cent had not looked at even one professional book in the preceding month and that ". . . two-thirds of the teachers . . . spent less than two hours per month on professional magazine materials. Approximately one in seven of the whole group spent no time at all on magazine reading." Simpson concludes that ". . . until teachers and administrators learn how to make reading function in the intelligent facing of their own problems it is unlikely that they will teach effective reading to their pupils" (1942, Pp. 11-13).

Experienced teachers enrolled in reading methods courses were found by Schubert (1960) to own few professional books and to subscribe to few professional journals. In his sample of 132, about one-third of the teachers subscribed to no professional journal and one-fifth reported owning no books on reading.

Fisher (1958) reported an intensive study of fifty teachers' reading patterns in relation to experience and education, interest in reading, curriculum committee service, and availability of materials. In schools where professional journals were regularly circulated and in schools where the principal called attention to recent literature at faculty meetings, almost all teachers had read some of the recommended materials. In two of the schools involved where the principal did not take an active role in seeing that materials were readily accessible, Fisher found the influence of the school environment on teachers' reading less marked. It was also noted that involvement on committees such as curriculum study groups caused teachers to make time for reading. Some teachers, notably those with advanced degrees, did substantial reading, even though they did not show high enthusiasm for it. Fisher asks if these teachers had not perhaps developed a sense of obligation to the profession.

One of the most recent reports concerning teachers' reading interests was published by Graves (1966). In a questionnaire survey, he sampled classroom teachers from kindergarten through grade fourteen. Almost half the teachers reported reading one daily newspaper regularly, and nearly half reported reading a weekly paper also. More than 90 per cent responded that they read both local and national news stories in the papers, and almost 90 per cent also reported the reading of international news stories and education news. Of all popular magazines, *Reader's Digest* and *Life* were read most regularly. The news journals most often ready by teachers were *Newsweek* (39.7 per cent) and *Time* (38.6 per cent). More serious journals—*Atlantic, Harper's Reporter*—were all read by considerably less than 10 per cent of the teachers surveyed. The results of the NEA Research Division's study as reported by Graves are not essentially different from the findings Waples reported more than thirty years earlier.

In professional reading, Graves states "... typical teachers consider the *Instructor*, *the NEA Journal*, and the *Grade Teacher* as 'the most helpful' professional periodicals" (1966, Pp. 17-19). In professional journals, teachers usually read material devoted to teaching aids (84.6 per cent) and articles on curriculum and instruction (81.3 per cent), controversial issues (77.4 per cent), status of the profession (70.7 per cent), and humor (70.6 per cent). An average of four professional books had been read by teachers during the three months prior to filling out the questionnaire.

Summary

Research over the past thirty-five years shows a rather consistent pattern of reading habits and interests on the part of classroom teachers. One may interpret the findings in several ways. It does appear that teachers do some reading, but the quality of this reading has been questioned by several investigators (Balow, 1961; Odland and Ilstrup, 1963; Simpson, 1942; Waples, 1933). The questions raised are yet to be answered. If we are to develop in our pupils the habit of reading, the desire to read to find answers to their problems, do we not need to set the example? Or is it enough to tell pupils to do what we say and not what we do? Each reader must answer these questions for himself.

Positive action on the part of administrators, supervisors and reading consultants appears to be one means of influencing teachers to read professional literature. Reference to a particular article, involvement in decision-making at the curriculum study level, and the simple accessibility of professional literature all are avenues to the same end—that of promoting reading by teachers. If the reading teacher is indeed a member of a profession, then his reading in the professional literature, his knowledge of current issues in reading, and his delving into the literature to seek solutions to his own teaching problems must be fostered. Pre-service programs need to build activities promoting this kind of active reading-behavior into their curriculum, and in-service programs must continue to promote it.

REFERENCES

1. **ASHEIM, L.** What do adults read. In N. B. Henry (Ed.). Adult reading. *Fifty-fifth Yearbook of the National Society for the Study of Education.* Chicago: University of Chicago Press, 5-28.

2. **BALOW, B.** Magazine readers among teachers and prospective teachers. *Journal of Teacher Education,* 1961, 12, 57-59.

3. **FISHER, HELEN.** Teacher differences in professional reading. *Educational Administration and Supervision,* 1958, 44, 282-89.

4. **GRAVES, W. A.** Teachers' reading and recreational interests. *NEA Journal,* 1966, 55, 17-19.

5. **JACOBS, L. B.** Goals in promoting permanent reading interests. In Helen M. Robinson (Ed.). Developing Permanent Interests in Reading. *Supplementary Educational Monographs, No. 84.* Chicago: University of Chicago Press, 1956, 20-25.

6. **ODLAND, NORINE and ILSTRUP, THERESE.** Will reading teachers read? *The Reading Teacher,* 1963, 17, 83-87.

7. **SCHUBERT D. G.** Do teachers read about reading? *California Journal of Educational Research,* 1960, 11, 94-96.

8. **SIMPSON, R. H.** Reading disabilities among teachers and administrators. *The Clearing House,* 1942, 17, 11-13.

9. **WAPLES, D.** Reading interests of teachers. *Special Survey Studies, Part V, National Survey of the Education of Teachers, Vol. 5* United States Office of Education, Bulletin No. 10, 1933, 247-84.

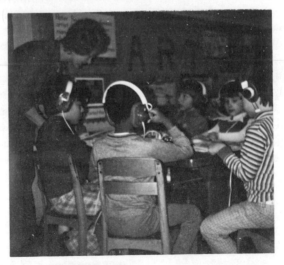

SCHOOL is for . . .
LISTENING ACTIVITIES

Communicating With Parents

JOHN M. DODD and NANCY S. DODD

Although parent-teacher cooperation in behalf of the child is a cherished ideal, it seldom works out that way. The most common situation is a kind of compartmentalization—the teacher takes care of the child during school hours; the parent takes care of him the rest of the time and never the twain shall meet (except, possibly, at short parent conferences each year). Other contacts may be dreaded, avoided, or postponed by parents and teachers alike. But if both shy away from something that could benefit the child, then it is worth examining some of the reasons behind this.

Why do teachers shy away from contacting parents? Primarily, because they expect the parent to react negatively. They fear that the parent will be angry, or insulted, or even deny the problem. There is also the lingering suspicion that the parent may challenge the teacher's competence: "If you were a better teacher, my child wouldn't be having such trouble in school!" There is even the fear that the parent may accuse the teacher of disliking the child. (Few teachers would feel comfortable with such a charge, even if the child was in fact dislikable.) Finally, the parent may force the teacher to defend school policies with which the teacher may have little sympathy. All of these possibilities are real; and the teacher's expectation of some negative reaction by the parents is well-founded. If the teacher understands *why* the parents react this way, and learns to ease the parents through the difficult initial contacts, the chances of helping the child are increased.

Why do parents shy away from contacting teachers? Because they are afraid of causing trouble for the child by mentioning some problem the teacher may not have noticed before. Moreover, no parent wants to seem interfering or demanding; they fear the teacher might resent the child in the future. Most parents do not want special attention for their child because they believe his classmates may reject him as a result.

Dodd, John M., and Dodd, Nancy S. "Communicating with Parents." *Academic Therapy*. Spring 1972. 7:277-283.

Finally, many parents dread schools and teachers both, because they feel inadequate. Thus, we have a situation in which teachers and parents are often reluctant to take the first step. Meanwhile, the child's problem continues.

When a conference is scheduled by the teacher, the parent may feel a strong urge to postpone or avoid it. After all, if a teacher asks for a special conference, it is almost certain to be something negative: either the child is not doing well academically, or he is a behavior problem—or both. Teachers seldom schedule special conferences to tell the parent that the child is doing well in school or behaving in class. If the parent does not know why the conference has been scheduled, the prospect is frightening. Even if the parent is aware that the child has a school problem, she is still anxious about its extent and seriousness. This anxiety can be expected to increase as the date for the conference approaches. When the time for the conference arrives, the parent (assuming she has conquered her resistance sufficiently to attend) has worked out some way of handling her anxiety. A good teacher can recognize several of these ways.

One way is to blame the teacher for not teaching the child appropriately or not giving him enough individual attention. Another way is to deny the existence of the problem, even in the face of overwhelming evidence. The parent may extravagantly blame herself or defend the child from accusations of academic failure by insisting that he is just stubborn or lazy. The teacher should realize that expressions of anxiety are not unusual: she should be prepared to deal with them.

HOW CAN TEACHERS HELP PARENTS reduce their anxiety about the conference? If the child is in a regular class and his academic or behavioral problem has never been discussed, the teacher can help most by being honest, specific, and calm when requesting a conference. Far too often the parent is informed of a special conference by a note sent home with the child which specifies only the time, date, and place of the conference and nothing else. The parent will immediately (and probably correctly) assume that the conference will be negative; and so she will begin to worry. One common, though regrettable, parental reaction is to ask the child what he has done, thereby involving him unnecessarily and destructively in the mounting anxiety of the parent. It would be impossible (and perhaps not even desirable) for the parent to dispense with all concern about the impending conference. It is wise, however, to allow the parent to focus her concern and to reassure her that she is going to the conference to communicate with a human being—not to fight an impersonal system. Simple changes in the note, however, can help allay the parent's anxiety. It might also help if the teacher can telephone the parent rather than send a note. Sometimes teachers hesitate to do this because they are afraid the parent will insist on discussing the problem on the telephone, but this seldom happens. When the parent does suggest this, the teacher can point out firmly that she feels it would be more helpful to discuss the child at a conference.

Whether the teacher telephones the parent or writes her a note, the wording is important. A sample telephone approach might be:

> Hello, Mrs. Jones? This is Mary Black, Donald's teacher. I've been concerned because Donald has been having some problems in reading. I'm interested in getting to know more about him and what he is like outside of class because that might help me and some of the other people here at the school to help Donald do better. Could you come in to talk with me on Thursday, October 3, at 3:15? Thank you. I'll see you on Thursday at 3:15 then.

This simple format says several extremely important things to the parent. First, it says, "I am a real person with a name and I am Donald's teacher, so I do have a legitimate reason for being interested in his progress." Second, it says that Donald does have a problem but it does so calmly. The message expresses interest without panic, and conveys the impression that there are steps to be taken to alleviate the problem. It focuses the parent's attention on a specific area—reading. The message conveys respect for the parent and expresses the feeling that the parent has a valuable contribution to make without shoving the entire responsibility—and therefore the entire blame—on to her. It conveys an interest in the child as a total person, not just as a class problem. Finally, the message states a specific time when the parent will be able to take constructive steps with another interested person to deal with the problem. That is a lot to say in a few words, but it will help to alleviate the parent's vague anxiety and help her to focus her thoughts constructively. It will not be necessary to ask the child what he has done. When the child asks about the coming conference, some parents will continue to say, "We're going to discuss your poor reading." Most, however, will be more likely to follow the teacher's lead in phrasing and say something like, "Mrs. Black says you're having some problems in reading and she'd like to talk to me to see if we can figure out some ways to help you read better.

NOW THAT THE TEACHER has lessened the parent's initial anxiety and negative feelings, the conference should go much more smoothly. If the parent does come to the conference anxious or hostile, the teacher needs to help her to overcome this. The teacher's ability to help the parent depends partly on her own ability to convey certain traits and attitudes. The teacher must convey a sense of confidence in herself as a person and as a teacher without becoming arrogant. She must convey her sincere interest in helping the child develop as a person and as a student. She must also convey respect for the parent. This means she must not be overly anxious or even hostile herself. A teacher can become so oriented to the child's problems that she does not realize the parent may have exhausting personal problems of her own—problems which may prevent full attention to the child's problem, no matter how all-important it may seen to the teacher.

The teacher's first duty at the conference is to determine the parent's present understanding of the child's school problem. If the parent is not aware of the problem, or actively denies the problem, or evades the problem ("If the school taught reading right, my child wouldn't be having this problem") the teacher must first deal with the parent's attitude. Misconceptions can often be clarified, but problems of attitude are more difficult. Above all, the teacher needs to be sure that the parent understands exactly what the teacher is trying to say, although teachers, like all professionals, lapse naturally into their own jargon and easily lose sight of the fact that "school words" may not be "household words." Impressing the parent—even for the legitimate purpose of establishing the teacher as an expert whose opinion is worth listening to—is seldom effective in the long run. An attitude of sincere interest and confidence in being able to help will do far more than any jargon to impress a parent.

The words the teacher chooses are just as important as they were in the teacher's initial note or telephone call. Words like *never* and *can't* should be avoided. If the parent gets angry at the school, it may be helpful for the teacher to say, "I understand that you feel angry." To say "I understand why you would feel angry" involves the teacher unnecessarily in an attack against the school that she probably never intended and, furthermore, it places her in a compromising position. For the teacher to reply by defending the school is equally unproductive, for it forces the parent into an emotional defense of her own statements—no matter how unreasonable.

At this point, the teacher can take several possible approaches to the parent, depending on how the parent understands the problem and how willing she is to cooperate. There is no pat formula for evaluating this but some general guidelines can be offered. If the parent seems able to concentrate on the problem without undue anxiety, to respond appropriately to the teacher's lead, and to be ready to work on ways of alleviating the problem, the relationship is probably on firm ground. The teacher, however, should continue to be sensitive to subtle forms of resistance. Overt hostility or denial are fairly easy to distinguish; but because the teacher is used to passive acceptance from her students, she may not recognize parental passivity as resistance. Thus, the teacher may move too quickly into a plan for helping the child when the parent is not yet ready to cooperate or may not even accept the necessity for cooper ation. One guide to passive resistance in the parent is not how much she accepts but how much she contributes to the mutual discussion of the problem. When the parent stops saying "I understand what you mean," and begins saying "I've noticed that he . . ." there is solid indication that the parent has begun to cooperate.

BECAUSE OF HER TRAINING and her regular professional responsibilities, the teacher is usually very confortable in the role of giving information and suggesting courses of action. However, people tend to be more receptive to ideas they have expressed themselves and more eager to work on plans they feel they have developed themselves. Thus, the teacher needs to encourage the parent to tell about related problems she has observed at home and develop suggestions for helping the child.

Parents of children with school problems sometimes contribute to those problems themselves. The teacher must be able to judge the severity of the parent's own difficulties and the parent's ability to modify either the home environment or her relationship with the child in realistic and constructive ways. Different parents are ready to respond to different approaches from the teacher. Some parents, particularly those who were already aware of the problem and were providing a healthy emotional environment at home, are able to respond constructively and quickly when provided with appropriate information about the child's difficulty and the resources available to help him. Teachers usually feel quite comfortable in this kind of situation, and handle it well. Unfortunately, however, many teachers fall into the trap of thinking that *all* parents respond to this approach.

The parent who is aware of the problem, either because she has discussed it with school officials in the past or because she has observed the child at home, may have become caught up in anxiety about the problem. Anxiety over an extended period, especially if the parent can find no solution, can leave her in an emotionally wrought-up state. If the teacher lets the parent talk about her anxiety, and accepts this as normal, many parents can begin to cooperate.

Another problem the teacher may encounter is the parent who is so concerned with some other problem that she has no emotional resources left to concentrate on the child's school problem. It is not the teacher's professional role to work with the parent toward solving the other problem unless it is unusually simple. The teacher may, of course, help the parent contact professional help. It *is* the teacher's role, however, to help the parent sort out the two problems, see how they interrelate, and work toward helping the parent develop a realistic perspective about the need for working on the child's school problem despite other worries.

Some parents have chronic and severe personal problems that require the help of a specialist, such as a psychiatrist, psychologist, or social worker. Teachers should learn to recognize such situations. The adjustment of people with emotional problems is often unstable, and the teacher should always remember that any attempt to modify the situation could aggravate the problem. If the teacher suspects a problem of this kind, she should seek the opinion of a qualified professional and concentrate on obtaining help for the parent rather than on solving the immediate school problem.

Sometimes a parent has ways of responding to her child which defeat her efforts to remedy the child's school problem. This can be seen particularly clearly in parents of children with learning disabilities. Such parents sometimes develop stereotyped ideas about what a child should be able to do, whether or not the child actually can. Comparatively, this is not a difficult problem to work with; but it can be extremely time-consuming, because the teacher must review the parent's responses step-by-step, using specific instances, until the parent can develop more appropriate responses and expectations.

ONE OF THE CRITICAL POINTS in communication between teachers and parents comes when they discuss the educational diagnosis. If the parent has been thoroughly briefed on the child's problems, the shock of the diagnosis may be less severe. All parents can be expected to have some reaction to the application of an unflattering label to their child. Some parents who are well prepared are, because of their own personality, able to handle this without further help. Some parents are not. In our society, a child reflects on his parent's status and self-concept. Once the label "Learning-disabled" has been applied, the parent has difficulty ignoring the implications. If the child is then assigned to a special class, it makes the problem seem even more irreversible to the parent—and to the child as well. The consequent relief from unrealistic demands made on him may compensate the child to some extent, but it can never undo the blow to the self-esteem of parent and child both.

Above all, even though the cause of learning disabilities is seldom known, and even though there often seems no way the parent could have avoided the problem, teachers must realize that parents often do feel responsible and even guilty for having caused the problem.

One common suggestion is that the parent help the child with school work. This is most likely to be the material with which the child has the most difficulty at school. Thus, the child is in the unenviable position of failing consistently in front of the most meaningful adults in his life. Furthermore, helping the child with material he finds difficult is extremely frustrating to most parents. This does neither the parent nor the child any good: it interfers with the role of the parent in helping the child develop a good self-image. If extra help is important, tutoring by someone besides the parents should be arranged.

Thus, developing skill in working with parents is not easy. Teacher-education programs should, therefore, consider making it part of the practical preparation, or at least provide simulated experiences. As for the teachers in the field, they need to overcome their resistance to calling the conference, to help parents overcome their resistance and, most important, teachers must learn how to promote cooperation in helping the child achieve.

SCHOOL is for . . .
PET SHOWS

The "In-Group" Is Interviewing

DR. R. C. BRADLEY

All teachers confer at one time or another with parents. Many teachers across this country are beginning to confer on a scheduled basis. There are many valid reasons for this trend. The traditional gradecard has become outmoded. Traditional classroom organization is being revised. Many school systems are adopting non-graded systems at elementary levels. Likewise, modified versions of self-contained classroom units are upward instructional moves.

There is growing interest in many school districts for the elementary principal to be held accountable for the instructional problems occurring in his building. Teachers and principals themselves desire help in becoming more adept in visiting with parents. Hence, one of the first programs often undertaken is upgrading the effectiveness with which the building staff reports progress of pupils to parents.

There is much discussion among prominent educators of the possibility that gradecards will soon be abandoned from our educational system. Several national and state organizations have indicated their willingness to support such a move.

Equally, if not more importantly, pupil instruction at the elementary level is becoming more highly *personalized*. The needs of pupils are met in a greater number of small-group and individual instructional settings.

One of the many faceted school tasks is—communication with parents. Therefore a major purpose of this Monograph is to help those who have any part in conferring with parents on the subject of pupil progress. It begins with ideas for those who have not had experiences in conference organization and ends with some creative conjectures to aid teachers who are already experienced in interview techniques.

Bradley, R. C. *The "In-Group" is Interviewing.* A Bassi Association Monograph Publication: Denton, Texas. December 1971. 1:1-4.

Tools for Effective Interview
Operation

Materials the Principal will need in Establishing an Interview Program. For brevity, it can only be stated that these materials* must be considered as essential to conference establishment.

1) Prepare a letter to parents indicating what the new parent-teacher interview system is all about. (What?   Where?   When?   Why?).

2) Prepare a second letter to go out a few weeks prior to the fall and spring conference sessions. This letter invites the parents to select a time and day that they would like to come for an interview.

3) Prepare short, ditto reminders for parents. These should be given to them just a few days before the regular conference session is to begin. Each parent will receive his assigned time, date, and place to appear for his conference. This affirmation can be sent home by his own child.

Teacher Materials. Most teachers will profit from the use of an interview guidesheet. These guidesheets can be prepared for uniformity purposes by the school district or by committees of teachers on respective grade level assignments (E.g.: kindergarten, primary, intermediate, upper, special education, and special services.) A carefully designed set of guidelines appears in the text, *Parent-Teacher Interviews, A Modern Concept.*

Guidesheets for actual interview purposes are important because they reduce to a minimum: oversights, forgetfulness, guesswork, admonitions, and feelings of inadequacy about what to report. The teacher who uses a guidesheet will know *what to report* because those kinds of suggestions and ideas are recorded on it. Beginning teachers, particularly, will know just what to do. Established teachers will find criteria with which to compare what they actually do to what is professionally recommended.

Moreover, guidesheets are helpful within the actual interview because there is no question as to where the conversation is at a given moment. That is, if parental questions or injections distract or divert the interviewer from earlier basic premises, it takes only a glance at the interview guide to see where the last pencil check was made at the time of departure. This allows one to immediately pinpoint the spot at which the structured interview should begin once again.

Experienced interviewers have found that talkative parents can be redirected to the guidesheets more effectively than in situations where they were not used. By simply saying, "I believe we should return to the guidesheet now in that I did want to be sure to tell you about this section," results not only in refocusing of the attention of the highly verbal parent to the current issue, but sharpens his listening pattern.

An *interview schedule sheet* is also needed. On this sheet the name of the parent and child, job occupation, time of conference, and related information are recorded. (See sample which follows):

INTERVIEW TIME SCHEDULE

MORNING _____
(date)

Time	Parent's Name	Occupation	Child
9:00-9:15			
9:15-9:30			
AFTERNOON			
1:00-1:15			
1:15-1:30			
NIGHT			
7:00-7:15			
7:15-7:30			

Listing the parent's occupation is important because likely it will indicate something of his educational background and the interviewer can couch his ideas in that frame of reference and pitch his conversation to the level of understanding of the participating parent. It is a good practice to list the child's name at the side of his parents to avoid giving the wrong report if there are two or more families with the same last name represented in the room.

A third type of record is needed by the teacher; namely, the *follow-up conference sheet*. After the initial parent-teacher conference is held, or immediately after all conferences are completed for the room, the teacher should jot down a practical report of each parent conference. It should be brief and specific in most cases. Only where unique problems exist does it need to be more elaborate. Particularly if suggestions for action were given, and in a few weeks a follow-up conference is to be conducted to determine the extent of progress, then that information should be *recorded. Interview caution:* In the case of possible failures, discipline cases, underachievers, gifted children, and problems appertaining to all areas of *exceptionality*, the principal should receive a carbon copy of your notations in the event that you feel his help will be needed. On any type of problem case the principal should be informed early regarding it—the problem, the recommendations, the progress, the receptiveness of the parent (or lack of it).

Interview Habits to be Cultivated

Collect and save a variety of classroom papers on each child. From a reservoir of daily papers collected from each child, select some representative ones for showing at conference time. After you have made your collection let the child see what you are going to display, then ask him to supplement your selection with five or six papers that he chooses.

This method insures some balance between (perhaps at times) divergent points of view.

Remember that any papers shown to parents should be carefully analyzed: (a) scoring should be correct, (b) misspelled words underlined, (c) grammatical usage corrected, and other routine matters commonly considered in scoring of papers should be accounted for wherein feasible. There is rarely anything more embarrassing to a teacher than to find, upon showing the paper to the parent, that "oversights" have resulted in scoring the paper improperly. To have a problem in arithmetic checked (√) incorrect, when it is right, is deemed equally as serious to the parent as would be his discovery of an unchecked problem which should have been marked wrong. *Interview caution:* It is wiser to have a few papers checked thoroughly and carefully for display and discussion purposes, than it is to show several samples which deserved closer analysis by the red pencil.

Designate a portion of the conference time to reporting similar information on each child. Conferences are used to *personalize* our conduct with both parent and child. That is, the setting is provided in which our carefully selected words tell a parent we care about his child, we expect good things of him, that his child has *worth.* Yet on the other hand interviews serve another major purpose: opportunity is provided to *individualize* our report about each child. However, individualization should not rule out the fact that parents will talk with one another as they leave school, carpool together, or meet at club activities and parties. Consequently, five minutes of any 15 minute conference period should be given to a structured schema of reporting for all grades and classes.

To illustrate, all primary teachers may decide that in the forthcoming report session each parent will receive a report of his child's progress on the use of the five major word attack skills in reading, while intermediate level teachers may select critical reading skills (inference-making, seeing relationships, cause-and-effect patterns) as the area in which commonality among reports will be sought.

The remainder of the conference time (10 minutes) might be given to personalized comments about a parent's child which are only characteristic in nature to his work habits, attitudes, and abilities. *Interview caution:* Conferring orally with parents provides opportunity to discuss their child's individual assets and liabilities quite thoroughly, but some conference time should be reserved for comparing him with his class, school norms, and national standards. Much of this information would come from standardized tests measuring intelligence or academic achievement, supplemented by results derived from teacher-made tests.

Seek "to get" information as well as "to give" it. In a typical 15 minute conference an upward limit of approximately 3250 words are exchanged. Each parent comes to the conference wanting to ask certain specific questions, yet sometimes, they cannot get up the nerve to do so. Some parents know what they want to find out but can't choose the right words to ask it. In this light, then, the competent interviewer will seek to trigger off some questions that will aid the parent in his effort to query about content subjects, behavioral traits, and the like which he wants to know about, but doesn't have the educators dialogue to express himself. Through the questions one devises to help parents get information from the interview, one receives insights into these same parents' knowledges, feelings, and beliefs about the subject at hand.

Information *to get* from parents becomes quite *individualistic* wherein their child is concerned. One may need to know why the child is so tired each day (as if he seemingly needs more sleep). Perhaps the child is crying profusely at school and the teacher needs the parent's opinion as to why or what might be causing this. *Interview caution:* Never have your feelings extended to be hurt when you query parents about problems of their children. They will tell you! Since not all parents have the education that you have, their frankness must be appreciated even though tactfulness is sometimes lacking.

Remember, for the child who doesn't want to come to school, the parent may unjustly place the blame upon the school. However, the school could be at fault. The child is having trouble with his peergroup or his classwork may be beyond his ability to cope with it. For those who truly want to know what the problem is, *then ask!* Consider this fact (lamentably) wherein the home is at fault, likely the problem will be more difficult to correct than if the condition is attributed to neglect of the school. Each school problem ought to be solved wherein negligence is determined as the major contributing factor.

Creative Conferring

Everybody likes to be creative. Be a creative interviewer. Try the following:

    1) Refrain from using names of pupils on charts and graphs for all parents to see. Use symbols instead of names: "On the spelling graph, your child's number is 5!" This technique allows you to place all children's work on a single sheet for composite work purposes but only the parent being interviewed knows the number you've assigned to his child.

    2) Hand out education materials that you want certain parents to read which really relate to problems of their child. These can range from free booklets to lists of books that would be good for them to purchase for birthday presents.

    3) Have a 3-way conference sometime. Let the child come and participate in some opening minutes of the conference.

    4) Bring children in on the planning for the conferences with their parents. Much can be learned during those planning moments regarding each child's anxiety, if any, toward his forthcoming interview.

    5) Recommend TV programs, special excursions, activities and events, development of parental school codes, and the related types of parent participation that makes for better schools. The learned parent is a voting parent.

Summary

Parent-teacher interviews are on the way "in" in most modern programs of public school education. To be counted among the IN-group one only has to abandon traditional forms of reporting and adopt the favored INTERVIEW SYSTEM. For too long the gradecard has reflected the faults, weaknesses, and handicaps of children in some weird statistical fashion from comparing youth to one another, down to forcing their abilities into some preconceived lettergrade mold.

The parent is still a major cog in an elementary school child's spin of his educational wheel of fortune, consequently he is entitled to learn firsthand of the factors contributing to his child's success at school. Nevertheless, an interview must be judged not so much by what it means to a parent as to what it does for his child.

Chapter VIII

The Teacher "Subbing" As Counselor And Guidance Specialist

Every teacher is of necessity a guidance specialist in function, with or without training. The idea that the teacher is the key person in a school guidance program and that he should work in close cooperation and harmony with the guidance specialist has received fairly wide acceptance. This concept attests to the fact that guidance and psychological services for children cannot be the function and prerogative of one group of professional specialists. Since most schools thus far at elementary levels do not have guidance and counselor specialists, then it behooves the teacher to function at times as if he were such a specialist but he should never lose sight of the "as if" quality.

The selections of this Chapter are based on the assumption that the school's function is to educate and the teacher's function is to facilitate learning; therefore, to be effective at times one must acquire the special tools of support personnel. In order to work through certain relationships with the child, a teacher often needs to view the child from the guidance specialist's vantage point.

SCHOOL is for . . .
CONFERRING

The Many Facets of a Child

MARTIN L. STAMM and BLOSSOM S. NISSMAN

The teacher and administrator realize that much is yet to be done in areas of human relationships, in improving the classroom climate, and in meeting the needs of the child as he functions both in and outside the school environment.

No longer are reading, 'riting and 'rithmetic completely adequate requirements in preparing a child for middle-school and high-school experiences in contemporary society. The understanding of human relationships is the passport to human effectiveness. Development of wholesome relationships enables each individual to function optimally within the school as well as within the ever-changing society of today.

There exists a keen awareness of the need to help children learn more about themselves and to increase the effectiveness of the instructional program within the elementary school. For obviously, awareness of the uniqueness of each child is necessary in determining and developing a well-rounded educational experience.

To improve a child's performance it is necessary to understand and consider the many facets that determine a child's actions, motivations, and the extent to which he uses his talents and innate abilities. How can the teacher learn more about the child? Other than through examination of testing results and cumulative records, how can the teacher find information important in determining the personal needs, deficiencies, talents, and experiences of the child? Without this information, how can the teacher really provide relevant educational information?

Many interesting techniques may be used to supply information for the teacher that will be helpful without making the child feel he is just answering meaningless questions on an application form.

One of the techniques involves the use of an outline map of the world as a backdrop for a bulletin board. This can be drawn easily by even the youngest student with the aid of the opaque projector. Infor-

Stamm, Martin L., and Nissman, Blossom S. "The Many Facets of a Child." *NJEA Review*. February 1972. 45:12-15.

mation gleaned about the children could include locating where they were born, locating the states they have visited, and locating where they have lived and attended school. It is not unusual, in this mobile society of today, to find children placing their pictures (a good source of identification) on practically every state in the United States as well as on foreign soil.

In addition, a small car, plane, and boat can be attached to the map by a long piece of elastic or string. Using each mode of transportation, the child can illustrate for the group how he crossed the country by plane or car, and how he would have to go if traveling by boat. This realistic lesson in geography, in addition to providing the teacher with clues as to the child's past experiences, shows his ability to communicate to the other children. The world map has endless possibilities of exploration for the creative teacher.

When studying about foods and vocations, the teacher can add to this map by encouraging the child to examine labels of canned goods and determine where the products originated. A variety of foods can be pasted in their state or country of origin to give a vivid and colorful picture to the child of the natural resources and industries of their state, country, and around the world. As each type of food or industry is explored, information about the occupations within their areas could be discussed. Each area of exploration leads to another of related interest.

Determine Environment

To determine family relationships and home environment, the teacher can develop a "family album" made up of five or six pieces of drawing paper stapled together in booklet form. Each page will illustrate some part of the family group. It is important to note that this does not mean identification of mother, father, sister, or other relatives, because there will be children within each classroom group who do not have this family arrangement.

Taking this into consideration, the teacher identifies family relationships in the following categories: 1.) The person who takes care of you. This can be any adult in the home, but not necessarily the parent. 2.) Children who live with you. This can be any child even though not a sister or brother. 3.) Your favorite pet. This can be anything from a stuffed dog to an elephant. 4.) My room. This will illustrate the part of the home the child feels is most important to him.

Children love this "family album," and parents usually save it for many years as the treasured collection of their child's thoughts in pictures.

Knowing the parents or guardians of a child is important. How many times has a teacher been heard to say, "Now that I've met Mary's mother I understand why Mary acts the way she does!"

To meet parents in a social setting, other than the formal parent-teacher conference, the teacher can provide a "Family Day." As a planned time, sweetened by treats prepared by the class, "family" is invited to come to school to share a treasure about which father, mother, or grandmother can tell a story. Children are fascinated when grandmother shows the class the tiny-size dress she made by hand for the child in the classroom. The old-fashioned doll saved by mother with its fragile face is a history lesson not easily forgotten. Yet, at the same time it tells the teacher a lot about the child's parent. This occasion has another vitally important aspect—that of pride in the family heritage.

Puppet shows are excellent mirrors of a child's thoughts and feelings. Here, he can act out in dramatic play his feelings about situations presented to him. Puppets can be made of simple materials. Clothespins, socks stuffed with paper or rags, balloons covered with papier mache, and toys tied to strings make wonderful actors in the empty carton cut out for a stage.

Records can be used for many activities in exploring a child's interpretation of life around him. Why does Jimmy always feel the person in the story must get hurt? Why does Susie never mention Daddy in a story about families? The teacher can learn much about the child from these creative verbal and manipulative expressions. The child can also learn about himself.

A well-known tale can be used effectively in its entirety as the children are encouraged to portray the parts spontaneously as the record plays. It is interesting to note the child who always wants to be the villain and the one who will volunteer only for sweet and gentle roles. It is even more interesting and revealing to the teacher to watch as the pent-up anger is often given an opportunity for release in an accepted manner.

Appreciated For Behaving

The child who always finds himself target of the teacher's reprimand because of his disruptive activity in class suddenly finds himself the "star" and highly appreciated for behaving in exactly the same manner with approval of all. What a triumph for that child! He has found a place within the group. He has found a way to make a unique contribution to the group. It is not surprising to find this child more willing to follow rules in anticipation of further rewards from the same group.

The teacher understands that a child's yearning for approval and success will increase once he has had a taste of it. The child who has seen nothing but failure and disapproval has nothing to strive for. It can probably be likened to the inability to eat just one potato chip: it is delicious; it is a satisfying experience; he will want to experience it again.

Pride is a powerful catalyst of motivation. When a child can share his successes with those whom he wants most to impress, he will have good reason to achieve. Usually his parents and peers are the ones from whom he seeks this approval. To learn for the sake of learning is an outgrowth of this feeling of pride.

Through display of his work in an attractive manner, this end can be achieved. One procedure could be used during the annual "open house" held at most schools. Using large sheets of brown frieze paper, the teacher has each child lie down on this paper as she traces around him with magic marker. This is cut out by the child who then draws himself within this life-size outline. This "image" is placed in the child's seat, and samples of work are displayed on his desk. As parents enter the room they try to identify their child by the drawing and then examine the child's work.

Child Has Talent

Every child has some talent in something of which his parent can be proud. This does not display the work in a comparative manner as on a bulletin board, but gives the parent an opportunity to see his child as an individual. It is also an attractive sight to see all those colorful "children" smiling a greeting to "their" parents. Most parents have little difficulty identifying their child's work because of hair color, coloring style, or clothes illustrated that they recognize. It also gives parents a vivid picture of the teacher's view of their child within the group.

A usual reaction is "I'm exhausted with two at home, how do you manage 25?" Appropriate understanding between parent and teacher is significant of the child's behavior. A child who realizes the teacher has a "direct line of mutual interest" with his parents concerning his work and his behavior will try a little harder to live up to the responsibilities he knows are expected of him.

Some children are very shy and hesitate to express themselves before the group. A good method of helping them become a part of the group situation is through the use of a tape recorder. The child is given an opportunity to describe himself over the tape in an effort to draw a verbal picture. After several children have done this, the tape is played to the class, and the children try to guess who best fits the description given.

This not only gives the child a chance to participate but gives the teacher some insight into the child's feelings about his own image. The class is encouraged to look for clues by listening to the voice, description, and personal comments. The shy child then realizes he is noticed by others in the class and in turn builds up his self-confidence. This can be done effectively in the beginning of the school semester and will help the class as well as the teacher get to know one another better.

As the children become acquainted, and begin to recognize one another's voices, a variation of the same procedure can be used—having each child describe another child in the class. Children then quickly realize how little they notice about their friends and will make a greater effort to show more interest in one another. With this awareness of others, the child also increases his awareness of things about him and in turn often becomes more attentive in class as well as more interested in his self-image.

Activities that highly motivate performance usually achieve the best results. It is not unusual for the teacher to use the autobiography to discover a child's interests, needs, and potential. The difficulty in the lower grades lies in the fact that the young child does not have sufficient writing skill to express himself.

To compensate for this, the teacher can set aside some time each day for each child to dictate this information. It is then typed on a primary typewriter and pasted on 9" x 12" construction paper. The child draws himself or illustrates his "story." All these autobiographies are combined into booklet form with yarn and a hard cover front and back.

The teacher keeps this until the middle of the school year and then adds it to the regular storybook collection on the library table. What an exciting experience for the child to see the story he once dictated and now can read on his own. It soon becomes the most popular "book" on the table. The children find great enjoyment in reading about themselves and identifying one another.

Concerned About Attitude

Every classroom teacher should be concerned about the development of attitudes of the children toward one another. Overt activity does not always tell a true story. At every level, the format of the sociogram can be used successfully in determining individual as well as group needs. Understanding of normal development is vital in determining the significance of response.

Often in the primary grades a child is "chosen" by other children because the children feel this is the teacher's choice. In contrast; in the older grades, a child is often looked upon negatively by his classmates because the teacher shows this favoritism. The teacher considers the emotional levels of the children when examining the results of group evaluation.

The procedure used is as follows: The children are given a list of character traits such as happy, sad, go-getter, moody, lazy, ambitious, reliable, and so on, and a list of responsibilities, such as chairman of a committee, president of the class, or song leader, and finally a complete relisting of all these traits and jobs. Next to the first set of words and responsibilities, each child places one or two names of children within his class he feels would best fit the description.

On the second listing, he would rate himself to show the areas in which he feels he rates highest and has the most interest, as well as the traits that describe him most accurately in his own estimation. From these listings, the teacher can discover much about the child and the interrelationships within the classroom.

As the child progresses in school, he is more capable of verbal expression but often less willing to reveal his problems, conflicts, or misunderstandings. This is probably because it becomes a threatening experience to admit faults or inadequacies. To meet this need, the teacher can use a technique within his language program of creative writing.

Express Themselves

Students are given various titles to expound upon that would permit expression not directly identified with themselves as a person. For example, the topic, "How would you feel if you were a bottle cap?" would permit varied creative thought. This type of composition often reveals what a child feels he cannot do and would do if he were someone or something else. It is the type of composition not limited by rules and regulations of society.

A first grader dictates: "If I were a bottle cap I would put all my toys in my bottle and close me up so my little sister can't wreck them when I have to go to school and she is home."

A third grader writes: "If I were a bottle cap I would collect all people that make wars and lead them into my bottle and close them up until they learned how bad it is to be a prisoner. Then they would be happy to be free and not fight anymore!"

A sixth grader writes: "If I were a bottle cap I would pop my lid!"

Another said, "I would just hope that the soda inside my bottle was the kind I like!"

As the children become more familiar with this freedom to write, their stories become more detailed and more significant of their real feelings.

When working with students on building vocabulary, the teacher can discover much about a child. With investigation into such areas as "What words make you think of happiness, fear, anger," much is told by the child. Not only will the teacher help strengthen vocabulary concepts, but he will see clearly the quiet child who makes illogical analogies and perhaps needs professional help.

The teacher is not playing the role of analyst or psychologist, but merely provides the opportunity for the child to express himself in an interesting and personal manner. The teacher is sensitive to the child, and the child is encouraged to think and put his ideas and feelings in their proper perspective. It is more than likely to lead to sound group discussions and give both teacher and child a chance to explore the child's success in his educational and social environment.

Such non-test techniques of appraisal can be used effectively within the elementary school. Variations of other techniques, such as anecdotal records, observations, cumulative records, rating scales, questionnaires for pupil data information, sociodrama, and case studies, are also effective methods to be used by the teacher for evaluation and appraisal.

Anecdotal records can be very helpful to the classroom teacher, counselor, and principal. Whenever the teacher feels something significantly important happens concerning a child, he jots it down. The teacher does not limit these comments to abnormal behavior, discipline problems, or other negative remarks. Interesting remarks and expressions of talent or concern for a specific area of the school program, as well as specific physical signs (such as a squint or tic), provides clues to the teacher.

The interesting remark is a treasure to be shared with the parent at a conference, the talent discovered helps the teacher understand the areas of learning that need deeper exploration, and the physical signs may be a signal that a follow-up by the nurse or family doctor is needed.

In the busy day of the teacher, many worthwhile experiences are forgotten. A short notation acts as a reminder and in turn gives the teacher a closer understanding of the child. Behavior patterns are seen in their proper perspective, and if other help is needed for the child, the teacher has objective information to give to the specialist.

Observe Child

Additional observation of the child can be achieved by the teacher or specialist during an activity in which the teacher does not play the role of leader. During committee reports, or when an art, music, or gym teacher is working with the class, the child can be observed casually. Relationships within the group as well as reactions to the group leader are significant in better understanding a child.

The technique chosen should serve a specific purpose and function. And secondly, the teacher should have the competencies to derive benefit from its use.

Understanding is the basis of learning. And, the teacher who understands the potential of a child can realistically plan a more meaningful instructional program. Pupil appraisal opens the doors for teachers to explore the most interesting aspect of education—understanding children.

SCHOOL is for . . .
PUPIL PERFORMANCE

The Teacher As Diagnostician

LUCY T. DAVIS and BARBARA BOINEAU

A teacher once asked a psychiatrist when young children really started to learn. He thought for a moment and then replied, "It's difficult to know what goes on in the mind of a child before birth, but a great deal of evidence shows that a child is learning as soon as he takes his first breath."

The idea that a child "learns" long before he enters school may seem surprising to some teachers. Too often educators think of "learning" as primarily reading, writing, and arithmetic or put another way—those educational skills that it is the school's business to teach.

For example, learning as defined by one teacher is the ability to write the letters of the alphabet and read independently, and to understand number values and computational skills. Another teacher may feel that the major learning for a child is to trust others, to make good choices, and to show initiative. A third teacher may say that social learning is the most important asset. Positive attitudes toward adults and peers, especially in regard to race, is the important learning.

Each of these teachers has a valid, though limited, opinion about learning; each approaches learning from his unique perspective. Each opinion contributes to a broader concept of school learning which can be defined to include the cognitive, social, expressive, emotional, and perceptual-motor abilities which the young child develops during his primary years.

Child specialists indicate that children, aged five to eight, are engaged in many types of maturation and growth. Physically and emotionally the child is moving ahead on several fronts, sometimes through major crises and in several directions. He steps away from home, sometimes before he has resolved his questions about his place in the family. In school he takes on another world of peers and experiences cooperation and competition. He has relationships with new adults who have authority over him. He learns new symbol systems and develops tools of language.

Davis, Lucy T., and Boineau, Barbara. "The Teacher as Diagnostician." *North Carolina Education*. March 1972. 2:16-17, 35-36.

Good teachers of young children have known intuitively what research reports now tell them. Experiences with deprived children have taught teachers that there are many strengths among children who carry impressive responsibilities for their ages. Experiences of teachers have also shown how difficult it is to reverse deficits which limit abilities and freedom to learn.

Most teachers develop ways of looking at groups of young children and accept that the range of normality is wide. Often after working with a class for a few weeks, a teacher can describe strengths and weaknesses of specific children. Many times, teacher opinions are as valid and useful as standardized testing results. If the learning of a child does not proceed along expected lines or within generally expected boundaries, usually the child's teacher is one of the first adults to know it.

Regardless of how simple or complex the learning problem is or how much experience or training the teacher has, the teacher plays a pivotal role in helping identify the learning problems of a child. He may ignore or deny the problems of the child, due to inexperience or to other reasons. He may become intensely involved and concerned about the problem, so much so that he is not able to perform a diagnostic, observational role with the child. Or the teacher, working with parents and with the school or community resources as needed, can help any child have a better chance to learn. These authors see the teacher as a key person in diagnosing learning problems of young children.

Educationally, the teacher is the best one equipped to assess the child's learning problem as manifested in the daily classroom. He may be the careful observer of the problem, and he can describe its nature and its relationship to the child's educational history. Until teachers feel confident and able to participate in the diagnosis of learning problems and to formulate instructional strategies for assisting the pupil in the classroom, diagnostic or prescriptive teaching and individualized instruction are empty phrases.

How is the teacher able to diagnose learning problems? First, and perhaps most important, the teacher is with the child each day. He implicitly understands his strengths and weaknesses. Most research results confirm that teachers can rate a child appropriately in regard to his cognitive development, his emotional maturity, his language abilities, his perceptual motor skills, and his social development.

It is important for a teacher to develop an initial evaluation procedure for a child or to participate in his school's assessment procedures for school beginners. Often in schools, more data are collected than used or than shared with or interpreted to teachers.

If the school collects data about school beginners, a teacher should have such information available to him about his pupils. An interpretation of the pupil data related to teaching and learning should also be available to the teacher. However, if information is not systematically collected on school beginners, a teacher can devise a program to help himself get answers to questions which seem important to him.

In a demonstration center where the authors worked with 50 young children, it was important to not only collect initial data, but to also formulate objectives to guide each child's progress in the program. After data collection, setting objectives was the second element related to diagnosing learning problems. Specification of objectives was based on the initial evaluation and data collections. Schaefer's "Classroom Behavior Inventory," a systematic method of observing and recording three types of behaviors (task orientation, getting along with others, feeling confident with self), provided a basis for formulating specific objectives for work with a child. Realistic objectives for each child in light of his characteristics, his strengths and weaknesses, represented the second factor in facilitating the learning process.

Allowing time for change to take place is the third crucial element of the teacher's diagnostic procedure. If learning involves a change in behavior, the initial observations and impressions should be followed by a period of time which allows the child to show changes in one or more areas in which he and the teacher are working.

After an interval of about six or eight weeks, the teacher may repeat the initial evaluation procedures. Such a procedure may be as formal as a test or a rating scale or it may be as informal as summarizing observations and impressions of the child's recent performance. By comparing the two evaluations made at separate time intervals, the teacher can determine whether the child is moving ahead, standing still, or moving backwards in regard to the objectives agreed on.

For example, a first grade teacher, Mrs. Adams, was concerned about Bobby. She described him as developmentally like a three-year-old rather than like the six-year-old which he was. Results from a test showed that he scored extremely low on the measures that indicate readiness for first grade instruction. Mrs. Adams individualized some of Bobby's instruction each day and encouraged him to participate in classroom activities in which he would be successful.

Each time Mrs. Adams sat down to re-evaluate Bobby's performance in learning, she noted substantial changes in several areas of his behavior. Bobby was still the slowest child in her class, but in her opinion, this was not a problem because of the growth and changes that she had noted. At the end of the year she repeated the original test, and the results confirmed her impression that Bobby had learned. At seven years of age Bobby scored at a five-year-old mental age. This was significant growth when compared to the ratio of mental age of three and chronological age of six that Bobby exhibited at the beginning of the year.

Alice was another child in Mrs. Adams' class. In contrast to Bobby, Alice scored in the top third of her class on the readiness test. But Alice's behavior had been of concern to Mrs. Adams. Alice consistently appeared tired and demonstrated a very short attention span in instructional periods as well as other times. She initiated no contacts with other children in the classroom and passively resisted the overtures other children made toward her. Mrs. Adams noted these impressions shortly after the beginning of school. Even when she attempted to interest Alice through informal conversations with her, Alice appeared non-committal.

Mrs. Adams described Alice as standing still in instructional areas. In contrast with other children who were steadily progressing over a period of time, Alice was getting further behind. Therefore, Mrs. Adams felt that Alice demonstrated a learning problem. She shared her information with Alice's parents, and with their support, referred Alice to the school counselor for a further evaluation.

Does the teacher identify or diagnose the learning problem? To identify a problem is to recognize its existence. Diagnosing a problem involves assessing, observing, and analyzing the information that has been gathered and formulating a professional opinion. Educators frequently question their ability to make an appropriate psycho-educational diagnosis from their work with a child in the classroom.

An example of the difference between identifying and diagnosing a learning problem was Mrs. Camp's work with her first grade pupils. Leslie's mother reluctantly released her six-year-old daughter on the first day of school to Mrs. Camp. She gave Mrs. Camp complete instructions on how to relate to Leslie. According to mother, Leslie was to be given "tender, loving care" with no academic demands. Mrs. Camp observed that Leslie regularly demanded hugs and kisses from all adults in the school. Her general behavior was similar to that of a very gregarious toddler. At this time Mrs. Camp could have identified Leslie as having a learning problem in growing up. Instead she chose to evaluate the child more thoroughly in a number of ways which seemed significant for teaching.

Leslie had low scores in the initial testing results, but Mrs. Camp felt that Leslie was capable of performing better. Mrs. Camp grouped Leslie with three other children and moved them into a small conference room for two short instructional periods each day, using some appropriate materials. The teacher's goal was to help Leslie feel that she could do "school type" work, that learning was fun, and that she could use her extrovertive, social assets in group learning activities.

Over a period of several months Leslie demonstrated very distinct positive changes, especially in the manner relating to adults. She also improved her gross and small motor coordination and showed increased ability to postpone immediate recognition and affection. She was able to sustain some frustration in a variety of new learning experiences.

What is the teacher's role? Most teachers are intrinsically rewarded by the progress of their pupils. When a teacher identifies a child with a learning problem, he can choose to ignore or reject the child, ignore or reject the problem, or attempt to act positively about the child's problem.

The teacher is in a unique position to observe the child in a group of children approximately his age. Also the teacher can utilize from his reservoir of experience all that he has come to know about that age and grade group. Frequently these observations are the most valuable data available for instructional planning and also for parents and clinicians who want to help the child.

The teacher and the parents can consolidate their efforts by selecting a few common objectives that can be implemented at home and at school.

If resources outside the school are needed, the teacher should be in position to help the parents understand the function of such resources or agencies, what to expect from such help, and how to initiate a request for assistance.

The wise teacher recognizes the other professional resources available for assistance about a child's learning problems. There are distinctive and essential relationships available to teachers from pediatricians, child psychologists, social workers, child psychiatrists, special educators, and other child care personnel. Also there are several problems related to learning which only selected specialists are trained to diagnose.

However, regardless of the severity of the learning problem, the child is still of central daily concern to his teacher and his parents. Developing skills and confidence in diagnosing learning problems of young children in the school setting should ease the teaching job for the teacher and should help the teacher act as a facilitator of learning for the child under his care.

Children See Themselves as Others See Them

PAUL MAZZA and CLARK TUFTE

How can elementary school children be assisted by schools to monitor their behavior independently? This question prompted us to examine the past processes by which we controlled the children in our classrooms. The methods we had used were difficult to face; yet in all honesty we had relied upon them exclusively. We were present, we scolded, we looked crossly at kids, we kept them after school, we pleaded, we reasoned, we used grades, we praised, we used privileges, we smiled, we laughed, we used parents, we ignored, and sometimes we used the principal to control behavior.

We did a lot of things, but what did the child do? The child's role in monitoring his behavior was always subordinate to an authority figure. Actually the child did not have to evaluate his behavior as this was done for him by the teacher. A child could behave in school in a given way for quite some time, and not be particularly conscious of his behavior until the teacher suddenly brought it to his attention. At this point the child had a decision to make. The decision was like a moment of truth.

> Teacher: "Albert, why are you making those faces?"
> Albert (to himself): "Oh-oh, she's mad. What did she say I was doing? Making faces. Yea, that's it. Wonder what kind of faces I was making, if I was!"
> Teacher (sternly): "Well, Albert, you haven't answered me."
> Albert: "I'm sorry."
> Teacher (relaxed): "That's better."
> Unfortunately the exchange does not end at this point.
> Albert (to himself): "She's nuts. I wasn't making any faces. Who does she think she is anyway?"

Mazza, Paul., and Tufte, Clark. "Children See Themselves as Others See Them." *Peabody Journal of Education*. April 1972. 49:235-238. Reprinted by permission of the author and George Peabody College for Teachers, copyright © 1972.

By acting as an interpreter of behavior the teacher is in a position of telling a student how he has acted. The student must decide: (1) if he did behave as the teacher indicated, (2) if the teacher operated with partial information, and (3) if the teacher were wrong. The student is in a position to either totally or partially accept or reject the teacher's interpretation of his behavior. It is quite possible that the student may even reject the teacher. How often is it that students reject teachers?

What a choice for the student! He must choose between accepting someone's interpretation of his behavior and in the process of that acceptance reject part of himself, or rejecting someone's interpretation of his behavior, thus being supportive of himself. One can easily imagine which choice has the greatest possibility of being made by the pupil.

Changes in behavior are dependent upon one of two sources, both of which are external to the child: teacher authority or peer pressure. The child is reacting to external stimuli rather than depending upon an initial self-evaluation of his behavior. We have become Pavlov's bell upon which the student could depend for control. He only has to learn how much external conformity would satisfy us. How are these processes helping him to monitor his own behavior? It seems that the approaches we have used actually have fostered a dependence on the part of the child. He is trying to please us, not himself, and too often when the bell is gone so is his desirable response.

What if a child could see his behavior as others see it? Would he react to his behavior as others had reacted to it when he saw himself through the impartial eye of a camera? Would this view of himself be enough to cause him to want to change his behavior? Our classroom for nine-, ten-, and eleven-year olds at Burris Laboratory School already had access to a video tape camera and recorder. A creative Teaching Grant from Ball State University financed the purchase of video tapes, and we were on our way to try an alternative approach to external reward and punishment as a means of changing behavior.

The basic idea was to permit the child to view himself from a different perspective than is usually available to him. Through the use of video tape his behavior would be recorded in as many different settings as possible within the classroom. This would allow the student the opportunity to view himself from a different perspective, and then to analyze his behavior for the purposes of self-assessment and establishment of behavioral goals. Through periodic recordings, progress toward the behavioral goals chosen would be evaluated by the student.

The following procedure served as the basic format in working with the child:

1. The child's behavior was video taped without his knowledge in a classroom situation chosen by the teacher.

2. Before viewing the tape, the child verbally assessed his own behavior as he perceived it during the time taped.
   a. Specific questions might be asked at this point to guide the child's assessment, but only when the child seemed to be unable to express his own perceptions of his behavior as he remembered it.
   b. This verbal assessment was tape recorded.
3. The child then viewed the video tape of himself. The teacher made no comments while the child viewed the video tape. In fact, the teacher did not need to be with the child during the viewing.
4. The child was asked to determine whether his assessment of his behavior was realistic. The child sometimes needed to listen to the tape recording made in Step 2.
5. The teacher asked specific questions about his behavior on the video tape to assist him in seeing where possible improvements might have been desirable. If the teacher was not careful he could easily lapse into the familiar role of interpreter of behavior and defeat the purpose of the video taping. If the child, even after reviewing the tape, saw nothing he wanted to change it would be wise to end the conference and try taping again at a later date.
6. Sometimes a re-viewing of the tape was desirable at this point.
7. The child would, with guidance from the teacher only where necessary, set goals for himself for changes he felt would be desirable. The teacher would help the child clarify a reasonable behavioral goal, not make a goal for the child.

The child's behavior was, at some later time and in some other situation, again video taped and the above procedure was repeated with major emphasis on the child's assessment or progress toward his chosen goals. Children became more adept at analyzing their behavior as they had more guided experiences in the process of self-analysis of their behavior.

There were no controls utilized by the classroom teachers who developed the technique of using video tape as a means of helping children become more responsible for their behavior. At this point in time the technique was being developed. Controls and experimentation would be the next logical step.[1] However, we did notice that substantial improvement occurred in several children who were utilizing the video tape self-assessment technique.

One boy almost completely monopolized class discussions. Apparently, he was oblivious to the fact that he monopolized class discussions. Then he saw and heard himself on the video tape. It was as if, for the first time, he realized how he appeared to others in the class. Con-

---

[1] A controlled study using the technique described in this article is currently being researched at Shippensburg State College under the auspices of Federal Grant No. OEG-3-71-0107.

sequently, he set a goal for himself to talk less and listen more. He was successful in meeting the goal which he had established for himself.

In one case, two girls were viewing the video tape of their behavior in the classroom. They discovered that their actions toward another girl in the room were not in keeping with their feelings toward that girl.

The video tape self-assessment technique can be used in any classroom that has access to a video tape recorder and play back unit. Either a teacher or a counselor can use the video tape equipment to help children become increasingly aware of and responsible for their behavior. Certainly the goals of a school should include helping children to become increasingly aware of and responsible for their behavior.

SCHOOL is for ...
ENCOURAGING

A Consultant Role in Elementary School Guidance: Helping Teachers Increase Awareness of the Behavior Dynamics of Children

MARY WEIKING FRANKEN

Consultation with teachers often includes an in-service experience between a teacher and an elementary school guidance consultant (Faust, 1968). The importance of this consultant role in elementary school guidance programs has been widely discussed by authorities in the field of elementary school guidance (Patouillet, 1968; Dinkmeyer, 1968; Faust, 1968; ACES-ASCA Position Paper, 1966). Teachers in a multicounty area of northeast Iowa are receiving consultant help through an in-service education program called Project ABC.

Project ABC received its name as a short way to remember the purpose of the project—increasing awareness of the behavior dynamics of children. During a time when curriculum, materials, and methods have been improving in the elementary school, the need was recognized for focusing on the most complex of all the ingredients in the teaching-learning process, namely, the child.

Sponsor of this three-year project is the Black Hawk-Buchanan County Board of Education, utilizing a Title III ESEA grant. The Project ABC staff presently includes a director, two elementary school guidance consultants, an educational media consultant, three media technicians, and a secretary. Evaluation of the services of Project ABC includes pre- and post-testing of randomly selected classes of children in the schools served by Project ABC, using the California Test of Personality to attempt to assess change in self-concept. Other data available on these children will also be utilized. The teachers of these children were also given an instrument designed to measure their attitudes toward the guidance needs of children, which will be repeated at the end of the project.

Informal evaluations include an opinionnaire sent out after the first year of the project as well as comments made by administrators and teachers. The high demand for Project ABC services and the enthusiastic response of teachers can be interpreted subjectively as a positive reception thus far in the project.

The underlying philosophy of Project ABC is to build effective learning climates for children. The role of the elementary school guidance consultant, to be enhanced in the next two years when local schools begin adding counselors to their staffs, is based on several premises:

1. The developmental approach to an elementary school guidance program, focusing on *all* children, could best be met through consultation with teachers and administrators.
2. The teacher, the most crucial agent of change for the child in school, has the most opportunity for affecting the learning climate of the classroom as well as the self-concepts of children in the class.
3. Learning climates that effectively meet the needs of students "free" a child to learn and develop according to his maximum potential.
4. Many children who can profit from counseling on a one-to-one or small-group basis can also be helped by a sensitive teacher providing a good climate for learning and human development.

Purposiveness of Behavior

One function of an elementary school guidance consultant is to help teachers identify the behavioral characteristics and needs of *all* children. A fundamental assumption for understanding behavior is the concept of basic needs (Dinkmeyer, 1965). Needs take the form of goals or motivating forces in the life of a child. When teachers stop to consider a child's behavior in terms of the child's goals and purposes, the action often makes sense. For example, a primary grade teacher may have become irritated with seven-year-old Susan for seeking approval for every answer that she completes in her workbook, even though she can do the work without help. While visiting with the elementary school guidance counsultant, the teacher may look for the motivations or meanings behind Susan's behavior. She may ask herself questions such as: "Could it be that Susan is really saying, 'I need the reassurance of your approval to know that I belong.' Or perhaps 'I am afraid of making a mistake because my sister always gets things right the first time.'?"

Once a teacher is able to identify the needs and purposes that a child's behavior is trying to fulfill, she is able to help change the direction of the motivating forces or the means and methods by which a student meets his needs or solves his problems. Four goals that a child may set for himself include attention-getting, power contest, revenge, and inadequacy as excuse (Dreikurs, 1968). An example of attention-getting behavior is given by Rudolf Dreikurs:

> Mary, a six year old girl, is shy, dependent, and charming. The oldest of three children, she has a 3 year old brother and 2 year old sister. The smallest child in the class, she was regarded by the others as the baby of the group. Mary accepted this role of baby and soon had her classmates doing for her things she felt she could (or would) not do as well as things she could do. Through a parent conference, the teacher learned more about the goals behind Mary's behavior. The teacher discovered that Mary's passive, but attention getting pleasant behavior made her the center of attention with her divorced mother and overprotective aunt, whom she stayed with during the week. Her behavior carried over into the classroom. When the teacher recognized Mary's behavior as a passive-constructive form of getting attention, the teacher thought of ways to help her gain recognition through doing—being a helper, having responsibilities, etc. When she experienced satisfaction through this "doing," it made it possible for Mary to give up the satisfaction previously obtained through passive provocation. Her attention getting behavior began to change (pp. 146-147).

When teachers become more sensitive to the feelings and needs that children express through their behavior, they are more likely to "tune in" on the things that are meaningful to each child. Learning climates improve when teachers recognize and provide for the needs that *all* children have: needs for belonging, achievement, security, love and affection, self-respect, understanding, and freedom from fear (Raths & Burrell, 1963).

During consultation with a Project ABC consultant, a teacher may explore various ideas for helping children meet their needs and may seek new approaches for working with children who are using inappropriate behavior to meet their needs.

Self-Concept and Behavior

The self-concept of a child is made up of the perceptions and convictions he has about himself. The self-concept is developmental because it continues to be influenced by experiences of the past and by anticipated experiences of the future (Dinkmeyer & Dreikurs, 1963). The cues received from "significant others" in the life of a child, including teachers, are very influential in the formation of a child's self-concept.

A child's basic need to belong is reflected in his self-concept, and a teacher has great opportunity to affect the way a child meets this need for belonging through his behavior. A Project ABC consultant has the opportunity to talk with teachers about ways a child can be helped to become responsible for his actions and can be recognized for his contributions, thereby enhancing his concept of self. A child's view of self may move from, "I am no good," "Nobody likes me," "I can't do it," to "I'm pretty good," "I can do it," "I'll get it done," "I'm pretty good at certain things and not so good at others" (Dinkmeyer & Dreikurs, 1963, p. 76).

Through consultation, teachers may come to recognize the cues they give to children that affect self-concept. They also learn how a child reveals his self-concept through his performance and behavior. Some teachers come to recognize that techniques they thought would curtail undesirable behavior instead reinforced a child's already low opinion of himself, thus provoking even more undesirable performance. They also come to realize how the children in a class imitate the teacher's cues to a child. For example, a teacher's remark, "Are you the last one done again?" is soon picked up by the whole class. If a teacher scorns or rejects a child, this can become a prevalent attitude of the entire class.

Figure 1 illustrates how the cues from "significant others" in a child's life can negatively influence his self-concept. Because behavior is a reflection of a person's self-concept, undesirable behavior is a probable outcome of low self-esteem. If most cues a child receives from "significant others" are anger, annoyance, ridicule, rejection, distrust, discouragement, or impatience, a child develops a feeling of failure and low self-esteem. His self-concept probably reflects itself in negative behavior—aggression, indifference, failure, withdrawal, tension, hostility, fear, guilt, or submissiveness.

By Contrast, Figure 2 depicts how positive cues from "significant others" in a child's life can give a child a sense of personal worth, which is reflected in positive behavior and performance. Cues like acceptance, love, concern, encouragement, security, empathy, sensitivity, and understanding give a child a sense of personal worth. His behavior and performance will more likely be characterized by success, creativity, achievement, belonging, interest, identification, co-operation, curiosity, and enthusiasm.

CHILD'S SELF-CONCEPT

Cues from "Significant Others"

Ridicule
Sarcasm
Annoyance
Rejection
Anger
Distrust
Discouragement
Impatience

Behaviors and Performances

Aggression
Indifference
Failure
Withdrawal
Tension
Hostility
Fear
Guilt
Submissiveness

Sense of Failure,
Low Self Esteem

FIGURE 1

CHILD'S SELF-CONCEPT

Cues from "Significant Others"

Acceptance
Love
Concern
Encouragement
Security
Empathy
Sensitivity
Understanding

Behaviors and Performances

Success
Creativity
Achievement
Belonging
Interest
Identification
Cooperation
Curiosity
Enthusiasm

Sense of Personal Worth

FIGURE 2

Project ABC consultants stress the importance of understanding children's self-concepts in their in-service work with teachers. Individual consultations between teacher and consultant, small and large group discussions, and the newsletter published by Project ABC provide opportunities for the teachers to share ideas about how they assess and enhance children's self-images.

Unfinished sentences and creative writing are useful in gaining insight into a child's concept of himself. The answers to the following examples of unfinished sentences may be very revealing: "I am happy when..., School makes me feel..., I worry when..., I'd like to be..., Other people think I'm..." Creative writing can be used to learn more about the subject a child knows most about—himself. Topics like "If I Had Three Wishes," "My Biggest Problem," "When I Grow Up," "If I Were the Teacher," may help a teacher understand a child's real or ideal self-image more clearly. This experience also gives the child the feeling that his teacher cares about him and his problems.

Other activities teachers use to establish good teacher-student relationships include creative art, group discussions in which children share their feelings and problems without evaluative comments, and role-playing, whereby children can try out what it feels like to take on roles different from their own.

Discussions following stories, films, or filmstrips that relate to children and their feelings are also excellent group mental health activities. Problem checklists are another tool for looking at the way a child feels about himself and others.

The Teacher's Reaction to Child Behavior

Serving a large geographical area and great numbers of teachers, the Project ABC consultants reach teachers through local and area-wide in-service meetings, workshops, and a monthly newsletter. With the help of an educational-media consultant and media technicians, the consultants present materials and lead discussions related to common developmental needs and problems of all elementary school children. The importance of the relationships between the teacher and the child and between the child and his peers is emphasized. Teachers are encouraged to explore new ways of observing and understanding the feelings of children—through observation checklists (Kough & DeHaan, 1955), sociometrics, role-playing, creative writing and art, and mental health materials (Ojemann, 1961; Mountain, 1965).

The consultants also establish relationships with individual teachers in the schools. The use of video tape has been invaluable in establishing meaningful dialogue between teacher and consultant. By teacher request, a technician takes a 20- or 30-minute tape of a classroom in progress, with an unobtrusive portable camera. Because the purpose is to help teachers be more aware of the feelings and behavior of the children, the camera focuses on the children and not on the teacher. Soon after the taping is over, the teacher and consultant view the tape together to discuss the children and their reactions. The teacher, now able to be a visitor in her own classroom, is quick to point out many things she was not aware of during the class—tone of the classroom climate and the facial expressions and feelings of individual children: discouragement, joy, boredom, tension, frustration, disappointment, pride, etc. Soon she starts analyzing the meanings of behavior, noticing and searching for ways to help children who do not have a positive self- concept or who have other problems.

The viewing of the video tape usually builds a bond of mutual concern for the children on the part of the teacher and consultant. Because there is no fear of evaluation, the teacher is also free to explore and better understand her own feelings about the children and the class. She may recognize some of the behavior cues she is giving the children and how these cues affect their self-concepts and thus behavior.

Being aware of the behavior dynamics of children does not guarantee that a teacher will be more effective. If a teacher does have a genuine concern for each child, the desire to help each child grow and develop to his maximum potential, and the willingness to make a personal investment in each child, increased sensitivity about the behavior of children is a very important ingredient in the classroom learning climate.

REFERENCES

1. **ACES-ASCA** Joint Committee on the Elementary School Counselor. Report of the ACES-ASCA Joint Committee on the Elementary School Counselor, Washington, D.C.: (Mimeo.) 1966.

2. **DINKMEYER, D.** *Child Development: The Emerging Self.* Englewood Cliffs, N. J.: Prentice-Hall, 1965.

3. **DINKMEYER, D.** The Consultant in Elementary School Guidance. In D. Dinkmeyer (Ed.) *Guidance and Counseling in the Elementary School, Readings in Theory and Practice.* New York: Holt, Rinehart and Winston, 1968.

4. **DINKMEYER, D. & DREIKURS, R.** *Encouraging Children to Learn: The Encouragement Process.* Englewood Cliffs, N. J.: Prentice-Hall, 1963.

5. **DREIKURS, R.** *Psychology in the Classroom.* New York: Harper, 1968.

6. **FAUST, V.** The Counselor as a Consultant to Teachers, in D. Dinkmeyer (Ed.) *Guidance and Counseling in the Elementary School, Readings in Theory and Practice.* New York: Holt, Rinehart and Winston, 1968.

7. **KOUGH, J. & DeHaan, R. F.** *Roster Workbook,* Vol. I, *Identifying Children with Special Needs,* and Vol. II, *Helping Children with Special Needs.* Chicago, Ill.: Science Research Associates, 1955.

8. **MOUNTAIN, L. H. & Mason, W. M.** *Challenge Readers.* Wichita, Kansas: McCormick Mathers, 1965.

9. **OJEMANN, R.** *A Teaching Program in Human Behavior and Mental Health.* Cleveland, Ohio: Educational Research Council of America, Rockefeller Building, 44113, 1961.

10. **PATOUILLET, R.** Organizing for Guidance in the Elementary School. In D. Dinkmeyer (Ed.) *Guidance and Counseling in the Elementary school, Readings in Theory and Practice.* New York: Holt Rinehart and Winston, 1968.

11. **RATHS, L. E., & BURRELL, A. P.** *Understanding the Problem Child.* West Orange, N. J.: The Economic Press, 1963.

The School's Role In Emotional Health

ALICE DANIELS

It's a small world, that of a child's school—a miniature reproduction of the friendships and hostilities, the successes and failures, the adventures and mishaps of the world outside. The school is the place in which for twelve years of his life the child lives, does jobs, has fun, absorbs knowledge, and develops attitudes that in most cases remain with him for life.

No wonder schools have great potential for protecting and promoting emotional health. Unfortunately, they also have great potential for damaging emotional health. Along with its main job—that of enabling a child to learn—the school has a responsibility to see that children stay healthy so they *can* learn. In the case of emotionally distressed children, the school has a further responsibility to see that steps are taken to help them. "Next to the family, the school is probably the most important unit of society as far as the protection of mental health is concerned," writes Dr. Robert H. Felix, former director of the National Institute of Mental Health.

The center of the school's role in achieving mental health is, of course, the teacher. Even though a teacher is busy introducing his charges to reading and arithmetic and social studies and physical education, there are many ways in which he can forestall mental disturbance and, if it comes, alleviate it. The most important is "to build a bridge of feeling," says psychiatrist William G. Hollister, M.D., a bridge built out of trust between teacher and pupil.

Such bridges are not new to teachers. Every teacher worth his salt tries to build one, for he knows how much easier it makes teaching and how much more effective it makes learning. Teachers know, too, that bridge building takes time. It also takes patience, genuine caring for

Daniels, Alice. "Emotional Health." *The PTA Magazine.* April 1970. 64:16-17, 36.

children, and a sure technique. Some teachers are born with these invaluable qualities. Most have to learn them, usually on the job. That is why it is so important for schools to provide in-service training to their teachers.

What are some of the elements in this bridge-building technique? Dr. Hollister tells us that one such element is establishing a good emotional climate in the classroom. This is done best not just through talk but through more subtle means of communication: tone of voice, facial expression, gestures, even ways of standing and walking.

Contrasting Climates

Miss Canfield always stood by the door in the morning as the children trooped in. She had a cheery word or at least a friendly smile for everyone. The children responded readily. "That's a pretty dress, Miss Canfield," one of them might say. Another might confide to her that his cat had had kittens last night. As the children settled into their seats, they looked forward with eager expectation to the activities of the day.

Mrs. Beaumont was usually seated at her desk when the children arrived. They never knew just what she was doing. Perhaps she was thinking up projects for today, or running over the names of those who hadn't done so well yesterday, so she could call on them first thing. Only if the children were noisy did she look up, to quell the disorder with a frown or a sharp word. The children sat down in their seats chastened, resigned, or rebellious, depending on their moods and their emotional stamina. The afternoon dismissal bell seemed impossibly far away.

Each of these teachers created an atmosphere that her class was to breathe all day, and it is not hard to see which atmosphere made a better climate for learning. Miss Canfield's students were willing, well disposed, and excited about the adventure of learning. Mrs. Beaumont's were bored, unhappy, and oppressed by the enormous weight of the learning task.

In both classes the usual discipline problems cropped up as each schoolday ran its course. As one would expect, the two teachers handled them very differently.

One day Billy was preoccupied during a unit on the geography of Greece. While Mrs. Beaumont was pointing out Greek cities on a wall map, he was playing—secretly, he hoped—with a small rubber ball in his lap. His activity didn't disturb anyone until the ball bounced out of his lap and rolled straight toward the teacher's desk. The whole class stiffened as Mrs. Beaumont turned from the map and, with majestic slowness, stooped and picked up the ball. There was breathless silence as she slowly and grimly walked over to Billy, ball in hand.

What she said to him doesn't particularly matter, for the impression had already been made. Mrs. Beaumont's gait, her demeanor, her expression all told the children, "Look here! What *I* say goes around here, and anyone who doesn't know that is going to find out. I have no respect for misdoers, nor am I their friend." No bridge here, only a gulf of resentment and fear.

Miss Canfield might have handled that incident something like this: She would finish talking about the historic Greek cities before she smiled at Billy and said, "Would you like to get your ball now and put it in your pocket, Billy? We wouldn't want anybody to stumble over it." The only reproof necessary would be her silence as she and the class waited while Billy sheepishly retrieved his property. After that the lesson would go on as before, with Billy—likely as not—looking rather shamefaced and feeling that the whole thing hadn't been much fun after all. Miss Canfield's behavior said as plainly as words, "Even when you make mistakes, I value you as a person. As you do me."

Every schoolday is filled with cues for such scenes: scenes of quiet drama and of growth, scenes that teach children that the teacher cares about them and is ready to respond to their needs.

Children's misbehavior—like that of grownups—is often due to uncomfortable inner feelings they themselves are only half aware of. A child may be puzzled and edgy because he doesn't understand what is expected of him, either by the teacher or by the class. Or he may not see any way to get himself out of a bind he has somehow gotten into. Again, he may be too excited and upset to think clearly. The sensitive teacher will recognize these difficulties and try to perceive what friendly suggestion or comment the child needs.

Unspoken Communication

"Heard melodies are sweet, but those unheard/are sweeter," said a great poet. Teachers sense those unheard harmonies (and disharmonies, too) in every classroom. That is the time for the teacher to "sing along with" Betty or Jimmie in an inaudible yet moving harmony of the spirit. In more matter-of-fact language, at these times the teacher *feels with* the child, sensing that behind his defiant words or disruptive actions there is insecurity, or anxiety, or hurt feelings. She conveys her feelings in a wordless way that is infinitely comforting and encouraging.

There are children in every classroom who desperately need this emotional support. There are children who cannot learn math or history or language because they are starved for love or recognition or security.

Their whole being is taken up in trying to get the missing emotional nourishment. For such children, acceptance by the teacher, and their awareness of her affection for them, can mean the difference between mental health and mental illness.

Only an empty classroom is without behavior problems. Experienced teachers have said that certain problems turn up each year as regularly as the common cold. Many of them could literally be plotted on the school calendar. And that is a blessing, for it gives teachers a chance to take preventive measures—not against the problems, for those nobody can prevent, but against their developing into major confrontations that will hurt the child and seriously disrupt the class.

For example, Mr. Rush, a science teacher, every now and then takes his pupils on a tour of the local science museum. All sorts of things can happen on a field trip, so Mr. Rush spends several days getting his class ready for the experience. He tells them what they will be able to see in the museum, then asks them which exhibits they most want to visit. He may draw on the blackboard a rough map showing the location not only of the major exhibits but also of entrance and exit, drinking fountains, washrooms, and lunchroom. He explains how the group is going to get to the museum and the rules to be followed so no child (and no child's mittens) will get lost.

Thus the children live through the trip ahead of time. This procedure not only extends the joy of the trip, but nips in the bud a number of anxieties that might otherwise cause problems.

Teachers can also contribute to their pupils' emotional security in another way—by giving each child an opportunity to find out what kind of person he really is. Through discussions of ethical principles and values, even young children can get some understanding of the diversity of values among their classmates. More important, they can begin to examine their own goals and standards.

The teacher can and should give all children an opportunity to relate their education to their own lives. Surely any school subject, if vividly presented, can be linked to children's experiences and interests. If Tommy cannot see what education means to him, he is likely to be an unhappy, unsuccessful student.

Another important step toward mental health that every teacher can take is to assure that each child succeeds at *something*. At school, as in the larger world, success breeds success. It builds the confidence and self-esteem that everybody needs for achievement and content. Continual failure, on the other hand, brings loss or lessening of self-respect. The wise teacher praises a child for what he does well—no matter if it's only for cleaning up the mess after a science demonstration. Then she encourages him to move toward something a little harder. Such a teacher does not expect either too much or too little of any child, for excess in either direction would jeopardize his self-confidence and eventually his mental health.

The School Administration

Next to the teacher, the school administration has the most important part in promoting mental health. Unfortunately, too many schools these days are looking the other way. They are putting dangerous pressures on children to excel, and at the same time blocking their paths with demands that breed learning difficulties. Result: The child's stability is shaken; his self-confidence shrinks. If every child is to experience in school the joy and stimulation of achievement, then the school must put less emphasis on grades and more on personality-building experiences.

Enterprising schools are offering students a chance to work in the community and to relate to adult society. The Joint Commission on Mental Health of Children urges that schools give children a role in the curriculum-planning and administrative work of the school; find ways for them to explore community activities; and involve adult community members within the school program, both as salaried employees and as volunteer workers. It is important that parents from all sorts of backgrounds become involved. When a child's parents are part of the things closest to him, he feels that home and school are connected and that he need not choose between loyalties to teachers and loyalties to parents.

When Mental Illness Looms

No matter how many preventive steps a school may take to establish a healthful educational environment, there will still be children in the school whose emotional health is already weakened. Experts estimate that 10 to 12 percent of elementary-school pupils suffer from serious emotional disorders. Charlotte Haupt, education consultant, sums up for teachers the effect of such upsets on the learning process: "If a child is loaded with anxieties when he comes to school in the morning and you cannot alleviate them, or at least let him know that you are in tune with him, he will learn nothing all day—no matter how hard you may try to teach."

Once again we must turn to the school's prime mover—the classroom teacher. That teacher must brace himself for an occasional confrontation with a severe emotional problem.

In dealing with an emotionally disturbed child, the teacher's first task is to discover what people and conditions are responsible for the problem. Many things shape children's lives—inborn characteristics, differences in cultural training, physical or developmental differences, parents' attitudes, conditions in the neighborhood and in the school itself. Once teachers understand the background from which undesirable behavior arises, they may be able to help the child cope with his problem.

At other times, group dynamics are involved. If a child has but a lowly status in the "pecking order" of the class, he may react negatively or angrily to almost everything that happens in the classroom. Not only is he emotionally upset himself; he creates unhealthy classroom situations that can leave an emotional mark on everyone concerned. Here the teacher can assist the low-status child by devising activities in which he can achieve some success and admiration.

Easing classroom pressures on a disturbed child can reduce his feeling of tension. Even a child whose emotions are at ease may under pressure practically go to pieces. For example, many a youngster who has been made unduly apprehensive about a test blanks out, giving wrong answers to questions he would ordinarily answer correctly.

Certainly regular classroom teachers cannot be expected to have the specialized training necessary for pinpointing each child's difficulty and designing a long-range program to aid him. Schools must see that teachers have an opportunity to consult with mental health specialists who, like school psychologists, understand the world of education and the problems of the school system. Thus the guidance and counseling service is one of the most important parts of any school's effort to keep its pupils emotionally healthy. The staff can spot emotional difficulties early, refer the child to community treatment facilities, and coordinate the child's education with recommended therapy.

Ideally, guidance programs at the elementary level should provide at least one full-time, fully qualified counselor for every 500 to 600 students, along with the part-time services of a psychologist. Social workers, psychiatric consultants, school physicians and nurses, and remedial teachers are all valuable members of guidance teams. And the Joint Commission recommends that classroom teachers, too, be regarded as full-fledged professionals working in partnership with other members of the guidance team.

In many schools, however, guidance services are less than ideal or are even missing entirely. Some districts are too small to provide them, and in large cities such services are frequently understaffed for lack of funds. Even if a school can afford an adequate staff, trained personnel are in short supply. Finally, the hands of even the best guidance staff are tied if there are no community facilities that can accept school referrals for treatment or therapy.

Inevitably there will be some children who are so disturbed that their regular classroom teacher, even with expert guidance, cannot provide sufficient help. In some schools, the next step is special classes for emotionally disturbed pupils.

In these classes, it is true, the disturbed child's behavior and achievement often improve. But the improvement may disappear when he returns to his regular classroom. Moreover, since the self-esteem of emotionally disturbed children is exceedingly fragile, it may be severely damaged by the stigma of being in a special class. A few school systems are developing programs that can help the emotionally disturbed child while keeping him at least part of the time in the normal classroom atmosphere. The success of this procedure depends, first, on early identification of emotional problems and, second, on close involvement of mental health specialists in planning and directing the child's program.

As long ago as the early 1960's California carried out a research project in which a screening procedure, easily administered by the classroom teacher, was used to identify children with emotionally based learning problems. Individual studies were then made of each child to determine the nature and extent of his difficulties, and a school program was planned to help him.

At about the same time, New York City instituted its Early Identifi-, cation and Prevention Program, in which a team including a guidance counselor, a psychologist, and a social worker, with the consultant services of a psychiatrist, spotted troubled children in the first three grades and planned help for them. In another New York City program, known as Play Group, an experienced play therapist meets with small groups of children once a week.

Other schools are experimenting with "crisis teachers"—specially trained teachers who work with children individually or in small groups at times when their behavior has made it impossible for them to remain in a regular classroom. The crisis teacher, in close liaison with the regular teacher, works with the child on both behavioral and academic problems until he has regained sufficient control to return to his class.

Important as its role is, the school cannot be held solely responsible for maintaining pupils' mental health. It would be unrealistic to expect any one institution to undertake that task alone, and by the time a child reaches school, his emotional patterns have already been set in the home.

Obviously schools can't force a child's family to change its attitudes or its child-rearing tactics. They can't supply magical solutions to the problems children face as they grow and develop; and they can't erase the influence on children of the culture in which they live. Amidst the upheaval and loss of morale that affect all our social institutions today some schools have been made the scapegoat for problems they reflect but have not created.

What can be done to help the schools fulfill their crucial role? A great need at present, says the Joint Commission on Mental Health of Children, "is a better meshing of school programs with other programs in the community, a greater understanding and trust between the various child- and youth-serving professions, and a greater involvement of the parents and young people themselves in the whole process of planning and carrying out programs aimed at enhancing the healthy growth and development of young people." As I understand it, this is the very need that the PTA Children's Emotional Health Project is designed to meet.

Nothing is more important than helping young people move into responsible adulthood. It would be difficult to overestimate the role of the school as a prime guarantor of emotional well-being—first in the climate it creates for children and second in transmitting the information young people need to see life sanely and whole. Children can come out of our schools with either a lifelong feeling of inadequacy and distrust or a lifelong sense of worth and responsibility—the key to emotional health.

SCHOOL is for . . .
DEVELOPING
RESPONSIBILITIES

Confidentiality of Student Records

The matter of confidentiality of student records encompasses two rather different relationships—the professional relationships among guidance personnel and other staff within a school system, and the relationships between school personnel and the community, particularly parents of attending students.

Two recent trends have brought into prominence the matter of confidentiality of records. The first is the rapid emergence of guidance and counseling and related specialties within our educational institutions. One of the hallmarks of an emerging profession is concern for its ethical responsibilities. Because of this concern, the membership of the American Personnel and Guidance Association adopted a set of ethical standards in 1961. These provide one type of guide to school personnel with regard to confidentiality.

The second trend is that of increased community interest in the schools—not only in their academic programs but in their pupil personnel programs and their modes of work with pupils. In the state of New York, this interest evolved into a legal issue over whether or not a parent had a right to inspect the school's records of his child. The judicial decision indicated that the parent was not a third party to the school's efforts to assist the child and hence did have such a right.

One of the critical points in this decision lies in the verb *inspect*, which is not synonymous with *learn about, consult,* or like verbs, which convey the idea that school personnel interpret records to parents in order that the latter may become maximally informed about their children's status. Of course, the typical interaction of school and parent would take the latter form of relationship, but the judicial decision made the parents rather than the school responsible for deciding the nature of the relationship.

Thus, we have rather sensitive issues involving transmission of infor-

---

Magoon, Thomas. "Confidentiality of Student Records." *NEA Journal* (now TODAY'S EDUCATION). December 1962. 51:29-30.

mation about students. And, of course, *information* as used here covers an extremely wide range of content—from that which is highly personal to that which is matter-of-fact and unemotional, from material gained in confidence to that gained in routine administrative fashion, and from material gained or used by a few persons with particular training and responsibilities to that which may be gained or used by all members of a school's staff.

When misunderstandings do develop within an institution as to what information should or should not be transmitted to whom and by whom, a paradox frequently develops. Staff Member A feels he cannot reveal to B certain information known to him about a student. Individual B feels that the effectiveness of his work with the student depends largely on the amount of knowledge he has of the student. The paradox here lies in the fact that both parties rest their positions on the same argument, namely, the best interest of the individual student.

In spite of the complexities involved in the matter of confidentiality of student records and the transmission of information, two generalizations can be made. First, problems of this nature will arise periodically—among the school staff and between school staff and parents or others in the community. Second, in these matters, decision making born of desperation in the face of a present crisis invites decisions of questionable quality for all concerned.

Administrators, teachers, and guidance workers in every school system should consider this question: "What is to be our position regarding matters of confidentiality in records and transmission of information?" Solutions will vary depending on particular locales, past precedents, and the orientation of those formulating the position. However, helpful guidelines have been laid down for the formulation of such a position.

Two of these are the Ethical Standards of the American Personnel and Guidance Association and a policy statement by the same organization regarding student records and their use, particularly with reference to relationships between school personnel and the parents involved.

The four points of this statement which are most germane to the issue of confidentiality of student records are as follows:

1. The best interest of the student is served when school record information is interpreted by appropriate professional personnel. Any decision as to the display of such information for visual inspection by the parent or guardian must rest with the professional judgment of the appropriate school personnel.
2. School record information may contain material prepared by other sources, such as clinics, physicians, psychiatrists, psychologists, etc. These records should be prepared in a form for use by appropriate

school personnel. It should be made clear whether such records are the property of the school or of the agency or clinic which was the source of the records. In the event of any doubt by school personnel as to their competence to interpret such material to parents, or in the event that the originators of such material do not expect it to be interpreted by school personnel to parents, then the parents should be referred to the originator of the material for consultation.

3. Education institutions are responsible for insuring that the content and manner of records gathered are limited to those materials which in the institution's judgment contribute to its efforts to educate the student. Records should differentiate between those entries which are observations and those which are inferential in nature.

4. Educational institutions are responsible for insuring through selection, training, and review of practices of their personnel that appropriate personnel are competent to use and interpret information.

The following suggestions may be useful to those who are uncertain as to the practical implication of this statement for their school system.

• Teachers and administrators should learn about and respect the ethical standards of the school counseling profession.

• Teachers, administrators, and counselors need to learn about the legal precedents in their own states regarding transmission of information. State laws and precedents vary considerably, and what may hold true in one state may have little relevance or validity in another.

• Teachers, administrators, and counselors should carefully review existing record-keeping practices. A school may well be gathering information which has little functional value.

• Teachers, administrators, and counselors should determine who within the school should have access to what kinds of records.

• Whoever is to have access to records (test scores, interview records, diagnostic reports, anecdotal records, etc.) should be systematically trained in their interpretation and use.

Setting up carefully thought-out principles and procedures regarding confidentiality and general transmission of information should result in (a) better understanding and acceptance by guidance workers, teachers and administrators of their respective contributions, roles, and prerogatives; (b) more purposeful record keeping; (c) more sophisticated use of records; (d) more effective consulation between school staff and parents of students.

It seems clear that achieving these results amply justifies the effort involved in working out wise principles and procedures for dealing with confidentiality of student records.

Chapter IX

The Teacher And His Psychological Expertise

A great teacher will have good general intelligence and an acceptable degree of intellectual brightness, but he must also have rich understandings of how to deal effectively with people. Obviously, we cannot control all the kinds of stimuli a child encounters, nor do we have the ultimate control in maintaining what gets inside his psychological or central nervous system. However, a teacher does have control over some things the child does and all of the things she says. If the classroom teacher finds positive, creative ways to provide the kind of image, the kind of stimulus, the kind of feedback that helps a child to become the type of person in him to become, likely that child is feeding upon the right type of psychological diet.

The current review of research reveals quite vividly: *Pupils tend to become the kinds of people their teachers are.* Psychologically a pupil can become the kind of person he perceives, therefore, a teacher has much to do with the kinds of perceptions a child will experience. The number of success and failures a child has in school is generally based upon the psychological expertise of his classroom teacher. In the subsequent articles information is provided which will enable the reader to improve his own self image as well as that of the pupil. Likewise some of the selected work illustrates the point that appropriate psychological behavior just doesn't happen automatically in school, it must be taught.

Fundamental Principles for Teaching by Objectives

RUSSELL N. CASSEL

During the past decade the systems analysis approach to education has served to yield new insights into the psychology of learning, and promises to bring new and higher credibility to our schools for reaching many of the usual school dropout students.[1] More recently, performance contracting, teaching accountability, and management by objectives serve to improve certain psychological dynamics introduced by systems analysis.[2] Still other writers have served to clarify certain aspects of individual differences, where lack of general intelligence has been attributed to the cause of school failure for too many of the disadvantaged, but where such lack of intelligence was mistaken for difference in background experiences.[3]

Fundamental Principles

As one examines critically the literature underlying newer teaching accountability concepts, 12 basic and rather fundamental principles emerge. Each one of these principles is related to the other in a hierarchial fashion so that succeeding ones cannot be expected to emerge effectively unless former ones are present.

Planned outcomes. The critical focus begins with clear identification of intended outcomes, and with the emergence of other principles largely dependent upon accomplishment of this first requirement. Such intended outcomes are to be stated in terms of actual performance of student expected, in terms of behavioral change, and not in terms of meaningless philosophical jargon so characteristic of the education pro-

Cassel, Russell N. "Fundamental Principles for Teaching by Objectives." *Peabody Journal of Education.* October 1972. 50:75-80. Reprinted by permission of the author and George Peabody College for Teachers, copyright © 1972.

fession, i.e., worthy home membership, good citizenship, or worthy use of leisure time, to name but a few of the meaningless ones. Without such clearly defined intended outcomes, there can be no meaningful planned learning activity or experiences. The principal focus has shifted from one of major attention to activity to one of major attention to outcomes. Not only has the attention shifted, but all other psychological aspects of the learning process are based on the presence of such expected outcomes as a necessary requisite.

Relevance. Many recent critics of present educational practices have challenged the relevance of curriculum offerings in the schools. Under the newer teaching accountability the question of relevance must be directed squarely at the expected student outcomes; under the newer individualized approach there may be an infinite number of unique activities to achieve clearly defined student outcomes. The question of relevance must always be evaluated in terms of the life-goals of the student, and school offerings must be available in terms of the individual needs of each and every student; nothing less will suffice. Teachers and guidance counselors must be able to demonstrate the relevance of specific school offerings to the pertinent life-goals of students to the respective student's satisfaction, and where such relevance is not present, other appropriate offerings must be provided so that every school may be adapted to the individual needs of each and every student.[4]

Motivation. Simply stated this means, does the student accept the stated student expected outcomes? Student goals and student motivation are, indeed, one and the same thing. Where student motivation is absent, it is evident that there is little or no personal involvement in the expected student outcomes, or it may be evidence of a physical problem of the student, i.e., glandular, mild neurological handicap, etc.[5] Self-participation in goal setting or establishment of expected student outcomes is an important aspect involved in student motivation, and where such motivation is absent it may be restored through the process of goal-setting activity.

Self-confidence. The first psychological requisite to learning or personal accomplishment of any type is the belief of the individual that such accomplishment is possible. Recent empirical findings in humanistic psychology demonstrate the importance of the learner's self-expectations in relation to learning success. The development of student self-imagery that is conducive to learning effectiveness is not an isolated phenomenon, but more often than not it is a social phenomenon that permeates a particular group. The important implication for the teacher is that the situational press, learning ecology or context in which learning occurs must reflect a positive social climate if effective learning is to emerge. Too often in the traditional classroom the comparison of success for some against the failure of others serves as the basis for developing self-confidence for select groups. It is this psychological on-slaught in the classroom which some consider to be the basis for many of the present school dropouts.[6]

Thrust. Schools have traditionally been the center of learning activity, but more often than not there was little or no relationship between such activity or school experiences and the planned student outcomes. Only through the recent systems analysis approach has the need for carefully stated student performance outcomes been accepted as a requisite.[7] *Thrust, then, means that certain activity is planned to accomplish well defined performance objectives, and that some meaningful relationship exists between such activity and the defined planned outcomes.*

Involvement. The trend towards greater emphasis on student involvement in the learning situation is longer than the recent past decade emphasis on systems analysis, and the newer teaching by objectives. More and more the teacher's function becomes one of guiding learning activity as opposed to the older notion of "dispensing of knowledge." Clearly now the emphasis is on learning with the nucleus or germ for such learning found in the personal adaptation of the student through planned learning experiences. The newer approaches emphasize the value of such involvement through gaming and simulation where students play surrogate roles, and where they can live a thousand lives of intrigue, immorality, and life and safety hazards without a single risk entailed. Such involvement serves to enhance learning, and to afford opportunities for application of learning in effective classroom situations.[8]

Variety of modes. The notion that only one type of learning activity is needed for all to achieve planned student outcomes is probably the greatest injustice to students imposed through the traditional schools. Unique and individual differences in relation to personal interests and to certain requisite experiences, dictate the utilization of different modes of learning for achieving the same planned performance objectives for different individuals.[9] The critical aspects of individual differences in relation to school dropouts is in relation to opportunities for a wide variety of modes to learning for accomplishing planned student outcomes, not in relation to the intellectual ability as measured by group intelligence tests.[10] Students are not naive, and they can easily see that the mode or type of learning activity is not important, but that the student outcomes are all that matter. For teachers to fail to provide enrichment through variety by adapting to the individual tastes and interests of, students, is to create distrust in the whole learning-management process. More often than not it is from this nucleus of distrust that increased disinterest in school activities emerge.

Knowledge of progress. Learning effectiveness is intimately related to some knowledge of progress, and knowledge of progress must always be in terms of expected student outcomes.[11] The knowledge of how well a student has mastered or accomplished planned behavioral performance is much more important, and to be preferred, than the degree of comparison of such accomplishment to other members of the learning group. In terms of the technical jargon of the measurement man, absolute norms are to be preferred to relative norms; and assessment of student outcomes is to be preferred to measures of proficiency with learning activity. Knowledge of progress must always be relative to the precise statement of the expected behavior outcomes, and if such expected outcomes are stated in a vague and ambiguous manner, the measures for knowledge of progress will be just as unclear and vague.

Dynamic assessment. Knowledge of progress is a general concept and often is not concerned with dynamic or cause-and-effect relationships that might exist in the learning situation. Continued and improved progress can only result if select aspects of learning activity or experience may be attributed directly to the aspects of the expected student outcomes. This aspect of learning necessitates critical observation on the part of the learner. Specific student outcomes may then be related to emerging anticipated outcomes or the absence of such outcomes to materialize.[12] The precise assessment of dynamics involved in cause-and-effect relationships between learning activities and planned student outcomes or select aspects of such planned outcomes is the most critical aspect of the learning process.

Feedback utilization. This implies provision for change in the learning activity as the basis for maximizing planned student outcomes. The student alone must be in a position to vary such learning activities or experiences in a direction that emphasizes that aspect of the learning activity that produces expected outcomes, and to minimize that aspect which fails to produce results. In a very real sense this entails hypothesis development and testing as an integral aspect of the regular and usual learning situation, and such process may begin even during the infant stage of development. Thus, self-observation suggests that a certain aspect of the learning activity yields desirable planned student outcomes, and further observation tends and seeks to confirm such fact.

Success. The basis for success and failure is contained in the principles that precede this, and reflect some comparative evaluation between expected and actual observed student outcomes. If the expected student outcomes are excessively high, failure alone can result. Failure may be changed to success through two variants: (1) increasing performance, and (2) lowering of goals. The absence of success is evidence of failure in one or more of the principles involved, and success alone is necessary for further success. Nothing succeeds like success; it is contagious. More often than not lack of success may be attributed directly to the selection of learning activity or experiences; what produces specific student outcomes for one person, may never be expected to produce similar outcomes for a different person or even for the same person at a different time. It would be naive, indeed, for a student to continue with learning activity that fails to yield expected outcomes. Often lack of success may be traced to an unwillingness to change such activity.

Impact. "The proof of the pudding is in the eating," is an old adage that seems appropriate for this principle in relation to teaching by objectives for effective thrust and impact; similarly, if there is no learning there could not have been any effective teaching. Learning, then, means effective educational development of the individual; development in terms of achieving expected performance behavior; and of developing proficiency or competency in select areas of endeavor. Impact means change and growth in relation to the student or learner. It does not mean proficiency in relation to select learning activity that may or may not be related to planned student outcomes. Only by teaching by objectives can one expect to have effective educational thrust that will lead to meaningful impact on the learner. Thrust without carefully planned direction or without precise expected student outcomes is chance impact. Only by chance could such an impact be expected to be articulated into any semblance of an integrated educational growth or development pattern.

REFERENCES

[1] W. W. Cooley and R. C. Hummel, "Systems Approaches in Guidance," *Review of Educational Research*, 39 (April 1969), 251-262; R. N. Cassel, "Systems Analysis in Our Schools and Colleges," *Education*, 90 (September-October 1970), 18-25.
[2] H. B. Gelatt, "Guidance Accountability and Management by Objectives," *Focus on Guidance*, 1971, Denver, Colorado; B. Rosenshine, "Evaluation of Classroom Instruction," *Review of Educational Research*, 40 (April 1970), 279-300; R. E. Schultz, "Measurement Aspects of Performance Contracting," *NCME Measurement in Evaluation*, 2 (March 1971), 1-4; D. D. Sjogren, "Measurement Techniques in Evaluation," *Review of Educational Research*, 40 (April 1970), 301-317.
[3] J. David, "The Clark Plan for Learning," *College Student Journal*, 5 (September-October 1971), 20-23; B. S. Bloom and J. T. Hastings, *Handbook of Formative and Summative Evaluation of Student Learning* (Manchester, Missouri: McGraw-Hill, 1971); R. N. Cassel, "Operant Conditioning Fails to Foster Self-direction and Tends Towards Enslavement of the Individual," *Psychology*, 8 (May 1971), 22-26.
[4] G. H. Copa, *Identifying Inputs Toward Production Function Application in Education*, University of Minnesota Technical Report, April, 1971; Bloom and Hastings, D. Lipe and S. M. Jung, "Manipulating Incentives to Enhance School Learning," *Review of Educational Research*, 41 (October 1971), 249-277.

[5] Copa; Lipe and Jung.

[6] A. W. Halpin and D. B. Crofts, *The Organizational Climate of Schools*, U. S. Office of Education, Department of Health, Education, and Welfare, Contract No. SAE 543 (8639), pp. 80-89.

[7] Cassel, "Systems Analysis in Our Schools and Colleges"; Rosenshine, "Evaluation of Classroom Instruction"; Schultz, "Measurement Techniques in Evaluation."

[8] Cassel, "Operant Conditioning Fails to Foster Self-direction"; V. C. Joe, "Review of the Internal-external Control Construct as a Personality Variable," *Psychological Reports*, 28 (April 1971), 619-640; Gelatt, "Guidance Accountability and Management by Objectives."

[9] Bloom and Hastings.

[10] Cassel, "Systems Analysis in Our Schools and Colleges"; M. C. Alkin, "Evaluation Theory and Development" *UCLA Evaluation Comment*, 2 (October 1969), 2-7.

[11] Alkin; Rosenshine; Sjogren.

[12] Schutz

SCHOOL is for . . .
CREATING JOY
AND HAPPINESS

The Helping Relationship As Described By "Good" and "Poor" Teachers

ARTHUR W. COMBS and DANIEL W. SOPER

A number of writers have suggested that the characteristics of the helping relationship may be the same wherever these relationships occur. In a previous experiment Soper and Combs[1] demonstrated that superior teachers describe the helping relationship in a fashion highly similar to the descriptions of expert therapists. They found the opinions of a highly select group of teachers in a university laboratory school correlated .809 with the ideal relationship Q sort of a group of expert therapists reported by Fiedler.[2] Apparently good teachers and therapists are in agreement about the nature of a helping relationship. But will the same condition hold true for poor teachers? Moreover since teaching is basically a relationship one would expect good teachers to know more about the nature of an ideal relationship than poor ones. This research was designed to test whether "good" and "poor" teachers differ significantly from expert therapists in their conception of the characteristics of the ideal relationship.

The "Good" and "Poor" Teachers

To test our hypothesis we were able to secure the cooperation of "good" and "poor" teachers nominated from two sources: (a) from

[1] D. W. Soper, and A. W. Combs. "The Helping Relationship as Seen by Teachers and Therapists." *Journal of Consulting Psychology* 26: 288; 1962.
[2] F. E. Fiedler. "The Concept of an Ideal Therapeutic Relationship. *Journal of Consulting Psychology* 14:239-245; 1950.

Combs, Arthur W., and Soper, Daniel W. "The Helping Relationship as Described by 'Good' and 'Poor' Teachers." *The Journal of Teacher Education.* March 1963. 15:64-67.

students who had been in their classes, and (b) from supervisors familiar with their work.

(a) Sophomore students at the University of Florida enrolled in their first course in professional education were asked to nominate for our study, (1) "the very best teacher you ever had," and (2) "the very worst teacher you ever had." Each of the teachers so nominated was then invited to participate in the study and, if she agreed, was sent a copy of the Ideal Relationship Q sort with the appropriate instructions.

Since the students nominated many more teachers from the secondary schools, which they had only recently left, we had too few elementary school teachers to comprise a sufficient sample.

(b) We therefore sought the help of teacher supervisors for additional nominations at the elementary school level. A similar panel of "good" and "poor" teachers was nominated by five supervisors in widely separated parts of the country. The teachers so nominated were invited to participate in the study in the same fashion as the student-nominated ones. Table I shows the number of teachers nominated and the extent of their participation in the study.

The Ideal Relationship Q Sort

Each teacher nominated for the study was told we were studying the nature of the Ideal Helping Relationship and was asked to help us by sorting out 75 Q items. The fact that two groups of teachers were included in our study was not mentioned. Each teacher who agreed to cooperate was then sent a copy of the modified Fiedler Q sort. This was developed as follows: In his study Fiedler had developed a composite Q sort or the Ideal Therapeutic Relationship as seen by his expert therapist subjects. In an earlier experiment, Soper and Combs modified this Q sort for use with teachers by the simple expedient of changing the word, "therapist," to "teacher," and the word, "patient," to "student." In this way a statement reading, "The therapist tries to please the patient" in Fiedler's scale became, "The teacher tries to please the student" in our scale. The 75 items were to be sorted into piles of 1, 7, 18, 23, 18, 7, 1 from the most characteristic of an ideal teacher-pupil relationship to the least characteristic.

When the sorts were completed, each teacher's Q was correlated with the Fiedler Ideal Relationship Composite. These correlations were then summed to provide the analyses we were seeking. Results are shown in Table II.

It is clear from this table that *both* good and poor teachers are in essential agreement with the expert therapists as to what an ideal relationship *ought* to be like. Apparently a knowledge of the nature of good helping relationships is not a distinguishing factor between good and poor teachers. The finding lends additional support to the observations of Combs,[3] Rogers,[4] and others that the nature of good helping relationships is generally recognized by everyone. Such knowledge is in the public domain and apparently any intelligent person can describe pretty well what good relationships should be like.

In Table III, the eight top and eight bottom items of the scale, as sorted by our teachers and by Fiedler's therapists, are compared. It can be seen in this table that the two groups show a high degree of similarity; they agree on three most ideal items and on six least ideal items. Teachers and therapists differ slightly, however, among the most ideal items; the teachers show more concern for guidance and direction while the therapists emphasize the importance of empathy and "being with" their clients. At the other end of the scale, the therapists again show this concern in giving low ratings to items that imply breakdown of empathy, while teachers repudiate rejection and seduction of students. The term "seduction" carries a milder meaning in the technical jargon of therapy than in common usage, and this probably plays a part in its failure to appear in the least ideal list for the therapist group.

TABLE I

TEACHER PARTICIPATION IN COMPLETING IDEAL RELATIONSHIP Q SORTS

Source	Invited to Participate	Agreed to Help	No. Teachers Who Completed Sorts		
			"good"	"poor"	Total
Supervisor-Nominated	78	51	21	13	34
Student-Nominated	182	97	43	35	78
Total	260	148	64	48	112

[3] A. W. Combs and D. Snygg. *Individual Behavior*. New York: Harper and Brothers, 1959.
[4] C. R. Rogers. The Characteristics of a Helping Relationship." *Personnel and Guidance Journal* 37:6-16; 1958.

TABLE II
MEAN CORRELATION COEFFICIENTS FOR "GOOD" AND "POOR" TEACHER Q SORTS CORRELATED WITH FIELDER COMPOSITE

	No.	"Good"	"Poor"
Supervisor-nominated elementary	34	.61	.62
Student-nominated elementary	19	.61	.59
Student-nominated secondary	59	.67	.64

Correlations are Pearson product moment.

TABLE III
THE EIGHT MOST IDEAL AND LEAST IDEAL ITEMS AS SORTED BY OUR 112 TEACHERS AND BY FIEDLER'S THERAPISTS

8 Most Ideal Items

Rank   Our Teachers

1. The teacher directs and guides the student.
2. The teacher sees the student as a co-worker on a common problem.
3. The teacher greatly encourages and reassures the student.
4. The teacher really tries to understand the student's feelings.
5. The teacher usually maintains rapport with the student.
6. The teacher is well able to understand the student's feelings.
7. The teacher is sympathetic with the student.
8. The teacher gives and takes in the situations.

Fiedler's Therapists

The therapist is able to participate completely in the patient's communication.
The therapist's comments are always right in line with what the patient is trying to convey.
The therapist is well able to understand the patient's feelings.
The therapist really tries to understand the patient's feelings.
The therapist always follows the patient's line of thought.
The therapist's tone of voice conveys the complete ability to share the patient's feelings.
The therapist sees the patient as a co-worker on a common problem.
The therapist treats the patient as an equal.

8 Least Ideal Items

Rank   Our Teachers

75. The teacher is hostile toward the student.
74. The teacher is rejecting to the students.
73. The teacher's own needs completely interfere with his understanding of the student.
72. The teacher is very unpleasant to the student.
71. The teacher feels disgusted by the student.
70. The teacher is seductive toward the student.
69. The teacher is punitive.
68. The teacher cannot maintain rapport with the student.

Fiedler's Therapists

The therapist shows no comprehension of the feelings the patient is trying to communicate.
The therapist acts in a very superior manner toward the patient.
The therapist is very unpleasant to the patient.
The therapist is punitive.
The therapist is hostile toward the patient.
The therapist feels disgusted by the patient.
The therapist's own needs completely interfere with his understanding of the patient.
The therapist cannot maintain rapport with the patient.

Some Implications

Quite frankly, the results of this study are not what the designers had originally expected would be the case. Indeed, we had hoped the results of this study might justify using the modified Q sort as a device to distinguish between "good" and "poor" teachers. From the results of this study, it is clear that this hope must be abandoned. "Good" teachers apparently cannot be distinguished from "poor" ones on the basis of their understanding of what a good helping relationship ought to be.

Although both "good" and "poor" teachers know what ideal relationships ought to be like, it is certain they do not equally well put these understandings into effect. The distinguishing factor lies not in what teachers know they ought to do but in whether or not they do what they know they ought. This has some interesting implications for teachers colleges. It means that, to be truly successful in turning out superior teachers, it is not enough to help students see more clearly what good helping relationships are like. Apparently, they know this already! Indeed, a college which goes no further than this in its program ought not to be surprised if students regard its offerings as "Pablum" or "Mickey Mouse" stuff. A college should be expected to teach more than "what everybody knows"! There is a great difference, it appears, between "knowing" and "behaving," and the successful teachers' college cannot be content with producing mere changes in "knowing"; its students must behave differently as a result of their exposure to the program. This is not an easy assignment for it means changing people, a much more difficult task than providing information.

Perhaps the agreement demonstrated in this study between the understandings of expert therapists and teachers may suggest possible sources of help for the teachers' college in the task of producing behavior change. Apparently, helping relationships are not markedly different wherever they are found. This means that training programs for counselors, psychotherapists, social workers, nurses, and all other helping professions, including teaching, are engaged in the same basic processes. This commonalty is rarely perceived, however. A clear recognition of this mutual stake might lead to much more interaction among the training supervisors in these groups and a sharing of ideas, methods, and policies that would redound to greater success for all of them.

Summary

Sixty-four "good" and forty-eight "poor" teachers were given a seventy-five item Q sort on the nature of the ideal teacher-pupil relationship. Their performance was correlated with a composite Q sort on the ideal relationship as defined by expert psychotherapists. Both "good" and "poor" teachers showed high agreement with the expert therapists. This suggests that good and poor teachers cannot be discriminated on the basis of their knowledge of what helping relationships ought to be like. The findings are interpreted as support for the existence of certain factors common to all helping relationships wherever found.

SCHOOL is for . . .
EVERYBODY

Development Of Attitudes!

R. C. BRADLEY

For years we have given special treatment to those students who have suffered physical disabilities, emotional disturbances, brain injury, and reading deficits. Now it seems time to add a new dimension to our list—children who have value-related disturbances. These children present idio-syncratic behavior patterns. Their apathy, flightiness, extreme uncertainty, and inconsistency are readily observable characteristics. Most teachers can identify children who drift, overconform, overdissent, underachieve, and role play beyond normal expectation. It is conceivable that "confusion in values" is a more serious malady than inability to read or to calculate mathematical problems.

Value—a definition. In this brief article the term value is used to mean "the process by which a pupil makes decisions that concern him; the moral beliefs he adheres to; the spirit with which he engages in making decisions regarding others; and the feelings and attitudes he holds toward life, mankind, his self, and his God."

What can a school do about a child's values? First, educators can seek to help a child answer the question, "How did I get my ideas?" Second, the school should help a child make a decision as to "What am I to do with my life and force?" It is a terrible thought to find that schools are not dealing with these two basic questions. A growing tragedy is that there is no school time set in many schools for what really counts—value development. Witness the pupil who beats up his brother at school only to hear the remark, *"For this you will be punished."* Generally, there is no discussion which deals with moral responsibility toward one's brother, nor is there an attempt to secure a closer tie between brothers. This task is left to the home which has already failed.

The school should help the child to find clear purposes for his life, to know what he is for and against, to know where he is going and why. If a child does not have this guidance then unclear values serve to

Bradley, R. C. "Development of Attitudes." *The Minnesota Elementary School Principal.* May 1972. 14:4-5.

promote lack of direction for his life. He fails to build the criteria which is essential to choosing what to do with his time, his energy, and his very being. A quick scanning of any local newspaper will indeed show that it is becoming increasingly apparent that all too few humans have clear values.

Is a school contributing to the value development of children if it allows the following to occur in selected settings: (1) defacing of school property (writing on rest room walls; marking desks; footprints on painted walls; littering schoolyards and walkways up to four blocks from school); (2) booing of referees at the local basketball tournament; (3) failing to recognize that in one out of every five families the mother is not at home when children return from school; (4) to avoid controversy, teachers are hired who won't rock the educational boat; (5) the certificate or diploma becomes more significant than the education attained; (6) the child is allowed to acquire the school atmosphere of "Don't stick out your neck," "Don't take a chance," "Play it safe," (7) the rate of suicide among children is growing; (8) in our rich society the number of very poor in our schools has changed hardly at all; (9) there is little attempt to help children deal with the modern complexities of living; and (10) the means for determining and identifying those who are having difficulty in forming values has made no great progress in this age of the computer than was already achieved thirty years ago.

Certainly not all schools are neglecting value development of their youngsters, but another author could supply a different list of values which deserves the attention of educators in any given locality.

"What can I do as a teacher?" We can help children learn to choose what is right, what Americans should prize, and to act once the choice has been made. One should learn to choose freely from alternatives after thoughtful consideration of the consequences of each alternative. As a student prizes his choice, he learns how to cherish his choice and to publicly affirm his choice when challenged. After making his choice and affirming it, a pupil must be expected to do something with his choice, repeatedly, in some experience provided by the school. The results of achieving these processes (valuing) are *values*.

Research findings suggest that many students in our schools do not behave in ways which they are proud (F. P. Dee, Rutgers University). Being proud of one's behavior is one of the criteria essential to value development and it is within the power of the school to develop.

Students must be urged to go beyond their assignments for there is little to be proud of if one merely is taught to do his duty. Research can be found to support the contention that teachers who attempt to help children clarify their value responses are indeed persons who have made a difference in what students come to value. They do influence in positive ways the attitudes and patterns of student behavior.

An attempt should be made to identify a series of value issues that would serve as the discussion base in social studies classes. These issues might well include: relationships between work and leisure; change vs. stability; relationships between self conduct and social well-being; acting on insufficient evidence vs. complete inaction; planning for a group with imposed restrictions vs. planning for individual freedoms with no restrictions; tardiness vs. promptness of action; slovenliness vs. neatness.

How do I know values of children are changing as a result of my instruction? The sense of progress comes from watching the pupils change in their reaction to one another. Some change can be noted in the way they discuss issues. Certainly the collecting of behavior profiles from time to time (e.g.; Super's *"Work Values Inventory,"* 1965) will provide not only evidence for others but evidence for a teacher's own sense of accomplishment.

Summary. When educators emphasize *thinking*, children are taught to observe, compare, interpret, deduce, criticize, analyze, and imagine. But when pupils are taught to study their *own values*, emphasis is given to a study of what they conform to and why; where they receive their attitudes, feelings, purposes, and aspirations.

Schools are doing a better job on intellectual skills than they are on values. Thinking without values, however, can be likened to a cart without a horse. Thinking takes on the dimension of the cart while valuing takes on the dimension of *"horsepower"* which makes the cart go.

Life for a child is less neat and simple than it was only a generation ago. As Raths, Harmin, and Simon have admonished in their provacative book, *Values and Teaching* (Charles E. Merrill, 1966), *"Could it be that the pace and complexity of modern life has so exacerbated the problem of deciding what is good and what is right and what is worthy and what is desirable that large numbers of children are finding it increasingly bewildering, even overwhelming, to decide what is worth valuing, what is worth one's time and energy (p. 7)?"* If the values of youth fail, so in the end will the nation, and it is the schools that will in part determine the ultimate outcome.

"It is conceivable that confusion in values is a more serious malady than inability to read or to calculate mathematical problems."

"The school should help the child to find clear purposes for his life . . . . . . to learn to choose freely from alternatives after thoughtful consideration of the consequences . . ."

". . . the pace and complexity of modern life has . . . exacerbated the problem of deciding what is good and what is right . . ."

Reality Therapy: An Approach to Encourage Individual and Social Responsibility in the Elementary School

RICHARD M. HAWES

Life Skills are important — *young teachers are more comfortable w/this b/c*

The technological and cultural forces of today seem to have a separating and depersonalizing effect. This situation causes people to experience the gnawing feelings of loneliness perhaps more frequently and more intensely than in the recent past. As authority, tradition, and conformity lose their potence to solve the problems of the day and to protect us from loneliness and uncertainty, self-esteem (to care for oneself—individual responsibility) and the capacity to love (to care for others—social responsibility) become more necessary for human survival.

In an attempt to *be* loved, many people learn ways to "make" people love them. These desperate power plays are sometimes successful in gaining respect, but respect is only a substitute for love, and the pains of loneliness remain. An alternative method is to learn ways to become more self-responsible (worthwhile) and socially responsible (the capacity to love).

This paper is based on the premise that these conditions (self-worth and the ability to love) are learned, that they are essential learnings for survival, and that the educational system needs to look at them as major educational aims. The following is a description of an attempt in that direction.

Hawes, Richard M. "Reality Therapy: An Approach to Encourage Individual and Social Responsibility in the Elementary School." *Elementary School Guidance and Counseling*. December 1969. 4:120-127. By permission of the author and The American Personnel and Guidance Association, © copyright 1969.

Teaching Self-Worth and Ability to Love

At 10:19 a.m. in the third grade class of the Eastern Elementary School, Mrs. McHenry has the following discussion with Jimmy, an eight-year-old boy who has a difficult time completing assignments even though the school records show him to have above average intelligence. Jimmy, slouched in his chair, is blowing on the edge of his science book when, with the rest of the class, he should be copying five arithmetic problems for his homework assignment. Usually, Mrs. McHenry tells him to get busy, but this time she begins by asking a question. In this approach, it's more valuable to ask questions than to make statements or give directions.

> Mrs. McHenry: Jimmy, what are you doing?
> Jimmy: (Startled, says nothing and shows that he's not sure what to say or do.)
> Mrs. McHenry: Show me—tell me what you are doing. It's important to me.
> Jimmy: I-I-I was blowing on the edge of the book like this. (He then demonstrates.)
> Mrs. McHenry: (Smiling) That's right, you were.
> Jimmy: (Smiles slightly.)

Their smiles suggest that Mrs. McHenry and Jimmy are experiencing a positive relationship and feeling good about it. A classroom situation that usually ends in a strained or distressful relationship has ended in a positive one. Mrs. McHenry has helped to make a potential minus into a plus and the therapeutic value is significant—for both parties. Another similar technique to help create a positive tone is making a "yes" out of a "no."

EXAMPLE: A child is raising his hand to ask permission to sharpen a pencil. The teacher feels this activity would disturb the class. In place of saying, "No you can't," she says, "Yes, you may when the bell rings."

A single incident of this nature is of little value, but when many people (children and adults) try to make a "yes" out of a "no," the effect on the school's atmosphere is great.

> Mrs. McHenry: (Continues by asking.) Does that help you complete the arithmetic problem?
> Jimmy: (Shrugging his shoulders.) No.

Mrs. McHenry without commenting, moves across the room to help another child who has her hand raised, leaving Jimmy with the choice of continuing the behavior discussed, doing something else, or copying the arithmetic problems.

In another classroom, Mrs. Jones' second grade class is lining up in the back of the room for recess. Tom and Sam get into one of their playful shoving matches, which usually results in a rather serious scuffle. This one is no exception, and one of the girls in the class is slightly injured by an unintentional kick in the shin.

> Mrs. Jones: What happened?

The children begin to talk all at once, creating a lot of confusion and noise.

> Mrs. Jones: I think we had better bring this up for discussion at our regular class meeting later this morning.

Later, after the class has returned from recess and about 20 minutes before lunch, the class moves into a circle for discussion.

> Mrs. Jones: Let's review in as much detail as possible what happened between Tom and Sam earlier this morning.

Tom and Sam reenact or "role play" the situation for the class.

> Mrs. Jones: What do you think? How do you feel it worked out?

The children begin to comment, express their opinions, discuss various ideas on how it worked out, judge how valuable it was, estimate the effects the incident had on the class, and suggest how a similar situation could be prevented.

> Tom: I guess it wasn't so hot, but we were just fooling around.
> Mrs. Jones: We've talked this over pretty well now and we've come up with several ideas on how to solve it. Tom and Sam, what's your plan? (The discussion is always directed toward solving the problem. It is not directed toward finding fault or deciding on punishment.)
> Sam: I guess we'll do our own idea of lining up at the ends of the line.
> Mrs. Jones: When?
> Tom: (After exchanging glances with Sam.) At lunchtime.

It's best to spend as little time as possible on classroom behavior problems. Too much concern can backfire and reinforce what you are trying to eliminate. Time is better used on open-end discussion sessions.

The open-end sessions, the most frequently used and perhaps the most valuable of class meetings, are designed to supplement the academic program by stimulating the children to think and respond. The sessions provide the children with a situation that gives each pupil the opportunity for intellectual success without the possibility of failure. The child makes no mistakes by his answers. Thinking rather than memory is accentuated. These regularly scheduled classroom discussions are the backbone of the program's attempt to encourage individual and socially responsible behavior.

The topic for open-end discussion may be introduced by any class member or the teacher. The topic for one day is introduced by a teacher as she asks the children the following series of questions. Enthusiastic discussion usually follows each question, such as What is play? What is work? Is play or work more important? Would you rather work or play? Is school work or play? Do you learn anything when you play?

Later in the afternoon, several teachers are enjoying coffee in the teachers' lounge. Bill, a sixth grade student who is well known for disruptive behavior, poor academic attitude, and a low achievement record is being discussed.

As in the class meetings, the teachers accentuate practical, reasonable, and realistic solutions rather than reasons (excuses) for his behavior, fault finding, where he can get help, or methods of punishment. They ask, "What can *I* do to make him feel worthwhile?" "Who has an idea that will help him to be more successful while he is in school?" "Of all the people available, who can work out something with Bill whereby he can begin to be more successful?" "Is school relevant to him?" "What can we do to make his time in school more important to him?" Before long, a specific plan is worked out which possibly will help him be more successful in school and lead him to more self-satisfying behavioral patterns.

The Plan: Mr. Ackley, third grade teacher who gets along well with Bill, will ask him to help as a teacher's aid during part of the school day. Bill will be given the responsibility of helping younger children to learn. A responsibility of this nature frequently has a very positive effect on the behavior of the pupil who is giving the help. It is far more effective than when one is lectured or punished.

Applying Reality Therapy

These are a few glimpses of how reality therapy may be applied in an elementary school. Reality therapy has been developed by William Glasser, a Los Angeles psychiatrist who has had considerable experience in private practice, correctional institutions, and as a consultant to various groups, schools, and organizations throughout this country and in Canada. Recently he has shown increasing interest in the schools and their relationship to mental health and human development.

Dr. Glasser's work in the schools over the last few years is reflected in a book entitled, *Schools Without Failure* (1969). His earlier books, are *Mental Health* or *Mental Illness* (1960) and *Reality Therapy* (1965).

Reality therapy is based on the idea that everyone needs to have an identity. For some, this may be described as a "successful" identity because the person is able to become involved with life in a manner that allows him to fulfill two basic needs: Feeling worthwhile toward himself and others; and to love and be loved. When one is unsuccessful in fulfilling any part of these needs he suffers. One suffers not only if he is unable to be loved, but also if he is unable to give love—it's a two-way street.

Dr. Glasser (1966), in a speech to primary reading specialists in the Los Angeles School District, has commented:

> These are two-way needs: to love and be loved implies someone to love and someone who loves me. If we don't have this we suffer. For some children the form of this suffering is not learning to read and they won't learn to read until they get the idea that someone is able to care for them and they *can* learn [p. 1].

Because these suffering children are in the process of developing failure identities by their very experiences, they are unable to make the kind of relationships with *responsible* people that are necessary for them to fulfill their needs. It then becomes the first responsibility of the teacher to make contact with them in a way that is open, transparent, honest, and congruent. One needs to meet them as a human being who cares. Without this type of encounter, their chances of shifting from a failure identity (characterized by delinquency or withdrawal) to a successful identity (characterized by self-esteem and love) will be slim indeed. People need people. As Glasser (1966) puts it:

> Children suffer by not learning or they get tired of suffering and cause others to suffer . . . The teacher's first job is to make contact with these children . . . as a person who cares . . . a person interested in them . . not as a teacher but as a person . . . Everyone is doing the best he can at the time. If he could do better he would. You can't convince them they can do better until they relate to you and begin to meet their needs [p. 1].

By making this authentic and personal contact, involvement is increased while loneliness is decreased. This personal involvement is reflected by the child's increased motivation to learn.

As the discussion so far implies, the first essential step in the application of reality therapy is to get personally involved. With little children particularly, it is important to use personal pronouns as Mrs. McHenry did with Jimmy, when she said, "It's important to me" (that you show and tell me what you are doing). It is important for the child to know that you are interested in him as a person, not only as a pupil in the class, a name on the attendance book, a 1.5 reading level, or a 107 IQ score. Casual, interested, and authentic conversation where you get to know one another as people is extremely important. It is important for *him* to know that you enjoy playing tennis, watching "Bewitched," have two boys and one girl, and a husband who sells carpets at Sears. It is important for you to know personal things about him. Spontaneous, casual give-and-take, one human being to another, creates a quality of involvement that causes one to hurt if the child is unable to read.

Our daily newspapers remind us with foreboding that one of our most serious problems today is lack of involvement or social responsibility. Arthur H. Brayfield (1968) suggests that we need to develop an environment"... that will foster the sense of personal worth and self-esteem required to sustain the human spirit, give meaning to our lives, and provide the energizing force to forge our personal destinies and to insure the emergence and survival of a humane society."

A second guideline of this approach is to accentuate the present time. Do not get involved in reinforcing the set that Jimmy is always doing something like blowing on the pages of his book when he is supposed to be doing arithmetic, that Tom and Sam have a past history of scuffles, that Bill has always been a behavior problem, or that Johnny was unable to read in the past. Being successful at not succeeding is a certain kind of success, and so we have some very successful failures. Do not reinforce past failure but rather expect Johnny to be successful at reading in the present, expect Jimmy to complete the arithmetic lesson successfully today, expect Tom, Sam, and the class to come up with a solution to their scuffling, expect Bill to be successful in helping a third grader to learn.

A third consideration is to deal with behavior. The purpose is not to search for *why* he is behaving the way he does or *how* he feels about it. The valuable point is to help the child become aware of *what* he is doing that is contributing to his failure. In the case of Jimmy, Mrs. McHenry was able to help him become consciously aware of his behavior, not by demanding that he stop and get busy (an approach designed to take responsibility for him, rather than his taking responsibility for himself), but by encouraging him in a nonpunitive manner to describe, as best he could, his actual behavior. The process of describing helps to bring the behavior to the most optimum conscious level.

These first three points, establishing personal involvement and accentuating present behavior, put the situation clearly in the open and set the stage for a fourth point, which is one of the most important, relevant, and meaningful learning opportunities anyone can experience: The opportunity for one to reflect upon and make a value judgment about his own behavior. The value of this experience of responsible self-evaluation and direction cannot be overemphasized. It is extremely important when working personally with individuals, small groups, or large classroom groups, to work toward their making value judgments. This is usually best accomplished by asking questions, not making statements. "Is it worthwhile to blow on the book or complete the arithmetic lesson?" "Is it worthwhile to learn to read?" "Is it worthwhile to help another student?" "Is it worthwhile to kick someone in the shin?" "Is it worthwhile to graduate from high school?"

On this point, Glasser (1966) states, "You can't tell them it is important to learn to read. They must make their own value judgments" (p. 3). When the child decides it is worthwhile to change his behavior, the teacher must work with him in an effort to come up with a specific plan and then encourage him to make a commitment to the plan. Making a plan and getting a commitment are steps five and six. The plan should be such that its fulfillment is guaranteed. Nothing succeeds like success. Once again, questions are important, rather than statements or directions: "What can you do about it?" "What is your plan?" "Will you commit yourself to the plan?" "Will you do it?" "When?"

Jimmy could choose to do the arithmetic lesson, Tom and Sam decide to line up at the extreme ends of the line, and Mr. Ackley is going to ask Bill to help in the third grade.

The seventh and eighth steps are to eliminate punishment and not to reinforce excuses. Punishment and excuses are of no value when working with children who already hurt.

As Glasser (1966) remarks:

> Discipline is hard because we not only deal with excuses, we ask for them. Discipline is poorly understood—it has nothing to do with hurting or harming children. It is teaching someone that the way he is going is not helping him and getting him to make better choices. It takes a long time for a child to fulfill his commitments. He will check you out. He will try to see if you will take excuses. If you accept excuses, it proves you don't really care and the old failure pattern recurs. If you accept excuses you are saying, "You are worthless." If the assignment is not done say, "When will you do it?" "Can you do it?" "Can you do it in school today?" "After school?" Not "Why didn't you do it?" If you don't ever accept excuses you are saying, "You are a worthwhile person and I'm waiting for you to complete your commitment" [p. 4].

It should be noted that the cumulative effect of many people becoming personally involved, dealing with present behavior, changing why to what, making plus out of minus or yes out of no, emphasizing thinking and value judgments through techniques such as regularly scheduled classroom meetings, accentuating and expecting successful experiences, eliminating excuses, and not resorting to fear or punishment, creates a distinct environment. This atmosphere itself becomes an added force toward responsible behavior, successful identity, mental health, overall human development, and the capacity to love.

REFERENCES

BRAYFIELD, A. H. Human Resources Development. *American Psychologist*, 1968, 23, 479-482.

GLASSER, W. How Can We Help Young Children Face Reality and Become Responsible Human Beings? Excerpts from a speech made by Dr. Glasser at the ESEA Workshop for Primary Reading Specialists, Los Angeles, Calif., August, 1966.

GLASSER, W. *Mental Health or Mental Illness?* New York: Harper, 1960.

GLASSER, W. *Reality Therapy.* New York: Harper, 1965.

GLASSER, W. *Schools Without Failure.* New York: Harper, 1969.

SCHOOL is for . . .
DECISION MAKING

Psychotherapy and Learning Therapy in the Special School

MARVIN WALDMAN

The child who is experiencing severe learning disability will receive his greatest help through services provided in the school. Children learn best from those people who are sensitive to both their ego needs and their academic problems. In a psychologically oriented school program it is important to differentiate the roles of psychotherapist and learning therapist. The latter is represented by the teacher who brings to his role a grasp of psychodynamics, an understanding of child development, and sufficient clinical sophistication to enhance his teaching and relationship effectiveness. The psychotherapist in the school situation supports the learning therapist, aids in crisis intervention, and generally attempts to establish an emotional climate in the school conducent to helping the child function more effectively.

After many difficult years of experience in special education, those of us working in this field have learned much about the world of the child with a learning disability. We have seen how his many problems have been compounded and distorted by conditions that have made him feel eons distant from his peers in status and achievement. Frustration and despair have followed him through his preschool years and continue to plague him as he meets the newer challenges of his schooling. Parental sensitivity, always so sorely needed, has been compromised by frustration, guilt, and anger. Already vulnerable and still heir only to denigration, this child attempts to meet the challenge of school that prophesies only failure. Rather than help, the teacher and the regular school too often perpetuate the deadly cycle already existing at home. And then we attempt to break this cycle through the special school with the special services not ordinarily available in regular schools.

Waldman, Marvin. "Psychotherapy and Learning Therapy in the Special School." *Journal of Learning Disabilities.* March 1972. 5:165-169.

The service that permeates all others, the one that touches the child through the entire course of his learning day, is the atmosphere of the school. While such a factor as physical plant contributes to atmosphere, we are most concerned with how the people who staff the special school behave, and to what degree they understand the child in their charge. At Parkway Day School there is a deep commitment to the belief that children learn best from those people who are most sensitive to their academic, social, and emotional needs. This belief seems especially relevant to the child who is a disabled learner. In many instances the child with a learning disability is the product of an atmosphere which, because of its insensitivity, acts before understanding, imposes rather than guides, and punishes, so that gentleness and respect go begging. At crucial points in his life the child with a learning disability has usually been exposed to the very bitter lesson that his desperately needed mentors and guides—parents and teachers—were his seeming enemies. To the degree that we who work with him are effective in reducing our insensitivity, to that degree do we succeed in changing his image of us from that of enemy to that of helping friend.

Sensitizing the child's world to him begins with the people chosen to teach and to help. Reasonable and comfortable spontaneity with children and adults; a strong desire to help children grow and to become independent; the ability and desire to learn about people and things; and the indispensable capacity to use oneself as a tool, to listen to those intuitive whisperings that teach us about insight and its use, are some of the characteristics typical of the teaching personnel most successful in our particular program.

Supplementing our efforts to maintain a high level of sensitivity at Parkway, a psychotherapist is employed on a full-time basis. He is available to the entire school population as needed. The decision as to when a child should be seen by him can be made by any staff member. The decision is usually based on whether the child is able to maintain a learning set in the classroom. Disruptiveness and behavior of a withdrawn nature, such as fantasizing and despondency, have been the usual reasons for referral.

A prime goal of the psychotherapeutic interview is to return the child to his classroom as quickly as possible. Consequently the contacts are usually short, lasting perhaps only a few minutes and seldom exceeding half an hour. When we first started our intervention program we almost invariably saw the child in the psychotherapist's office. Finding that we achieved as good if not better results when we saw the child in a corner of his classroom, we changed our emphasis for some children from privacy to expediency.

While the etiology, history, and indeed the personality structure of children with learning disabilities are quite different, they usually show patterns of behavior that lend themselves to grouping.

One group of children often seen in special schools is the latency-aged labile group; these children feel and show their affect in quite intense and confused form. Denial and projection are their prime means of dealing with a devastatingly poor self-image. They constantly see challenges in the world and react in a manner to provoke power struggles. Rather than try to learn they seek to control; rather than try to achieve they attempt to live out fantasies in which they have supreme power. As these children grow older without appropriate academic and psychotherapeutic intervention, they become increasingly embittered, manipulative, and distrustful. The earlier affectualizing turns into pseudo-sophistication. But while the child of this group no longer wears his heart on his sleeve, tears of regression are not far beneath the surface.

Yet another group of children becomes despondently quiet in class without apparent provocation. Without warning these children may simply lower their heads and cry; they may also stare off into fantasy land. On investigation these children are usually found to have been teased or threatened by a peer; they may also be worrying about their school performance.

To approach these hurt children we utilize our total school setting; our aim is to ensure that their painful upsets are met and dealt with, not wasted. Our staff responds by appreciating the many dishonest, hurtful, double-binding, and growth-denying situations that have become their heritage. Knowing the child's history, being familiar with his test data, observing his behavior carefully, and discussing his problems with other staff members places everyone in the position of preventing those incidents which have plagued his life from recurring. For example, we place great emphasis on not giving him work to do that is beyond his ken; hence, he is not set up to fail. Also, we ensure that his feelings are addressed, not ignored; therefore, he has not been demeaned. Our focus is on sharing knowledge with the child. In this process we look to the point in time when we can let him know that there are many, varied reasons for his inability to learn—*not* because of retardation or stupidity.

In clarifying our program, differentiating the roles of psycho-therapist and learning therapist will be helpful. We all have different specific ideas about what a psychotherapist is and does, but his general role is well understood and need not be gone into here. But the role of the learning therapist does need clarification. To us the learning therapist is a teacher who brings to his role a grasp of psychodynamics, and understanding of child development, and enough clinical sophistication to enhance his teaching and relationship effectiveness. In our setting the learning therapist has a number of functions which further clarify his role. These functions we have tentatively categorized into the following four strategy groups: Preventive, Defusing, Integrative, and Maintaining Contact.

Strategy Groups

By *preventive* techniques we mean those which the learning therapist utilizes to maintain the child's learning set. His prime asset in reaching this goal is knowing the child. Knowing his moods, his tolerance levels, his strengths and weaknesses is indispensable in preventing ego disruption from occurring. Commendation, support, appropriate preparation for work and for social challenges are his stock in trade. The psychotherapist's direct role in this area is quite minimal, although he may function in an advisory capacity.

When prevention fails we are faced with the very difficult task of employing techniques to help the child regain the integrity of his ego. For this purpose we employ a number of *defusing* techniques designed to restore the child's equilibrium. Prime among these is an approach which does not blame or provoke additional arguments or discomfort in the child. Rather, we accept the child's feelings about his reality as he sees it, no matter how distorted, until he is able to enter into more rational discussion with us. Separating the child from his peers or asking him to leave the class to be with the psychotherapist are other defusing approaches. While the learning therapist has a large responsibility in this area, when the situation promises to be too time-consuming and involved, the psychotherapist is asked to intervene.

By *integrative* techniques we mean those which enlist a child's judgment and emotional appreciation in order to examine a string of incidents that deepen his insight. We also mean various approaches that help a child to achieve short range goals while on the way to more distant ones. Although the learning therapist has a role in this area, the psychotherapist becomes more actively engaged with the child at this level for a while once the program is under way. This is also the area where learning therapist and psychotherapist can supplement each other. For example, with the child's full knowledge and cooperation, the psychotherapist may set up a program with the learning therapist whereby he carefully makes clear to the child the particular behavior which is of a defensive nature or provokes others into attacking him.

By *maintaining contact* we mean those informal social amenities that help the child to feel that he is part of different social relationships which he is thought of and respected. The learning therapist may take a snack with a child; the psychotherapist may stop him in the hallway to discuss a recent camping trip. Such contacts often serve as a helpfully supportive framework within which difficult episodes and situations find more comfortable resolution.

To know the child and to understand relationship problems means that we must also know the learning therapist. We are well aware that such factors as inexperience and ignorance can interfere with therapeutic effectiveness. To minimize these negative factors a formal training discussion program is included. This interlocks with individual conferences and preceptor situations between more experienced staff and the psychotherapist on the one hand and new teachers on the other. Since our emphasis is always on more and not less knowledge, it is also realized that just as a psychotherapist's effectiveness can be compromised by countertransference, just so can the learning therapist find himself caught up with feelings which undermine his role. In our seminars, as well as in individual conferences, the phenomenon of countertransference is made as clear as possible. We focus on anger, overprotectiveness, resentment, seductiveness, guilt, jealousy—the very same problem feelings seen in parents—when they serve to distort the relationship between teacher and child. To cope with this problem, we first move in the direction of exposing its presence, and then take whatever measures are necessary to neutralize the situation.

Much of our emphasis on increased sensitivity toward the child is motivated by our awareness of the enormity of the impact of what adults do and say to them. Impressing our learning therapists with this fact is an important facet of our training program. For example, we know that inexperienced and novice psychotherapists may clumsily approach their clinical responsibilities by basing their interpretations on unwarranted assumptions; they also may make premature comments which do much to muddy issues and upset their patients. Similarly, the inexperienced learning therapist may zealously misinterpret his role and freely interpret a student's behavior; he may also mistake tactlessness for frankness and hurt a student by showing insufficient awareness of the disrupting impact his words can have. With time and seasoning both psychotherapist and learning therapist change their ways: the psychotherapist becomes more conservative, less inclined to be weighty and pompous, and more inclined to learn about his patient; and importantly, he also starts paying much closer attention to feelings. The developing learning therapist, in our view, shows that he too is learning many of the same things.

There are a number of important differences. Where the psychotherapist probes and interprets, the learning therapist teaches and focuses on those aspects of the classroom situation which prevent loss of the learning set. Where the psychotherapist may be guided by a particular theory of personality development, the learning therapist knows much about the kinds of learning skills and behavior characteristic of different age levels. Where the psychotherapist is skilled in the technique of carefully dealing with emerging defenses, the learning therapist is skilled in the technique of structuring lesson plans and in selecting those approaches most relevant for specific academic deficits. Where the psychotherapist clarifies his patient's feelings, the learning therapist may utilize reading materials to discuss and clarify the feelings of characters in stories.

We have found that there is much potential in an approach which utilizes classroom material to clarify feelings. First by dealing with the story characters and then by inviting class discussion, the material often becomes affectively charged because of its personal meaning. Since handling such class discussions requires considerable tact and skill, we see it as an area most worthy of exploration and application. In fact, with carefully chosen class groups, we see this approach as one in which a psychotherapist and learning therapist can work together as co-therapists.

Our interest is not to demean teachers by turning them into junior psychotherapists; our goal is to develop better teachers. For example, our intent is not to teach a teacher to make a correct interpretation; we simply feel that there is danger is not helping a teacher recognize what a clumsy interpretation sounds like and why it has a particular impact on a child. Similarly, when we talk with our learning therapists about their feelings toward the children and about themselves, our intent is not to use psychotherapy on them; we simply do not want our teachers to act on feelings not really relevant to their contemporary relationship with a particular child. Consequently we see danger in not helping a teacher to understand and affectively appreciate what countertransference is all about.

Essentially we believe that what we are doing is surrounding the child who has suffered from a lack of understanding with people who are sensitively capable of reacting to him free of guilt and conflicted animosities. In this process our philosophy is seen as providing the child with a more hopeful and helpful picture of the world; our approach is one which opens the child's view of himself in relation to others without the need to be hurtfully defensive. One of the major goals in this particular approach is to help the child live without the expectation that he will be demeaned, attacked, misunderstood, that he will fail or be socially unacceptable. Too often we have seen that the expectations prophesy the outcome.

Detecting Psychological Symptoms of Brain Injury

HARRY S. BECK

During the past ten or fifteen years educators have become increasingly aware of the existence of the brain injured child, especially in association with remedial and special education programs. There has been a growing awareness, too, of the need for better program planning for these children in both academic and non-academic areas, in and out of school.

Although a medical diagnosis of brain injury may not be of great importance, from a strictly pedagogical point of view, it is important from the standpoint of medical therapy which may make the child more accessible or amenable to learning, and in terms of prognosis for development.

As educators we are particularly interested in the psychological symptoms in terms of planning an educational program for these children. It should be pointed out that there are both psychological and physical symptoms associated with brain injury, and that traditionally the diagnosis has been based primarily upon the physical symptoms (i.e., neurological examinations, electroencephalograms, pneumoencephalograms, x-rays, etc.).

In effect, then, a medically diagnosed brain injured child will usually display some psychological symptoms, but a child displaying these symptoms may not necessarily be brain injured from a medical viewpoint. This is certainly not the most desirable state of affairs, but it nevertheless represents the present situation. This point is brought up because it may well be that any correlation which exists between the so-called psychological symptoms of brain injury and medically or physically determined brain injury is an associative relationship, rather

Beck, Harry S. "Detecting Psychological Symptoms of Brain Injury." *Exceptional Children.* September 1961. 28:57-62.

than a cause-effect relationship.

This article is primarily concerned with the effects of brain injury in children who show no gross muscular involvements such as some of the cerebral palsied. The emphasis is upon those cases that Strauss and Lehtinen (1950) refer to as exogenous, and Doll (1951a) classified under neurophrenia. In these children the injury usually occurs before, during, or shortly after birth, and the children are more often than not considered to be problems of behavior or learning. According to Bender (1956) they usually are referred to clinics for some reason other than the brain injury itself.

The problem is, of course, to gain a better understanding of the particular symptoms which these children present and to determime whether there is a definite syndrome of symptoms characteristic of brain injury in children. Another aspect of the problem is concerned with the validity, in terms of medical agreement, of psychological tests for detecting this condition.

It was felt that the best approach would be to survey the literature and summarize the findings of some of the outstanding writers in this area. In this way it could be determined, to some extent, the amount of agreement among those writers concerning the symptoms of brain injury and their detection.

Extent of Problem

Although it is becoming more and more apparent that the brain injured child exists in greater numbers than was suspected a few years back, the full extent of the problem is not known. Beck (1956) estimates that at least 60 to 70 percent of all educable mentally handicapped school children are brain injured, and Gesell and Amatruda (1954) estimate the the brain injured comprise one-fifth of all cases of amentia and over one-third of the motor disabilities of crippled children. The number of cases having normal or better intelligence whose difficulties are manifested by personality problems, reading disabilities, and the like is unknown. Courville (1950) states that some degree of injury occurs during delivery in probably more cases than is commonly appreciated.

In reading literature describing the brain injured child, it is not difficult to see that the various writers are talking about the same type of child. In other words, it can be readily seen that the child being described is one whom we know from experience to be brain injured. Yet when listing the actual symptoms described by these authors, no two lists are exactly alike. In all, 43 symptoms were found, with one writer listing 32, and another mentioning only six.

This, however, does not represent as great a diversity as it would appear on the surface. A great deal of the disparity results from the fact that some writers use very specific terms such as dysphasia and dysarthria, while another groups them together under language disorders. Another source of difficulty results from the fact that different authors are writing for different purposes. Strauss and Lehtinen (1950), for example, are quite definitive and describe a number of brain injured children displaying different symptoms. Yacorzynski (1951), on the other hand, describes some specific disabilities such as those found in cases with frontal lobe involvements. As a consequence, it is almost impossible to compare these writings for the purpose of making a normative study. However, these different authors would probably be in agreement on any given case.

By grouping some of the more specific symptoms under more general headings, one finds that the majority of writers are fairly well agreed on 15 categories. List No. 2 indicates the symptoms most commonly agreed upon by Strauss and Lehtinen (1950), Doll (1951a), Carmichael (1954), Tredgold (1952), Goldstein (1954), Bender (1956), Gesell and Amatruda (1954), and Yacorzynski (1951).

LIST NO. 1
Symptoms Ascribed to Brain Injured Children
by Various Writers

distractibility
perseveration
catastrophic reaction
temper tantrums
disorganization
visual perceptual difficulties
conceptual difficulties
detail consciousness
difficulty in spatial visualization
concrete thinking
difficulty in auditory perception
dysarthria
dysphasia
agnosia
apraxia
impulsiveness
compulsions
disinhibition
poor motor coordination
poor ability to anticipate
over-responsive to stimuli

disparity in development
hyperactivity
difficulty in symbolization
animistic thinking
emotional instability
insecurity
daydreaming
irritability
difficulty in forming associations
confused laterality
poor retention
convulsions
mental deficiency
lack of insight
fatigability
rigidity
abnormal stimulus boundness
poor body image and identification
anxiety
clinging behavior
destructiveness

LIST NO. 2
Symptoms of Brain Injury Indicated by the
Majority of Writers

perseveration	disparity in development
distractibility	hyperactivity
disorganization or lack of integration	emotional instability
perceptual difficulties	insecurity
conceptual difficulties	irritability
language disorders	convulsions
motor incoordination	mental deficiency
	poor retention

Doll (1951a) has summed up the situation rather well with his statement that it is not feasible at this time to delineate either the neurological antecedents or the behavior sequelae with definitive exactness, but rather, this must be left to further experience, observation, and research.

Although there is considerable agreement as far as the various symptoms are concerned, there is no indication that any given symptom must of necessity be present in any given case of brain injury. Kephart states, "In general the association of specific psychological symptoms with brain pathology has not been successful. It would appear that brain damage, except in specific motor and sensory areas, leads to a disturbance of the integration of behavior rather than to the development of isolated symptoms."[1]

This is not too surprising, when one stops to consider that in most cases the injuries are minimal and diffused and that different areas and functions of the brain are affected to differing degrees in various individuals. Then, too, the inherent make up of the brain and its ability to resist, repair, or compensate damage varies from one child to another. Gesell and Amatruda (1954) indicate that the consequences of very slight injury are greatly aggravated by emotional sensitivity in the child and by faulty environment and care. They further state that in infants and young children the symptomatology of nervous disease tends to be diffuse rather than localized, and it is this diffuseness that accounts for the injury to intellect and to personality that so often accompanies affections of the nervous system in infancy and childhood.

This then brings us to Strauss and Lehtinen's (1950, p. 4) definition: "A brain injured child is a child who before, during, or after birth has received an injury to or suffered an infection of the brain. As a result of

---

[1] This statement was taken from a personal communication with Dr. N. D. Kephart.

such organic impairment, defects of the neuromotor system may be present or absent; however, such a child may show disturbances in perception, thinking, and emotional behavior, either separately or in combination." It seems to the writer that this definition is a good summary of the situation as it presently exists.

Since, as we have seen, the symptoms of brain injury can be quite varied, and as they do not necessarily fall into any given pattern, certain implications become apparent with regard to psychological testing. To begin with, we are faced with the problem of determining whether any of these symptoms exist, which means that an extremely large number of abilities and a wide range of behavior need to be sampled and evaluated. This would imply that a shotgun type of approach be used in the beginning, followed up by more specific techniques in those areas which are suspected as pathological. If this be true, then it becomes necessary to evaluate both general tests or test batteries, and specific tests or tests of specific functions.

General vs. Specific Tests

With regard to general tests, Strauss and Lehtinen (1950) have stated that, with few exceptions, there does not exist at this moment, a pattern or a type of response characteristic and specific for the brain injured defective child on standardized tests of intelligence, academic achievement, and visuo-motor performance. Beck and Lam (1955), using a public school group of mentally handicapped children, found that the WISC Performance IQ's and WISC Full Scale IQ's of organics were significantly lower than those of non-organics. In the organic group the Performance IQ's tended to be lower than the Verbal IQ's, whereas the non-organics showed a reverse pattern. There was no characteristic patterning of subtest scores, however.

On the other hand, Newman and Loos (1955), using an institutional population, found that organics show no difference in WISC Verbal and Performance IQ's but that organics do have lower Performance IQ's than do familials and undifferentiated groups. Haines (1954) did a study using the Merrill-Palmer Scale of Mental Tests and concluded that it was not useful for the differential diagnosis of brain injured children from problem or foster home children. Berko (1955) found that exogenous mentally handicapped children had a significantly larger scattering of misses on the Stanford-Binet items than endogenous mentally retarded children. On the basis of these studies, it would seem that disparities in the child's development are reflected in the child's performance on the WISC and Stanford-Binet, which may suggest, to the examiner, the possibility of brain injury.

On tests designed to evaluate more specific functions, there is also more doubt than certainty as to their validity in differentiating between brain injured and non-brain injured. Most of them do not stand up under rigorous statistical analysis. Yates (1954) reviewed some of the more commonly used qualitative and quantitative tests and noted that most of them are subject to criticism. He found only two tests that seemed to differentiate organics consistently. One was the Block Design Rotation Test, and the other was the Manual and Finger Dexterity Tests of the U.S. Employment Service Battery. Unfortunately these tests are designed and/or standardized on adults and not children. Strauss and Kephart (1950) also studied some of the tests commonly used with children and concluded that the validation of tests of this sort was still incomplete. One of the main objections was that there had been no systematic attempt to differentiate brain injured from emotionally disturbed children. Of all the tests studied, the two most promising were the Ellis Visual Designs and the "Method" or "Approach" score on the Marble Board Test. These two were far superior to the others.

Inasmuch as most tests are lacking in statistical validity as predictors or indicators of brain injury, it is interesting to note Goldstein's (1954, p. 114) comment on this situation: "In pathology, results of examinations can be evaluated only by analyzing the procedure by which the patient has arrived at his results. This precludes any statistical comparison with the results of normal subjects. Any quantitative rating, as to success and failure by use of the usual tests, constitutes an infinite source of error." It would seem then that diagnosis is, at its present stage of development, more of an art than a science, and consequently the diagnosis must necessarily be a function of the examiner and not the tests.

Yates (1954) feels that the basic flaw in most of the tests of brain damage lies in the theoretical approach. Instead of employing the theory that brain damage results in deterioration, he suggests that what is needed is a theory which is exclusive to brain damage. Strauss and Kephart (1950), on the other hand, seem to feel that what is needed is further development and refinement of some of the tests presently in use.

The big problem in differential diagnosis seems to lie in the ability, or lack of ability, of tests to distinguish between organic brain damage and emotional disturbances. This, however, assumes that the symptoms are the same, or can be the same, in both conditions. If this be so, then it would seem impossible to devise a test to distinguish between the two conditions, since the overt behavior which the test measures would be the same in either case.

Functional Brain Impairment

At this point the writer would raise the question as to whether or not it is actually possible to get the same identical symptoms, or constellation of symptoms, in both conditions, or whether the apparent confusion is the result of our inability to make an adequate medical diagnosis. This also brings up the question of the possibility of functional brain impairment. If, for example, an individual developed an emotional disturbance, which resulted in some change in body chemistry, this might conceivably result in electrical changes in the brain, which in turn might affect its functioning.

In fact, Darrow (1950, p. 59) states, ". . . feed back effects which, when they act moderately, appear to provide regulation of the central nervous system, but which, when they become excessive in strong emotion, may produce relative functional decortication." Darrow (1950 a, p. 248) also states, "Furthermore, if these mechanisms are operative during the child's early stages of rapid growth and development, it is easy to understand how chronic states of emotional perturbation not only may alter the normal activity of the brain but may even prevent its normal development." If this is possible, then final diagnosis may depend upon the determination of the reversibility of the condition.

It would seem that Yates (1954) has put his finger on the crux of the whole situation. If psychological tests are going to be employed to determine the etiology of malfunction, then it is necessary to determine functions which are characteristic of, and peculiar to, the precise etiological factor in question. This may prove to be a formidable problem in the light of present knowledge. This is particularly true, when even medical or physical diagnosis of brain disorder is based on inferences as the result of the neurologist's evaluation of the individual's functioning. Actually medicine is, to some extent, faced with the same problem as psychology, and until better means are found to make the medical determinations, it is doubtful how far psychological testing can be extended.

From a practical point of view, the outlook perhaps is not as dismal as the theoretical considerations would suggest. In the case of a child we are concerned with several problems, all of which can be dealt with fairly well regardless of the theoretical problems. For example, neurological examination, plus E.E.G.'s, X-rays, penumoencephalograms, etc., can determine fairly well whether or not there are any major injuries, tumors, convulsive disorders, etc., and, if so, the proper procedures can be instituted. If medical evaluation definitely reveals damage then, of course, there is no problem of diagnosis. The problem then becomes one of determining the desirability of medication or other therapy, and the prognosis for future development.

If, on the other hand, the medical diagnosis is uncertain or negative, then the problem is whether or not there is damage which is medically undetectable. This is the dilemma with which we are faced in trying to prescribe adequate emotional and educational procedures, therapy, rehabilitation, and the like. Actually this doesn't present too great a problem, since the same procedure can be used in either case. The greatest difficulties resulting from this sort of situation might be some loss of time, and injury to the ego of the psychologist, if after treatment, the diagnosis turned out to be different than he predicted.

If the child displayed emotional or behavior problems, they would be handled about the same in either case. If he displayed learning difficulties suggestive of brain injury, he would be taught with techniques designed to overcome these difficulties. If a child displayed difficulty in perception or concept formation, the teaching techniques would be the same whether he turned out to be brain injured or not. When one considers the practical aspects of the situation, it then becomes apparent that present psychological techniques, especially if they can be more fully developed and refined, can be of real value as far as treatment is concerned.

REFERENCES

1. BAKER, H. J. *Introduction to Exceptional Children.* New York: MacMillan, 1945.

2. BECK, H. S. The Incidence of Brain Injury in Public School Special Classes for the Educable Mentally Handicapped. *J. ment. Def.,* 1956, 60, 818-822.

3. BECK, H. S., & LAM, R. L. Use of the WISC in Predicting Organicity, *J. Clin. Psychol.,* 1955, 11, 154-158.

4. BENDA, C. E. *Developmental Disorders of Mentation and Cerebral Palsies.* New York: Grune & Stratton, 1952.

5. BENDER, LAURETTA. *Psychopathology of Children with Organic Brain Disorders.* Springfield, III.: Charles C. Thomas, 1956.

6. BERKO, M. J. A Note on "Psychometric Scatter" as a Factor in the Differentiation of Exogenous and Endogenous Mental Deficiency. *Cerebral Palsy Rev.,* 1955, 16, No. 1.

7. BUROS, O. K. (Ed.) *The Fourth Mental Measurements Yearbook.* Highland Park: The Gryphon Press, 1953.

8. CARMICHAEL, L. *Manual of Child Psychology.* New York: John Wiley & Sons, 1954.

9. COURVILLE, C. B. *Pathology of the Central Nervous System.* Mount View: Pacific Press, 1950.

10. **DARROW, C. W.** A Mechanism for "Functional" Effects of Emotion on the Brain. In W. C. Halstead (Ed.) Brain and Behavior. *Comp. Psychol. Monogrs.*, 1950, No. 2.

11. **DARROW, C. W.** A New Frontier: Neurophysiological Effects of Emotion on the Brain. In M. L. Reymert (Ed.) *Feelings and Emotions.* (Mooseheart Symposium). New York: McGraw-Hill, 1950, Chapter 20. (a)

12. **DOLL, E. A.** Mental Evaluation of Children with Expressive Handicaps. *Amer. J. Orthopsychiat.*, 1951, 21, 148-154.

13. **DOLL, E. A.** Neurophrenia, *Amer. J. Psychiat.* 1951, July. 108, 50-53. (a)

14. **DOLL, E. A.** Varieties of Slow Learners. *Except. Child.*, 1953, 20, 61-64.

15. **DOLL, E. A.** Mental Deficiency vs. Neurophrenia. *Amer. J. ment. Def.*, 1953, 57, 477-480.

16. **DOLL, E. E., & WALKER, MABELLE S.** Handedness in Cerebral Palsied Children. *J. Consult. Psychol.*, 1951. 15, 9-17.

17. **GESELL, A., & AMATRUDA, C. S.** *Developmental Diagnosis.* New York: Paul B. Hoeber, 1954.

18. **GOLDSTEIN, K.** In H. Michal-Smith, *Pediatric Problems in Clinical Practice.* New York: Grune & Stratton, 1954.

19. **GRASSI, J. R.** *The Grassi Block Substitution Test for Measuring Organic Brain Pathology.* Springfield, Ill.: Charles C. Thomas, 1953.

20. **HAINES, MIRIAM S.** Test Performance of Preschool Children With and Without Organic Brain Pathology. *J. Consult, Psychol.*, 1954, 18, 371-374.

21. **HUNT J. Mc. V.** *Personality and the Behavior Disorders.* New York: The Ronald Press, 1944.

22. **LOUTTIT, C. M.** *Clinical Psychology.* New York: Harper & Brother, 1947.

23. **MIKESELL W. H.** *Modern Abnormal Psychology.* New York: Philosophical Library, 1950.

24. **NEWMAN, J. R., & LOOS, F. M.** Differences Between Verbal and Performance IQ's with Mentally Defective Children on the Wechsler Intelligence Scale for Children. *J. Consult. Psychol.*, 1955, 19, 16.

25. **PENFIELD, W., & RASSMUSSEN, T.** *The Cerebral Cortex of Man.* New York: MacMillan, 1952.

26. **PENNINGTON, L. A., & BERG, I. A.** *An Introduction to Clinical Psychology.*

27. **PENROSE, L. S.** *The Biology of Mental Defect.* London: Sidgwick & Jackson Ltd., 1949.

28. **SARASON, S. B.** *Psychological Problems in Mental Deficiency.* New York: Harper & Brothers, 1949.

29. **STRAUSS, A. A., & KEPHART, N. C.** *Psychopathology and Education of the Brain-Injured Child.* Vol. 2, *Progress in Theory and Clinic.* New York: Grune & Stratton, 1950.

30. STRAUSS, A. A., & LEHTINEN, LAURA E. *Psychopathology and Education of the Brain-Injured Child.* New York: Grune & Stratton, 1950.

31. TREDGOLD, A. F., & TREGOLD, R. F. *Mental Deficiency.* Baltimore: Williams & Wilkins, 1952.

32. WHITE, R. W. *The Abnormal Personality.* New York: Ronald Press, 1948.

33. YACORZYNSKI, G. K. *Medical Psychology.* New York: Ronald Press, 1951.

34. YATES, A. J. The Validity of Some Psychological Tests of Brain Damage. *Psychol. Bul.*, 1954, 51, 359-377.

SCHOOL is for . . .
SPECIAL STUDY

Chapter X

The Teacher as an Exceptionality Diagnostician

Education of children with special learning difficulties and handicaps is undergoing a rapid, decisive change in the United States. In the past, attempts have been made to group pupils homogeneously in special self-contained classrooms. Instruction has been provided by a teacher who has had special training related to teaching children with a particular handicap. In recent years it has become evident that the special class with its special teacher is no longer the single most appropriate response of the school for meeting needs of these special children.

Certainly special schools and classes are needed and necessary for some exceptional children but the majority of cases would profit much more from the understanding and guidance of a regular classroom teacher for at least a portion of the school day. It is likely that every classroom teacher will have some type of exceptionality case assigned to her room. The scope of this textbook would not allow each type of exceptionality case to be thoroughly discussed. However, the areas selected for presentation are representative samples of the types of problems a teacher must be able to diagnose and deal with as handicapped pupils become an integral part of the regular classroom.

The Exceptional Child— A Modern Concept

DR. R. C. BRADLEY

An historical approach would show that the entire concept of educating each child to the height of his ability is relatively new. In days gone by, the "exceptional" child was one who was exceedingly bright or extensively talented. Today the child who is bright is simply a member of a category making up the many categories of exceptional cases. Most authorities now accept the definition of the exceptional child as that pupil who deviates from the average or normal child in mental, physical, emotional, or social characteristics to such an extent that in order to develop in strong measure his capacity to learn, a modification of school practices is necessary.

No longer do educators suggest that an exceptional child receives special school treatment only for the major purpose of developing him to his maximum capacity or potential. All of us know what would happen to our cars if we drove them to the full limit that the speedometer readings indicate possible for an extended period of time. By the same token, one would not want to drive the child to the utmost (maximum) capacity even for short periods of time, nor in all subjects. Therefore, a child is considered educationally exceptional if his deviation is of such kind and degree that it interferes with his being taught under regular classroom procedures.

For the most part, educators accept the fact of individual differences. This would mean that the child is more advanced or less advanced than another child of the same grade. Although an exceptional child does differ from the average in class, this is only one of the factors to be taken into account. Within this category one would find children who are intellectually inferior or superior, those who may not see or hear as well, those who lack mobility, or pupils who don't have adequate language or

Bradley, R. C. "The Exceptional Child—A Modern Concept." *The Oklahoma Teacher*. December 1967. 49:12-13, 14.

speech skills as does the average child. Moreover, a child in this category may be deviant in interpersonal relations. Teachers know that not only is it important "how well" a person relates to others, but also to the "manner or ways" in which he approaches them.

The second category that the classroom teacher must consider in his analysis of children deals with how the exceptional child, after having been identified, seems to grow unevenly. These children differ markedly from the average child in many characteristics and, in addition, vary in growth within themselves. This category certainly includes the gifted, mentally retarded, auditorily handicapped, visually handicapped, speech handicapped, crippled, socially maladjusted, and multiply handicapped. Yet, the major consideration in a study of this category would be the ways that each of the aforementioned factors represented "discrepancies" in a particular growth pattern.

What is Special?

What is "special" about Special Education? Special education is not a total program entirely different from the education of the ordinary child within the regular classroom. Special education becomes special because it is an aspect of a child's training which is unique or in addition to the regular program for all children. For example, the general educational program for a child who is bright is carried out in all phases of learning by the regular classroom teacher. The **special** part of his education may come when he meets 15 minutes a day with persons who are trained in working with the special talents of the gifted. Naturally, some need more special help than others—the training of the deaf and blind suggest this fact. The child becomes a member of a special classroom primarily because the special class teacher is trained in methods not used by the regular teacher or special equipment is needed for training purposes.

Although the many "special programs" coming into existence might suggest the thought that there must be a trend toward educating most children in some special class, such is not the case. Generally authorities agree that most exceptional children need to have some time in a pleasant association with regular school children. This association is best engendered in the regular public school setting. Certainly special schools and classes are necessary for **some** exceptional children, but the majority of cases would profit much more from the understanding and guidance of a regular classroom teacher at least a portion of the school day. When exceptional children can attend a special class, the regular classroom teacher does not have to worry about giving the major portion of her teaching time to those cases, possibly neglecting the larger number of her students of normal abilities.

Since the writer has suggested a description of the exceptional children to whom he refers, and further has indicated that regular classroom teachers tend to have the greater impact upon the vast number of exceptional children who still find themselves in regular classrooms, the following suggestions are given to aid classroom teachers in dealing with certain cases of exceptionality.

1. In enriching the program for gifted children, one cannot enrich simply by asking another set of questions. The ability to recognize and memorize facts is important, but productive thinking is more so. The school program must develop these pupils' abilities to create new ideas, evolve new concepts, and perceive contrasting relationships.

2. If we cannot identify or find a place for a particular child with some type of problem, all too often he is labeled "brain injured" and goes to that respective class. Before a child is labeled as brain injured he should have a proper examination by a competent neurologist and an accompanying psychological examination.

3. To know that there are three children in a class who are hard of hearing does not necessarily mean that much is being done about it. It is sound practice for the teacher to check hearing aids for weak batteries, excessive wax in the hearing plug, defective wiring and the like. Some children simply need a seat where they can view the teacher's lips, or perhaps it is by demand of the teacher they continue wearing a hearing apparatus.

4. Although it is important that weaknesses be identified, certainly those weaknesses should not determine the program for exceptional children. What happens to the child who is labeled as a "retarded reader?" Usually, he is given **more** reading. If he doesn't like reading to begin with, certainly he isn't going to do well by having more of it. Teachers need to search out new or different avenues to accomplish the same thing. There are many ways of learning to read without having to use the textbook. Films, over-head projectors, and science experimentation are examples of this fact. The brain is like a gigantic switchboard. It doesn't matter about the sensory organ used to transmit the idea; what matters is whether or not it has been perceived in the central nervous system.

5. Sometimes we operate between two extremes in dealing with exceptional children. We feel sorry for them and expect too little; or we know what is going to be demanded of them in job situations in the future and then we expect too much. Possibly the better approach would be, "treat them gently, yet firmly." Goals must be set and deadlines met.

6. Tests for diagnosing specific problems of exceptional children must be selected with extreme caution. For example, screening tests are

given to identify the presence of any visual difficulties. If observations or screening tests suggest a defect, the teacher refers the child to an eye specialist for extended examination. The Snellen Test is most widely used for visual screening. However, the Snellen chart measures central distance acuity only. If a child stands at 20 feet away as the directions indicate, then only far point acuity is measured. In reality, particularly for school purposes, a measurement of 14 to 18 inches (near point acuity) would have more merit. This is not meant to discourage the use of the Snellen Chart by any means, but it is to indicate other tests are also needed which would determine near point vision, peripheral vision, convergence ability, muscular imbalance, or fusion ability.

7. Unless children are going to be taught differently, then there is little need of special classes for them. All too often special classes for exceptional children are organized in the physical setting, but the same methods and procedures are carried over from the regular classroom. The special classroom teacher should have a thorough understanding of the Fernald technique, Doman-Delacato Developmental approach, Operant Conditioning procedures, and the like, plus the fact that he must be well grounded in those procedures basic to good classroom instruction.

In summary, if exceptional children are going to enjoy aspects of life that are basically normal for most children, then they must have some daily association with normal children where possible. It is strongly recommended that school vision screening programs be expanded to include tests in other areas to supplement the Snellen chart. Rather than to debate whether one should organize the curriculum to allow emphasis of either "strengths" or "weaknesses" in the teaching of exceptional children, possibly greater attention could well be directed toward achieving a proper balance of emphasis between the two factors. Although the selection of experienced teachers whose personality and interests are suitable for the teaching of exceptional children is of utmost importance, strong or at least equal consideration must be given to the fact that persons working with exceptional children should have experience in clinical and group-work procedures of a very high order.

Is There A Handicapped Child In Your Class?

TONY and MARTY DEAHL

The prospect of having a handicapped child in a class with thirty "normal" demanding children need not be frightening. Many handicapped children are more like their peers than different. They have the same physical, intellectual, and emotional needs as other children, plus additional special needs resulting from their handicap. With competent medical care, good environments, and suitable educational programs, many of them will become mature, contributing members of society.

It is often assumed that the social and physical environments, and therefore the educational programs, of the normal and the exceptional child are vastly different. However, in many cases with a few adjustments they can complement each other. The exceptional child needs empathy, not sympathy. Once the child and the problem are understood, the child will not seem so frightening, or the problem so overwhelming.

The necessary adjustments may be as beneficial to the normal child as the exceptional one. For example, the hard-of-hearing child misses so much of what is being said that he may just stop paying attention. Inattentiveness may be just as great a problem with the normal child, for a variety of reasons such as lack of interest. For both, inattentiveness may become a habit; and for both, activities using auditory discrimination and the following of oral directions may help to alleviate the problem. Again, tapes and records, which are valuable tools in the education of the visually handicapped, may be just as valuable for other students who may retain auditory information better than visual.

But not all the adaptations required for exceptional children will benefit other children in the class. The teacher should expect that the exceptional child will require additional attention and should provide for flexibility in planning.

A teacher's understanding and acceptance of the child will influence not only his attitude toward his peers, and toward society in general, but also their attitude toward him. In this series we will discuss how children handicapped in various ways can be handled in the regular classroom, including concrete suggestions which the teacher can use with both exceptional and normal children.

The Visually Handicapped

Cindy, a ten-year-old fourth grader, is a fairly typical partially sighted student who might be found in a regular classroom. She has three visual defects; nystagmus, a continual wandering or searching movement of the eyes; astigmatism, which prevents her eyes from focusing properly and causes a blurred image; and esotropia, a turning in of the eye—in other words, people describe her as "cross-eyed." To further complicate the situation, Cindy is a partial albino. With this condition, seeing in bright light is very difficult, and long periods of time in the sun will result in sun poisoning unless protection is used.

But in spite of Cindy's visual handicaps, she can handle most classroom activities, with some special adaptations. She reads large-print books, or small-print books with the aid of a magnifying glass. Talking books, books recorded on records, and tapes are useful. A special seat placement helps Cindy make good use of what vision she has. Perhaps she can also benefit from special paper with heavily printed lines spaced further apart.

Each specific subject may require some adaptations. Art is an area often overlooked for the visually handicapped. Here we will suggest several art experiences which will be beneficial not only to Cindy, but to the rest of the class.

If one word could describe an attitude to adaptive art for the visually handicapped child, it would be *macro.* Emphasis should be placed on large manipulative materials, methods, and techniques. Paper-bag art, nature mobiles, and pebble sculpture are examples.

Paper-bag art utilizes common everyday materials, and lends itself to self-expression and creativity, which are essential components of a good art project. Materials include a paper bag or two for each member of the class, scraps of cloth or leather, and assorted buttons, washers, ribbons, pressed leaves, or other decorative materials. Let the paper bags soak in warm water for approximately fifteen minutes. Carefully open each glued edge, and crumple the bag as the water is being wrung out. After spreading and drying, the paper will resemble tapa cloth. Simple articles of clothing may then be cut out, glued together, and decorated. The simplest and most popular articles are vests, skirts, shirts, and aprons.

Nature mobiles give opportunity to utilize art and science in one project. Nature mobiles can be constructed from a combination of almost any natural objects. Twigs and well pressed leaves can be made into a very interesting mobile, and also lend themselves well to the teaching of basic science. During the fall months children may collect and press leaves of different colors and shapes.

Pebble sculpture is another example of "macro" art. Often children make collections of rocks selected for their shape, color, or resemblance to animals or people. By gluing different sizes and shapes of pebbles together with epoxy glue, and adding wire for hair, pipe cleaners for limbs or tails, and buttons for eyes, the children can create any number of fanciful characters.

A Hearing Impaired Pupil in the Classroom

WINIFRED H. NORTHCOTT

A teacher confronted for the first time with the presence of a severly hearing impaired child in the classroom may not know how to handle the situation in such a way that the child will be effectively integrated into the class. A balance must be achieved so that the hearing impaired child will have the opportunity to receive the maximum benefit from the experience and the normal classroom procedure will not be impeded. To help the teacher who may be facing this experience in her classroom, I have set forth these guidelines, which were originally written for use in the Minnesota public schools.

Conditions Affecting Hearing And Learning

The audiogram, in itself, does not determine the hearing impaired child's potential for success or failure in an integrated setting in a local school district. Some of the contributing factors are: age at onset of loss, degree of loss in the speech range, quality of parent-child relationships, lipreading ability, personality, and availability of supplemental instruction services provided by an academic tutor or developmental reading specialist as well as the services of a speech clinician.

Full-time use of an individual hearing aid, when prescribed, is essential for effective classroom participation. It enables a student to hear individual speech sounds more adequately, makes their production more accurate, and supplements the limited clues supplied by lipreading. An extra hearing aid battery should be kept in school at all times.

Northcott, Winifred H., Ph.D. "A Hearing Impaired Pupil in the Classroom." Reprinted by permission from *The Volta Review*, 74, 2, February 1972, pp. 105-108, copyright © The Alexander Graham Bell Association for the Deaf.

A pupil's hearing loss will fluctuate, complicated by severe colds in wintertime. The thresholds of audibility will vary sharply during a school day. The reverberations of sound present in a group discussion make listening difficult in contrast to the one-to-one relationship when supplemental instruction is being provided. The hearing aid magnifies all sounds equally and auditory discrimination of speech sounds is a gradual developmental process. Afternoon fatigue, particularly in young children, often contributes to added difficulty in comprehension during the afternoon hours.

The result of a fluctuating acoustic environment is that the hearing impaired child may require good lipreading clues and more repetitions than usual in certain situations. When the vocabulary and conceptual content of your conversation are familiar to him, his response will be more appropriate. At other times, when he misses the substance of what is being said, he will appear to be inattentive or misbehaving.

Securing Class Cooperation

Your tolerance, humor, and affection for children are essential for successful integration of the hard of hearing or deaf child in social and academic activities. The other pupils in your class will be quick to mirror your attitudes toward him. The expression on your face, your muscle tension, and subtle actions will be eloquent silent testimony as to whether you regard this youngster as an interloper or an interesting addition to the class.

In the primary grades, children respond quickly to a simple explanation of the problems that accompany a hearing loss. In the upper grades, the student should be consulted about his role and his wishes in such an undertaking. You might read in a whisper from an unfamiliar book to demonstrate the difficulty of relying on lipreading clues and imperfect hearing. A class might enjoy compiling a list of "look alikes" for the word *pan (p, b, m and t, d, n,* are identical on the lips.) Other words are invisible on the lips *(onion, king, egg)*. A sentence should be rephrased, if it is not understood initially, to include words with higher visibility.

A pupil, not hearing the total conversation, may make an inappropriate remark or give an answer not pertinent to the topic under discussion. Children may have to wait until the hearing impaired classmate looks at them before speaking.

Let your pupil share in the original decision of classroom seating, with opportunity to change if his first choice has proved unwise. Ideally, the seating should be flexible, with one desk located near the blackboard for the pupil to slip into when oral demonstrations are being given. For the music period, let the hearing impaired pupil stand near the piano, his hand resting lightly above the keyboard, facing the piano player and the class. In this way, he can keep pace with the words and music.

If there is a unilateral hearing loss, the pupil should be seated so that the ear with normal hearing is toward the majority of the class.

Optimum Conditions For Learning

Appoint a "listening helper" (to be rotated) to sit next to the hearing impaired pupil to ensure his turning to the correct page in a workbook or textbook. Homework assignments should be kept in a small notebook, with the pupil being responsible. This will be reviewed by you at the end of each day for accuracy.

Good lipreading conditions require that the light be on your face and out of the pupil's eyes; your hands be away from your face; and that there be a distance of three feet between you and the child. Eighteen inches is an ideal listening distance for the child.

Although you are proceeding at the pace appropriate for the average student in your room, it will help the hard of hearing child if you write key phrases or vocabulary words on the blackboard. At times, you may wish to rephrase the material to ensure greater comprehension.

When dictating spelling words, use them in sentences to provide additional clues for comprehension.

Expect your hearing impaired pupil to contribute to oral discussions daily, in reduced and appropriate degree. Accept his imperfect expressive language, repeating it with corrections, or making mental note to discuss the problem with the supplemental tutor and speech clinician.

Encourage your hard of hearing pupil to let you know when he doesn't understand. A nod or smile does not always indicate comprehension; a periodic check is necessary in the form of a question requiring a substantive reply.

This youngster may need extra help in understanding the rules of a game in physical education or on the playground. He should not be permitted to have the passive role of a bystander in group activities.

Successful integration into a class of hearing children requires that a hard of hearing or deaf child be independent, persistent, adaptable, and socially mature as well as academically competitive. Your influence should be strong in every facet of his growth and development.

Parental Responsibility

Invite the pupil's parents to visit school regularly so they can realistically assess their child's abilities and appreciate the extra guidance and support you provide him in the classroom.

Members of the family should reinforce, through home stimulation, the vocabulary and concepts encountered in school. The emphasis should be on useful, idiomatic language and natural conversation revolving around attitudes, activities, and interests of the hearing impaired child. Parents will vary in their ability to cope with these challenges or to follow your recommendations.

Regular visits to the school and neighborhood library are desirable. It is also well to encourage hobbies which promote resourcefulness and creativity. At the secondary level, a student must supplement the incomplete notes and understanding of a day's teaching by reading the assigned textbook chapters at home. Reading for pleasure and comprehension is necessary also.

An Annual Evaluation

It is essential that the classroom teacher, supplemental tutor-audiologist, and speech correctionist participate in a comprehensive evaluation of the hearing impaired child each spring to determine appropriate placement for the following academic year. Consideration of the social maturity, academic achievement, intellectual potential, hearing aid usage, and personality of the pupil will highlight the appropriateness of the present academic environment or the need for change.

The Epileptic Child in School

PHILIP T. WHITE, M.D.

Great advances have occurred in the treatment of epilepsy in the past few decades. Many drugs are now available and with the proper drug, or combination of drugs, most children can enjoy a relatively normal unrestricted life. In about half of the children seizures can be completely controlled, and in another 30% seizures can be controlled to the point where they represent no severe handicap.

The epileptic child may represent a problem in school. However, the majority of such children are capable of attending school regularly, of enjoying a normal healthy life, and of looking forward to becoming worthwhile contributing citizens. Children with epilepsy, like healthy ones, display a wide range of intelligence—the average epileptic child without severe injury belonging to the so-called "normal" population.

Some epileptic children are superior; some are of low intelligence. Some children with epilepsy are intellectually handicapped and will need to attend special classes. Each case must be individually assessed and blanket restrictions cannot be laid down.

The need for special classes should be dictated by the pupil's abilities rather than by the fact that he is subject to seizures. Fortunately, most youngsters with epilepsy can continue in regular classes. This often requires cooperation and understanding between the parents and the teacher.

Often the teacher can help the parents accept a handicap. In turn the parents should be willing to inform the teacher as to any special needs and restrictions that apply to their child. It is helpful if the teacher knows the type of seizure that the student is likely to have and a knowledge as to the effects of the medicine the child is taking. In counsel with the family physician, the school health personnel and teacher can often help insure regularity of medication and any special attention the child might or might not need.

White, Philip T. "The Epileptic Child in School." *Arizona Teacher*. November 1964. 53:12-13. Copyright © 1964 by the Arizona Education Association.

The occurrence of a convulsion may disrupt not only an entire classroom but also the entire future of a child, unless the incident is handled intelligently by the teacher. It is well to know the causes for epilepsy; they are many and varied. In some youngsters no definable cause is apparent, and these are sometimes said to have idiopathic epilepsy.

In other children, infections, injuries, congenital defects, or growths on the brain may cause seizures. Disease elsewhere in the body may result in seizures; for example, diabetes, poisonings, heart disease, allergies, and kidney disease. Seizures from whatever cause may be aggravated under certain circumstances such as periods of emotional tension or stress, undue excitement or during simple infections of the type affecting children. Any person can suffer seizures—they can occur at any age—often without warning.

Witnessing a seizure, especially the first time, is often dramatic and frightening. It is, therefore, important for the welfare of the child and the subsequent attitude of his classmates, that the teacher act in a calm manner. Fortunately, a seizure of the "grand mal" or major type usually lasts only a short time and does not require expert care. A few simple procedures are often helpful.

What to do for an Epileptic Seizure

1. Ease the child to the floor and loosen his clothing.
2. Use gentle restraint to prevent the child from injuring himself by striking objects with his head or arms. Keep the child away from radiators and other hot objects.
3. Turn the child on his side so that the saliva can flow out of his mouth. It is not necessary to insert a mouth gag and one should *never place a finger in the mouth or try to force open the clenched jaws.*
4. After the movements stop and the child is relaxed, he should be allowed to sleep or rest, preferably in a quiet area.
5. If the seizures are mild, school attendance for the rest of the day may well be possible. If the child shows persistent after effects, he should probably be accompanied home.
6. The parents should be notified that a seizure has occurred, particularly if this is the first such seizure. Even in the known epileptic such information should be relayed to the parents so that the physician in charge of the case may have knowledge of these events.
7. The occurrence of a seizure in the classroom can be used by the teacher as an object lesson. Her calm and competent manner will help other students to understand and accept this illness in their classmate. A simple brief explanation that this is a form of illness over which the pupil has no control will usually suffice. Older pupils may benefit from a more detailed explanation. The older pupils can often learn a great deal from a child with a handicap. Children should not be isolated from unpleasant and unsightly aspects of life. They should be taught to help others less fortunate than themselves. The teacher can

often be instrumental in preventing the epileptic child from becoming isolated and the subject of cruel taunting from the other pupils.

An accurate description by the teacher of any seizures that occur is often very helpful to the physician treating the student. This type of cooperation is highly commendable and of inestimable value to the community eventually.

In general, physical activity has a favorable effect on epilepsy. It is generally not necessary to restrict participation in the usual physical activities about a school. The student should be made to feel as much a part of the group as possible and restricting him from activity will set him apart. Certain obvious restrictions must be observed. Climbing to heights, power machinery, and hot equipment may have to be avoided. Swimming may or may not be restricted, depending upon the frequency and severity of seizures. Close supervision of the latter is always advisable. For the older student participation in driving education courses is often possible.

Some epileptic children present problems not because of seizures but because of behavioral difficulties. Parental and playmate attitudes often result in isolation of a handicapped child, and behavioral disturbances may be a reaction to this isolation. This requires an understanding on the part of the school authorities. If such difficulties are not recognized, the child may not be given the help and understanding that is necessary and may develop behavioral aberrations. The treatment of seizures depends largely on a variety of medicines, and unfortunately, these medicines may in some cases induce behavioral changes.

To summarize, medical treatment can often perform wonders in the control of epilepsy, but this is only one aspect of the proper treatment of the epileptic student. The attitudes of parents and teachers and classmates are of paramount importance in establishing this pattern by which the child develops in the future.

SCHOOL is for . . .
DEMONSTRATING
PERSONAL POWER

Therapeutic Role Of The Teacher Of Physically Handicapped Children

MYRON SWACK

Each member of the habilitation team, acting as a specialist, makes a unique contribution in a cooperative effort for the benefit of a handicapped child. In addition, team members as generalists do some of the work of the other specialists.

For the most part, physical therapists have discarded the notion that therapy ends when the student patient leaves the department. The locus for physical therapy may be defined as the total geographical area in which the handicapped child is functioning rather than just the site of the department. Thus, one test of good therapy might be the extent to which it is carried on by other workers outside of the physical therapy department. Physical therapists should assume responsibility for teaching desirable therapeutic techniques to persons who are within the sphere of influence of the physically handicapped child, such as the classroom teacher who is in an ideal position to aid in the determination and attainment of objectives.

Classroom teachers of orthopedically handicapped children are an integral part of the habilitation team. These teachers have more influence than any other team member in a school setting on how children ambulate outside the physical therapy department. By the same token, teachers can, through observation and appropriate action, insure safety practices throughout the child's school environment. The teachers can be the determining factors regarding whether a given child will be oriented towards passive roles or towards active participant roles.

Swack, Myron. "Therapeutic Role of the Teacher of Physically Handicapped Children." *Exceptional Children.* January 1969. 35:371-374.

General Objectives

Habilitation specialists working with physically handicapped children are concerned with the establishment of desirable habit patterns in three basic areas:

1. Consistent use of the method of locomotion which would enable the handicapped child to ambulate at his highest level of capacity.
2. Observation and inspection of a child's therapeutic equipment to insure proper functioning.
3. Classroom safety practices which would decrease accidents and injuries in the school environment.

These areas represent behaviors in which the whole habilitation team could focus its attention. In helping to implement these objectives, the classroom teacher would become a full member of the habilitation team, with the following possible results:

1. Throughout the school environment, physically handicapped children would utilize gait patterns considered optimal, and carryover to the home would be enhanced.
2. Children would become more independent in attitude and thought if the classroom teacher participated actively to achieve this basic objective of therapy.
3. Teachers would respond to a handicapped child or children rather than be constantly reminded by the physical therapist.
4. Classroom teachers would have a better understanding of where any given child was located in the ambulation sequence. The teacher would also recognize his role in this locomotion continuum.
5. By observing the state of a child's therapeutic equipment, the teacher could extend safety practices to all parts of the school environment.
6. Stressing independent action could carry over to other phases in the educational scene, e.g., the role of a handicapped person in society, home, peer group, etc. Teaching units regarding safety in a variety of situations—home, community, and school—could be initiated in the classroom.
7. Relationships between classroom teachers and physical therapists could improve as each gained insights and understandings of the others' role as members of the educational team.

Specific Objectives
Methods of Locomotion

Handicapped children who are in the process of a gait sequence may have two types of ambulation patterns which are being used simultaneously. The primary gait pattern is the method of locomotion the child utilizes in the school day and the secondary pattern is the pattern which he is learning in physical therapy and which needs to be reinforced away from the physical therapy department. For example, a child may be propelling himself in a wheelchair at the same time that he is learning a four point crutch gait in physical therapy.

The critical points in the locomotion sequence may be placed on a continuum from the least desirable form to the most desirable method of ambulation. These are: (a) a child being pushed in a wheelchair; (b) a child propelling himself in a wheelchair; (c) a child ambulating with a walking aid; (d) a child walking with crutches but needing aid in standing and sitting; and (e) a child ambulating with crutches without any additional help. An analysis of each category follows:

A child being pushed in a wheelchair. This method of mobility allows a child to be a passive participant in the locomotion sequence. While it is true that some children are so severely involved that they cannot help themselves, it should be recognized that this method of locomotion is undesirable and usually indicates a poor ambulatory prognosis. Whenever possible, this behavior should be discouraged by the classroom teacher and the student's fellow classmates.

A child propelling himself in a wheelchair. A handicapped child using this method of mobility is assuming more responsibility for himself than the child in a wheelchair. The reach, grasp, strength, and endurance of the upper extremities are being perfected. The child has independent control of movement. He cannot negotiate stairs but he can learn appropriate behavior for use of elevators and ramps.

Negative aspects of this method of mobility include the fact that the sitting position is conducive to the development of muscular contractures and that standing tolerance, standing balance, and reciprocal leg motion are not being attained.

A child who can ambulate with a walking aid. In this phase, there is increased opportunity for the child to assume more responsibility in weight bearing, standing tolerance, standing balance, endurance in mobility, and confidence in himself with regard to ambulation. He may be pushing a weighted wheelchair with a bar located between the wheelchair handles or using a variety of other walking aids. The key factor is that the child is in a standing position, which can relieve and alleviate muscular contractures resulting from remaining in the sitting position. The psychological implications of independent action could spur the child to greater attempts and subsequent success.

The child should be taught by the physical therapist and reinforced by the habilitation team to rise from the sitting position, attain a standing balance, reach a desired destination, and return to a sitting position. One of the greatest fears of the novice teacher is the thought of the child walking toward some objective and falling. There is a strong tendency for habilitation team members to pick the child up rather than allow the child to do what he has been practicing and in certain instances to use what he already knows. When a child reaches this level, he should make use of his physical gains whenever and wherever possible, e.g., when going from classroom to library, classroom to cafeteria, classroom to bus, classroom to outside activities, and when participating in activities within the classroom.

A child who can ambulate with crutches, but needs help in attaining the standing position or in sitting when he reaches his destination. This phase of the gait sequence can be a highly critical area. In many instances a child may be classified as being in a dual developmental stage, for, in an effort to reach his optimal method of ambulation, he may be using one type of gait pattern while learning another more desirable gait pattern. The over-all transfer objective in gait training is the attainment of a consistent and optimal gait pattern wherever and whenever possible. This enigmatic goal should allow the child to be given the benefit of the doubt as to whether attainment is possible.

Standing balance and locomotion from the standing position are usually taught in advance of rising and seating. Consequently, there occurs the time when the child can ambulate to chosen destinations but needs help in rising and in being seated. This period usually is of relatively short duration. In certain instances, the child is allowed to ride in a wheelchair or revert back to using a less desirable walking aid when no one is around to supply the needed help. This regression may also occur when the child is poorly motivated toward independent action or is oriented toward passive roles. Habilitation team members can and should in this phase aid the child to rise and upon reaching the desired destination regain the seating position. The physical therapist should teach the various techniques to classroom teachers. It is imperative that communicative lines be open between the teacher and the therapist in order to coordinate the degree of help the child may require.

A child who can ambulate with crutches without any aid. The child, to be totally independent, must be able to reach and grasp his crutches and protective equipment (helmet, face guards, etc.). To facilitate this, classroom furniture must be modified to accommodate crutches and protective equipment. For example, equipment holders must be located near the classroom desk or wheelchair.

Observation and Inspection of a Child's Therapeutic Equipment

The inspection of a child's therapeutic equipment constitutes a response to a discriminative stimulus—a handicapped child with his braces, crutches, protective helmet, etc. Many therapists prefer to make this inspection themselves; however, the teacher can aid by insuring a constant surveillance throughout the school day. Braces must be able to support weak musculature, crutches must be sound, helmets must be protective. By this attention, unnecessary hardships and accidents in the school environment can be alleviated.

Ideal behavior would be for the handicapped child to be able to recognize and isolate defects in his equipment. When a child senses a lack of support or control, he should be encouraged to seek the aid of the teacher and/or physical therapist. The reduction of uncertainty concerning his therapeutic equipment would be reinforcing. A teacher asking a child as to the status of his bracing and crutches can stimulate a self evaluation of his equipment. This practice could be integrated at a regular time in the school day as part of his educational program.

When the child demonstrates apprehension about his therapeutic equipment, the teacher could examine braces and crutches. There are certain conditions, e.g., spinal conditions, in which physical sensations are lacking or missing. Consequently, an inspection must be made by direct observation by the teacher as well as by the child. With braces, the following possible problems should be checked: brace straps too tight or too loose, brace joint blocked by foreign materials, shoe laces missing or tied short, braces misaligned, braces not attached to shoes, straps broken, or screws loose. A child's crutches should be checked for screws loose, rubber crutch tips missing or loose, or hand grip loose.

Classroom Safety and Use of Therapeutic Equipment

There are many instances in which a handicapped child's therapeutic program can be augmented and implemented in the classroom. Suffice to say that the following suggestions should be analyzed according to the needs of a particular program and implemented as the need arises.

Braces. Basically, the classroom teacher should be able to remove and replace the various types of braces used by orthopedically impaired children. When the teacher can do this, it is a relatively simple matter to lock hip and/or knee joints and place the appropriate individual in a standing table, or to lock knee joints of a child sitting at his desk. The locking of knee joints while the child is in a sitting position may require additional support to maintain a comfortable sitting position. The key issue is the graduated increase of time spent in either the locked braces position or the standing table. Communication between the teacher and the physical therapist can clarify and regulate the graduation of the time element.

Protective helmets. Safety is not the domain of any particular therapy or person. The implementation of desirable safety practices is a function of the total habilitation team. Running in the halls and speeding wheelchairs are examples of behavior which must be controlled. A child who wears a protective helmet should wear the helmet properly when ambulating. Some helmets have modifications for additional protection, e.g., face guards, chin guards, etc. The helmet should be worn with maximum protection to the wearer. Some children wrongly prefer to wear the helmet cocked to one side or on the back of their head, the chin straps open instead of closed, and are thus afforded no protection. Helmet modifications should be intact and in place, e.g., the chin strap should cover the chin, nose guards should protect the nose, and supportive straps should be closed. Implementation of these suggestions can decrease unnecessary accidents and harmful effects of needless injuries.

Wheelchairs. Accidents in wheelchairs come primarily from two basic causes: (a) classmates pushing wheelchairs at a very rapid rate of speed, and (b) wheelchairs rolling away because the child cannot help himself due to severity of his handicap. Constant surveillance by the habilitation team and reinforcement of the following two practices can neutralize or ameliorate these conditions:

1. Promote the rule, "Running in or around the school premises will not be tolerated." Discussions led by the teacher in the classroom would help. The establishment of safety patrols in schools for physically handicapped children could also be of value.
2. Strictly enforce the rule, "Wheelchairs when not in motion will be locked." This rule will not only prevent rolling away but will also furnish a stabilized base for those children who can transfer from the wheelchair to a desk, toilet, or another type of seating.

Conclusion

Due to the fact that a variety of approaches are being utilized in treating physically handicapped children, especially the cerebral palsied, this article was limited to those therapeutic programs which use braces, crutches, wheelchairs, and other therapeutic equipment. It would be highly desirable for each school program to adapt some of the aforementioned comments to its own setting. In the last analysis, if there exist any tasks or behaviors which are important enough to warrant their being transferred from the physical therapy department to other pertinent sites, they must be taught by the appropriate therapists to other persons within the sphere of influence of the handicapped child.

Responsibility of Public Education For Exceptional Children

RAY GRAHAM

Lincoln Steffens in his autobiography tells the story of a man and the devil walking together down the street of a busy city. They saw a man reach out and grasp a fine and worthy idea—right out of the air. The man said to the devil, "Did you see that? And aren't you afraid of it? A worthy idea can grow and grow until it becomes so powerful it will destroy you." The devil replied, "No, I am not afraid of it. First they will give it a name. Then they will organize and promote it—and then there will be so many ideas of how to handle it that they will become confused and controversial among themselves and the worthy idea will weaken and destroy itself. No, I am not afraid of it."

The history of education is replete with many fine ideas. In spite of the devil many have grown and endured—the steadfast belief in public education in a democracy; the growth of colleges and universities; a dedicated faith in children and youth; worthy objectives of education; and high professional standards. In the development of every one of these ideas, it has been necessary to whip the several devil's advocates: (1) misconception as to purpose and plan, (2) conformity to past patterns and established beliefs, and (3) lethargy of action. One of the more recent (in terms of the long history of public education) is what is commonly referred to as special education for exceptional children.

It is not easy to determine just when this worthy idea was "plucked out of the air." Possibly it was when special institutions for handicapped were developed, first in Europe and later in this country. Possibly the idea began with the adoption of our state constitutions guaranteeing an

Graham, Ray. "Responsibility of Public Education for Exceptional Children." *Exceptional Children.* January 1962. 28:255-259.

educational opportunity to all the children. (I have never been able to find any interpretation that said these state constitutions meant to say "all the children but those who were mentally retarded, or severely crippled, or totally blind, or brain-damaged, or deaf, or bed-fast, or delinquent and incorrigible." The interpretation is that *all* means *every* child.)

The idea may have been born again as various states passed compulsory attendance legislation. Or it may have developed naturally through the processes of conception of an idea, pregnancy, birth, and growth from the emergent democratic philosophies that have been the seeds of all progress in government and politics, in culture, in economics, in science and in education. For instance, the children's charter which said in Article XIII: "For every child who is blind, deaf, crippled, or otherwise physically handicapped, and for the child who is mentally handicapped, such measures as will early discover and diagnose his handicap, provide care and treatment, and so train him that he may become an asset to society rather than a liability. Expenses of these services should be borne publicly where they cannot be privately met."

Suffice it to say that in the middle of the twentieth century it has become an accepted responsibility, with special legislation enacted in every one of the states, to set up a plan whereby all the children including the handicapped may secure a school opportunity. It is not an opportunity for the mentally retarded child if he is expected to do the same work with the same achievement that is required of children with average ability. It is not an opportunity for the physically handicapped child who is limited in physical performance to have to adjust to the same curricula in every detail as does the non-handicapped. It is not acceptable opportunity to deprive the superior child by limiting him to an average program. It is not an opportunity for a child to learn to adjust to all the complexities of the society in which he must live if we isolate and segregate him by placing him only with the handicapped of his own type.

Education today has a major challenge to find the ways and means, and to develop the philosophy and the facilities, to provide for this rather new adventure in education—a group that is by no measure insignificant in numbers or in the kinds and degrees of their complex problems.

Acknowledging the Problem

In 1958-59, the State of Illinois conducted an exhaustive survey in an attempt to assess the scope of this problem. Every teacher, administrator, and agency dealing with children participated. It was found that of the approximately two million children of school age in Illinois, 390,000 represented exceptionalities of some type or degree. This is nearly 20 percent. Ninety-six thousand were receiving some special education—that is about 25 percent of those needing it. We found that there were nearly 12,000 children outside of Chicago who were not in school (not even in a regular class) because their handicap seemed to be the basic reason for denying them any educational opportunity. There is no evidence to support any thinking that conditions are much better in other states.

The Illinois study indicated that approximately five percent of the total school enrollment were classified as slow learners or children with educational handicaps. There were about 25 percent of the total number of exceptional children listed as having exceptionalities of sufficient importance as to be counted. Four percent were found to have speech defects. Two and one-half percent of all children were listed as having emotional disturbances or social maladjustments. Two per cent were listed as gifted; 1.8 percent were mentally retarded; one percent had visual problems; and three-fourths of one percent had orthopedic or other physical handicaps. One-half of one percent, or five children out of every 1000, had hearing handicaps; and one percent were multiply handicapped to an extent that they could not be adequately provided for in a special class for children with one major handicap.

Defining the Responsibility

In the United States responsibility for education is a state function. Under our system of government local school districts derive their authority from their state legislature. Local districts may do what they are given legislative permission to do. For many years—and especially in the 19th century—the only specific legislation for the education of the handicapped provided for state institutions or residential schools. In a vague way the legislative provisions for common schools may have been interpreted as providing for the handicapped along with all other children.

But realistically they could not fit into the regular classes and make progress. As a result most of them made no attempt to attend school. It is true that in larger centers of population local boards of education provided some special classes and facilities long before legislation began to develop specific provisions. For instance, the first day school classes for blind children were opened in Chicago in the year 1900.

Today all states have some legislation that defines the responsibilities of local districts for exceptional children. Most of the states have specialists in the state department of education giving leadership at that level. A majority of the states appropriate funds for assisting local districts in meeting the increased costs of such programs.

The federal government has taken cognizance of the problem and some financial help is available from that source. Generally this has been emphasized in the area of mental retardation and is providing money for research, and fellowships designed to develop leadership in these newer developments of education.

As a rule, the authority for establishing and maintaining special education is left to the local district. The progress that has been made is generally proportionate to the understanding, acceptance and readiness of the local community and district. Of course there are problems of financing the programs, of finding suitable building facilities in these times of expanding school populations, and of recruiting, selecting, training and placing adequately trained personnel. Too often it is urged that the development of special services is retarded because of these problems of finance, building, and personnel. But I am proposing that in my opinion the basic road blocks are in the lack of understanding, acceptance and readiness.

I am amazed to note that when the local community opinion becomes strong enough, or the parents apply the pressures of their organized group, the ways and means are found. The community of the concerned generally finds ways of setting the objectives of education and the policies of a board of education. Where understanding of the children, their problems, and the advantages to both the children and society are clearly set forth we find progress. Where the community accepts these children and its responsibility to them we find results. Where the professional staff understands and accepts we always find readiness to do the job.

Essential Aspects of Administration

In evaluating any educational program I am interested in four aspects:

● *Philosophy.* A person or a community, functions no better than the philosophy that motivates. If a school administrator, teacher, or community believes in children and education, and if their concepts of service are triggered by attitudes that include acceptance of handicapped children they will generally provide most acceptably for them. But if they go no further than to question whether this is a problem of education or welfare; or if they ask "we must first take care of the regular children;" or "we will do the job if the state pays for it," then they will generally do nothing, or do it inadequately. If the philosophy is one of getting out of accepting responsibility, the individual or community can generally find a way to realize the objective.

● *Leadership.* A team may have great players, but their winnings are pretty much determined by the caliber of coaching and quarterbacking. A business generally pays dividends in proportion to the quality of its directing executives. A school board turns to its professional leadership. A mediocre teacher with a good principal may be more effective than an excellent teacher with a poor building leader. Leadership sets the pace, coordinates the programs, interprets within and without the school. Leadership inspires. It supports the discouraged as well as the ambitious. Leadership is creative and creativity is contagious. Leadership gives status and balance. Leadership gets results.

● *Organization.* In special education organization starts with objectives. It includes lines of authority and methods of communication. It is much more than providing facilities and assigning personnel. In special education it includes such intricate details as identification of pupils, determinations of their eligibility through careful study, diagnosis, and proper placement. In identifying one handicapped child a whole chain of reactions is set in motion of telephone calls, visitations to home and to clinics, conferences with doctors, psychologists, community agencies, principals, nurses, teachers, and others. Organization of special education is concerned with pupil-teacher ratios, or class size, that in turn are related to age range, grade levels and types and degrees of handicaps. Organization is concerned with equipment, materials of instruction, curriculum, teacher selection and supervision, and school-home relationships. In special education this means making special education as definite, as accepted, as permanent, and as respected as is the third grade, reading, or geometry.

● *The Look Ahead.* No special education program can succeed if it is designed to meet only an immediate condition. The handicapped child that is six today will be 16 in 10 years. The exceptional children in special classes today will be reaching forks in the road ahead. Some will still be handicapped when they are adults. Some will improve, some will regress. Some will go through high school, some to college, and some will find work. Even in school the roads will fork. Some will be in a special class all day. Some will be integrated gradually into some regular classes, and finally into all.

Planning for the future is two fold. It includes the future of each child. It includes the expansion of programs within the school. Each type of handicapped child has special needs. As the school develops services for one type it creates awareness of the needs of others. A small program managed by the superintendent or principal may grow into one where specially qualified directors and supervisors will be needed. The look ahead means planning for the future—planning for buildings, rooms, surveys, financing, personnel selection. Future planning is evidence of growth. Lack of growth is evidence of decay.

Current Trends

Three noteworthy considerations stand out among others in developing a good special education program.

1. *Legislation.* In most states the existing legislation for special education has been enacted within the last decade. In all states it has developed piecemeal. In some instances it is quite limited in that it may apply to only certain types of exceptional children. The patterns of authority for administration and the patterns of reimbursement vary greatly. In some states legislation requires rather high standards and in some they are very weak and would be difficult to defend professionally. The provisions for special education vary in order to coincide with legislative patterns for regular education in the same state. Since special education in most states has developed within the last decade or two this has been beneficial in some respects. It has enabled the state and local districts to study their situations and develop slowly but more soundly.

However, children are children the world over. Education and special education represent a rather definite philosophy whether in one state or another, and medical, social, educational and rehabilitation needs are similar because the kinds and degrees of handicaps are much the same wherever they are found.

Special education has reached a stage of national development where it seems reasonable to assume that it would be most profitable to make a study of legislation in all states so that the best points of each could be evaluated and considered. Such a study should include a comparative study of total legislation. What are essential patterns in all special education legislation? How does legislation relate special education to all education? What are the administrative responsibilities at state and local levels? What administrative rules, regulations and standards are necessary to supplement the legislation? Which features should be permissive and which ones mandatory? What patterns of state financial aid are most appropriate? How does the legislation for day school programs integrate with those for public residential schools? How do they integrate with programs for private schools, and also with other public and private services such as medical and social agencies?

2. *Status of Special Education.* The rapid growth of special educa-

tion programs has often resulted in a growing apart instead of together with the total education framework. Special education developed because regular educators were concerned about children with problems. And they asked for those special facilities to be furnished to supplement the regular facilities. Too often we find them operating entirely unrelated to each other. This leads to misunderstandings and poor functioning. We should probably return frequently in our thinking to the original premise that "special education has no justification for existence except as special facilities not available in the regular school are needed."

Special education needs status. Status comes only from understanding and acceptance. It is easy to set up special services that are so separate in administration, in housing, and in program that it soon becomes a school within a school. No child should be in a special class if he can be fairly and adequately served in a regular class. He should be returned to that regular class for any part of the program where he can adjust to it. Special education should never become possessive of these children, nor should regular education ever totally release them.

Status of special education will be attained when it is considered a definite part of the regular school faculty in the building where he teaches. Special education should have no better—and no worse—rooms or equipment than other classes. Exceptional children should not be pampered in school anymore than they should at home. They should be given work they can do and then be expected to do it. Special teachers should be on the same salary schedule as any other teacher with similar amounts of training and experience. If differentials of salary are given for extra work or responsibilities they should be defined and made available to all who qualify—whether special or regular teachers.

Most fundamental to this problem of status is the acceptance of the exceptional child and the special education program by the school in which the class is located, by the Board of Education, and by the local community. Too often the statement comes from the local community that "this is a state function," or "the state should pay most or all of the costs." This is rejection—not acceptance. Status will be attained only when the local community recognizes the handicapped child as one of its precious possessions—a child. And when they have a desire to meet his needs they will tackle the job whether the state has a little Marshall Plan or not to bail them out as to extra costs. The community that accepts the child and the job of serving him gives status to the program.

Only when special education earns status will it have status.

3. *A Balanced Program.* Balance in program means many things. It means not just programs for one or a few types of handicapped, but for any and all children who need special services. Balance means an adequate and appropriate program at all levels—primary, intermediate,

and high school. Balance means a total program, not just one in academic training.

Handicapped children need attention to their growth and development in physical fitness, social adjustment, emotional security, spiritual welfare, and mental growth. Handicapped children need extra curricular activities, vocational or prevocational training, counseling and all other resources of the school. A balanced program relates the school program with the child's program in the home and community. A balanced program coordinates the special with the regular classes. It coordinates the educational services with those given by the nurse, the guidance staff, the psychologist, the school social worker, and the total staff. A program—like a person—that loses its balance will fall.

A Credo of Faith

This I do believe:
- That every child is important.
- That every child is basically a normal child and that even the so-called handicapped child is rather a normal child with a handicap.
- That public education can and should render a service to all children including those with handicaps.
- That the basic consideration is not the lowness of the child but rather the highness of our ability to help him.
- That special education is *a part of* and not *apart from* regular education.
- That every child is entitled to a program of education wherein he can experience success.
- That in education it is not as important what we do for a child as it is what we do to him.
- That laws do not so much give schools the authority to serve children as it does give opportunity.
- That our success in special education should be measured not in the numbers we have served, but in the degree of our success with the most difficult ones.
- That no reward in life surpasses that spiritual reward of helping the child to overcome his handicap by adjusting to it.

Yes, special education is a worthy idea. Those of us who work in the field can become confused and controversial, and thus destroy it. Or we can be so clear and so united that together we can make it grow in stature and favor with God and man.

Chapter XI

The Teacher As An Evaluator

Evaluation has long been recognized as an essential phase of the educational program in the elementary school; yet, rarely are teacher biases discussed openly in seminars for beginning elementary teachers. Consequently a critical analysis of teacher bias in pupil evaluation is submitted for review and analytical study in this chapter.

Before one can evaluate effectively, he must first make some rather refined observations about his pupils. His evaluation will only be as accurate as are his data from which projections are gleaned. Therefore, one article has been included in this chapter for the purpose of illustrating that testing and diagnosis should precede evaluative techniques in selected situations. There are times when the teacher must evaluate each case individually so that proper class placement and personalized programs of education might be planned.

The recent emphasis upon personalized programs of instruction necessitated the inclusion of some comments about ways in which the school should measure and assess a child's rate of learning when he is provided with optimal learning conditions in his classes. Conventional procedures typically used in evaluating children will not work in modern classroom settings.

The challenge to becoming a professional teacher is the willingness to analyze yourself in light of what the experts say as contrasted with what you believe now regarding the evaluation of the mental, social, emotional, and physical attainments of both boys and girls. It is believed that the selections found in this chapter will broaden one's perspective as he sets out to evaluate children individually or collectively.

What Is Evaluation?

L. L. BOYKIN

EVALUATION, as applied to education, is a relatively new technical term. It is believed to have originated as a part of the Progressive Education revolt against the traditional curriculum.[1] It gained wide acceptance through the work of Wrightstone in the appraisal of new educational practices in the schools of New York City, and of Tyler, Smith, and others in connection with the Eight Year Study.[2] Commenting upon the origin of the movement, Smith and Tyler observe,

> Most of the achievement tests then on the market measured only the amount of information which students remembered or some of the more specific subject skills like those of algebra and the foreign languages. The new courses developed in the Thirty Schools attempted to help students achieve several additional qualities, such as more effective study skills, more careful ways of thinking, a wider range of significant interests, social rather than selfish attitudes. Hence, the available achievement tests did not provide measures of many of the more important achievements anticipated from these new courses.[3]

As originally conceived, evaluation included the concepts of measurements as used in psychology and education; however, the term implied a more comprehensive program of appraisal than the more conventional testing and examination programs.[4]

Since its inception the term "evaluation" has been defined and interpreted in a number of ways. According to Quillen and Hanna, "evaluation is the process of gathering and interpreting evidences on changes in the behavior of students as they progress through school."[5] Torgerson and Adams state, "that to evaluate is to ascertain the value of some process or thing. Thus educational evaluation is the passing judgment on the degree of worthwhileness of some teaching process or learning experience."[6]

The following observation concerning measurement and evaluation

Boykin, L. L. "What Is Evaluation?" *Journal of Educational Research.* March 1958. 51:529-534.

is made by two well known authors on the subject,". . . Measurement, however, does not necessarily imply evaluation. Evaluation assumes a purpose, or an idea of what is 'good' or 'desirable' from the standpoint of the individual or society or both."[7] Ross and Stanley also state:

> As used in education, 'evaluation' is a far more inclusive term than measurement. Two aspects of evaluation may be distinguished: (1) data relating to some important aspect of the school, such as it organization, program, or results and (2) a set of values or standards against which these data are interpreted and appraised. Furthermore, the evaluator's philosophy and sense of values will determine what objectives of the school program he considers to be important, as well as what data he will look for, or regard as relevant in the situation. It is apparent that while measurement may be highly mechanical and at times a routine, evaluation can never be; at every stage evaluation requires the exercise of mature judgment.[8]

According to Barr, Davis, and Johnson,

> The investigator used measurement to determine status, but he is not interested solely with status itself. Measurement is also used to ascertain relationships; cause and effects relationships and concomitant variations which are only a part of a longer process . . .
> Appraisal (evaluation) is thus a much broader term than measurement since it involves not only the collection and analyses of data but the placing of some value upon it or the reaching of a conclusion regarding its worth.

They further state:

> All appraisal and research as contrasted with mere measurement or data gathering should be made in the light of objectives either stated or assumed. Whether the means, processes, and products of a given educational program are adequate will depend upon the objectives sought in each situation.[9]

The modern concept of evaluation stem from a newer philosophy of education which call for the development of more adequate techniques of assessing pupil growth and development.[10] It emphasizes the responsibility of the educator not only for the development of concepts, information, skills, and habits, but also for the stimulation of pupil growth in attitudes, appreciations, interests, powers of thinking, and personal-social adaptability.[11]

Modern evaluation differs from older forms of appraisal in several ways. First, it attempts to measure a comprehensive range of objectives of the modern school curriculum rather than subject achievement only. Second, it uses a variety of techniques of appraisal, such as achievement, attitude, personality, and character tests. Included also are rating scales, questionnaires, judgment scales of products, interviews, controlled-observation techniques, sociometric techniques, and anecdotal records.

Third, modern evaluation includes integrating and interpreting these various indices of behavior into an inclusive portrait of an individual or an educational situation.[1][2]

While each of the above statements helps to sharpen the meaning of the term and to provide a foundation for deciding a "true definition," it is apparent after careful and thoughtful consideration that evaluation is not just a testing program, is not a synonym for measurement, is not an administrative means or technique for gauging good teaching or end product or culminating activity. Rather it is a comprehensive, cooperatively developed, continuous process of inquiry which, in the final analysis, must be interpreted and defined in terms of its principles, functions, characteristics and purposes. What, then, are the more important of these principles, characteristics, functions, etc.? Briefly stated they are as follows:

I. *A clear concept of the aims of society, of education and of the school, is basic to evaluation.* Evaluation of the work of a school is made in terms of the philosophy of the school and objectives which the school is expected to attain. Evaluation validates the hypotheses upon which the school operates. It is descriptive as well as quantitative.

II. *A program of evaluation must be comprehensive.* It should not be limited to a few isolated goals, or objectives, but should include all the major objectives of instruction. Evaluation is concerned with all aspects of pupil behavior and with all the objectives which the teacher, the school and society hope to achieve.

III. *Evaluation is concerned with the study, status, and/or changes in, pupil behavior.* It is more concerned with pupil growth than with where pupils stand in relation to their peers or to national norms. It is concerned primarily with the growth of pupils in learning to satisfy needs in a socially accepted manner, rather than with subject-matter facts, concepts and information per se.

IV. *The methods for summarizing and interpreting the evidence obtained from a variety of appraisals are a fundamental part of the evaluation program.* No longer do tests of intelligence and subject matter achievement alone meet the needs for appraisal of the aims of a comprehensive educational program designed to meet the varying needs, abilities, interests and purpose of children and youth. Such newer techniques as anecdotal records, observational methods, questionnaires, inventories, interviews, checklists, rating scales, personal reports, projective methods, sociometric methods, case studies, and cumulative records are required to assess such objectives as knowledge and understandings, skills, interests, aptitudes, attitudes, personal-social adjustment, critical thinking, and health and physical development. In addition, techniques are needed to evaluate such correlative factors as the social and economic backgrounds of pupils and the educational climate in which classroom and school activities are conducted. Such data are derived from papers, observation, conferences, class work, library, and social situations.

V. *Evaluation is a continuous process, an integral part of all learning.* It is the starting point in instructional planning. It broadens the teacher's awareness of the child in a total environmental situation. It promotes individualized classroom instruction. As pupil behavior and its meanings are studied, evaluation focuses the teacher's attention upon the developmental changes in pupils. It familiarizes the teacher with the tools and techniques used in studying and analyzing the nature and causes of behavioral changes. It makes provision for gauging the growth of pupils without primary emphasis upon academic achievement alone. Evaluation as a continuous process demands constant curriculum revision which is in step with changing times, thus lessening the frequently cited lag between social change and the school program.

VI. *Evaluation involves an approach that leads to improvement.* Adequate evaluation leads to improvement of the learning situation, to the growth of the teacher, to better administration and supervision, to new and improved curriculum practices and guidance service. An essential purpose of evaluation is to make a periodic check on the effectiveness of the school and thus to indicate points at which improvements in the program are necessary.

VII. *An effective evaluation program provides information basic to effective guidance of all pupils in the school.* It is adjusted to the needs and abilities of the individual pupil.

VIII. *Evaluation is a group endeavor.* It is a cooperative process involving pupils, parents, teachers, principals and supervisors. Service, custodial, and lunchroom personnel also play important roles in the evaluation process. From its inception, evaluation makes use of group techniques and approaches—group discussion, group leadership, group planning, group organization, group decisions, socio-drama, role playing, group guidance. Evaluation sensitizes teachers both to the subtleties and importance as well as increases skill in the interaction process. Evaluation provides a high level of on the job education. It strengthens democracy because it is, dependent upon the use of democratic procedures for its successful fulfillment.

IX. *Evaluation provides a sound basis for public relations.* It improves public relations because its process involves parents and other members of the community. Cooperatively evolved evaluation programs based upon commonly accepted values enjoy the support of the community to the extent that its members have shared in the valuing, planning, and executing which is entailed. A sound evaluation program provides a certain psychological security to the staff, to the students, and to the parents of a given community.

X. *Self analysis and appraisal are essential parts of the evaluation program.* In fact, the trend toward self-evaluation is one of the significant features of recent developments in evaluation. Such a procedure includes: (a) cooperative establishment of goals; (b) cooperation in determining present status with respect to these goals; (c) cooperation in the activities required to secure the desired growth; and (d) cooperation in securing evidence as to progress in the fulfillment of goals to be realized.

XI. *Educational evaluation or appraisal is a much broader term than measurement.* The term "evaluation" as distinguished from measurement, is used to refer to the process of appraising the "whole child" or an entire educational situation. It involves not only the collection and analysis of data but the placing of some value upon it or the reaching of a conclusion regarding its worth. It is the process of assigning value to the results of measurement or to other data. Definitions vary, but, in general, measurement is thought of as precise quantitative description, while evaluation is described as appraisal in terms of some criterion of excellence. Measurement is often a means for evaluation, but evaluation usually goes beyond measurement in its use of the value concepts. Measurement is always a means to an end, never an end in itself. The significance and educational implications of measurement are rarely self-evident or automatic. As a rule, the true significance of measurement can be determined only when it is seen in relation to other relevant factors. While measurement is never everything in evaluation, measurement in some form is implicit in the evaluative function. Properly used, measurement is a valuable aid to analysis and educational evaluation. Measurement, as related to evaluation, performs a useful function in determining what alleged facts really are facts, as well as providing an exact method of describing them. It is also indispensable in the final stage of evaluation and appraisal. However, at best measurement merely provides data needed for evaluation; it is not evaluation per se.

XII. *A sound program of evaluation requires the use of both qualitative and quantitative data.* One of the most important requirements in evaluation is the use of quantitative as well as qualitative data. Qualitative data merely indicates the presence or absence of acts, components, and aspects of things, whereas quantitative data indicates their amounts. Much of the material needed for comprehensive evaluation requires the use of data which have not as yet been reduced to a quantitative basis. Among qualitative types of data are those found in behavior descriptions and the so called intangibles such as attitudes, appreciations, loyalties, beliefs, etc. In time, it may be expected that many qualitative types of data will be quantified. In fact, promising beginnings have already been made along this line.

In more recent years, the following trends in evaluation have become evident: (a) The modern teacher and the supervisor are concerned with important functional learning outcomes, many of them less tangible and less easily measured than the subject-matter concepts, skills, and abilities of previous decades; (b) an increasing emphasis on the measurement of understanding and interpretation rather than upon isolated information skills, and abilities as particularly observable in present-day tests of general educational development; (c) the increased use of informal, or teacher-made test exercises for instructional purposes to supplement formal or standardized tests is also characteristic of recent evaluation programs; (d) the development of factor analysis of mental abilities may also be cited as an important new approach in measurement and evaluation; (e) the development of techniques for measuring role of the individual, as well as of small groups in studies of group relationships; (f) increasing attention has been given to the development and refinement of unstructured, or projective, tests of personality.

FOOTNOTES

[1] Prior to, and during the early phases of this revolt there were a number of important attempts to use evaluative techniques. See H. A. Carroll "A Method of Measuring Prose Appreciation," *English Journal,* 22:184-89, 1933; W. W. Charters, "Education and Research at a Mechanical Institute: A Character Development Study." *Personnel Journal* 12:119-23, 1933. L. M. Heil, "Evaluation of Student Achievement in the Physical Sciences, The Application of Laws and Principles," *American Physics Teacher* 6:62-66, 1938; J. M. Stalnaker, "Validity of the University of Chicago's English Qualifying Examination," *English Journal* (College Edition) 22:561-67, 1933. J. B. Tharp "A Modern Language Test," *Journal of Higher Education* 6:103-104, 1936. J. W. Wrighstone, "Measuring Some Major Objectives of the Social Studies," *School Review* 43:771-779, 1935.

[2] J. Wayne Wrightstone, *Appraisal of Newer Elementary School Practice.* New York: Bureau of Publications, Teachers College, Columbia University, 1938; R. W. Tyler, "Evaluation: A Challenge to Progressive Education." *Progressive Education* 12:552-556, 1935; Wilford M. Aiken, *The Story of the Eight Year Study,* New York: Harper and Brothers, 1942.

[3] Eugene R. Smith, Ralph W. Tyler and the Evaluation Staff, *Appraising and Recording Student Progress,* New York: Harper and Brothers, 1942, p. 4.

[4] J. Wayne Wrightstone, "Evaluation." *Encyclopedia of Educational Research,* New York: The MacMillan Company, 1950, p. 403.

[5] I. James Quillen and Lavone A. Hanna, *Education for Social Competence,* Chicago: Scott Foresman Company, 1948, p. 343.

[6] Theodore L. Torgerson and Georgia S. Adams, *Measurement and Evaluation,* New York: The Dryden Press, 1954, p. 9.

[7] H. H. Remmers and N. L. Gage, *Educational Measurement and Evaluation,* New York: Harper and Brothers, 1955, p. 21.

[8] C. C. Ross and Julian C. Stanley, *Measurement in Todays Schools,* New York: Prentice Hall, Inc., 1954, p. 373.

[9] Arvil S. Barr, Robert A. Davis and Palmer O. Johnson, *Educational Research and Appraisal,* Philadelphia: J. B. Lippincott Company, 1935, pp. v, 7, 10, and 11.

[10] J. Wayne Wrightstone, "Recent Developments in Evaluative Procedures," Chicago: University of Chicago Press, 1940, pp. 12-29.

[11] J. W. Herrick, "Outcomes of Systematic Evaluation," Chicago: University of Chicago Press, 1940, pp. 30-44.

[12] See Pedro T. Orata, "Evaluating Evaluation," *Journal of Educational Research* 33:641, May 1940; P. B. Diedrich, "Design for a Comprehensive Evaluation Program," *School Review,* 58:225-232, April, 1950; W. G. Findley, "Educational Evaluation Recent Development, *Social Education,* 14:206-210, May, 1950. Ralph W. Tyler, "The Place of Evaluation in Modern Education,"*Evaluating the Work of the School.* Proceedings of the Ninth Annual Conference for Administrative Officers of Public and Private Schools (William C. Reeves, Ed.), Chicago: University of Chicago Press, 1940, pp. 3-11.

Teacher Bias in Pupil Evaluation: A Critical Analysis

Critics of American education claim that American students are not evaluated according to their merits and capabilities but rather the biases and prejudices of their teachers. Professors of sociology, such as Patricia Cayo Sexton of New York University and Edgar Z. Friedenburg of the State University of New York at Buffalo, maintain that the middle-class values and prejudices of teachers impel them to reward students on the basis of how closely they adher to middle-class standards, without reference to their true achievements, capabilities, and potential.

This teacher attitude, the critics feel, encourages mindless conformity while unfairly discriminating against pupils from economically deprived social groups. Jonathan Kozol and Herbert Kohl, who taught for a short time in ghetto areas, feel that a heavily racial bias undermines any true evaluation of pupil progress in deprived sections of many cities. There also exists a persistent bit of educational mythology to the effect that girls get all the breaks in teacher grading and boys are unjustly downgraded merely because they are boys and act in a masculine manner not appreciated by feminine teachers. In addition, there is the possibility that children may have grades unfairly awarded because of a "halo" effect: students with "good" reputations get undeservedly good grades while students with "bad" reputations get undeservedly bad grades.

How true are these claims and opinions? Are teachers really biased in their evaluations of children? There is enough evidence in the research literature to help answer these questions with empirical light rather than passionate heat.

Metzner, Seymour. "Teacher Bias in Pupil Evaluation: A Critical Analysis." *The Journal of Teacher Education.* Spring 1971. 22:40-43.

Socioeconomic Bias

There is no doubt that when achievement is objectively measured by standardized tests there is a strong relationship between socioeconomic status and test scores. Davidson and Lang (2) found that the higher the socioeconomic level of school children the better their test achievement, a finding completely typical of many others in the field. In the wide-ranging domains of education and sociology, there are few conclusions quite as consistent as the close connection between social status and objectively tested academic achievement. Although these scores are outside the direct influence of the teacher, some observers claim that the lower expectations teachers have for lower social class children, and teacher attitudes and actions based on these expectations, give the children a diminished sense of self-esteem that indirectly influences their achievement on objective tests. This seemingly logical extrapolation falls apart in face of the evidence from all early childhood education studies, showing that these socioeconomic differences in performance exist between the children upon their entrance into school and before the teachers have had any chance to affect them in any manner whatsoever. Class differences reflected in objective tests may have their genesis in genetics, social-environmental differences, or the vagaries of test construction; but only someone with a deep-seated anti-teacher bias could place the blame for this on teacher influence.

The possibility of teacher bias influencing the subjective evaluations of students via grades awarded directly by the teacher has more substance. Studies (2, 6) reveal that when teachers are asked to indicate the children of whom they most approve those from higher social strata get a disproportionately large share of high approvals and those from lower socioeconomic groups a disproportionately large share of low approvals.

One of the reasons for this seems to be a reflection of teachers' tendencies to favor children who are high academic achievers. The finding by Cawley (1), that teachers have positive attitudes toward high-achieving pupils and negative attitudes toward low achievers, is reinforced by the Davidson and Lang (2) study revealing that children decline in a teacher's favor as their achievement declines. Since middle-class children, objectively rated, have better achievement than lower-class children, this would seem to give them a distinct edge in any competition for teacher approval, since the main reason for teacher approval is achievement rather than social class perception per se.

Nonacademic Biases

There is reason to believe that the grades awarded by teachers reflect facets of school life other than academic achievement. Analyses of factors influencing school grades indicate the heavy influence of such pupil variables as school attitudes, interest shown in studies, conscientious effort, and general citizenship, all of which influence the grade that presumably reflects school achievement only (7, 3). Here again, the middle and upper social classes have an advantage, since children from these homes are more oriented toward teacher-conforming values and attitudes than lower-class children.

The tendency toward awarding grades that are presumably influenced by miscellaneous attitudinal and citizenship variables is not likely to be restricted to past and present teachers. An investigation by Harris (5) showed that teacher education students, who will be the teachers of tomorrow, used the same teacher-conforming, work-oriented value and attitude bases as experienced teachers in expressing approval or disapproval of students. In this case, the pattern of the past is an excellent indication of prospects for the future.

Influence of Teacher Socioeconomic Status

One might think that this middle-class bias could be avoided by having more teachers recruited from lower-class families; presumably, they would be more appreciative of lower-class values and aspirations and less likely to denigrate lower-class children for not living up to middle-class standards. In view of Hart's (6) study, this is a forlorn hope. Hart found that teachers from lower-class family backgrounds not only showed the same pattern of approval and disapproval in evaluating middle- and lower-class children but were actually more authoritarian and unsympathetic. It is possible that the entire concept of schooling is so middle class that only those who embrace the appropriate values and attitudes, either by family background or personal endeavor, can hope to succeed either as student or teacher.

Racial Bias

It is impossible in any empirical, scientific fashion to show a racial bias existing in teacher evaluations. Anecdotal reminiscences of specific teacher bias show only that some teachers are racially biased, and this claim could be made of any group in the world. The poorer grades given to Negro children can be very adequately explained by the overwhelming middle-class orientation of the school in conflict with the equally strong lower-class orientation of most Negro pupils. These grades might also reflect the much lower achievement of Negro children than of white children on objective tests. It is, therefore, impossible to determine what part racial bias might play in teacher evaluation of Negro pupils.

Sex Bias

Although racial bias is difficult to prove, this difficulty does not exist with sexual bias. All studies are in agreement that girls get a better break from teachers than do boys. Not only do they get more teacher approval (8) but they are also marked in a decidedly unfair manner as compared with achievement grades given boys. Hadley (4) found that girls were consistently given grades higher than warranted by their objective achievement on standardized tests, while boys were consistently given grades lower than indicated by achievement test results. This is easily understood in view of the previously mentioned tendency of teachers to award approval on the basis of factors other than objective achievement. Teachers and prospective teachers give approval to students based on student acceptance of school routine and conformity to teacher-dictated work habits (5). The more conforming behavior of girls in these matters would make a definite sexual bias quite logical. Possibly the present trend of boys and girls to dress and look alike may confuse teachers to the point where they will not be able to differentiate between them and will thus do away with the present sexual bias!

Halo Effect

Human frailty in the teaching faculty is the best explanation for the tendency of teachers to mark papers by student reputation rather than by more objective criteria. Morris (9) found that knowledge of a student's reputation as a "good" student unduly raised that student's grades on an English test. This same halo effect was found by Wodtke (10), who noted that teachers' behavioral ratings of students were influenced by knowledge of their aptitude scores. The many halo effect studies in psychology lead to the conclusion that a planned absence of information is the only effective way to counter this very human bias.

The Role of the Teacher in Evaluation

In view of the many ways in which subjective biases may color a teacher's perception of any individual student, what should be the place of the teacher in pupil evaluation? The proper role of the teacher is to be primarily responsible for the evaluation of a student's social and emotional growth: this would include effort, citizenship, work habits, and attitudes. The evaluation of academic achievement should be based solely on the results of standardized tests or other norms not open to teacher interpretation. Only in this way can grades that presumably refer to academic achievement be reasonably interpretable while still giving full due to the just province of the teacher, the important task of evaluating the social adjustment aims of the school.

REFERENCES

1. CAWLEY, JOHN F. "Inter-Group Comparisons Among the Expressed Attitudes of Teachers and Bright, Average, and Slow-Learner Children at the Fifth- and Ninth-Grade Level." Doctor's thesis. Storrs: University of Connecticut, 1962. (Unpublished)

2. DAVIDSON, HELEN H., and LANG, GERHARD. "Children's Perceptions of Their Teachers' Feelings Toward Them Related to Self-Perception, School Achievement and Behavior." *Journal of Experimental Education* 29:107-18; December 1960.

3. DOHERTY, WILLIAM V. "A Survey of the Evaluation of Pupil Progress in Selected Elementary Schools of Ohio." Doctor's thesis. Columbus: Ohio State University, 1954. (Unpublished)

4. HADLEY, S. TREVOR. "A School Mark: Fact or Fancy?" *Educational Administration and Supervision* 40:305-12; May 1954.

5. HARRIS, DALE B. "How Student-Teachers Identify Responsibility in Children." *Journal of Educational Psychology* 45:233-39; April 1954.

6. HART, JOE W. "Socially Mobile Teachers and Classroom Atmosphere." *Journal of Educational Research* 59: 166-68; December 1965.

7. JACOBSON, MORRIS ALEXANDER. "The Relationship of Creative Thinking, Ability, Intelligence, and School Performance." Doctor's thesis. Los Angeles: University of Southern California, 1966. (Unpublished)

8. MEYER, WILLIAM J., and THOMPSON, GEORGE C. "Sex Differences in the Distribution of Teacher Approval and Disapproval Among Sixth-Grade Children." *Journal of Educational Psychology* 47: 385-96; November 1956.

9. MORRIS, GLENN L. "A Study of Some Determinants of Teacher Marks." Doctor's thesis. Houston, Texas: University of Houston, 1965. (Unpublished)

10. WODTKE, KENNETH H., and WALLEN, NORMAN E. "Teacher Classroom Control, Pupil Creativity, and Pupil Classroom Behavior." *Journal of Experimental Education* 34:59-65; Fall 1965.

Evaluation Under Individualized Instruction

MARGARET C. WANG and JOHN L. YEAGER

During the past decade, increasing attention has been given to the development of instructional systems designed to accommodate the individual needs of the pupil (1). Many classroom teachers are seeking new techniques and materials that are responsive the the the needs of individual pupils. Large-scale classroom innovations are being introduced to meet individual needs. Among these innovations are programmed instruction, individually prescribed instruction, and Project PLAN.

Because of the increasing emphasis on the individualization of instruction, methods of assessing pupils' learning need to be revised. Under conventional instructional procedures, pupils are required to master particular lessons within a given time interval, and each pupil is expected to proceed at the same pace. Conventional procedures do not take into account individual differences in rate of learning. A pupil's success or failure in school learning is judged in terms of his achievement when learning time is held constant. Achievement is usually measured by standardized achievement tests or by tests that the teacher has constructed.

The recent emphasis on programs that provide for individual differences has resulted in a number of procedures which permit pupils to progress through a given set of learning tasks at individual rates. In a discussion on individualization of instruction, Bloom calls attention to one basic assumption in these programs: if we can find ways and means of helping each pupil, all pupils can conceivably master a given learning task (2). It must be recognized that some pupils will require more effort, more time, and more help to achieve mastery than other pupils, but given sufficient time and appropriate types of assistance, the majority of pupils can achieve mastery. Under these circumstances, individual differences are expressed in the amount of time the learner requires to master a particular learning task. Under most plans of individualized instruction, the level of mastery each pupil exhibits on a test does not provide a valid indication of the pupil's progress, since all pupils are required to attain a specific level of mastery before continuing in the program.

Let us say that a criterion level of 80 per cent is specified for a particular test: all pupils must achieve a minimum of 80 per cent before moving on to a new area of study. Under this arrangement, variability in achievement is limited. However, since each pupil is permitted sufficient time to meet this criterion level, the amount of time pupils require to meet the criterion varies. Some pupils may require three days; other pupils may require ten. One reasonable solution to the problem of measuring pupil achievement when individual rates of progress are permitted to vary is to use rate of learning as an achievement measure— that is, to use the number of lessons mastered, the number of tests passed, or the amount of time required to complete a given task. In brief, a pupil's achievement can be measured by his performance on a particular test and the amount of time required to master the given activity.

Research studies on learning, in particular, report substantial differences in rate of learning among pupils. The differences have been found in school situations as well as under experimental laboratory conditions (3-7). These differences in individual learning rates are related to characteristics of the learner, to the learning task, and to the learning environment (8-13). Some studies indicate that learning rate is related to typical aptitude measures (14-16). Other investigations indicate that rate does not have any simple relationship to measures of aptitude and is not consistent over many units of work (17, 18).

Why do some studies show no relationship between a given rate measure and pupil's aptitude and no consistency of the rate measure over a number of tasks? Perhaps the materials and the lessons are more suited to some pupils than to others. Under these circumstances, a measure of learning rate may be biased.

The writers working in an individualized instructional program—the Individually Prescribed Instruction Project (17)—investigated the relationship between a number of indices of pupil's rate of learning and selected measures of pupil aptitude, and achievement, as well as certain measures of classroom performance.

The results of these studies indicate that no one measure of learning rate is superior to any other; nor does there appear to be any simple relationship between rate of learning and selected pupil characteristics. On the basis of these studies, it would seem that rate of learning is specific to a given task and is not a general factor that characterizes pupil performance in all learning situations. Furthermore, the results suggest several possible reasons why various measures of rate of learning have not been found to be consistent and why related or predicting factors have not been clearly identified.

School learning situations are complex. This fact poses many problems in measuring learning rate. The problems can usually be classified into two major categories: problems associated with the measure used and problems associated with the many variables that probably affect rate of learning.

A major problem in measuring rate of learning arises from the definition of *rate*. *Rate* may be defined as the amount or degree of anything in relation to units of time, that is, rate $= \frac{\text{amount or degree}}{\text{time}}$. The main problem here is to determine the amount or degree of learning (the numerator in the equation).

Should the amount to be learned be specified in terms of the number of discrete skills to be mastered over a short period of time, such as a few hours of work? Or should the amount to be learned be represented by longer periods of time covering larger areas of content? Should the skills and the attitudes that the pupil brings to the learning situation be taken into account? What type of measure should be developed to account for and describe the learning rate of two pupils, each working on the same task, when one pupil has mastered 40 per cent of the task before he began work and the other pupil had mastered none of the task before he started? These are technical problems associated with the development of any measures of achievement; yet the classroom teacher must recognize the difficulties when evaluating pupils' performance.

The writers believe that the basic problem in studying pupils' rate of learning and the factors related to it is to specify the characteristics of the learning situation itself. In the writers' judgment, before any consistent relationship can be established between measures of rate and the learning task and pupil variables that might be related to these measures of rate, a careful study should be made of the nature of the learning task itself. In other words, it is essential to examine the learning objectives and the types of skills to be learned in each unit of the individualized curriculum. After this step has been taken, the relationship between pupil's rate of learning and the type of tasks to be learned can be specified.

Once the nature of the task to be learned is specified, the next major problem is to identify classroom procedures that will help each pupil master the specified task to a degree commensurate with his abilities. It should be recognized that the relation between pupil variables and rate of learning may be influenced greatly by the effectiveness of the instructional system. Pupil's rate of learning in school varies with the nature and the quality of instruction. Carroll has suggested that the effectiveness of instruction determines rate of learning (9).

Therefore, one major task in solving the measurement problems in assessing pupil's rate of learning in school is to develop an instructional system that provides optimal learning conditions for each pupil. Only when each pupil has maximum opportunities to learn can one realistically investigate the pupil's rate of learning in school situations. Only then can one study the nature of the relationship between rate and factors related to pupil's rate of learning in schools under an individualized instructional system.

In summary, scores on achievement tests, by themselves, do not describe the progress of pupils in an individualized system of instruction. The seemingly obvious alternative—to measure learning rate—also poses major problems. Even so, teachers who are working in classroom settings that permit each pupil to progress individually through a sequence of learning experiences must consider two measures of pupil progress— degree of mastery achieved on tests and the rate at which the pupil masters a given task. If one or the other of these measures is missing, there is little chance that the assessment will be meaningful.

NOTES

1. The research reported herein was supported by the Learning Research and Development Center supported as a research and development center by funds from the United States Office of Education, Department of Health, Education, and Welfare. The opinions expressed in this publication do not necessarily reflect the position or policy of the Office of Education.

2. B. S. BLOOM. "Mastery Learning for All." An invited address presented at the American Educational Research Association Annual Meeting, Chicago, February, 1968.

3. J. O. BOLVIN. "Report on Individualized Instruction Project." Presented at the Board of Visitors Meeting, Learning Research and Development Center, University of Pittsburgh, April, 1965 (mimeographed).

4. R. KALIN. "Development and Evaluation of a Programmed Text in an Advanced Mathematical Topic of Intellectually Superior Fifth- and Sixth-Grade Pupils." Unpublished doctoral dissertation. Tallahassee: Florida State University, 1962.

5. D. L. NICHOLAS. "The Effect of Pacing Rate on the Efficiency of Learning for Programmed Instructional Material." Unpublished doctoral dissertation. Bloomington: Indiana University, 1967.

6. P. SUPPES. "Modern Learning Theory and the Elementary School Curriculum," *American Educational Research Journal, 1* (March, 1964), 79-94.

7. J. L. YEAGER. "Measures of Learning Rates for Elementary School Students in Mathematics and Reading under a Program of Individually Prescribed Instruction." Unpublished doctoral dissertation. Pittsburgh: University of Pittsburgh, 1966.

8. R. B. ALLISON."Learning Parameters and Human Abilities." Unpublished doctoral dissertation. Princeton, New Jersey: Princeton University, June, 1966.

9. J. B. CARROLL. "A Model of School Learning," *Teachers College Record, 64* (May, 1963), 723-32.

10. J. P. GUILFORD. "Three Faces of Intellect," *American Psychologist, 14* (August, 1959), 469-79.

11. D. D. SJOGREN. "Achievement as a Function of Study Time," *American Educational Research Journal, 4* (November, 1967), 337-43.

12. J. T. SMITH, M. D. RUTER, F. M. LACKNER, and D. S. Kwall. "Academic Sociometric and Personality Variables in the Prediction of Elementary School Achievement," *Proceedings of the 75th Annual Convention of the American Psychological Association,* Vol. II, pp. 339-40. Washington, D.C.: Merkle Press, 1967.

13. C. J. SPIES. *Some Non-Intellectual Predictors of Classroom Success.* Technical Report No. 10, Office of Naval Research, Contract No. NOR816 (14) Naval Air Technical Training. Washington, D.C.: Department of Naval Research, October, 1966.

14. A. JENSEN. "Learning Ability in Retarded, Average, and Gifted Children." In *Educational Technology,* pp. 356-76. Edited by J. P. DeCecco. New York: Holt, Rinehart and Winston, 1964.

15. R. GLASER, J. H. REYNOLDS, and M. G. FULLICK. *Programmed Instruction in the Intact Classroom.* Project No. 1342, Cooperative Research, United States Office of Education, Pittsburgh, Pennsylvania. December, 1963.

16. G. L. GROPPER and G. KRESS. "Individualizing Instruction through Pacing Procedures," *Audiovisual Communication Review, 13* (Summer, 1965), 165-82.

17. M. C. WANG. "An Investigation of Selected Procedures for Measuring and Predicting Rate of Learning in Classrooms Operating under a Program of Individualized Instruction." Unpublished doctoral dissertation. Pittsburgh: University of Pittsburgh, 1968.

18. C. M. LINDVALL and J. O. BOLVIN. "Programmed Instruction in the Schools: An Application of Programming Principles in Individually Prescribed Instruction," *Programmed Instruction,* p. 217. Sixty-sixth Yearbook of the National Society for the Study of Education, Part II. Edited by Phil Lange. Chicago: National Society for the Study of Education, 1967. (Distributed by the University of Chicago Press.)

Early Indentification of Learning Disabilities

WILLIAM E. FERINDEN, JR. and SHERMAN JACOBSON

Most state laws require a child to enter school at a particular chronological age. However, not all children are ready to cope with the learning situation at such a time due to organic, environmental, or intrapsychic conditions. As Careth Ellingson states in her book *The Shadow Children*, many learning disorders are often the result of sheer immaturity, and a child who has not reached a stage of neurological development comparable to his chronological age level may be defeated before he starts. If it is required that all children go to school, then appropriate education must be provided for every child, and the concept of individual differences must be understood.

If children with learning disabilities are correctly diagnosed before they have suffered the trauma of continued failure, and if they receive skilled help from properly motivated and trained educators, they can lead happy and productive lives.

Procedures

The objective of this study was to compile a test battery which would be valid in diagnosing potential learning disabilities at the kindergarten level. To obtain this objective we had to be able to identify those children who would experience the greatest difficulties in learning to read.

The source of subjects was ten kindergarten classes, eight located in schools which included a high percentage of culturally deprived youngsters, and two classes in a school containing mostly middle-class students.

Ferinden, William E., Jr., and Jacobson, Sherman. "Early Identification of Learning Disabilities." *Journal of Learning Disabilities.* November 1970. 3:48-52.

Teachers were requested to choose those students whom they believed to be high risk in the probability of developing learning problems and also to select those students whom they believed would be most capable of performing at the first-grade level.

A total of 67 children were studied. A team composed of a school psychologist and two learning disability specialists administered a battery of tests and made clinical judgments concerning the discrepancies in the performance of each child. Forty-five children were diagnosed as suspected potential learning problems. The entire population was retested after a four-month exposure to the first-grade curriculum. First-grade teachers were not informed which children were suspected potential learning problems for fear that special attention would be given to these children, thus contaminating the findings.

Test results were compared with each student's post-testing reading grade level.

Four diagnostic instruments were employed in the testing program:

(1) The Wide Range Achievement Test (WRAT). The reading section of the WRAT was included in the experimental battery because of its extensive use in the field of special education. It is readily administered and samples word recognition and visual perceptual skills.

(2) The Evanston Early Identification Scale (EEIS). This test is a simple *screening* device for identifying those children who can be expected to have difficulty in school. The EEIS is not a *diagnostic* instrument, as children who perform poorly may possibly have emotional, perceptual, or other problems. The child is required to draw the figure of a person. The figure is scored through the use of a 10-item weighted scale resulting in either a low risk, middle risk, or high risk drawing.

(3) The Bender Gestalt Visual Motor Test. The Bender Gestalt test is highly rated and among one of the most widely used clinical tests. It consists of nine figures which the subject is asked to copy on a blank piece of paper. The test is used to measure visual-motor perception.

(4) Metropolitan Reading Readiness Test Form R. This test was devised to measure the traits and achievements of school beginners that contribute to their readiness for first grade instruction. The test is administered in group form.

Results

Experienced kindergarten teachers can select with extreme accuracy those children who will experience difficulty at the first-grade level. As seen in Table I, which gives data on the four test instruments used, the teacher-referred group was below the reading-readiness level of the non-referred group on all four test instruments. The Evanston Early Identification Scale means scores for the referred group on both the pre- and post-test fell within the middle-risk area while the non-referred group means fell within the low-risk category. The Wide Range Achievement Test depicted a difference of 3.94 or almost 4 months between the two groups on the pre-test results and a difference of 4 months on the post-test results. The mean scores for both groups on the pre- and post-tests of the Bender Gestalt Visual Motor Test were considerably higher for the referred group, suggesting a greater level of maturation or visual motor readiness. The Metropolitan Readiness Test for both groups showed a mean difference of 54.5 in favor of the non-referred group.

The standard deviations on the Bender Gestalt Visual Motor Test and Metropolitan Readiness Test were extremely high. This suggests some doubt as to their validity in predicting first-grade readiness.

The authors evaluated each case individually with regards to the students preference in reading at the first-grade level and ascertained that overall the teachers were 80 percent effective in predicting potential learning problems at the kindergarten level employing subjective judgment alone.

In Tables II, III, and IV the relation between readiness status, as determined by the total score on the various tests, and grade achievement at the fourth month of the first grade is shown in the form of bivariate distributions. The kindergarten grade "success" of pupils in each April readiness status category is shown by the frequencies at each one-month grade-equivalent interval. (See Tables II, III, IV.)

Table II results indicate that some children in the low and middle-risk groups eventually will be referred (50%), although they were not initially identified by the Evanston Early Identification Scale. However, a high-risk drawing, with a cut-off point of 8 or above, correctly identified 99 percent of those children who experienced poor success in reading at the first-grade level. These results are similar to those found by Landsman and Dillard (1967).

In Table III the results of the Wide Range Achievement Tests depict a 93 percent accuracy in correctly identifying those youngsters who will experience poor success in reading at the first-grade level. Of the 28 children who scored at the norm of kindergarten grade .8 during April achievement testing, only three were not on grade level upon follow-up in December. Thirty-nine children scored below the norm of kindergarten .8 during April testing; however, only four cases were on grade level, 1.4, at the time the December achievement test was administered.

The results of the Metropolitan Readiness Test in Table IV suggest that when utilizing the total percentage test score the only effective

TABLE I. *Teacher Ratings*

Group	No. of Subjects	EEIS Pre-test Mean	SD	EEIS Post-test Mean	SD	WRAT Pre-test Mean	SD	WRAT Post-test Mean	SD	BENDER GESTALT Pre-test Mean	SD	BENDER GESTALT Post-test Mean	SD	METROPOLITAN READINESS TEST Mean	SD
Referred	45	6.03	3.31	7.01	3.55	Kg.542	.193	1.03	1.03	81.9	27.4	95.3	15.7	27.7	22.7
Non-referred	22	3.07	2.64	3.00	2.60	Kg.936	.164	1.46	.424	109.2	17.7	116.8	23.5	82.2	26.1

TABLE II. *Distribution of December Grade Equivalents on the WRAT Reading for Pupils**

Readiness Status in April of Kindergarten (EEIS)

Grade Equivalent Reading (WRAT)	Low-Risk Score 1	2	3	4	Middle-Risk Score 5	6	7	High-Risk Score 8	9	10	11	12	13	14
2.4-2.5						1								
2.2-2.3														
2.0-2.1														
1.8-1.9														
1.6-1.7	3			1		2								
1.4-1.5	3	3	1	3	1	6	1			1				*
1.2-1.3	6	1	1	1	1	3	1		4	1	1			1
1.0-1.1				2		1	1		1				1	
Kg.8-Kg.9							1	1		1				
Kg.6-Kg.7								1				1		
Kg.4-Kg.5	2					2			1	2				
Kg.2-Kg.3				1				1	1					
TOTAL	14	4	2	8	2	14	5	2	6	3	4	1	1	1

*The dotted line divides those who scored at or above norm (1.4) from those who failed to read the norm on the December achievement test.

predictor for screening potential problems in reading at the first-grade level is a score which falls below the 30th percentile (97 percent). Such results are dissimilar from the findings of Landsman and Dillard (1967) who reported that the Metropolitan Reading Readiness Test did not predict serious learning problems.

Table V depicts correlations between the Bender Gestalt Visual Motor Tests and Reading Achievement on both the kindergarten and first-grade level. Such results suggest that because of the maturational factor the Bender Gestalt is not a valid test for predicting first-grade success in reading. However, the higher correlation between the Bender Test and first-grade reading ability would suggest that the instrument is a better predictor if administered at the first-grade level. Such findings are in agreement with those of Koppitz (1964) who suggested that good school achievement can be predicted with some assurance if a child does well on the Bender Test at the beginning of the first grade, and also

TABLE III. *Readiness Status in April of Kindergarten (WRAT)*

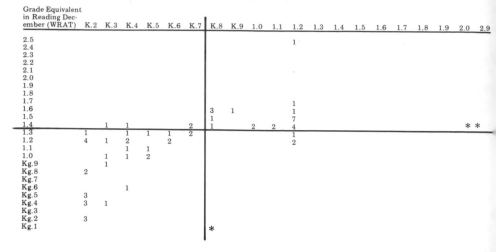

Grade Equivalent in Reading December (WRAT)	K.2	K.3	K.4	K.5	K.6	K.7	K.8	K.9	1.0	1.1	1.2	1.3	1.4	1.5	1.6	1.7	1.8	1.9	2.0	2.9
2.5											1									
2.4																				
2.3																				
2.2																				
2.1																				
2.0																				
1.9																				
1.8																				
1.7											1									
1.6							3	1			1									
1.5							1				7									
1.4		1	1			2	1		2	2	4								*	*
1.3	1		1	1	1	2					1									
1.2	4	1	2		2						2									
1.1			1	1																
1.0		1	1	2																
Kg.9		1																		
Kg.8	2																			
Kg.7																				
Kg.6			1																	
Kg.5	3																			
Kg.4	3	1																		
Kg.3																				
Kg.2	3																			
Kg.1							*													

*This line represents those who scored at or above norm (Kg. 7) during April kindergarten testing.

**This line divides those who scored at or above norm (1.4) from those who failed to read the norm on the December achievement test.

TABLE IV. *Distribution of December Grade Equivalents on the WRAT Reading for Pupils**

Readiness Status in April of Kindergarten (MRT)

Grade Equivalent in Reading (WRAT)	E Low	D Low Normal	C Average	B High Normal	A Superior
December	(F) 0-7%	(F) 8-30%	(F) 31-61%	(F) 62-68%	(F) 69%-Above
2.4-2.5					1
2.2-2.3					
2.0-2.1					
1.8-1.9					
1.6-1.7			3	1	2
1.4-1.5		3	5	1	12 *
1.2-1.3	2	8	6	2	1
1.0-1.1		3	2		1
Kg.8-Kg.9	1	2			
Kg.6-Kg.7	1				
Kg.4-Kg.5	2	5			
Kg.2-Kg.3	2	1			
TOTAL	8	22	16	4	17

*The dotted line divides those who scored at or above norm (1.4) from those who failed to reach the norm on the December achievement test.

TABLE V. *Correlations Between Bender Gestalt Test and WRAT Reading (April) and WRAT Reading (December).*

Bender Gestalt Visual Motor Test

WRAT Pre-test	WRAT Post-test
.280	.760

similar to the findings of Keogh and Smith (1961) who reported that children who performed well on the Bender in kindergarten tended to be good school performers but that poor Bender performance was non-predictive.

Conclusions

The teacher has a key role in the early identification of children with learning disabilities. Individual behavior analysis done by the teacher was effective 80 percent of the time. However, the clinical team involved in this study feel that the validated abbreviated WRAT and EEIS could be taught to the kindergarten teacher who could administer them to the children obtaining almost 90 percent or more accuracy in screening for potential learning disabilities. More important is the fact that the clinical team would thus be freed from this testing and could spend a greater amount of time in consultation and remediation.

Early identification and screening of potential learning disabilities is not only desirable but a necessity. If children with learning disabilities continue to attend school without being diagnosed and given special attention, they eventually become frustrated and develop negative attitudes toward the learning situation. Such anti-academic attitudes are consequently carried over from grade to grade and often result in emotional difficulties and eventually referral to psychological services.

REFERENCES

1. ANASTIASI, A.: *Psychological Testing*, New York: Macmillan, 1954.

2. DILLARD, H. K., and Landsman, M. *The Evanston Early Identification Scale: Prediction of School Problems From the Human Figure Drawings of Kindergarten Children. Clin. Psychology*, 1968, 24 (2), 227, 228.

3. ELLINGSTON, CARETH: *The Shadow Children*, Chicago, Ill. Topaz Books, 1968.

4. HARING, N. G., and RIDGWAY, R. W.: *Early Identification of Children With Learning Disabilities. Exceptional Child*, 1967, 17, 172-175.

5. JASTAK, J. F., and JASTAK, S. R., *The Wide Range Achievement Test.* Wilmington, Del.: Guidance Associates, 1965.

6. KEOGH, B., and SMITH, C.: *Group Techniques and Proposed Scoring System for the Bender Gestalt Test With Children. J. Clin. Psychology*, 1961, 17, 172-175.

7. KOPPITZ, E. M.: *The Bender Gestalt Test for Young Children.* New York: Grunet Stratton, 1964.

8. LANDSMAN, M., and DILLARD, H.: *The Evanston Early Identification Scale.* Chicago, Ill.: Follett Publ., 1967.

9. MITCHELL, D. C.: *The Metropolitan Readiness Tests as Prediction of First Grade Achievement. Educ. and Psychol. Measure.*, 1962, 22, 765-772.

10. ROBINSON, H. A.: *Reliability of Measures Related to Reading Success of Average Disadvantaged and Advantaged Kindergarten Children. Reading Teacher*, 1966, 20 (3), 203-209.

If I Have But One Life To Live, Let Me Live It ABOVE The Median

ELDON E. GRAN

"Promise her anything but give her Arpége!" Promise students anything, but give them standardized tests! It's amazing how we can go about, proudly clucking that the modern school respects the dignity of the individual, then march all those individuals into some sterile central spot, slap a standardized test before them, snap on the stopwatch, and complacently sort and classify children by percentiles, grade placements, deciles, stanines, and all the other little bins and boxes contrived to house individuals. The only way open to a child to succeed with a standardized evaluation is to follow a standardized curriculum—and this is *not* individualization.

Having 50 percent of a population below the median is the kind of illness that has no cure. There cannot be 50 percent above the median unless there are 50 percent below it. That's what the median is. We dreamed up the concept, coined the term—and it survives to haunt us at every turn. Of course, one way to eliminate the median is to make everybody exactly alike so that no median exists. The standardized curriculum, measured by the standardized test, thus far has not accomplished this. But we do keep on trying. We even have an A-B-C-D-F grading scale which is useful in reporting degrees of deviation either above or below the standard.

Do we really need to know into what percentile a child falls, or how many standard deviations above or below the mean his test score falls? This information, of course, makes a lovely matrix or chart; however, it does little for the child. What we really need to find out about a child are his needs; then we need to get busy and meet them. We need to find the success level of the child—every child has one—begin with it, and then remember there is no such thing as remediation, only progress on an individualized basis.

However, this can never happen as long as teachers are led to feel that their job is to make all their little lambs nibble at the same grass in tidy groups of thirty. It will never happen as long as the equation remains *listening + remembering = learning.* It will never happen as long as we are more concerned with test performance than with progress. Nor will it ever happen as long as we continue to apply child to curriculum instead of curriculum to child.

Consider the physician who would require all his patients to undergo a tonsillectomy at age 6.6, since this has been the age established as readiness for tonsillectomies. Absurd? Unreal? Then why is it that teachers are asked to hammer and tong children into reading at this age? Why is it that most school entrance age requirements are based on this bit of standardization?

Imagine a lawyer who tells you that today everyone will be tried for petty larceny, for this is the day he has decided to offer that particular experience—even though what you want is help with your income tax. Ridiculous? Then go into a fifth grade and watch some of the children scratch and claw at operations with fractions before they have mastered operations with whole numbers. Why are they doing this? Because Book 5 is prescribed for Grade 5. It contains work on fractions. This is the right time. Work on fractions now. Next year is the time for decimals. That's standard. Do you want to be below the median?

There is more respect for individuality at a Sunday smorgasbord than in the majority of our public schools. After all, at a smorgasbord you don't get clobbered if you select pickled flounder in preference to smoked turtle, or if you take potatoes without gravy and substitute butter, or if you take just a smidgin instead of a whole platter of something you never saw before in order to find out whether it will get along with your stoney gallbladder.

But just let our boy Herkimer apply the same principles to the learning process. Suppose he decides the story in his reader is not for him and pulls out his copy of *Popular Science* as a substitute. "Oh, no, Herkimer, today we read 'Bubbles Meets a Bear' in our reader. You are not to read about the moon landing—that's for out of school. Besides, there's a space unit in seventh-grade science; wait for that. If you miss 'Bubbles Meets a Bear,' you may never learn the six new words it contains. You won't pass our standardized test. You will be below the median. You want to be promoted, don't you? Well, then, get busy and read to find out what Bubbles said when she first saw the bear smelling the baked beans."

Picture a dialogue between doctor and nurse. The doctor has taken the temperature of Clatimore Coolblood and reported to the nurse, "His temperature is two points too low." The nurse inquires, "What does he need?" The doctor replies, "He needs to have his temperature raised." The nurse wonders, "How? What is your prescription?" But the doctor merely barks, "I told you to raise his temperature. You're the nurse. Take him to your ward and get busy."

In school we do things like that; we get the temperature but not the cause. Herkimer scores 3.9. This is the fifth month of fourth grade so he should be scoring 4.5. Did anybody find out what Herkimer has instead of what he hasn't? Probably more homework, maybe a tutor, better study habits, an eye check, and improved home conditions are prescribed. Did anyone try having a nose-to-nose talk talk with Herkimer and saying to him, "Look, Herk, you don't know your multiplication tables. Let's quit stumbling around and clean up that little problem. Here are some materials you can use. When can you have them down pat? Maybe next Tuesday? Good boy. See me then." This means, of course, that Herkimer will not be on the right page. It also means his activity won't match the Tuesday square in teacher's plan book, which in June must be carried on high for inspection and filing. And it means something else, too: no standards—only needs.

Do we ever stop to recognize that most of the students who grab off an *A* on the Friday spelling test knew most of the word list on the Monday trial? Do a little classroom action research if you doubt this point. Arbuckle got an *F* this week. Smartacia got an *A*. On the Monday trial, Arbuckle could spell only two of the words. That's because he had never had an occasion before to use the other 18. So on Friday he could spell only 10, and there were 20 on the list. Shame on Arbuckle! Smartacia already knew 15 of the 20 on Monday. On Friday she knew all 20. Bless Smartacia! We need more like her. She makes teaching easy; she is above the median. *A* for Smartacia."Both Arbuckle and Smartacia take Lesson 19 next week. Next week is the 19th week, isn't it? Arbuckle, you study harder. You have a problem, you know. Smartacia, you're a good speller. Next week we'll find something interesting for you to do. Arbuckle, when you can spell, you may also do something interesting; for now, keep gnawing away at the impossible, please."

Yes, Arbuckle is in the lower 50 percent, but his contribution is what makes the upper 50 percent possible. Bless Arbuckle, too. He makes Smartacia look first-rate. Maybe he should have an *A*, too, even if the teacher knows it really means "awful" by comparison with Smartacia.

Next time you shop for shoes, ask the salesclerk to consider your age and the number of years you have worn shoes. Insist on the standard size for that age and the number of years of being shod. If the miserable things fall off or pinch, don't complain. If you don't like the style, keep still. Wear the shoes. After all, they're standard and right for your age and period of nonbarefootedness. The problem is not the shoes; it's your feet. This exercise in discipline and standardization will put you in just the right frame of mind to bludgeon children into doing the standard thing at the standard time with the standard attitude. Anyway, eventually your feet will become so numb you won't notice them or even care about the shoes. Eventually, they'll take on some kind of bizarre shape that fits the shoe. The shoe is the important thing. Adjustment is up to the individual.

Standardization is the key. Above the median is the place to be.

SCHOOL is for . . .
EXPERIMENTING

Chapter XII

The Teacher As A Research Analyst

During the 70's increasing numbers of teachers, both experienced and inexperienced, have taken on an "experimental attitude" in an effort to provide more meaningful learning experiences for pupils in their classrooms. A research analyst is viewed in this Chapter as any teacher who desires to become actively engaged in problem solving (research) activities in his own classroom or who is interested in analyzing the research results of other teachers and researchers. The articles in this Chapter provide the beginning teacher with some ideas which might lead him to instigate or replicate some action research project with his own pupils.

Those of you who feel that you have acquired the competency for analyzing research should, after reading this Chapter, divert your efforts toward "in-depth" research appearing in the *Journal of Reading, The Teacher's Handbook, The Encyclopedia of Educational Research*, and other similar sources.

What Research Says To The Classroom Teacher

R. C. BRADLEY

As teachers we are busy people. Sometimes it is difficult to read and study as widely as we would like. On many issues facing us, it is not necessarily that we don't know better; it is simply that conditions or facilities prevent us from doing better. This article purports to deal with some significant facts which would be pertinent to us if we but could find time to look further into their rather startling implications. Among these significant research findings are found certain "hints for improving our teaching":

1. By the age of ten or eleven years the child has ordinarily reached a plateau in artistic maturity. The child is likely to remain on this plateau **throughout** adult life unless given special art training of an effective type. This art training demands deeper understanding than can be acquired by drill on draftsmanship and pattern work alone. Therefore, some time should be given to the study of great works of the masters, and provisions made for art work in all elementary classes of the creative and teacher-directed types.

2. When asked to select the brightest child in our room without the aid of intelligence tests, we are prone to select the child who has a higher chronological age. The older one is selected because he has learned the social amenities of life and the like; therefore, we think him to be the brightest, when actually this is not the case. We are correct in judging by guessing the child's mental capacity only about 57% of the time; and in our judgment concerning relationship of achievement to mental ability only 25% of the time. Hence, some thought must be given to using the IQ score as related to scores obtained on achievement tests.

3. Children can identify the child who is best accepted or rejected by their group than can the classroom teacher. Unless socio-metric data are available, we teachers tend to misjudge time after time who actually is accepted in a group when only personal observation criteria were applied. Therefore, sociometric devices of the teacher-made and commercially developed types should be administered to our groups of youngsters.

Bradley, R. C. "What Research Says to the Classroom Teacher." *Alabama State Teachers Association Journal.* May 1965. 6:36-38.

4. Delinquent conduct of a student is the result of frustration, and is believed to be frequently caused or brought about by the school. For example, many children drop out of school simply because they did not learn to read at their teachable moment. Possibly, more attention should be given to the non-reader than has ever been given to him before. This would include taking him through the "readiness materials" at a pace commensurate with his abilities.

5. Under threatening conditions, children do less well on tests and also do less well in remembering that information at a later time. Test anxiety seems to occur with equal frequency in different social classes. Research provides abundant evidences that performance and behavior in a situation in part depend on attitudes held toward the test situation by both pupils and teacher. It would be well that teachers use tests as learning devices rather than to use only the results of what has not been learned. Praise for the job well done should come generously.

6. Teachers who work consistently and tactfully with pupils to help them feel free, secure, and successful; to want to learn and like school, will have a classroom in which attendance will increase markedly. The one who gives several daily responsibilities to their children for carrying on routine matters of the classroom develops a keen sense of responsibility as well as good attendance practices.

7. If the teacher contributes a higher percentage of work-centered and friendly remarks than the group of children whom she teaches, the group's percentage of friendly remarks to each other and to their teacher will increase significantly. In other words, to be a model or an example as a teacher brings rewards to the group as various individuals select the teacher as "the model to live by."

8. Concepts that refer to classes of material objects are more thoroughly understood when the student has an opportunity to manipulate and study the objects than when only factual information is given in daily lectures. In modern mathematics for example, it would be better that drawings, cutouts, pictures, and the like be used both as demonstrative materials and self-study materials.

9. Teachers estimate that children listen only about 75 minutes out of the school day, when in fact as much as 160 minutes are so consumed in listening activities. Some thought should be given by all teachers as to the significance of every verbal comment used for instructional purposes in their classrooms.

10. Orally presented materials by the teacher should be less difficult than material to be read, if it is to be comprehended with equal effectiveness by the children. This suggests that those of us who have been reading materials to children because they couldn't read them for themselves may not be tenable.

11. For group reading purposes, as an individual reads orally to the group all listeners should have their books closed so that emphasis is placed upon effective listening. With books closed in the group, the reader interprets with better expression and reacts more critically to what he actually is trying to impart.

12. If more than 15 minutes per day is being devoted to a formalized spelling program in the elementary school, important time for other educative purposes is being unwisely consumed. About one third of a class will know the words in a list of twenty spelling words anyway; therefore, they shouldn't be expected to study words they already know. Another one-third of the group will be working on words above their abilities. Hence, teachers directing spelling lessons should give more time to providing opportunity for children to contract for words during the week. This would mean that some children might

take five or most lists of words per week. While on the other hand, a few youngsters would not take more than five words per day.

The dozen points mentioned above can become important guidelines to elementary teachers. We cannot expect children to become artistic without education in the arts; to be achieving to their capacity, if we cannot relate their actual IQ's to achievement test data; to become skilled listeners if material presented orally is too difficult; nor to become competent spellers if they are superficially studying words in a list which they already know. We have heard much about adjusting our programs to the child. Possibly, we need to make more adjustments in our own thinking relative to the problems and issues in our hands at the moment. A knowledge and review of the current and practical research going on in our field, should be of considerable assistance to our many educational endeavors.

SCHOOL is for . . .
ACTION RESEARCH

The Classroom Teacher In Action Research

ANNA L. BREWER

Action research is a term which is bandied about a good deal. In some quarters it is described in glowing, although somewhat vague terms, as a panacea for our educational ills. Elsewhere its proponents, its terminology, and its rather inconclusive results are scoffed at.

While many questions about research remain unanswered, we cannot help but ask ourselves a few more questions:

What sensible meaning can be attached to the term "action research"? Who should undertake it? What can research "tell" the teacher?

In attempting answers to such questions, this is addressed neither to the enthusiast nor to the professional. Rather, it is addressed to that somewhat conservative group of teachers who constitute the main care of the teaching profession and who are being oriented to the idea of action research and relating it to their classroom work. This choice of audience reflects a belief that without the interest and intelligent participation of the classroom teacher, action research stands little chance of becoming a dominant or even an effective force for educational change.

Action research in education is research undertaken by practitioners in order that they may improve their practices. Practitioners are those people who actually teach children or supervise teachers or administer school systems and who attempt to solve their problems by using the methods of science. They are the curriculum builders in our schools. They recognize that a change needs to be made. They accummulate evidence to define their problems more sharply. They draw upon all the experiences available. They test out promising procedures on the job, in the heat of combat, and again accumulate the best evidence possible. They try to generalize in order that their research will contribute to the

Brewer, Anna L. "The Classroom Teacher in Action Research." *Michigan Education Journal.* October 1964. 42:15.

solution of future problems or eliminate certain phases of future problems.

To further emphasize the foregoing let us recognize that action research offers two avenues of growth to the teacher. In the first place it is the means by which the teacher can demonstrate his professional competence to make intelligent and independent classroom decisions. But more than this, the creative function in action research provides an avenue of personal growth without which the teacher's work would be intolerable. Because action research undertaken by the classroom teacher offers so much to the teacher as an individual and to the pupils with whom he or she works, a re-emphasis of the "steps" which would be commonly recognized in the research approach will be made.

The logical sequence in action research probably begins with a feeling (perhaps vague) of dissatisfaction regarding the effectiveness of some aspect of the educational program. There must then follow a process of clarification in which the aims and free variables are identified and the situational givens recognized. At this point a specific problem has emerged—to make that assignment of the values to free variables which will produce the greatest increase in the effectiveness of the program. As the problem emerges, the teacher may refer to the research literature to ascertain what manipulations of the free variables have been tried, under what combination of "givens" they were tried, and with what results. At this point our knowledge of the process becomes thinner. After the critical requirements of the problem have been studied at the conscious level, they appear to be retained in the subconscious levels of thought, even if the attention of the teacher is temporarily turned elsewhere (one writer described this process as "incubation"). Then in some manner—as yet unknown—there tends to emerge an "hypothesis"—a suggestion or insight as to a possible solution. This hypothesis may take the form of a "guess" about the most fruitful manipulation of variables, or about the probable relationship of two previously unrelated variables. In a final stage, this hypothesis must be verified.

The practice of conducting research in order to improve decisions, practices and procedures that have to do with educational activities is certainly not new. The term "action research" is comparatively new and means much the same as the term "practical research" or the term "operational research."

A psychological value in action research is that the people who must—by the very nature of their professional responsibilities—learn to improve their practices are the ones who engage in the research to learn what really represents improvement. They have the thrilling experience of learning through trying out their own ideas and testing their work.

Without doubt, many people have personal preferences for one kind of research as opposed to another. This preference can be explained by differing personalities, training, experience or situations. However, few people would hazard the claim that one kind of research is intrinsically of more value than another. Whether the research is pure, applied, formal, informal, or whatever other label one may wish to attach, the ultimate criterion of its "value" is the degree of improvement it leads to in educational programs. From the point of view of impact, no doubt many of us can recall some rather informal and "unrigorous" research done by us in our classrooms that has been of great value in making constructive changes.

If action research seeks to maximize the rationality of educational decision-making, then perhaps one might suggest that there must be knowledge, for how can a teacher test the effectiveness of competing alternatives if he is unaware of the existence of these alternatives? There are many dimensions of the student personality and the classroom learning situation which are unknown to a minimally-trained teacher. Thus a teacher would not likely suspect that the social structure of a classroom could profoundly affect learning outcome unless he had some acquaintance with sociological theory. And again, the teacher must be familiar with the work of Piaget relative to a well-defined sequence of qualitative levels in the child's thinking if he expects to pick out the significant variables in the learning situations in order to be in a position to control or manipulate them.

It is also apparent that the teacher who wants to "do research" should have a high tolerance for ambiguity—such is the nature of research.

Finally, the researcher (action or traditional educational) should bring a certain amount of humility to his work, realizing that conclusions are always somewhat tentative, and that, on the basis of our present knowledge, dogmatic assertions are more than slightly ridiculous. There is something unpalatable about the individual who keeps reminding us what research "says" when we know perfectly well that the very highest level of research can, at best, only suggest.

Student Teachers Try Action Research

ALEX F. PERRODIN

" . . . Learning that changes behavior substantially is most likely to result when a person himself tries to improve a situation that makes a difference to him."[1]

A full-time student-teaching experience has become widely accepted as a vital part, if not the climax, of the preservice preparation of teachers. For it is during this extended period of daily contact with a school, a teacher, and a group of children, that the would-be teacher has an opportunity to test theory in action, to discover his own strengths and weaknesses as a teacher, and to develop some minimum competences that will bolster his self-confidence as he goes on to "real" teaching.

Carbon Copies

Sometimes, however, those responsible for teacher education programs note the student's tendency to develop as somewhat of a carbon copy of his constant associate, the supervising teacher. This is understandable, for the supervising teacher has been selected on the basis of certain criteria, the chief of which usually is some years of highly successful teaching. On the other hand, another factor, that of grading the student on his student-teaching experiences, enters the picture. Frequently the achievement of the student teacher is measured by the degree to which he can adopt the methods successfully being used by the

---

[1] Stephen M. Corey, *Action Research to Improve School Practices* (New York: Bureau of Publications, Teachers College, Columbia University, 1953) p.9.

Perrodin, Alex F. "Student Teachers Try Action Research." *The Journal of Teacher Education.* December 1959. 10:471-474.

supervising teacher in this particular situation. Any great variation from the existing practices may upset the smooth functioning of the classroom so carefully developed by the supervising teacher, who must maintain responsibility for the class before, during, and after the student teacher's participation with the group. Also the introduction of a second teacher in the classroom who successfully uses a method differing from the current classroom practices, may unintentionally threaten the security or prestige of the supervising teacher. The combination of these factors with the student teacher's intense motivation to succeed in this large segment of his professional preparation perhaps is a just explanation of the possible development of "carbon copies," or as some educators lament—the perpetuation of existing teaching practices.

Individuality Through Action Research

In an effort to encourage individual differences and at the same time to contribute to the development of problem-solving skills, elementary-school student teachers at the University of Georgia were encouraged to try a simplified version of action research. During the quarter preceding student teaching these students, in addition to the usual study of elementary-school curriculum and methods, had an opportunity to observe and participate for 10 to 12 half-days in several nearby schools where teachers were engaged in co-operative action research. The students were oriented to the over-all purposes of the co-operative study underway, saw educational research activities in progress in the various schools, and before entering student teaching had obtained, through college class discussions, information as to basic procedures of action research.

With this background the students began their fulltime student teaching extending over a period of 11 to 12 weeks, many of them working in classrooms where they had earlier spent 10 to 12 half-days of observation and participation. As they were gradually inducted into teaching, they became more sensitive to educational problems, and some developed a readiness to launch out on their own into simplified action research.

The following are brief summaries taken from student accounts of their experiences:

EXAMPLE 1

Grade Level: First.
Problem: How can I obtain information concerning this group of children which will aid me in improving my teaching with this group?
Hypothesis: If a survey is made of reading and television interests, this information will serve as a guide to improve my teaching.

Action Taken: (1) Studied cumulative records to determine socio-economic status and intellectual ability of children involved in study; (2) developed an interview guide containing questions on reading and television interests; (3) interviewed the 22 first-graders using this guide; and (4) tabulated these data and attempted to draw implications for teaching.

Findings and Evaluation: (1) found information on books children had at home, children's interests in these books, magazines in the home, and indications of interest in parts of newspapers; (2) children indicated interest in books with color pictures, yet some preferred to read or hear the story without looking at the pictures; (3) boys preferred animal and western stories but girls preferred fairy tales and travel; (4) all children had TV at home; viewing habits varied greatly, but comedies and westerns were their favorite types of programs; and (5) this information enabled the student teacher to become better acquainted with her class group and served as a valuable guide to her planning of learning experiences.

EXAMPLE 2

Grade Level: First

Problem: How can a first-grade teacher obtain information which might help in the prevention of mental-health problems?

Hypothesis: If a standardized test of personality is given, a study of the results will help the teacher to obtain a better understanding of her group.

Action Taken: (1) The California Test of Personality was administered individually by supervising teacher and student teacher to each first grader; (2) tests were scored and summary sheets prepared; (3) test scores were compared with student-teacher and supervising-teacher observations of the children.

Findings and Evaluation: (1) A total picture of each child's personal and social adjustment was obtained and studied; (2) when test scores indicated adjustment problems, the student teacher and the supervising teacher studied possible causes and tried to find ways to provide beneficial classroom experiences; (3) test scores helped the student teacher and the supervising teacher to determine children who should be given priority in making home visits.

EXAMPLE 3

Grade Level: Second (last months of school year).

Problem: What teaching procedures and materials should be used with the advanced group of children who completed the second-grade basic reading program by the end of March?

Hypothesis: If these children are guided in reading books of their own choice, they will continue to gain in reading skills and will develop further interest in reading.

Action Taken: (1) Both student teacher and supervising teacher read widely available materials on "individualized reading programs"; (2) collected books from a variety of sources; (3) made plans for. and explained proposed program to children; (4) prepared individual record sheets entitled "My Reading Record"; (5) allowed minimum of 30 minutes per day for individualized reading and developed with the children guides to selection, reading, reporting, and recording.

Findings and Evaluation: (1) The twelve students involved read more books in 20 days than the entire class of 25 pupils had read in the previous nine weeks; (2) children and teachers were very enthusiastic about this type of reading program; (3) children improved in ability to select books that they could read independently; (4) other children became more interested in reading (5) teacher and student teacher plan to continue this procedure in combination with the standard basal reading program.

EXAMPLE 4

Grade Level: Third.

Problem: How can the tape recorder contribute to a sound educational program?

Hypothesis: If a tape recording is made of parts of a unit of work, children will be helped to improve in their writing and speaking.

Action Taken: (1) The student teacher planned with the pupils for a program based on the on-going unit theme; (2) children wrote paragraphs from which selections were made for the recording; (3) children of varying abilities were selected to do the recording; and (4) the tape was played back for group evaluation.

Findings and Evaluation: (1) All ability levels took part and profited from the experience; (2) children were enthusiastic in their desire to improve writing and speaking; (3) all children had an opportunity to learn from the sharing of information; and (4) the student teacher gained new insights into behavior of the children involved.

EXAMPLE 5

Grade Level: Fourth.

Problem: How can I best help to improve the reading of the slow reading group?

Hypothesis: If children are provided interesting reading materials at their reading level and are given daily guided instruction in word recognition skills, they will gain confidence and skill in reading.

Action Taken: (1) Checked on children's reading-grade placements and ability levels; (2) provided basic reading materials at their reading levels; (3) used teacher's guide materials from publishers of basic reading series to aid in developing daily plans; (4) used phonics, recordings, and accompanying cards in relation to daily reading program; (5) developed daily mimeographed teaching and drill materials.

Findings and Evaluation: (1) Through conferences, teacher observation, and teacher-prepared tests, evaluation of children's progress was continuous; and (2) children gained in confidence, gave evidence of improved attitudes toward reading, and scores on teacher-prepared reading-achievement tests showed improvement.

EXAMPLE 6

Grade Level: Fourth.

Problem: How can the natural curiosity of children be encouraged and utilized to contribute to a planned school program?

Hypothesis: If a procedure involving the solving of the "Mystery of the Week" is used in the classroom, children will be encouraged to manifest and explore the questions about which they are curious.

Action Taken: (1) Class situations were noted in which children indicated a curiosity regarding something beyond the immediate situation; (2) From these a "Mystery of the Week" was selected and listed on the chalkboard reserved for this purpose (*e.g.*, "How much is one peso?"—suggested from a filmstrip on Mexico; "How was soap made in olden days?"—from a story read by one reading group; "How do you make the word 'calf' plural?"—from a spelling list; "Why do we observe

Valentine's Day?"—from a class discussion of the need for a Valentine box; and (3) children were encouraged to act as detectives and try to obtain clues providing answers to questions such as these, but kept answers to themselves until the end of the week.

Findings and Evaluation: (1) Children made more frequent use of dictionaries, encyclopedias, and other resource materials; (2) children indicated wider variety and larger number of curiosities than previously.

EXAMPLE 7

Grade Level: Fifth (last part of year).

Problem: What methods and materials can I use to guide the reading development of 12 advanced readers selected from three fifth grades who have completed all basal reading materials?

Hypothesis: If these children are provided a variety of historical biographies to read, they will continue to develop their interest in and achievement in reading.

Action Taken: (1) Studied test data from *Weekly Reader Tests, California Reading Achievement Tests,* and group intelligence test scores and observed children in a variety of situations; (2) obtained copies of an adventure series of biographies of heroes of the wild west; (3) prepared with the group some guides to keeping records of reading; (4) met the group for 45 minutes a day on three days of each week for nine weeks in whatever school space was available; (5) developed procedures for silent reading, exchange of books, and individual reading to the student teacher; (6) the student teacher kept individual anecdotal-type records of each student's reading as observed in individual conference.

Findings and Evaluation: (1) Children appeared to enjoy the reading time; (2) children maintained consistent gains in reading and achievement as measured by standardized tests; (3) the student teacher gained much insight into the reading interests, problems of advanced readers, and developed skills of anecdotal record keeping; and (4) the student teacher recognized the need for better facilities for class and for a greater number and variety of materials.

The preceding are not suggested as examples of or as substitutes for a planned research program. Neither are they intended to take priority over the primary functions of a student-teaching experience.

These experiences have provided an opportunity to encourage the growth of the student teacher as an individual, an opportunity to try something not ordinarily associated with the supervising teacher's successful procedures. Careful preplanning with both the college supervisor and the supervising teacher was done to avoid any threat to the security of the established procedures of the supervising teacher.

At the same time both student teacher and supervising teacher have had an opportunity to develop a better understanding of the basic skills of action research. They have been sensitized to problems of teaching; helped to define these problems; enabled to state hunches as hypotheses; provided with some opportunity to test these beliefs, and then to try ways of evaluating the findings and the procedures used.

Sufficient time has not elapsed to determine whether the learnings involved in these experiences will be tried again in the solving of new problems as the students continue in the teaching profession. However, it is hoped that the interest which has developed, the skills that have been obtained, and the satisfactions which have accrued from solving smaller problems, will give the neophyte sufficient confidence and under-standings of a useful method to attack larger problems as they arise.

SCHOOL is for . . .
RESEARCH PROJECTS

Research On Teacher Evaluation

N. A. FATTU

Studies on teacher effectiveness have been summarized and reviewed periodically since 1926. While empirical study of teacher effectiveness be said to have begun about 1891, it was not until the period 1913-17 that some momentum was attained. This momentum continued for almost twenty years. The advent of Gestalt psychology and the organismic point of view was reflected by a significant decrease in the number of studies based upon empirical data. Tomlinson has told the story of this movement in detail.[1]

Two major reviews of the literature on teacher effectiveness are those by Domas and Tiedeman[2] and by Morsh and Wilder.[3] These summaries by no means list all of the publications on teacher effectiveness. They exclude the vast majority of the publications which were not empirical in some way. These two summaries cover the literature on quantitative studies up to 1952.

Other reviews and summaries that should be read by anyone seriously interested in further exploration of the field are the Mitzel and Gross review of the pupil growth criterion;[4] the series of reviews by Barr over a period of more than thirty years, of which only those in the period 1940-58 are indicated here;[5] the annotated bibliography by Castetter and others;[6] the Leiderman and others summary of teacher behavior studies;[7] the Levin and others comments on the questions asked about, and the reasons for, unproductive studies;[8] the McCall,[9] Mitzel,[10] Remmers and others[11] studies; the American Educational Research Association's *Review of Educational Research* triennial summaries; the Ryans,[12] Tiedeman and Cogan,[13] and Watters[14] studies.

No one seriously interested in teacher evaluation can afford to

Fattu, N. A. "Research on Teacher Evaluation." *The National Elementary Principal.* November 1963. 43:19-27. Reprinted by permission of the author and The National Association of Elementary School Principals, © copyright 1963.

neglect to read—diligently and frequently—the *Handbook of Research on Teaching*.[15] This book began in 1950 with the appointment of a Committee on the Criteria of Teacher Effectiveness by the American Educational Research Association. In 1956, the Committee, then called the Committee on Teacher Effectiveness, proposed the development of the handbook. In 1957, N. L. Gage, chairman of the Committee, was named editor. Most relevant to the present discussion are segments of Parts II, III, and IV in the *Handbook.* In Part II on *Methodologies in Research on Teaching*, the following chapters may be most useful to elementary school principals and supervisors: chapter 6, "Measuring Classroom Behavior by Systematic Observation" by Donald Medley and Harold Mitzel; chapter 7, "Rating Methods in Research on Teaching" by H. H. Remmers; chapter 8, "Testing Cognitive Ability and Achievement" by Benjamin S. Bloom; and chapter 9, "Measuring Noncognitive Variables in Research on Teaching" by G. C. Stern. In Part III on *Major Variables and Areas of Research on Teaching*, chapter 11, "The Teacher's Personality and Characteristics" by J. W. Getzels and P. S. Jackson is recommended. Part IV, *Research on Teaching Various Grade Levels and Subject Matters*, is addressed largely to high school and college people. Elementary school principals and supervisors would find chapter 15, "Research on Teaching in the Nursery School" by Pauline Sears and Edith Dowley, and chapter 16, "Research on Reading" by David Russell and Henry Fea, most useful.

Obviously, what research says about teacher effectiveness cannot be summarized in a few words. One who wishes to understand the findings should consult the sources indicated, especially the *Handbook of Research on Teaching.*

What is Effectiveness?

A difficult problem in the study of teacher effectiveness has been whether to assume that effectiveness is a statement about an attribute of the teacher in a particular teaching situation or to assume that it is a statement about the results that come out of a teaching situation.

It appears, as indicated by Barr, that most studies of teacher effectiveness are searching for a property of the teacher. As indicated by Remmers, the search has not been successful. But the assumption on which this search is based has not been tested. To do so would require a longitudinal study with repeated measurement of the same teacher on the same criteria under a wide range of teaching conditions. Such a study has not been conducted.

In examining the assumption that effectiveness is an attribute of the teacher, one should recognize that it lies along a continuum of assumptions. At one end is the assumption that effectiveness is determined almost wholly by the teacher, that it is one of his attributes, and that it depends very little on the variables within the situation. At the other end of the continuum is the assumption that effectiveness is almost wholly determined by the particular variables operating in the situation where teaching occurs.

One is free to choose his assumption anywhere along the continuum, but in choosing he implicitly makes a hypothesis about the adaptability of teachers to teaching situations. If he assumes that effectiveness depends on the particular variables operating in a situation in which a teacher teaches, he is saying that teachers simply react without close regard to the appropriateness of that behavior with respect to the variables in the situation. If a teacher happens to react properly for a particular set of conditions, then he is effective.

Or if one proceeds on the assumption that effectiveness is almost wholly attributable to the teacher, he claims that teachers are adaptive in their teaching behavior so that they react with a close regard to its appropriateness. He states that teachers are capable of fine discriminations in their environment and have available the responses appropriate to those discriminations.

Apparently a choice of one assumption or the other is not desirable, because the very act of choosing makes it necessary to exclude one of the assumptions. There is no reason to think that effectiveness depends entirely on variables operating in the situation or that it necessarily depends on the teacher. Perhaps both assumptions are valid, depending on differences among teachers. Some teachers are no doubt capable of producing desirable pupil behaviors in a wide variety of teaching situations. The behavior they display, of course, depends on the situation, but this is not the point. The point is that their behavior is appropriate to that situation and that desirable pupil behaviors result because it is appropriate. These teachers do not have some sort of magical property called "effectiveness," but they are characterized by adaptability to teaching situations, or they have developed a high level of skill in dealing with the problems which arise in the course of their professional work.

There are other teachers who no doubt are capable of producing desirable pupil behaviors under more limited teaching conditions. These teachers are effective within the range of teaching situations for which their responses are appropriate.

Finally, there are no doubt teachers whose patterns of teaching behavior are so poorly developed that they can succeed in only a very few teaching situations or not at all.

In other words, effectiveness has several meanings, and no harm is done in using the term if one is clear as to which meaning is intended.

Teacher Characteristics

The purpose of teacher characteristics studies is to discover which traits or combinations of traits are closely enough associated with teacher competence to permit prediction of such competency. Among these traits are intelligence, knowledge of subject matter, scholarship, educational background, age and experience, professional knowledge, cultural background, socio-economic background, teaching attitude and interest, and voice and speech characteristics.

Intelligence and success. Whether or not intelligence is an important variable in the success of the instructor apparently depends upon the situation. In general, there appears to be only a slight relationship between intelligence and *rated* success of an instructor. Correlation coefficients for high school teachers tend to be somewhat higher and somewhat less variable than those reported for elementary teachers. For all practical purposes, however, this variable appears to be of little value as a *single* predictor of rated instructor competence.

This does not mean that teachers do not need to be intelligent. Rather, those who teach have been selected on the basis of intelligence, and within the range of scores characteristic of teachers, differences in intelligence have not been shown to be crucial. In more refined research where variables are more carefully controlled, intelligence test scores are more closely related to teacher performance.

Knowledge of subject matter and success. A common misconception is that knowledge of subject matter is a major factor in teaching performance. Except for occasional studies in mathematics, chemistry, and physics, research findings report little relationship. Again, whether or not knowledge of subject matter is related to instructor competence seems to be a function of the particular teaching situation and is generally a complex interaction rather than a simple variable.

Professional knowledge and success. It appears that a teacher's rated effectiveness at first increases rather rapidly with experience and then levels off at five years or beyond. The teacher may show little change in rated performance for the next 15 to 20 years, after which, as in most occupations, there tends to be a slow decline.

Cultural background and success. There is no substantial evidence that cultural background is significantly related to teaching effectiveness. Studies reviewed indicate the relation of Cooperative General Culture Test scores to instructor effectiveness is congruent with results reported for other subject-matter areas.

Socio-economic status and success. The relationship of socio-economic status (as measured by such devices as the Sims Socio-Economic Scales) to criteria of instructor effectiveness is low. The research suggests, however, that those from higher groups usually have greater probabilities of success in life than those less fortunate.

Sex and success. No particular differences have been shown when the relative effectiveness of men and women teachers has been compared.

Marital status and success. Despite some prejudice to the contrary, there appears to be no evidence that married teachers are in any way inferior to single teachers.

Teaching aptitude and success. Results obtained from measures designed to predict teaching ability show great disparity. Data thus far available either fail to establish the existence of any specified aptitude for teaching with any degree of certainty or indicate the tests used were inappropriate to its measurement.

Teaching attitude and success. Attitude toward teachers and teaching as indicated by the Yeager Scale, which was devised for its measurement, seems to bear a small but positive relationship to teacher success measured in terms of pupil gains.

Job interest and success. In most of the studies reviewed, interest in teaching was measured by interest test scores which indicated similarity between the interests of teachers and the interests of persons undergoing the test. Correlations resulting from the use of several standard interest tests either cluster around zero or are so inconsistent as to render such tests of doubtful value as predictors of teaching success. The common factors that were found through factor analyses to underlie the reasons given for choosing the teaching profession are perhaps provocative of further research, but are based on too few cases to justify any clear-cut interpretation.

Voice-speech and success. On the basis of studies reviewed, it appears that the quality of the teacher's voice is not considered very important by school administrators, teachers, or students. In one study, however, certain speech factors were found to be correlated significantly with student gains and with effectiveness ratings of supervisors. The intercorrelations of the speech factors, however, were so high that general speech ability based on a single factor is probably as useful as a composite of judgments based on several speech factors.

Special abilities and success. Such instructor factors as empathy, professional maturity, general knowledge, mental ability, and social adjustment have been identified through factor analyses by various investigators. The statistical analyses so far reported, however, suffer from inadequacies of criteria, testing instruments, or number of cases.

Teacher failure. In most of the studies of unsuccessful teachers, it has been found that poor maintenance of discipline and lack of cooperation tend to be the chief causes of failure. Health, educational background, preparation, age, and knowledge of subject matter, on the other hand, appear to be relatively unimportant factors in terms of teacher failure.

The attempts made to identify characteristics of successful and unsuccessful instructors by making lists of traits based on opinion appear largely sterile in terms of usability for evaluation or selective purposes.

Ryans' Study of Teacher Characteristics

Perhaps the most extensive study of teacher characteristics ever carried out is that by Ryans.[16] More than a hundred separate research projects were conducted. About 1,700 schools, involving 450 school systems and 6,000 teachers, took part.

Factor analyses of data revealed three patterns of teacher behavior:

Pattern X_0 —warm, understanding, friendly vs. aloof, egocentric, restricted teacher behavior. Pattern Y_0 —responsible, businesslike, systematic vs. evading, unplanned, slipshod teacher behavior. Pattern Z_0—stimulating, imaginative, surgent vs. dull, routine teacher behavior.

Among elementary school teachers, X_0, Y_0, Z_0 patterns were positively correlated and each seemed to be correlated with pupil behavior in the teachers' classes. X_0, Y_0, Z_0 patterns for married elementary teachers tended to be higher than for single elementary teachers. Patterns did not vary significantly with Minnesota Multiphasic Personality Inventory scores or the Allport-Vernon-Lindzey Study of Values.

Other results were: 1) Educational views of secondary teachers appeared to be more traditional—those of elementary were more permissive; 2) Attitudes of elementary teachers toward pupils, administrators, fellow teachers, and non-administrative personnel were distinctly more favorable than were those of secondary teachers; 3) Male teachers, both at the elementary and secondary school levels, appeared substantially more stable emotionally than female; 4) Observer assessment of pupil behavior in the classroom did not seem to be related to teachers' attitudes; 5) Verbal understanding scores (on vocabulary and verbal analogy problems) of secondary teachers were significantly higher than those of elementary teachers.

Much of the study was devoted to determination of correlates of teacher classroom behavior. A 300 item multiple-choice and checklist self-report inventory of personal preferences, self-judgments, activities, and biographical data—called the Teacher Characteristics Schedule—was developed. Numerous item analyses were done using observer assessments and direct-response scales as criteria. Scoring keys were developed for a large number of teacher groups.

Comparing characteristics of teachers gave the following results:

- Elementary school married teachers attained more favorable scores on these variables.
- Teachers from large universities achieved higher scores on stimulating classroom behavior and child-centered views.
- Teachers who had been outstanding students scored higher than other groups on most scales. The only exception dealt with emotional stability.
- Teachers who claimed they entered teaching because they liked school and because of its social service usually scored higher on most of the characteristics. Teachers who entered the profession because they were advised to do so or because of favorable prospects for advancement generally scored lower.
- Teachers who reported childhood activities as "reading to children" or "playing school," etc., had higher scores on "friendly, responsible, stimulating" classroom behavior, favorable attitudes toward pupils, and democratic classroom procedures than others.
- Scores of the older teachers (age 55 and over) were not as favorable as those of younger teachers except on warm, understanding, friendly behavior and tradition centered behavior. Trends for experience were like those for age.
- At the elementary school level, men and women teachers differed in only four of the personal-social characteristics studied. Men were less responsible and businesslike in classroom behavior and more favorable toward democratic classroom practices, more inclined toward permissive, child-centered educational viewpoints, and more stable emotionally.
- Teachers from larger schools and larger communities scored substantially higher than others on friendly, stimulating classroom behavior, favorable attitudes toward administrators, verbal understanding, and emotional stability. As a rule, teachers from smaller communities scored lower than those from larger communities, except for teachers from the largest cities (1,000,000 and over) who scored about as low as teachers from very small communities.

Teachers were classified as "high" (at least a standard deviation above the mean) and "low" (at least a standard deviation below the mean) on characteristics. Results are summarized by Ryans as follows:

There was a general tendency for high teachers to: be extremely generous in appraisals of behavior and motives of other persons; possess strong interest in reading and literary affairs; be interested in music, painting, and the arts in general; participate in social groups; enjoy pupil relationships; prefer non-directive (permissive) classroom procedures; manifest superior verbal intelligence; and be superior with respect to emotional adjustment. On the other hand, low teachers tended generally to: be restrictive and critical in their appraisals of other persons; prefer activities which did not involve close personal contacts; express less favorable opinions of pupils; manifest less higher verbal intelligence; show less satisfactory emotional adjustment; and represent older age groups. (pp. 397-98).

The Teacher Characteristics Study was an impressive enterprise, but it is obvious that the author's cautions relative to conclusions are justified.

Personality Patterns

For many years, research on personality characteristics was conducted through opinion studies. On the whole, such studies failed to obtain anything more than agreement on a few general trait designations, such as "interested" and "sympathetic." These provided little insight or help; Guba and Getzels in 1955 commented, "Despite a large number of investigations, relatively little more is known now than in 1900."[17]

Recently, emphasis has shifted to greater use of psychological theory and carefully planned measurement devices. Cook and others developed the Minnesota Teacher Attitude Inventory. Studies by Gage and Cronbach (1955)[18] and Ryans (1960)[19] are recommended for reading. Chapter 11 of the *Handbook of Research on Teaching* summarizes a good deal of the literature.

Results obtained with personality tests of teachers have shown wide variation when correlated with other measures. However, until carefully controlled, well-designed studies employing adequate numbers of instructors have been made, the problem of determining the personality patterns of effective teachers must still remain unsolved.

Assessing Teacher Behavior

Teacher behavior in the classroom obviously would seem to be the most useful source of data on teacher effectiveness, since it would appear to have an authentic on-the-job performance type of validity. Again, the problem is to obtain accurate and comprehensive measures. These measures usually consist of some kind of ranking or rating procedure.

Rating devices. Rating scales are the most frequently used devices for assessing teacher behavior. In practice there is usually no clear delineation regarding what relevant behavior is. Rather, an attempt is made to use rating as a widespread net in the hope of catching some of the unsuspected variables. Rating scales and observation scales exhibit the characteristic features of common sense formulations—vagueness of definition, lack of specificity regarding the range of applicability, and absence of means of determining the invariant rather than the merely immediate and specific features.

In a sense, the use of rating scales to measure behavioral features tends to emphasize the subjectivity that characterizes broad definitions of behavior, interpretation or inference of goals from actions. Add the "natural" variability among raters, and the residue that is free of experimental error and errors of measurement becomes relatively small.

Surveys of appointment blanks and rating scales in use have failed to provide means for identifying the significant items to be used in setting up rating devices for teacher effectiveness. Frequently mentioned qualities on existing teacher appointment blanks are disciplinary ability, teaching ability, scholarship, and personality. There is no general agreement about what constitute the essential characteristics of a competent teacher. Similarly, items on rating scales tend to be subjective, undefined, and varied; there is little consistency as to what traits a supervisor might be expected to observe and evaluate. Chapter 7 of the *Handbook* contains a comprehensive summary of rating methods.

Administrative ratings. Over-all administrative opinion constitutes the most widely used single measure of teacher competence. Available studies have shown in general that teachers can be reliably rated by administrative and supervisory personnel (usually with correlations of .70 or above). For the most part, administrative ratings do not produce very high correlations with measures of student gain. Intercorrelations of rated traits or categories indicate that traits that are more objectively observable, or are more independent of opinion, tend to be less prone to logical error or halo effect than those traits that are more intangible and more subjectively estimated. Findings suggest that ratings made by a single person are apt to be contaminated by halo effects and that, in many such instances, a single rating of over-all effectiveness is useful only when based on a composite of a number of ratings of separate traits.

Peer ratings. Peer ratings are little used. For administrative purposes they are probably not very useful since teachers tend to have certain misgivings about expressing judgment on fellow teachers. As a rule, ranks probably give better results than ratings. Studies have shown substantial agreement between supervisors and fellow teachers in ratings assigned to teachers. As in the case of administrative ratings, substantial correlation is found among ratings given different traits by the same peer raters. In other words, halo effects influence peer ratings just as they do administrative ratings.

Student ratings. When student ratings are compared with other measures of teacher effectiveness, varying results are found, depending in part upon the criteria employed. Considerable halo effect is usually noted when students rate their instructors on several traits. Results suggest that if the instructor favors the brighter students, he tends to be approved by them and a positive correlation between student ratings and grades results. If he teaches for the weaker students, he is not approved by the brighter students and a negative coefficient tends to be obtained. By and large, such factors as size of class, sex of students, age or maturity of students, and intelligence or mental age of students seem to have little bearing on student ratings. Research has been too sporadic and results too diverse to generalize about the influence of other factors on student ratings.

Self-ratings. Instructors tend to overrate themselves. Self-ratings show negligible relationships with administrative ratings, student ratings, or measures of student gains. On the basis of the few available studies of self-ratings of instructors, the obvious, undisguised self-rating technique appears to offer little encouragement for evaluative or research purposes.

Systematic observation. Systematic observation techniques to determine differences in performance of effective and ineffective teachers were largely neglected until rather recently.[20] Most of the observations seem to depend upon the subjective judgment of the observer. In the case of planned observational recording, the reliability compares favorably with other methods of teacher evaluation. The most general criterion of validity of observation appears to be face validity. No single, specific, observable teacher act has been found whose frequency, or per cent of occurrence, is invariable and significantly correlated with student achievement. There seems to be a suggestion, however, that questions based on student interest and experience rather than on assigned subject matter, the extent to which the instructor challenges students to support ideas, and the amount of spontaneous student discussion are related to student gains. Also, there seem to be no optimal time expenditures for particular class activities; a good teacher could apparently function successfully within a wide range of time distributions.

Critical incident technique. The critical incident technique described by Flanagan (1949) has been used in an attempt to describe teacher behavior. Observers and teachers reported anecdotal incidents in which they thought teachers were particularly effective or ineffective. Incidents were then classified in an attempt to isolate patterns. While many useful incidents were obtained, it has been difficult to put them into significant categories.

Other approaches. Students have been asked to describe their best and poorest teachers; parents and teachers have been asked to recall the behavior of teachers they remembered as being effective; leaders in education have been asked to describe what they regarded as effective and ineffective behavior. These approaches have not been rewarding. The time and effort could better be spent in more precise definition, observation, and analysis of the network of relationships among teacher behaviors, instructional goals, and pupil characteristics.

Pupil Growth and Achievement

Pupil growth and achievement in relation to teacher performance has been reviewed by Ackerman,[21] McCall,[22] Medley and Mitzel,[23] Mitzel and Gross,[24] Morsh and others,[25] Taylor,[26] and Webb and Bowers.[27] If the purpose of teaching is to attain objectives by bringing about desired changes in pupils, the obvious measure of teacher effectiveness is the extent to which the teacher actually produces such changes. Unfortunately, some difficulties intrude upon this happy prospect: 1) It is difficult to measure pupil growth, and 2) it is difficult to determine precisely how much change can be attributed to a particular teacher. It is not surprising that the number of student gain studies is rather low. The great discrepancies in findings of the studies using student gains criteria emphasize the complexity of their relation to instructor performance.

The central difficulty is establishing sufficient experimental controls to show that certain changes in pupil behavior occur if, and only if, these changes are preceded by actions of a teacher.

To attain precise controls is probably impossible, although various statistical controls including matched groups, analysis of covariance, and various randomized and similar designs serve as approximations. A further difficulty in the matter of demonstrating that particular pupil behaviors are associated with actions of a particular teacher lies in the amount of confidence that can be placed in the criterion measure of pupil behavior. For instance: the immediate goal of a teacher may be to get the pupils to perform long division problems of a given level of difficulty. If the pupils learn to do such problems, one has some confidence that the teacher has achieved the goal; but if at a later time the pupils have difficulty in learning to do more difficult problems in division, or have difficulty in learning to use division in algebra, or can't use division to solve elementary science problems, confidence in the criterion is not as firm.

At this point, an interesting paradox appears. As one moves from the more immediate and more convenient criteria for assessing pupil achievement to those that are more distant but more valid, the pupil behavior attributable to a given teacher becomes increasingly confounded with the effect produced by other teachers. Thus, as one's confidence in the criteria of effectiveness increases, the likelihood of being able to attribute it to any one teacher correspondingly decreases. A reason for this is not hard to see. The more distant criteria depend on the transfer of learning. Transfer depends both on initial learning and on what is done later. One of the criteria for how well a fourth-grade teacher teaches arithmetic depends on how well his students learn fifth-grade arithmetic, while one of the criteria of how well a fifth-grade teacher teaches arithmetic is the extent to which he can create situations to which the pupils coming from the fourth grade can transfer their knowledge. The fourth-grade and fifth-grade teachers here become interacting units, and to which of them the arithmetic behavior at the end of the fifth grade is to be attributed is a very interesting problem in logical and statistical analysis.

The problem of inter-teacher influence is further complicated by the other influences that shape pupil growth: home, community, clubs, communication media, books, magazines, and libraries, to name a few. Considering the theoretical importance of pupil gain criteria for the assessment of teacher effectiveness, it is surprising that so few studies have used this measure. Barr's 1948 summary lists only 19 investigations that could possibly be said to use student gain as a criterion. In 1956, Mitzel and Gross found only 20 studies which had used student gain as a criterion. These studies exhibited conflicting results.

The criterion has been used most effectively by Morsh, Burgess, and Smith (1956). However, it should be indicated that the objectives of concern were strictly limited to subject-matter achievement in an Air Force technical specialty school. Mastery involved simply rote learning rather than cultivation of higher mental processes. In this restricted case, clear demonstration of pupil gains in relation to teacher activity was possible.

The Administrator and Teacher Effectiveness Research

So far we have considered only the point of view of researchers. When talking about teacher effectiveness, it is equally important to consider the concerns of teachers and administrators.

Within the arena of practical affairs, concern about teacher effectiveness is frequent. By virtue of local control, it is the responsibility of school officials to obtain an estimate of teacher effectiveness in order that decisions on retention, promotion, salary, or helping teachers to improve may be made.

School officials cannot make a decision as to how well a particular teacher performs without defining, however loosely, the teacher's job. When the job is loosely defined, school officials may base their evaluations on how well they like the teacher; or the number of complaints or commendations received about the teacher from parents; or the extent to which the teacher disrupts or facilitates smooth operation of school machinery.

At a slightly more organized level, administrative officials may work with the school board, the teachers, and the community in attempting to determine what the functions of a teacher in the local schools should be. Decisions of such groups may range from so rigidly specifying the functions and activities that little autonomy is left to the teacher, to stating functions so vaguely that virtually all is left to the judgment of the teacher. Whatever the position of the group, the definitions refer to teacher function only within a limited geographical area.

Under local control, teacher function is free to vary from school system to school system. The job of the teacher thus varies with its location. Given that the functions a teacher should perform are well defined within a particular school system, one must consider the further complication that while first-grade teachers and senior high school teachers perform the same general functions, their specific responsibilities are quite different. Thus the teacher's job also varies with the grade.

Because most administrators are responsible to a local board of education, they can assess teacher performance by reference to locally defined functions. Generally speaking, all evaluations can be categorized as either formal or informal. Within this context, three techniques for local appraisal of teacher performance are typically used—ratings, observations, or student gains measured by standardized tests.

Ratings may consist of an over-all estimate of teacher effectiveness or of separate evaluations of specific teacher behaviors or traits. Self-ratings may be used, or ratings may be determined by the teacher's peers, by students, or by administrative personnel.

Ratings may involve ranking per cent of efficiency, indication of the level of a trait, forced choice, or any of the devices indicated in the *Handbook of Research on Teaching.*

Observation of teachers in the classroom may be used by local school officials; in practice, this technique is seldom the only one used for judgments of teacher effectiveness, and it is rarely used in an objective, scientific fashion.

Student gain, as measured by standardized tests, may be used appropriately to evaluate teacher effectiveness only if extensive controls and adjustments are made to recognize and compensate for factors other than teacher influence.

From the standpoint of the local school administrator, the extent to which any or all of these procedures are used depends on how much and what kind of evidence is desired in making decisions about local school personnel.

If one wants only to make a decision, ratings may be sufficient. If one wants to provide for in-service training and upgrading, ratings are not sufficient. It then becomes necessary to search for more explicit connections between attainment of objectives, teacher behaviors, characteristics and education. The process of joint inquiry, involving both the teachers and administrators, has much to recommend it. Administrators and teachers can help each other clarify their thinking and knowledge, and in the process both gain something in professional fulfillment.

[1] Tomlinson, L. R. "Pioneer Studies in the Evaluation of Teaching." *Educational Research Bulletin* 34:63-71; March 1955.
Tomlinson, L. R. "Recent Studies in the Evaluation of Teaching." *Educational Research Bulletin* 34: 172-86; October 1955.

[2] Domas, S. J., and Tiedeman, D. V. "Teacher Competence: An Annotated Bibliography." *Journal of Experimental Education* 19: 101-218; December 1950.

[3] Morsh J. E., and Wilder, E. W. *Identifying the Effective Instructor: A Review of Quantitative Studies, 1900-52.* Research Bulletin No. AFPTRC-TR-54-44. San Antonio, Texas: USAF Personnel and Training Center, 1954. 151 pp.

[4] Mitzel, H. E., and Gross, C. F. *A Critical Review of the Development of Pupil Growth Criteria in Studies of Teacher Effectiveness.* Research Series No. 31. New York: Office of Research and Evaluation, Division of Teacher Education, Board of Higher Education of the City of New York, 1956. 28 pp.

[5] Barr A. S., and Jones, R. E. "The Measurement and Prediction of Teaching Efficiency." *Review of Educational Research* 28: 256-64; June 1958.

[6] Castetter, D. D.; Standlee, L. S.; and Fattu, N. A. *Teacher Effectiveness: An Annotated Bibliography.* Bulletin of the Institute of Educational Research, Vol. 1, No. 1. Bloomington: Indiana University, 1954.

[7] Leiderman, G. F.; Hilton, T. L.; and Levin, H. "Studies of Teachers' Behavior: A Summary Report." *The Journal of Teacher Education* 8: 433-37; December 1957.

[8] Levin, H.; Hilton, T. L.; and Leiderman, G. F. "Studies of Teacher Behavior." *Journal of Experimental Education* 26: 81-91; September 1957.

[9] McCall, W. A. *Measurement of Teacher Merit.* Publication No. 284. Raleigh, N.C.: State Superintendent of Public Instruction, 1952. 40 pp.

[10] Mitzel, H. E. "Teacher Effectiveness." *Encyclopedia of Educational Research.* Third edition. (Edited by Chester W. Harris.) New York: Macmillan Co., 1960. pp. 1481-85.

[11] Remmers, H. H., and others. "Report of the Committee on the Criteria of Teacher Effectiveness." *Review of Educational Research* 22: 238-63; June 1952.
Remmers, H. H. and others. "Second Report of the Committee on Criteria of Teacher Effectiveness." *Journal of Educational Research* 46: 641-58; May 1953.

[12] Ryans, D. G. *Characteristics of Teachers.* Washington, D.C.: American Council on Education, 1960. 416 pp.
Ryans, D. G. "Prediction of Teacher Effectiveness." *Encyclopedia of Education Research.* Third edition. (Edited by Chester W. Harris.) New York: Macmillan Co., 1960. pp. 1486-91.

[13] Tiedeman, D. V., and Cogan, M. "New Horizons in Educational Research." *Phi Delta Kappan* 39:286-91; March 1958.

[14] Watters, W. A. "Annotated Bibliography of Publications Related to Teacher Evaluation." *Journal of Experimental Education* 22: 351-67; June 1954.

[15] Gage, N. L., editor. *Handbook of Research on Teaching.* (A project of the American Educational Research Association, NEA.) Chicago: Rand McNally, 1963. 1218 pp.

[16] Ryans, D. G. *Characteristics of Teachers.* Washington, D.C.: American Council on Education, 1960. 416 pp.

[17] Guba, E. G., and Getzels, J. W. "Personality and Teacher Effectiveness: A Problem in Theoretical Research." *The Journal of Educational Psychology* 46: 330-44; October 1955.

[18] Gage, N. L., and Cronbach, L. J. "Conceptual and Methodological Problems in

Interpersonal Perceptions." *Psychological Review* 62: 411-22; 1955.

[19] Ryans, D. G. "Prediction of Teacher Effectiveness." *Encyclopedia of Educational Research.* Third edition. (Edited by Chester W. Harris.) New York: Macmillan Co., 1960. pp. 1486-91.

[20] Medley, D. M., and Mitzel, H. E. "Measuring Classroom Behavior by Systematic Observation." *Handbook of Research on Teaching.* (Edited by N. L. Gage.) Chicago: Rand McNally, 1963. pp. 247-328.

[21] Ackerman, W. I. "Teacher Competence and Pupil Change." *Harvard Educational Review* 24: 273-89; Fall 1954.

[22] McCall, W. A. *Measurement of Teacher Merit.* Publication No. 284. Raleigh, N.C.: State Superintendent of Public Instruction, 1952. 40 pp.

[23] Medley, D. M., and Mitzel, H. E. "Pupil Growth in Reading—An Index of Effective Teaching." *The Journal of Educational Psychology* 48: 227-39; April 1957.

[24] Mitzel and Gross, *op. cit.*

[25] Morsh, J. E.; Burgess, G. G.; and Smith, P. N. "Student Achievement as a Measure of Instructor Effectiveness." *The Journal of Educational Psychology.* 47: 79-88; February 1956.

[26] Taylor, H. R. "Teacher Influence on Class Achievement: A Study of the Relationship of Estimated Teaching Ability to Pupil Achievement in Arithmetic." *Genetic Psychology Monographs.* 7: 81-175; 1930.

[27] Webb, W. B., and Bowers, N. D. *Student Performance as a Measure of Instructional Proficiency.* Research Project No. NM001077-01-06. Washington, D.C.: U.S. Naval School of Aviation Medicine, 1957. 7 pp. "The Utilization of Student Learning as a Criterion of Instructor Effectiveness." *Journal of Educational Research* 51: 17-23; September 1957.

SCHOOL is for . . .
COMMITTEE INVESTIGATION

Chapter XIII

The Teacher And School Organization

A school is organized so it can be administered and administered by a principal in order that its students might be taught. The organizational matrix in which teachers and pupils are brought together so that instruction can take place is called *organization for instruction* and it will vary from school to school. This list is by no means all inclusive but some of the widely used organizational schemes include: self-contained classrooms, nongraded plans, team teaching, open concept schools, departmentalized plans, and multi-age grouping.

Research evidences indicate that no one plan in and of itself can acclaim an educational product superior to those produced in other designs of school organization. In any schema where pupils in an experimental study did in fact academically surpass achievements of control groups, it was the *teacher variable* which made the difference. In other words, although much can be said for adopting the type of school organization that best meets the needs of pupils, the extent to which that program works and children succeed within it, depends on the expertise of the classroom teacher. The articles which follow will serve to acquaint the beginning teacher with some of the more timely forms of school organization and a cursory mention of a few of the considerations which must be entertained if the schemas are to function properly.

"The Open Classroom"

By VERL M. SHORT

Magic answers? Total chaos? Just a fad? The open classroom movement is in serious danger of being misunderstood because so few people know what it is really all about.

Everybody who has an interest in education has probably heard by now some mention of the open classroom. Modelled on the British infant schools, the open classroom has become the latest educational fad, a new kind of magic answer to meeting the individual needs of young children.

In my current role as principal of a teacher education institution and as an instructor of young children, I have had considerable exposure to open classrooms in various parts of North America and Europe over the past five years, and I believe that the movement is already in serious danger of being misunderstood because of a minimal understanding of what open classrooms are all about. Many schools undoubtedly advertise to the effect that they possess an open classroom program without really understanding the true meaning of the terminology.

The area of early childhood education itself often requires definition so that the terms of reference for the ages of the children involved become more specific. Most early childhood educators consider that children from birth to approximately eight or nine years of age are within this type of programming. However, one must fully realize that some people still remain more childlike after the age of nine, and some people never lose their childlike qualities at all. This may or may not be a positive value for the individuals concerned but if a little of the child is left in teachers, it often helps them to better understand the children they work with in the classroom.

Short, Verl M. "The Open Classroom." *Education Canada*. June 1972. 12:4-9.

Psychology has demonstrated rather clearly what the young child should have included in his program to make his education more meaningful. Educators, however, have been very slow to adjust to the various concepts presented. There is thus a tremendous credibility gap between what we know we should be doing and what our practices actually consist of in our school classrooms. This misunderstanding is quite prevalent among adults in general, and we are still seemingly quite interested in making children into little adults and preparing them for some future endeavour without really understanding children and their needs of today. We know, for example, that young children need plenty of freedom of movement to insure a responsive learning atmosphere. The educator, on the other hand, continues to devote a great deal of classroom time to taming the young child and to gluing him to his seat.

To examine this concept, let us take a look at some of the characteristics of the young child and relate them to the "sitting still" concept that many of us hold as an ultimate value in education today. We might consider the following:

The young child is blessed with high energy. He runs, jumps, pushes, pulls, and makes a lot of noise.

He has tons of imagination. Any adult trying to get a straight story from a young child will find himself revolving around in circles. The child, although he may have a complete understanding of what took place, has not always the ability to separate what happened from what should have happened. Vocabulary limitations, too, hamper the child's ability to express himself properly.

He is largely muscle oriented, and this makes him somewhat clumsy in his movements. He literally bounces off the furniture and walls as he moves about in his home and school environments.

The young child also burns with curiosity. He has the fever to touch, see, smell, hear and to actually learn all about his world, *first hand!*

In consideration of the foregoing it is not too surprising that more and more teachers of the young child are becoming concerned about trying out other varieties of programming and thus reducing the gap that exists between our understanding of child development and actual classroom practices. One of the concepts being considered is the open classroom.

What exactly is an open classroom? First of all, it is definitely not a traditional one. At times, the open classroom can be the antithesis of the traditional classroom. However, even when teachers "open" their classrooms only to a limited extent, they are tacitly agreeing with those education critics who argue that the traditional classroom is outmoded and irrelevent.

The basic difference between the traditional and the open classroom is one of structure. The traditional classroom is teacher-oriented and, even at its most benevolent, authoritarian. Traditional teachers rely heavily on prescribed curriculum and lock-step advancement according to achievement testing. The main axiom of their educational philosophy is that children must learn a given body of knowledge and that they, the teachers, are best qualified to direct children in absorbing that knowledge, preferably in a preordained sequence. These assumptions are reinforced by the physical arrangement of the traditional classroom. Usually desks are placed in rows, with students facing a teacher who instructs the entire class as a group and decides which children may talk at any given time

Some people insist that open classrooms, in contrast, have no structure and are utterly chaotic. They can, in fact, get pretty messy at times, with too much noise and not enough learning. But these conditions are also true of some traditional classrooms. Open classrooms do indeed have structure, although it is dramatically different from the structure of the traditional classroom.

Having observed open-classroom programs in several places, including California, Florida, England, Germany and Nova Scotia, I find very few outstanding differences among open classrooms in widely separated parts of the world. Most of the programs I have observed have large worktables instead of desks, and cubbyholes for the children's belongings. There is no front of the room in the traditional sense. Upon entering an open classroom, one often has to look around for awhile to find the teacher who may be sitting on the floor with a small group of students, playing a game or conducting a mini-lesson.

Invariably the room is divided into separate areas, often called interest centres. These represent such aspects of the curriculum as math-science or language arts. In the best open classrooms that I have viewed, each of these areas is filled with thought-provoking learning materials. For example, a language arts corner might contain word-games and books for a variety of reading levels. Other interest centres might include such common items as animals, plants, balancing and measuring equipment for math, Cuisenaire rods, games, blocks, water and sand tables.

In open classrooms children usually work independently or in small groups. They are free to move about the room, talking to others and exploring interest centres until they find some project with which they can become really involved. They work in corridors, libraries, and other common meeting areas. In many schools special rooms are set up to form a "complex of work opportunities". The children use these with poise and serious purpose because their learning experiences are suited to their own interests and their own levels of ability. The fluid nature of this approach to learning erases the dividing line between "teaching" and "non-teaching" and designates the teacher a guide rather than a taskmaster.

A successful open classroom teacher must be able to do the following:

Accept all children as individual and be responsive to their different needs.

Respond to a child's annoying behaviour as a symptom of need rather than one of willful meanness.

Accept patiently each child's rate of learning and permit him to go at his own rate.

Enjoy the hum of a busy classroom environment and the exclamations of discovery of success without worrying about the outworn idea that children must be silent in school.

Deal effectively with adults in order to obtain their support.

Accept parents as people concerned about their children whether these parents punctuate their sentences with profanity, live ostentatiously, or push the school for unrealistic achievement for their children.

See the world through children's eyes.

The philosophy of the open classroom is as radically different from that of the traditional one as is its physical appearance. A basic tenet of this philosophy is that children learn even such basic skills as reading in an almost seemingly random way and at their own pace. They cannot, therefore, be programmed to learn according to a predetermined sequence. One child might be reading on a second grade level in kindergarten, while another might only be ready to start reading at the end of the first grade. This type of reading gap can also occur in the traditional classroom but in that instance both children are generally labelled as gifted or retarded. Also paramount in the open classroom philosophy is the idea that the child's motivation is a crucial factor in the retention of what he learns. Teachers who follow this method tend to encourage play, spontaneity, and individual creativity much more than those who adopt a traditional approach.

The open classroom is so multi-dimensional that it is difficult to give to any one individual or country complete credit for the idea. With its stress on Dewey's concept of experimental learning and exploration, its roots can be traced to the progressive education movement of the twenties and thirties. The extensive use of various objects and games as instructional materials stems partly from the work of Montessori. Interest in a freer approach to learning in England sprang originally from the innovative work of Susan Isaacs at the Malting House School in Cambridge. Dorothy Gardner, who worked in London, was responsible for the idea being carried to other schools in England. Faith in the child's natural curiosity and growth represents a mode of educational thought reaching back at least to Rousseau and, in this century, to such advocates as Dewey, A. S. Neill, Bruner, and John Holt. Each of these authorities, although in basic agreement, has proposed varying schemes to achieve their common end. Proponents of the open classroom often cite the psychological and educational studies of Jean Piaget, whose research substantiates the idea that children learn through direct experience and in varying stages.

The open-classroom or integrated-day approach of roughly half the infant schools in England, evolved more or less independently of any major theorist, was not recognized as a significant educational phenomenon until it was documented in the studies of a British government advisory commission. Published in 1967, these studies are commonly known as the *Plowden Report.* Shortly afterwards, Joseph Featherstone began in *The New Republic,* a series of articles about the British infant schools. These virtually opened the floodgates for the movement in North America.

Although the number of open classrooms in Canada is small, extensive and rapidly growing programs are evolving in selected regions in this country. Furthermore, in almost any school one visits these days, one is likely to find at least one or more teachers who are either experimenting with the open-classroom approach or thinking about trying it. Charles E. Silberman's best-selling *Crisis in the Classroom* has given the movement a tremendous boost. The book, which resulted from a three-and-a-half year study of American schools, advocates "informal" education on all levels as a remedy for what Silberman describes as the dreariness and boredom of the majority of the public schools in North America.

Every open classroom I have seen has the identical problem. Parents begin wondering, "Is my child really learning? It seems to me that all he does is play!" And then at the slightest suggestion that a child might fall behind—even temporarily—they push the panic button. Are these fears justified? If, indeed, the open classroom has really failed to provide children with basic skills essential to their survival, it could hardly have progressed as far as it has today. In fact, teachers of open classrooms go out of their way to prove that they are teaching basic skills at least as effectively as they would by traditional methods. It is an obvious fact, however, that the more freedom a teacher allows a child, the more he is likely to do only what pleases him. Obviously, some kind of balance must exist between required and free activities. A child who is never required to do anything is going to suffer as much as a child who has no freedom at all. It must be realized, too, that some children require more structure than others. It is here that the teacher plays her most important role.

In the best open classroom, the teacher is the patient guide who is always sensitive to what each of his students is doing at any given time. He cares as much about their total development as he does about their skills. In short, he stresses affective growth at least as much as cognitive growth. Thus, it is obvious that the teacher's role in the early childhood environment requires continuous adjustment to meet the ever-changing needs of the individual child. Recent studies of child development have emphasized the importance of maturation in learning. The corollary is not to make the teacher's role passive but to underline the importance of diagnosing children's needs and potentialities. Teachers face the difficult task of assessing individual differences, appraising effort in relation to them, and avoiding the twin pitfalls of demanding too much or expecting too little. Teachers must support apathetic children until they gain a momentum of their own. They must challenge and inspire children who are too readily satisfied and, on occasion, force independence on those children who wait to be prompted. They must sometimes recognize a child as being more gifted than they are themselves and be perceptive enough to provide through books or by invoking the help of another teacher the stimulus which they cannot themselves furnish.

If, today, the emphasis is on children learning rather than on ourselves as teachers, the demands made on teachers appear extremely high. The school curriculum must touch on the scientific and mathematical knowledge on which the modern world depends and in which children are particularly interested. The teacher who used to give set lessons could manage on a little knowledge, and use it over and over again. Far more knowledge, both about subject matter and about how children learn, is called for in teachers who have continually to exercise judgment, to "think on their feet," to keep in mind long term and short term objectives. They have to select an environment which will encourage curiosity, focus attention on enquiries which will lead to useful discovery, collaborate with children and *lead from behind.*

Teachers cannot escape the knowledge that children will catch values and attitudes far more from what teachers do than from what they say. Unless teachers are courteous, they cannot expect courtesy from children. When teachers are eager to learn and turn readily to observation and to books, their children are likely to do the same. There is little hope that children will come to an appreciation of order and beauty either in nature or in what is man-made, unless these qualities are enjoyed by their teachers and exemplified in our schools.

The era of the self-contained class sitting quietly in rows while the teacher offers group instruction is ever so slowly coming to an end.

Individualization of instruction through a variety of means has become the major innovation in education in the last decade, and the open classroom is only one manifestation of this trend. The 70's, we can be certain, will see many others make their appearance.

SCHOOL is for . . .
GAMES AND THINGS

Is Specialization the Answer?
The Departmental Classroom
Revisited

R. RUEL MORRISON, JR.

The impact of curriculum revision on the elementary school in recent years has generated renewed interest in classroom organization. Increased pressure on teachers to be adept in teaching the rapidly expanding areas of knowledge has once again focused attention on the relative merits of the self-contained classroom and the departmental program. The issue can be stated simply: Is one teacher teaching all subjects more effective than several teachers teaching separate subjects?

Statistical studies of the effectiveness of departmentalization and the self-contained classroom often report findings that are contradictory and inconclusive. Investigations first by Gerberich and Prall, and later by Gibb and Matala, indicated some advantage for departmentalization, particularly in arithmetic and science (1, 2). Studies by Rouse, Spivak, and Woods, however, pointed to a somewhat generalized superiority for the self-contained plan (3, 4, 5). Studies by Jackson, Hosley, and Coffin found no significant differences favoring either group (6, 7, 8).

The purpose of the study reported here was to compare, over a two-year period, 1963-65, the achievement in arithmetic computation and arithmetic reasoning, of sixth- and seventh-grade students in departmentalized schools with the achievement of students in comparable self-contained classrooms. All students attended white elementary schools in Atlanta, Georgia (9). This part of the study will be called the "two-year study." Since scores from tests administered to sixth-grade classes in departmental and self-contained classroom schools during the 1964-65

Morrison, R. Ruel, Jr. "Is Specialization the Answer? The Departmental Classroom Revisited." *The Elementary School Journal.* January 1968. 68:206-212. Reprinted by permission of the author and The University of Chicago Press, © copyright 1968.

school year were available, these data were analyzed as a part of the total test design. This part of the study will be called the "one-year study."

The investigation also sought to answer the following question: Is there a relationship between socioeconomic class and achievement in either of the two types of classroom organization? Do upper-, middle-, or lower-middle-class students perform better under one type of classroom organization than under the other?

The subjects of the study were 1,346 sixth- and seventh-graders. They were divided into two experimental groups and two control groups. Experimental Group 1 (two-year study) consisted of 336 students and Experimental Group 2 (one-year study) consisted of 376 students from seven elementary schools where arithmetic, language arts, and social studies were taught by special teachers. The experimental groups spent fifty-minute periods with these teachers each morning and then returned to their homerooms for the remainder of the day. Control Group 1 (two-year study) consisted of 269 students and Control Group 2 (one-year study) consisted of 365 students from seven elementary schools that had self-contained classrooms. While weekly time allotments for each subject area are suggested in Atlanta curriculum guides, no daily time sequences for subjects were required for the control group.

All schools involved in the study chose their patterns of organization. Patterns were not imposed on the schools. Six of the seven schools in the experimental group had been departmentalized for a number of years before the investigation. This feature of the study was considered important in reducing the Hawthorne effect and in ruling out the possibility of teacher antagonism toward a particular type of organization.

Arithmetic instruction in the schools in the experimental and the control groups, as in all schools in the Atlanta system, was under the supervision of the co-ordinator of mathematics. The Georgia Mathematics Curriculum Guide, developed by a committee of teachers and consultants at the state level, provided the general guidelines for concepts and skills introduced in each grade. The suggested topics in the guide are similar to those found in other systems. For example, the sixth-grade program includes the extension of work with large and small fractions, the use of ratio in per cent, the extension of ideas of measurement, and selected concepts of geometry. The seventh-grade program includes the introduction of negative numbers, the use of the metric system, work with equations, and the construction and interpretation of graphs. In both grades stress is placed on discovery, seeing relationships, and the making and the testing of generalizations from specified data.

A committee of Atlanta teachers, working with the co-ordinator of mathematics, periodically selects three or four standard textbooks deemed most appropriate to achieve the objectives stated in the Georgia curriculum guide. School faculties then choose a single series from the list to be used at each grade level. During this study, no special arithmetic programs or projects were under way in the schools in the experimental or the control groups.

Experimental and control schools were matched on the basis of certain demographic and academic characteristics. A descriptive study that the Community Council of the Atlanta Area made of recent census tract data was used to equate groups with regard to educational level of parents, family income, occupation of parents, home ownership, housing soundness, and overcrowding (10). This information also provided the basis for subdividing the schools into upper, middle, and lower-middle socioeconomic levels for part of the statistical analysis. The Kuhlmann-Anderson Intelligence Tests, Sixth Edition, were administered to students in the experimental and the control groups to determine equivalence in ability. Tables 1 and 2 indicate that, with one exception, no statistically significant difference existed between experimental and

TABLE 1. *Means and Mean Differences for Kuhlmann-Anderson Intelligence Tests for Experimental and Control Groups in Upper, Middle, and Lower-Middle Socioeconomic Classes—Grade 6, October, 1963, Two-Year Study.*

Category	Experimental Group	Control Group	Difference	Standard Error of Difference	
All Classes	106.90	107.60	− .70	.92	.76
Upper	•114.19	113.58	+ .61	1.29	.31
Middle	104.15	104.95	− .80	1.29	.62
Lower-middle	98.90	101.22	−2.32	2.18	1.06

TABLE 2. *Means and Mean Differences for Kuhlmann-Anderson Intelligence Tests for Experimental and Control Groups in Upper, Middle, and Lower-Middle Socioeconomic Classes—Grade 6, October, 1964, One-Year Study*

Category	Experimental Group	Control Group	Difference	Standard Error of Difference	
All classes	107.45	108.05	− .60	.98	6.1
Upper	114.70	112.80	+ 1.90	1.33	1.43
Middle	106.10	106.98	− .88	1.34	.66
Lower-middle	94.85	101.58	−6.73	2.73	2.66*

*Significant at the .01 level.

control schools when considered as total groups or when subdivided by socioeconomic levels. The one exception occurred at the lower-middle socioeconomic level in the one-year study. This category was deleted from the study.

All sixty-two teachers in the combined experimental and control groups had professional elementary-school certificates and degrees from four-year colleges. Teachers in the experimental group averaged six years of experience and teachers in the control schools, four and a half years. About half of the teachers in both groups were in their first three years in teaching.

The study used the pre-test-post-test design and adhered to the normal testing schedule and procedures of the Atlanta public school system. The sixth-graders of Experimental and Control Groups 1 (two-year study, 1963-65) were administered Form A, Intermediate Battery of the Metropolitan Achievement Tests in October, 1963. Although the study was concerned chiefly with gain over a two-year period, an alternate form of the Metropolitan Achievement Tests was administered to these same groups in October, 1964, to determine how much gain took place during each of the years. The sixth-graders of Experimental and Control Groups 2 (one-year study, 1964-65) were administered Form A, Intermediate Battery of the Metropolitan Achievement Tests in October, 1964.

The post-test for both studies was given in May, 1965. At this time experimental and control groups were administered alternate forms of appropriate batteries of the Metropolitan Achievement Tests.

To evaluate the results, analyses of covariance were computed for

TABLE 3. *Adjusted Means for Arithmetic Computation for Two-Year Study (Grades 6 and 7)*

Category	Two-Year Study (1963-65) Experimental Group	Control Group	First Year (1963-64) Experimental Group	Control Group	Second Year (1964-65) Experimental Group	Control Group
All Classes						
Number of pupils	333	263	333	263	333	263
Mean	8.56	9.07*	7.33	7.71*	8.77	8.91
Upper						
Number of pupils	139	134	139	134	139	134
Mean	9.37	9.60	7.64	7.91†	9.45	9.47
Middle						
Number of pupils	149	106	149	106	149	106
Mean	7.90	8.89*	7.09	7.66*	8.20	8.64†
Lower-middle						
Number of pupils	45	23	45	23	45	23
Mean	7.97	7.40	6.95	7.09	8.06†	7.34

*Significant at the .01 level.
†Significant at the .05 level.

the test scores of experimental and control groups. Adjusted means were obtained for the three subgroups with respect to socioeconomic class, and for all sub-groups combined.

Table 3 reports the findings in arithmetic computation for the students in the experimental (departmental) and control (self-contained) groups who participated in the two-year study. Results for the first and second years are shown separately so that the amount of gain for each of the years can be determined. It will be noted that there is a difference between the post-test adjusted means for the second year of the two-year study and the post-test adjusted means for the two-year study taken as a whole. This difference results from the difference in covariates used in the analyses. Covariates for the second-year comparisons were the pre-test scores obtained in the fall of 1964, while the covariates for the two-year study as a whole were the pre-test scores obtained in the fall of 1963.

The control group obtained higher adjusted means than the experimental group in three out of four comparisons. Two of these comparisons, for the middle class and for all socioeconomic classes, were significant at the .01 level. Only in the lower middle socioeconomic class did the experimental group obtain a higher adjusted mean, and the difference was not significant.

The gains of the control group were made primarily during the first year of the two-year study. By the end of the second year, only the control group in the middle socioeconomic class continued to significantly outgain the experimental group. One significant difference favoring the experimental group appeared in the lower-middle socioeconomic class. The departmental students were clearly reducing the difference between the groups.

TABLE 4. *Adjusted Means for Arithmetic Computation for One-Year Study (Grade 6)*

Category	One-Year Study Experimental Group	(1964-65) Control Group
All classes		
Number of pupils	379	367
Mean	7.48	7.44
Upper		
Number of pupils	152	139
Mean	8.20*	7.70
Middle		
Number of pupils	197	176
Mean	7.18	7.41

Significant at the .01 level.

As Table 4 shows, the one-year study did not follow the pattern set by the two-year study. The experimental group received higher adjusted means in two of three comparisons. For one of these, the difference was significant at the .01 level. Only in the middle socioeconomic class did the control group outgain the experimental group, and this difference was not significant.

One fact, then, seems clear in regard to arithmetic computation. The self-contained group from the middle socioeconomic class consistently performed better than either group from any other socioeconomic class. Not only did the self-contained group achieve higher adjusted means in both the two- and the one-year studies, but this was the only group to achieve significantly higher adjusted means in both the first and the second years of the two-year study.

Tables 5 and 6 present more substantial evidence favoring the self-contained classroom in arithmetic reasoning than was found in arithmetic computation. Four out of seven comparisons in the combined two- and one-year studies favored the control group, with three of these being significant. Two differences favored the experimental group, but only one was significant. As in arithmetic computation, the departmentalized

TABLE 5. *Adjusted Means for Arithmetic Reasoning for Two-Year Study (Grades 6 and 7)*

Category	Two-Year Study (1963-65) Experimental Group	Control Group	First Year (1963-64) Experimental Group	Control Group	Second Year (1964-65) Experimental Group	Control Group
All classes						
Number of pupils	333	263	333	263	333	263
Mean	8.58	9.08*	7.95	8.20*	8.64	8.92*
Upper						
Number of pupils	139	134	139	134	139	134
Mean	9.22	9.55†	8.68	8.69	9.30	9.61†
Middle						
Number of pupils	149	106	149	106	149	106
Mean	8.03	8.76*	7.47	7.98*	8.25	8.60†
Lower-middle						
Number of pupils	45	23	45	23	45	23
Mean	8.03	7.81	7.19	7.33	8.03	7.81

*Significant at the .01 level.
†Significant at the .05 level.

students performed better in the one-year study than in the two-year study, the greatest gain being by those from the upper socioeconomic class. But contrary to results in arithmetic computation, the departmentalized students did not reduce the difference from their control counterparts during the second year of the two-year study; the self-contained group obtained two significantly higher adjusted means the first year and three significantly higher adjusted means the second year.

Again, the students in the self-contained classrooms from the middle socioeconomic class consistently performed better than either group from any of the other socioeconomic classes. In all four comparisons for the middle socioeconomic class in both the two-year study and the one-year study, the students in the self-contained classrooms achieved higher adjusted means. Two of these were significant at the .01 level and one at the .05 level.

While a majority of the significant differences obtained in this study favored the self-contained classroom, the inconsistency of the data makes it appear unwise to ascribe an over-all superiority to either type of organizational arrangement.

The most decisive evidence obtained was that middle-class children learn arithmetic computation and arithmetic reasoning more effectively in a self-contained classroom than with special teachers. This finding was borne out in both the first year and the second year of the two-year study, and in the one-year study.

Evidence from the two-year study indicated that upper-class children learn arithmetic reasoning better in self-contained classrooms, but this finding was contradicted by the one-year study. Less evidence supported the self-contained classroom as the most effective method for teaching upper-class children arithmetic computation.

TABLE 6. *Adjusted Means for Arithmetic Reasoning for One-Year Study (Grade 6)*

Category	One-Year Study Experimental Group	(1964-65) Control Group
All classes		
Number of pupils	379	367
Mean	7.61	7.52
Upper		
Number of pupils	152	139
Mean	8.61*	7.97
Middle		
Number of pupils	197	176
Mean	7.19	7.47

*Significant at the .01 level.

While there was no significant differences favoring either the departmental or the self-contained groups in arithmetic computation or reasoning in the lower-middle-class children, the majority of the non-significant differences favored the departmental program.

The following implications seem to be justified:

In the middle-class schools, the self-contained classroom is to be preferred to departmentalization in teaching arithmetic computation and arithmetic reasoning.

In upper-class schools, results are inconclusive. There is more evidence to support the self-contained plan in teaching reasoning than in teaching computation, possibly because the teacher in the self-contained classroom has more time to devote to problem-solving. Schools that have departmental programs should consider increasing the block of time allotted to arithmetic to permit more opportunity for teaching reasoning skills.

In lower-middle class schools, the non-significant differences favored the experimental (departmental) group. However, because a comparatively small number of children were involved in this socioeconomic category of the study, generalization is hazardous. Prudent teachers should await further evidence before considering change in either direction.

1. J. R. GERBERICH and C. E. PRALL. "Departmental Organization versus Traditional Organization," *Elementary school Journal, 31* (May, 1931), 761-77.

2. E. G. GIBB and D. C. MATALA. "A Study of the Use of Special Teachers of Science and Mathematics in Grades 5 and 6," *School Science and Mathematics, 112* (November, 1962), 565-85.

3. MARGARET ROUSE. "A Comparison of Curriculum Practices in Departmental and Nondepartmental Schools." *Elementary School Journal, 47* (September, 1946), 34-42.

4. M. L. SPIVAK. "Effectiveness of Departmental and Self-contained Seventh- and Eighth-Grade Classrooms," *School Review, 114* (December, 1956), 391-96.

5. ROY C. WOODS. "Relative Merits of Departmental and Non-departmental Elementary Schools," *Peabody Journal of Education, 37* (November, 1959), 161-69.

6. JOSEPH JACKSON. "The Effect of Classroom Organization and Guidance Practices upon the Personality Adjustment and Academic Growth of Students," *Journal of Genetic Psychology, 83* (May, 1953), 159-70.

7. CHARLES T. HOSLEY. "Learning Outcomes of Sixth-Grade Pupils under Alternate Grade Organization Patterns." Unpublished doctoral dissertation. Stanford, California: Stanford University, 1954.

8. G. C. COFFIN. "The Effect of Departmental Teaching on Academic Achievement of Children in Grades 4, 5, and 6." Unpublished doctoral dissertation. Storrs, Connecticut: University of Connecticut, 1964.

9. Desegregation of high schools began in 1961, but did not extend to elementary schools until 1965.

10. Community Council of the Atlanta Area, Incorporated. *Atlanta's People: A Study of Selected Demographic Characteristics of the Population in the Atlanta Metropolitan Area, by Census Tracts, 1960.* Atlanta, Georgia: Community Council of the Atlanta Area, 1963.

Individualization of Instruction vs. Nongrading

WILLIAM P. McLOUGHLIN

A review of the basics of viable individualized instructional programs

Articles on individual differences and individualization of instruction are frequently written as if these were new educational problems. Of course they are not. Nearly every prominent educator from Plato to the present has commented on the implications of human variability for instruction.

We are prone to forget that American schools began as *ungraded* schools. Children of different ages met in one room with one teacher and progressed at their own rate through the few instructional materials available. I do not mourn the passing of the one-room schoolhouse nor opt for its return. I merely wish to point out that even in the one-room school the instructional implications of individual·differences were recognized.

As enrollments grew and the inability of the one-room school to deal effectively with individual differences became increasingly apparent, the graded school seemed a more effective way of dealing with these problems. By 1871 virtually every school in America, even the one-room rural school, was a graded school. But by the end of the nineteenth century efforts were already under way to "break the lockstep approach to education" found in the graded school. The emotional and psychological carnage left in the wake of relentless conformity to procedures developed by the graded school to reduce learner variability screamed out for more viable and humane alternatives. In 1888, for example, Preston Search was developing procedures for the individualization of instruction in the schools of Pueblo, Colorado, and by 1911 Frederick L. Burke and his associates at the San Francisco State College Training

McLoughlin, William P. "Individualization of Instruction vs. Nongrading." *Phi Delta Kappan.* February 1972. 53:378-381.

School were individualizing instruction in all curriculum areas requiring the least amount of group contact. This was the precursor of a number of "laboratory approaches to education" like the Winnetka Plan.

After the floodgates for "plans" to individualizing instruction were opened, American education soon became inundated with such propositions. The St. Louis Plan, the Dalton Plan, the Batavia Plan, the Elizabeth Plan—and plans far too numerous to list—became *the* educational innovations of the late nineteenth and early twentieth centuries. More than a decade ago, Harold Shane identified 35 such attempts at individualizing instruction.[1]

All these efforts, and many which followed, had two things in common. First, they were not thoroughgoing rejections of the basic approach of the graded school for individualizing instruction through group teaching of children assumed to be similar. At best they were well-intentioned but faulty attempts at vulcanizing the holes in such an approach for coping with individual differences. Second, each of these plans sought new organizational devices for adjusting the child to the instructional offerings of the school but never looked for ways of adjusting the instructional offering of the school to the child.

The Nongraded School

Perhaps the most viable alternative to the graded school has been the non-graded school. Unlike the other educational propositions purporting to recognize individual differences and individualize instruction accordingly, the nongraded school does not seek to bolster the sagging graded school. Rather, it begins by suggesting that children's progress through school should be continuous and devoid of artificially induced skips or lags.

Though this approach was first tried in Bronxville, New York, in 1925,[2] it did not receive critical acclaim until the late 1950's. While well-intended, the message of the nongraded school is at best vague and its translation into practice leaves much to be desired. Almost without exception, converts to the non-graded school rely on one or more of the organizational schemes mentioned by Shane. Also, and again virtually without exception, *no substantial changes in instructional procedures accompany comtemporary plans to non-grade the graded school.* Reliance is placed on *group instruction* as the method of ministering to individual differences. Viewed from this vantage point, most efforts made to nongrade the elementary school are little more than tired reruns of inefficient and ineffective administrative gambits at grouping away the influence of individual differences on instruction.

A casual analysis of the characteristics of most efforts at nongrading reveals a hierarchy, not a quality but of organizational complexity, in the schemes developed to individualize instruction:

> 1. Without altering so much as a grade label, some schools simply announce they are henceforth nongraded. Teachers are instructed to take children where they find them and bring them as far as they can go during the year. Visitors to these nongraded programs frequently observe no differences from the typical graded school. Class organization, teacher and pupil assignments, and, lamentably, instructional practices are unchanged. This approach, I suppose, simply verifies the adage that a graded school by any other name surely smells.

There is something inherently reprehensible in such an approach to educational change. Essentially, it maintains that teachers all along have the ability to individualize instruction under the present educational arrangement but simply withhold this type of instruction until they receive administrative approval. I do not believe this to be the case, any more than I believe programs founded on this approach to the individualization of instruction are effective.

> 2. The next procedure used for non-grading a school and individualizing instruction is only modestly more complex. The basic design of the graded school is retained—one teacher for one self-contained class for one year—except that children of similar achievement and/or ability are grouped for instruction. Utilizers of this procedure are vehement in their denials that their nongraded plan is homogeneous grouping revisited. They justify such an arrangement of children by observing that it greatly reduces the range of differences within the class, eases the teacher's job, and makes individualization of instruction not only feasible but attainable.

It may be graceless to observe that the major purpose of nongrading and other respectable efforts to individualize instruction are not to ease the job of instruction for the teacher but to facilitate learning for the child. They are not designed to mask individual differences among children by bringing children of assumed likenesses together for instruction but to create an instructional setting which will magnify each individual's uniqueness bigger than life, so that something may be done to capitalize on those differences. Additionally, these efforts, which are at best thinly disguised homogeneous grouping schemes, have been exquisitely distinguished in the past by their failure to influence either student achievement or adjustment. Even more discouraging, however, is the fact that those espousing this brand of nongrading seem marvelously unaware that what they have done is introduce into their schools in the name of nongrading an organizational scheme developed to preserve the graded school from complete collapse.

3. Large schools frequently use "cross-class grouping" to produce nongrading and individualize instruction. Essentially, the grade structure is preserved and children "on the same level" are regrouped for instruction in reading and sometimes in arithmetic on the basis of their past achievement in these subjects. These procedures are obviously more concerned with *group* learning needs than with *individual* learning needs; they are simply another effort to individualize instruction within the framework of group instruction.

4. Smaller schools use an adaptation of cross-class grouping to nongrade their schools and individualize instruction. Typically, the primary grades are viewed as a single instructional unit. During the day children from these classes are regrouped for instruction in reading and sometimes in arithmetic. Again, the single requirement for inclusion in any group is similar achievement in reading and/or arithmetic. It goes without saying that a mere willingness to transgress established grade lines to form classes for instruction in reading is a poor guarantee that instruction in these classes will be individualized.

Even if this were an effective way of organizing children for individualized instruction, few schools would be willing to undertake the massive reassignments of children such a plan dictates. If in grade five, for example, a class of 34 pupils is to be formed so the range of reading achievement falls between 5.1 and 5.4, the class would probably contain: eight second-graders, eight third-graders, seven fourth-graders, nine fifth-graders, and two sixth-graders. Furthermore, it is educational folly to pretend such rearrangements of children accomplish anything. About the only way a homogeneously grouped class can be kept homogeneous is to teach them nothing, for the differences in learning rates alone assure us that children will differ greatly after instruction is begun.

5. Lastly, interage grouping—assigning children of different chronological ages to one teacher in a self-contained classroom for more than one year of instruction—is also found in nongraded schools. This, of course, is the condition that prompted the conversion of the pre- 1850 ungraded schools into graded schools. Remember, while this organization of children may teach teachers a considerable amount about child growth and development, it in no way provides them with additional instructional resources for coping with these differences. At best, such procedures do little more than complicate the instructional problems faced by most teachers.

The affinity for the graded structure of those who would nongrade is reminiscent of the problem faced by the Australian bushman who received a new boomerang—he couldn't throw the old one away. The nongraded school, while an agreeable enough education idea, is so vague and chameleonic that it makes a poor blueprint for building a thoroughly new instructional program. The answers to the instructional problems produced by individual variabilities are not to be found in unique groupings of students but in unique instructional practices. This article is intended to suggest the banning of innovations that simply rediscover past educational failures. Too many innovators are little more than educational archeologists who delight in resurrecting moldy plans for individualizing instruction, Without a doubt, education would be better off if these schemes had been left to mold in peace.

Planning for Individual Instruction

Hastily conceived programs for individualized instruction will probably rediscover many of the ineffectual educational practices detailed above. Viable individualized instructional programs emanate from carefully planned strategies for educating each individual to the fullness of his potential. Basic to such planning are these goals:

1. The individual instructional programs must be developed to deal with individual differences, not group similarities.
2. The individual instruction program is at least a schoolwide program, and hopefully a districtwide program. Most homegrown educational innovations are underplanned and oversold and eventually die from an acute attack of administrative jitters. Apparently administrators fear direct confrontations with incompetent instruction and justify their "hands off" approach to educational improvement by pointing to anticipated adverse teacher reactions. More often than not they simply meet the instructional problems produced by individual learner differences by pledging support to any teacher willing to try to individualize instruction in his classroom. Effective programs of individualization of instruction must be considerably more than a *tour de force* for an occasional willing and competent teacher, a random, uncontrollable occurrence available to a limited number of children on an unpredictable schedule in an indeterminable number of classes.
3. A basic recasting of the role of the teacher in the instructional process is necessary for development of effective and durable programs for individualized instruction. In such a program increasing responsibility and accountability for learning must be placed on the instructional materials used. It is clearly impossible for a teacher, even the most dedicated teacher, to satisfy all the individual learning requirements of all of the children in all learning areas of the school curriculum. We must demand much more teaching effectiveness from the instructional materials in use and require teachers to become increasingly proficient in recognizing and supporting the learner's expanding capacity to become an independent learner.
4. *Systematic* development of individualized instructional programs must relate the purposes of instruction, the instructional procedures developed for realizing these purposes, and the evaluation procedures employed to assess the adequacy of instruction and the scope of learning.

Implicit in this systematic approach is the interchangeability of instructional materials, a requirement that should discourage schools from undertaking the production of these materials. The question, "Why can't teachers produce these materials?," assumes that teachers have both the expertise and the desire to do this job. But such undertakings require the use of rather sophisticated constructs about teaching and learning, constructs which the typical teacher has not developed.

More mundane reasons for discouraging teacher production of these instructional materials include cost (teachers often demand and receive compensation for the work done to produce instructional materials) and the inability to integrate such materials into the school's instructional program. Administrators know that teachers, even beginning teachers, are hesitant to use instructional materials developed by other teachers. The discouraging legacy of local efforts to develop materials for an individualized instructional program is an enormous, disorganized, underutilized collection of ditto masters that are considerably more trouble to locate and run off than they are worth.

5. A carefully developed and continuous in-service program for introducing teachers to individualization of instruction must be an integral part of the school program. Too often schools undertake pervasive educational changes without developing procedures for the preservation and refinement of these innovations. The schools cannot assume that the staff which plans the innovation will implement and operate it. If the typical school has a 70-80% staff turnover in a 10-year period, it means that teachers with little of the understanding of the programs as developed by their creators are expected to operate these programs. Lack of effective and efficient indoctrinating procedures is one of the most serious shortcomings of most innovative efforts.
6. Detailed evaluation procedures should be formulated concurrently with program development. Too often the intense desire to put an educational idea into practice is so overpowering that little or no attention is given to developing procedures for evaluating the efficacy of the innovation introduced. Programs worthy of introduction into schools should also be worthy of the best possible evaluation available, not an unsystematic, uninterpretable collection of teacher and administrator opinions about the presumed merits of the program. This requires ongoing and pervasive evaluation of all aspects of the innovation.

Some Specific Procedures

I hope that what I have been giving the reader is a tall order and not simply a tall story. Here is a list of specific references to procedures helpful in filling this order:

Behavioral Objectives—Virtually every serious effort at individualization of instruction uses behavioral objectives. The works of Mager[3] or Vargas[4] or the Vimcet[5] materials developed for group instruction are useful guides for the purposes and preparation of behavioral objectives. Other sources include the 4,000 or so behavioral objectives developed for PLAN (Planned Learning in Accordance to Need); they are available from the Westinghouse Learning Corporation for under $60. The Instructional Objectives Exchange of UCLA's Center for the Study of Evaluation sells numerous lists of behavioral objectives in a wide range of instructional areas at minimal cost.

Commercially Prepared Programs—Schools seriously considering individualizing instruction should look carefully at commercially prepared programs. I.P.I. (Individually Prescribed Instruction), from the University of Pittsburgh and Research for Better Schools in Philadelphia, and PLAN, the Westinghouse Program, are perhaps the two most ambitious works in this area. Programs of this type are not giveaways. PLAN, for example, costs a school district approximately $100 a year per child to operate after initial fees have been paid. A complete breakdown of the costs looks like this:

	Annual Charges For a School of 400 Pupils
Teaching Learning Units ($6/child/month)	$24,000
Computer Control ($2.80/child/month)	11,200
Computer Line and Terminal Charges ($2/child/month)	8,000
Total	$43,200
Initial Sign-up Charges (one time only)	$ 5,000
Supervisor Training Chart (one-time-only charge)	500
Teacher Training Chart ($300/week/teacher)	4,800
Total	$10,300
Support Material Charge (varies with amount of equipment and utilization patterns of the school)	$53,500

Some educators seeing these program costs for the first time think, "My board will never buy it." Possibly we are overquick to diminish the efforts made to support education and even use our fiscal woes as reasons for doing nothing. We point with almost masochistic pleasure to the fact that in a recent year the world only spent $100 per child on education but $7,800 per soldier. While allocating $110 billion of its resources to education, it invested a whopping $159 billion in armament.[6] We are quick to conclude from these and similar data that schools are not getting their fair share of the tax dollar.

This is far from the whole story of educational support. In the past two decades education spending in the U.S. increased fivefold[7] while personal consumption merely doubled.[8] In the same period school enrollments increased 88%, but school expenditures, in *constant dollars*, increased 350%.[9] While employment in private industry increased 38%, employment in public education increased 203%.[10] The public has not been unwilling to support education.

Taxpayers may be justified in digging in their heels to resist school tax increases, for there is virtually no relation between the money spent on education—per-pupil expenditures, community tax rates, teacher salaries, pupil-teacher ratios, number of administrators per 100 pupils—and educational attainment.[11] Even the feeble relation between grade six reading achievement and educational expenditures virtually vaporizes by the tenth grade. About all that increases in staff size and salaries seem to do is increase the size of the educational tax bill.

I have no desire to dazzle the reader with fancy statistical footwork. I merely wish to replace the conjecture and wishful thinking that shroud discussions of the efficacy of increased educational spending on education attainments with hard data on this point. Traditionally, the public has been led to believe that money was the cure-all for instructional ills and that the yellow brick road to educational excellence is paved with smaller classes and larger and better paid staffs. Taxpayers once endorsed this solution but are now disappointed with its attainments. Most of them, too, do not necessarily demand more bang for the buck; they would gladly settle for an occasional pop.

Suggesting the merits of the "big package" of commercially developed instructional materials as the starting point for a local effort to individualize instruction is often characterized and rejected as the impossible educational dream. Solutions short of this are solicited. Inherent in this quest is tacit recognition of the merits of the big-package approach but a willingness to make do with second-best solutions. I do not countenance reckless educational spending, but I suggest that those coveting educational innovation be innovative themselves. I feel the time may have come when we must stop asking boards of education what they can do for our instructional program and start asking ourselves what alternatives to increased spending we can develop for these programs.

Innovation, like charity, begins at home. In the days of tight money, unique solutions should be developed for obtaining the innovations desired and creative use of resources placed at our disposal is imperative. I know one administrator, for example, who filled one first-grade teacher opening with two half-time teachers. Besides providing valuable opportunities for using unique staffing patterns, this departure from tradition saved money which otherwise would have gone to auxiliary compensation, retirement funds, medical insurance, etc. The money saved was used to purchase additional instructional supplies and services. Boards of education must be presented with alternatives to the funding needs of innovative schools. They simply cannot be asked regularly and relentlessly to dig deeper and deeper into the taxpayer's pocket for more dollars for these programs.

Taxonomies of Education—Essentially, most available solutions to the instructional problems resulting from individual differences focus on a single aspect of learner differences—differences in learning rates. Qualitative differences are known to exist among learners, too. Space does not permit a critique of available references, but I would like to draw attention to the works by Bloom and Krathwohl.[1][2] Together with other relevant studies, these taxonomies could provide a framework for assessing the scope of the learnings provided by the school curriculum. They will not provide cures for ills plaguing a school but may help explain what is killing the school's individualized instructional program.

Systems for Evaluation—Because evaluation is related to the goals and procedures used to achieve specified outcomes, it is not possible to provide a system for evaluation prior to program development. However, CAM (Comprehensive Achievement Monitoring) has an overall assessment design which may provide schools interested in individualizing instruction with a framework for developing a sound procedure for program assessment.

Elixir for the Individual

The discussion of individual differences and individualization of instruction has come full circle. While the instructional difficulties produced by individual learner differences are clearly not new educational problems, viable solutions to these problems are still urgently needed. What has been learned about individual differences from earlier efforts to deal effectively with the instructional problems they produce fills many volumes. The yet unanswered questions about individual differences, however, would fill many more. If indeed the past is truly prologue, it must be scrutinized, for educators can ill afford to accept its errors as their truths. The time for stockpiling outmoded organizational gimmicks and empty dictums about individual differences has passed. Both the public and the profession have drunk too long and too deeply of this old wine in new bottles to mistake it as an elixir to cure the instructional problems produced by individual differences. A brave new world of procedures for working effectively with individual differences is being built; it could decline and fall for want of brave new educational leadership.

[1] Harold G. Shane, "Grouping in the Elementary School," *Phi Delta Kappan*, April, 1960, pp. 313-19.

[2] William P. McLoughlin, *The Nongraded School: A Critical Assessment.* Albany: New York State Education Dept., 1967, p. 2.

[3] Robert F. Mager, *Preparing Instructional Objectives.* Palo Alto, Calif.: Fearon Publishers, 1962.

[4] Julie S. Vargas, *Writing Worthwhile Behavioral Objectives.* University of West Virginia, no date.

[5] Vimcet Associates, *Vimcet Filmstrip-Tape Programs*, Vimcet Associates, P.O. Box 24714, Los Angeles, Calif. 90024.

[6] "The Cost of World Armaments," *The UNESCO Courier*, January, 1970, p. 13.

[7] U.S. Office of Education, *Digest of Educational Statistics*, 1970 ed., Table 25.

[8] *President's Economic Report*, January 1971, pp. 197-98.

[9] U.S. Office of Education, *op. cit.*

[10] Office of Business Economics, *The National Income and Product Accounts of the United States*, 1929-65, p. 100.

[11] California State Dept. of Education, *California State Testing Program, 1968-69: An Analysis of Reading Test Scores and Other School Factors*, Sacramento, 1970.

[12] Benjamin S. Bloom, ed., *Taxonomy of Educational Objectives, Handbook I: Cognitive Domain.* New York: David McKay, 1956, and David R. Krathwohl, ed., *Taxonomy of Educational Objectives, Handbook II: Affective Domain.* New York: David McKay, 1964.

[13] William Gorth, *Comprehensive Achievement Monitoring (CAM).* Amherst: University of Massachusetts Press, 1970.

SCHOOL is for . . .
INDIVIDUAL DEVELOPMENT

Team Teaching:

A Study Of Team Development And Interpersonal Functioning

JUNE GALLESSICH, IRA ISCOE and SHERRY PAYNE

Team teaching, a structural reorganization requiring teachers to work very closely together, is now widely practiced in elementary schools. Reports of team teaching, however, have had very little to say in regard to teamwork processes.[1,2]

A major goal of a three-year study by the Research and Development Center for Teacher Education of The University of Texas was to investigate team development, dynamics, and problems.* The subjects of this investigation were members of 24 elementary school teaching teams in six school districts. The organization of the teams studied was more collaborative than hierarchical.[3] The team leaders received no extra pay but were relieved of some teaching tasks in order to have time to coordinate team activities. Most teams were composed of teachers of only one grade level. The primary objective of the team organization was individualization of instruction.

The present report is based on clinical assessment of case studies of 24 teaching teams. The major sources of data were the records of three years of extensive observations and interviews by the six psychologists who formed the research team. The data included 40 videotapes of teams in planning sessions and informal interviews and 12 audiotaped exit interviews with teachers who resigned. Notes from structured interviews with team leaders and principals were also available. From these case studies, some critical issues in team development and interpersonal functioning were identified.

*This research was supported by U.S.O.E. Contract 6-10-108.

Team Developmental Stages

Between the first serious consideration of reorganizing for team teaching and successful, well-organized team functioning, several discernible stages of team development take place:

The period of stimulation and contemplation. First of all, a stimulus of some kind is required, such as a challenging article in a professional journal or a personal contact with a teaching team, followed by a period of open-minded and thoughtful consideration of possibilities. There must be an atmosphere that encourages collaboration and change. Potential team members need ample time and freedom to explore the potential consequences for themselves and their pupils.

Team initiation. The next stage is one in which a tentative decision is made to team, to invest energies in disturbing the status quo. Team formation is facilitated when members of the emergent team have developed a very strong interest in team possibilities and when teamwork meets some important emotional or intellectual needs. A high degree of trust in fellow team members is necessary for open, candid exchanges of ideas and feelings. A stable catalyst—a teacher or principal who provides continuing encouragement and challenge during this anxious period—can be very helpful.

The actual decision to team may come from a group of teachers, a principal, or an administrative official such as the school superintendent or director of curriculum. The *position* and *style* of the initiator, however, have important implications for the success of the planned changes. A transition period is imperative. There must be ample opportunities for conflicting opinions to be elicited and discussed. Furthermore, it is very important for the teachers, who must carry the responsibility for accomplishing the change, to have some freedom of choice as to whether to innovate or not. Transfers to traditional schools should be accepted without stigma. When the decision to team comes in the form of a directive, resistance is almost certain to occur and to inhibit team development. Attrition in this case can be very high and will continue unless care is taken in selecting and training new team members. The following examples of patterns of introduction of team teaching illustrate typical processes and problems.

Team teaching was introduced by fiat in a district whose superintendent, through discussions at a regional conference, became convinced that team organization was "the answer." He directed the principals and teachers in his system to adopt the team approach. From the beginning, confusion and covert resistance were apparent. Two years later, "team teaching" was said to be practiced in the system, very few actual changes had occurred.

Successful team teaching was introduced in another school by several teachers who had taught in adjacent rooms for a number of years. One was intrigued by a journal article describing team teaching. She discussed this approach with her colleagues, and slowly several teachers of the same grade level became interested in collaboration. They decided to begin team teaching for a part of each day. Full-fledged team teaching resulted and spread throughout the other grades with the principal's encouragement and support. There was some attrition due to the project, but most of the teachers of other grade levels voluntarily teamed. Three years after teaming was first begun, each grade level was team organized.

The bright, young, charismatic principal of another school introduced and guided his teachers in reorganizing for team teaching. This project progressed successfully during the first year. The second year, following the principal's resignation and move to another city, the new structure quickly collapsed. Obviously, the teachers had depended on the initiating principal for inspiration and guidance. Morale deteriorated rapidly with loss of his leadership, and most of the team teaching features were abandoned.

Establishing successful interpersonal relationships. The next developmental stage is a critical, tense, emotionally draining period during which the major task is to establish group cohesiveness. Norms—such as mutuality as opposed to "pecking order" relationships—are set during this period. This is the most difficult developmental stage. Many teams never establish the successful interaction needed to continue with team teaching and eventually return to modified self-contained classroom arrangements.

An example of a team stuck at this stage is the Eastwood Team, which was observed over a three-year period. Significantly, the leader, Mrs. Adams, is the only surviving original team member. The remaining four positions have been occupied by a dozen teachers. While many of these resignations were because of pregnancy or out-of-town moves, a considerable number were attributable to dissatisfaction with the team.

Eastwood has two widespread age groups: Two members are in their 20's, and the others are 40 or older. Mrs. Adams and one other older teacher form a dominant subgroup. The two young teachers form an alliance based on youth and disenchantment with the team leader. The fifth team member is not closely identified with either group. The team atmosphere is tense and anxious; conflict is continuous. The leader's struggle for control is the most obvious dynamic and is infectious. Two members react by attempting to capture some control of their own. The other two psychologically withdraw from involvement. Curricular responsibilities are ostensibly divided, with area chairmen self-selected according to interests. Little responsibility, however, is actually assumed by any of these "chairmen." The team meets frequently, almost daily, in hour-long conferences after school.

In private interviews, exiting teachers described their disappointments. They complained about lack of courtesy among team members and of the authoritarian, controlling tendencies of the leader. They were unable to establish any team commitment to standards of behavior for pupils. The inconsistent requirements of the conflicted teachers resulted in disturbing and unruly behavior. These teachers considered most planning sessions to be a waste of time. It seems predictable that Eastwood Team, under the present leadership, will not be able to develop workable teacher relationships.

Structural tasks. While intra-team relationships evolve, certain structural tasks must be accomplished. Immediate procedural decisions such as degree of collaboration, scheduling, division of curricular responsibilities, criteria for grouping pupils, and definition of the leadership role must be made. A tremendous, concerted effort is required for the team to make well-considered decisions on these issues, which have far-reaching implications. Mechanisms should be established for obtaining continuing feedback to modify policies and procedures whenever indicated by further experience.

Development of creative capacities. After working through the preceding stages, a team can focus on long-range concerns such as careful diagnosis and planning for individual and small-group instruction, curricular revision, building media banks, devising new forms of reporting to parents, and working on multi-disciplinary approaches to skill building and social development of pupils.

The Willowcreek Team is an effective, well-organized team that has experienced and solved major interpersonal and procedural problems during its four years of development. This team is now focusing on long-range curricular planning and a multidisciplinary approach to promote academic and social growth. It has been strengthened by selective processes. Two original team members had many conflicts that disrupted team functioning; one transferred to another school, and another dropped out of teaching after being asked to resign.

The average age of the team is about 40—with a range of more than 25 years. The more experienced teachers tend to sit together in meetings, slightly apart from the two younger ones. The leader and another senior teacher form a distinct, close alliance, which does not appear to affect team harmony. Although there is a detectable informal power hierarchy, leadership is shared to a large degree. Any of the five teachers could easily be visualized in the leader role. Each seems autonomous; yet they are interdependent. Interaction between members is unusually free. All members are articulate and uninhibited in team discussions. Moreover, there is an unusual equivalence of talking and listening, perhaps an important ingredient of a successful team.

One team member described this team as involved in a "creative process in which everyone contributes ideas and develops them," a process also noted by observers. Team members readily acknowledge that they "learn from each other." They point out that, although they work harder and longer than they would in self-contained classrooms, the satisfactions are worthwhile. Each member has chosen the area in which she wishes to specialize and leads the group in this curricular area. However, all members teach all subjects. The team is working toward integration of content areas, procedures for increased individualization of instruction, and special media centers.

Conflicts Within the Team

Team relations are frequently marred by conflicts between the "ingroup" and the "outgroup." These groups differ on a number of dimensions. The ingroup members, typically the original team members who remained with the new structure while their less enthusiastic colleagues dropped out, tend to be more zealously committed to the team organization, more experienced, and considerably older than outgroup members.

The ideal condition for team integration is the presence on each team of a core of mature, professionally earnest teachers who are firmly committed to the team teaching philosophy and goals and at the same time open to new ideas from others—those within the seasoned, stable nucleus as well as new team members. These two conditions—dedication to the project and continuing openness to suggestions—appear somewhat incompatible. Few teachers are both devoted to this new organization and truly receptive to critical comments, even when these comments are carefully and tactfully presented. Teachers who create a team and foster its development usually have such strong involvement that they are unable to view the team approach objectively. They tend to over-emphasize advantages and to negate flaws. Especially threatening to these ardent innovators are new team members who, even though acknowledging the advantages of the team organization, comment frankly on problems or weaknesses. A spiral of growing animosity and cleavage begins as the older members become increasingly defensive in their commitment to the team. The rift widens when the newcomers become passively or actively resistant to the whole concept of team teaching.

A principal humorously described this tendency of teachers who have worked together in evolving a team to resist suggestions for modifications. She recalled an exasperating situation in which the original members of a team looked on their new, tentative procedures as the "dogma" and refused to consider minor procedural changes. It is as though the equilibrium of a newly achieved structure is precarious and must be defended against even small changes. The "bible" has been written.[4]

At first glance, it would seem that it is the team *leader* who must be dedicated and open. But leadership is seldom vested solely in the team's formal leader. Instead, leadership is generally shared among all senior teachers. They are often observed watching each other for verbal or nonverbal cues. They seem to reinforce each other's rigidities and beliefs. Together, they present a united and controlling clique. Conflicts within this alliance are subordinate to the conflict between subgroups. Probably the subgroup conflict is to some extent the direct cause, as well as the product, of the cohesiveness within the senior group.

The tendency toward polarization or the team-patriotism axis is aggravated by other differences typically found between the major subgroups. The mean age of the ingroup tends to be considerably greater than that of the outgroup. Often a range of more than 20 years divides these groups. There are predictable differences in social activities, values, and jargon. In addition, indications of generation rivalry are sometimes observable. Some older teachers are envious of the youthful good looks and energy of the junior group. Also, teachers many years out of college may be threatened by confrontation with current professional ideas introduced by young people fresh out of training. Younger teachers often react negatively to the authority, professional poise, and security of the seasoned older teachers. They often have not outgrown adolescent rebelliousness, and this dynamic is mobilized by the controlling tendencies often found in teachers.[5] An authoritarian stance by the older teachers tends to widen the group schism by generating hostility.

The predisposition of teams to fissure on the team-loyalty dimension is due to the normal attrition processes of school faculties, as well as to the selective screening that takes place when there is a marked change in a school milieu. Many teachers in schools that are moving toward team teaching transfer out in advance of the reorganization or screen themselves out, often under pressure from teammates, in the early planning stages or as the team progresses and their incompatibility becomes increasingly evident. Therefore, team replacements are continually needed. Recruits for team teaching schools are rarely drawn from the ranks of senior teachers, who are usually well established in conventional schools. The new team members are usually inexperienced teachers, new to the school system. Actually, the age distribution found in teams is only an exaggerated reflection of the discrepancies often found in public schools. Teachers in their middle 20's often resign to have babies and remain at home until their children enter school. Consequently, many faculties tend toward a bimodal age distribution.

In some schools, administrators planning for team teaching have "stocked" teams with young, comparatively inexperienced teachers. In other instances, teams consist entirely of older teachers past 40 years of age. In these teams, the subgroups described earlier may be non-existent or scarcely perceptible. Nevertheless, special problems occur in these more homogeneous teams. The younger teams seem to be open-minded and enthusiastic but seem to require strong administrative support and guidance. Otherwise, they tend to become disorganized, and their energies are dissipated. In teams composed entirely of older teachers, traditions are, of course, more entrenched, and inertia may impede innovation.

Problems of the New Teacher on the Team

The novice teacher's response to confrontation by a strong, cohesive clique is a significant predictor of his acceptance or rejection. Two young teachers, newcomers to the same teaching team which was beginning its third year, illustrate personality differences that are related to professional acceptance.

The team to which these new teachers were assigned was functioning with moderate effectiveness. The efficient, pleasantly assertive leader is a task-oriented person who briskly moves business ahead in team meetings. However, she was observed to encourage other team members to express their ideas and reactions. She and another charter member of this team form a strong alliance and share the leadership role. Their staunch loyalty to the team project is evident in their quick defense of any criticism, especially when it comes from the new teachers. Faced with this authoritative, close-knit clique, the two new teachers responded with vastly different styles.

Mrs. Kennedy, a young and pretty teacher with two previous years in a self-contained classroom, reacted to the team with a passive, conforming manner which scarcely covered her negativism. In team interaction, the appeared anxious and progressively withdrawn and rarely exhibited any kind of positive coping. She spoke very little, but it was clear to everyone in the school that she was increasingly unhappy in team teaching. She confided to the principal that she was emotionally upset by the team environment, but she remained psychologically distant from all team members. After four months, she resigned.

Mrs. Ingram is an example of a new teacher with the professional expertise and the skill in human relations to achieve acceptance by older colleagues. She had no previous teaching experience but had received student teacher training in a team teaching school. She coped with the team situation with unusual flexibility. Enthusiastic and assertive, she was still able to yield gracefully to the older teachers when, according to observers, she perceived herself in a position that was logically tenuous or psychologically threatening. She appeared to assert herself when sure of support from members of the dominant subgroup or when sure of her own knowledge of a subject.

In an early interview with the team, older members clearly perceived Mrs. Ingram as a professional subordinate. At that time, she was subdued and participated very cautiously. Several months later, Mrs. Ingram, with obvious pleasure and competence, led the team in a planning session discussion of two important subject areas. She appeared to have the complete approval of the older team members. Several times, she clarified issues for the group's benefit. By the end of the year, she appeared to be completely integrated into the older group as a genuine colleague.

Two teachers assigned to another team, entirely different in its interpersonal climate and teaching effectiveness, further illustrate personality characteristics and interpersonal dynamics involved in the conflict between new teachers and the "old guard." The team to which these teachers were assigned was crippled by strife. Two senior members dominated team conferences. Neither of the two new team members was successful in working out a satisfying position in this team.

Mrs. Page, young and pretty, hypersensitive and shy, was highly respected by many faculty members and by all the student teachers who were assigned to the team. Undoubtedly a creative teacher with unusual sensitivity to children's needs, Mrs. Page never felt comfortable or accepted within this team situation. She spoke very little in team interviews without explicit encouragement from the interviewer. Questioning revealed that she found team teaching confusing, involving endless time spent in planning. She would have preferred to spend this time with children or "browsing through the new media." During the year, Mrs. Page became increasingly silent and withdrawn in team planning sessions and resigned after one term. She is a vivid example of the excellent teacher who works well alone and for whom team teaching—at least with this particular team—was anathema.

The other new member of this team was Mrs. Nelson, a bright and poised young teacher. She had taught previously in another team teaching school and began the year optimistically excited about team teaching. She was brimming with ideas on improving teaching through the team approach. Her suggestions, however, were not used by this team to any extent. She received outstanding approval from student teachers assigned to this team and to other teams within the school, but approval from senior teachers was withheld or slowly and begrudgingly given, in spite of Mrs. Nelson's strenuous efforts.

Midway through the year, Mrs. Nelson was observed, in a videotaped planning session, to be initially quite restrained, solemn, and attentively listening to the leader. She nodded frequently as though in agreement. After a few minutes, however, she began to participate actively insisting on expressing her ideas. Often, the older, dominant members interrupted to modify or subtly denigrate Mrs. Nelson's comments. Nonetheless, she persisted, several times out-talking these teachers, who eventually appeared to accept her ideas. But the team climate prevented professional and personal satisfaction, and Mrs. Nelson left at the end of the school year, disappointed in the functioning of this team and doubtful about the future of team teaching.

Discussion

From the instructional viewpoint,[6] there are many potential advantages in successful team action. More effective decision making and problem solving can be expected through the pooling of ideas and exploration of alternatives. Possibilities for redeploying pupils, teachers, and material resources are multiplied, so that endless grouping arrangements can be made as needed to suit instructional needs and teacher abilities and preferences. Through group strength, teachers are encouraged to greater boldness in innovative activities.[7] Change is not only more likely to occur but more likely to be of a permanent nature when it is attempted through a team rather than through separate individuals.[8]

Effective team functioning, however, is not easily accomplished. The manner in which the decision to team is made is a crucial issue. Teachers should be fully involved in the decision process and encouraged to express their ideas and feelings freely in discussions with the principal. A supportive administrative milieu is very helpful in providing material and emotional assistance.[9] A long period of planning and transition is essential.

Individual differences create widely different teacher reactions to the team approach. Many teachers who work well with children are not happy in a team organization, while others find team contact very stimulating. We know very little about the characteristics needed for good team relationships. One study[10] suggests that successful teams are composed of teachers with low needs for reassurance and approval. At any rate, careful selection of teachers for teams is needed, and teachers who are reluctant to team should be allowed to remain in a self-contained classroom.

The team's interpersonal functioning is a sensitive and critical area. While total agreement among team members is not necessary,[11] cooperative attitudes are essential. The divisiveness in some cases serves a useful function in the initiation of new teachers who, after demonstrating competency during an "apprenticeship" period, are incorporated into the ranks of the senior faculty. But rifts may seriously obstruct constructive and integrated team-work. The tendency of any working group to splinter is antithetical to the development of cohesiveness, a factor demonstrated to be closely associated with high morale and achievement[12] and effective problem solving.[13] When a serious cleavage exists on a teaching team, communication will be poor and the teachers immobilized as their energies are drained into nonproductive conflict.

Another problem area is team leadership. Teachers find it difficult to accept peer leadership. They resent the disturbance of the traditional quality-autonomy-isolation pattern.[14] Lortie questions the viability of team teaching, describing it as an attempt to combine two unstable elements, hierarchical rank and close working relationships.

If the decision is made to team teach, teachers need to be trained in group processes. Laboratory experiences such as those described by Bradford, Gibb, and Benne[15] would facilitate communication and constructive interaction. Blake[16] pointed out the need to utilize such techniques in team teaching. The *Dundee Report*[17] of a team teaching project contended that systematic training in group processes would have minimized or prevented the interpersonal difficulties of teams in that project. Our intensive case studies of 24 teams lead us to a similar conclusion.

FOOTNOTES

[1] Heathers, G. "Research on Team Teaching." In Shaplin, J. T., and Olds, H. F., Jr., editors, *Team Teaching.* New York: Harper & Row 1964. pp. 306-44.

[2] Heathers, G. "Team Teaching and the Educational Reform Movement." In Shapin, J. T., and Olds, H. F., Jr., editors, *Team Teaching.* New York: Harper & Row, 1964. pp. 345-75.

[3] Lortie, D. C. "The Teacher and Team Teaching: Suggestions for Long-Range Research." In Shaplin, J. T., and Olds, H. F., Jr., editors, *Team Teaching.* New York: Harper & Row, 1964. pp. 270-305.

[4] Bion, W. R. *Experiences in Groups.* New York: Basic Books, 1961.

[5] Minnis, D. L. "Rebellion in Teacher Education: Requiem for a Fossil in White-Tie-and-Tails." *California Journal for Instructional Improvement* 12: 181-91; October 1969.

[6] See footnote 2.

[7] *Dundee Team Teaching Project.* New York: Institute of Field Studies, Teachers College, Columbia University, 1965.

[8] Levin, K. "Group Decision and Social Change." In Swanson, G. E., and Newcomb, M. M., editors, *Readings in Social Psychology.* Henry Holt and Co., 1952. pp. 330-44.

[9] Davis, H. S. *The Effect of Team Teaching on Teachers.* Doctoral dissertation. Detroit, Mich.: Department of Education, Wayne State University, 1964.

[10] Reasoner, R. W., and Wall, H. R. "Developing Staff Interaction in Team Teaching." *National Elementary Principal* 44: 84-86; January 1965.

[11] Anderson, R. H. "The Organization and Administration of Team Teaching." In Shaplin, J. T., and Olds, H. F., Jr., editors, *Team Teaching.* New York: Harper & Row, 1964. pp. 170-215.

[12] Cartwright, D., and Zander, A. "Group Cohesiveness: Introduction." In Cartwright, D., and Zander, A., editors, *Group Dynamics.* New York: Harper & Row, 1960. pp. 69-94.

[13] Kelley, H., and Thibaut, J. "Experimental Studies of Group Problem Solving and Process." In Lindzey, G., editor, *Handbook of Social Psychology, II* Cambridge, Mass.: Addison-Wesley Publishing Co., 1954. pp. 735-85.

[14] See footnote 3.

[15] Bradford, L. P.; Gibb, J. R.; and Benne, K. D. *T-Group Theory and Laboratory Method.* New York: John Wiley & Sons, 1964.

[16] Blake, R. F. "Small Group Research and Cooperative Teaching Problems." *National Elementary Principal* 43: 31-36; February 1964.

[17] See footnote 7.

ADDITIONAL REFERENCES

GIBB, J. R. "Climate for Trust Formation." In Bradford, L. P.; Gibb, J. R.; and Benne, K. D., editors, *T-Group Theory and Laboratory Method.* New York: John Wiley & Sons, 1964. pp. 279-309.

SHAPLIN, J. T. "Toward a Theoretical Rationale for Team Teaching." In Shaplin, J. T., and Olds, H. F., Jr., editors, *Team Teaching.* New York: Harper & Row, 1964. pp. 57-98.

Teacher Aides: Their Role In The Schools

FRANCES P. FRIEDMAN

Lawyers have secretaries, doctors have nurses and technicians, college professors have graders and assistants; but teachers have only themselves, which is not enough. The need for sub-professionals exists.

This is the rationale put forth in the experiment using teacher aides conducted by the University of California, Riverside Campus.

Known also as auxiliary personnel, paraprofessionals, sub-professionals, school aides and most typically as teacher aides, their purpose, according to the NEA Educational Research Service, is to relieve the teacher of non-teaching duties.

The job of today's teacher has become almost unmanageable. Unless something is done to remedy the situation, creative, competent teachers will find themselves hopelessly bogged down in technical and clerical duties which could be performed by others.

You will recall the TV commercial, using fast action camera, picturing the harried housewife running from chore to chore all day long, when suddenly she collapses. There's a hammering in her head! But ah! Anacin to the rescue! Fade in. Relief! The charming gracious wife smilingly greets her husband after an impossible day.

Picture now if you will, in the same speedy motion, the daily duties of the average school teacher. She is attendance taker, computer, hostess, clerk, wet nurse, ticket seller, counsellor, cashier, housekeeper, decorator, policeman, surveyor, administrator—to name but a few. When does she have time to teach? Is she not wasting her true professional ability, which is her talent to teach and inspire?

The problem of how to get quality education as the numbers of students increase and the number of good teachers decreases dates back

Friedman, Frances P. "Teacher Aides: Their Role in the Schools." *Education Canada.* June 1969. 9:2-9.

to World War II. Today, staff projection figures for the future indicate that, by 1970, two million classroom teachers will be needed in the U.S. In England and Wales, it is estimated that, by 1980, if they are to adhere to the traditional staffing organization of the public school, 50 percent of the current school population must enter teacher training institutions. Our position in Canada is not dissimilar.

Precisely what is happening? The teacher is frustrated and dissatisfied. Parents are unhappy about the lack of quality education their children are receiving, and to many a student, school has become a place where he is a number instead of an individual. The quantity of student casualties at all educational levels causes grave concern.

In the 1950's, some American schools, aided by the Ford Foundation, experimented with the problem of meeting the shortage by using the available teachers more effectively and efficiently through the use of teacher aides. Preliminary analysis revealed that teachers were spending anywhere from 21 to 69 percent of their time in non-teaching tasks.

One of the earliest R and D projects in the use of teacher aides sponsored by the Ford Foundation took place at Bay City, Michigan. It was reported in *Decade of Experiment*, a Ford Foundation publication, as follows:

"If educators all over the country recognize the name of Bay City, Michigan, it is very likely because of an experiment that started there in the early 50's. This, the Fund's first venture in teacher utilization, consisted of a grant in 1952 to Central Michigan College of Education (now Central Michigan University) in support of a joint proposal from the college and the public schools of nearby Bay City. The idea was to have carefully selected and supervised non-professionals in a few Bay City elementary classrooms take over some or most of the teachers' tasks, such as keeping records, readying classroom equipment, collecting lunch money and the like.

"The College and the Schools proposed first to analyze the average teacher's activities, and then to try out the use of aides in Bay City; if this proved out, the plans would be applied to other Michigan cities, and perhaps throughout the States. After preliminary analysis had revealed that teachers were spending anywhere from 21 to 69 percent of their time on non-teaching chores, Bay City hired housewives and other women in the community as teacher aides to perform some of the housekeeping, bookkeeping and papercorrecting chores. This freed the teachers to devote more time to preparing lessons, leading discussions, counselling and performing other skilled professional duties. Modest in scope though it was, the experiment generated nationwide interest and comment, and the "Bay City Plan" soon became the generic term for any similar arrangement using teacher aides.

"Other early teacher aide projects were carried on in Fairfield, Connecticut; and in New York City. The project in New York City, sponsored by the Fund and the Public Education Association, began with 20 volunteers in a single school in 1956 and grew by 1960 to nearly 250 volunteers in 12 schools, performing 175 different kinds of activities and working a total of over 17,000 manhours during the year."

The Fairfield, Bay City, and similar experiments have demonstrated that most objections to the use of teacher aides arise from their misuse in the past, and that a well-planned, carefully supervised program can avoid the risks inherent in the use of non-professionals in the classroom.

Teacher education programming for teacher aide use. One of the early studies reporting on the use of teacher aides in a teacher education program appeared in 1960. In the magazine *Arithmetic Teacher*, two University of South Florida professors reported a study which involved a randomly selected group of 23 students and a control group, formed by individually matching the members of the experimental group to other students in the "Arithmetic for Elementary Teacher" course.

Members of the experimental group were asked to work in the local public elementary schools as teacher aides for a minimum of two hours per week for ten weeks. They were assigned by the principal to teacher aides for a minimum of two "get acquainted" weeks with the stipulation being that they participate in some phase of developing arithmetical concepts while in attendance. Otherwise the experimental and control groups participated equally in regular class activities.

Two criteria were used to evaluate the teacher-aide experience: (1) Did the experimental program improve the students' achievement of arithmetic concepts and skills? (2) Was the program of value in developing understanding of teaching procedures?

The first question was investigated with a post-treatment test, the Cooperative Mathematics Test (Form X); it was concluded that the experimental program *did* improve arithmetic understanding and skill.

The second question was investigated by the classroom teachers and the teacher aides, all of whom were asked to evaluate the teacher aide experience. The classroom teacher was asked to assess the benefits to the teacher aide and to the pupils.

This teacher aide program, taken in the second of a four-year teacher preparation course, was of particular value to the students in that it introduced them to the classroom experience before they took their formal period of student teaching. The project was the first of many which changed the traditional student teaching experience of the past to the many-faceted sequential program of field work in classrooms and elsewhere that has resulted in reform in teacher education programming.

The Rutgers Plan. One of the bestknown teacher aide plans is the use of lay readers, also known as the Rutgers Plan; it was developed at summer workshops (financed by The Ford Foundation) for high school teachers, at Rutgers in 1959 and 1960.

Qualified housewives were employed to read papers, direct independent study reading programs, and conduct periods of "self-correcting homework" (programmed exercises with immediate feedback), thereby releasing the English teacher to lead class and small group discussions, plan individualized instructional programs for the very slow and the very fast learner, and do research for class presentations.

One evaluation study of lay reader use for English classes reported:

(a) Students approved the program in a ratio of 15:1.

(b) A great majority of the students reported that they felt their writing had improved.

(c) There were no critical losses in the quality of student writing.

(d) Student writing was more varied and intensive.

(e) Student conferences to discuss the individual students writing assignments were increased.

The American use of teacher aides has been greatly increased as a result of funds made available by the Economic Opportunity Act of 1964, and the Elementary and Secondary Education Act of 1965. Under Operation Headstart, preschool centres were set up in the deprived neighbourhoods of Indianapolis to help small children overcome their lack of socio-economic opportunity before entering the public school system. An attempt was made for community involvement.

One teacher aide was placed in each of 40 classrooms. All the aides lived near the workshop centre. Many were mothers receiving public assistance, and most had less than grade 10 education. The child-adult ratio was 7½:1, the centres were open four days per week, and teachers visited the homes of the children on the fifth day.

The teacher aides were given extensive in-service training to help them perform more efficiently as aides; those who had not completed high school were required to attend formal school through the Indiana public schools.

From this project it was found that:

(a) Some of the aides were "naturals" in that they could often communicate better with the children than could the professional teacher who came from a different cultural background.

(b) These indigenous teacher aides often served to bridge the communication gap between the shy, low socio-economic parent and the middle class teacher. They helped the professional teachers to a better understanding of the value patterns which motivate the behaviour of the culturally disadvantaged.

(c) When the classroom teacher was absent, the teacher aide was able to give valuable assistance to the substitute teacher.

Another extensive project on teacher aides was conducted by the University of California. Each teacher was assisted by a team made up of a local housewife, a college student, a high school student and a high school dropout. The study indicated that teacher aides could be used to great advantage in low income areas, and that the number of school dropouts decreased.

A similar finding was reported by the *Teenager Teacher Aide Program*, which started in June of 1966, where 133 teenage trainees were recruited in 11 counties of Ohio and West Virginia and given an intensive five-week training in working with pre-school children. It was reported that not only did many dropouts return to school, but the program developed motivation for meaningful living among the teenagers.

Dr. Gordon Klopf, reporting on *Project Aware* in 1966, noted that, in order to properly train sub-professionals to work in anti-poverty programs, many variables have to be considered. The functions they might be required to perform must be defined and isolated and the particular level of educational preparedness they possess should be considered so that a realistic and significant training program can be designed and implemented. Dr. Klopf felt that paraprofessionals could be trained as members of an instructional team which would include teachers from the school system.

In an analysis of the Huntington Beach, California, program, another writer concurred with Dr. Klopf that the teacher's responsibilities will disclose many different levels of skill. Some require advanced professional knowledge of a high order; others require professional skill at a rather modest level. Still others seem primarily technical in nature, while some appear to be of a quite routine clerical character. However, all need to be planned and co-ordinated by an experienced and professionally competent teacher, but *all* of these skills need not be carried out by the *same* individual.

The teacher aide movement has obviously gone through a number of stages in its historical development.

Following the baby boom of the post World War II years, the need for professional teachers became crucial. The Ford Foundation hypothesized several solutions with its staff utilization studies of which Bay City, Michigan, and Fairfield, Conn., projects in teacher aide use were a part. These reforms were based on the idea that, through the use of aides, the teacher would be freed to better play his role as a professional.

Dissatisfaction was expressed with the traditional teacher education programs, and new ways of providing more involvement of the teacher-preparation student in school settings were researched. Teacher aide experience was one of the solutions investigated.

Studies of the work load of teachers of secondary school English indicated that this group of teachers were in much need of help if students were to have effective programs in composition and literature. English teachers were in short supply, so the solution was found in the hiring of paraprofessionals—lay readers, as described in the Rutgers Plan.

In the 1960's, numerous studies made us painfully aware of the plight of the poor. The U.S. Anti-Poverty Program came into being. Financed by the office of Economic Opportunity, Operation Head Start and Operation Bootstrap were aimed at giving employment to the poor to help upgrade the education of the culturally disadvantaged. It was during these experiments that the use of teacher aides was given the greatest opportunity to develop. Across the country paraprofessionals of a variety of types were hired. In 1965, 46,000 teacher aides were used in pre-school programs alone in the United States.

As we look at the sequence we realize that whenever there were not enough teachers to fill the demand, teacher aides were hired. In each instance, the social climate of the times brought forth its own solution.

It may well be that the recruiting and training of teacher aides will increase at an amazing rate within the next decade so that eventually the paraprofessional may outnumber the professionally trained teacher.

The NEA survey of teacher aide use in the United States. In April of 1967, the Educational Research Service of the American Association of School Administrators and the National Education Association published the results of a descriptive study of the use of teacher aides in large school systems. The use of teacher aides by 217 large American school systems for the 1965-66 term was reviewed. For the purposes of the study, aides were defined as "all non-professionals who relieve regular teachers of some non-teaching duties, whether they are paid or volunteer their time."

The study showed that the use of teacher aides has developed largely within this decade. Teacher aides introduced into the school systems were surveyed as follows: 1930-39, 1.8 percent; 1950-59, 16.6 percent; 1960-64, 36.4 percent; 1965-66, 40.1 percent (no reply, 5.1 percent).

Of the 217 systems surveyed, 161 made no use of volunteer teacher aide workers. The greatest number of aides were used in the elementary school.

The duties performed by aides were numerous and varied. The most frequently mentioned duties were, in order of their frequency: (1) preparing report cards, (2) supervising study halls, (3) corresponding with parents, arranging conferences between parents and teachers and guidance counsellors, (4) assisting in the school laboratory, (5) corridor monitoring, (6) administering tests, (7) reading and correcting student themes, (8) helping with discipline, (9) ordering and setting up AV materials and other supplies, (10) supervising the loading and unloading of buses, (11) recording data in student files, (12) keeping attendance registers and preparing attendance reports, (13) supervising cafeteria, and (14) tutoring individual students.

Most volunteer aides worked less than six hours per week, whereas the paid aides usually worked 20 or more hours per week.

Payment to aides was made in a variety of ways. Hourly rates ranged from $1.35 to $3.15 an hour with the average hourly rate being $1.83.

Little difficulty has been experienced in the recruitment of aides in the United States, either paid or voluntary. In about two-thirds of the systems employing aides, a high school education was listed as a requirement. Aides were usually selected by central office personnel, occasionally by principals. Teachers were directly responsible for their supervision.

In eight out of ten of the systems surveyed, the aides received on-the-job-training from the supervising teacher. Almost half of the systems used written materials as guides for the teacher aides, one-third used pre-school institutes and slightly more than half used in-service workshops. A few junior colleges have developed courses for the training of the teacher aides. Only 16 of the 217 systems indicated that they used no formal training procedures, and many of the systems used more than one of the methods reported above.

The NEA report concludes with a number of open-end statements from the survey respondents. On the whole, these are most enthusiastic, indicating the great amount of good that teacher aides bring to a school system. Here is a sample statement:

"The paid aide program has been accepted by the teaching staff as the greatest single effort that has been made to facilitate improved teaching. They are exuberant in their rating of the services rendered."

Teacher aide use in Canada. An early review of teacher aide use was published by the Alberta Teachers' Association in 1960. Written in non-support of the use of teacher aides in schools, it noted that "no evidence has been produced to show that the students learn more or less of the basic subjects in classes with teacher aides than they do in classes without teacher aides. Neither has any evidence been put forth to prove that the use of teachers aides is helpful or harmful as far as the pupils' happiness and adjustment are concerned."

It suggests that a greater effort be made to investigate the advantages of the use in the schools of clerical assistance to teachers, teaching machines, student assistance and a student teacher internship program.

Despite the lack of positive support for teacher aide use found in the 1960 report, the use of teacher aides in Canada is definitely on the increase. A 1967 Information Bulletin of the Canadian Education Association, *The Use of Teacher Aides in Canadian Schools*, presents some interesting statistics.

Questionnaires were sent to 576 school systems to determine where teacher aides were being used. Returns were received from 487 systems, of whom 126 reported use of teacher aides in their systems. About 1,200 teacher aides were employed during 1967, the majority of them in the secondary school.

A follow-up questionnaire was sent to the 126 systems employing aides; the result was a survey of the use made of 980 teacher aides in 94 school systems.

Eighty-three percent of the teacher aides were being used in secondary schools. They were usually recruited through local press advertisements, and hired on the advice of the principal to whom they were responsible. No pre-service training was provided. The salaries ranged from $1.65 to $3.00 per hour, $45 to $85 per week, and $200 to $400 per month.

Teacher aides in Canadian schools performed in a variety of roles:

(1) *Classroom assistant.* These teacher aides worked as kindergarten assistants or as aides to special education teachers with three exceptions: two grade 12 students working with a primary teacher on a part-time basis, and an adult doing marking and record-keeping duties for a Quebec high school teacher.

(2) *Lab assistant.* Six out of ten were adults; the rest were senior students. They looked after equipment, kept the lab area in order, cared for live specimens, set up demonstration equipment, and took inventory.

(3) *Lay readers.* 172 lay readers were employed in Canada in 1967. The readers analyzed and evaluated essays, working directly with teachers.

(4) *Noon hour activity supervision.* 58 aides were employed to supervise the lunchroom and the playground, being directly responsible to the principal. Fifteen were employed in elementary schools, 43 in secondary.

(5) *Audio-visual assistant.* 51 AV assistants were reported, all except three being in secondary schools. Their duties varied according to the school system.

(6) *Study supervision.* 34 teacher aides were employed as study hall, library and cafeteria supervisors under the direction of the principal.

(7) *Library assistant.* Seven full and part-time aides were employed as library clerks, aides or pages.

(8) *Other.* 23 teacher aides held such diverse positions as lab book marker, business manager, data processing assistant, storekeeper or group organizers of social activities.

More study of teacher aides is needed. Over the past decade, significant studies have been made in defining and clarifying the role of the teacher aide in the school community. It is now time for those who are interested in research to search out answers to the school employment of paraprofessionals, and assess the teacher aide idea in its current stage of development.

Undoubtedly, when the teacher aide is brought into the personnel structure of the school organization, there will be much need for care and planning so that the best interpersonal relationships result. Placing the right aide with the right teacher, and finding satisfactory expression for the special talents of the teacher aide, as well as the teacher, will be of most importance.

We need basic research evidence in interpersonal relations from our educational sociologists and psychologists to help us define teacher role change, the shifting patterns of instructional style, and student acceptance of this paraprofessional that we are adding to the teaching team.

Studies could also be made of the use of paraprofessionals by members of other professions (e.g. doctors, lawyers, nurses and engineers) and applications of the findings made to formulate hypotheses for using teacher aides in schools.

Studies similar to the time and motion studies of industry are needed to help us decide what might be omitted from the "job description" of that increasingly rare member of the school work force, the expert professional teacher.

Who should and who can decide what an adequate training program might be for the teacher aide? Should the university be involved in this training program? What will be the role of government? Of the professional organization? Of the employing school board? We need research evidence to help us find answers to these and other questions.

What happens to the grade 4 teacher of 20 years' experience when she is told that she must learn to work with a teacher aide? What are the threats to the classroom teacher's concept of status when the teacher aide arrives on the scene? Again, we need research evidence to help us make wise administrative moves as we bring about these changes in the staff's role.

Is there a possibility that we might devise a teacher aide program to train the young spirited Indian boy to act as a teacher aide to bridge the gap between his culture and that of the white teacher? Could we make use of the older members of the community as aides?

The day of the teacher as an independent operator in the classroom is past. The day when he could close his classroom door and be the only arbitrator within the confines of his "egg-crate" is gone.

Research workers, along with school administrators and supervisors, must work co-operatively to help the classroom teacher realize his professional potential in the new organizational structures when teacher aides become a part of the school staff.

There is much to be done if this new development in staff utilization is to be instituted economically and effectively in Canadian school systems.

SCHOOL is for . . .
GROUP INSTRUCTION

Utilizing Teacher Aides In The School

WILLIAM R. SPEER and LLOYD L. LEONARD

Much has been said and written about the teacher aide movement in the United States in the past three or four years. Not satisfied with mere words alone however, a sizable number of schools across the country have capitalized upon the whole idea of teacher aides as one means of helping to free teachers to do the job for which they were employed—to teach. In the state of Illinois, in fact, hundreds of teacher aides are assisting many hundreds of classroom teachers and many more thousands of children. It has been predicted that by 1972 teacher aides in the nation's schools will number approximately a quarter of a million and will eventually outnumber certified staff members.

The teacher aide idea is really not a new one. The public schools of Bay City, Michigan, did the first major experimentation in the utilization of auxiliary personnel some seventeen years ago with a grant in aid from the Ford Foundation. Although the teacher aide idea has been somewhat slow to catch on, an analysis of this more recent trend in our changing times indicates that several convergent forces—social, educational, economic, and political—are giving a renewed thrust to the teacher aide movement.

Although American educators, particularly classroom teachers and principals, have for years realized that teachers have been saddled with many activities, chores and duties not directly related to the teaching act, it has been only recently that funds in any significant amount have become available to study the problem of the over-burdened classroom teacher.

The availability of federal funds for the employment of low income nonprofessionals from such sources as the Office of Economic Oppor-

Speer, William R., and Leonard, Lloyd L. "Utilizing Teacher Aides in the School." *Illinois Principal.* May 1970. 5:10-12.

tunity, Title I of the Elementary and Secondary Education Act, and programs, institutes and workshops sponsored by professional organizations such as the National Commission on Teacher Education and Professional Standards and the National Classroom Teachers Association have helped to focus the attention of educators upon the use of auxiliary personnel in the schools. Furthermore, it has been rather clearly demonstrated by schools that have enlisted the help of teacher aides and other auxiliary personnel that many of the menial tasks customarily performed by the regular classroom teacher are being handled effectively by nonprofessionals.

Still another factor which undoubtedly helped to focus renewed attention on the teacher aide movement is the fact that teaching has in recent years become a much more complex process than it has ever been in our history. Team teaching, the non-graded school, auto-instruction and programmed learning, the use of educational television and other learning media, learning centers, independent study and other teaching-learning concepts which have been implemented in many of our schools in recent years have placed many new and different demands upon teacher time. Consequently, many schools have turned to the utilization of teacher aides, clerical aides, library aides, and other auxiliary personnel as one means of relieving the professional staff of non-instructional tasks.

A question frequently asked of teachers who utilize aides is "What do your teacher aides do to help you to do a more effective job of teaching?" The question is as pragmatic as it is natural and reasonable. Fortunately, studies have been made which furnish some clues to the answer to this question. Two such studies which reveal useful information about the kinds of work auxiliaries can do in schools under the direction and supervision of the professional staff are the study completed by the Bank Street College of Education and the more recent investigation undertaken by the Illinois TEPS Commission. The Bank Street Study of Auxiliary Personnel in Education was undertaken in 1966 in response to a request by the Office of Economic Opportunity and the U.S. Office of Education. Exploratory and developmental in nature, the study embraced three specific areas of inquiry: role definition, training, and institutionalization of auxiliaries in school systems. A 200 page report and a 21 page pamphlet, describing the study and its findings, are available from Bank Street College of Education.[1]

---

[1] Bowman, Garda W. and Klopf, Gordon J. *"New Careers and Roles in the American School,"* A REPORT ON A STUDY OF AUXILIARY PERSONNEL IN EDUCATION, Bank Street College of Education, September, 1967, pp. 3-5.

The findings in the Illinois study were based upon the replies to a questionnaire by 762 Illinois school superintendents. The study revealed that approximately 20 per cent of the public school districts in Illinois utilized teacher aides. Concerning the type of work they performed, the majority of the aides performed what was classified as general type work. Thirty per cent assisted in one way or another with instruction, and 35 per cent were classified as activity or clerical aides. It is significant to note that, while only 20 per cent of the school districts utilized teacher aides, 50 per cent of the 762 school administrators reporting indicated that they believed that teacher aides could be used effectively in their schools.[2]

Teacher-Learning-Oriented Activities

Some examples of activities that have been reported as being successfully performed by teacher aides which support the teaching-learning process either directly or indirectly are:

1. Taking charge of a small group working on a special project while the teacher works with another group.
2. Listening to children tell stories.
3. Telling stories to the children.
4. Reading stories to the children.
5. Helping children improve upon special skills.
6. Guiding children in learning how to look up information.
7. Preparing bulletin boards, displays, and exhibits.
8. Making arrangements for field trips.
9. Showing absentees, upon their return, what they have missed.
10. Helping pupils with practice and drill activities.

The examples above merely illustrate the wide range of teaching-learning activities which are frequently appropriate and desirable, depending upon the background of the teacher aide, the particular needs of the pupils, and the leadership of the teacher, his purposes, objectives, and beliefs.

Routine Activities

In schools where teacher aides have been utilized, certain more or

[2] Leonard, Lloyd L. *"Teacher Aides in Illinois Public Schools,"* EDUCATION, Vol. 57, No. 4, December, 1968, pp. 143-145.

less chore activities performed by the teacher aides have proved helpful to teachers. Some examples of activities which help teachers by relieving them of some of the "non-instructional" duties are:

1. Preparing audio-visual materials.
2. Making arrangements for the use of equipment and facilities.
3. Typing, filing, and cataloging materials.
4. Checking, inventorying, and requisitioning supplies.
5. Keeping attendance and health records and other appropriate records.
6. Operating machines, projectors, and other audio-visual equipment used in the school.
7. Supervising pupils during recess and lunch periods, in the corridors, restrooms, on buses.
8. Checking equipment used by children in the school and on the playgrounds.
9. Collecting monies paid in by pupils for such things as milk, lunches, pictures, books purchased or rented.
10. Doing routine errands and carrying messages.
11. Distributing and collecting materials.
12. Administering simple first aid.

Most if not all of these more or less routine tasks have for years been considered as part of the regular teacher's normal day. They were taken for granted as being simply part of his job. Yet, by their very nature, they are the kind of tasks that can be easily delegated to the noncertified person who may perform them more efficiently than the regular teacher.

Home-Community Oriented Activities

It has been found that some of the most important activities performed by teacher aides are those which help to improve school-home and school-community relations. In some communities, a few teacher aides have been selected to serve because of their sensitivity to children's special needs and their demonstrated skills and abilities in working with pupils individually and communicating with parents. Such auxiliary personnel usually possess some special qualifications by virtue of their preparation or experience in educational guidance, psychology, or social work. The following activities are illustrative of those which have been performed to improve school-home and school-community relationships:

1. Visiting parents of children who are new to the school and welcoming them to the school and community.
2. Reporting to school authorities problems observed in home visits so that appropriate steps may be taken to solve them.
3. Taking children to their homes when they become ill in school.
4. Working individually with children who for one reason or another become too disturbed to remain in the classroom.

5. Helping to plan and organize either individual or group meetings with parents.
6. Helping to recruit and pre-register pupils before the opening of school.
7. Conferring with parents, providing them with information and help, referring them to other appropriate sources for further help.[3]

Some aides have special skills which are valuable for use in the school. In some communities auxiliaries who speak another language as well as English serve as interpreters for parents who speak English with difficulty or who feel sensitive or embarrassed about their language problem.

There have been some teacher aides who have demonstrated extraordinary skill and ability to help children to become increasingly more self-directing in the learning process. With special attention being given recently to independent study, and learning or resource centers, such schools are indeed fortunate to secure the services of auxiliary personnel who possess these special skills and competencies.

Special Need-Oriented Activities

According to the findings in the study of auxiliary personnel in education by Bank Street College, many disadvantaged children have special needs which auxiliary personnel can help the school to meet. Examples of situations, conditions, and circumstances under which teacher aides may be helpful in classrooms with disadvantaged children are:

1. Both teachers and auxiliaries may establish relationships with the learner different in both character and quality and more pertinent to the child's peculiar needs when there are two or more adults in the classroom.
2. Auxiliary personnel aiding the regular classroom teacher enables the teacher to permit a freer movement about the room and a greater diversity of activities geared especially to those disadvantaged children with a high anxiety level. More activities of a small group nature are naturally made easier when the teacher has the assistance of additional adult help.
3. If the aide should happen to live in the same neighborhood as the child, as is sometimes the case, he can communicate with the child in

[3] Bank Street College of Education, A STUDY OF AUXILIARY PERSONNEL IN EDUCATION, *"New Partners in American Schools,"* published by Bank Street College of Education, November, 1967, pp. 12-13.

a manner which is neither threatening nor strange to him and possibly in a way which the classroom teacher could never hope to do. In addition, the aide may be of special help to the child by helping to interpret some aspects of the child's life or behavior to the teacher who may live in a different type of community.

4. Frequently aides are parents who reside in the attendance area or school district. The involvement of such parents as aides in the classroom can be a help in supporting children's learnings. Parents who understand accurately and well the school's goals and the real problems in realizing their goals are frequently good interpreters of the school to the community.[4]

General Recommendations

1. The aims, goals, and objectives of the auxiliary aide program should be thought out clearly and soundly, preferably in writing.
2. When defining and describing the duties, responsibilities, and performance tasks of the auxiliary aide, limits should be set on the activities of the aides, but within these stated limits the role of the aide should be a flexible one and one which takes into account his qualifications and limitations.
3. All professionals who will be working with auxiliary aides in any way should receive proper and adequate orientation to the auxiliary aide program and how it will operate in the school system to ensure maximum effectiveness of the efforts of the aides serving in the system.
4. All auxiliary aides should receive preservice training and preparation for the various kinds of services they will be performing and the rationale underlying their work.
5. Inservice institutes should be planned and developed for the team preparation of administrators, other professionals, and the aids themselves.
6. Ways and means should be found for securing feedback from the aides concerning the success of their efforts or lack thereof as they see it, and their views should be received with sincerity, an openness of mind, and with sympathetic understanding.
7. The effective use of auxiliary aides at various grade levels and in a variety of situations should be explored and investigated.
8. An advisory committee of school administrators, other professionals, auxiliaries and other laymen should be established for the purpose of evaluating and improving the effectiveness of the auxiliary aide program.

[4] Bank Street College of Education, op. cit., pp. 6-7.

Chapter XIV

The Teacher and School Law

Having a knowledge of school law has long been relegated by teachers as an administrative responsibility and not a concern of theirs personally, with the exception of teacher tenure and contracts. However, a significant increase in the number of cases filed in the courts by parents, as well as groups attempting to protect the rights of the individual, make it mandatory that the elementary teacher candidate of the 70's have some understanding of his legal status in the educational setting.

Articles in this Chapter dealing with the lack of legal status for an individual during his student teaching experience should be of personal interest to all teacher education majors. Becoming knowledgeable about one's lack of legal authority for conducting classes, but understanding the possibility of being held legally responsible for negligent acts therein should prove helpful to the reader in preparing himself for his student teaching assignment.

Legal rights and responsibilities are presented from several vantage points for examination by the beginning teacher. It is anticipated that the articles contained in this Chapter will stimulate the reader to examine more fully what he believes to be best educational practice for classroom learning with the realities of the risks of legal challenges to his operational decisions. The authors of this textbook do not wish this Chapter to be interpreted as a threat or an excuse for not teaching to the best of your ability and convictions. Rather, their concerted opinion is that you must become more aware of the total implications of the decisions which the teacher must make in his classroom every day of the year.

Statutory Hearing Rights of Nontenure Teachers

NATIONAL EDUCATION ASSOCIATION

NEA CONTINUING RESOLUTION C-36 on the subject of continuing employment and fair dismissal practices, adopted by the Representative Assembly in 1970, expresses the belief that "laws in each state must provide for continuing employment of educators," and that "provisions in state laws and master contracts must afford educators, before demotion, dismissal, or nonrenewal of contracts for good and just cause" the following procedures:

    a. Timely and adequate notice of hearing, including a statement of charges
    b. A fair hearing with opportunity to confront and cross-examine witnesses and to present argument and evidence in defense
    c. Representation by legal counsel
    d. A decision based upon the evidence adduced at the hearing, with a statement of the reasons for the decision and evidence relied upon by an impartial decision maker.

In the light of this resolution, and based on the NEA Research Division's recently completed (October 1970) state-by-state summaries of teacher tenure or fair dismissal laws, and statutory provisions relating to employment contracts of teachers in nontenure states, this article explores the statutory hearing rights, if any, accorded to probationary teachers in tenure states and to teachers employed in school districts not governed by tenure laws. While the discussion is limited to the state statutes, mention should be made of some recent court decisions that are according substantive and procedural due process rights of nontenured teachers despite the absence of statutory protection. (See NEA RESEARCH BULLETIN, October 1970, p. 90.)

National Education Association. "Statutory Hearing Rights of Nontenure Teachers." *NEA Research Bulletin.* March 1971. 49:17-20.

Tenure Laws—National Picture

As of October 1970, a teacher tenure or fair dismissal law was in effect state-wide (with some exceptions as noted below) in 39 states and the District of Columbia. This represents a growth of five states since 1966, the latest enactments being in Nevada and Wyoming (both in 1967), Virginia (1968), Missouri (1969), and Arkansas (1970). In 37 states the laws are mandatory and apply to all school districts in the state without exception, although the provisions may vary according to size or class of school district. As to the other two states, New York excludes rural districts from tenure law coverage, but the law must be observed everywhere else; the California law prescribes tenure throughout the state except that adherence to the provisions is optional in districts with under 250 pupils in average daily attendance.

Besides these 39 states, the Texas permissive tenure law, enacted in 1967, gives all school districts the option of coming under its provisions. Also, five other states have tenure laws that apply either to certain designated cities, or counties, or school districts. These states are Georgia, Kansas, Nebraska, Oregon, and Wisconsin. Thus, there remain five states with no tenure laws whatsoever, namely, North Carolina, Mississippi, South Carolina, Utah, and Vermont.

Probationary Teachers

With rare exceptions, teachers in tenure states must serve a probationary period and other requirements must be met before tenure benefits are conferred. The pertinent statutory provisions relating to probationary teachers may be summarized as follows:

Most prevalent is a probationary period of three years. Two years is not unusual and is found in at least 10 states. The period is as long as four years in Kentucky and five years in Indiana and Missouri except for St. Louis. At the other extreme, four states—Arkansas, Iowa, North Dakota, and Washington—make no mention at all of probationary service.

Usually tenure teachers lose all tenure rights and must again serve a full probationary period when moving intra-state to another school system. Some states, however, allow school boards to shorten or to waive probationary service if the teacher was tenured elsewhere in the state. Pennsylvania is most unusual in that tenure, once earned, is retained when the teacher transfers to another school district.

In a number of states, teachers do not attain tenure status automatically on completion of probationary service. Other requirements may be imposed, among them, that the teacher be re-appointed for the next succeeding school year or that the school superintendent recommend that tenure be granted the teacher.

Typically, employment of the probationary teacher is on an annual contract, often under statutory provisions for automatic renewal of the contract if notice of nonrenewal is not given by a specified date. Non-re-employment of the probationary teacher is in the discretion of the employing school board, but this power is limited by the principle that the decision of the board may not be for constitutionally impermissible reasons.

Rights of Probationary Teachers

In view of this wide discretion on the part of school boards, what rights do probationary teachers have under tenure or fair dismissal laws with respect to notice, statement of reasons, and a hearing in the event employment is terminated? Although there is considerable variation from law to law, an over-all look at the laws reveals these distinct patterns:

- Of 41 state laws (including California, New York, Oregon, and Texas) nearly half are silent on hearing rights of probationary teachers, even when dismissal occurs during the school year. A few of these states, however, require that the probationary teacher be apprised of the reasons for dismissal. Under express provisions in some laws, as for example, in New York, probationary teachers may be dismissed at any time on recommendation of the school superintendent, and in Oregon, probationary teachers may be dismissed at any time for any cause the school board deems sufficient.
- The statutes in 12 states differentiate between dismissal during the school year and nonrenewal of the contract at the end of the school year. These statutes provide due process rights to probationary teachers only in case of dismissal during the school year. For the most part, due notice, causes for discharge, and the hearing procedures parallel those that apply to tenure teachers.
- In Arkansas, Iowa, North Dakota, and Washington, the four states whose statutes do not mention probationary service, all teachers have hearing rights at the time of dismissal during the school year and at the time of nonrenewal of their contracts.
- Five states whose laws require service of a probationary period expressly entitle probationary teachers to a statement of reasons and a hearing in either situation—when the contract is not renewed at its expiration date or when discharge occurs during the school year. These states are Alaska, California, Connecticut, Rhode Island, and Texas. Even so, some distinctions are made between tenure teachers and probationary teachers, with less exacting statutory standards enacted for the latter group. For instance, the Alaska statute enumerates the specific causes on which nonretention of tenure teachers may be based. But as to probationary teachers in Alaska, nonretention may be for any

cause the board deems adequate, and they, unlike tenure teachers, are not entitled to a judicial review.

● Besides the nine states named above, the law of one other state (Nevada) merely provides that the probationary teacher who is dismissed or is not re-employed, has the right to appear before the next regular meeting of the school board to learn why and is to be given an opportunity to reply. Lastly, in a few states the laws provide that on request of the probationary teacher, the reasons for nonrenewal of the contract must be supplied, but no hearing rights are granted.

Nontenure Jurisdictions

In the five states where tenure laws are limited in application to designated school systems, all but Kansas provide some statutory rights to teachers employed in nontenure areas. In Georgia, a teacher suspended for cause is entitled to a written notice with enumeration of charges, and a hearing at which he may present evidence and witnesses in defense. A 1969 amendment to the Oregon statutes on employment contracts in nontenure districts (those with fewer than 4,500 pupils in average daily attendance) provides that a school district wishing to dismiss a teacher during his contract term must give the teacher written notice of charges and opportunity to be heard in his own defense; grounds for dismissal in such an instance are the same as under the tenure provisions. In Nebraska, teachers in nontenure areas may ask for a hearing on receipt of notice of nonrenewal of their annual contracts; after the hearing the board must supply reasons. Under the Wisconsin statute, teachers outside the tenure areas have the right to a private conference if notified by the employing school board that contract non-renewal is being considered.

North Carolina and Vermont, two of the five states without any tenure legislation at all, have statutory provisions that specify the causes for which a teacher may be dismissed during the contract term, require that the teacher be given proper notice with grounds for the con-templated board action, and provide the teacher with an opportunity for a full hearing.

In summary, examination of the existing statutes shows that there is some semblance of due process for nontenure teachers in a number of the states. But most state laws have a long way to go to measure up to the standards expressed in the NEA Continuing Resolution C-36 at least with respect to nontenure teachers.

For details see: National Education Association, Research Division. *Teacher Tenure and Contracts.* School Law Summaries. Washington, D.C.: the Associaton, 1971.

Student Teaching–A Legal Vacuum

LARRY E. LONGSTRETH and BOB L. TAYLOR

Although qualification for a teaching certificate in the United States is usually dependent upon the completion of a student-teaching program, many of the states make no legal provision for such a program. Hence, student teaching functions in a legal vacuum. It seems incredible that state legislators require student teaching for certification and yet fail to include legal provisions for such a practice. The alternatives are either to rely on case law or to hope that the legal status of student teaching is not challenged in the courts. A review of case law in those states not making statutory provision for student teaching reveals the importance of this issue. If educators hope to secure a legal status for student teaching commensurate with the needs of the teaching profession, it is imperative that they work for favorable legislation.

The authority of the student to teach in the absence of statutory provision has been the subject of some controversy. One theory holds that a school district may participate in such a program as a part of its implied powers, KENTUCKY ATTORNEY GENERAL, No. 269 (1963). Yet, a court in New York held that the power to conduct a student-teaching program could not necessarily be regarded as an implied power of the local board, *McGilvra v. Seattle School District No. 1*, 118 Wash. 619, 194 Pac. 817. Nevertheless, there is some precedent supporting the authority of the student teacher to teach. It was held in one case that a school board was within the powers granted by the state legislature when it established a model school for student teaching in a public school, because student teaching was merely a variation of method through the use of an assistant teacher, *Spedden et al. v. Board of Education of Independent District of Fairmont, et al.*, 74 W. Va., 81 S.E. 724. In a

Longstreth, Larry E., and Taylor, Bob L. "Student Teaching—A Legal Vacuum." *The Journal of Teacher Education.* Spring, 1971. 22:48-50.

similar case, the court upheld the practice of student teaching if such was done under the supervision of a regular teacher, *Clay v. Independent School District of Cedar Falls et al.*, 187 Iowa 89, 174 N.W. 47 (1919). Thus, the authority of the student teacher to teach in the absence of statutory authority has not been clearly established.

There is little precedent relevant to the authority of the student teacher to regulate pupil conduct in the absence of legal provision; however, what precedent there is would seem to deny such authority. The court in *Spedden et al. v. Board of Education of Independent School District of Fairmont et al., supra*, specified that the student teacher, although having the right to teach, did not have the authority to control pupil conduct. In the Opinion of the Kentucky Attorney General, *supra*, a regular teacher may not delegate authority for supervision, nor may the student teacher exercise authority in the control of the class. This would seem to be consistent with the ruling that a student teacher is not a teacher within the meaning of the law, *State v. Preston*, 79 Wash. 286, 140 Pac. 350 *acquiescing in School District No. 20 v. Bryan*, 51 Wash. 498, 99 Pac. 28.

The question of legal liability for pupil injury is difficult. Though the student teacher may not possess the authority to regulate pupil conduct, he may be held liable for pupil injury. A student teacher in New York was found negligent in an injury resulting to a pupil who tried to do a headstand in a physical education class. *Gardner v. State of New York* 256 App. Div. 385; 10 N.Y.S. 2d 344 (1939). Consequently, it seems likely that student teachers can be held liable for pupil injury and should protect themselves with appropriate insurance coverage.

The supervising teacher would seem to be particularly vulnerable, since it was held in *Spedden et al. v. Board of Education of Independent School District of Fairmont et al., supra*, that a regular teacher may not delegate supervisory responsibilities. Negligence on the part of a teacher has been determined by this standard: "the ability of a prudent teacher, in the exercise of ordinary care, to foresee that harmful results will follow the commission of the act."[1] Liability is based on a want of proper care and is a matter that must be determined by a jury. It seems clear that the teacher who remains in the room taking reasonable and prudent care in the supervision of his charges assumes little risk.

---

[1] Cited from *Black's Law Dictionary* (1951 edition) as reported in Gauerke, Warren E. *Legal and Ethical Responsibilities of School Personnel.* Englewood Cliffs, N. J.: Prentice-Hall, 1959, p. 260.

However, good practice dictates that the supervisory teacher, after having ascertained the competency of the student teacher, should leave the class in his charge at certain times. The risk that a teacher incurs in leaving the room seems inversely related to such variables as the maturity level of the class and the nature of the classroom activity; for example, a senior high school history teacher could feel more secure in leaving than could a first-grade or a shop teacher. Though leaving a classroom may or may not in itself constitute negligence, a court has held that a class supervised solely by a student teacher does not comply with the legal provisions for supervision in a classroom, *Gardner v. State of New York*, *supra*. Thus it seems likely that leaving a student teacher in charge of a classroom may be somewhat akin to providing no supervision. The conclusion is that, in the absence of statutory provision, a supervising teacher who leaves the classroom under the supervision of a student teacher does so at his own risk. Possible liability may also extend to the school district and the teacher education institution.

Another perplexing question is the responsibility of the teacher education institution and the school district for the welfare of the student teacher; that is, who is responsible if a student teacher is injured in the course of his duties? There is a dearth of legal authority on this question, and responsibility is difficult to ascertain.

Most educators maintain that student teaching is the most important and meaningful experience in the teacher education program. Student teachers themselves verify this conclusion. Yet, student teaching has remained low man on the prestige pole in terms of assignments of university and college personnel and has received like consideration from the legislatures of most states. The preparation of teachers is obviously vital to education and the education profession, as well as to the general welfare of America. It seems rather ludicrous that student teaching should be regarded as a "variation of method" in an effort to find legal justification. A valid student-teaching experience is, in fact, a teaching experience, and this should be so reflected in the law. Although many states have legalized the sale of alcoholic beverages and some have even legalized gambling, few have seen fit to legalize student teaching. This is a tragic situation; the student teacher, the supervising teacher, the school district, and the teacher education institution are entitled to status and protection under the law. The State of California grants legal status to student teachers through temporary certification, and a few other states have done the same through general legislation of one kind or another. It is imperative that the many other states which have ignored the problem should take action to legalize student teaching.

Adequate legislation can be obtained only if the teaching profession is willing to establish this as a high priority goal and work for the imple-

mentation of laws equal to the needs of teacher education. The failure to
do so may result in the eventual emergence of additional case law that
will be highly detrimental to such needs, in which case, educators have
only themselves to blame. It is time to fill this legal vacuum with suitable
legislation. Student teaching rates better treatment than it has received,
and now is the time to legalize it in all of the fifty states rather than in
just a few.

SCHOOL is for . . .
PROVOCATIVE
FIELD TRIPS

May Parent Legally Criticize Teacher?

M. CHESTER NOLTE

Teachers and other school employees are protected by the doctrine of privileged communications when, in the line of duty, it becomes necessary for them to release information about one of the students.

However, just how free is a parent to criticize the teacher, even though it is later proved that the parent's accusations are false? This question was placed before the court in an interesting case which arose in New York in 1965.[1] The court's decision, and the reasoning supporting it, are of more than passing interest to school boards and administrators today, since parents are taking a more active part in school affairs than ever before, and often are prone to make complaints to school officials.

When parents act in good faith, it appears that they may make defamatory remarks about the teacher, so long as they believe the statements are true, even though, in fact, they are false. The case represents a legal extension of the time-honored "doctrine of privileged communications" to include not only school personnel who have been covered in the past but parents as well.

Freedom of speech is a cherished birthright guaranteed under the First Amendment. The courts have interpreted this right to mean that one can tell the truth and comment fairly on the facts, but a person is barred from circulating falsehoods and from personal attacks upon others in the guise of the role as public servants. Under the law of defamation, one who falsely or maliciously damages the good name of another may be held to account in damages to the injured party and, in extreme cases, may be held guilty of criminal libel.

---

[1] Segall v. Piazza, 46 Misc. 2d 700, 260 N.Y.S. 2d 543 (1965).

Nolte, M. Chester. "May Parent Legally Criticize Teacher?" *The American School Board Journal.* October 1966. 153:66-67.

Facts of the Case

Plaintiff had been an industrial arts teacher in the New York City school system for 17 years. The defendant was the mother of one of plaintiff's former pupils. Plaintiff sought damages for "injury to his credit and reputation and his standing in the community," and "great mental pain and anguish."

Defendant visited the school principal in his office to complain and to investigate an incident which allegedly took place in plaintiff's classroom the day before. The principal called the teacher into his office. In the presence of the defendant and her son, the plaintiff was informed by the principal that he had received an oral complaint from the mother that on the previous day he, the teacher, while correcting the schoolwork of the boy, had grabbed him by the neck and pushed his head onto the desk, causing his nose to bleed. Plaintiff denied the incident took place. The principal then requested the mother to write a letter concerning the incident and submit it to him. This she did, as follows:

February 15, 1964

To Whom It May Concern:
   On Thursday, Feb. 13, 1964, my son . . . arrived from school hysterical and upset. His nose was bleeding profusely. Before I could ask him what had happened, he begged me to come up to his school . . . as his shop teacher . . . had banged his head against the desk several times, thus causing his nose to bleed . . .
   He told me that he had received instructions during his eighth period from Mr. S. on mechanical drawing. His assignment was to make something 2¼ in. wide. When he had completed the assignment, Mr. S. came to check it. Charles was off on his measurements slightly, whereupon Mr. S. started to pound his head against the desk, saying, "I am very surprised at you, Charles."
   Charles' nose began to bleed, but he remained seated and said nothing until it was time to be dismissed, which was approximately 15 minutes. He then came home, his nose still bleeding badly.
   On Friday, February 14, 1964, I went to the school to speak to the principal and to investigate the matter further. Mr. S. was called in. Immediately after hearing my son's account of the incident, he asked my son, 'Did you report the fact that you had a bloody nose to me?' My son replied that he had not. . . .
   I have heard that children who have been pupils in Mr. S.' class in the past, that he has been abusive to his pupils on other occasions. However, this is hearsay and I cannot attest to these allegations.

The letter was placed in the teacher's personal file. The teacher then brought suit against the mother, alleging that the accusation was false; that since the incident he had suffered mental anguish with many sleepless nights; that teachers were discussing the incident and saying he was in trouble; that teachers withdrew when he approached them; and that he feared that the false statement would interfere with his promotional opportunities and pay increases.

Witness Testifies

A student who sat next to Charles in class testified at the trial, which was tried without a jury. The boy said he did not see plaintiff beat Charles, that he and Charles returned to their homeroom together and he did not see Charles' nose bleed, and that he did not see the boy holding a handkerchief to his nose.

The court held that (1) the accusations about the teacher were false, and (2) that the letter and its contents were libelous. The next question then became: "Was the communication (contained in the letter) privileged?" The court gave the following test for a privileged communication.

> The test of privilege is "a communication made bona fida upon any subject-matter in which the party communicating has an interest, or in reference to which he has a duty; . . . privileged, if made to a person having a corresponding interest or duty, although it contained criminating matter which, without this privilege, would be slanderous and actionable."

The rule of law that permits such publication, said the court, grew out of the desirability in the public interest of encouraging a full and fair statement by persons having a legal or moral duty to communicate their knowledge or information about a person in whom they have an interest to another who also has an interest in such person. Such privilege is known as a "privileged communication" and is a "qualified privilege." It is qualified because it does not extend beyond such statements as the writer makes in the performance of such duty and in good faith, believing them to be true.[2]

When defendant's statements are presumptively privileged, as in this case, the rule is that, in order to render them actionable, it is incumbent upon the plaintiff to prove that they were false and that the defendant was actuated by express malice or actual ill will.

Reasoning of the Court

The court held that although the accusations against the teacher were false, they were privileged. The plaintiff had failed to prove malice and ill will on the part of the defendant. His case therefore failed.

[2] Bingham v. Gaynor, 203 N.Y. 27, 96 N.E. 84 (1911).

The court held that the teacher could not recover damages. Said the court:

> Unquestionably, the defense of "privilege" is applicable here and the court so holds. Therefore, in order to recover, plaintiff must prove by a fair preponderance of the credible evidence not only that the statement is false but that the defendant, in making it, was actuated by express malice or actual ill will. This the plaintiff has failed to do.
>
> Accordingly, judgment is granted to defendant for dismissal of the complaint.

The defense of qualified privilege is a major protection for school personnel in the exercise of duties in connection with handling confidential information about students. So far as the author knows, this is the first case in which the privilege has been extended to a parent.

The obvious "interest" which the parent has in his child, and in his education, makes him legally covered by the privilege, so long as (1) he complains to the school official qualified to receive such a complaint, and (2) he acts not with malice and ill will, but in good faith. Whether or not the accusation is true or false has little to do with proof of damages incurred, apparently being transcended by the motives of the accuser.

SCHOOL is for . . .
RECESS BREAKS

Are Teachers Citizens of their Communities?

EARL HOFFMANN

The rights of teachers, as seen and understood by the public, have changed somewhat during the past decade or two. But the rights of teachers, as perceived by teachers, have changed radically during that same period of time. This disparity in the perception of roles, rights and responsibilities of teachers has created tensions heretofore unknown in the educational profession.

It is a matter of record that undue, inhibiting restrictions regarding their social and personal activities have been placed on teachers in many communities. Recently, however, these restraints have been modified in many districts. Teachers are becoming quite vocal in their efforts and demands to gain a greater influence in the development and implementation of school curriculum; they are active in social and civic organizations; they have entered the political arenas. In some cities, teachers serve as aldermen or mayor with considerable influence on the public.

What has caused this recent change? A number of factors can be named as having some degree of responsibility. Among them are:

1. General relaxation of social restraints on all people.
2. Improved educational standards of teachers and administrators.
3. Organizational efforts of the teaching profession and the usurpation of responsibilities.
4. Decisions in various court cases which have confirmed many common rights for teachers.

One of the hardest fought cases involving a teacher's right to assume some of the prerogatives of a citizen was *Pickering v. Board of Education of Township High School District No. 205* in Illinois (391 U.S. 563). The case was heard by the United States Supreme Court in 1968, and the litigation offers guidelines for administrative and teacher behavior.

Hoffmann, Earl. "Are Teachers Citizens of Their Communities?" *School Management*. April 1972. 16:10.

In 1961, the Lockport, Ill., district presented to the voters a bond issue for two new high schools. The proposal lost, but a subsequent modified proposal was passed 11 months later. In May and September of 1964, the board presented tax referendums for educational purposes, and both were defeated. It was then that Mr. Pickering, a teacher in the district, wrote his "letter to the editor" that resulted in his confrontation with the board. In this letter, Pickering criticized the school board and administration for mismanagement of school funds and for the control of information given to the citizens of the district. He accused them of over-emphasizing the athletic program at the expense of the academic program. Specifically Pickering claimed:

1. Construction of the two new high schools deviated from the promises made by the board prior to the bond issue.
2. The total of teachers' salaries reported to the public was incorrect and exaggerated.
3. School athletes were receiving free lunches on away-from-home athletic dates and an additional $20,000 was being spent for athletics during the fiscal year while classroom materials were not being supplied.
4. Teachers were required to submit publicity items through the superintendent's office and their freedom of speech was thereby being unduly suppressed.

The Board of Education dismissed Pickering as a result of his letter on the grounds that its publication was "detrimental to the best interests of the schools." In a hearing which followed, the board charged that numerous statements made by the teacher were false and that they "unjustifiably impugned the motives, honesty, integrity, truthfulness, responsibility, and competence of both the board and the administration."

Appeal

Pickering felt strongly that his constitutional rights as a private citizen had been violated, but his appeal to the Circuit Court of Will County fell on unsympathetic ears. The court's review found sufficient evidence to determine that his letter was detrimental to the interests of the school system, and therefore the rights of the school system overrode his rights as an individual under the First Amendment.

Pickering's attorneys appealed this decision to the Illinois Supreme Court where again, the judgment was affirmed. The court examined the specific charges of misrepresentation and mismanagement and found them to be substantially false or misleading. It agreed that the letter was detrimental to the functioning of the system, and that the Board members had acted reasonably and within the scope of their responsibility. The court re-emphasized that the administration of the schools was within the domain of the local school board, and in the absence of impulsive or capricious action, it refused to interfere.

However, two of the seven justices dissented (225 N.E. (2d) 7). They stated that no evidence was presented to show that the contents of the letter "had any effect whatsoever upon the teachers, the people of the school district, or anything else." As a result, the justices felt that the board had overstepped its authority and had abridged the right of Pickering to speak out and to inform the citizens of his community of his thoughts and views.

Pickering still insisted that he had been wrongfully dismissed and was granted a hearing by the United States Supreme Court in 1968. The body recognized the two main points of dispute as being the statements concerning allocation of monies between athletic and educational programs and the methods of informing (or not informing) the public of facts, actions or opinions. In each instance the Supreme Court found that the teacher was indeed protected by the First Amendment inasmuch as no harm seemed to have been done to any person or the school district, and no proof had ever been offered by the board to that effect.

Encouraging free and open debate on controversial issues, the court emphasized that a teacher has no less a right of expression than any other citizen. In its summation, the Court said, ". . . we hold that, in a case such as this, absent proof of false statements knowingly or recklessly made by him, a teacher's exercise of his right to speak on issues of public importance may not furnish the basis for his dismissal from public employment." The judgments of the lower courts were reversed and the school district was ordered to reinstate Pickering.

Great care must be exercised by boards of education when disciplinary measures are initiated against a teacher because of his out-of-school activities. His personal rights may not be violated.

In another instance, an Ohio teacher wrote letters to a former pupil that allegedly contained vulgar and offensive language. These were used as the basis for the attempted dismissal of the teacher on grounds of immorality. The teacher sued for reinstatement and the court noted, "The private conduct of a man, who is also a teacher, is a proper concern to those who employ him only to the extent it mars him as a teacher, who is also a man. Where his professional achievement is unaffected, where the school community is placed in no jeopardy, his private acts are his own business and may not be the basis for discipline." (*Jarvella v. Willoughby-Eastlake City School District*, 233 N.E. (2d) 143.)

Of course, it is possible to dismiss nontenured teachers at the end of a contract period with or without cause so long as the provisions of established and recognized policies and procedures are adhered to.

The Pickering case will continue to serve as a model for the courts as they consider dismissal cases. The courts are aware of the rights and responsibilities of school boards to administer their schools, but they must also be zealous in protecting the rights of individual teachers who teach in these districts.

SCHOOL is for . . .
SHARING CONFIDENCES

What Teacher Aides Can–And Cannot–Do

S. KERN ALEXANDER

Nearly half the teacher aide programs now operating in large public schools are less than three years old. Using a sample of large school districts, a recent report found that 40 per cent of all teacher aide programs were started in the 1965-66 school year and 36 per cent between 1960 and 1964.[1] Because of the comparative recency of the use of teacher aides, their function in our educational system is ill-defined. There are no concrete definitions or measures of established practice which state and local school districts can use as guidelines.

Most states do not have specific statutory provisions pertaining to teacher aides. The majority of the school districts operating aide programs are doing so under general legislative provisions for operating and maintaining public school systems.

The legal question is: "Does a school district have the authority to expend public funds for teacher aides in the absence of statutory authority?"

A case which may serve as precedent was decided in Minnesota involving the employment of a school nurse. The board of education employed a nurse for one month to make an inspection of the physical condition of the pupils in certain schools. The board's authority to take this action was challenged. The court held that the board exercised an implied power and said:

'The purpose of the corporation is to maintain efficient free public schools . . . and, unless expressly restricted, (the school board) necessarily possesses the power to employ such persons as are required to accomplish the purpose. Education of a child means more than merely communicating to it the content of textbooks".[2]

---

[1] "Teachers Aides in Large School Systems," Circular, Educational Research Service, No. 2 AASA–NEA, Washington, D.C., April 1967, pp. 1-2.

[2] State v. Brown, 112 Minn. 370, 128 N.W. 294.

Alexander, S. Kern. "What Teacher Aides Can—and Cannot—Do." *Nation's Schools.* August 1968. 82:23-25, 46.

Other courts have rendered similar decisions concerning student teachers. In a West Virginia case, a school board consented to provide practice schools for college teacher training. The authority of the school district to provide supervision and facilities for the student teachers was challenged. The court held for the school district saying where a board of education has powers and discretion for the conduct and management of the public schools, the board has the authority to determine the mode and course of instruction.[3]

Although some conflicting cases exist regarding the power of boards of education to expend public moneys for certain purposes, the weight of judicial authority, as the above cases show, seems to support the general premise that in the absence of statutes to the contrary, the power to hire and pay teacher aides is within the authority of local school districts.

Recent legislative action: While there seems to be no great trend in this direction, some state legislatures in recent years have enacted statutes providing for the employment of teacher aides. Some of these statutes provide for teacher aides for specific purposes, while others are rather comprehensive and provide a very realistic legal and broad-scale basis for such employment.

During 1965, the *Washington*[4] and *Massachusetts*[5] legislatures passed laws authorizing local school districts to employ noncertificated personnel to supervise pupils in noninstructional activities during regular school lunch services. The Washington provision was made in order to provide teachers with a 30 minute duty free lunch period.

In 1966, the *California* legislature authorized approval of projects for noncertificated school aides for use in compensatory education programs in Grades K-6. Such aides may be high school students in Grades 11 and 12 and college students. The legislature felt that it was necessary to make provisions for employment of aides to reduce the ratio of pupil to aide/teacher in order that compensatory classes not exceed 20 to 1.[6]

Nevada[7] and *Illinois*[8] in 1967 enacted legislation which provided for

---

[3] Spedden *v.* Board of Education, 74 W. Va. 181, 81 S.E. 724.
[4] Washington Code, Chapter 18, 1965.
[5] Massachusetts Code, Chapter 164, Acts of 1965.
[6] California Legislature, Senate Bill No. 28, 1966.
[7] Nevada Code, Chapter 201, 1967.
[8] Illinois Legislature. House Bill 1107 and House Bill 1889, 1967.

more general use of teacher aides than did either the California or Washington statutes.

The Nevada statute is probably the most comprehensive and grants boards of education the power to employ teacher aides and other auxiliary nonprofessional personnel. These personnel must be directly supervised by certificated persons when assisting in instruction, but may not be under such supervision when performing noninstructional duties. The legislature in this state had the good foresight to require that local boards of education, employing aides or auxiliary personnel, develop written policies governing their duties.

State education agency provisions: In recognizing the need for teacher aides, several state boards of education and state departments of education have published statements concerning the use of aides in our public schools. Generally, these provisions have not been adopted as official state regulations and, therefore, do not carry the weight of law, but they do lend guidance and direction in the employment and use of teacher aides.

A recent study by the New England Educational Assessment Project pointed out that the state departments of education in New England have not licensed or certified teacher aides but have issued general statements regarding duties and qualifications of aides.[9] *Maine*, for example, defined a teacher aide as a noncertified person whose duties are limited to assisting a certified teacher. This department of education describes the types of responsibilities which aides may assume in assisting the regular teacher. This statement places limitations on the use of teacher aides in saying that, "aides shall not be used as substitute teachers, to relieve teacher overload, or to replace teachers on leave." Qualifications for aides are also detailed. They are: Aides must be at least seventeen years old, be a graduate of secondary school, have the moral character required of teachers.

Federal programs

Although teacher aides or auxiliary personnel have been used for a number of years by many school districts, a giant step forward was taken

[9] "Teacher Aides in the Classroom, A New England Study," New England Educational Assessment Project, Funded under Title V, Section 505 of the Elementary and Secondary Education Act of 1905, Providence, Rhode Island, November, 1967, pp. 23-27.

in this area by the passage of the Elementary and Secondary Education Act of 1965. This Act provided many school districts with the necessary funds to employ teacher aides to assist with programs for culturally deprived children.

In 1965, the U. S. Office of Education published guidelines[10] which suggested the use of subprofessional personnel for assisting teachers in educating culturally deprived children. The guidelines pointed out that parents may be employed and this might help bridge the communication gap between home and school.

In 1967, the Congress enacted the Education Professions Development Act.[11] This Act provides for state education agencies to submit state plans which include programs to obtain services of teacher aides and to provide them with preservice or inservice training which will enable them to better perform their duties. In order to participate in this program, the state education agency must establish certain standards for teacher aides and should indicate the scope and nature of the duties expected of teacher aides. Also, this Act requires that in order to participate, states must designate the program of state supervision and leadership to be used and develop short and long-range policies and procedures on the use of these federal funds to obtain and train teacher aides.[12]

Authority of Teacher Aides

Teaching: All states have certification laws which require persons to meet certain minimal qualifications before they may become teachers in the schools. Therefore, unless there are statutes providing to the contrary, a teacher aide is not authorized to perform instructional duties or to teach.

The attorney general of at least one state has held that a school district cannot receive state aid allotments for the time pupils spend under the lone supervision of noncertificated persons such as a student teacher or teacher aide. This decision would probably apply to most states that distribute funds on pupil-teacher ratios or classroom units based on the number of teachers employed.[13]

---

[10] "Guidelines, Special Programs for Educationally Deprived Children," Draft, October 8, 1965, Office of Education, H.E.W., p. 20.
[11] Education Professions Development Act. P.L. 90-35, Sec. 520 Title V, Part B. Higher Education Act of 1965, as amended.
[12] "Guide for Preparing a State Plan for Attracting and Qualifying Teachers to Meet Critical Teacher Shortages," Under Part B, Subpart 2 of the Education Professions Development Act (Title V of the Higher Education Act of 1965).
[13] Kentucky, O.A.G. No. 269, 1963.

Regulation of pupil conduct: Some teacher aide duties include situations which require direct contact with pupils and may render the aide at least partially responsible for the conduct and control of pupils. These activities include supervising playgrounds, cafeterias, study halls, the loading and unloading of school buses, and corridor monitoring. Many of these duties formerly belonged to the teachers and administrative personnel.

Unless it is specifically provided for in statute or by state board of education regulation, the teacher aide probably does not have the authority to regulate pupil conduct. There is little case law relating to this problem, but decisions concerning the use of student teachers may be used as a guide. For example, the Supreme Court of *West Virginia* upheld the use of student teachers in the classrooms but ruled they had no authority to control pupil conduct. The court in this case said:

> "The law requires the employment of competent teachers, but there is no express exclusion of assistant or underteachers. The student teachers are not employed, nor have they a particle of authority in management and control. While they are dealing with classes, the regularly employed, competent teachers stand over them and see that recitations are heard and instruction given according to their own judgment, will and discretion. This involves no delegation of their powers".[14]

Swalls, after extensive research concerning the legal status of student teachers, concluded that the weight of evidence seemed to indicate that the student teacher had no authority to regulate pupil conduct.[15] While student teaching activities and teacher aide duties do not precisely coincide, especially where student teachers are allowed to conduct regular class work, a general area of nonprofessional duties and activities exists which would place the two under the same umbrella of common law reasoning.

Liability for Pupil Injury

When teacher aides are assigned tasks involving supervision, they are placed in positions of potential liability for pupil injury. In such a situation, liability is likely to arise out of negligence on the part of the aide. Any person assigned such responsibilities is ignorant at his own peril. If

---

[14] Spedden et al. *v.* Board of Education of Independent School Dist., 81 S.E. 724 (W. Va.).

[15] Swalls, Fred, "Legal Aspects of Student Teaching." Cooperative Research Project, S-075 (Order from the Interstate Printers and Publishers, Inc., Danville, Illinois).

he is not qualified to supervise playgrounds, then he should not try to do it.

In cases involving pupil injury, the courts have traditionally held the teacher to a higher standard of care than that owed to the general public. Likewise, a teacher aide, when placed in a supervisory capacity, owes the pupils a greater standard of care than is normally required in other personal relationships.

Liability of administrator or supervisor: Where the administrator or supervisor appoints a well qualified person to perform certain functions about the school and injury results, the administrator is not liable for negligence. The general rule of law is that in the public school situation the master is not liable for the commissions or omissions of his servant. In a *Rhode Island* case illustrating this principle, the court held that a school principal, who had authority over a school janitor, was not liable for injuries to a school teacher when he failed to warn her of a slippery floor in the school building.[16]

Therefore, a teacher or a principal is not liable for the negligent acts of a properly appointed and qualified teacher aide. On the other hand, if a teacher or a principal assigns duties for which the teacher aide is not qualified and the purposes of which do not fall within the scope of the aide's employment, the teacher or the principal may be liable for negligent acts by the aide.

In a *New York* case,[17] a child was injured during lunch hour in the school gymnasium while under the supervision of the school janitor. The school district was found negligent on the theory that the duty to provide competent supervision had not been met. The court said:

> "By common practice the only supervision, direction or control provided was that of a janitor. It might well be that one employed as a janitor would be competent to direct athletic activities. But the proof here is that the one to whom supervision was entrusted was in fact, a janitor, and nothing else .... It is our view that this was a palpable failure to meet the requirements of the common-law rule, as well as an evident neglect of the duty imposed by the student."

[16] Gray v. Wood, 64 A. 2d 191 (1949).
[17] Garber v. Central School District, 251 App. Div. 214, 295 N.Y. Supp. 850 (1937).

Are You Risking An Arrest And/ Or A Court Suit?

RICHARD D. GALLIAN and R. C. BRADLEY

An Ounce of Prevention is Worth
A Day in Court Any Day

The common law doctrine of governmental immunity, often phrased as "The king can do no wrong," has been an acceptable rule for many years. Schools have been favored by such a belief but the times are changing regarding it. Regardless of change, no one has been immune from the law wherein negligence and/or injury to others could be proven. School people must prepare themselves for many different types of legal battles as legal opinions will be sought on many issues, particularly when one's rights have been breached.

Presently there are some misunderstandings arising with respect to the general ongoing business of the school, and it is clarifying selected aspects of these legal encounters that the major portion of this article will be directed.

Out-of-School Behavior. School people, generally have more concern for the conduct of pupils within the confines of school property than when away from school premises. Especially is this true when it is presumed that the child is under the control of his parents. A quick perusal of court cases reveals that far too many teachers and principals were not knowledgeable of the fact of their responsibilities for the health, safety and welfare of the children in the public school, not only normal school hours, but also encompasses the time from the point at which the child leaves his home until the time the child reaches home again. The amount of time enroute from home to school, and school to home, of course, will depend upon the various circumstances within each school situation. A number of schools throughout the country, in an

Gallian, Richard D., and Bradley, R. C. "Are You Risking An Arrest And/Or A Court Suit?" *The TEPSA Journal.* April 1972. 3:14-16.

effort to decrease the chances of injury as much as possible, advises parents that children are not to ride bicycles to school. In addition, school personnel on their way to school, or on the way home from school, who observe for example, a fight between two school children in which an injury occurs, could conceivably be held responsible for not stopping the fight. This refers back to the belief that the school is responsible as much as possible for the health, safety and welfare of the child.

Parental Notes and Field Trips. Merely to have a note from a parent, which indicates that their child may go on a field trip and releaving the school of responsibility and liability in the event an accident occurs, has little meaning. Although it is advisable that schools obtain whenever possible a written consent from parents or legal guardians to permit the child to go on the field trip, school personnel must remember that they can still be held accountable in the event an accident should occur.

To illustrate, suppose a teacher obtains from parents written permission for their children to go on a field trip away from the school property. Let's further assume that that teacher has enlisted the help of a number of parents to help supervise the children. In the event of an accident a parent can then file suit against a teacher and the school in the name of the child. And the suit does not have to wait until the child reaches the age of twenty-one. A parent waiting until a seven year old reaches twenty-one will surely have exceeded the time provided for in the statute of limitations. Secondly, although a teacher enlisted the help of parents and assigned them the authority to supervise children, this in no way means that the school can escape responsibility in the event of an accident. Primarily, the reason is that parents are not state certificated teaching personnel and as such are not "supposed" to know how to supervise children. This is a school function and a school responsibility and not one wherein responsibility can be delegated.

Leaving Classrooms Unattended. When a teacher leaves a classroom unattended he immediately subjects himself to a charge of negligence in the event a child is injured. Too often when a teacher leaves the room, children (at times) will be prone to sword fight with rulers or poke at one another with pencils, or scissors, or engage in some other enjoyable activity only to injure someone. Should a suit arise over the injury of a child under this set of circumstances the teacher simply has no defensible grounds. If a teacher must leave the room for any reason, then, the teacher should somehow contact the school principal and either get his expressed permission to leave the room, or have him provide a substitute in the room for those minutes the teacher is gone. A school secretary is not a state certificated teacher and thereby cannot be delegated the responsibility for supervising children.

Playground supervision. It is estimated that some 95 percent of all injuries to school children occur on the school ground. Furthermore, there is reason to believe that if the parents wanted to pursue the matter in a court, a good number of suits would have been won by parents. Playground supervision means just what it says. A teacher is to be on the school ground, . . . out watching children play, being ever on guard for any kind of situation that may arise wherein a child could possibly be injured. A teacher who is late to duty, spends time talking to others on the playground or spends time playing games with children is not supervising his assigned area and therefore is open to a charge of negligence in the event of an accident. Often times the occasion arises when a teacher is not feeling well or for some reason or another is unable to be on the school ground play area for supervision. In this instance, it is the responsibility of that teacher to inform the principal that he or she will be unable to be on the assigned duty so that another teacher may be assigned to cover the assigned area. Here again if an accident occurs when no teacher is at an assigned area this leaves that teacher, that principal, and that school district wide open for any court suit that may follow. Accurate, written records of playground and lunchroom rosters are strongly favored here, rather than scheduling or changing daily work schedules by "word of mouth."

Standing Children in the Hallway as Punishment. In view of what has been said in the preceding paragraphs it would seem that the reader has now drawn a conclusion that placing a child in a hallway makes it extremely difficult for that teacher to supervise that child. If a child must be removed from a classroom he should be removed to the principal's office for proper supervision.

Sending Children on Errands. It is rather common practice for teachers to send children on errands not only within the school building but across the street either to a drugstore, dime store, or some other errand;—even to the child's home to pick up some papers that were forgotten. Now the questions here are: (1) In the event of an accident was that child supervised? (2) Did that child leave the teacher's supervision of his own volition or was he sent out on an errand by the teacher? The reader can see the answer to these two questions poses a very serious threat to the teacher's defense.

School Patrols. Although many schools have school patrols the danger of this practice is so enormous the continued practice of the use of school boy patrols fully escapes our understanding. The reason for this is that if a crossing is so dangerous that there must be a crossing guard of some type why must we assign a child to do an adult task? Where dangerous crossings do exist the local police department should be encouraged to provide personnel to cross children at these intersections.

If this is not feasible then an attempt should be made to encourage parents to volunteer to help children cross those areas where mature judgment needs to be exercised. In any event, patrol children should not be directing traffic or moving children into busy interesections.

Corporal Punishment. Corporal punishment is a means of punishment used by many schools. Far too often the punishments chosen go beyond the wisdom engendered to teachers and principals, violating what is generally known to be sound principles of child growth and development. Aside from the emotional trauma involved, consider the legal point of view for a moment.

Although many states in their state codes (or local school board rulings) have something to say about corporal punishment in that a teacher may paddle when a witness is present, the fact remains that any time a teacher or principal strikes another human being, student or not, they run the risk of being arrested for assault and battery. Immediately the question arises from a great many people to the effect that if one cannot paddle how can he maintain order or teach anyone anything? Our courts response to this is, namely: *A teacher is hired to educate, not discipline.*

If one can accept the philosophy of John Dewey, then, paddling and coercion is not education, it is training. If a situation arises and little cooperation is shown after counseling with a child and the parent, then, suspension of a child to the custody of the parents seems to be the best plausible answer. One may argue, "Well, what happens to the child when he is sent home?" An answer to that is, every state has a compulsory education law. It merely states that every child shall be educated. It does not dictate to the parent *where* that child shall be educated. If the presence of that child and his behavior causes disruption or injury or harm to other children or to teachers then that child should be removed to the custody of the parent. If a parent sees fit to spank a child then that is his prerogative—not the schools.

Summary and Recommendations. Some rules adopted by boards of education unfortunately, or perhaps fortunately, are in conflict with state and federal constitution. Some local policies, if upheld by a court, do little to diminish the mental anguish of teachers during the ensuing months before final court decisions are made. Another point to ponder is, suppose that there is some sort of legal litigation. Who pays for legal counsel for the teacher? Often teachers are led to believe that the school district will pay for the teacher's attorney. This is misleading to say the least. Generally, school districts *shall* pay the legal fees if teacher and district are named together. However, if a school employee is named in a suit without the district being named, the district may at its own discretion provide legal service for the teacher. At any rate, the teacher suffers mental anguish and emotional strain even if the problem is solved out of court.

In the event of injury to children, one of the first questions to be asked will be "Was there a competent professional certificated person on duty supervising the children's activity?" Secondly, was the danger foreseeable and had the children been properly warned? If the answer to those two questions is negative then there is very little hope for an adequate defence in court. All of us who have worked within public schools know that accidents will incur. Indeed, even if each child has a supervisor by his side invariably some accident could occur. But it must be shown that adequate and competent supervision was available and on duty.

In order to insure the teacher of some sort of financial aid should a court case arise it is strongly urged that teachers and principals obtain a professional liability insurance policy. Indeed, a number of districts suggest that their teachers and student teachers obtain professional liability insurance. Moreover, some superintendents do not accept student teachers into their programs unless that student teacher has a state issued substitute credential and professional liability insurance. Members of Texas State Teachers Association have some protective insurance provided them; however, it is not always enough.

These are only a few of the many hundreds of questions asked about teachers and school personnel liability in working with children. Hopefully this short discourse will interest the reader enough to want to pursue the matter further. It must be realized that in spite of all the different opinions expressed by those interested in law and teaching, the final definite decision rests in a court. Are you willing to continue the risk? What school policies do you have now that the strongest legal encounterment would affirmatively support? What policies need modification and clarification with your staff?

SCHOOL is for . . .
FORMING LASTING
FRIENDSHIPS

Chapter XV

The Teacher As A Community Leader

The initiative for a sound public relations program for the schools obviously rests with teachers and administrators. Since the public estimate of any profession is roughly an accurate one, each teacher will want to improve his public image. But moreover, the teacher should assume a citizen's rightful responsibility in the life of the community in the school area which he serves. Perhaps it is only when a teacher does not participate in social, civic, and community affairs that he is considered different.

The good teacher must not only be good in the classroom but consistently good as a leader outside the confines of the school. The merits, accomplishments, and total program of the school should be common knowledge to all teachers of the school district. It is always easier to assume leadership responsibilities,—to defend practices, to promote new programs, or merely tell the story of the school—when one has already analyzed the strengths and weaknesses of his school.

More and more communities are seeking school direction in community activities, and all teachers are being given credit for their share in undertaking community responsibilities. Helping the teacher find meaning in the opportunities for helpfulness and leadership which life in the community affords, is the purpose with which the following selections purport to deal. But knowledge of strategem without the concomitant understandings as those that students have beliefs, feelings, and worth can be likened to a ship without a sail. The teacher who is able to anchor his thoughts to both *strategy* and *love* will not only have smooth sailing with children but will know the harbors into which he sails and more likely reach the distant ports. Commitment to teach goes much beyond the written contractual agreement. Commitment is the extent of one's willingness to share himself with pupils, parents, community and his profession.

Teacher–Community:
Surveying Three Worlds

SISTER MARIAN LEONA TOBRINER, SNJM

Contemporary American Society has emerged as a competitive, pluralistic, dynamic polity, quivering with the glory and the challenge of a summer stroll on the Sea of Tranquility. Nevertheless, the nation remains morosely inert and discouraged at the illogic and disorder of perennial ghettos and barrios. Problems and possibilities come in such staggering sizes that, among others, teachers suffer the symptomatic inertia of a cultural lag.

They find they are not appropriate to co-existent crises. Their actions, repetitive and non-functional, appear meaningless to students and society alike (even if for contrary reasons); and they almost suspect (shocked!) that their lessons reflect only another era. Responding creatively to an entire age may mean, rather, living creatively for a single moment; comprehending the society may mean coming to understand the local community for the microcosmos which it is, here and now, for teacher and learner alike.

One-fifth of all Americans this year will move their residence. Mobility at that rate would keep a teacher from assuming that his community can be "caught" and studied like a frozen specimen under a microscope. However, in the history of American education, perhaps even to the beginning of the twentieth century, schools were so much a part of communities that each were almost interchangeable. The boy-apprentice in the butcher's, the baker's, and the candlestickmaker's workroom participated simultaneously in the social, economic, and educational systems of the society.

Almost three-quarters of a century ago men like Francis Parker and John Dewey plotted a new direction for education in a new era: the

Tobriner, Sister Marian Leona. "Teacher-Community: Surveying Three Worlds." *The Clearing House.* March 1970. 44:391-394.

school should be a small duplicate of the larger society. From his earliest years in the schools, the American child was to *live* his society. Its components were the classroom's components; in a sense, this arrangement almost inverted the historical form. Where once the school existed within the society, now the society existed within the schools, with the largest emphasis placed on the American orientation to democracy.

Whatever the motive, the contemporary school entering the Seventies has assumed the role of acting, and re-acting, agent in the community. The school knowingly acts upon the society and, in turn, is consciously receptive to society's press. Such complementary growth profits both structures in their organized, cohesive, and rational responses to each other, transforming each other into the new mode requisite for the twenty-first century.

Further, in sheer defiance of the faceless bulk of big government, big business, big industry, and big society in megalopolis, men and women have turned to the local community in affirmation of their very smallness and their individuality. The people of the disadvantaged communities, never having departed from their extended families in the first place, have viewed the local community as an intrinsic means of coping with society's rejection. And significantly, ethnic minorities have parried the thrust of closed-circuit white racism by demanding local exclusivism for their children in their constraint toward racial self-awareness.

Because of this drift to local control, the contemporary teacher must look upon the task of studying his local community as one of strictest obligation. The teacher new to a locality, yet understanding himself in his three-fold role—transmitter of culture, interpreter of the present, change-agent for the future—will look to himself, his school, and its neighborhood with its concentric enlargements as areas of introspection and research.

In the first place, his survey will undoubtedly begin in the small world of himself. He was, and is, himself a learner: of what education is he a product? Which era was his "present"? For which future was he prepared? What is his own culture, in its anthropological sense? To which socioeconomic class, with its attendant value system, does he belong? Is he geographically and socially mobile? What roles does he play in the school in his relations with students, other teachers, administrators, supervisors, community members, parents, his own family and friends, his own local community (if he is not a member of the community in which he teaches)? Answers to such questions locate the boundaries of one's personal commonwealth.

Secondly, the teacher will turn to the topography of his school community. It would be a truism to define the school as a society, replete as it is with a culture and a social structure uniquely its own.

Bimodal in its age levels—that is, with a statistical "generation gap" separating two normal curves of faculty and student age-distributions—the society is further structured by time: the number of years of schooling provided by the school, the number of grades required for graduation, the number of days per school year, minutes per day, minutes per class-subject period. The very school building itself molds the learning-teaching society: its rigidity or flexibility of space, its allowance for flow in the grounds and in the classrooms, the physical locale of the institution, its architecture, and aesthetic inner and outer environment.

The teacher's interactions with school personnel necessarily form into "political" and social configurations, giving evidence of a four-quadrant human interplay. The traditions, mores, and folkways of the school further reveal the educational community in its own unique existence.

Diversity characterizes the ordinary school. Socially distinct groups form, each with their own subculture. Codes of governance, written and unwritten, rise in response to the need for dialog between authority and the governed. Beliefs about what "should" be done conflict with practice. Motivations of parents and children color the directions taken in day-to-day schooling. Ethnic groups enter the social arena with urgencies both human and political.

The concerned teacher sensitizes himself to these realities, aware of their dependencies, cross-purposes, and intrapolations. He becomes skilled in assessing movements of persons and conformations of ambitions. He participates in the formal power structure—whether political or social—as a concerned citizen and private individual, both for his own purposes and as a teaching situation for students and community. He searches out the informal power structures—not necessarily visible—because he has learned that *where* the last word was spoken, and *who* said it, is frequently a clue to the significant utterance.

Widening his scope from self to school, and from school to community, the vigilant teacher finds that honest altruism (plus a hint of professionalism) will provide strategies for measuring the community geography. For example, he might graphically inscribe on a street map the existence of subcommunities, neighborhoods, and subcultural centers, visually providing for himself the gross community in which his students are situated. Then his specific options for plotting his young population include the use of flagged pins to indicate simply the presence of a child in that location, colored dots to indicate the number of children in a family, colored pins to show the school-grade level, or a variation and combination of still other signals.

As an alternative, if not a companion-piece, he may make an

informal demographic study of the community. Census Tract Summaries, available from federal or state population survey offices, proffer a wealth of socio-economic statistics. The blocks reviewed by a Census Tract analysis are so specific that the teacher finds available a summary of the very area and inhabitants of his community. To cite the general type of information thus accessible, he will note such factors as the infant mortality rate, ethnicity, marital status, income distribution, types of occupation, rate of employment, condition of housing, and levels of education in the community.

The decennial federal census is taken early in 1970, with computers producing some statistics by the fall of the same year. Unless the teacher's own locale has conducted an interim census (as some of the larger metropolitan areas have done), he may discover that the conditions of the 1960 census have changed radically, even to the point of being descriptively valueless. However, the new results in 1970 should be ready shortly for profitable investigation.

State or county population offices, social planning groups both private and public, commissions on human relations, and similar bodies concerned with the human condition regularly publish predictions and analyses. And finally, information can be garnered from regional and local banks in their economic studies of communities.

Again, the teacher's determination to know his community might lead to an informal sociological study accomplished through self-structured observation. If he were to make his school the center of an imaginary circle, he would personally drive the circumference within which he defines the local community. He would literally travel up one street and down another, noting the distinctions of class and culture perceptible even one block away from each other. Here is where the children of his classroom dwell; here is where he learns *who* and *why* they are, in much the same way in which the children learn these very concepts themselves.

Knowing that he is not a professional researcher, he takes the freedom of the amateur in looking for significant clues, valuable to himself rather than to formal investigators. He will note the kind of homes, whether single family, duplexes, or multiple family dwellings; whether they show signs of dilapidation or deterioration; whether possession is by rental or ownership. Further observations focus on cars typical of the neighborhood, the number in each family, their condition, and the other transportation available to a non-driver; the normal noise level of the area; the proximity of industry; kinds of food served in local restaurants; kinds of food available in the ordinary stores of the community (often a hint to the strength of ethnic traditions and customs); apparent leisure time activities of the men and women of the neighborhood; play habits of the children; status and activities of adolescents; senior citizens' facilities; the authority exerted by parents (as, for example, the apparent obedience of children when called in from play); the visibility of cigarettes, drugs, narcotics, and alcohol among children, teen-agers, and adults; number and location of churches; garbage pick-up; kinds of reading favored at the public library or purchased from magazine and paperbacks racks; and other typical social (that is, human) interests, concerns, or drives manifested publicly.

Growing in functional insight into his local community fulfills one of the teacher's largest obligations to society and himself. In time, the community may come to study its own past, examine its means of coping with the present, and set its directions for a deliberately selected future. If both teachers and community consciously scrutinized the structure and culture of their mutual society, the center of erstwhile conflicts between school and community might well evolve into a meaningful education for the child, ultimately the professed ambition of both bodies.

The growing trend toward local control of education within the larger school system—as evidenced by experiments in New York, Chicago, Oakland, and to a lesser extent Los Angeles—gives hint of the future of governance and responsibility. If the experiments grow into wider practice, knowing his local community will be crucial to the teacher's professional and teaching competence. If the experiments fade into failures, the continuing need for tempering the anonymity of metropolitan or megalopolitan education with local acquaintance will be crucial to both the students' and the teacher's social and psychological durability.

In any case, awareness of the relation between school and community remains in the best American tradition, not as though the school were a mirror of the larger society, but rather as a human agent. Together, positively and affirmatively acting and reacting *in* and *with* and *through* each other, school and society enhance their mutual task of enculturating the young citizen in his past, interpreting his present, and readying both him and his future.

Public Relations for Today's School

IRA WILDER

Maintaining a friendly and favorable attitude of the public toward the schools is a never-ending job. What the public in one community thinks of the schools affects the attitude of the larger public in the nation.

Public relations means the winning, or retaining, of the good will and friendship of the public as a whole. "The art of winning friends" is an excellent description, but not an adequate definition. To understand public relations, it is as important to tell what it is *not* as to tell what it is. For it is more than the winning of friends among the people of the community, although that has a very important bearing upon public relations. It is more than the winning of supporters for the policies and goals of the public schools.

With most private business firms public relations is applied largely toward protecting the right of the institution to exist or to operate under certain favorable conditions. That right may be threatened by legislation, public condemnation, or conflicts and disturbances in which the public attitude, as expressed in police protection, may be the deciding factor. Not only private business firms but all institutions exist under sufferance of the public, even the most despotic dictatorships.

There is a new public every day. Every day more than 20,000 people in America become 21 yeas of age; more than 13,000 die and are a part of the public no longer. Furthermore, the shape and structure of the public changes daily. New leaders arise and old ones are pushed aside. The school has an excellent opportunity to sell itself to the boys and girls who will be the public. We, as educators in the public schools, must demonstrate every day that we are acting in the public interest.

Anybody who does business with the public is in a public business

---

Wilder, Ira. "Public Relations for Today's School." *The Clearing House.* May 1971. 45:537.

and subject to regulation by the public in many ways. The public lays down the rules for its service, partially in laws and partially in public opinion. At any time the public opinion may crystallize into a law or decree.

It is becoming a truism to say that in a democracy all public schools exist and continue to operate by virtue of meeting the needs of all of the children of all of the people. This era in history is already being termed the "era of the crowd." More and more the public is having a voice in determining how our schools, business, and governments are conducted. Strong, intelligent, courageous leadership is more than ever a necessity today in order to guide the public and create the right attitudes toward schools.

If we, in educational institutions, have a large measure of public approval and if the public has a large measure of confidence in us (confidence meaning that we are conducting our schools in the public interest), schools will be given ample freedom. The public can, and must, in its own interest, judge wisely the amount of control it wishes to retain over its schools.

As some regard it, the basic problem of public relations is to reconcile or adjust in the public interest those aspects of our personal and institutional behavior which have a public significance. The business of educating boys and girls of all interests, abilities, and aptitudes must be studied in relation to the total needs of our youth. The faculty, administration, and board of education should be assisted and advised by a good public relations official who is something more than a publicist, a journalist, or a statistician. The importance of such an individual to a modern school system cannot be overestimated. If any school person says, "I do not care what the public thinks about my school," that teacher, administrator, or board member is a liability to all of the schools. No public school has any moral right to allow itself to be unexplained, misunderstood, or publicly distrusted.

In our public relations we must try to get favorable public opinion by three definite steps. The first is to find out what the public actually thinks about our schools. The second is to change the practices or policies to which the public objects, provided these objections are reasonable, and to emphasize more those practices to which the public gives approval. Third, we must supply complete information to the public and map a program of enlightenment aimed to dissuade the public of unfavorable attitudes and to encourage favorable ones.

Politics is for Everyone Especially Teachers

MRS. WATKINS C. SMITH

When an educator accepts his professional responsibilities with pride and really cares about his community, he will become a "political citizen." He will express his concern, whether it be for educational improvement or for action that will help make our country a better place for all of us.

The National Education Association has by formal resolution stated its belief: that every educator has not only the right but also the obligation to be an informed and active citizen. NEA's Citizenship Committee states: "Many good people look with distaste on politics. To disparage the political processes necessary to democratic government is to deny and to destroy the very foundations upon which this country rests. Our nation cannot afford to have teachers with this attitude."

For a long time many school divisions forced employees who became involved in politics to give it up or lose their jobs. Then, too, it has been my observation as a teacher that the great majority of educators have been all too willing to "let George do it," and the few who were active in political matters seemed to have little influence.

It need not be this way.

NEA has recommended consistently that every educational system guarantee to all its employees full equality with other citizens in exercising their political rights and responsibilities. Involvement in public decision-making is an exciting, challenging adventure. Teachers should be among the best qualified to lead and, above all others, they are in a position to speak about the needs of the schools.

Smith, Watkins C. "Politics is for Everyone—Especially Teachers." *American Vocational Journal.* May 1972. 47:47-48.

Basic Political Skills

In order to be effective, we must have basic political information and develop basic political skills. How?

First, each of us should be registered and vote in all elections. We should discuss, help formulate policy in groups such as the local education association, openly and energetically support candidates and platforms, distribute information, and write letters to editors and government officials. We should take a position when there is a referendum and work tirelessly for what we think is right.

Teachers, however, must be careful to influence by example and indirection—never by coercion. We should keep the teaching function and personal participation in politics scrupulously separated. There should be no partisan advocacy and political activity while on school premises during school hours. In the classroom, we must conscientiously strive to give a balanced presentation of issues.

Today, it is recognized that the best leadership in political matters is provided by groups such as education associations, League of Women Voters, local newspapers, and retired citizens—to name only a few. The individual should align himself with an action group, be outspoken as it formulates its program of action, then help promote the plan until what he wants becomes a reality even if it takes a while.

Keep Working at It

Some persons are easily discouraged. If a matter they have gotten all fired up about doesn't materialize immediately, they lose interest and spend their time and effort berating those who seem to be blocking it. Keep working at it. Here are several suggestions.

- *Choose your candidate and work for him.* It's fun, especially organizing "meet-the-candidate" meetings. Even if you are able to influence only a few votes for him, it is a thrill to help him celebrate his victory. If he loses, commiserate with him; everybody can't win. Better luck next time.
- *Know your elected officials, how they stand on pending legislation,* and how they voted on past legislation. Personal visits are effective if you keep the conference friendly, personal and informal. Invite a legislator to have lunch with you at school. It is extremely important that we help keep our lawmakers informed. Teachers can do this in all levels of government.

    Most public officals are conscientious public servants who deserve respect. They are trying to do a good job, and they will give serious consideration to any matter that they are convinced enjoys widespread support among their constituents. They want us to make a clear distinction between fact and argument. We should not burden them with matters that we would not consider if we were in their places.

● *Write your legislators.* But there is a right time to write—maybe when a bill is being formulated, sometimes to a committeeman while a bill is being considered, and, the best time of all, when a bill is headed for floor action.

Keep your letters short and sincere. Clearly state your position and your reasons. One U.S. representative commented that it is not enough to know who is for or against a proposed law; legislators need to know *why* this stand was taken.

Legislators say that form letters are not as convincing as personal letters. One representative went so far as to state that "one thoughtful, factual, well-reasoned letter carries more weight than 100 form letters or printed post cards."

● *Be tactful.* Don't approach a winning candidate (even if you worked hard for his election) with a platform immediately. Give him time to catch his breath. Write him if there is something you especially want him to remember; you can't bank on his having taken notes in previous discussions.

When you write, you can be informal; if you forget the proper form and don't have a ready reference, write anyway. It is good, however, to know that you address elected officials as "The Honorable (full name)—Dear Senator, Mayor, etc., or Dear Sir." "Yours sincerely" is always in good taste as a close. If you use the title "Miss" or "Mrs.," enclose it in parentheses.

● *Ask your legislators for progress reports.* Share these with your associates. You can have access to copies of all printed bills so that you can better express your views on them. Get on your legislators' mailing lists. They like to send you their newsletters.

Don't forget to write that "Thank-you" letter.

Contributions, of any size, are always gratefully accepted and add to the aggregate; running for even a small office is expensive.

● *If you have the qualifications and the desire, don't hesitate to run for public office.* Educators throughout the country are now serving on city councils, boards of supervisors, in State legislatures. In order to become elected, you must create an organization and be willing to spend some money—the amount will no doubt depend on the backing you can get from your party.

Remember, your willingness to assert yourself fully as a citizen, including active participation, is vital to the pursuit of high quality education and to the continuance of good, democratic government.

You, Too, Can Be A Leader

LAUREL M. PENNOCK*

Few things in this world are admired more than leadership. Have you ever wondered if you, too, qualify to be a leader? Of course, you have. Almost everybody asks himself, one time or the other, what it takes to be a leader?

I do not believe that people are born leaders.

The five qualities of leadership, which I consider most important, are within the reach of most everyone. You, too, can be a leader, if you really want to.

1. *The leader cares deeply*

First of all, the leader is a person who cares. He has a concern about something. The popular view of a leader is that of a good talker. Of course, it helps to be able to speak well, but before you can say anything, you've got *to have something to say*. There must be something on your mind, something that moves you, excites you or bothers you. All progress begins with someone troubled. Thomas Surgrue remarked:

> "If man had not been troubled millions of years ago, he would still be living in caves. If he is not troubled now, and does not remain troubled, he will soon be back in the caves."

Leaders in all walks of life are those who are dissatisfied with the way things are. The automobile was invented only because somebody was no longer satisfied with the speed of the horse and buggy. Every political reform originated with some discontent. Leaders are those who have a special sensitivity that tells them that something is wrong or not quite as good as it can be and want to do something about it.

---

*Laurel M. Pennock, a native of Minnesota, was named Assistant Executive Secretary of the National Association of Elementary School Principals in February 1968. In September 1969 he was promoted to the position of Associate Executive Secretary and in September 1971 to Deputy Executive Secretary.

Pennock, Laurel M. "You, Too, Can be a Leader." *ODESP Journal*. November 1971. 7:23-24.

Annie Besant, one of the first great leaders in the movement for the Independence of India, put it this way:

> "Someone ought to do it, but *why should I?*
> Someone ought to do it, so *why not I?*"

Between these two sentences lies the difference between the non-leader and the leader. The leader responds to a need. He takes personal responsibility for meeting it because, deep down in his heart *he cares.*

2. *The leader is in contact with people*

There must be many compassionate and concerned people, but they do not become leaders for one good reason: they never tell anybody. Leadership is being with the people, knowing them and being known by them. Before anybody can march in front of the people, he has to walk among them. The leader must mingle and not with just one clique. He must lend a willing ear to everybody and not mind talking to anyone. Someone said that leaders are like the long nails that hold various boards together. Leaders must be broadminded enough to associate with all kinds of people. He can hold them together in a group only because he has contact with each of them.

3. *The leader is a step ahead*

The third leadership quality in initiative. Simply and plainly defined, a leader is a man who has followers. He is followed not because of mysterious power or force but simply because he keeps a step ahead of the rest. He is a pace-setter who is usually the first to offer an idea or suggestion. He is a "self-starter." He does not wait for others to push him. He has plans and talks about them and tries to set them in motion. The one who makes the first good suggestion is usually the one whom the group wants to follow. This truth a veteran leader, who had more than his share of leadership, stated in poetic form:

> At every meeting I attend,
>   Temptation is attractive
> To stand and let them know my thoughts—
>   But I remain inactive.
> Although I'm full of good ideas
>   And wonderful suggestions
> I swallow them and say no word,
>   Refrain from asking questions.
> For each time that I've had my say,
>   I always came to rue it—
> *They praised my fine suggestion and*
>   *Appointed me to do it!*

An old French definition of leadership is:

> *"To Govern is to Foresee."*

In plain words, the leader keeps a step ahead.

4. *The leader does not "boss" but encourages his followers*

A popular misconception of leadership is that he must be a boss. The truth—and this is the fourth characteristic of good leadership—is that the leader does *not* say, "Get going!" Instead he says, "Let's go!" and leads the way. He does not walk behind with a whip; he is out in front with a banner. He leads by example. He does not coerce—he inspires. He assumes that his followers are working *with* him, not for him. The leader respects the people around him. He has faith in their responsibilities.

John Buchanan, author, general of the army and later Governor General of Canada, who was an outstanding leader himself, said:

> "The test of leadership is not to put greatness into humanity, but to elicit it, for the greatness is already there."

A truly great leader is a man builder. He helps those under him to grow big. He does not hold down those who rival his own abilities, but he lifts them up higher still so that they, too, might scale the peak of leadership.

Great leaders rid themselves of envy. They encourage an idea even if it is not their own. A good leader takes a little more than his share of the blame when things go wrong—and a little less than his share of the credit when things go well.

5. *The leader does not hate his critic*

Finally, the good leader accepts criticism. He knows that leadership is like trying to dance in a nightclub. No matter what you do, you rub somebody the wrong way. It is not necessary for him to win every argument. He can live with himself and others when he makes mistakes, for he knows that leaders, too, are human. He is humble enough to pay attention to the critic and sincere enough to put the cause above personal pride or sensitivity.

None of the leadership qualities I have mentioned are beyond the reach of normal people. If you are the kind of person,

who cares deeply about something,
who likes to mingle with people,
who is quick to volunteer ideas and help,
whose example is good enough to inspire others
and who can listen to criticism without hating
the critic.

—if you fit this description, you, too can be a leader!

Chapter XVI

The Teacher and Commitment

The old-style, prim and proper *schoolmarm* is gone from the educational scene, her replacements strategists of a new breed. Her demise is not an unmixed blessing. Certainly there has been need of change in education. The subject of education now is immersed in how best to anchor oneself to "the changing world", and an educational system that failed to adapt to it would stagnate and fall short of its teaching goals.

But accompanying this change is an unfortunate trend, in teaching, as in all fields, to act on the mistaken belief that the need for change requires a rejection of all that has been accomplished in the past. The major purpose of this Chapter is to help effect certain changes, but these authors would not want any beginning teacher to turn his back on the good which has been brought forth by established field teachers during the past decades.

The schoolmarm was overworked and underpaid, but she was also respected, honored, loved. She was dedicated and this commitment molded her community, our country, and the world. Most educators know that the appreciation shown for her was not expressed by high salary, shorter working hours, or low teacher-pupil ratio. What she did was based primarily on personal dedication and professional commitment.

Likewise it should be remembered that the school teacher of yesteryear may not have been adequately progressive in failing to use the best sellers in her literature classes, but she did manage to teach English, spelling and penmanship. She may not have participated in street marches to symbolize her concern for human rights, but she did impart to her students an understanding and regard for the law and the need for the type of citizens who would go on protecting the rights of others. She may not have been properly conversant with behavioral modification experts or those more learned today about behavioral objectives, but she managed to teach decency, justice and selfless citizenship exemplified by example of her own behavior. Thus in many ways the experienced teacher has set excellent exemplars for new teachers to study and follow.

Consequently it is hoped that the contents of this Chapter will be used not only to improve one's commitment to teaching tasks and roles but to increase the attraction of the beginning *teaching specialist* to what great teachers have done for pupils for many, many years,—*increased their love of learning* and provided them with *a sense of pride, respect* and *accomplishment.*

Teaching should always be a human relationship. To behave effectively first year teachers must possess precise understandings about pupils and their capabilities. To be sure if one is truly a good teacher he must have *instructional power:* the kind derived from knowledges of a variety of teaching strategies.

SCHOOL is for . . .
PUPILS TEACHING
ONE ANOTHER

The Challenge of Teaching

BRUCE B. CLARK

Many years ago, when I was an unmarried young man, I used to give a series of lectures on marriage and parenthood. Now that I have been married more than twenty years and am the father of six children, I wouldn't dare pose as an authority on either marriage or parenthood.

Perhaps I should have the same reluctance to discuss teaching now that I have been a professional teacher for some twenty years also. But through these years, both as a teacher and as a supervisor of teachers, I have arrived at what seem to me some useful conclusions which I would like to share.

In doing so I want it clearly understood that I regard teaching, at whatever level, from kindergarten through college, as one of the world's great professional challenges. Indeed no role, unless it is parenthood, provides a more awesome challenge. The responsibilities resting on the shoulders of a teacher, as all good teachers know, are both frightening and wonderful.

Because I am an English teacher, what I say will apply especially to the teaching of English. I hope, however, that I have spread the focus enough to cover the broad field of teaching as a whole.

As a beginning let me describe seven types of teachers that I feel a young teacher should determine with all his willpower never to become:

(1) First is the sentimentalist—the teacher who reacts emotionally to everything and everyone he teaches. I don't believe a teacher can get away with gushy sentimentality even in grade school. The children will see through it and mock it. Certainly in junior high and high school the weepy or saccharine teacher will be looked on by students as both shallow and weak. The ineffectiveness, indeed the harm, of such a teacher in college is so obvious as to need no comment. We cannot teach those who do not respect us, and no one respects the sentimentalist, not even his fellow sentimentalists. (I am not, of course, talking against genuine sentiment, which has its place in education as in life and lies at

the center of literature. The difference between sentiment and sentimentality is the difference between emotion that is honest and emotion
that is cheap, surfacy, and false.)

(2) Second is the cynic—the sophisticated intellectual egotist who
believes in nothing, not even the subject that he teaches. He analyzes to
scorn and examines to ridicule. Criticism for him means hyper-criticism.
He is skilled at finding fault with all that he reads and with all of the
students he teaches. In his role as teacher he is at the opposite extreme
from the sentimentalist, scorning all forms of sentiment, both the true
and the imitative; and in his dread of being regarded as "soft" or "wholesome" he sustains a pose of flippancy and snobbish boredom. Students
may learn from such a teacher, but often he will do them harm greater
than the help he gives.

(3) The third undesirable type, the sadist, is a first cousin of the
cynic. His attitude towards everything, including especially his students,
is negative always, and he prides himself in failing as many students as
possible, justifying himself by his "high academic standards." He delights
in student blunders because they give him an opportunity to ridicule. His
students are in the grip of his power, and he punishes them without
mercy, finding fault equally with all that they do and all that they don't
do, much like a Setebos delighting in the plight of a Caliban. He enjoys
the suffering of others and seems even to get a masochistic pleasure out
of his own sour attitude. Pessimism is his dominant mood, sarcasm is his
main weapon, low grades are his principal threats, and his students are his
victims.

(4) Fourth is the egoistic show-off, the teacher who uses his classroom mostly as a theater in which to parade his personality before a
captive audience. He is so interested in himself that he has little concern
for others, including especially his students. Whether they learn or don't
learn, whether they fail or pass, is secondary to the marvelous experience
they have of seeing and hearing him, and he hopes that they appreciate
him as he deserves to be appreciated. In my criticism of such a teacher, I
don't want to imply that teaching should be dull and flat. Quite the
contrary, it should be as vivid as possible, and every good teacher is
properly part showman, perhaps even with a tinge of the prima donna in
his nature. But teaching that focuses on the teacher's desire to display
himself rather than on the needs of the students will always, I think, be
bad teaching.

(5) Fifth is the faddist, the hobbyhorse rider, the teacher with
narrow interests who cannot see beyond his own myopia. Here we find
the classicist who sees nothing of value in modern literature and art, and
the modernist who views all literature and art before 1900 as uselessly
old-fashioned; the American enthusiast who won't waste his or his
students' time on foreign works, and the traditionalist who feels that
only the uninformed will stoop to read an American book; the preacher-
type teacher who turns art into a tool for instruction, using only those
works that are explicitly didactic, and the obscurantist who scorns anything that can be understood; the scientist who sees nothing worthwhile
in art, the artist who sees nothing worthwhile in science, and the moralist
who sees nothing worthwhile in either art or science. Narrowness and
prejudice can ruin an otherwise able teacher, who in his limited vision
often becomes a cultist crusading to shape his students in his own narrow
image and labeling as evil anyone who doesn't share his constricted views.
In religion and philosophy such narrowness can be especially dangerous,
for one narrow man's orthodoxy may well be another narrow man's
heresy. In religion, as in philosophy, as in literature, as in art, as in
education, as in the whole of life itself, the broad view should be culti-

vated, not at the sacrifice of truth or of critical standards, but with the reward of truth and of deepened critical standards.

(6) Sixth is the information-giver, the teacher who deludes himself into believing that he is fulfilling his teaching role when, like a machine, he feeds students a mass of facts and has them parrot the information back in examinations. Years ago I took a course in Shakespeare from a famous Shakespearean scholar. I looked forward to the course with excitement—and left it with disappointment. In it we learned every detail of Shakespeare's life, every date in and around his career, multitudinous facts about the publication of all his plays, and about their sources, innumerable items of information about the Shakespearean theater, and the language of Shakespeare's London, and the politics of Shakespeare's England. Everything, in short, except an understanding of Shakespeare's writings. We had missed the most important thing; and with this missed, all of the other things were of little importance. I am not suggesting that knowledge is unimportant. It is very important, both as an end in itself and as a tool. But beyond knowledge lie principles and relationships and thought-processes and value-judgments that should be the ultimate concern of both a teacher and his students. Ignorance is dangerous, but knowledge without responsibility may be more dangerous. More than to give information, a teacher needs to help guide a student's mind to think, and even beyond that, to help him shape his character. Giving information is easy. Forming a thinking mind is hard. And shaping a strong character is hardest of all, partly because it must be shaped mostly from within. Giving information is only the beginning of a teacher's responsibility; the end is to stimulate, excite, motivate, lift, challenge, inspire.

(7) Seventh is the "wage-earner teacher," the person for whom teaching is primarily just a job, just a way to make a living. I am not implying that a teacher should work for a sub-standard salary; he should not. As a highly trained professional person, he is worthy of an adequate salary and should get it. But if he is a first-quality teacher he will work for higher wages than money. His reward will be the growth of his students' and of his own vision, and the satisfaction of unselfishly giving himself in the service of the human struggle upward. As teachers we must resist the trend of our time to demand more and more money for less and less work, and we should also resist a growing tendency among ourselves to waste our energy in complaining about salaries and about the burden of papers to correct and students to advise and committees to serve on. We need to subdue any feeling within us that teaching is just a job and cultivate an attitude of dedication in our work. At least we must do this if we want to rise above being mere wage-earners and become great teachers.

Up to this point I have been talking mostly about extreme attitudes that as teachers we should avoid. Let me shift ground a little now and talk more directly about our goals in teaching. First, I believe, we should recognize that above all else we exist professionally to serve our students. This means that we should be concerned about them and available to them, outside the classroom as well as in it, for much of our best teaching is done outside the classroom. If we hide from our students, making ourselves as inaccessible as possible, we are neglecting one of our major responsibilities.

Some say we should be as objective as possible in teaching, treating each student impersonally. To the extent that this applies to standards of grading, I agree that it is the proper and necessary attitude; but to the extent that it applies to our relationship with the personalities of the students, I am convinced that complete objectivity is inadequate, harmful, and also, fortunately, impossible. We must see them as individuals! Every student is a unique personality and must be approached uniquely. The right way of handling one student may well be the wrong way for another, and we must treat each as sensitively and wisely as possible.

I remember a boy suffering from cerebral palsy whose brilliant mind was hampered with spasms that weakened the control of his body. He needed special arrangements to complete his examinations, and I would have been inexcusably unfair if I had treated him the same as the other students.

That boy's uniqueness was, of course, visible and invited immediate sympathy. Sometimes the injury is hidden inside. I remember a Freshman English student who was so torn emotionally that she could not complete some of her assignments. A few months earlier her father had shot her mother and stuffed the body down an abandoned well because the mother had caught the father molesting this girl, his own daughter. The father then shot himself as a posse approached his hideout in a clump of mountain trees. This girl had seen too much of life and too little of love. She needed the special understanding that a teacher can give when the parents have failed.

Sometimes, too, we must be firm and seemingly harsh. It is easier to be tenderly considerate than to be rigid, but sometimes rigidity is needed. I remember a boy who asked me to falsify a grade because he said he was suffering from an incurable disease and did not want to die with a "D" on his record. He was a brash boy who had never learned to be honest with himself; always he had found a way to maneuver around the truth. I told him that it was better to die with a "D" on his record than with a lie on his conscience. This is the cruellest thing I have ever told a student, but it was right. At least I *think* it was right.

These are dramatic examples. But, in less extreme ways, all of our students are unique personalities and need to be treated as such if we are to influence them beyond just feeding them information. I shall never forget the student who came to my office several years ago and said, "You are the worst teacher I ever had, and I've had some bad ones." I was stung by his comment, not by the falseness of it but because, as I thought the course over, it was true. I *was* his worst teacher. At least I was for him a bad teacher. He had special academic problems and I had failed to help him overcome them. I may have been a good teacher for other students in the class, but I was a bad teacher for this particular student. Our responsibility is not only to teach *part* of the students but to teach *all* of them who come to us. And when a student fails, a teacher fails also.

I suppose there has never been a teacher skilled and powerful enough to reach all his students, but we need to try. There is the student who sleeps with bored or weary eyes, and the one who sleeps with eyes open but mind closed; the one who says "I dare you to teach me," and the one who, like a sponge, uncritically absorbs everything; the girl who has learned to use her body more than her mind, and the boy who spends his time looking at her; the would-be writer who thinks that his small talent excuses him from learning anything, and the memorizer who mistakenly assumes that an accumulation of facts equals genuine knowledge; the girl who always has a sympathy-winning explanation for her failure to learn, and the boy who has brilliant possibilities but is so torn in the depths of his own thoughts that all we can see is a tangled mass of potentiality; the student who tries very hard and is very sweet and very wholesome but just doesn't have the mental strength to come through, and the one who terrifies because he is obviously brighter than the teacher; the gregarious student whose personality makes him always the center of a circle, and the one who is a misfit in all groups and all situations; the student who never speaks because he has nothing to say, and the one who never speaks although he has much to say, and the one who speaks often even though he has little to say. All of these and the hundreds of others equally diverse, all must be reached. At least we should try.

Part of our responsibility is to help students enjoy the excitement of learning. Perhaps teaching should at times be painful, but it should never be dull. I came out of high school hating English, although I had loved it in earlier years. A succession of dull teachers had poisoned me against it, the worst of whom was the football coach who taught English to round out his schedule and who spent one full semester reading to us *The Bridge of San Luis Rey* in the flattest, most drearily monotonous voice I have ever heard in a classroom. The only things that saved me from hating the whole world of literature were a mother who encouraged me to love books and an inner compulsion that caused me to write dozens of grim short stories and romantic poems in secret, and to read endlessly. It wasn't until I was lucky enough to have Wallace Stegner as a Freshman English teacher in college that I rediscovered a pleasant relationship between the formal study of English in the classroom and the things I was reading and writing in secret. Even then I was so conditioned against English that three more years were needed to get the poison, and my passing desire to be a chemist, out of my system so that I could return to the first love of my boyhood, literature, and could decide that teaching English would be my life.

Therefore, I repeat: Perhaps teaching should at times be painful, but it should never be dull. The best guarantee against poor discipline is good teaching. And this is true at all levels of teaching. If the teaching is good enough, the students will be attentive and responsive. When students are bored and unruly, the best solution is not harsher rules but better teaching.

I would like to say a little more about the hard work of being a good teacher, because I think it *is* hard work—hard and long. Anyone who thinks otherwise can probably find and keep a job teaching, but he won't be a good teacher. One of the unfortunate things about teaching as a profession is that all teachers, whether strong or weak, energetic or lazy, inspired or dull, are paid about the same. Oh, we hear talk of merit pay, etc., but the truth is that the best teachers aren't paid much more than the worst teachers. They may be worth several times as much, but they won't be paid according to their worth. The strong ones will be paid too little, and the weak ones will be paid too much. Therefore, the rewards for a good teacher must be other than money. Fortunately, the rewards are abundant, and they are available daily, including the wonderful pleasure of teaching itself.

If we are good teachers we will have to work hard just to complete our daily tasks. Even so, I don't think most of us ever reach our potentiality as thinking, creative human beings. Most people, including both those of us who are teachers and those who are students, operate at about half efficiency, I fear. We sleep too much, eat too much, idle too much, and waste too much time in trivia. We need to work harder, think deeper, exchange ideas more constructively, and create more abundantly. One of our special problems as teachers is that we talk constantly about the need to do scholarly and creative work—and then spend hours of precious time explaining why we don't have time to do these things. I am convinced that we do have time if we will organize and discipline it. Many years ago I planned to do a great deal of writing. In fact, I thought writing would be my central career. Then came doctoral work and teaching, and writing was forgotten. Well, not really forgotten but pushed to some indefinite time in the future. Then, about nine years ago, I read some place the awful comment that if one has not published by the time he is forty he will never publish. I was annoyed by the statement, partly because I was already a little past forty. And I determined to write. Now, in the past eight years, which have been the most crowded of my life, I have made time to write, in spite of increasingly extensive administrative responsibility, and without giving up teaching, even for a semester, because teaching is the relaxation that keeps me sane in an otherwise too tense existence. And if I can do it, so can most other teachers—at least all who are willing to pay the price through hard work.

As a final point, I want to comment on what I feel is the valid privilege, indeed the responsibility, of a teacher who has genuine religious convictions. Unless we are teaching in a denominational school, we should not, of course, indoctrinate our students with our private views. On the other hand, to hide completely our basic religious position is not altogether honest either. Our students are entitled to know where we stand. They should not be obliged to agree with us, and should in no way be penalized for disagreeing; but it is only fair that we honestly and simply acknowledge the basic beliefs which, intentionally or unintentionally, will inevitably shape our teaching—just as an atheist or a communist should have the privilege, indeed the responsibility, to make his position clear. This is not only academic freedom but also intellectual honesty. And if we are believers, in a nation with a great heritage of religious freedom, including the freedom of expression, our students are entitled to be aware of our interest in religious matters to sense our faith in religious principles, even to hear our convictions. I do not mean that we should spend class time preaching to our students, which would be highly improper. Our responsibility is to teach the subject matter for which we are professionally trained, and besides, preaching tends only to alienate the most sensitive of the students. But occasionally we need to let students know where we stand on the vital issues of the spirit. They need to know that we have studied philosophy, literature, and science and remained strong in our religious faith. They need to know that we have explored the unanswerable questions with our spiritual convictions intact. I am not asking that we betray our integrity. I am asking only that we fulfill and share it.

As I say all of this I hope no one feels I am denying my loyalty to the world of literature and art that I respect so much. I believe we have a solemn obligation to teach in harmony with the fundamental principles of our religious convictions; I believe we also have an equally solemn obligation to be defenders of liberal culture and the humanities. And, which is most important of all for me, I believe we can keep both loyalties strong, without hypocrisy, double-talk, or double-think. Through the centuries literature, and especially poetry, has been the bulwark of man's faith and the guardian of his spiritual ideals, as well as the goad to his conscience. That there should be, or seem to be, a battle between religion and art is most regrettable. Of course there are extremists on both sides, but we should lament them, not extol them. We should pity the men of religion who see art as an obstacle to their faith, and we should pity the men of art who see religion as an enemy to their ideals. Many have deplored the rift between religion and art, and many have pleaded for an armistice. But too often the crusader for religion has been willing to compromise only on his terms, with the bulk of art thrown out of his ideal republic and only that left which can be turned into the handmaiden of religion; and too often the crusader for art has been willing to compromise only on his terms, with religion knuckling under to acknowledge not only its supposed sins and prejudice but also the ultimate supremacy of art. If the war between religion and art is lamentable, the efforts to end the war with such unequal compromises are hardly less lamentable. As teachers, we need to speak courageously our confidence that liberal education and religion are comrades in arms against the common foes of selfishness, materialism, and all things maudlin, superficial, and gross. This is the goal of education, and this is the challenge of the first-quality teacher.

I have been talking about the ideal teacher. My students will testify that as a teacher I too fall short. My only plea is that I too am human, and that, however inadequate, I see the vision.

SCHOOL is for . . .
CLASS PLAYS

Helping Young People Discover Commitment

ARTHUR W. COMBS

I am much concerned these days with the question of commitment and involvement. Finding satisfying commitments has become almost a casualty of our way of life, so that many social scientists are studying this question. For example, Rollo May discusses the problem of encounter. Carl Rogers talks about involvement. Martin Buber speaks of dialogues, Maslow talks about commitment, and Victor Frankl is concerned with the problem of helping people discover meaning. I have been using all of these terms interchangeably.

What I mean by commitment and involvement is the ability to enter into meaningful relationships. It is a question of the discovery of purpose and point in life and the finding of fulfillment in the things that one is doing. We know there is simply no action and no learning of any consequence without some kind of involvement on the part of the individual.

Once it was easier to develop involvement. In a frontier society, with not enough food, clothing and shelter, involvement was *given* to people and they were firmly committed without much choice. The problem is different in a replete society. In a society so wealthy it has the majestic impertinence to believe it can eliminate poverty—the problem of finding something to be committed to, something to be involved with, something that makes life worth while becomes a much more difficult question. What shall man live for in so rich a society? What shall he die for? What shall he work for? What shall he give himself to?

Combs, Arthur W. "Helping Young People Discover Commitment." *Educational Leadership*. December 1964. 22:164-169.

Tough Questions

These are tough questions for adults. They are terrible questions for young people because they find themselves confronted with a society which has entered into a conspiracy to keep them from getting involved or committed to anything. We are embarrassed by our overproduction of children. We cannot very well plow them under like we do with cotton, or bury them in caves like we do with butter, or sell the surplus to the Russians like we do with wheat. We do not know what to do with them and, as a result, they are having a hard time finding any place where they belong. For example, we have five percent unemployment among our adult population, while with young people it is 18 percent! Our young people find themselves in a world which rejects them right and left. We prepare them better and better to do less and less. We keep them out of adult things just as long as possible. We tell them to go away and don't bother us.

The matter is especially difficult with teen-agers. The very word "teen-ager" is practically a "cuss word" in our society. We just don't like them. We have practically driven them out of our society. Their reaction to this is to build a society of their own, with their own music, their own language, their own dress, their own codes of ethics, their own traditions, their own customs, their own symbols of prestige and status. They have developed their own because there is no place for them in the society in which we are living.

We cannot afford this waste. On humanitarian grounds the loss in human potential involved in this rejection is tremendous. The loss in human happiness is even greater. If it is not enough to be concerned about the matter because we love and respect our young people, there is another very practical reason why we had better be interested. That is, because it is downright dangerous not to be concerned.

One of the things we found out about the young men in Korea who succumbed to brainwashing was, that those who did give way were young men who *had no commitment or involvement of their own*. If you have to argue with the Russians, for whom their way of life is practically a religion, and you do not have a strong commitment of your own, then you are a sitting duck to be changed.

People who do not feel they really belong to our society see no reason why they should support it. If you do not feel that you belong to the club, there is no reason why you should pay your dues or look out for the members. If the club we are talking about happens to be the human race, and young people feel they do not belong, that is a very dangerous condition indeed.

Young people do not *want* to be uncommitted. They want to be involved. They want to be committed, and they seek such commitment when it is possible for them.

At our university, many young people have offered their help with problems of cultural deprivation in the Negro children of the community. They have volunteered many hours to help some Negro child enrich his experiences and pick up some of the cultural aspects that he is not getting elsewhere. These young people are having the time of their lives. The other day one of these young ladies came to see me after class and said: "When I entered this class, I listened to a lot of these people and the things they say about education. I don't think it would be worth much. But two weeks ago I started working with a little Negro girl on the other side of town, and I have decided that teaching is for me!" Her eyes were shining and the look on her face expressed the joy she felt in being committed to something.

Principles of Commitment

I believe our schools are crucial in helping children find commitment. We cannot wash our hands of our responsibilities. I am not talking just about mental health ideas. Youngsters cannot even learn mathematics without being committed to it, or English or any other subject. Even the child's grasp of the curriculum cannot come about without some opportunity really to get committed to the subject matter. Somehow we have to find better ways of developing this commitment and of filling this gap which has come about in our society. Unhappily, much of what we do in schools seems almost expressly designed to discourage children from getting committed. I would like to suggest four principles about commitment which may help to point some directions.

Commitment and Discovery

First, commitment is a matter for discovery. It cannot be given. It cannot be taught. It has to be learned. It is a personal matter. It is a personal discovery that some idea, some person, some thing is enhancing and fulfilling. It is a question of being challenged but not threatened.

There is a difference between being challenged and threatened. An individual feels challenged when he confronts a situation he thinks he has a chance of dealing with. He feels threatened when he is confronted with a demand that he does not feel he is capable of fulfilling. Our problem is how to help him feel challenged without feeling threatened. Yet this is not a question of how it looks to you and me. It is a question of how it looks to him! We need to understand that what is challenging is not determined by some outsider, but by how it seems to the individual.

Here is one source of the dropout problem. Dropouts are young people who are not finding anything to commit themselves to in school. Perhaps sadder still are the ones who sit in classes day after day but for all practical purposes have dropped out because they have no commitment left to the program in which they are trapped. Whatever threatens or embarrasses, whatever degrades, whatever cuts down a person's conception of himself, is not only humiliating; it is also stultifying and stupefying. Such acts actually destroy intelligence and have no place in our public schools.

Eliminating Barriers to Commitment

A second principle: We must systematically search out the barriers that lie in the way of people getting committed. People will become committed if they can but we have erected an unbelievable number of barriers that stand in the way of getting committed.

One way to find out about these barriers is to listen to young people. As part of my homework for this paper, one of the things I did was ask my sophomore students at the university: Why is it so hard to become committed? How is it that young people in other countries riot over politics and foreign affairs but our young people riot over co-eds' panties? I was astonished at the list these young people gave me. They said:

"The reason we don't get committed is that nobody ever believes we are important or count. Nobody has any respect for our beliefs. The only choices we are confronted with demand conformity. They feed us a 'pablum' diet; it is all chewed over and there is nothing left in it of any interest.

"Everybody is afraid to let us try. Nobody really cares. Students and teachers are enemies; they behave as though they didn't like each other. We never talk about ideas, only about more and more details. Grades, grades, grades! That's all we hear, and everybody behaves as though that's all that matters. A college education is only of value to get your union card. You don't ever dare to question the teachers' ideas."

Most shocking of all was this statement which all agreed upon: "The things that are worth getting committed to are not the things that get you ahead!" I think that is a terrible indictment of our world.

We must find ways of searching out barriers to commitment and of rooting out these barriers. Years ago I discovered, quite by accident, how to do this. I was adviser for the High-Y in our high school. The school had a regulation that any money obtained from students during the year had to be returned to the students somehow before the end of the year. So, our club came up to the end of the year with $35 in the treasury. What could we do with it?

Somebody suggested that we could give a party for the school. Another said, "Well, it ought to be for everybody." I said, "Let's see if we can figure out a way of getting everybody into the act." Someone else suggested, "Well, we could have a dance, but if we do have a dance, the people who can't dance won't come." Then another person said, "Well, maybe we could have a dance that everybody will come to."

We thought: "What kind of dance would that be?" This was a large city high school and nobody in this high school knew how to square dance, so far as we knew, so somebody came up with the idea, "Let's have a square dance." And that is what we agreed upon.

Then somebody said, "Well, even if we have a square dance, some people won't come because they don't have the right clothes." The reply was, "Well, this is a country dance; we won't let them in if they look too sharp." Somebody else said, "Well, they won't come if they aren't able to get a date," and somebody else suggested, "Well, we could let the boys in one door and let the girls in the other on opposite sides of the gym, and nobody would know who had a date."

Then somebody suggested: "Some of the people won't come because they won't have enough money and they would want to buy the girl they were with something after the dance was over." So we said: "Let's feed them at the dance." A committee was set up to enlist the aid of mothers in baking cakes. When we got all through with this, someone said, "We've still got the problem: Some won't come because they can't afford it."

So after much figuring, we found out how much it would cost us for the band, made an estimate of how many people we thought would come, and finally got the price of the dance down to eight cents.

Everyone told us, "It will never work!" but when the night of the dance came, we had the largest crowd that had ever been in the gymnasium since the school was built. In fact, we had so many people that nobody could dance because there was not any room and instead of losing $35 we made $50.

I have tried a similar approach with my classes at the University of Florida asking, "What are the factors that get in the way of student commitment to these ideas?" This has resulted in major changes in the traditional practices of lecturing, grading, assignments and discussion programs. It has also produced innovations like personal letters to the instructor, planning committees which tell me what to lecture about, individual projects of great ingenuity and the creation of an atmosphere as free of threat and full of challenge as we can make it. The result has exceeded my fondest hopes in student commitment even in classes as large as one hundred and fifty.

Commitment from Relationships

A third thing we know about commitment is that it comes about through relationships with significant people, especially people who care. Every psychotherapist knows this.

It is no accident that the very best cure we have found for juvenile delinquency is marriage. Of all the things associated with delinquents who get better, getting married seems more effective and more certain than any other one thing that we know about. When you have somebody who cares, somebody to live for, somebody to share things with, you are taken out of the boredom that is the basis of most delinquency. Juvenile delinquents are simply bored to death. The reason they are bored is that they cannot find anything that is meaningful with which or with whom to find satisfying and fulfilling relationships.

All this is not only true with respect to people. It is true of ideas and of subject matter, too. Learning itself is a social process. The youngsters know this, too. Despite our best efforts to tell them to work on their own, they still insist on sharing things with each other, in spite of our apparent determination to make education a solitary business. They know you cannot get along that way and so they share things with each other, sometimes, even in spite of us, answers on examinations.

We are beginning to discover that human interaction is not just a nice idea. Satisfying human relationships are not just a nice way to live. They are vital to living. In recent experiments, it has been found even monkeys who have never seen or entered into relationships with other monkeys cannot be made to reproduce. Apparently, they do not know they are monkeys, unless they have some kind of experience with another monkey that helps them to discover who they are and what they are.

We cannot afford dehumanized schools. We have sold ourselves on the idea that in order to have a rich curriculum we must have large schools, and I guess that is true. The only difficulty is that people get lost in large schools, lost and lonely. We must find ways of reintroducing human relationships on a person-to-person basis, in our beautiful, huge new plants. When I was at Syracuse University years ago, we used to have a winter carnival. All the fraternities would build snow sculptures on the lawn. I remember one that showed a large building marked "Syracuse University." Going in one door was a freshman with his little green cap on his head, and coming out the other side was an IBM card complete with a diploma. This was a cry of protest from the young people who were going through this great university!

Commitment and Responsibility

It is necessary for us to recognize that teaching for commitment is a relationship. I would point out, however, that you cannot have a relationship with a nonentity. Teachers have to *be* somebody and have to *act* like somebody and have to *stand* for something and to share their humanness with young people. Encouraging young people to get involved is not going to get results unless we ourselves value involvement, because each of us behaves in terms of what he thinks is important in spite of himself. As the old Indian said, "What you do speaks so loudly I cannot hear what you say."

A beautiful example of this occurred recently in a fifth grade. At the end of the day the youngsters in the class got to talking about love for half an hour or so. Following this the teacher said to the youngsters, "For tomorrow, I want you to write me a letter about our discussion and what you think about it." One of the letters she got from a little boy said: "Dear Miss X: It sure surprised me when we talked about love in our class today. I learned a lot of things about how people feel about each other. It sure surprised me, though, to talk about love in our class. I never knew you could talk about things in school before that you didn't get grades for!"

I think it is a sad commentary when what is perhaps the most important subject in the world is not regarded as part of the curriculum. If we do not think it is important for young people to become involved, they simply will not do so, at least not about what we hope they will.

We have to find ways of giving young people responsibility for their own learning and for their own direction. This means we have to involve them in planning. It means our schools must become more and more and more child-centered rather than less and less as some people would have us believe. A well-known educator once said, "Isn't it interesting that we give children more choices in kindergarten than at any other time they are in school?" Presumably the younger a child is, the less he is capable of making intelligent choices, and the older he gets and the further he goes through school, the less choices we give him until by the time he is working for a doctor's degree he hasn't got any choice whatever.

Responsibility and involvement are learned from being *given* responsibility. They are never learned from withholding it. Let us take the example of the teacher who leaves the room and goes down to the office. She says to the youngsters, "I'm going to leave you for a few minutes. I want you to be good kids till I get back." She comes back to find the room is in bedlam. She walks in and says, "I will never leave you alone again!" By this act she has robbed these children of their only opportunity to learn how to behave when the teacher is not there. You cannot learn how to behave when the teacher is not there if the teacher never leaves you! When we are too afraid that children may make mistakes, involvement does not happen, because we do not dare let them try.

Building Confidence

Sometimes students back away from responsibility and involvement when we try to give it to them. They do not want to take it. We must not be misled by this. It only means that they have not had enough responsibility. Responsibility and involvement are learned like everything else. You have to have simple responsibilities to build up confidence to deal with big ones. Even an adult who is given a responsibility that he has not had an opportunity to build skills and confidence for handling, is quite likely to feel anxiety-stricken and to back away from it. Involvement and commitment are learned from having opportunities adjusted to the individual's state of readiness.

One of the things that have been said about a genius is that "a genius is a guy who likes to get in trouble for the sheer joy of getting out again." I think we need to encourage our young people to get into more trouble. I mean this very seriously. I think we have leaned over so far in the opposite direction in not ever giving them opportunities to try, that for a while it would be good to go in the other direction, good for all of us concerned.

Somehow we have to find better ways of getting across to young people the idea that it is good to look and fun to try and that it is all right to be different. We are not doing this well at the present time.

Outstanding Teachers: Who Are They?

By MANUEL ZAX

The adjective "outstanding" is meaningless out of context. The person who is rated as the best of one group of teachers may be rated as being much less than best when considered in relation to another group of teachers. The use of different criteria to determine outstandingness will produce different selections of persons of the same group. Whether one or more judges make the selection also makes a difference as to who is selected.

These few aspects of the problem of determining outstandingness among teachers indicate what a great variety of approaches may be used in most accurately identifying those who are outstanding among a given group of teachers. This is an old problem, though, which many investigators have tackled in the past. What light did their inquiries shed on this problem?

Wilson's study[1] furnishes evidence indirectly that administrators may have unique ideas about what kind of teacher is a most effective teacher. In his study, two groups of high school teachers were involved— one group chosen randomly and the other made up of teachers who were chosen as being most effective by seniors with high scholastic achievement records. They were compared on eight different indices, one of which was ratings by principals. It was in this category that the least difference between the two groups of teachers was found. The findings suggest that the principals did not agree with the high achieving students that the teachers chosen by the students were the most effective teachers. Hedlund, on the other hand, identified effective teachers by combining the judgements of students, principals, and college observers;[2] while Johnson and Radebaugh used students, teachers, and administrators, finding that teachers and administrators were in greater agree-

Zax, Manuel. "Outstanding Teachers: Who are They?" *The Clearing House*. January 1971. 45:285-289.

ment of identification of "excellent teachers" than were students and teachers or students and administrators.[3]

The selection of outstanding teachers need not be mysterious, however. Hawkins approached the question of identification of outstanding elementary teachers by subjective and objective means and found that "there is substantial agreement in the identification of outstanding teachers by methods representing formal evaluation, informal evaluation, and current salary practice."[4] Of course, agreement need not mean that the identification of the outstanding teachers had been made. As Chrisman found, a variety of criteria are used to identify superior teachers, but the one most frequently found was a teacher's willingness to assume extra duties. Paradoxically, Chrisman learned that more than 75 per cent of the superintendents in his study gave as a reason for their loss of superior teachers: left to receive more money.[5]

An attempt at identifying attitudes and traits of the excellent teacher was made by Avent, who in 1927 announced in the educational journals of the United States that certain prizes were to be awarded to those who sent the largest and best lists of "Excellences and Errors in Teaching." The result was that 1,002 teachers sent in lists ranging from 78 to 8,770 items in length.[6] The large number of items may of course be ascribed to the contest aspect, but Avent's classification of the items produced 1,513 topics,[7] indicating the degree to which he consolidated the returns.

That widely divergent views are held as to what attitudes and traits are those of the excellent or outstanding teacher was agreed to in 1961 by the American Association of School Administrators (A.A.S.A.), the Department of Classroom Teachers of the N.E.A., and the National School Boards Association on the basis of a comprehensive review of studies dealing with effectiveness in teachers.[8] They stated, "The notion of the 'good teacher' so basic to the study of teacher effectiveness turns out to be almost as vague and diffuse as the range of human experience relative to teaching."[9] However, they did make the observation:

> Overall administrative opinion constituted the most widely used single measure of teacher competence. Available studies showed in general that teachers could be reliably rated by administrators and supervisory personnel (usually with correlations of .70 or above).[10]

But it must be noted that agreement as to ratings of teachers does not guarantee that the choices made are valid ones.

Accounts of great teachers, such as those by Peterson[11] and Highet,[12] reveal the variety of types of teachers considered by various people as great teachers. The elusiveness of the ingredients which make these teachers great is exemplified in the following quotation by Walter

Dyer in his description of Charles E. Garman, one of his teachers:

> It would be possible, doubtless, to analyze scientifically Garman's methods of teaching, to reduce them to a working formula, and to arrive at a more accurate appraisal of the work he did, but such an analysis would surely fail to explain his extraordinary influence in many noteworthy individual cases. It was a matter of personality, and such a personality as his was and must always remain a mystery.[13]

Lathrop felt that there would be some value for teachers of his day (1930) to be made aware of the characteristics and practices mentioned most frequently in connection with teachers rated as great by their students. He listed the following characteristics in order of frequency on the basis of students' views of 50 teachers, including such great teachers as Mark Hopkins, William James, Woodrow Wilson, and Oliver Wendell Holmes: clarity of expression, humor, enthusiasm, insistence on high standards, sympathy, interest in students, expressive voice, cordiality, patience, impressive physique, tolerance, and enjoyment of teaching.[14]

In like manner Lathrop listed the most frequently mentioned practices in order of their frequency: use of effective illustration, provision for activity of the learner, careful preparation for each teaching exercise, encouragement of efforts of students, drawing upon fields other than the special field, statement of all sides of a question, avoidance of adherence to the text, provision for teaching students to think, seizing upon a few essentials, and iteration and reiteration.[15]

Perhaps one would not quarrel with most of these characteristics and practices as being appropriate to today's teachers, but Getzels and Jackson point out that "the image of the teacher has undergone significant change so that many images of the 'good' teacher exist today."[16] It may be that there are fewer images of the most outstanding teacher, but that there exists a plurality of images appears evident from the above studies by Chrisman, Avent, the American Association of School Administrators, and the writings of Peterson and Highet.

If an investigator were to consider teachers from the viewpoint of their effectiveness, he might encounter one or more of the problems discussed by Rabinowitz and Travers:

(1) context
(2) variability of pupils
(3) time
(4) teacher behavior and pupil reaction to it not necessarily linear in correspondence
(5) behavior of teacher may be function of pupil behavior
(6) contaminations of other influences impossible to control[17]

If an investigator were to attempt to identify the best teacher among a group of teachers on the basis of personality, he might agree with

Symonds: "I doubt if we shall ever know enough to say that this or that personality type is most desirable to teach our children."[1] [8] Among the reasons given by Symonds for his arriving at this conclusion is the following:

> I have seen successful teachers with loud, harsh voices, also with very soft, indistinct voices. I have seen successful teachers who were lax, easygoing, highly permissive and others who were strict and restrictive. I have seen successful teachers who were effusive in giving praise, but I have also seen successful teachers who never seemed wholly satisfied with what the children in their classes do.[1] [9]

In a study conducted by Gowan, 20 elementary teachers were selected as outstanding from nearly 3,000 teachers of Southern California who had been observed by "trained, competent observers" as part of the Teacher Characteristics Study by Ryans.[20] These 20 teachers were labeled "outstanding" on the basis of their having been rated "considerably above average on each of the three factors identified in the main study and on total assessment."[21] It is important to note that in the main study, "the assessments were not accomplished primarily for the purpose of picking out 'effective' or 'ineffective' teachers, but with the intent of describing certain behaviors of teachers."[22] The three factors to which Gowan referred, are:

(1) a factor contributed to by understanding, friendliness and responsiveness on the part of the teacher;
(2) a factor contributed to by systematic, responsible, organized teacher behavior; and
(3) a factor contributed to by the teacher's stimulating and original behavior.[23]

It is conceivable that a teacher may have been rated high in all three of the above factors and not have been outstanding as a teacher, unless it is by such a high rating that the outstanding teacher is defined. Gowan's personal choice of subjects, in fact, might have been different from the 20 teachers whom he did use. He stated that he had a "distinct impression" that four of his subjects were "less outstanding teachers than the others."[24] How much less outstanding these four were was not stated, but for Gowan to have registered this impression lends support to the opinion that the determination of outstanding teachers is extremely difficult.

The above review of literature may be summarized as follows:

(1) It is likely that students and administrators will select different teachers as being outstanding (Wilson, Johnson and Radebaugh).
(2) Subjective or objective means of selection may be used with equal success (Hawkins), but must be adequately qualified (Gowans, Ryans).

(3) Varieties of criteria are used for such selection by administrators (Chrisman, Avent, A.A.S.A.).

(4) Administrative selections have been reliable (A.A.S.A.).

(5) Great teachers are of quite different types (Peterson, Highet).

(6) Great teachers exhibit similar characteristics and practices (Lathrop).

(7) There are many images of the good teacher (Getzels and Jackson).

(8) Selection of such teachers on the basis of their effectiveness is accompanied by problems of control (Rabinowitz and Travers).

(9) The use of personality as an identifier is highly questionable (Symonds).

The advice included in 2, 3, 4, 5, and 7 indicates that the best method of selection might be one which did not dictate the qualities of the subjects and which utilized administrators as the choice-makers. Such was the method used in a study I made, in which 46 secondary school teachers were identified by their respective principals as being outstanding.[2 5]

On the basis of about 500 pages of data gained through open-ended, semi-structured interviews, I drew a composite picture of my subjects, stemming from that data which was representative of the majority of the teachers of the study. Perhaps this composite picture answers the question posed in the title of this article: Outstanding Teachers: Who Are They?

(1) These teachers enjoy teaching in general, and enjoy teaching their subject matter in particular. They may have had ideas about following different careers earlier in their lives, but now they are committed to the career of teaching.

(2) The classroom is their base of operation, and although this room filled with students is theirs to control, the teachers admit to, and appreciate, an unpredictability about the events which occur in the classroom. Change in the classroom is expected and produced by these teachers.

(3) The teachers report that there are restrictions imposed upon them, but they describe these as being not very serious. If possible, however, these teachers would like some clerical help, and would like to be freed from non-teaching duties.

(4) Of real concern to the subjects is the improving of their effectiveness in teaching their students. They work hard at communicating with their students through enthusiasm, variety, and acting. In this effort the teachers consider that though they are successful in communicating with most students, they are aware of a small number of students with whom their success has been minimal or nil. The teachers are convinced that part of the reason why they have not been successful with these students is that they do not know enough about most students, particularly the ones who constitute perennial problems.

(5) Toward the problem- and non-problem students alike, however, the teachers express positive feelings of affection. These feelings are extended to those students whom the teachers consider as being misplaced ability-wise, even though the presence of these students complicates the teachers' self assessment of their teaching effectiveness. The complication arises since the students' responses and reactions are viewed by the teachers as key determinants of their

teaching effectiveness.

(6) Although the teachers of the study expressed views which they held with vigor, they gave evidence of being teachers who are nonetheless anxious to hear from their colleagues, and wish to have administrative support.[26]

Missing from the picture is a comment relative to competency of the teachers in terms of their subject matter. There are doubtless some other missing components in this word picture; and doubtless, too, some components do not apply to some outstanding teachers. They do apply to the majority of teachers in the above study. As such the picture is a guide, which is the intent of this article: to serve as a guide in considering the question of outstandingness in teachers, and in doing so to reveal the impreciseness of any such guide.

FOOTNOTES

[1] Garfield W. Wilson, doctoral dissertation, *A Study of Differences in Teacher Effectiveness Between STAR Teachers and a Random Selection of Teachers in Georgia*, Florida State University, 1964.

[2] Paul A. Hedlund, "Cooperative Study to Predict Effectiveness in Secondary School Teaching." *The Journal of Teacher Education*, IV (September, 1953), pp. 231-32.

[3] James A. Johnson and Byron F. Radebaugh, "Excellent Teachers—What Makes Them Outstanding?" *The Clearing House*, XLIV (November, 1969), pp. 152-156.

[4] Edward E. Hawkins, doctoral dissertation, *Identification of Outstanding Elementary Teachers by Subjective and Objective Means*, University of Southern California, 1963.

[5] Charles M. Chrisman, doctoral dissertation, *Current Administrative Practices Used to Identify and Reward Superior Teachers in Selected Missouri Public School Districts*, University of Missouri, 1961.

[6] Joseph Avent, *The Excellent Teacher*, Joseph E. Avent, publisher, 1931, p. 1.

[7] *Ibid.*, p. 4.

[8] American Association of School Administrators, Department of Classroom Teachers of the N.E.A., and National School Boards Association, *Who's a Good Teacher?*, 1961.

[9] *Ibid.*, p. 37.

[10] *Ibid.*, p. 32.

[11] Houston Peterson (ed.), *Great Teachers*, Rutgers University Press, 1946.

[12] Gilbert Highet, *The Art of Teaching*, Alfred A. Knopf, 1951.

[13] Peterson, *op. cit.*, p. 119.

[14] F. W. Lathrop, *The Characteristics and Practices of Great Teachers*, paper presented before the American Association for the Advancement of Agricultural Teaching, Nov. 17, 1930, Washington, D.C., p. 6.

[15] Ibid., *p. 8.*

[16] J. W. Getzels and P. W. Jackson, "Research on the Variable Teacher. Some Comments," *School Review*, LXVIII (Winter, 1960), p. 460.

[17] William Rabinowitz and Robert M. W. Travers, "Problems of Defining and Assessing Teacher Effectiveness," *Educational Theory*, III (July, 1953), p. 217.

[18] P. M. Symonds, "Reflections on Observations of Teachers," *Journal of Educational Research*, XLII (May, 1950), p. 690.

[19] *Ibid.*, p. 691.

[20] David G. Ryans, "The Investigation of Teacher Characteristics," *Educational Record*, XXXIV (October, 1953), pp. 371-96.

[21] J. C. Gowan, "A Summary of the Intensive Study of Twenty Highly Selected Elementary Women Teachers," *Journal of Experimental Education*, XXVI (December, 1957), pp. 115-24.

[22] Ryans, *op cit.*, p. 386.

[23] *Ibid.*, p. 387.

[24] Gowan, *op. cit.*, p. 119.

[25] Manuel Zax, doctoral dissertation, *Perceptions of Teaching Held by Outstanding Secondary-School Teachers*, Cornell University, 1968.

[26] *Ibid.*, pp. 111-13.

SCHOOL is for . . .
PRAISE AND LOVING
KINDNESS

The Rewards and Results of Teaching

KAORU YAMAMOTO

We are teachers and teaching is our business. This is obvious between you and me, right? Now, let us ask ourselves a question: "Why are we interested in teaching and why are we engaged in this act?"

Undoubtedly, we will try first to trace the origin of such interest to our earlier experiences and to explain our persistence in the profession by the current challenges and satisfaction and by future aspirations and goals. We may concede that, at least partially, we were favorably influenced by the "occupational label" (31) or the "occupational type" (30) of the teacher, although studies (15, 26) have revealed surprisingly self-disparaging attitudes among active teachers. We may also mention the desires and opportunities for working with youngsters, for pursuing a favorite academic subject, for devoting life to a worthy social cause, or for securing a stable but flexible job, as some of the motivating factors (9, 32).

We may further insist (21) that basically we entered and have remained in education "for personality (value-oriented) reasons rather than specific external rewards" (8), even though "very little is known for certain about the nature and measurements of teacher personality" (13). Or, else, how could we stay on teaching, knowing that the profession offers but limited income and restricted opportunity for advancement (3, 6, 17, 24)?

Shift in Emphasis

All these answers are indeed pertinent and informative. Nevertheless, they will not completely clarify the gist of the problem, namely, "When

Yamamoto, Kaoru. "The Rewards and Results of Teaching." *Education.* October 1966. 87:67-72.

a person *teaches* someone else, what does this really mean in terms of the basic human relationship?" or, "What is involved in one individual's taking a position *to teach* in relation to another?"

Let me explain this a little. Margaret Mead, in one of her fascinatingly written articles, contrasted education in our society with that in contemporary primitive societies and pointed out some striking differences, the most important being "the shift from the need for an individual to learn something which everyone agrees he would wish to know, to the will of some individual to teach something which it is not agreed that anyone has any desire to know" (22, p. 164).

Assimilation of members of other cultures, proselytization of people of different ideas and attitudes, colonization of the natives to assure communication through the colonist's language, and compulsory schooling of the immigrant masses to maintain and enhance national identity and loyalty in discontinuity with the previous generations'—all these stem from the idea of Truth, or the idea that one set of cultural beliefs is definitely superior to another. The net result is the transfer of emphasis from the desirability of *learning* to that of *teaching*, from changing of *self* to changing of *others*, from what a person *does* to what *is done to* him, and from the *learner* to the *teacher*.

The implications of such differences observed between the American society and the people of, for example, Manus, Arapesh, Iatmul, Bali, Mundugumor, or Samoa are explained thus:

> The attempt to assimilate, convert, or keep in their places other human beings conceived of as inferior to those who are making the plans has been a boomerang which has distorted our whole educational philosophy; it has shifted the emphasis from one of growth and seeking for knowledge to one of dictation and forced acceptance of cliches and points of view. Thus we see that the presence of one element within our culture—a spurious sense of superiority of one group of human beings over another, which gave the group in power the impetus to force their language, their beliefs, and their culture down the throats of the group which was numerically, or economically, or geographically handicapped—has corrupted and distorted the emphasis of our free schools (22, p. 171).

It is easy for you and me to raise a voice of protest against such an uninvited indictment of our educational system whose innovative roles as a medium of social change have been increasingly emphasized over its conservative roles in contemporary America (14). Nevertheless, it would seem quite worthwhile for us to consider the matter carefully and soberly.

Teaching and Learning

Naturally, the problem has not entirely escaped the keen observers of our day. The rather belated discovery (or, rather, rediscovery) of the concept of competence (18, 34) was a good reminder of the fact that there is indeed such a thing as a self-motivated, curious, exploring learner not entirely definable by environmental variables.

The realization that teaching is one thing and learning is quite another (10, 11, 29) also stimulated studies of human instruction as such and not as an incidental adjunct of the pure and rigorous laboratory experimentation whose transfer value to the actual classroom learning has been questioned even by the learning psychologists themselves, e.g., Bugelski (5).

When, accordingly, a close look is taken at what really is involved in imparting knowledge through the vehicle of the school, a picture quite similar to that described by Mead appears. Thus, for example, it was pointed out by Bruner (4) that, among the Kung Bushman of the Kalahari, southern Africa, there is virtually no instance of "teaching" or "telling" taking place outside the situation where the behavior to be learned is relevant and learning is in fact mediated by "showing" and imitative playing in the actual life of the tribe, characterized by constant adult-adolescent-child (vertical) interactions.

> The change in the instruction of children in more complex societies is twofold. First of all, there is knowledge and skill in the culture far in excess of what any one individual knows. And so, increasingly, there develops an economical technique of instructing the young based heavily on telling out of context rather than *showing* in context. In literate societies, the practice becomes institutionalized in the school or the 'teacher.' Both promote the necessarily abstract way of instructing the young. The result of 'teaching the culture' can, at its worst, lead to the ritual, rote nonsense . . . (4, p. 1009).

Unfortunately, moreover, there are indications that the very worst result of "teaching the culture" out of context is characteristic of the current American schools. Speaking of college curricula, for example, Katz pointed to the prevalent attitudes among many serious institutions concerning the attainment of the curricular goal by their students within a brief period of four years. By offering courses in every imaginable art and science, institutions expect some miraculous learning taking place among these 17 to 21 year-old adolescents, "who seem by their very developmental status barred from a proper appreciation of the material" (20, p. 380).

Probably the most telling index of the meaninglessness of "teaching" from students' viewpoint is the ratio of school dropouts. It is obvious that when 35 per cent of youth drop out of school before high school graduation (16, 23) and when 40 to 60 per cent of students leave colleges (19), we cannot easily convince ourselves of the exciting learning opportunities provided through our educational institutions.

Another observation comes from a questionnaire survey of two suburban public school systems near Boston conducted by Wilson and Goethals (35). These authors reported that, in spite of the general agreement on the most valued techniques (small group interactions) of instruction between teachers and students, the most commonly used teaching method was one on which they both placed a low value. Teachers and students alike reported that "the school ethos retains the conventional assign-study-recite technique" (2, p. 275).

This entire situation was cogently summarized by Waller (33, p. 202) in his now classic analysis of the sociology of teaching.

> The characteristic mode of social interaction of the school, an interaction centered about the giving and receiving of instruction, determines the political order of the school. The instruction which is given consists largely of facts and skills, and of other matter for which the spontaneous interests of students do not usually furnish a sufficient motivation . . . The political organization of the school, therefore, is one which makes the teacher dominant, and it is the business of the teacher to use his dominance to further the process of teaching and learning which is central in the social interaction of the school.

Preoccupation of Teachers

Why are we, as teachers, so preoccupied with "telling" someone something, even though the matter does not interest the person at all? Seemingly, we often forget that our specialty has given us, but not others, a primary focus under which to organize our life, but not theirs, and make it meaningful. Thus, we tend to be little disposed to see our students, who are non-specialists, in their own perspective, or to distinguish clearly between our function to preserve and advance knowledge and that to educate (20).

I am not castigating teachers, including myself, concerning their enthusiasm and dedication. Instead, I am suggesting a time out to consider a possible negative side-effect of teachers' "teaching" orientation. A teacher may be a "shaman" (a charismatic type), a "priest" (an agent of the collective identity of academic disciplines), or a "mystic healer" (a false altruist), as schematized by Adelson (1). Either way, his preoccupation with himself is frequently quite patent although he is unaware of this.

In view of the recent findings concerning the relationships between a man's personality and his vocational choice, e.g., Roe (27), it is easy to hypothesize that teaching also serves to satisfy some people's basic motives which may include needs for status, affection, security, power, leadership, and guaranteed superiority. Naturally, there is nothing inherently good or bad about this. "What led a person to enter a profession is significant only if it increases our understanding of his present actions and feelings" (25, pp. 482-3).

It may help in this context, nevertheless, to observe among all these different motives one common thread, a single basic force which *compels* us to teach, whether we are professional teachers or not. Erikson described this in stating that "adult man is so constituted as to *need to be needed* lest he suffer the mental deformation of self-absorption, in which he becomes his own infant and pet" (7, p. 130). He continued further:

> And man *needs* to teach, not only for the sake of those who need to be taught, and not only for the fulfillment of his identity, but because facts are kept alive by being told, logic by being demonstrated, truth by being professed. Thus, the teaching passion is not restricted to the teaching profession. Every mature adult knows the satisfaction of explaining what is dear to him and of being understood by a groping mind" (7, p. 131).

In other words, we *have* to teach, "for we are the teaching species" (7, p. 130).

Teaching at Its Worst and Best

At its best, therefore, teaching is an embodiment of human concern and care, of mutuality of partners in a shared identity. At its worst, however, teaching may be nothing but an act of self-righteousness, indoctrination, and manipulation on the part of the teachers. It seems to be this latter kind of consideration which induced Rogers (28) to acknowledge that the outcomes of teaching are either damaging or inconsequential and which motivated Wrenn (36) to emphasize the fact that what is right for one person is right for him only and not for anybody else.

The American faith in education as a creator of something new and desirable in *our* definition and belief should be carefully scrutinized. So long as the children are instructed to build a new social order *according to our blueprints and dreams,* the basic tenet of education becomes nothing more than a technique with which one human being exploits another. If, under the disguise of preservation of truth, liberty, and justice, we try to insure through our teaching that the citizens of the next century will follow no path over than that which we have laid down, this will be a mockery of human love.

No matter how uneasy it makes us feel today, we should discard the idea that our children's task is to stand a dreary watch over the ancient values which we cherish and instead convince ourselves that each generation has to "re-create those values continuously in their own behavior" (12, p. 126), to fight their own crucial battles to establish the moral order, and to bring new vitality to the ideals or drop them at their discretion. The task is a challenge to both the old and the young, both the teacher and the learner. We must, in other words, care, share, and dare *together*. And,

> We must concentrate upon teaching our children to walk so steadily that we need not hew too straight and narrow paths for them but can trust them to make new paths through difficulties we never encountered to a future of which we have no inkling today (22, p. 173).

REFERENCES

1. ADELSON, JOSEPH. "The Teacher as a Model." *The American College*. (Edited by Nevitt Sanford.) New York: Wiley, 1962. Pp. 396-417.

2. ALLINSMITH, WESLEY, and GOETHALS, GEORGE W. *The Role of Schools in Mental Health*. New York: Basic Books, 1962.

3. BECKER, HOWARD S. *Role and Career Problems of the Chicago Public School Teacher*. Doctoral Dissertation, University of Chicago, 1951.

4. BRUNER, JEROME S. "The Growth of Mind." *American Psychologist* 20: 1007-1017; December 1965.

5. BUGELSKI, B. R. *The Psychology of Learning Applied to Teaching*. Indianapolis: Bobbs Merrill, 1964.

6. DUTTON, WILBUR H., and KEISLAR, EVAN R. "Attitudes Toward Teaching." *Journal of Teacher Education* 12: 165-71; June 1961.

7. ERIKSON, ERIK H. *Insight and Responsibility*. New York: Norton, 1964.

8. FISCHER, LOUIS, and THOMAS, DONALD R. *Social Foundations of Educational Decisions*. Belmont, California: Wadsworth, 1965, p. 313.

9. FOX, RAYMOND B. "Factors Influencing the Career Choice of Prospective Teachers." *Journal of Teacher Education* 12: 427-32; December 1961.

10. GAGE, N. L. "Paradigms for Research on Teaching." *Handbook of Research on Teaching*. (Edited by N. L. Gage.) Chicago: Rand McNally, 1963. Pp. 94-141.

11. GAGE, N. L. "Theories of Teaching." *Theories of Learning and Instruction*. (63rd NSSE Yearbook, Part I, edited by Ernest R. Hilgard.) Chicago: University of Chicago Press, 1964. Pp. 268-85.

12. GARDNER, JOHN W. *Self-Renewal*. New York: Harper, 1963.

13. GETZELS, J. W., and JACKSON, P. W. "The Teacher's Personality and Characteristics." *Handbook of Research on Teaching* (Edited by N. L. Gage.) Chicago: Rand McNally, 1963, p. 574.

14. GOSLIN, DAVID A. *The School in Contemporary Society*. Chicago: Scott, Foresman, 1965, 173 pp.

15. GRAMBS, JEAN D. "Teachers as a Minority Group." *Journal of Educational Sociology* 22: 400-5; February 1949.

16. HAVIGHURST, ROBERT J. "Youth in Exploration and Man Emergent." *Man in a World at Work.* (Edited by Henry Borow.). Boston: Houghton Mifflin, 1964. Pp. 215-236.

17. HILLS, JOHN R., and DOWNS, HARRY S. "College Students' Attitudes Toward Teaching as a Profession." *Journal of Teacher Education* 13: 396-401; December 1962.

18. HUNT, J. McV. "Experience and the Development of Motivation: Some Reinterpretations." *Child Development 31: 489-504; September 1960.*

19. IFFERT, ROBERT E. *Retention and Withdrawal of College Students.* (U.S. Office of Education, Bulletin No. 1958-1.) Washington: Government Printing Office, 1957.

20. KATZ, JOSEPH. "Personality and Interpersonal Relations in the College Classroom." *The American College.* (Edited by Nevitt Sanford.) New York: Wiley, 1962. Pp. 365-395.

21. LLOYD-JONES, ESTHER, and HOLMAN, MARY V. "Why People Become Teachers." *The Teacher's Role in American Society.* (Edited by Lindley J. Stiles.) New York: Harper, 1957. Pp. 235-46.

22. MEAD, MARGARET. "Our Educational Emphases in Primitive Perspective." *Anthropology: A Human Science.* (Authored by Margaret Mead.) Princeton: Van Nostrand, 1964. Pp. 162-174.

23. MILLER, CARROLL H. *Foundations of Guidance.* New York: Harper, 1961, 464 pp.

24. PETERSON, WARREN A. *Career Phases and Inter-Age Relationships: the Female High School Teacher in Kansas City.* Doctoral Dissertation, University of Chicago, 1956.

25. REDL, FRITZ, and WATTENBERG, WILLIAM W. *Mental Hygiene in Teaching.* (2nd edition) New York: Harcourt, Brace and World, 1959.

26. RETTIG, SALOMON, and PASAMANICK, BENJAMIN. "Status and Job Satisfaction of Public School Teachers." *School and Society* 87: 113-6; March 1959.

27. ROE, ANNE. "Personality Structure and Occupational Behavior." *Man in a World at Work.* (Edited by Henry Borow.) Boston: Houghton Mifflin, 1964. Pp. 196-214.

28. ROGERS, CARL R. "Personal Thoughts on Teaching and Learning." *On Becoming a Person.* (Authored by Carl R. Rogers.) Boston: Houghton Mifflin, 1961. Pp. 273-278.

29. SMITH, B. OTHANEL. A Concept of Teaching." *Language and Concepts in Education.* (Edited by B. Othanel Smith and Robert H. Ennis.) Chicago: Rand McNally, 1961. Pp. 86-101.

30. TERRIEN, FREDERIC W. *The Behavior System and Occupational Type Associated with Teaching.* Doctoral Dissertation, Yale University, 1950.

31. THOMAS, DONALD R. "Who Wants to Be a Teacher?" *Teachers College Record* 60: 164-71; December 1958.

32. TINK, ALBERT K. *Factors Related to Students Choosing or Not Choosing Teaching as a Vocation.* Doctoral Dissertation, Northwestern University, 1960.

33. WALLER, WILLARD. "The Sociology of the School." *Education and Society.* (Edited by W. Warren Kallenbach and Harold M. Hodges.) Columbus, Ohio: Charles Merrill, 1963. Pp. 201-215.

34. WHITE, ROBERT W. "Competence and the Psychosexual Stages of Development." *Nebraska Symposium in Motivation.* (Edited by M. R. Jones.) Lincoln: University of Nebraska Press, 1960. Pp. 97-140.

35. WILSON, W. CODY, and GOETHALS, GOERGE W. "A Field Study." *The Role of Schools in Mental Health.* (Edited by Wesley Allinsmith and George W. Goethals.) New York: Basic Books, 1962. Pp. 173-277.

36. WRENN, C. GILBERT. "The Culturally Encapsulated Counselor." *Harvard Educational Review 32:* 444-9; Fall 1962.

SCHOOL is for . . .
PLAYGROUND
SOCIALIZING

PTA to Classroom Teachers

ELIZABETH MALLORY

No enterprise is so crucial to the goodness and greatness of a nation as the education of its young citizens. That is why, as the school year rounds to a close, I would salute the nation's teachers, many of whom are our co-workers in the PTA, and devote this page to an issue that is of immediate concern to us all.

The PTA is disturbed, as are professional teachers organizations, at the crisis in public confidence in public education, which is, in part at least, responsible for the financial plight of some school systems. We are particularly disturbed at the apparent erosion in parent-teacher relations, for parents are the most powerful generators of public confidence in schools. When teachers stay away from PTA meetings, when teachers are hard to reach, trust and confidence in them decline, no matter how excellent their classroom performance.

Teachers are overmodest in estimating their attractiveness. Of course the program at a PTA meeting is important, but their presence is more important. Parents want to meet them and talk with them. The ominous communication gap between school and the public cannot be closed by public relations. It can be narrowed by parents who know their teachers.

Research like the Coleman study points up the influence of parents on children's success in school. Knowledgeable educators urge involving parents in their children's education. Parent involvement is a requisite for Title I funding under the Elementary and Secondary Education Act. Most parents are eager to become involved or more involved. And the PTA exists to bring parents and teachers into closer, more productive relations. What are we waiting for?

Surely, parents and educators, thinking together in the PTA, can work out meaningful forms of parent involvement that benefit parents, teachers, and, above all, children. The PTA Action Program offers various suggestions for parent involvement. For example, the PTA

Mallory, Elizabeth. "PTA to Classroom Teachers." (Editorial). *The PTA Magazine.* April 1972. 66:15.

Project RISE, Reading Improvement Services Everywhere, offers abundant opportunities for home-school cooperation in this important area of children's learning.

Through tranquil and tempestuous times, teachers and parents have worked together. We have worked for higher teachers' salaries and better working conditions as well as for better education for all children. Together we have helped to resolve educational crises and together we will surmount the present crisis.

Bigness has become an obsession in our country. I would urge teachers, however, not to think big. Think small. Think not in terms of masses of people but of individuals—individual parents and students. Think not in terms of public relations gimmicks (they only widen the credibility gap) but in terms of human engagements—sensitive, significant encounters with parents and students. With your help, we can make the parent-teacher partnership grow and glow across the land, so that all children may feel at home in school and therefore more ready and more eager to learn.

Every teacher with professional skills and the love of children is worthy of the highest respect a community can give that teacher. Yet somewhere along the line teachers have lost some of that respect even as they have gained through negotiation so much of what was rightfully due them. The more one thinks upon the role that teachers play in our children's lives, the more painful it is to realize that they are not given the respect they richly deserve. There should be no prouder designation in introducing a person than to say, "This is my child's teacher." Wouldn't it be great if we could restore that sense of pride in their children's teachers among all the nation's parents?

Let's use the PTA extensively and imaginatively to accomplish this worthy goal.

Chapter XVII

The Teacher And The Road Ahead

If we could first know where we are,
and whither we are tending we could better
judge what to do, and how to do it.—Abraham Lincoln

The teacher who is entering the profession now does so at an exciting time. The account that follows will support this contention. The tempo of change for the teacher may be expected to accelerate in the coming decade. Oppenheimer has expressed the break with former eras in these terms:

> This world of ours is a new world, in which the unity of knowledge, the nature of human communities, the order of society, the order of ideas, the very notions of society and culture have changed, and will not return to what they have been in the past. What is new is new not because it has never been there before, but because it has changed in quality. One thing that is new is the prevalence of newness, the changing scale and scope of change itself, so that the world alters as we walk in it, so that the years of man's life measure not some small growth or rearrangement or moderation of what he learned in childhood, but a great upheaval (1, p. 5).

It will suffice to say that the concluding articles are compelling and that they carry some sense of urgency. But in no sense do these textbook authors mean that the ideas should be implemented on a crisis or crash oriented basis. Rather, it would be their concerted opinion that the best ideas be facilitated in the sense that former President Johnson has stated: "If we are learning anything from our experiences, we are learning that it is time for us to go to work, and the first work of these times and the first work of our society is education."

1. Ways, Max. "The Era of Radical Change." *Fortune Magazine.* May 1964. 58:5.

The road ahead for teachers seems to be lined with signposts labeled "open schools", "accountability", "competency-based instruction", "value clarification", "schools of perception", and the "systems" approach to education. A word of caution seems in order regarding the use of a *behavioral objectives system* of instruction. In any behavioral objectives system acquired from an industrial group the emphasis is upon the product;—the *worker* is the way you get to the product. In education, the *worker* (pupil) is the product. Consequently, one *should not* use solely any behavioral objective system, purposefully avoiding *perceptual* models, since it is the humanistic model which works upon the pupil.

The behavioral objective system of instruction guarantees your goals will be accomplished. The criteria of a well-written instructional objective indicates what the pupil is to do, under what conditions he is going to do it, and the time and extent of accuracy expected in the doing of the chosen objective. What one chooses to do, may cause a child to become quite narrow in what he does do because he will do anything to please his teacher. It may well be that many purposes of education are to be broad, not narrow. When ideas are too concrete and exact, the school is teaching the child to zero in on narrow ideas, specific facts, insignificant minutiae; anxieties are threatened and as a consequence the child merely tries to get by without thinking.

On the other hand, if the system of instruction becomes immersed in how a child feels about himself (his self concept) and what the school might do to enhance such feelings, then it is conceivable that clear-cut instructional purposes would emerge regarding the *affective domain* (values, attitudes, beliefs) to become behavioral guidance tools of every classroom teacher. In any event, with or without behavioral objectives, helping a pupil reach his needs and to identify problems of self which he never knew he had, should still be a primary goal of educators in the schools of the future.

A Concept of the "School" in 2000 A.D.

JOHN I. GOODLAD

In a nation that speaks of inalienable rights, the right to learn must be paramount. Yet that right, in its full meaning, has been denied to many in this nation. It has been denied because of color and religion, because of poverty and infirmity, and because of place of abode. And it has been denied because of our mindless adherence to unproductive teaching concepts and practices.

The right to learn is the goal we set for the 21st century. We want for our children a range of learning opportunities as broad as the unknown range of their talents—and a learning environment that nurtures those talents. We want them to have freedom, and the order, justice, and peace that the preservation of their freedom demands.

Yet we scarcely know the meaning of these grand words, let alone how to give them body and substance. Clearly, then, we must engage in great experiments encouraging alternatives and diversity throughout what must become a much more varied and comprehensive educational system. This must involve: 1) the reconstruction of existing schools, 2) the creation of new schools free of the present system, and 3) above all, the expansion of "school" into the world.

A Narrow Concept

Schools and teachers have been with us for so long that we now equate them with education and, worse, with learning. The infant learns to walk and to talk, to trust and to distrust; he learns fear and love and hate—all without benefit of school. The tragic irony is that we know all this and still equate learning with school. By age 5, the child has sat before a television set for at least the number of hours he will spend in the first three grades of school. And still we equate learning with school.

The first difficult step toward achieving our goal is acceptance of

Goodlad, John I. "A Concept of the 'School' in 2000 A.D." *The National Elementary Principal.* January 1971. 50:2-4, 86-88. Reprinted by permission of the author and The National Association of Elementary School Principals, copyright © 1971.

what should be obvious: School is but a part of the learning environment. Until recently, we believed that it was the most powerful part of that environment; we now know that it is not.

We have only begun to question the outworn notion that certain subjects or concepts are to be learned by all individuals, at successive stages of growth, at stipulated times, in sterile places. Reading is for the first grade, long division for the fourth, and fractions for the fifth and sixth. All this takes place between the hours of 9 and 3 in a big box divided into cells.

In this lockstep, as in so many other ways, we teach that each phase of life is instrumental to the next, rather than of ultimate value in itself. We see the man we want the child to become rather than the child seeking to become himself. In the words of Hannah Arendt, "Man sees wood in every tree." Perhaps this is one reason why more than half of all Americans over 50 say that they find their lives to be disappointing, unrewarding, unfulfilling, and find, when they come to die, that they "never had lived at all."

This is the winter of our educational discontent. Until recently, we believed that we had only to inject some new subject matter here, a heavier dose of phonics there, tighten the discipline a little, to improve both the system and society. Better schools (defined largely in quantitative terms) would mean more jobs, a brisker economy, safer cities, and more aware and dedicated citizens.

Or so we thought. Dwindling confidence in these relationships reflects both declining confidence in the schools and the tenacity with which we cling to the "learning equals school" equation. Painfully, we are coming to realize that grades predict grades, that success in school begets more success in school but is not a guarantee of good workers, committed citizens, happy mothers and fathers, or compassionate human beings.

For a brief span of years, we believed that the sickness spread only through the schools of our great cities. Increasingly, however, we have come to understand that suburban and, to an even greater degree, rural schools do not assure the diet nor provide the vitality our children deserve. Even the middle-class school around the corner reveals ragged edges surrounding a soft center. The overall failure is glaringly apparent in dropout rates, in barely minimal learning on the part of many who do remain in school, and in growing alienation among the young of all colors and classes.

Winners and Losers

At the root of the problem is an implicit denial of diversity. The schools have become great sorting machines, labeling and certifying those who presumably will be winners and losers as adults. The winners are disproportionately white and affluent; the losers, too often, poor and brown or black or red.

But many of the winners are losers, too. For they are shaped, directed, and judged according to a narrow conception of what is proper. This process begins very early; the environment of expectations, rewards, and punishments is established before mother and child leave the hospital. And in the home, infants are encouraged in their efforts to walk and talk, but their responses to sound, color, and smell are ignored or stifled.

This process of channeling energy and talent is refined and perfected in the schools through a network of expectations, rules, grades, required subjects, and rewards for what is wanted and the subtle extinction of the great range of talents and achievements that are not wanted.

A massive task of change lies ahead. We cannot point pridefully at those who have "made it" while half of us believe that life has passed us by.

Among many of our people there is a sense of outrage induced by the discrepancy between what is and what could be. We [the committee] share that outrage, but we have more than a little hope that a new era can be both described and created. At the core of this hope is a fresh awareness of children—of their intrinsic rather than instrumental value, of their ability to learn, and of the kind of learning they could and should have going into the 21st century.

Other generations believed that they had the luxury of preparing their children to live in a society similar to their own. Ours is the first generation to have achieved the Socratic wisdom of knowing that we do not know the world in which our children will live.

All that we can predict with certainty is that the central issue of the 21st century, as it is of this one, will be the struggle to assert truly human values and to achieve their ascendancy in a mass, technological society. It will be the struggle to place man in a healthy relationship with his natural environment; to place him in command of, rather than subservient to, the wondrous technology he is creating, and to give him the breadth and depth of understanding which can result in the formation of a world culture, embracing and nurturing within its transcending characteristics the diverse cultures of the world of today.

The education of 21st century man is necessarily an enabling process rather than an instructional one. It requires opening the whole of the world to the learner and giving him easy access to that world. This implies enormous respect for the child's capacity to learn, and with the granting of respect goes, by implication, the granting of freedom.

Learning as an End

When we look to education in the century to come, we see learning not as a means to some end but as an end in itself. Education will not be an imitation of life, but life examined and enjoyed. A prescribed age for beginning to learn—or for ceasing to learn—will be meaningless. So will age as a criterion for determining what needs to be learned. And so will the standard school day and academic year.

Compulsory education—or compulsory attendance, as it might better be called—will be a thing of the past. School as we know it will have been replaced by a diffuse learning environment involving homes, parks, public buildings, museums, business offices, and guidance centers. Many such resources that are now unofficial, unrecognized, unstructured, or unsupervised—and unused—will be endorsed and made fully available for learning. There will be successors to our present schools—places designed for people to gather for purposes of learning things together.

Children and their families will be responsible for setting educational goals and mapping the route toward them. Plentiful assistance and advice will be available, if desired, in planning highly flexible and individualized schemes for learning, but it will be left to the learner—and, when he is very young, his family—to choose among alternatives.

The very availability of a great range of options will represent what we believe will be an important and essential change in our national value system. "Success" will have been redefined, and a wide range of studies, tastes, careers, and "lifestyles" will be legitimized and praiseworthy. Boys will not be made to feel that they must grow up to be aggressive—or even affluent—men. Girls will not need to feel that domesticity is the necessary be-all and end-all of their existence; a career in science will not have higher status than a career in the creative arts. We will, in short, give substance to our longstanding but never fulfilled commitment to honor and develop the entire range of human talent.

Modern technology will help us realize our goals. The profound significance of the computer, when properly used in learning, is that it introduces an entirely new source of energy into the educational process. It is energy that is not affected by the night before, by viruses or by unmanageable children. Subjects missed this year can be picked up next year. Single subjects can be pursued intensively for periods of time governed only by the whim of the learner.

It is possible that advanced technology will return the family to center stage as the basic learning unit. Each home could become a school, in effect, connected via an electronic console to a central educational computer system, a computer-regulated videotape and microfilm library and a national educational television network. Whether at home or elsewhere, each student will have, at the touch of a button, access to a comprehensive "learning package," including printed lessons, experiments to be performed, recorded information, videotaped lectures, and films.

The moment so much teaching energy is made available throughout the 24-hour span of the day to all individuals at any place, school need no longer be what we have known it to be. It may be used for other functions not fully recognized until now. It will be the place where human beings come together not for the formalities of learning subject matter but for the higher literacy going far beyond reading, writing, and arithmetic.

Heavier stress will be laid on learning different forms of rationality and logic and on dealing with crisis and conflict. The individual will be helped to develop a greater consciousness of his thoughts and feelings, so that he may feel and experience life and at the same time "stand outside" his immediate experience. For 21st century man would be a sentient being with both the freedom that comes from understanding and the accompanying control of impulse.

In such an educational world, everyone will be, from time to time, both teacher and learner, but there will still be great need for teachers who, for the first time, will be free to engage in truly human tasks. No longer will they need to function as ineffective machines imparting "facts" by rote—real machines will have taken over that function. Some will spend many hours preparing a single lesson to be viewed by thousands or even millions of individuals of all ages; others will evaluate such counseling centers. Others will be engaging with groups of all ages in dialogue designed to enhance human communication and understanding.

The entire educational enterprise will be directed toward increasing the freedom and the power of the individual to shape himself, to live at ease in his community and, in doing so, to experience self-fulfillment.

Achieving Utopia

We have sketched a kind of learning Utopia; achieving it will not be easy. In fact, without massive, thoughtful social reconstruction, we will not get there at all. To stand aside—unconcerned, uncommitted, and unresolved—may very well be to assure no 21st century and, least of all, no Utopia.

The first step is moral commitment. Like all moral commitments, it must be backed by resources and action. We sound a special call for full and genuine commitment to the right to learn.

The signal announcing his commitment will be the long-awaited injection of large-scale government funds into learning: for encouraging experimentation in existing schools, for the creation of experimental schools, and for transcending the schools by bringing new learning into them and taking children to the range of resources outside them. For a time, at least, we must infuse these funds as though we were at war—because we are at war—with ignorance, prejudice, injustice, intolerance, and all those forces crippling and restricting young and old alike.

The first phase of reconstruction involves the schools we have. Supposedly, the decade of the Sixties was one of school reform: in the curriculum, in the organization of school classroom, and in instruction. But recent studies reveal that the appearance of change far outruns the actuality of it.

Despite emphasis on the need for identifying goals, few schools have a clear sense of direction. Despite the obvious futility of "teaching" the world's knowledge, schools still emphasize the learning of facts rather than how to learn.

Despite this golden era of instructional materials and children's literature, the textbook is still the prime medium of instruction. Despite gaining knowledge about individual differences in learning, what children are to learn is still laid out by grades, years, months, and even days. Despite increased insight into how learning occurs, teaching is still largely telling and questioning. In a diverse, complex society, our schools demonstrate almost monolithic conformity and enormous resistance to change; close scrutiny reveals a deep-seated impotence, an inability to come to grips with the acknowledged problems.

Investing in the Unknown

The top agenda item, then, in seeking to enhance learning in the Seventies is unshackling the schools. The process must begin by decentralizing authority and responsibility for instructional decision making to individual schools. Simply dividing large school districts into smaller districts is not the answer. Schools, like individuals, are different: in size, problems, clientele, and types of communities served. They must create programs appropriate to their local circumstances. Many schools are not ready to take quick advantage of such sudden freedoms. Too long fettered by the large system, their staffs will be timid and uncertain.

We recommend, therefore, that substantial federal funds be allocated for the deliberate development of schools whose sole reason for being is experimental. Designed to provide alternatives, such schools could provide options in the community and thus would attract a more supportive parent group. In time, such schools would provide models for replication in networks of cooperating schools seeking to learn from each other.

Such schools need not arise solely within "the system." The need to break out of established patterns has never been more critical. We need alternatives whereever we can find them. Some of the "free" schools springing up around the country offer diversity and should be encouraged to the point where their practices truly reflect their underlying philosophies.

We urge that schools be given support for abolishing the grade levels, developing new evaluation procedures, using the full range of community resources for learning, automating certain kinds of learning, exploring instructional techniques for developing self-awareness and creative thinking, rescheduling the school year, and more. Most of all, we urge substantial financial support for schools seeking to redesign their entire learning environment, from the curriculum through the structure of the school to completely new instructional procedures.

Especially needed are well-developed models of early learning. We know now that the first five years of life largely determine the characteristics of the young adult. Yet we fail these years shamefully either through neglect, through narrow, thoughtless shaping, or through erratic shifts from too little to too much concern.

Two successive administrations have promised and failed to deliver on a national effort for expansion and improvement in the education of young children. A National Laboratory in Early Childhood Education suffered a crippled birth under one administration and is now starving to death under another. We need research on what we now know; we need thousands of adequately prepared teachers to staff nursery and play schools, and we need exemplary models of programs stressing cognitive, esthetic, motor, and affective development.

Remaking Our Teachers

High on our list of "old business" is the overhaul of teacher education from top to bottom. The continuing debate over the value of "methods" courses, whether to have more or fewer of them, and how to regulate teacher education by legislative fiat only reveals the poverty of our approaches to the problem. Shuffling courses about is not the answer. Required are strategies that take account of the fact that preservice teacher education, inservice teacher education, and the schools themselves are dependent, interrelated, and interacting components of one social system.

It becomes apparent, therefore, that financial resources must be directed toward those strategies that link schools seeking to change with teacher education institutions seeking to shake out of established patterns. The teacher for tomorrow's learning must be prepared in school settings endeavoring to create a new kind of tomorrow; most of today's teachers are prepared for yesterday's schools.

The tasks for the Seventies may not have the heady appeal of the slogans for the Sixties, but they have a meaty substance about them, an "action" appeal for students, teachers, parents, private foundations, and all levels of government.

But we need not wait for the 1980's to get a good start on other components of our visions for 2000. In fact, some roots already are taking hold.

School, however reformed, is but one of the child's resources for learning. Children spend more time, perhaps learn more, for better or for worse, in the electronic embrace of television. Television, however, is but one of several powerful teachers of the electronic genre. The computer has even greater potential because of its ability to coordinate an array of devices for sight, sound, touch, and even smell.

We must stop talking about the possibilities and engage in experimentation on a much broader scale. To date, educational television has teetered on the brink of disaster, its limp fare failing to compete with commercial products, especially advertising. "Sesame Street" demonstrates vigorously that this need not be. It also demonstrates that successful use of television for desirable learning by children requires substantial financial backing—for air time, for production, for evaluation, and especially for research into what constitutes appropriate subject matter. Ten years from now, initial use of television to teach children numbers and the alphabet will probably appear primitive.

One of the major tasks involved in bringing electronics productively into children's learning involves a kind of research; namely, determining appropriate roles for human and machine teachers. The cant of audio-visual education insists that equipment be only an extension of human teachers. For computers, for example, to be mere aids of human teachers is to cripple both. We must recognize the fact that electronic devices constitute a new kind of instructional energy—indefatigable, relatively immune to changes in the weather, and contemptuous of time of day or day of week.

The human teacher, on the other hand, is sharply limited in energy pattern, highly susceptible to chills, immobile in times of flood and snow, and sensitive to time of day. Clearly, the tasks for human and machine teachers should be both differentiated and complementary.

When we come to recognize fully the characteristics and possibilities of electronic energy, most of the "givens" of schooling collapse. Learning need not take place in a box, from 9 to 3 each day, five days a week, 180 days per year. There need not be a school beginning at age 5, a graded school, or a "balance" of subjects throughout the day. Nothing need be "missed" because of absence, for it can be picked up tomorrow by asking the machine to retrieve whatever is wanted.

Experimentation is needed, beginning now and continuing unabated into the 21st century, to create and legitimize options for schooling. Soon it will be common practice to show a variety of cassette tapes through a home television set. Cable television promises a new set of options. And just behind both of these developments lies the home computer television terminal plugged into several video outlets, capable of playing its own records and cassettes, and providing printouts of the learning and cultural options currently available in the community. Taking advantage of these alternatives must be accepted and encouraged.

One way for us to begin to grow accustomed to this nonschool freedom is to use the learning resources lying outside school much more vigorously. Children should be excused from school for blocks of time to gain access to a nonschool teacher, to serve as apprentice to an artisan, or to practice a hobby in depth.

The Role of Drugs

We had better begin now, because we will need all our imagination and wisdom to cope with some of the critical moral questions soon to be thrust upon us. We do know that drugs are being used deliberately, under medical supervision, to intervene in the learning processes of children. Electronic means are being used to assist in the treatment of childhood disorders. Independent of these activities, drug use, ranging from mild exploration to dangerous abuse, is now a fact of life. Who are to be judged deviant and needful of chemical or electronic treatment? What restraints are to be placed upon the use of drugs for educational, self-serving, or destructive purposes?

And who is to make what decisions for whom? That question is probably the most pressing educational question for both today and tomorrow. It is at the core of any minority group demands for self-determination and equality. Ultimately, it brings us into the matter of who owns the child and who is to determine his freedom. To return where we began, the right to learn means the freedom of each individual to learn what he needs in his own way and at his own rate, in his own place and time.

This interpretation of the right to learn will not be easily understood. Nor are we likely to come easily to full acceptance and support of the flexibility and experimentation required to design the future of learning. We urge our leaders at all levels to work toward public understanding and support. We recommend that celebration of this nation's 200th birthday in 1976 be taken as the occasion for a nationwide dialogue about, and assessment of, our entire learning enterprise.

Teaching: An Educational Adventure

My many teachers have been of one general model, *dispensers of information.* This teaching model has a tremendous quality of perseveration as we continue to teach as we are taught. I would propose that the conditions of public and private education will now support, perhaps even demand, a *change* to teaching as an educational adventure.

There is becoming an ever increasing awareness that teaching must become a significant and real agent for positive change of behavior. Behavior change based on societal reality must become part of the curriculum of every classroom.

Becoming a member of the teaching profession is not synonymous with becoming a teacher. It is this awareness of what becoming a teacher should mean which is the thesis of this essay. The teacher who begins to see teaching as an adventure in changing behavior toward positive societal reality will need to identify at least three major teaching roles. The teacher will need specific professional skill to complete his functions in each of these roles.

Three Faces of Teaching

The teacher who will accept the challenge of an educational adventure must see teaching as (1) educational management, (2) educational interaction, and (3) educational therapy.

The expectation must be that teachers will, in fact, become managers, interactors, and therapists of professional quality and that the concept of teaching as telling will be replaced with the concept of teaching as an adventure in positive human change.

Myers, Kent E., "Teaching: An Educational Adventure." *The Clearing House.* November 1971. 46:131-135.

Teaching as Educational Management. The learning experience in school is a management process performed by the teacher. Yet, we seldom find the teacher being trained with management skills except as these skills are incidentally learned in teaching methods classes or as by-products of practical experience. The concept of management makes a teacher face the challenge of answering the key question, "Why am I teaching what I am teaching?"

It becomes apparent that as a teacher designs an instructional sequence the question he usually answers is, "What am I going to do?" This leaves the *why* unanswered and often leads to unreal and artificial curriculum content which may or may not produce positive change in behavior and seldom leads to behavior which is useful in the larger society outside the walls of the school.

Management implies a basic skill in the decision-making process. Teachers who have had little or no practice in this process in an educational setting need training in the skill of making appropriate decisions.

MODEL FOR INSTRUCTION

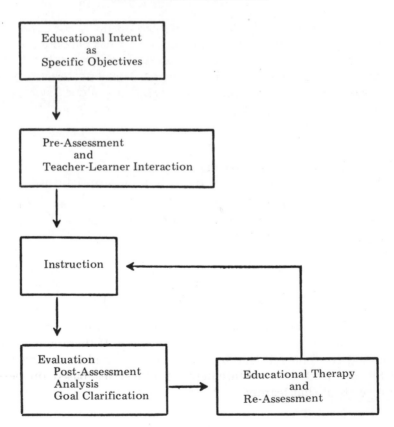

Management of appropriate learning experiences for every student will demand some method of individualized instruction. Appropriateness is possible, but only if decisions about instruction are based on the individual needs, capacities, and present abilities of the learners and the planned educational intent of the teacher.

Teaching as educational management implies that a teacher is accountable for educational results. An educational management model for instruction would have five basic operations.

The first educational decision comes from the question, "How can I state what is to be learned as objectives in terms of learner behavior?" Because the teacher's expectation is such an important motive to learners, the teacher must always consider the *why* of each objective and be able to state substantial personal and societal reasons for including specific objectives in the design. Developing reasons for why an objective should be reached gives purpose to learning and can therefore increase motivation.

Second, pre-assessment will give the teacher data on each student and should allow for counselling and clarification of each learner's need for instruction. It is amazing how many students will already have the skills, concepts or attitudes desired as outcomes of a particular lesson or unit of instruction if the teacher decides to find out who can perform and who cannot. Pre-assessment can and should be more than paper and pencil tests, especially if the objectives call for performance skills. Pre-assessment followed by teacher-learner interaction will give the teacher the opportunity to help each learner utilize the assessment of that learner's current knowledge and skills in the selection of appropriate instruction. It will also allow the learner who has already reached the objectives to move to new objectives immediately.

Third, instruction must be based on individual needs developed in the pre-assessment. Instruction must include appropriate use of space, materials and technology for independent study with the teacher as a basic resource person. More than *one* way should be provided for the learner to receive instruction. Choice of mode of instruction should be made by the learner whenever possible.

Fourth, evaluation should determine if the objectives have been attained by each learner. It should also allow the learner to perceive, by comparison with pre-assessment analysis, just how great the change has been. Teacher-learner counselling should determine the next step.

Fifth, the learner and teacher must decide if educational therapy is needed or if a new cycle of instruction can begin. If therapy is indicated, its form and content will lead to new instruction and further evaluation. It might also lead to a restatement of objectives based on personal, realistic needs of that learner.

Teaching as Educational Interaction. Educational management with educational interaction makes learning a real and individualized experience. Without the personal counselling which is possible in direct human interaction, teaching becomes routine and global rather than personal and individualized.

Suitability of instruction depends on the needs and the motor, perceptual, and cognitive abilities of the learner as well as a host of affective variables. Personal interaction gives the teacher the information and the insights needed to make the most of each learner's assets.

The teacher as a counselor must deal with the paradox of emotional feelings and objective thoughts. The counselor-teacher must find the appropriate balance so that the interaction relationship is real and dynamic. The feelings of the teacher must be genuine and sincere and information used in counselling must be clear and objective.

Personal teacher-learner interaction exemplifies the positive growth of the individual toward a position of self-respect and self-determination. Because each learner is unique, each relationship will be unique. Teachers already know that the same techniques of instruction will not fit every student. The same is true of the personal relationships developed in sessions of teacher-learner interaction.

The major problem to solve is to have the teacher see himself in the counselor-teacher role and to develop the skills to approach teaching with a counselor point-of-view.

Perhaps the most important characteristic the teacher will need to develop is that of *acceptance.* To accept a human being for what he is and lead him to a positive change means placing extreme value on the unique self which each learner will bring to the interaction moments.

Interaction and counselling in the model of instruction is shown as part of the pre-assessment and evaluation operations, but it should be understood that personal interaction is on-going throughout the learning process. Teacher counselling becomes a guiding of learning experience which is a key responsibility of teaching.

Teaching as Educational Therapy. Even under the most systematic management system there will be a need for special therapeutic measures for some learners. The system must not only allow for these measures, it must be made to enhance them.

"Therapy" as a word can take on many meanings, but here it means simply the restructuring of instruction to induce success rather than failure for the learner.

When evaluation reveals a marked difference between what was intended and what was achieved, therapy is indicated. This might include teacher-learner counselling, tutoring, establishing pre-requisite skills, or simply choosing a different mode of instruction. It may also include a review of the objectives in keeping with unique previous experiences of that learner to see if stated objectives are real and have meaning in *his* society.

Educational therapy should bring to bear all the expertise of the educational community and it must necessarily imply that all teachers need to develop skills in educational and psychological diagnosis. Appropriate skill levels will depend on the placement of the teacher, but basic diagnostic skills which will allow a teacher to make sense of test data, observations, and reports of others is imperative. Skill in the use of diagnostic instruments and techniques are requisites of educational therapy.

The concept of educational therapy is as applicable to a so-called normal classroom as it is to a classroom for remedial or special students.

The management of instruction will become individualized only when the teacher has attained skill in therapeutic diagnosis, personal interaction relationships, and programming of instruction which allows for the wide range of differences between and within learners.

The consequences of adequate adjustment to school as a part of society must not be underestimated. The adventure of school can end in tragedy as well as success if appropriate life-style adjustments are not made. Therefore, management, interaction, and therapy should be teaching tools which produce dynamic human relationships as well as academic progress.

Implications

In summary, the discussion of teaching roles will permit the statement of the following implications for education:

(1) Teacher education should be reorganized on the basis of proficiency of skills in educational management, interaction, and therapy.
(2) Teachers should develop a teacher-counselor *point-of-view* which can be used to develop relationships which give sincere indications to the learner that the teacher cares about him.
(3) The management and therapy techniques and skills will allow the teachers to provide effective instruction across a wide range of individual differences.
(4) Education can be an adventure which is deeply motivating to both teacher and learner if the learner is given responsibility for the success of his experience with expert guidance from a professional teacher.
(5) The model of "teaching as telling" must be replaced or modified to allow the model to be one of educational management through effective guidance of individualized learning experiences.
(6) Teachers can and should be held accountable for results and should be rewarded on the basis of proficiency in achieving results.
(7) Techniques of educational diagnosis, previously reserved for specialists, must become part of the professional training of all teachers.

REFERENCES

1. McCARTHY, JAMES J. and JOAN F. McCARTHY, *Learning Disabilities.* Boston: Allyn and Bacon, Inc., 1969.
2. OTTO, WAYNE and RICHARD A. McMENEMY, *Corrective and Remedial Teaching.* Boston: Houghton Mifflin. 1966.
3. POPHAM, W. JAMES and EVA L. BAKER, *Systematic Instruction.* Englewood Cliffs, N.J.: Prentice Hall, Inc., 1970.
4. STRANG, RUTH and GLYN MORRIS, *Guidance in the Classroom.* New York: The Macmillan Co., 1964.

SCHOOL is for . . .
DAYDREAMING

Shaping Our Image

R. C. BRADLEY

Now let us be honest with ourselves. Our concern with improved public relations grows out of enlightened selfishness. We think we know how a change will affect us, thus we are willing to work in order to get what we want. What we want, of course, is the unquestioned support of our citizens for their schools. Since we are a vital part of these schools, this school support means also support for us, appreciation of what we have done, approval of what we now are doing, and encouragement for what we plan to do in the future.

An interesting point to remember, however, is that every citizen in the community also wants something, and he will trade with us—give us what we want if we will give him what he wants. And this exchange seems fair. What he wants, of course, is a feeling of importance. He, too, wants to be accepted. He wants to be heard, as indeed he should.

With all this philosophy clearly understood by all parties concerned, the opportunity to improve our public image as teachers and as a profession becomes a challenge, and especially to the teacher. As trite as it may seem to report what is so often said, I must insist that school public relations (good or bad) start in the classroom.

The teacher who keeps his facts current, accurate, and specific regarding school and community issues of local, state, or national origin has found one of the secrets to success in public relations. A recognition of competence and thoroughness builds confidence and establishes reliability, both of which are essential to sound public relations.

Not an Administrative Exclusive

The school public relations program should not be left solely to administrative procedure. More than administrators must function

Bradley, R. C. "Shaping Our Image." *North Carolina Education*. February 1968. 34:15, 35-36.

actively in the on-going PR program. Obviously, therefore, the classroom teacher is in a strategic position for taking a look at what is actually happening and for identifying what groups are making it happen. Someone is going to make things happen in education and teachers generally know the makers. In fact, the teachers themselves are often the force behind the happening. The late President Kennedy hit the spot when he said to an assembly of education association leaders: "Things don't happen. They are made to happen. And in the field of education they are made to happen by you and your members."

What then, can the individual teacher do as a private contribution to a public relations program? He has two approaches. Approach number one deals with an external effort, meaning that as a private citizen he should seek to be well informed about general policies, practices, and beliefs of the governor, legislators, and statewide organizations toward educational issues that will affect schools and youth. Approach number two deals with an internal effort, meaning that he should strengthen teacher-parent partnership! This he can do through (a) the public relations clinic in which the entire staff conducts a self-evaluation project and identifies ways of improving school public relations. One such way, for example, is to do a better job of making school visitors feel welcome. (b) The regular faculty meeting, at which each person is asked to contribute new public relations ideas. (c) Self-image measurement, by which you try to determine how the public sees you as a teacher. (d) Building public relations coordinator, whose responsibility it will be to collect effective public relations ideas from all members of the faculty, using them in a faculty bulletin.

Without anybody's help, however, you can consider these three suggestions: You can invite knowledgeable parents to speak at assemblies and faculty meetings. This partnership will help to build a good relationship. Too, many speaker-parents will find out for the first time how the school performs. Parents nights when they assume the roles of students have proved to have special PR value. Without genuine teacher enthusiasm for this occasion, however, a negative attitude may be revealed.

Personal Letters

Other projects include an improvement in appearance of the school entrance, school hallway, or reception room, clean-up campaigns and landscaping activities on the school-ground, a personal letter to parents outlining your goals and ambitions for your class, and, frequently, a complimentary note about some deserving child.

Of course, a public relations gimmick can be too self-revelatory. Remember that most men select a new necktie and women an Easter bonnet pretty enough to win attention, but not so startling as to attract shocked stares. So it is with the public relations program. The story-telling classroom bulletin board is really a better step toward sound public relations than is the mimeographed faculty bulletin which may be collecting dust on the bookshelf. Eternal vigilance must be the watchword, for your school may be the next to be criticized publicly for not teaching the fundamentals, using the public dollar wisely, or providing space-age education for youth. Too, you may be lambasted for overemphasis on new concepts of human dignity, rights of labor, or the social significance of democracy; hence all classroom teachers must be prepared to reply to such attacks and further educate themselves so as to understand these issues.

Finally, a part of your responsibility in school public relations is to understand fully the current issues in education. Parents need to know that the present demands upon the classroom teacher are tremendous. It is your duty to be ready at all times with Henry Steele Commager's declaration: "No other people ever demanded so much of education as have the American. None other was ever served so well by its schools and educators."

SCHOOL is for . . .
COOPERATION

Some Basic Concepts

■ What precisely is performance-based instruction? One can search dictionaries indefinitely without finding a satisfactory definition of the term *performance-based*, the reason being that it is a coined term—a sort of trade name which also represents a new movement in education. Another term might have been equally suitable. Indeed, some people prefer *competency-based*, and the two terms are used interchangeably.

What, then, are people talking about when they refer to performance-based or competency-based instruction? Essentially they are saying that all learning is individual—that the individual, whether teacher or learner, is goal-oriented.

They are saying that the teacher-learning process is facilitated if the teacher knows what he wants the pupil to learn and if the learner is aware of precisely what is expected of him or what he expects of himself. Precise knowledge of results also enhances learning.

Finally, they are saying that the learner or teacher is most likely to do what is expected of him and what he expects of himself if he is accountable for doing what he undertakes.

Understanding the performance-based movement presents some difficulties. For one thing, not everyone is saying the same thing with regard to it. For another, people have a tendency to mix the concept of performance-based with other concepts closely related to it. Attempts to develop a precise definition have led some educators to use a model composed of three concentric circles.

Howsam, Robert B. "Performance-Based Instruction—Some Basic Concepts." *Today's Education*. April 1972. 61:35-39.

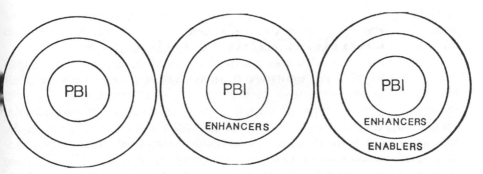

The inner circle represents performance-based instruction (PBI), which has four essential elements. These elements are: (a) precise objectives, stated in behavioral terms; (b) performance criteria, indicators of performance, modes of assessment, and criterion levels specified and made public along with objectives; (c) instruction pertinent to the criteria; and (d) learner accountability in terms of the criteria.

The second circle represents ideas and practices so closely identified with performance-based instruction that they tend to be mixed up with it. They are often the means by which PBI is implemented. We can term these ideas and practices *enhancers.*

Some of the enhancers are: (a) individualization and personalization of instruction, (b) modularized instruction, (c) multiple alternative learning opportunities, (d) use of technology, (e) use of the open-space concept, and (f) instructional teams.

The outer ring of the three circles represents less closely related but important considerations that may be thought of as *enablers.*

A few examples of enablers are (a) application of systems, principles, and techniques; (b) participative management (involvement processes); (c) effective teacher personnel procedures; and (d) management by objectives.

There has long been a tendency in teaching to be relatively imprecise about objectives—those specific objectives which identify the target. Even if a teacher is conscious of specific objectives, it has not been customary for him to share these objectives with his students. The result has been confusion and lack of purpose for many learners.

Teaching is, by definition, a process of deliberately managing the learning environment and learning activities in such a way as to bring about desired behavior. The proponents of PBI believe that teaching cannot take place in the absence of specific objectives nor can the results of teaching be known unless the desired behaviors are identified and assessed.

Accordingly, performance-based instruction concentrates on

identifying objectives and stating them in behavioral terms—in terms of what the learner is able to do. Let's compare this type of instruction with the traditional variety.

For example, traditional instruction might aspire to have pupils "know about the native trees, plants, animals, and birds in their locality." The teacher would "cover" the material and then use a test to determine by some kind of sampling what proportion of the material each pupil learned. Normally, student strengths in one area (for example, animals) would counterbalance weaknesses in another (plants). Performance would consist of recall or recognition on written tests. Grades based on some kind of distribution of scores would be given. Certain students would be deemed to "fail."

PBI might have the same goal and objectives as traditional instruction. It would, however, proceed quite differently.

In the first place, it would divide the material into smaller instructional units, often called modules. It would state the objectives for each module in terms of what the learner must be able to do before *his* responsibility is met. For example, he might be expected to:

1. Identify not less than 16 birds in his area from colored pictures, models, or specimens—with the correct name, pronunciation, and spelling.

2. Identify the songs of 15 (out of 20) birds from recordings.

3. Participate in a bird-watching field trip or provide evidence of a personal activity of equal value.

4. Describe, either orally or in writing, the feeding and nesting habits of 10 birds.

5. Identify the natural enemies of five birds, indicating how people can protect these birds.

Note that in each case the objective is stated in terms of performance—*identity, imitate, participate.* The performance criteria are, therefore, specific. Also, the criterion level (15 out of 20) is indicated and the means by which the competence will be assessed are clearly stated.

Since all of this is made known in advance, both the student and the teacher have shared knowledge of the performance criteria, the criterion levels, and the methods assessment. This specificity sharpens the focus of both teacher and learner. Above all, however, it makes possible new levels of independent and interdependent pupil behavior. It permits accountability for results on the part of both learner and teacher.

Since the performance level is established for each objective, accountability applies to each one. A learner cannot come out "satisfactory" or "average" by excelling in one objective and doing poorly in another. This principle of establishing the performance level for each objective is termed *criterion referenced* in contradistinction to the present widespread use of *norm referenced* assessment.

Whatever the respective strengths and weaknesses of PBI and of more traditional instruction, it becomes increasingly apparent that truly individualized and personalized instruction can come about only if education provides independent learning activities. This, in turn, depends upon the ability to package learning activities effectively and to make them available through a sort of educational smorgasbord.

Precision, as against vagueness, is the key to preparing instructional modules. The pupil will move from the feet of the master only if his dependence on the master can be reduced.

The performance-based idea can be used with any kind of teaching from strict lecturing to the most advanced and sophisticated forms of self-directed and individualized instruction. *Any teacher at any level and under any set of circumstances can, if he wishes, move his instruction toward conformity with the four essential elements of performance-based instruction.*

The real potential of PBI, however, will not be fully realized with traditional forms of instruction. Use of enhancers and enablers will greatly enlarge PBI's utility and effectiveness.

One needs to understand the concept of PBI and its methods, but he doesn't have to deal with all the methods at the beginning. As a matter of fact, presenting the full array of elements, enhancers, and enablers to teachers at one time might so discourage them as to cause them to abandon the concept altogether. The teacher who wishes to try PBI techniques can do so without the need to have a differentiated assignment on a teaching team in an open-concept school equipped with a full array of educational technology. Indeed, most of us couldn't use these resources all at once even if we had them. Nor does the teacher have to have extensive formal preparation, useful though this might be.

What the teacher *does* need is understanding and commitment. Beyond that, many alternatives are available. You, the teacher, may find some of the following suggestions useful:

• Be sure that you understand the basic principles or elements of PBI. Then, form (or join) a group of teachers with which to share the experience. A group within your school would be most useful, and it will be helpful if the principal wants to be included.

• Avoid having administrative or group pressures applied to teachers who are reluctant to participate. Also, avoid letting your group become a clique within the staff.

• Gain experience in writing instructional objectives in behavioral terms—with mutual in-group help, with outside assistance, or with both.

Excellent materials, some in self-instruction form, are available. As you achieve basic competence with instructional objectives, begin to apply it to your day-to-day teaching.

● Select one unit of work (not too involved or lengthy) and redo it, applying PBI principles. One or more modules will result. Ask other teachers in the group to react to your materials.

● Prepare the module(s) with more than the usual degree of care, using every teaching strategy and all the materials available to you.

● Be sure to provide at least two optional modes by which students can meet each of the behavioral objectives (your lesson, designated sections of workbooks and textbooks or other reading materials, cassette or tape recordings, slide-tape materials, and so on). Ensure that it is possible for the learner, by exercising his options, to gain the expected level of performance on each criterion.

● Add other units to your repertoire and expand the use of PBI as you gain experience and confidence. At the same time, refine your initial efforts based on results of your experiences.

● Develop related parts of the instructional system, such as grading and promotions, since many established procedures will not fit in with your new efforts. However, because your efforts might upset the larger system, be sure to consult with your principal before you try to effect any basic changes.

● Prepare your students for the PBI experience. Traditional teaching modes do not fit the student for specific performance accountability and for the role of responsible independent learner. This does not imply making a big production of it. It does imply specific instructions and careful but unobtrusive management and supervision.

● Be patient with students, other teachers, administrators, and above all with yourself. What you're attempting demands a lot of behavior reorganization and relearning.

● Be aware that eventually it will be desirable to inform and involve the school community. It is not necessary, and probably not advisable, to do this before the initial stages of development and experience are successful. Curriculum change implies public involvement, but individual or group experimentation on a small scale with instructional strategies does not. Premature publicity and inflated expectations are not useful; neither is large-scale change without public support and understanding.

Performance-based teacher education (PBTE), as its name indicates, is the application of the principles and practices of performance-based instruction to teacher preparation. Such instruction appears to be well suited to educational training programs.

For one thing, it has the precision necessary to the training task and the flexibility needed to preserve the individuality of the practitioner. In addition, it is thoroughly consistent with the avowed principles upon which our society is based. It is rooted in respect for the individual. It gives a fuller measure of equality of opportunity. It encourages both independent and interdependent behavior—and it is efficient.

In applying the principles of PBI to its training programs, the teaching profession first proceeds to develop specific objectives. Such efforts have led to the derivation of five categories of objectives for teacher education, based on the kinds of performance criteria used in determining whether the objective has been met. The five kinds of objectives are:

1. Knowledge objectives, for which the criteria are concerned with what is to be known or understood.

2. Performance objectives, for which the criteria are concerned with what a person is able to do.

3. Consequence objectives—the highest order of objectives—which use as criteria for successful teaching the performance or behavior of the individuals being taught. In other words, the focus is on results. For example, if the objective in a college laboratory class is to have each student teacher develop a given level of ability to ask higher order questions in a microteaching setting, the professor would be accountable for attaining this result (consequences of his· teaching) and each student teacher would be held to this criterion (performance objective).

4. Affective objectives, which are concerned with feelings, attitudes, values, and beliefs. Criteria for these objectives are difficult to define. Because of their nature, attainment of these kinds of objectives often has to be inferred from other evidence. For example, appreciation of literature may be inferred from an increase in the voluntary reading of literature or from membership in a literary club.

5. Experience objectives, also known as expressive and exploratory objectives, for which performance criteria cannot be determined before the act. Expressive objectives are concerned with the experience rather than with the intended learning. They represent recognition that not enough is known—at this time or in the foreseeable future—about learning to program it all. Thus, experiences are provided on the assumption that valuable learnings will occur even though it cannot be stated what they will be.

Students in teacher education may live or work in ghetto communities or tutor in the children's ward of a hospital. In such cases, the performance criteria consist only of requirements that the opportunity for the experience is exercised. In many respects, student teaching is an exploratory experience, since both its conditions and its outcomes are largely uncontrolled.

Clearly, the criteria levels represent a hierarchy of utility and difficulty of application. Knowledge criteria are the easiest to apply. Next comes performance and then consequence criteria. The affective, which is present in all activities, is both most elusive and, perhaps, most important. Experience objectives provide a broad tent within which one can pursue activities that appear valid and worthwhile even though their value cannot be proved. Obviously, the higher the order of the criterion, the longer the period of time over which data relevant to it must be gathered.

In analyzing or describing performanced-based teacher education (PBTE), one can again use a model based on three concentric circles.

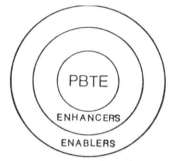

The essential elements are the same as those of PBI, with special emphasis on education for the profession and on the five categories of objectives.

The most exciting developments in teacher education have been taking place in the area of the practices that enhance the effectiveness of PBTE. The enhancers include (a) individualization and personalization; (b) modularized instruction; (c) use of technology with delivery systems and feedback; (d) use of behavior-laboratory techniques, such as simulation, microteaching, and performance analysis to develop specific teaching skills; and (e) field-based experience where participation, observation, tutoring, serving as aides, student teaching, and internship teaching are among the alternative approaches.

The same kinds of resources that PBI needs also facilitate performance-based teacher education—which is most effective when system approaches are used and when the management and personnel subsystems are well developed. Some PBTE enablers are (a) systems applications, (b) management systems, (c) personnel systems, (d) collaborative relationships, and (e) teacher centers.

The last concept, that of teacher centers, is rapidly emerging as one of the most potentially significant enablers of effective performance-based teacher education. It brings into working partnership those who are concerned with teacher education, both preservice and continuing. All of the following are involved in various ways: teacher education institutions; the organized teaching profession; public and private schools, as employers of teachers and providers of training situations; the public; state education agencies; other agencies, such as intermediate governmental units; and the federal government.

Up to now, teacher certification has been based on imprecisely defined criteria. Training has been general rather than specific. The technical arsenal of both teaching and teacher education has been scanty. Thus, completion of a specified number of knowledge courses and the student teaching experience have been the basis for certification. Professional examinations, based on the assumption of knowledge and behavioral performance, have long been in disfavor.

The development of the performance movement has opened new avenues of approach to teacher education. If objectives can be defined and if performance criteria can be established, certification can be based either on completion of a performance-based program or on meeting the criteria levels through an examination procedure.

A number of states are already committed to performance-based certification. Within this decade most, if not all, states are expected to place their certification processes on a performance basis. The impact of such a step will force institutions to revise their traditional programs to incorporate the elements and enablers of performance-based instruction.

Teacher education stands at the source of the mainstream of professional practice. Further downstream is the mighty river, comprised of all who practice. Given limited resources, it would seem the better strategy to concentrate on quality control at the source, where the problem is manageable. The best hope for the teaching profession at this time seems to be in two companion developments:

• The move to integrate the teaching profession and its training components.

• The focus of the teaching profession on improvement of the quality of teacher education.

Strong forces are working in contrary directions. Some would eliminate teacher education institutions and transfer the functions to school-based units. Others would open the schools to talent regardless of certification or training.

Never has there been a greater need for responsible professional attention to the concerns of teacher preparation and of teaching. Performance-based instruction, with its essential elements, enhancers, and enablers, provides an analytic vehicle for such a careful look.■

ISSUES TO BE CONSIDERED*

■ Participants in the Classroom Teachers National Study Conference identified issues that performance-based instruction raised for them and their professional associations. These issues, which have been synthesized to eliminate duplication, are grouped below under eight broad headings.

It should be emphasized that this list represents the perceptions of conference participants and does not, therefore, purport to be all-inclusive. Also, no attempt has been made to evaluate issues, elaborate upon them, or suggest solutions.

1. Decision Making at the Institutional Level

● Should the professional education association have parity with institutions of higher education and local school systems?

● To what extent should teachers be involved in planning and decision making through their professional education association?

● To what extent should the professional education association be involved in writing the objectives to establish performance-based programs?

● To what extent should the professional education association negotiate on matters of instruction?

● What should be the role of the Student NEA and its chapters in guaranteeing student involvement in the teacher preparation process?

2. Interpersonal Relationships

● What are the rights and responsibilities of classroom teachers, students, and parents in performance-based instruction?

● How should the roles of the public school classroom teacher and the college professor be redefined in performance-based instruction?

● What are the rights and responsibilities of classroom teachers, students, and parents in performance-based instruction in the elementary and secondary schools? In higher education?

● To what degree should students be involved in determining curriculums in elementary and secondary schools? In higher education?

● At what point should students be involved in determining performance criteria in elementary and secondary schools? In higher education?

---

*"Issues to be Considered" were synthesized from The Classroom Teachers National Study Conference and are reprinted as they appeared in *Today's Education*, April 1972, 61:39-40.

3. Teaching Competencies

- What competencies will be measured?
- Who will identify these competencies?
- Who will determine criteria and behavioral objectives?
- How can the affective domain be maintained as a viable part of the curriculum?

4. Evaluation

- What will be the purpose and use of evaluation?
- Who will be evaluated? Students? Teachers? Administrators? College personnel?
- Who will do the evaluation?
- What criteria are relevant in evaluating student performance, teacher performance, and administrator performance?
- Should all evaluative criteria be specified in advance of evaluation? Might the evaluator use some hidden criteria?
- Who determines what will be evaluated and how?
- What role does the individual play in his own evaluation?

5. Conditions of Work

- Will adequate time be provided for teachers to perform the essential tasks of planning and preparation?
- Will adequate services, materials, and supplies be provided for implementation of performance-based programs?
- Will the in-service needs of educators be provided for when a program is initiated and maintained?

6. Costs and Funding

- What are the potential costs of performance-based teaching? What are the comparative costs of a performance-based vs. a traditional program?
- Will adequate funding be provided for performance-based instruction?
- What are the attitudes of the state department of education, state legislature, and community toward financial support of innovation, particularly performance-based instruction?

7. Certification

- How does performance-based teacher education relate to certification?
- What are the implications of existing credit vs. performance-based requirements for certification?
- What legislation is needed to establish new requirements for certification of graduates of performance-based education programs?
- Will recertification of current staff be required? If so, what are the implications?
- What are the implications of performance-based certification for teacher mobility?

8. Impact on Higher Education

● What are the implications within the total realm of higher education of moving from the current course and credit approach to a performance-based approach? What are the implications in the school of education?

● How will performance-based teacher education affect transfer of students among institutions?

● How will performance-based teacher education affect placement of student teachers?

● What are the implications of performance-based teacher education for accountability of schools of education and college faculty for the quality of teacher education? □

STEPS TO BE TAKEN

■ What are the next steps that should be taken in the performance-based instruction movement? Conference participants recommended certain basic steps to be taken by all individuals and groups involved in performance-based instruction: federal, state, and local education agencies; institutions of higher education; professional education associations; and/or other organizations of educators or educational institutions. It also recommended additional steps to be taken by professional associations and by the Student NEA.

Recommendations to All Individuals and Groups Involved in Performance-Based Instruction

1. Identify and define terms; standardize terminology.

2. Create parity among public education, higher education, and the United Teaching Profession; establish the professional education association as a full partner with the school system and the university in all phases of performance-based instruction—exploring, planning, decision making, implementing, evaluating, and redesigning.

3. Develop and disseminate widely a clear, concise statement setting forth the fundamental concepts of performance-based instruction and answering the following questions: What is it? What are its implications for education, school administration, public school finance, and teacher education institutions? What are the roles and responsibilities of the various institutions involved—the public school, institutions of higher education, professional associations? What are the roles and responsibilities of the various individuals involved—classroom teachers, and administrators, higher education faculty, auxiliary personnel, parents, and students?

Recommendations to the Professional Association

1. Assume greater responsibility for performance-based instruction.

● Establish and disseminate widely a resolution and/or official policy statement setting forth a position with regard to PBI.

● Launch an action program: Assign responsibility to staff and/or committee; provide consultants; sponsor conferences; disseminate information through news articles, pamphlets, and publications; establish a clearinghouse of information; conduct research.

● Take the initiative in establishing a partnership with the local school system, the state department of education, and institutions of higher learning. Seek agreement regarding exploration, planning, implementation, and evaluation. Refuse to participate in any program in which the local association is not appropriately involved in all phases from inception of the idea through evaluation.

2. Assume greater responsibility for the climate in the school system.

● Negotiate for teachers. Establish parity for the professional association in decision making; provide for the effective and appropriate participation of all segments of staff, students, parents, and minority groups.

● Seek appropriate conditions of work—time, materials, personnel, facilities, in-service education opportunities, protection of teacher rights, financial resources.

3. Assume greater responsibility for improvement of preservice teacher education.

● Take the initiative in establishing a cooperative relationship with colleges of teacher education.

● Refuse to cooperate in any program of teacher education that does not provide parity for the professional association.

● Take the initiative in establishing a cooperative relationship with Student NEA.

4. Assume greater responsibility for improvement of certification. Take the initiative in establishing a cooperative relationship with the state department of education; initiate appropriate state legislation; take steps to provide for mobility of teachers across state lines.

Recommendations to the Student NEA

1. Seek to represent all education students.

2. Develop and disseminate widely policy statements with regard to (a) the appropriate role of teacher education student in determining individual and course goals, behavioral objectives, performance criteria, and evaluation standards and procedures; and (b) the appropriate role of college faculty and public school cooperating teacher.

3. Seek to establish a cooperative relationship with education associations at national, state, and all levels. ■

What Will the Schools Become?

HAROLD G. SHANE and OWEN N. NELSON

If the future is what we make it, and since we will all spend the rest of our lives there, much can be said for the current interest in future-peering. Here are the results of the peering of 333 school persons into school problems a quarter of a century hence. The findings are encouraging.

Man has always had a keen interest in his future. In the present climate of speculation, how does the U. S. educator perceive our changing schools in the interval between 1975 and 2000? *What* does he believe may happen, *when* it is likely, and does he *like* what he anticipates? What changes seem likely to come about easily, and where will the schools resist change most vigorously?

In an effort to obtain thoughtful conjectures about developments just over the horizon, the authors invited 570 persons* to react to 41 possible educational futures, all of them discussed in more than 400 books and articles dealing with alternatives for the next 30 years. Of the respondents, 58% answered 205 queries which dealt with 1) curriculum and instruction, 2) new organizational patterns and pupil policies, 3) economic and political influences, 4) teacher preparation and status, 5) the school's relationships to society, and 6) biological intervention and mediation tactics such as the use of drugs to increase children's teach-ability.

The responses reveal the status and direction of educators' thinking. They merit added consideration because of the "self-fulfilling prophecy" phenomenon, which suggests that the beliefs of our sample, if widely held, could perceptibly influence future developments in education. A

---

*Respondents were selected from among five occupational categories: school administrators (72), subject matter specialists (42), curriculum professors (37), doctoral students (87), and a random sample of public school teachers (95).

Shane, Harold G., and Nelson, Owen N. "What Will the Schools Become?" *Phi Delta Kappan.* June 1971. 52:596-598.

few of the questions in all six areas have been selected for discussion here.

Curriculum and Instruction

Multimedia. Almost all of the educators (93%) anticipate that a mix of learning resources will replace the traditional monopoly that the textbook has enjoyed as a mainstay of instruction. Virtually everyone (96%) agrees that a multimedia approach is desirable, that such approaches would be fairly easy to bring about, and that they will become prevalent between 1975 and 1985.

Student tutors. The use of student tutors (for example, 11-year-olds working with six-year-olds in reading) will be commonplace if not a standard procedure by the early 1980's, in the opinion of almost three-quarters of the survey participants. Four out of five feel the idea is excellent, and two-thirds think it would be easy to start such programs.

A new English alphabet. The predictions and enthusiasm of a few linguists notwithstanding, most respondents are pessimisitc about the prospects for a phonetic alphabet of approximately 45 letters, which more nearly coincides with the number of phonemes (significant speech sound units) in English. While three out of four concede the virtue of such a change, over half think it is unlikely to be adopted and assign a low priority to the task.

Increased time for the expressive arts. Teachers of drama, art, and music will be cheered to know that over half of their fellow educators participating in the survey are convinced that work in the expressive arts will double its present time allotment in the curriculum within 10 to 15 years. Seventy-five percent also believe the 100% increase is desirable.

Controversial issues. An overwhelming 91% of the educators feel that, before 1980, instruction in the social studies will come to grips with controversial topics (activist movements, discrimination, and so on), and over 90% think that is high time to give top priority to the forthright study of these social issues. Opinion is split as to how much public resistance there might be to controversial content and issues on which the schools took a stand.

With reference to sex education, and despite the fact that 60% feel it would be difficult, 89% of the educators believe that comprehensive study of human sexuality in all its aspects should begin in the primary years. Four-fifths urge that the introduction of sex education programs receive high priority.

Organization and Pupil Policies

A 12-month-year and personalized programs. The organization of

U. S. education and many of its long-familiar policies are due to change sharply and rapidly if the views of professors, teachers, and administrators are accurate. No later than the mid-Eighties, 84% believe, our schools will be open for 12 months and students' programs will be so personalized that the individual can leave school for three months each year, choosing both the time and the length of vacations. Educators concede, however, that the public will be reluctant to accept such flexibility. Noncompetitive "personalized progress records" are endorsed, but a strong minority (38%) foresee that grades will be used to report pupil achievement for another 10 to 15 years.

Early childhood education. Respondents were optimistic when asked whether school services would extend downward to enroll three-year-olds and to provide health services for babies no later than at age 2. Three-quarters of the replies favor such early childhood programs. Some 73% further urge that high priority be assigned to early childhood education and estimate that programs for the youngest will be a universal reality by around 1985. A large majority of the sample is convinced that the British infant schools will influence practice, and they believe this is a good thing.

Revision of compulsory attendance laws. Opinions of the survey population are almost evenly divided on whether compulsory attendance laws will be relaxed, although 63% favor the idea if exit from and reentry into school can be made more socially acceptable, personal, and flexible. Attendance policies will be hard to change, 60% said, although most feel that they ought to be eased to permit students to leave school sooner to enter the world of work.

Funding and Financial Policies

Governmental agencies. The respondents forecast (62%) and endorsed (88%) rapid consolidation of federal education programs. Strong and united professional action is required to accomplish this goal, and 82 out of 100 urge a high priority for coordinated action by school officials. Even so, 10% of the respondents conjecture that it will be the year 2000 before cooperation among governmental agencies replaces duplication and competition. One extreme cynic cast a write-in vote for 2500 A.D. as the probable year of consolidation for overlapping agencies.

Differentiated staffing. Despite heated opinions on differentiated staffing, 74% of the educators favor differentiation with teacher-pupil, *ratios*, but with paraprofessionals and educational technology utilized to decrease teacher-pupil *contact hours*. This is viewed as a means of increasing productivity, efficiency, and wages. Another large group, 66%, indicate that differentiated staffing probably will be accepted, though not without a struggle. If the respondents' hunches prove accurate, a substantial degree of differentiation will be attained within the decade.

Performance contracting. The average respondent is opposed to the idea of corporation management of school systems, but feels there is an even chance it will be more widely adopted. Estimates on when business may engage in increased school management responsibilities vary somewhat, but four out of five educators feel it could occur quickly. Ten percent believe that the purchase of instruction from corporations will be far more widespread as soon as four years from now.

Vouchers for tuition payments. Little enthusiasm is indicated for a voucher system. Seventy-one percent of the sample feel that such a plan will not get off the ground, and 67% condemn the idea. If vouchers ever are distributed, fewer than 15% see them coming into general use before 1985.

Salary and teacher performance. The antipathy toward merit rating which teachers have expressed for many years apparently has transferred to salary schedules based on teaching performance. Nearly 54% feel that performance-based wages and increments are not likely in the future. However, two-thirds of the replies acknowledged the desirability of basing salaries on competence.*

Teacher Preparation and Status

Teacher education and certification. Major changes in the preparation and licensing of teachers are widely accepted by those polled. For example, 92% feel that teacher education will be drastically modified to prepare pre-service students to work in teams or partnerships, to individualize instruction, to make use of educational technology, and to encourage greater pupil participation in the process of education. Routine use of sensitivity training in teacher education is foreseen by 64% of the respondents. Virtually all respondents (98%) favor major changes. There is also a pronounced feeling (82%) that alternatives to state-controlled teacher licensing are desirable, that they will be instituted (73%), and that they will be widely accepted by 1980 or 1985.

---

*This does not necessarily accurately reflect classroom teachers' attitudes. Only 95 of the 333 respondents were employed as teachers.

A strong current of opinion suggests that ways of obtaining teaching certificates should be liberalized (67% said "yes") and that few if any of the new avenues should involve merely adding courses in professional education. Major changes are presumably to be inaugurated in the immediate future and, for the most part, completed in 10 to 15 years.

The self-contained classroom. "One teacher-one group" instruction is on the way out, according to 69% of the respondents predicting the shape of the future. Another larger group (75%) apparently say "good riddance" to this venerable institution.

In place of the self-contained classroom, 67% of the educators see (and 79% cheerfully accept) some form of "flexible teaching partnerships." Presumably, such partnerships would be an extension of the team concept, but would involve greater "horizontal" and "vertical" deployment of a differentiated staff; that is, a given teacher would work "vertically" with more children of different ages and "horizontally" in more varied capacities.

The School and Society

Societal services. The school is viewed as an agency responsive to social change by most of the participants. Judging by majority opinions of social engineering, we can anticipate 1) psychiatric treatment without cost to students (76% said "yes," 87% "desirable"),* 2) massive adult education and vocational retraining programs (92% said "yes," 95% "desirable"); and 3) school programs designed to help adults adjust to increased leisure and longer periods of retirement (85% said "yes," 94% "desirable").

Mandatory foster homes. Respondents were asked whether they thought that children, before age three, might be placed in foster homes or kibbutz-type boarding schools to protect them from a damaging home environment. Opinions are about evenly divided on whether this is a good or bad policy, but the likelihood of such development in the U. S. is rejected by over 70%.

---

*Most (76%) of the educators expect public schools to assume routine responsibility for identifying and treating incipient mental and psychological disorders or problems beginning in early childhood; 89% favor the idea.

Intervention and Mediation

One of the more controversial items among the 41 in the educational futures instrument is whether or not, in the years ahead, schools should and will use chemical compounds to improve the mood, memory, power of concentration, and possibly the general intelligence of the learner. Most of the respondents feel that what is measured as intelligence can be increased substantially. Ninety percent of the survey participants consider it appropriate to try to increase the IQ through such mediation tactics as enriched environment in early childhood, and 82% also express confidence that measurable intelligence will be increased by or before 1990.

However, the use of drugs to increase "teachability" was labeled as both unlikely (57% say it will not occur on a widespread scale) and a bad practice to boot. Fifty-six percent rejected the idea of using stimulants, tranquilizers, or antidepressants.

"Intervention" in early childhood. The presumed importance of education under school auspices in the learner's early years is supported by survey respondents. Over 70% feel that "preventive and corrective intervention" before age six might, within the next 25 years, make the annual per-pupil expenditures for the early-childhood group even higher than per-student costs at the university level.

Conclusion

Our small sample—directly or by implication—expresses great confidence in the influence of and financial support for education between 1975 and 2000. The respondents expect and desire substantial educational changes; their dissatisfaction with the status quo comes through clearly. If the 333 respondents who struggled patiently through the survey instrument represent U. S. educators as a whole, then the coming decade should attain levels of humaneness and educational zest and venturesomeness reminiscent of the 1930's, the heyday of the progressive education movement.

Code of Ethics of the Education Profession

Approved by the Representative Assembly of the National Education Association July 5, 1968, and amended June 30, 1972.

PREAMBLE

The educator believes in the worth and dignity of man. He recognizes the supreme importance of the pursuit of truth, devotion to excellence, and the nurture of democratic citizenship. He regards as essential to these goals the protection of freedom to learn and to teach and the guarantee of equal educational opportunity for all. The educator accepts his responsibility to practice his profession according to the highest ethical standards.

The educator recognizes the magnitude of the responsibility he has accepted in choosing a career in education, and engages himself, individually and collectively with other educators, to judge his colleagues, and to be judged by them, in accordance with the provisions of this code.

PRINCIPLE I

Commitment to the Student

The educator measures his success by the progress of each student toward realization of his potential as a worthy and effective citizen. The educator therefore works to stimulate the spirit of inquiry, the acquisition of knowledge and understanding, and the thoughtful formulation of worthy goals.

In fulfilling his obligation to the student, the educator—

1. Shall not without just cause restrain the student from independent action in his pursuit of learning, and shall not without just cause deny the student access to varying points of view.

2. Shall not deliberately suppress or distort subject matter for which he bears responsibility.

3. Shall make reasonable effort to protect the student from conditions harmful to learning or to health and safety.

4. Shall conduct professional business in such a way that he does not expose the student to unnecessary embarrassment or disparagement.

5. Shall not on the ground of race, color, creed, sex, or national origin exclude any student from participation in or deny him benefits under any program, nor grant any discriminatory consideration or advantage.

"Code of Ethics of the Education Profession." *NEA Handbook for Local, State, and National Associations.* NEA 1201 16th Street, N. W., Washington, D. C. 20036. 1973. Pp. 41-43.

6. Shall not use professional relationships with students for private advantage.

7. Shall keep in confidence information that has been obtained in the course of professional service, unless disclosure serves professional purposes or is required by law.

8. Shall not tutor for remuneration students assigned to his classes unless no other qualified teacher is reasonably available.

PRINCIPLE II

Commitment to the Public

The educator believes that patriotism in its highest form requires dedication to the principles of our democratic heritage. He shares with all other citizens the responsibility for the development of sound public policy and assumes full political and citizenship responsibilities. The educator bears particular responsibility for the development of policy relating to the extension of educational opportunities for all and for interpreting educational programs and policies to the public.

In fulfilling his obligation to the public, the educator—

1. Shall not misrepresent an institution or organization with which he is affiliated, and shall take adequate precautions to distinguish between his personal and institutional or organizational views.

2. Shall not knowingly distort or misrepresent the facts concerning educational matters in direct and indirect public expressions.

3. Shall not interfere with a colleague's exercise of political and citizenship rights and responsibilities.

4. Shall not use institutional privileges for private gain or to promote political candidates or partisan political activities.

5. Shall accept no gratuities, gifts, or favors that might impair or appear to impair professional judgment, nor offer any favor, service, or thing of value to obtain special advantage.

PRINCIPLE III

Commitment to the Profession

The educator believes that the quality of the services of the education profession directly influences the nation and its citizens. He therefore exerts every effort to raise professional standards, to improve his service, to promote a climate in which the exercise of professional judgment is encouraged, and to achieve conditions which attract persons worthy of the trust to careers in education. Aware of the value of united effort, he contributes actively to the support, planning, and programs of professional organizations.

In fulfilling his obligation to the profession, the educator—

1. Shall not discriminate on the ground of race, color, creed, sex, or national origin for membership in professional organizations, nor interfere with the free participation of colleagues in the affairs of their association.

2. Shall accord just and equitable treatment to all members of the profession in the exercise of their professional rights and responsibilities.

3. Shall not use coercive means or promise special treatment in order to influence professional decisions of colleagues.

4. Shall withhold and safeguard information acquired about colleagues in the course of employment, unless disclosure serves professional purposes.

5. Shall not refuse to participate in a professional inquiry when requested by an appropriate professional association.

6. Shall provide upon the request of the aggrieved party a written statement of specific reason for recommendations that lead to denial of increments, significant changes in employment, or termination of employment.

7. Shall not misrepresent his professional qualifications.

8. Shall not knowingly distort evaluation of colleagues.

PRINCIPLE IV

Commitment to Professional Employment Practices

The educator regards the employment agreement as a pledge to be executed both in spirit and in fact in a manner consistent with the highest ideals of professional service. He believes that sound professional personnel relationships with governing boards are built upon personal integrity, dignity, and mutual respect. The educator discourages the practice of his profession by unqualified persons.

In fulfilling his obligation to professional employment practices, the educator—

1. Shall apply for, accept, offer, or assign a position or responsibility on the basis of professional preparation and legal qualifications without discrimination on the ground of race, color, creed, sex, or national origin.

2. Shall apply for a specific position only when it is known to be vacant, and shall refrain from underbidding or commenting adversely about other candidates.

3. Shall not knowingly withhold information regarding a position from an applicant, or misrepresent an assignment or conditions of employment.

4. Shall give prompt notice to the employing agency of any change in availability of service, and the employing agent shall give prompt notice of change in availability or nature of a position.

5. Shall adhere to the terms of a contract or appointment, unless these terms have been legally terminated, falsely represented, or substantially altered by unilateral action of the employing agency.

6. Shall conduct professional business through channels, when available, that have been jointly approved by the professional organization and the employing agency.

7. Shall not delegate assigned tasks to unqualified personnel.

8. Shall permit no commercial exploitation of his professional position.

9. Shall use time granted for the purpose for which it is intended.

Code of Ethics and Standard Practices for Texas Educators

Adopted by the Professional Practices Commission April 5, 1971

Preamble

The Texas educator strives to create an atmosphere that will nurture to fulfillment the potential of each student.

The educator is responsible for standard practices and ethical conduct toward students, professional colleagues, parents, and the community.

The Code is intended to govern the profession, and interpretations of the Code shall be determined by the Professional Practices Commission.

The educator who conducts his affairs with conscientious concern will exemplify the highest standards of professional commitment.

Principle I
Professional Ethical Conduct

The Texas educator, in maintaining the dignity of the profession, shall respect and obey the law, demonstrate integrity in personal business, and exemplify honesty in words and deeds.

1. The educator shall not intentionally misrepresent the views of the school district or organization and shall clearly distinguish those views from his personal attitudes and opinions.
2. The educator shall honestly account for all funds committed to his charge and shall likewise conduct his personal and official business with integrity.
3. The educator shall not use professional privileges for personal advantage.

The educator has a right to express an opinion, but he should specify whether he is stating the opinion personally or as a representative of a school district or educational organization.

The conduct of financial business alludes to the expectation that each educator should care for personal obligations in a manner to preclude personal or institutional embarrassment.

Principle II
Professional Practices and Performance

The Texas educator, after qualifying in a manner established by law or regulation, shall be judged on performance and shall continually strive to improve competence and to demonstrate effectiveness.

1. The educator shall apply for, accept, offer, or assign a position or a responsibility on the basis of professional qualifications and shall adhere to the terms of a contract or appointment.
2. The educator shall possess mental health, physical stamina, and social prudence necessary to perform the duties of his professional assignment.
3. The educator shall organize instruction to accomplish objectives related to learning activities.

4. The educator shall continue professional growth through study, experimentation, and participation in professional activities.
5. The educator shall comply with local school board policies, Texas Education Agency regulations, and state law.

The educator should be mentally and physically capable to perform duties daily and should separate himself from areas of social imprudence which could bring criticism or legal action—more specifically, social imprudence relates to the misuse and abuse of drugs, alcohol, and to moral propriety.

The right of academic freedom is recognized, but only to the extent that effective instruction occurs.

In recognizing that education is a continuous process, regular programs for self-improvement should be followed and efforts should be made to assist those in training or new to the profession. ○

Principle III
Ethical Conduct Toward Professional Colleagues

The Texas educator, in exemplifying ethical relations with colleagues, all accord just and equitable treatment to all members of the profession.
1. The educator shall not reveal confidential information concerning colleagues unless disclosure serves professional purposes or is required by law.
2. The educator shall adhere to local school board policies and legal statutes regarding dismissal.
3. The educator shall not willfully make false statements about a colleague or the school system.

Fair and accurate evaluation of colleagues should be based on performance so that recommendations are made with integrity. The educator should be prepared to perform any duties, such as offer testimony, requested by authorized bodies of professional inquiry.○

Principle IV
Ethical Conduct Toward Students

The Texas educator, in accepting a position of public trust, measures success by the progress of each student toward realization of his potential as an effective citizen.
1. The educator shall deal considerately and justly with each student and resolve problems including discipline according to law and school board policy.
2. The educator shall not intentionally expose the student to disparagement.
3. The educator shall not reveal confidential information concerning students unless disclosure serves professional purposes or is required by law.
4. The educator shall make reasonable effort to protect the student from conditions detrimental to learning or to health and safety.
5. The educator shall endeavor to present facts without distortion.

The educator should exhibit no prejudices toward students, and he should treat all individuals with equal consideration.

The educator should strive to build the confidence and self-esteem of students and embarrassment before peers should not be used as a form of punishment.

The malicious use of confidential information should not occur.

The educator should be aware of health, safety, and learning hazards and should attempt to build positive conditions in these areas.

This precludes presenting biases or misinterpretation of facts to students. ○

Principal V
Ethical Conduct Toward Parents and Community

The Texas educator, in fulfilling citizenship responsibilities in the community, cooperates with parents and others to improve the public schools of the community.
1. The educator shall communicate to parents information which should be revealed in the interest of the child.
2. The educator shall endeavor to understand community cultures and relate the home environment of all students to the school.
3. The educator shall have rights and responsibilities as a citizen.
4. The educator shall have a positive role in school public relations.

★ ★ ★ ★ ★ ★ ★ ★ ★

The educator is a citizen and in many instances a parent, and has all rights and responsibilities as such within the limitations of the law. Colleagues should not interfere for any reason in the exercise of these rights.○

○ **Clarification of Points**   Prepared by the Texas Education Agency—1971

Bill of Teacher Rights

Preamble

We, the teachers of the United States of America, aware that a free society is dependent upon the education afforded its citizens, affirm the right to freely pursue truth and knowledge.

As an individual, the teacher is entitled to such fundamental rights as dignity, privacy and respect.

As a citizen, the teacher is entitled to such basic constitutional rights as freedom of religion, speech, assembly, association and political action and equal protection of the law.

In order to develop and preserve respect for the worth and dignity of man, to provide a climate in which actions develop as a consequence of rational thought, and to insure intellectual freedom, we further affirm that teachers must be free to contribute fully to an educational environment which secures the freedom to teach and the freedom to learn.

Believing that certain rights of teachers derived from these fundamental freedoms must be universally recognized and respected, we proclaim this Bill of Teacher Rights.

Article I—Rights as a Professional

As a member of his profession, the teacher has the right:

Section 1. To be licensed under professional and ethical standards established, maintained and enforced by his profession.

Section 2. To maintain and improve his professional competence.

Section 3. To exercise his professional judgment in presenting, interpreting and criticizing information and ideas, including controversial issues.

Section 4. To influence effectively the formulation of policies and procedures which affect his professional services, including curriculum, teaching materials, methods of instruction, and school-community relations.

Section 5. To exercise his professional judgment in the use of teaching methods and materials appropriate to the needs, interests, capacities and the linguistic and cultural background of each student.

Section 6. To safeguard information obtained in the course of professional service.

Section 7. To work in an atmosphere conducive to learning, including the use of reasonable means to preserve the learning environment and to protect the health and safety of his students, himself and others.

Section 8. To express publicly his views on matters affecting education.

"Bill of Teacher Rights." *NEA Handbook for Local, State, and National Associations.* NEA 1201 16th Street, N. W., Washington, D. C. 20036. 1973. Pp. 44-45.

Section 9. To attend and address a governing body and be afforded access to its minutes when official action may affect his professional concerns.

Article II—Rights as an Employee

As an employee, the teacher has the right:

Section 1. To seek and be fairly considered for any position commensurate with his qualifications.

Section 2. To retain his employment following entrance into the profession in the absence of a showing of just cause for dismissal or non-renewal through fair and impartial proceedings.

Section 3. To be fully informed, in writing, of rules, regulations, terms and conditions affecting his employment.

Section 4. To have conditions of employment in which his health, security and property are adequately protected.

Section 5. To influence effectively the development and application of evaluation procedures.

Section 6. To have access to written evaluations, to have documents placed in his personnel file to rebut derogatory information and to have removed false or unfair material through a clearly defined process.

Section 7. To be free from arbitrary, capricious or discriminatory actions affecting the terms and conditions of his employment.

Section 8. To be advised promptly in writing of the specific reasons for any actions which might affect his employment.

Section 9. To be afforded due process through the fair and impartial hearing of grievances, including binding arbitration as a means of resolving disputes.

Section 10. To be free from interference to form, join, or assist employee organizations, to negotiate collectively through representatives of his own choosing, and to engage in other concerted activities for the purpose of professional negotiations or other mutual aid or protection.

Section 11. To withdraw services collectively when reasonable procedures to resolve impasse have been exhausted.

Subject Index